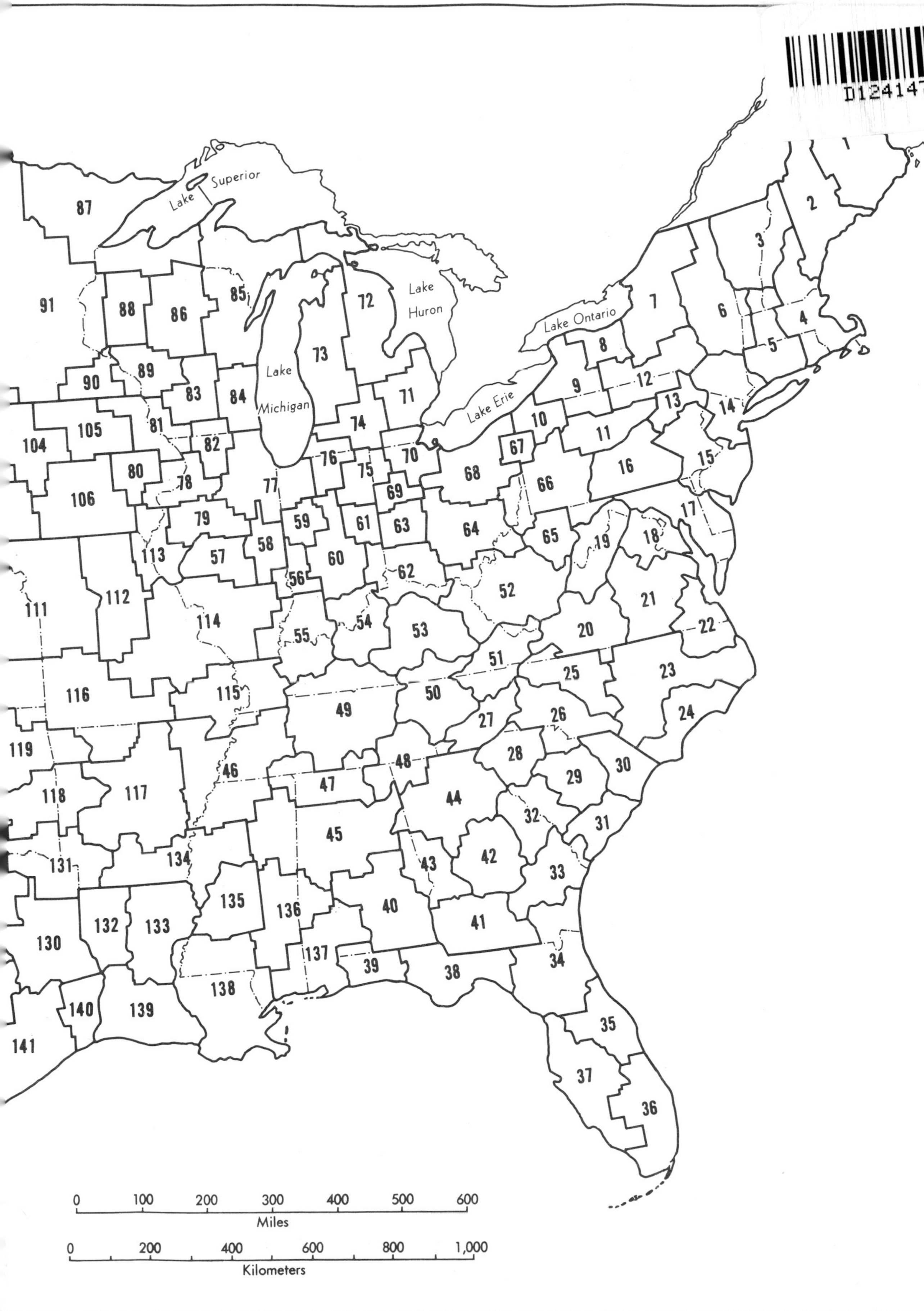

Lake Superior
Lake Michigan
Lake Huron
Lake Ontario
Lake Erie
1
2
3
4
5
6
7
8
9
10
11
12
13
14
15
16
17
18
19
20
21
22
23
24
25
26
27
28
29
30
31
32
33
34
35
36
37
38
39
40
41
42
43
44
45
46
47
48
49
50
51
52
53
54
55
56
57
58
59
60
61
62
63
64
65
66
67
68
69
70
71
72
73
74
75
76
77
78
79
80
81
82
83
84
85
86
87
88
89
90
91
104
105
106
111
112
113
114
115
116
117
118
119
130
131
132
133
134
135
136
137
138
139
140
141
0 100 200 300 400 500 600
Miles
0 200 400 600 800 1,000
Kilometers

The Development of

THE U.S. URBAN SYSTEM

Volume II / Industrial Shifts, Implications

The Development of
THE U.S. URBAN SYSTEM

Volume II / Industrial Shifts, Implications

EDGAR S. DUNN, JR.

Published by Resources for the Future, Inc. / Washington, D.C.
Distributed by The Johns Hopkins University Press / Baltimore and London

Published by Resources for the Future, Inc., 1755 Massachusetts Avenue, N.W., Washington, D.C. 20036
Distributed by The Johns Hopkins University Press, Baltimore, Maryland 21218
The Johns Hopkins Press, Ltd., London

Library of Congress Catalog Card Number 79-2180
ISBN 0-8018-2638-1
Library of Congress Cataloging in Publication Data will be found on the last printed page of this book.

Resources for the Future is a nonprofit organization for research and education in the development, conservation, and use of natural resources, including the quality of the environment. It was established in 1952 with the cooperation of the Ford Foundation. Grants for research are accepted from government and private sources only on the condition that RFF shall be solely responsible for the conduct of the research and free to make its results available to the public. Most of the work of Resources for the Future is carried out by its resident staff; part is supported by grants to universities and other nonprofit organizations. Unless otherwise stated, interpretations and conclusions in RFF publications are those of the authors; the organization takes responsibility for the selection of significant subjects for study, the competence of the researchers, and their freedom of inquiry.

This book is a product of RFF's Renewable Resources Division, Kenneth D. Frederick, director. It was funded by Resources for the Future, the National Science Foundation, and the Richard King Mellon Foundation. Edgar S. Dunn, Jr., is a Senior Fellow at Resources for the Future. The black and white maps were drawn by Art Services. The index was prepared by Florence Robinson. The book was edited by Sally A. Skillings.

Contents

PART TWO

List of Color Plates (following page 144)

All plates contain "Leading and Lagging Competitive Shifts"

List of Maps

Figure

List of Tables

Acknowledgments

The preface to volume I of this study included acknowledgments. In an effort as lengthy as this, the cast of characters changes in course. I am pleased to recognize once more those who have contributed so much to this program of work. In the administrative structure of Resources for the Future, Emery Castle and Kenneth Frederick were most supportive. Bruce Levine, Ronald Catzva, and Jamila Bomani in the Bureau of Economic Analysis of the U.S. Department of Commerce did most of the number crunching. They were unfailingly pleasant and cooperative. William Alonzo, Lowden Wingo, Sterling Brubaker, and Lowell Ashby were patient and constructive manuscript readers. Eldon Weeks, of the U.S. Department of Agriculture, cheerfully suffered through many conversations as the chapter on agriculture took shape. These people will forgive me for reserving the most heartfelt thanks for three special women. They were real "partners in crime," and they became good friends. Anne Price and Sylvia Steadham contributed to every aspect of the production short of drafting the manuscript. Sally Skillings repeated her skillful and supportive role as editor. Though Lorraine Van Dine was not a member of the official team, she shared office space and volunteered to serve as a cybernetic link and morale booster so often that she must not be overlooked.

Though they were not directly involved in the preparation of this manuscript, I would like to acknowledge my debt to two special colleagues. I began my work on developmental problems as a collaborator with Harvey Perloff and others in *Regions, Resources, and Economic Growth* (Resources for the Future, 1960). He was directly responsible for my returning to the work that led to these volumes. Walter Isard first introduced me to regional and urban issues and concepts. I tagged along as he established the Regional Science Association and its journal. To paraphrase a current song, we were "regional and urban" before "regional and urban" was "cool." However, it is more than my professional debt that compels me to acknowledge these two men. They are both "old school" gentlemen. They have each led and supported a lifetime of organizations and ventures, both academic and civic. They both display unusual human qualities that have given professional association an extra dimension. They both have wives who have added much to the experience. I feel fortunate to have been listed among their friends.

The preparation of the second volume of this study was aided by grants from the Richard King Mellon Foundation and the National Science Foundation.

November 1982 Edgar S. Dunn, Jr.

The Development of

THE U.S. URBAN SYSTEM

Volume II / Industrial Shifts, Implications

1

Recalling Volume I

This is the second of two volumes about the development of the U.S. urban system. It is a continuation of the concepts, representations, and explanations set forth in the first and thus can only be understood with volume I as background. To this end, we recall the highlights of the study thus far.

In volume I, which began with an attempt to reorient customary ways of looking at urban systems, a basic distinction was made between classificational and relational modes of observing urban regions. We distinguished, further, between different levels of behavioral observation: the object and activity levels of physical processes and the managerial and developmental levels of information processes (see figure 1 in volume I). In turn, each mode of observation was shown to be associated with a representational technique: boundary networks that classify, or relational networks that trace paths of connectivity. The existence of a hierarchy of observational levels yields two conceptual distinctions that shape the entire study. The first recognizes that empirical representation at a single level is merely descriptive. Explanation, however, requires each level to be viewed in the context of other levels (for example, behavioral artifacts explained by the physical activities that produce them; physical activities explained by the managerial processes that regulate them; artifacts, physical activities, and managerial processes all explained by the developmental processes that design and initiate them). A second distinction made in volume I differentiates between the *growth* of urban regions (which is based on scalar changes in the mix and level of established ways that households and enterprises behave) and the *development* of urban regions (which involves new ways of doing things triggered by new technologies and extraordinary environmental challenges).

When the relational mode of observation is emphasized, it leads to an activity network image of urban structure in which the transformation and transfer of material, energy, and information form a complex systemic network, the total field of which is taken in this study to correspond to the U.S. economy. In this way, urban centers or regions are viewed as subfields within which activity linkages tend to close into internalized circuits (in contrast to the cross-boundary extensions of tree networks).

Sources of change in this patterned network can be differentiated according to the basic distinction between growth and development. Changes in the scale and mix of activities associated with the management of performance do not alter either the logic of urban networks or their characteristic patterns. As the total urban system grows in scale, activities tend to intensify at established sites, which in turn upsets the balance between intensive and extensive margins. Although generating a more dense and spatially extended transaction network, growth does not change the relational logic of the established programmatic base. In contrast, developmental activities that change ways of valuing and doing things tend to transform the topology of the entire system. Developmental changes exert a much more direct and dramatic effect on network patterns. For example, the development of a new type of transport like the airplane dramatically alters transfer networks in a way that favors certain fields of connectivity relative to others. In a similar fashion, the development of a new energy resource such as oil favors oil fields and their connective networks relative to the transaction complex associated with coal.

When, in volume I, we turned our attention to the explanation of urban-system changes, the importance of the distinction between growth and development became apparent. It was concluded that growth effects can be explained in terms of preprogrammed managerial responses to scalar changes in final and intermediate demands as the economy acts to take up the productivity slack implicit in established technologies. But the productivity slack that educes growth is itself a product of historical developmental factors. Thus, while preliminary and proximal explanations based on scalar changes have meaning, ultimately all explanation comes down to developmental factors. This is consistent with the hierarchical nature of observation and explanation set forth in volume I.

At first pass, the changing connective patterns of urban systems are explained by the development of physical- and information-processing technologies and their effects on the relationships formed by production, transport, and communication linkages. Such technological changes can be viewed, in turn, as developmental, adaptive responses to a group of problems characteristic of an historical era—problems for which no preadapted managerial responses exist.

Beyond explaining the changes in urban transaction networks, there is the question of whether these changes pass through a recognizable sequence in time. The formulation of "developmental stage" theories has been a sometime vocation of urban-region scholars. But the conceptual framework of volume I reveals this to be a futile exercise except in the context of simple growth sequences. Such sequences can be fuzzily recognized in the historical record, but their nature can only be understood as a consequence of the way in which scalar growth progressively articulates the activity structure of a recognizable urban center. Thus, we can visualize the way in which scalar growth might change a localized hamlet into a convenience center and a convenience center into a shopping center, with each pattern progression representing an increase in complexity of function and an increase in network articulation. But that progression moves along a growth track defined by the urban-system logic of existing technology. Developmental adaptations progressively shift this track and redefine the fields of network closure that constitute recognizable urban entities of these types.

It follows that to generalize about a sequence of change, one must be able to recognize recurrent developmental sequences over some significant historical period. Patterns formed by sequences of problems and developmental solutions are recognizable in the historical record. But these historical sequences are unique and nonrecurrent, as are all evolutionary processes. We may be able to generalize about the process, but not about the future patterns of its behavioral consequences. This further emphasizes the importance of understanding the problems of an era when attempting to explain its structural changes.

When we turn to the empirical representation of these network images, we look in vain for adequate activity data. Almost all publicly available data are classificational statistics. Therefore, throughout this study I have attempted to shape such data into forms that facilitate inferences about underlying activity networks. By the use of commuting statistics, boundary networks were set up to designate urban regions that appear to display a significant degree of closure on household-linked activities (see the map on the front endpaper or map 1 in volume I). This exercise was extended to identify counties that belong to large, medium, and small urban centers which were, in turn, designated by transaction-field characteristics (color plate 1 in volume I). In addition, counties were identified with the trading characteristics of the highest order trade centers they contained (volume I, table 2). Finally, the industrial structure of employment was developed for each category. The entire empirical study covered the record of a generation (1940–70).

Employing these representational compromises, we inferred what we could about network patterns. The procedure was to deduce which settlement patterns one might expect to be associated with urban network concepts, then to compare them with observed patterns. We began by showing that the population-employment pattern implicit in conventional central place theory fails to correspond to the U.S. experience. Next we inferred that a more realistic image of the urban system would suggest a number of network consequences: (1) An off-centered distribution of population densities tends to emerge from regionally off-centered transaction fields formed by prominent intermediate production activities. (2) Where higher population densities occur, the interpenetration of household-oriented transactions tends to yield fewer trade centers of a given type, and each tends to display larger populations. (3) Variations in resource and intermediate activity linkages also lead to (within-class) variations in the observed sizes of trade center types. (4) Further variations in size and number can be related to the degree to which topographical and boundary constraints force the normal cobweb form of transaction networks into linear form. (5) The interpenetration of the transaction fields of conventionally identified urban centers often tends to yield multinodal, spread-density, symbiotic clusters of centers (in contrast to the more common image of single-centered urban regions associated with hierarchically subordinate trade centers). (6) The size and numbers of trade centers of a given type are related to the degree to which localized "warehousing" of populations takes place. (7) Differences in the pattern of transaction networks and their associated settlement patterns are associated in an important way with variations in the developmental history of differently connected urban regions. We saw in part two of volume I that a carefully structured representation of settlement patterns is consistent with these deductive inferences.

The next logical step leads one to examine changes in settlement patterns over time as a basis for inferring changes in underlying network patterns. In 1966, Hodge attempted this for Saskatchewan, Canada. He revealed a decline in the total number of trade centers, with the reduction concentrated in lower order centers. Over half the centers existing in 1941 either disappeared or changed their status by 1961. New trade centers emerged. Small centers close to a large center experienced a regression incidence twice as large as those further from its functional shadow. Convenience centers appeared particularly vulnerable to the way that developmental factors (for example, the automobile) redefined the logic of the transaction network.

It was not possible to extend this longitudinal analysis to the total U.S. urban field, so we turned to a different way of shaping classificational data to represent changing urban structures. First, we took data on employment by industry (for each of three urban-field classifications) to represent changing industrial profiles between 1940 and 1970. These profiles allow us to compute the weighted index of regional specialization for each type of regional classification. The fact that the weighted index declined for every urban transaction field suggests that the transaction network became more highly articulated during the study period.

Next, changes in the industrial profiles were examined over time. Because of the mass of detail, it was apparent that a summarizing device was required. It also became apparent that a change in the industrial profile between two time periods can be a consequence of several factors. It may be a result (1) of a change in the national comparison structure, (2) of the differential impact of a changing national structure on differently structured regions, (3) of a quasi-independent regional dynamic, or some combination of all three.

The shift-share technique helps resolve these two problems. In the technique, the three sources of structural change are specifically computed for each industry sector. The components of change turn out to be the familiar effects of national growth, industrial mix, and region share. Once computed for each industry, these change elements are summed to represent the composite effect in terms of changes in total employment. Although the limitations of the method were made plain in volume I, it was also suggested that these elements have a preliminary and proximal correspondence with our basic distinction between growth and development. The national growth and industrial mix components represent the direct impact of two dimensions of scalar growth on employment patterns. The region share component tends to capture more of the direct effects of developmental factors.

In volume I, two codes were employed to generate descriptive and quasi-explanatory tables and maps. The first, a summarizing code (code A), identified change patterns formed by the national growth effect and the total regional differential (the latter being the sum of the mix and share effects). The second, a differential code (B), identified change patterns formed by the industrial mix effect and the regional share effect. (These codes are defined in the glossary in this volume.) The summarizing code (A) reveals that urban-region differentials (20 percent) were variations riding on the surface of the great flow of change identified with the national growth effect (80 percent). We also discovered that many urban regions experiencing a differential disadvantage were carried along by the momentum of national growth more strongly than some regions that experienced differential gains.

It is the differential code, however, that generates the most interesting part of the study. It shows how the differential experience of an urban region is distributed between industrial mix effect (our crude estimate of the direct differential effects of growth) and the regional share, or competitive, effect (our crude estimate of the direct differential effects of development). From it, we learn that the regional share, or developmental component, was the larger source of change overall, and increasingly so in recent times. We also learn that 161 B1 and B2 counties (mix and share effects both positive) accounted for half of the total employment change between 1940 and 1970 (although they accounted for only 5 percent of all counties and 30 percent of the total population). At the opposite end of the scale, 1,324 B7 and B8 counties (mix and share effects both negative) displayed negligible or even negative employment changes (half of all counties but only 13 percent of total employment). These and the other change patterns each tell a distinctive story of the regionally differentiating effects of both a national and regional dynamic at work. The spatial patterns formed by these patterns of change were developed in more detail than can be reviewed here.

Because these change patterns were computed for each of the three decades, we can, for the first time, examine patterns of change in the change patterns; that is, we can consider sequences of change for each type of urban field. A three-decade cross-classification of differential codes reveals that over half of all conceivable sequence paths never occur, while a little over 10 percent of all possible paths account for 85 percent of observed sequences. Clearly the dynamic performance of each urban region in any time period was heavily conditioned by its antecedent performance. In addition, half of the sequences were either repetitive or oscillated between two states. By deducing the sequence pattern an urban region would experience if it were to follow a growth-cum-development path, we find that the remaining sequence patterns tended to track along that theoretical path in either an emergent or regressive direction. Thus, there is evidence of a substantial ebb and flow at work in the dynamic fortunes of urban regions—one largely governed by a developmental process.

When we turned our attention to trade centers and transaction fields, we discovered that the largest centers dominated the mass of change while the middle-sized centers proved to be most dynamic in relative terms. The dominant differential shifts have been from the most remote transaction fields (and lower order trade centers) to the urban cores (and higher order trade centers). This can be clearly traced to the mix effect which, in its turn, is primarily traceable to a dramatic decline in agricultural employment. In contrast, competitive shifts have been primarily between large urban cores and small and medium cores (along with their primary transaction fields).

In moving from description to explanation, we recalled the fact that the growth-induced patterns of change are the indirect consequences of development—development being the source of the system slack that feeds growth. For example, the differentiation of total industry sector growth rates lying behind the mix effect is largely determined by developmental factors. Thus, upon closing volume I with an examination of industry growth rates, we rediscovered a classic dichotomy. Rapidly growing regions tended to specialize in rapid-growth industries: (1) urban services, (2) urban-oriented transportation and communication activities and their related manufacturing supply sources, (3) high-technology industries, and (4) armed forces employment. Slowly growing regions tended to specialize in the slow-growth industries: (1) resource industries, (2) second-stage resource processors including the historically basic industries, (3) resource-oriented transportation, and (4) traditional daily household trade and service activities.

The developmental explanations for these differential industry growth rates and the attendant mix effects can be summarized as follows: Technological changes in production processes increased the number and complexity of the intermediate steps between the resource base and final demand. The information content of both processes and products increased relative to their material and energy content. Both developments increased the degree of articulation and roundaboutness of the total urbanized network. New techniques reduced the proportion of labor and material inputs. Developments encouraged the substitution of oil for coal. The nature and availability of materials was redefined. Thus, nonferrous metal and plastics became realistic substitutes for ferrous metals, and synthetic fibers were substituted for natural fibers. New technology altered the content of industry classifications (for example, many activities once considered as purely agricultural show up in food manufacturing). The increased information content of economic activity plus the increased complexity of transaction networks induced technological changes enabling transportation, wholesaling, warehousing, communications, and information-processing activities to play larger roles. The development of new consumer products (household appliances, automobiles, electronic appliances) created a redistribution of final demand. The increased complexity of the system led to an increasing role for public activities as social requirements shifted from "goods" production to "bads" avoidance. The increased articulation of the transaction network on an international scale, and the attendant conflicts of interest, led to larger armed forces and stimulated additional technological and developmental changes. These developmental explanations of the mix component of interregional shifts brought volume I to a natural close.

When we attempt to explain the direct developmental sources of the regional share, or competitive effects, our discourse must undergo a major shift in style and content. We leave the safe waters of *ceterus paribus* to swim in the turbulent surf of a large, complex dynamic system. Explanation is forced to deal with the *regionally differentiating,* rather than the *regionally common,* aspects of change.

This complicates the task unmercifully. Explaining a single national growth rate in terms of the developmental sources of change only requires us to examine the general productivity effects. Explaining the industrial mix effect requires us to consider how developmental sources of change affect thirty-one industry sectors differently. Explaining the regional share effect requires us to consider the way developmental factors reflect the different adaptive requirements of thirty-one industry sectors in 171 different regions. We are progressively faced with the need to explain first one, then 31, then 5,301 elements of change. And each step increases complexity many orders of magnitude! It is clearly impossible to perform this final explanatory task in any complete way. So, as we move to volume II, we shift our attention from the industrial characteristics of interregional shift patterns to the interregional characteristics of industrial shift patterns. Only in this way can we link the descriptive pictures of comparative shifts to powerful sources of developmental explanation.

Once we arrive at this level, we have turned the sequence of explanation quite around. Our shift-share technique permitted us to begin explanation with the growth factors. This can now be seen as a way of sweeping complexity "under the rug" until we can get a preliminary grasp of the nature of change. In the end we must understand fully that developmental sources are the prime movers of all changes and their initial effects are always localized. They are always initiated in specific industrial sectors of specific urban regions. The task in volume II is to deal with this shift in perspective, and with the change in order of complexity.

Part One

BRIDGING THE TWO PERSPECTIVES

2

Industry-Sector Shifts

We begin volume II with an understanding that a change in perspective is required. In volume I, the explanation of a changing urban system could proceed no further than a consideration of the sources of change that are shared by all regions: the consequences for each localized region of differences in national industry growth rates. This only permits one to explain the general developmental factors operating *indirectly*, and equally, on all regions through the instrumentality of growth. And this sort of explanation remains flat and two-dimensional until we reorient our approach to take account of the interregional shifts in activity experienced by each industry sector. Only then can the aspects of change that *directly* affect transaction patterns be accounted for.

Part one of this volume is devoted to building two bridges between the two perspectives. In this chapter, I will discuss the first bridge—the gross shifts between all regions experienced by each industry sector. The second bridge—the way specific industries lead and lag behind the overall competitive shifts experienced by specific regions—is discussed in the remaining chapters in part one. In chaper 3, we investigate the way these leads and lags emerge for broad geographical regions. Chapter 4 applies the study concepts to the pseudoregions formed by the now-familiar trade-center and transaction-field classifications. Chapter 5 considers the way these leads and lags form dynamic sequence patterns.

Industry detail was largely passed over in volume I. That is, after all, one purpose of the shift-share method—to summarize the net effect of changes affecting all industry sectors without becoming lost in detail.[1] Thus, the summarizing growth, mix, and competitive components of each region's total employment shifts have been generated, described, and analyzed. In tables 17 and 24 in volume I (pp. 121 and 133), each of the shift components was summed across all regions to provide the gross (growth, mix, and competitive) shifts across all regions. Our vehicle for beginning a consideration of detailed industry-sector shifts is the provision of gross mix and competitive shifts across all regions for each sector in the same fashion.[2]

We computed these summary representations for thirty-one industry sectors and for each of four time periods (1940–50, 1950–60, 1960–70, 1940–70). The results are presented in appendix II-A, which will serve as a bank of information throughout volume II. (Note to the reader: to distinguish the tables, maps, color plates, and appendixes in this volume from those in volume I, their numbers and letters will be prefixed with II.) Tables II-1 and II-2, which summarize data from appendix II-A, present an industry-sector array of the absolute and relative gross shifts. Table II-3 records the beginning and terminal indexes of industrial concentration. These are the first of a series of detailed industry-sector tables that will appear throughout part one. You should be aware that their role in part one will be restricted to illustrating and documenting the shift in perspective as we move from volume I to volume II. The tables are also being introduced as primary reference tools that will invite further study as we consider the detailed industry record in part two. These tables help bridge the volume I and volume II perspectives by providing both backward and forward linkages.

A Link Backward

Table 24 of volume I presented the all-sector gross mix shifts (summed across all regions, see footnote 2). The A panels of tables II-1 and II-2 break down this all-sector aggregate into the gross mix shifts characteristic of each industry sector. The reader is thus provided with a link backward to corresponding tables and discussions in volume I (chapters 11 and 13). It is especially interesting to note that agriculture, machinery manufacturing, the armed forces, and other manufacturing accounted for half of the aggregate interregional shifts attributable to the mix effect. In fact, only ten sectors account for over

TABLE II-1. Ranking of gross interregional employment shifts by industry, 1940–70

Panel A. gross industry mix shifts						Panel B. gross competitive shifts					
Rank	Sector no.	Industry	Industry mix shift	Percent of total	Cumulative percentage	Rank	Sector no.	Industry	Comp. eff. gross shift	Percent of total	Cumulative percentage
U.S. Total			±10,268,899[a]	100.00		U.S. Total			±12,688,367[a]	100.00	
1	1	Agriculture	2,049,799[b]	19.96	19.96	1	29	Prof. serv.	1,565,389	12.34	12.34
2	11	Mach. mfg.	1,205,406	11.74	31.70	2	14	Other mfg.	1,210,431	9.54	21.88
3	31	Armed forces	944,672	9.20	40.90	3	11	Mach. mfg.	1,003,411	7.91	29.79
4	14	Other mfg.	841,024	8.19	49.09	4	23	Other retail	857,217	6.76	36.55
5	29	Prof. serv.	795,056	7.74	56.83	5	31	Armed forces	694,717	5.48	42.03
6	24	F.I.R.E.[c]	516,968	5.03	61.86	6	30	Civ. gov.	669,334	5.28	47.31
7	13	Trans. equip.	437,063	4.26	66.12	7	1	Agriculture	594,955	4.68	51.99
8	30	Civ. gov.	376,074	3.66	69.78	8	24	F.I.R.E.[c]	581,367	4.58	56.57
9	12	Mot. veh. mfg.	330,780	3.22	73.00	9	4	Construction	510,479	4.02	60.59
10	23	Other retail	282,953	2.76	75.76	10	13	Tran. equip.	465,898	3.67	64.26
11	20	Whole. trade	273,680	2.67	78.43	11	7	Apparel mfg.	463,376	3.65	67.91
12	7	Apparel mfg.	213,516	2.08	80.51	12	26	Bus. & repair	453,770	2.79	70.70
13	4	Construction	192,285	1.87	82.38	13	20	Whole. trade	340,485	2.68	73.38
14	9	Chem. mfg.	178,343	1.74	84.12	14	21	Eat & drink	309,419	2.44	75.82
15	17	Other trans.	175,276	1.71	85.83	15	6	Textile mfg.	294,154	2.32	78.14
16	21	Eat & drink	172,618	1.68	87.51	16	25	Lodg. & pers.	292,630	2.31	80.45
17	3	Mining	172,203[b]	1.68	89.19	17	12	Mot. veh. mfg.	246,162	1.94	82.39
18	8	Print. & pub.	167,925	1.64	90.83	18	22	Food retail	237,931	1.88	84.27
19	26	Bus. & repair	147,420	1.44	92.27	19	3	Mining	226,437	1.78	86.05
20	28	Priv. hsehld.	146,959[b]	1.42	93.69	20	5	Food mfg.	221,526	1.75	87.80
21	18	Communication	114,769	1.12	94.81	21	9	Chem. mfg.	194,736	1.53	89.33
22	15	R.R. trans.	88,439[b]	0.86	95.67	22	17	Other trans.	190,260	1.50	90.83
23	6	Textile mfg.	80,012[b]	0.78	96.45	23	28	Priv. hsehld.	179,059	1.43	92.96
24	19	Utilities	66,540	0.65	97.10	24	19	Utilities	178,174	1.40	93.66
25	5	Food mfg.	61,549	0.60	97.70	25	18	Communications	173,709	1.37	95.03
26	16	Truck & whs.	59,033	0.57	98.27	26	10	Lumber & wood	162,744	1.28	96.31
27	25	Lodg. & pers.	51,243	0.50	98.77	27	8	Print. & pub.	152,942	1.21	97.52
28	22	Food retail	48,740	0.47	99.24	28	16	Truck & whsg.	139,185	1.10	98.62
29	27	Amuse. & rec.	39,785	0.39	99.63	29	27	Amuse. & rec.	81,465	0.64	99.26
30	10	Lumber & wood	31,757	0.31	99.94	30	15	R.R. trans.	65,987	0.52	99.78
31	2	Forest. & fish.	7,121[b]	0.06	100.00	31	2	Forest. & fish.	30,922	0.22	100.00

[a] All entries in table carry the ± sign indicating positive or negative shifts across all regions (see note 2 at the end of this chapter).
[b] Industry growth rate is negative.
[c] F.I.R.E. = Finance, insurance, and real estate.

TABLE II-2. Industry-sector arrays of mix and competitive shifts as a percentage of 1940 industry-sector employment

		Panel A				Panel B				Panel C	
Rank	Sector no.	Mix (percent)[a]		Rank	Sector no.	Competitive shift (percent)[b]		Rank	Sector no.	Ratio of gross competitive and mix shifts $\frac{R_{ij}}{K_{ij}}$[c]	
1	31	Armed forces	309.2	1	31	Armed forces	227.4	1	25	Lodg. & pers.	5.71
2	13	Trans. equip.	140.3	2	13	Trans. equip.	149.6	2	10	Lumber & wood	5.12
3	11	Mach. mfg.	110.9	3	11	Mach. Mfg.	92.3	3	22	Food retail	4.88
4	12	Mot. veh. mfg.	56.9	4	7	Apparel mfg.	56.9	4	16	Truck. & whsg.	4.79
5	9	Chem. mfg.	39.9	5	29	Prof. services	46.3	5	2	Forestry & fish.	4.34
6	24	F.I.R.E[d]	34.7	6	30	Civilian gov.	44.7	6	6	Textile mfg.	3.68
7	17	Other transp.	31.9	7	9	Chem. mfg.	43.6	7	5	Food mfg.	3.60
8	18	Communications	28.7	8	18	Communications	43.5	8	23	Other retail	3.03
9	7	Apparel mfg.	26.2	9	12	Mot. veh. mfg.	42.4			*Total retail*	2.83
10	8	Print. & pub.	26.1	10	26	Bus. & repair	40.1	9	19	Utilities	2.68
		Total mfg.	25.4	11	24	F.I.R.E.[d]	39.1	10	4	Construction	2.66
11	30	Civilian gov.	25.1	12	17	Other transp.	34.6	11	26	Bus. & repair	2.40
12	29	Prof. services	23.9			*Total mfg.*	34.2			*Total services*	2.26
13	1	Agriculture	23.6	13	14	Other mfg.	33.5	12	7	Apparel mfg.	2.17
14	14	Other mfg.	23.3	14	19	Utilities	32.3	13	27	Amuse. & rec.	2.05
	All-sector	**average**	22.6	15	2	Forestry & fish.	28.0	14	29	Prof. services	1.97
15	20	Wholesale trade	27.4		**All-sector**	**average**	27.9	15	21	Eating & drinking	1.79
16	3	Mining	18.6	16	20	Wholesale trade	27.8	16	30	Civilian gov.	1.78
17	26	Bus. & repair	16.7	17	16	Truck & whsg.	27.1	17	18	Communications	1.51
18	19	Utilities	12.1			*Total services*	26.3	18	14	Other mfg.	1.44
		Total services	11.8	18	6	Textile mfg.	25.2			*Total mfg.*	1.35
19	21	Eating & drinking	11.6	19	3	Mining	24.4	19	3	Mining	1.31
20	16	Truck. & whsg.	11.5	20	4	Construction	24.1		**All-sector**	**average**	1.24
21	27	Amuse. & rec.	9.8	21	8	Print. & pub.	23.8	20	20	Wholesale trade	1.24
22	4	Construction	9.1	22	23	Other retail	22.6	21	28	Private hshlds.	1.22
23	15	R.R. transp.	7.7			*Total retail*	21.1	22	24	F.I.R.E.[d]	1.12
		Total retail	7.5	23	21	Eating & drinking	20.8	23	9	Chem. mfg.	1.09
24	23	Other retail	7.4	24	22	Food retail	20.3	24	17	Other transp.	1.09
25	6	Textile mfg.	6.9	25	27	Amuse. & rec.	20.1	25	13	Trans. equip.	1.07
26	2	Forestry & fish.	6.4	26	5	Food mfg.	19.7	26	8	Print. & pub.	0.91
27	28	Private hshlds.	6.2	27	10	Lumber & wood	17.3	27	11	Mach. mfg.	0.83
28	5	Food mfg.	5.5	28	25	Lodg. & pers.	16.9	28	15	R.R. transp.	0.75
29	22	Food retail	4.2	29	28	Private hshlds.	07.5	29	12	Mot. veh. mfg.	0.74
30	10	Lumber & wood	3.4	30	1	Agriculture	06.9	30	31	Armed forces	0.74
31	25	Lodg. & pers.	0.6	31	15	R.R. transp.	05.7	31	1	Agriculture	0.29

[a] K_{ij} divided by total 1940 ind. employment multiplied by 100.
[b] R_{ij} divided by total 1940 ind. employment multiplied by 100
[c] Industry sectors in panel B of table II-1 divided by corresponding sectors of panel A in table II-1.
[d] F.I.R.E. = Finance, insurance, and real estate.

75 percent of the shifts. Thus, the sources of change at work in these activities carry more weight in accounting for the mix effects displayed in volume I.

But how does one explain these dynamic differences? In part, by going back to the computational root of the mix effect. It can be seen that the absolute size of the mix shifts in table II-1 are determined by three things: (1) the absolute size of the industry sector's 1940 employment, (2) the degree of industrial concentration in 1940, and (3) the size of the positive or negative employment growth rate between 1940 and 1970. Thus agriculture, which made the largest absolute contribution to the all-sector gross mix shift, had more than twice as many employees in 1940 as any other sector. It was also substantially more concentrated than total employment, and it experienced the largest negative growth rates of any sector. But the size factor is to a considerable extent an arbitrary artifact of the classificational system. So the array in table II-2 expresses the mix shift of table II-1 as a percentage of each industry's 1940 employment. Notice that agriculture moves from first to thirteenth position in the array. Other quite large industry sectors (like retail trade, other manufacturing, construction, and civilian government) also shift to lower ranks.

TABLE II-3. Ranked indexes of industrial concentration,[a] 1940, 1950, 1960, and 1970

1940 (1)		1950 (2)		1960 (3)		1970 (4)		Change in Index 1970–40 (col. 4 − col. 1) (5)		(1970–40)/1940 (6)	
Mot. veh. mfg.	.671764	Mot. veh. mfg.	.633306	Mot. veh. mfg.	.602092	Textile mfg.	.608817	Textile mfg.	+.05211	Pvt. hshld.	+.34016
Mining	.589943	Mining	.597707	Textile mfg.	.596682	Mot. veh. mfg.	.581070	R.R. trans.	+.05080	Bus. & repair	+.30516
Textile mfg.	.556712	Textile mfg.	.583864	Mining	.573618	Mining	.541884	Pvt. hshld.	+.04591	R.R. trans.	+.27517
For. & fish.	.551127	Armed for.	.518150	For. & fish.	.479455	Armed for.	.478484	Bus. & rep.	+.02938	Civ. gov.	+.09662
Armed for.	.539474	For. & fish	.505732	Armed for.	.461715	For. & fish.	.448439	Civ. gov.	+.01280	Textile mfg.	+.09359
Tran. equip.	.494975	Tran. equip.	.453078	Tran. equip.	.412151	Tran. equip.	.393255	Food mfg.	+.00691	Food mfg.	+.04100
Apparel mfg.	.434049	Apparel mfg.	.412674	Apparel mfg.	.387121	Lum. & wood	.378246	Lum. & wood	+.00539	Truck & whsg.	+.02366
Mach. mfg.	.391947	Lum. & wood	.391109	Lum. & wood	.383608	Apparel mfg.	.375768	Truck & whsg.	+.00216	Lum. & wood	+.01425
Lum. & wood	.372855	Mach. mfg.	.370239	Agriculture	.362451	Agriculture	.347714	Chem. mfg.	+.00142	Chem. mfg.	+.00829
Agriculture	.353566	Agriculture	.362931	Chem. mfg.	.297590	Chem. mfg.	.293863	Construc.	−.00467	Agriculture	−.01655
Other mfg.	.306429	Chem. mfg.	.284677	Mach. mfg.	.291615	Other trans.	.238870	Agriculture	−.00585	Construc.	−.05827
Chem. mfg.	.291446	Other mfg.	.270675	Other trans.	.240054	R.R. trans.	.235433	Amuse. & rec.	−.02915	Mining	−.08146
Other trans.	.273112	Other trans.	.221601	Other mfg.	.214561	Mach. mfg.	.229969	Lodg. & pers.	−.03416	Armed for.	−.11305
Wtd. index	**.23228**	**Wtd. index**	**.21055**	R.R. trans.	.214400	Other mfg.	.196583	Other trans.	−.03424	Other trans.	−.12538
Pr. & pub.	.219719	Pr. & pub.	.198536	Pvt. hshld.	.181662	Pvt. hshld.	.180855	Prof. serv.	−.02811	Apparel mfg.	−.13427
F.I.R.E.[b]	.212869	R.R. trans.	.196716	**Wtd. index**	**.17792**	Food mfg.	.175354	Other retail	−.03821	Mot. veh. mfg.	−.13501
R.R. trans.	.184629	Pvt. hshld.	.177302	Pr. & pub.	.168946	Pr. & pub.	.161646	Communic.	−.04345	Amuse. & rec.	−.16709
Amuse & rec.	.174425	F.I.R.E.[b]	.170967	Civ. gov.	.146416	**Wtd. index**	**.15499**	Mining	−.04806	For. & fish.	−.18632
Food mfg.	.168447	Food mfg.	.168941	Amuse. & rec.	.142656	Amuse. & rec.	.145280	Food retail	−.04819	Tran. equip.	−.20551
Communic.	.152508	Civ. gov.	.157218	Food mfg.	.136540	Civ. gov.	.145140	Eat. & drink.	−.05567	Pr. & pub.	−.26431
Whol. trade	.138605	Amuse. & rec.	.130168	F.I.R.E.[b]	.132763	Bus. & repair	.125640	Whol. trade	−.05774	**Wtd. index**	**−.33274**
Pvt. hshld.	.134950	Whol. trade	.116142	Bus. & repair	.110857	F.I.R.E.[b]	.122436	Pr. & pub.	−.05807	Lodg. & pers.	−.34259
Civ. gov.	.132352	Communic.	.115514	Whol. trade	.098950	Communic.	.098163	Apparel mfg.	−.05828	Communic.	−.35634
Utilities	.130275	Truck & whsg.	.090981	Truck & whsg.	.094252	Truck & whsg.	.093373	Armed for.	−.06099	Other mfg.	−.35847
Eat. & drink.	.124508	Construc.	.081522	Communic.	.088597	Whol. trade	.080863	Utilities	−.06278	Prof. serv.	−.36263
Lodg. & pers.	.099695	Eat. & drink.	.076649	Construc.	.070424	Construc.	.075827	**Wtd. index**	**−.07729**	Mach. mfg.	−.41327
Bus. & repair	.096264	Bus. & repair	.074414	Utilities	.066807	Eat. & drink.	.068836	F.I.R.E.[b]	−.09043	Whol. trade	−.41659
Truck & whsg.	.091215	Utilities	.073409	Lodg. & pers.	.065926	Utilities	.067499	Mot. veh. mfg.	−.09069	F.I.R.E.[b]	−.42483
Food retail	.086231	Lodg. & pers.	.073196	Eat. & drink.	.064646	Lodg. & pers.	.065540	Tran. equip.	−.10172	Eat. & drink.	−.44714
Construc.	.080519	Prof. serv.	.063314	Prof. serv.	.052531	Prof. serv.	.049398	For. & fish.	−.10269	Utilities	−.48187
Prof. serv.	.077503	Food retail	.049342	Food retail	.049444	Food retail	.038039	Other mfg.	−.10985	Other retail	−.54130
Other retail	.070597	Other retail	.040321	Other retail	.036040	Other retail	.032383	Mach. mfg.	−.16198	Food retail	−.55887
Range of Index	.60117		.59229		.56605		.57078				
Relative Dispersion	2.59		2.82		3.18		3.68				

[a] Sometimes called the index of regional localization.
[b] F.I.R.E. = Finance, insurance, and real estate.

Having thus eliminated this arbitrary element from the explanation, we consider the systematic effects of (1) the degree of industrial concentration and (2) the rates of growth displayed by each industrial sector. The array of growth rates was provided in table 37 in volume I. The array of indexes of industrial concentration are in column (1) of table II-3. This index of industrial concentration has a specific meaning. It says, for example, that in 1940 two-thirds of the employment in motor vehicle manufacturing would need to be redistributed among 171 urban regions before all such regions would contain the same relative share of motor vehicle employment. In contrast, only 7 percent of other retail employment would need to be redistributed to achieve the same result.[3] The most concentrated activities tend to be resource and manufacturing activities, while the least concentrated are the urban-servicing, trade, service, utility, and governmental activities.

Consider the table II-2 mix array in the light of the growth rates and the indexes of concentration. Observe that, of the fourteen industrial sectors that experienced above-average relative mix shifts, nine display both high relative growth rates and high indexes of industrial concentration. Thus, the armed forces, which is ranked first, has the highest growth rate and the fifth largest index of industrial concentration. There are three industry sectors (motor vehicles, apparel, and other manufacturing) for which substantial mix effects depend a great deal more on high degrees of concentration than on dynamic growth. Conversely, there are two sectors (civilian government and professional services) that experienced relatively heavy mix effects largely because of rapid growth rates. They are not highly concentrated.

In the end, these preliminary explanations must be backed up with developmental explanations. A summary explanation of the developmental factors underlying the differences in national industry growth rates has already been provided in chapter 14 of volume I. A developmental explanation of the differences in industrial concentration requires us to consider the technological changes that shaped these industries, not just during the study period but over a span of developmental history leading up to 1940. That, of course, carries us into the perspective and mode of explanation special to part two of volume II.

A Link Forward

By now we have come by several different routes to the same view of the remaining explanatory tasks—a consideration of the developmental sources of change. This brings us to the need to explain changes in the structure of transaction networks that generate changes in interregional comparative advantage, and hence, to an explanation of interregional competitive shifts by industry. As a link to this new perspective it is helpful to observe which of the industry sectors made the greatest contribution to the all-sector developmental dynamics reflected in the summary-line competitive shifts of volume I. The B panels in tables II-1 and II-2 provide the absolute and relative competitive shift arrays by industry. Specifically, table II-1 reveals that eleven industries account for two-thirds of the gross all-sector competitive shifts. But once again the array is heavily influenced by an arbitrary industry-size factor. Table II-2 corrects for this by providing an array of those industries undergoing the greatest relative changes.

The relative array gives us an interesting link forward to the explanatory enterprise of part two. There is a strong relationship between the industry sectors that experienced dynamic growth rates overall (table 37 in volume I) and those that displayed the greatest relative competitive shifts (table II-2). Thus, the armed forces, transportation equipment, and machinery sectors, whose gross competitive shifts are equal to or greater than their 1940 employment, are ranked one, three, and four, respectively, in the industry growth-rate array. Conversely, the railroad, agriculture, and household sectors, whose competitive shifts are all less than 8 percent of 1940 employment, are placed at the bottom of the array by large employment declines. We are brought to a meaningful generalization. The factors that generate large industrial growth rates are not often simple scalar changes in final demand unrelated to changes in production processes. They are more characteristically the result of a strong developmental dynamic reflecting technological inventions and innovations in the broadest sense. Therefore, large industry-sector growth rates also tend to be associated with major product and process changes that redefine the structure of urbanized activities and change the competitive position of different segments of the urbanized transaction field. To explain how and why that is so is, again, the task of part two, where we will consider the competitive interregional shifts experienced by each industry sector.

A closer examination of these competitive shift and growth-rate arrays reveals some instructive exceptions. There are two groups of industries for which this typical association between growth rates and gross shifts breaks down. One set displays relatively large gross competitive shifts, in spite of low growth rates. In the case of sectors like forestry and fisheries, mining, and other manufacturing, this is partly because of the heterogeneous nature of the classifications. In such cases, the low growth rates partly result in within-class offsets, like the substitution of rapidly growing oil mining for declining coal mining. However, there can be a substantive reason. Some industries undergo substantial structural changes, not so much because of a major internal developmental dynamic, but because of the necessity to adapt to the developmental dynamic of externally linked activities. Thus, textile and apparel manufacturing underwent substantial interregional competitive changes even though their growth rates were low relative to total employment. This was largely (1) because of the development of major interregional labor cost differentials stemming from externally induced changes in labor markets, and (2) because of major shifts in the industry's markets. With respect to (2), we shall see that the relative decline in styled goods in apparel manufacturing and the advent of new fabrics (both exogenous developments) altered the market location factors affecting the apparel business. There is the additional factor that some industries (like motor vehicle manufacturing) undertake technological developments that are primarily directed to improving labor productivity, thus depressing employment growth rates in an industry otherwise undergoing dynamic changes in transaction linkages that redefine the location matrix.

A second set of industries does not experience major interregional structural changes in spite of displaying very high growth rates. The list of these sectors (eating and drinking places, other retailing, wholesale trade, trucking, printing and publishing, construction) is our clue. The changes taking place in the external operating environments of these sectors did not operate so much to alter their interregional competitive advantages as they did in the cases above. Instead, the changes tended to increase their interindustry competitive advantages, hence their industry growth rates. By virtue of being major linkage and urban-servicing sectors, all these sectors experienced major scalar changes in the demand for their services that attended major developmental changes of external origin.[4] This is not to deny that they underwent substantial internal developmental changes as well, as we shall soon see. Here a second explanatory factor comes into play. Even substantial internal changes did not generate major locational differences between different regions or different urban fields because all of these sectors are heavily oriented to final demand. They are highly associated with the interregional distribution of total employment and population. In short, for these activities, there was not the same opportunity for developmental changes to alter regional comparative advantages.

Still another indication of the reorganizational ferment affecting the urbanized transaction system can be read from table II-3. The weighted index of industrial concentration declined progressively by two-thirds of its initial value. (This is the counterpart to the observation on p. 105 in volume I that regions were, on the average, becoming less specialized.) This reflects a degree of structural change beyond the capacity of simple scalar changes to effect. Substantial developmental changes are clearly at work. As was the case with the index of regional specialization, there is room for substantial individual sector variations. Nine industry sectors actually became more concentrated, several substantially so (railroad, household and business services, textiles, and civilian government). The trades and other urban-servicing activities experienced large declines relative to their initial period concentrations, but it is the heavy fabricating industries (machinery, transportation equipment, other manufacturing) that are chiefly responsible for the decline in the weighted index.[5]

All of these exercises bring us repeatedly to the same end point. Explanation can only proceed by examining the change factors at work as they affect each industry sector, and particularly as they change the comparative positions of each region for that activity. In the three chapters that follow we construct a second bridge taking us a step closer to this level of explanation.

Notes

1. Even though the contribution of each industry sector to the region's total employment shift (plus or minus) is specifically calculated and taken into account.

2. When we sum the all-sector and industry-sector components of shift-share across all regions, the mix and competitive components net to zero precisely because of the way they are defined. The shifts of employment out of one set of regions has to equal the shift into another set. The gross shift is, therefore, computed by adding these industry components without regard to sign and then dividing by two. The gross total employment shifts in table II-1 do not correspond with those recorded in tables 17 and 24 in volume I because the differences in the order of aggregation net out some of the shifts that are included in table II-1.

3. The index of industrial concentration is subject to the same limitations as the index of regional specialization described in volume I. By definition, the weighted index of industrial concentration is the same as the weighted index of regional specialization considered in chapter 7 of volume I. It turns out that the weighted index reported here is slightly different. There are two reasons. (1) There can be a difference in the accumulation of rounding error. (2) Most important, the two indexes were computed at widely separated points in time. In the intervening period, a slight change was made in the allocation formula producing the base data.

4. Construction may seem like an exception, but a major part of its growth had its origin in the demand increase associated with the booming road construction of the epoch.

5. The range (separating the smallest from the largest index in each period) barely changed, so the interindustry variation in industrial concentration did not materially change. In fact, with the declining index, the relative dispersion actually increased by half.

3

Leading and Lagging Industry Sectors

As we move to consider the nature of interregional shifts in employment for each industry, we need to carry along a bit of interpretive information derived from the region-by-industry cut. For example, it would be most useful to know whether an industry sector's competitive gain (or loss) for a region is greater (or less) than the all-sector competitive gain (or loss). In this way we can identify those sectors tending to lead, lag behind, or counter the competitive (developmental) tendencies of its region, taken as a whole. It would also add to our understanding of dynamic patterns if we could know whether or not a leading or lagging performance issues from a sector in which a region was initially specialized.[1]

Regional Developmental Profiles

To illustrate this leading and lagging characterization, we combine the 171 urban regions into 12 broad regions.[2] In this procedure, industry-sector and all-sector competitive shifts are normalized by expressing them as a percentage of their total interregional shifts (minus to plus). The results are depicted in table II-4. Thus, the Southeast[3] captured 24 percent of the gross all-industry competitive gains for all regions. The region's most dramatic leading sector was textiles (+92 percent of gross, all-region textile shifts). This procedure, basic to the work of volume II, gives us a summary perspective of the industry-sector contributions to the all-sector, interregional shifts examined in volume I.

There were no surprises in these shifts. The major overall losers were the Mid-Atlantic and Midwest–Great Lakes regions. Even so, in keeping with the fact that these regions are positioned differently in the total transaction network, the list of leading decliners was quite different for each. Highly specialized automobile, machinery, food, and furniture manufacturing led the relative declines of the Midwest region, while highly specialized transportation equipment, textile, and apparel manufacturing led the declines in the Mid-Atlantic region. Upper New England, the two Appalachian regions, and the Northern Plains registered only mild all-industry competitive losses. Leading decliners were concentrated in the service and transportation sectors for all four, because these transaction servicing activities tended to find greater advantage in more densely configured network fields. Upper New England and Upper Appalachia experienced lagging manufacturing declines overall, partially offset by a handful of countervailing gainers concentrated in resource and resource-processing activities. Lower Appalachia and the Northern Plains, in contrast, displayed countervailing gains in manufacturing overall, and close to half of their industries displayed offsetting gains.

There are several particularly interesting comparisons in the profiles of the regions displaying net, all-industry competitive gains. The leading gains of peninsular Florida and the Southern Mountains obviously stemmed from a similar tourist and retirement dynamic in which amusements and recreation, lodging, real estate, and retail trade are the leaders. Florida showed a greater lead in transportation because of its water and air links to Latin America. The Southern Mountain region showed greater overall strength in urban services, as historically its transaction network became progressively closer to forming a typical urban field. In both cases, manufacturing activities were lagging all-sector gains.

Metropolitan California experienced especially dramatic competitive gains overall. At first glance, the leading gains in services, trade, and transportation—along with lagging gains in manufacturing—seem to portray a dynamic mix similar to Florida and the Southern Mountains. On closer inspection, however, one sees that the leading sectors were concentrated in those services (business and professional, and government), transportation, and communication activities that are best characterized as servicing urban linkages. California is seen to have been led by its emerging role as a major national

TABLE II-4. Leading and lagging industry-sector competitive shifts in employment for twelve geographical regions, 1940–70

Upper New England		
Industry rank	S or U	Percent shift[a]
Countertrend		
Food mfg.	U	+1.2
For. & fish.	S	+1.0
Eat. & drink.	U	+0.5
Apparel mfg.	U	+0.3
Mining	U	+0.1
Mot. veh. mfg.	U	+0.1
Agric.	U	0.0
Lagging decliners		
Print. & Pub.	U	−0.1
F.I.R.E.	U	−0.2
Chem. mfg.	U	−0.3
Mach. mfg.	U	−0.6
Contr. const.	U	−1.0
Tot. retail	U	−1.0
Other trans.	U	−1.3
Other retail	U	−1.3
Food & dairy	U	−1.3
Lodg. & per.	U	−1.3
Total mfg.	U	−1.4
Amuse. & rec.	U	−1.4
Other mfg.	S	−1.6
All-sector total		−1.7
Leading decliners		
Utilities	U	−1.7
Priv. hsehold.	S	−2.0
Communic.	U	−2.3
Whole. trade	U	−2.3
Prof. serv.	S	−2.3
Total trans.	U	−2.4
Total serv.	U	−2.5
Civ. gov.	U	−2.5
Trans. equip.	S	−2.5
Truck. & whsg.	U	−3.4
R.R. trans.	U	−3.8
Textile mfg.	S	−4.3
Bus. & rep.	S	−4.7
Armed for.	S	−4.7
Lum. & wood	S	−13.7

Mid-Atlantic		
Industry rank	S or U	Percent shift[a]
Countertrend		
Bus. & rep.	S	+8.5
Agric.	U	+6.0
Lagging decliners		
Mot. veh. mfg.	U	−1.5
Whol. trade	S	−17.6
Lum. & wood	U	−19.5
Mining	U	−23.5
Mach. mfg.	S	−26.7
Civ. gov.	S	−27.2
Communic.	S	−31.8
For. & fish.	U	−36.2
Total serv.	S	−41.8
Truck & whsg.	S	−43.0
Food mfg.	U	−43.2
Armed for.	S	−43.9
Prof. serv.	S	−44.8
Amuse. & rec.	S	−46.9
Food & dairy	S	−49.4
Other mfg.	S	−51.3
All-sector total		−52.1
Leading decliners		
Chem. Mfg.	S	−52.9
Total mfg.	S	−53.1
Total trans.	S	−53.1
Other trans.	S	−53.3
Print. & pub.	S	−54.4
Total ret.	S	−55.5
R.R. trans.	U	−57.9
Other retail	S	−60.4
Contr. const.	S	−60.8
Utilities	S	−60.9
Priv. hsehld.	S	−61.5
Lodg. & per.	S	−63.2
F.I.R.E.	S	−68.0
Eat. & drink.	S	−70.8
Apparel mfg.	S	−73.9
Textile mfg.	S	−74.6
Tran. equip.	S	−96.7

Upper Appalachia		
Industry rank	S or U	Percent shift[a]
Countertrend		
Mot. veh. mfg.	U	+4.8
Lum. & wood	U	+3.2
For. & fish.	U	+2.3
Agric.	U	+1.8
Print. & pub.	U	+0.5
Lagging decliners		
Food mfg.	S	−0.2
Whol. trade	U	−0.4
Apparel mfg.	S	−0.7
Tran. equip.	U	−0.8
Eat. & drink.	U	−0.8
F.I.R.E.	U	−1.3
Amuse. & rec.	U	−2.5
Communic.	U	−2.7
Truck. & whsg.	S	−2.9
Other trans.	U	−3.0
Lodg. & per.	U	−3.1
Total retail	U	−3.6
Prof. serv.	U	−4.0
Contr. const.	S	−4.2
Total mfg.	S	−4.3
Other retail	S	−4.3
Food & dairy	U	−4.3
All-sector total		−4.4
Leading decliners		
Total serv.	U	−4.5
Priv. hsehld.	U	−5.1
Utilities	S	−5.5
Civ. gov.	S	−5.5
Mach. mfg.	S	−6.0
Chem. mfg.	U	−6.3
Other mfg.	S	−6.3
Mining	S	−6.4
Armed for.	U	−6.5
Total trans.	U	−6.8
Bus. & rep.	U	−7.5
Textile mfg.	S	−8.7
R.R. trans.	S	−27.9

Lower Appalachia		
Industry rank	S or U	Percent shift[a]
Countertrend		
For. & fish	U	+8.[illegible]
Chem. mfg.	S	+7.[illegible]
Mot. veh. mfg.	U	+7.[illegible]
Apparel mfg.	U	+6.[illegible]
Print. & pub.	U	+4.[illegible]
Mach. mfg.	U	+4.[illegible]
Total mfg.	U	+3.[illegible]
Food mfg.	U	+2.[illegible]
Textile mfg.	U	+2.[illegible]
Utilities	U	+2.[illegible]
Communic.	U	+1.[illegible]
Contr. const.	U	+1.[illegible]
Other mfg.	U	+1.[illegible]
F.I.R.E.	U	+0.[illegible]
Whole. trade	U	+0.[illegible]
Other retail	U	+0.[illegible]
Trans. equip.	U	+0.[illegible]
Armed for.	U	+0.[illegible]
Lagging decliners		
Lodg. & per.	U	0.[illegible]
Other trans.	U	−0.[illegible]
Total retail	U	−0.[illegible]
Amuse. & rec.	U	−0.[illegible]
Food & dairy	U	−0.[illegible]
All-sector total		−0.[illegible]
Leading decliners		
Eat. & drink.	U	−1.[illegible]
R.R. trans.	S	−1.[illegible]
Total trans.	U	−1.[illegible]
Priv. hsehld.	U	−1.[illegible]
Truck. & whsg.	U	−3.[illegible]
Total serv.	U	−3.[illegible]
Civ. gov.	U	−4.[illegible]
Prof. serv.	U	−4.[illegible]
Bus. & rep.	U	−5.[illegible]
Lum. & wood	S	−5.[illegible]
Agric.	S	−8.[illegible]
Mining	S	−28.[illegible]

Notes: S = Specialized; U = Unspecialized, 1940. F.I.R.E. = Finance, insurance, and real estate.

[a] $\frac{\text{Regional competitive shift}}{\text{Gross competitive shift}}$ (that is for the summary line and each industry line).

metropolitan region linking the Pacific nations and subordinate western regions into the national transactions network. There were gains in all manufacturing sectors, but these were lagging sectors with a single exception.

In many respects the developmental dynamics of the Southeast and Southern Plains regions were similar. Both displayed strong all-sector competitive gains, amounting to about a third of the U.S. total. Both displayed leading gains in manufacturing and countervailing losses in agriculture, forestry, and fisheries. They shared leading gains in food, automobiles, transportation equipment, and other manufacturing sectors, along with construction and utilities. There were significant differences, however. The Southeast was led by gains in the textile-apparel industrial complex, while the Southern Plains were led by the

'ABLE II-4. Leading and lagging industry-sector competitive shifts in employment for twelve geographical regions, 1940–70 (*Continued*)

Midwest-Great Lakes		
ıdustry rank	S or U	Percent shift[a]
Countertrend		
gric.	U	+4.5
or. & fish.	U	+4.0
rans. equip.	U	+1.4
Lagging decliners		
.R. trans.	S	−9.0
extile mfg.	U	−11.0
rmed for.	U	−15.3
ruck. & whsg.	S	−16.9
at. & drink.	S	−20.2
rof. serv.	U	−23.1
.I.R.E.	U	−24.7
odging	U	−25.3
pparel mfg.	U	−25.4
ontr. const.	U	−25.6
ther retail	S	−28.1
otal serv.	S	−28.5
riv. hshld.	U	−29.2
otal trans.	U	−30.1
otal retail	S	−30.3
tilities	S	−31.4
'hole. trade	U	−33.8
ood & dairy	S	−33.9
ll-sector total		−36.0
Leading decliners		
ining	S	−37.0
iv. gov.	U	−38.3
musc. & rec.	U	−38.4
hem. mfg.	S	−40.5
ther mfg.	S	−40.9
otal mfg.	S	−41.3
ther trans.	U	−41.5
rint. & pub.	S	−42.3
ommunic.	S	−43.3
us. & rep.	S	−49.1
um. & wood	U	−49.2
ood mfg.	S	−53.5
ach. mfg.	S	−66.7
ot. veh. mfg.	S	−98.5

Southeast		
Industry rank	S or U	Percent shift[a]
Leading Gainers		
Textile mfg.	S	+91.9
Armed for.	U	+67.3
Apparel mfg.	U	+62.5
Whole. trade	U	+42.1
Utilities	U	+39.6
Food mfg.	U	+37.5
Total mfg.	U	+36.2
Mot. veh. mfg.	U	+34.5
Truck. & whsg.	U	+31.9
Other mfg.	U	+28.6
Contr. const.	U	+27.5
Communic.	U	+25.8
Trans. equip.	U	+24.1
All-sector total		+23.8
Lagging Gainers		
F.I.R.E.	U	+23.6
Mining	U	+23.6
Mach. mfg.	U	+23.3
Other retail	U	+23.2
Total trans.	U	+22.9
Food & dairy	U	+21.3
Other trans.	U	+20.5
Total retail		+20.0
Print. & pub.	U	+18.6
Lum. & wood	S	+17.3
Priv. hshld.	S	+16.9
Chem. mfg.	U	+16.1
Lodging	U	+16.1
Eat. & drink.	U	+12.9
Civ. gov.	U	+11.5
Total serv.	U	+10.5
Amuse. & rec.	U	+9.1
Prof. serv.	U	+9.0
Bus. & rep.	U	+7.3
R.R. trans.	U	+2.4
Countertrend		
For. & fish.	S	−40.3
Agricul.	S	−79.1

Peninsular Florida		
Industry rank	S or U	Percent shift[a]
Leading Gainers		
Amuse. & rec.	S	+25.4
Other trans.	S	+25.0
Armed for.	U	+24.0
Contr. const.	S	+23.5
Lodging	S	+22.6
Total trans.	S	+21.6
Communic.	U	+21.4
Food & dairy	S	+21.2
Total retail	S	+20.7
Bus. & rep.	S	+20.8
Other retail	S	+20.3
Total serv.	U	+19.5
Eat. & drink.	S	+19.3
Prof. serv.	U	+18.5
F.I.R.E.	S	+17.6
Print. & pub.	U	+16.5
Truck & whsg.	U	+16.4
All-sector total		+15.7
Lagging Gainers		
R.R. trans.	S	+14.2
Whole. trade	S	+13.9
Priv. hshld.	S	+13.1
Agricul.	U	+12.3
Utilities	U	+12.3
Civ. gov.	U	+12.1
Food mfg.	S	+10.8
Other mfg.	U	+6.9
Mach. mfg.	U	+6.4
Total mfg.	U	+6.2
Trans. equip.	U	+5.9
Apparel mfg.	U	+5.8
Mining	U	+4.2
Chem. mfg.	U	+3.4
Mot. veh. mfg.	U	+2.4
Textile mfg.	U	+1.1
Countertrend		
Lum. & wood	S	−9.2
For. & fish.	S	−18.1

Southern Plains		
Industry rank	S or U	Percent shift[a]
Leading Gainers		
Chem. mfg.	U	+42.9
Mining	S	+41.0
Trans. equip.	U	+33.7
Utilities	U	+17.9
Contr. const.	S	+16.5
Other mfg.	U	+16.1
Total mfg.	U	+15.8
Food mfg.	U	+15.1
Civ. gov.	U	+14.4
Mach. mfg.	U	+13.6
Priv. hshld.	S	+12.6
F.I.R.E.	U	+12.3
Mot. veh. mfg.	U	+11.8
All-sector total		+11.7
Lagging Gainers		
Apparel mfg.	U	+11.7
Print. & pub.	U	+10.7
For. & fish.	U	+9.2
R.R. trans.	U	+8.8
Food & dairy	S	+8.0
Lodging	S	+8.0
Other retail	U	+7.9
Total retail	S	+6.6
Total serv.	U	+5.7
Prof. serv.	U	+5.4
Other trans.	U	+4.0
Total trans.	S	+4.0
Armed for.	S	+3.5
Amuse. & rec.	U	+3.2
Whole. trade	S	+2.1
Textile mfg.	U	+1.8
Truck. & whsg.	S	+1.5
Eat. & drink.	S	+1.1
Communic.	U	+0.7
Bus. & rep.	S	+0.7
Countertrend		
Lum. & wood	U	−4.9
Agricul.	S	−11.3

Notes: S = Specialized; U = Unspecialized, 1940. F.I.R.E. = Finance, insurance, and real estate.

[a] $\frac{\text{Regional competitive shift}}{\text{Gross competitive shift}}$ (that is for the summary line and each industry line).

petroleum-chemical-machinery industrial complex. In the Southeast the leading dynamic importance of urban-linkage services (wholesale trade, trucking and warehousing, communication) shows how its transaction field became more rationalized, articulated, and integrated with the total U.S. urban system. The developmental role played by the armed forces likewise attracts attention.

The reader can, of course, use table II-4 to spin out the tale in greater detail. More important, one can see how similar profiles for specific urban regions, counties, or any combination thereof (and for each of three decennial periods) allow one to trace the developmental dynamics of any region. The data are all readily available.[4] However, to extend this perspective here requires an additional summarizing device.

TABLE II-4. Leading and lagging industry-sector competitive shifts in employment for twelve geographical regions, 1940–70 (*Continued*)

Northern Plains

Industry rank	S or U	Percent shift[a]
Countertrend		
Agricul.	S	+31.9
Mot. veh. mfg.	U	+12.8
Mach. mfg.	U	+11.9
R.R. trans.	S	+11.8
Other mfg.	U	+9.9
For. & fish.	U	+7.1
Mining	U	+6.9
Total mfg.	U	+6.6
Armed for.	U	+5.3
Trans. equip.	U	+4.5
Other trans.	U	+3.2
Priv. hshld.	U	+2.6
Chem. mfg.	U	+1.8
Lum. & wood	U	+0.5
Lagging decliners		
Textile mfg.	U	−0.2
Apparel mfg.	U	−0.3
Utilities	U	−0.9
Print. & pub.	U	−2.6
Food mfg.	S	−2.9
All-sector total		−4.9
Leading decliners		
Other retail	U	−6.4
F.I.R.E.	U	−6.9
Contr. const.	U	−7.0
Total trans.	U	−7.5
Eat. & drink.	S	−8.7
Lodging	U	−9.3
Total retail	U	−9.9
Food & dairy	S	−11.1
Amuse. & rec.	U	−11.4
Total serv.	S	−19.9
Communic.	U	−21.8
Prof. serv.	S	−22.2
Civ. gov.	U	−24.5
Truck. & whsg.	S	−31.1
Bus. & rep.	S	−32.3
Whole. trade	S	−47.4

North. Mtn. & Pacific N.W.

Industry rank	S or U	Percent shift[a]
Leading Gainers		
For. & fish.	S	+47.7
R.R. trans.	S	+24.3
Priv. hshld.	U	+11.2
Agricul.	U	+10.6
Trans. equip.	S	+9.9
Food mfg.	U	+7.9
Eat. & drink.	S	+7.2
Chem. mfg.	U	+6.1
Prof. serv.	S	+5.9
F.I.R.E.	U	+5.2
Total serv.	S	+4.9
Other mfg.	U	+4.7
Whole. trade	S	+4.2
Total mfg.	U	+3.8
All-sector total		+3.8
Lagging Gainers		
Total retail	S	+3.7
Other retail	U	+3.6
Amuse. & rec.	S	+3.2
Mot. veh. mfg.	U	+3.1
Lodging	S	+2.8
Food & dairy	S	+2.7
Total trans.	S	+2.5
Mach. mfg.	U	+2.3
Lum. & wood	S	+2.0
Utilities	S	+1.8
Communic.	S	+1.7
Truck. & whsg.	S	+1.4
Apparel mfg.	U	+1.0
Countertrend		
Textile mfg.	U	0.0
Civ. gov.	S	−0.2
Print. & pub.	U	−0.9
Bus. & rep.	S	−1.7
Contr. const.	S	−2.5
Other trans.	S	−2.9
Mining	S	−4.8
Armed for.	S	−11.8

Southern Mountains

Industry rank	S or U	Percent shift[a]
Leading Gainers		
Amuse. & rec.	S	+40.3
Lodging	S	+24.2
Mining	S	+21.5
Eat. & drink.	S	+21.2
Civ. gov.	S	+18.3
Total serv.	S	+16.9
Prof. serv.	S	+15.4
Total retail	S	+14.9
Contr. const.	S	+13.7
Food & dairy	S	+13.5
Whole. trade	S	+13.2
F.I.R.E.	U	+13.1
For. & fish.	U	+13.1
Bus. & rep.	S	+13.0
All-sector total		+12.9
Lagging Gainers		
Other retail	U	+12.6
Print. & pub.	U	+12.4
Other trans.	U	+12.4
Total trans.	U	+11.6
Utilities	S	+11.4
Priv. hshld.	U	+10.9
Lum. & wood	U	+10.8
Truck. & whsg.	S	+10.2
Armed for.	S	+9.7
Communic.	S	+8.8
Mach. mfg.	U	+8.5
R.R. trans.	S	+7.7
Agricul.	S	+7.1
Chem. mfg.	U	+5.8
Total mfg.	U	+5.8
Trans. equip.	U	+5.5
Food mfg.	U	+5.4
Apparel mfg.	U	+5.0
Other mfg.	U	+5.0
Mot. veh. mfg.	U	+2.1
Countertrend		
Textile mfg.	U	−1.1

Metropolitan California

Industry rank	S or U	Percent shift[a]
Leading Gainers		
Lum. & wood	U	+64.
Bus. & rep.	S	+49.
Prof. serv.	S	+45.
Total serv.	S	+41.
Civ. gov.	S	+41.
Communic.	S	+38.
Truck. & whsg.	S	+38.
Print. & pub.	S	+36.
Eat. & drink.	S	+36.
Total trans.	S	+36.
Total retail	S	+33.
Priv. hshld.	U	+33.
Other trans.	S	+32.
Food & dairy	S	+32.
All-sector total		+32.
Lagging Gainers		
Other retail	S	+31.
R.R. trans.	U	+30.
Mach. mfg.	U	+29.
Other mfg.	U	+27.
Agricul.	U	+26.
F.I.R.E.	S	+26.
Lodging	S	+24.
Total mfg.	U	+22.
Whole. trade	S	+22.
Mot. veh. mfg.	U	+21.
Food mfg.	S	+19.
Amuse. & rec.	S	+17.
Contr. const.	S	+16.
Chem. mfg.	U	+16.
Trans. equip.	S	+14.
Utilities	S	+14.
For. & fish.	S	+12.
Armed for.	S	+7.
Apparel mfg.	U	+7.
Mining	U	+3.
Textile mfg.	U	+2.

Notes: S = Specialized; U = Unspecialized, 1940. F.I.R.E. = Finance, insurance, and real estate.

[a] $\frac{\text{Regional competitive shift}}{\text{Gross competitive shift}}$ (that is for the summary line and each industry line).

Classifying the Developmental Role of Industries: Code C

The concept of leading, lagging, and countervailing industries has been introduced here with a special purpose. Because it is necessary for volume II to move to a greater emphasis on developmental explanations at the level of specific industry sectors, it is necessary to focus more intensively on the regional share, or competitive, component of change. The just completed narrative (based on table II-4) demonstrates that categorizing the competitive component in this fashion adds descriptive, quasi-explanatory detail. At the same time, the mix component shrivels to a vestigial role when we consider specific industries. The mix-effect computation for a specific industry is principally valuable as an element in

TABLE II-5. Description of developmental code C

	Specialization role of industry in region	
Developmental role of industry in region	Specialized (1940)	Unspecialized (1940)
Strong leading or countertrend competitive gain	C1	C5
Weak or lagging competitive gain	C2	C6
Weak or lagging competitive loss	C3	C7
Strong leading or countertrend competitive loss	C4	C8

determining the all-sector mix effect so important in the earlier differential code profile of each region (code B). At the level of the industry sector, the mix component only tells us whether or not the industry is concentrated in the region (or conversely, whether the region specializes in the industry). It is better to factor this out for the reader and indicate it simply.

This means that we need a new way of representing change patterns corresponding to this change in emphasis. The differential code that carried us so ably through volume I does not convey the information we need at the industry-sector level. Accordingly, a new summarizing code (code C) is introduced. This developmental code is explained in table II-5. For each industry in each region, it indicates whether the region is specialized in the industry or not and whether the industry is a leading or lagging competitive gainer or a leading or lagging competitive loser.

Developmental Code Patterns

Apart from the use of historical materials, the empirical base of volume II consists of a series of maps and tables resulting from using the developmental code to classify a series of regional or county industry items. The geographical pattern formed by the county-level developmental dynamic for each industry is recorded in a corresponding color plate (following page 144). The frequency count of the number of counties in each developmental code category is detailed on the corresponding lines of table II-6. The proportion of the total (positive or negative) competitive shift accounted for by the county frequencies in each category is shown in table II-7.[5] Other representations will follow in succeeding chapters. These maps and tables point to the salient explanations needed to understand urban-system dynamics at a deeper level.

Panels B and C of table II-6 illustrate how different arrangements can highlight different combinations of attributes. All of this yields so much detail that the kinds of generalizations appropriate in an introductory chapter such as this are difficult to perceive. The reader should understand that, like other materials in part one, these tables and maps are intended to serve as basic reference tools throughout the balance of the study. The detail is necessary and appropriate because we will be moving directly to an explanation of the developmental dynamics at an industry-sector level. We pause here only to illustrate how these materials can be employed.

First, note that in panel B of table II-6, 70 percent of the county-industry items register competitive gains. Clearly the developmental effects were widely distributed during this period (both functionally and geographically). The most extensive experience of competitive gains was in the resource and manufacturing sectors (plus other transportation, utilities, finance and real estate, and the armed forces), while the most extensive experience of competitive losses was in the urban-servicing trade and service activities. Thus during this era, the resource and intermediate processing activities of society became more widely dispersed, while the final demand, urban-servicing activities became more tightly concentrated in the urban centers and their associated primary transaction fields. Key information-processing sectors (business, professional, and governmental activities) were particularly inclined to restrict their gains to a smaller number of centers. The first eight columns in table II-6 indicate that while the spread of manufacturing was taking place at a declining rate at the close of the period, the concentration of urban-servicing activities was actually accelerating.

In 1940, slightly under 20 percent of the county-industry observations revealed the county to be specialized in the industry under examination (panel C, table II-6). It is not surprising, therefore, that the largest incidence of gains (59 percent) was in unspecialized counties. The reverse was true for the unspecialized items. In short, in 1940 the odds of experiencing future competitive gains were substantially greater for those activities in which the counties were not specialists. The upshot of this is that, by 1970, the proportion of county-industry items recording specializations had increased from almost 20 percent to almost 30 percent. In chapter 5, we will inquire whether there might be some clue about the nature of the developmental process lurking here.

There were exceptions to the overall frequency patterns just noted. For agriculture, wood products manufacturing, and business and professional services, specialized counties experienced a higher incidence of gains as well as losses. Thus, for these sectors, the likelihood of experiencing a competitive gain was higher within existing regions of specialization than for the unspecialized regions.

Nor is this the whole story. So far, we have been focusing on the frequency counts exclusively. If we shift

TABLE II-6. County frequency tabulations, industry × code C, 1940–70

Panel A: basic code tabulation

Industry	Specialized strong gain[a]	Specialized weak gain[a]	Specialized weak loss[a]	Specialized strong loss[a]	Unspecialized strong gain[a]	Unspecialized weak gain[a]	Unspecialized weak loss[a]	Unspecialized strong loss[a]	Total counties
1. Agriculture	**1,003**–	**249**–	**71**–	**1,202**+ +	253+	143+	67+	77–	3,065
2. For. & fish.	**306**+ +	80+	17–	**361**+ +	**1,083**–	899– –	138– –	181+	3,065
3. Mining	**226**+	56+ +	33+ +	**400**+	**1,018**+	**1,186**– –	51– –	95–	3,065
4. Contr. const.	**172**+ +	**313**+ +	**50**+ +	**443**+ +	821– –	585– –	**318**– –	363–	3,065
5. Food mfg.	**184**+ +	69+ +	30+	184+	**1,101**– –	1,000– –	**238**+	259+ +	3,065
6. Textile mfg.	**161**+	19+	11–	172+	**1,078**+	**1,462**– –	64+	98+	3,065
7. Apparel mfg.	93+ +	24+ +	26+	162+	**1,477**– –	**1,152**– –	60+	71+ +	3,065
8. Print. & pub.	44+	34+ +	30+	71+	783+	**1,443**– –	**355**+	305+ +	3,065
9. Chem. mfg.	65+	25+ +	23+	207+	**1,058**+	**1,325**–	149+	213–	3,065
10. Lum. & wood	**329**–	**126**+	19+	**679**+ +	**873**+	737– –	129+	173+	3,065
11. Machinery mfg.	61+	21+ +	23+	113+	**1,341**+	**1,426**– –	50+	30–	3,065
12. Mot. veh. mfg.	57+	9+ +	6+	41+	**1,252**+	**1,626**– –	46+	28+ +	3,065
13. Trans. equip.	31+ +	17+	13+	71+	**1,217**+	**1,606**– –	67+	43+ +	3,065
14. Other mfg.	105+ +	46+ +	**61**+ +	218–	**1,424**+	**1,095**– –	60+	56–	3,065
15. R.R. trans.	**264**+	82–	**51**+ +	**386**+	559+	768–	**227**– –	**728**–	3,065
16. Truck. & whsg.	120+	133–	**63**+ +	**826**+	458+	625–	**226**– –	**614**–	3,065
17. Other trans.	47+	34+ +	19+	159+	981– –	**1,292**– –	**259**+	274+ +	3,065
18. Communication	59+	86+	34+	246+ +	568– –	994– –	**318**– –	**760**+ +	3,065
19. Utilities	127+ +	**138**+ +	**83**+ +	248+ +	**1,398**– –	721– –	190– –	160+ +	3,065
20. Whole. trade	53+	69–	25+ +	**326**–	541–	**1,055**+	**301**+	695–	3,065
21. Food & dairy	95+ +	147+ +	**85**+ +	200+ +	480– –	**1,260**– –	**428**– –	370+ +	3,065
22. Eat. & drink.	138+ +	181+ +	**91**+ +	201+ +	779– –	997–	**364**– –	314–	3,065
23. Other retail	73+	**143**+ +	**98**+ +	267+ +	671– –	970– –	**313**– –	**530**+	3,065
24. F.I.R.E.	44+	40+	25+	40+	821– –	**1,554**– –	**402**+	139+ +	3,065
25. Personal serv.	134+	**150**+ +	**73**+ +	166+ +	720–	**1,052**–	**390**– –	**380**–	3,065
26. Bus. & repair	56–	**138**–	37–	**747**–	106– –	578+	213+	**1,190**+ +	3,065
27. Amuse. & rec.	72+	**119**–	42+	232+	564– –	910–	**392**+	**734**+ +	3,065
28. Priv. hsehld.	**339**+ +	**156**+ +	**46**+ +	250+ +	**961**+	634– –	**265**– –	**414**–	3,065
29. Prof. serv.	133+	**148**–	**80**+	**427**+	187+	749+	210– –	**1,131**–	3,065
30. Civ. gov.	71+ +	**151**+	**67**+	285–	304+	743+	**438**– –	**1,006**–	3,065
31. Armed forc.	20+	6+	2+	107+	**1,073**–	**1,814**–	18+	25+ +	3,065
Total (1940–70)	4,682	3,009	1,334	9,437	25,950	32,401	6,746	11,456	95,015
Average	151	97	43	304	837	1,045	218	370	3.065
Percent	4.92	3.17	1.40	9.93	27.31	34.10	7.10	12.05	100.00
Intermediate aggregates (%)[b]									
Total resources (ind. 1–3)	**16.69**–	**4.19**–	1.32+	**21.35**+	25.60+	24.23–	2.78–	3.84–	100.00
Total manufact. (ind. 5–14)	3.69+	1.27+	.79+	6.26+	**37.86**+	**42.00**–	3.97+	4.16+	100.00
Transaction serv. (ind. 15–20)	3.64+	2.95	**1.50**+	**11.91**+	24.50–	29.66–	**8.27**+	**17.57**+	100.00
Retail trade (ind. 21–23)	3.33+	**5.12**+	**2.98**+	7.26+	20.99–	**35.10**–	**12.02**–	**13.20**+	100.00
Total services (ind. 24–29)	4.23+	**4.08**–	**1.65**+	**10.13**+	18.27–	29.78–	**10.18**–	**21.69**+	100.00

Notes: Boldface numbers indicate cell counts that are above the all-sector average. Table II-6 is a table of county frequencies corresponding to the color plates.

[a] Indication of gains or losses in cell frequency between first and last decade of period. Double sign indicates above or below average change; in effect, the sign and rough magnitude of the rate derivative.

[b] Intermediate aggregates expressed as percentage distribution of frequencies to facilitate comparison.

TABLE II-6. County frequency tabulations, industry × code C, 1940–70 (*Continued*)

Panel B: gain and loss tabulations

Industry	Strong gain 1 & 5[a]	Weak gain 2 & 6[a]	Weak loss 3 & 7[a]	Strong loss 4 & 8[a]	Compet. gain 1,2,5,6[a]	Compet. loss 3,4,7,8[a]	Total counties
1. Agriculture	**1,256** –	392 –	138 –	**1,279** + +	1,648 – –	**1,417** + +	3,065
2. For. & fish.	**1,389** + +	979 – –	155 –	542 + +	**2,368** – –	697 + +	3,065
3. Mining	**1,244** + +	**1,242** – –	84 +	495 +	**2,486** –	579 +	3,065
4. Contr. const.	**993** + +	898 –	**368** +	**806** +	1,891 –	**1,174** +	3,065
5. Food mfg.	**1,285** + +	1,069 – –	**268** + +	443 +	**2,354** –	711 +	3,065
6. Textile mfg.	**1,239** + +	**1,481** – –	75 + +	270 +	**2,720** –	345 +	3,065
7. Apparel mfg.	**1,570** + +	**1,176** – –	86 + +	233 +	**2,746** –	319 +	3,065
8. Print. & pub.	827 + +	**1,477** – –	**385** + +	376 +	**2,304** –	761 +	3,065
9. Chem. mfg.	**1,123** + +	**1,350** –	172 + +	420 +	**2,473** –	592 +	3,065
10. Lum. & wood	**1,202** –	863 – –	148 +	852 + +	2,065 – –	**1,000** + +	3,065
11. Machinery mfg.	**1,402** + +	**1,447** – –	73 + +	143 +	**2,849** –	216 +	3,065
12. Mot. veh. mfg.	**1,309** + +	**1,635** – –	52 + +	69 +	**2,944** – –	121 + +	3,065
13. Trans. equip.	**1,248** + +	**1,623** – –	80 + +	114 +	**2,871** – –	194 + +	3,065
14. Other mfg.	**1,529** + +	1,141 – –	121 + +	274 –	**2,670** +	395 –	3,065
15. R.R. trans.	823 + +	850 –	**278** –	**1,114** –	1,673 +	**1,392** –	3,065
16. Truck. & whsg.	578 + +	758 –	**289** –	**1,440** –	1,336 +	**1,729** –	3,065
17. Other trans.	**1,028** –	**1,326** – –	**278** + +	433 + +	**2,354** – –	711 + +	3,065
18. Communication	627 –	1,080 – –	**352** –	**1,006** + +	1,707 – –	**1,358** + +	3,065
19. Utilities	**1,525** –	859 – –	**273** +	408 + +	**2,384** – –	681 + +	3,065
20. Whole. trade	594 + +	1,124 +	**326** + +	**1,021** –	1,718 +	**1,347** –	3,065
21. Food & dairy	575 –	**1,407** – –	**513** –	570 + +	1,982 – –	**1,083** + +	3,065
22. Eat. & drink.	917 –	**1,178** – –	**455** + +	515 + +	2,095 – –	**970** + +	3,065
23. Other retail	744 –	1,113 – –	**411** –	**797** + +	1,857 – –	**1,208** + +	3,065
24. F.I.R.E.	865 –	**1,594** – –	**427** + +	179 + +	**2,459** – –	606 + +	3,065
25. Personal serv.	854 + +	**1,202** –	**463** –	546 +	2,056 –	**1,009** +	3,065
26. Bus. & repair	162 –	716 –	250 +	**1,937** + +	878 – –	**2,187** + +	3,065
27. Amuse. & rec.	637 –	1,029 –	**434** + +	**966** + +	1,665 – –	**1,400** + +	3,065
28. Priv. hsehld.	**1,300** + +	790 – –	**311** –	664 –	2,090 +	**975** –	3,065
29. Prof. serv.	320 + +	897 +	**290** –	**1,558** –	1,217 +	**1,848** –	3,065
30. Civ. gov.	375 + +	894 +	**505** –	**1,291** –	1,269 +	**1,796** –	3,065
31. Armed forc.	**1,093** –	**1,820** –	20 + +	132 + +	**2,913** – –	152 + +	3,065
Total (1940–70)	30,632 +	35,410 – –	8,080 +	20,893 + +	66,042 – –	28,973 + +	95,015
Average	988	1,142	261	674	2,130	935	3,065
Percent	32.24	37.27	8.50	21.98	69.50	30.49	100.00
Intermediate aggregates (%)[b]							
Total resources (ind. 1–3)	**42.29** –	28.42 –	4.10 –	**25.19** +	**70.71** –	29.29 +	100
Total manufact. (ind. 5–14)	**41.55** +	**43.27** –	4.76 +	10.42 +	**84.82** –	15.18 +	100
Transaction serv. (ind. 15–20)	28.14 –	32.61 –	**9.77** +	**29.48** +	60.75 –	**39.25** +	100
Retail trade (ind. 21–23)	24.32 –	**40.22** –	**15.00** –	20.47 +	64.54 –	**35.46** +	100
Total services (ind. 24–29)	22.50 –	33.87 –	**11.83** +	**31.81** +	56.36 –	**43.64** +	100

Notes: Boldface numbers indicate cell counts that are above the all-sector average. Table II-6 is a table of county frequencies corresponding to the color plates.

[a] Indication of gains or losses in cell frequency between first and last decade of period. Double sign indicates above or below average change; in effect, the sign and rough magnitude of the rate derivative.

[b] Intermediate aggregates expressed as percentage distribution of frequencies to facilitate comparison.

TABLE II-6. County frequency tabulations, industry × code C, 1940–70 (*Continued*)

Panel C: Specialized and unspecialized combinations

Industry	Specialized 1–4[a]	Unspecial-ized 5–8[a]	Specialized Gains 1 & 2[a]	Specialized Losses 3 & 4[a]	Unspecialized Gains 5 & 6[a]	Unspecialized Losses 7 & 8[a]	Specialized net gains & losses[a]	Unspecial-ized net gains & losses[a]	Total net gains & losses[a]
1. Agriculture	**2,525** −	540 +	**1,252** −	**1,273** + +	396 +	144 −	− **21** −	+ 252 +	+ 231
2. For. & fish.	**764** + +	2,301 − −	**386** + +	**378** + +	**1,982** − −	319 −	+ **8** + +	+ **1,663** − −	+ **1,671**
3. Mining	**715** +	2,350 −	**282** + +	**433** + +	**2,204** −	146 −	− 151 +	+ **2,058** −	+ **1,907**
4. Contr. const.	**978** + +	2,087 − −	**385** + +	**493** + +	1,406 − −	**681** −	− 108 + +	+ 725 − −	+ 617
5. Food mfg.	467 + +	**2,598** − −	**253** + +	214 +	**2,101** − −	497 + +	+ **39** + +	+ **1,604** − −	+ **1,643**
6. Textile mfg.	363 +	**2,702** −	180 +	183 +	**2,540** −	162 + +	− 3 +	+ **2,378** −	+ **2,475**
7. Apparel mfg.	305 + +	**2,760** − −	117 + +	188 +	**2,629** − −	131 + +	− **71** + +	+ **2,498** − −	+ **2,427**
8. Print. & pub.	179 +	**2,886** −	78 +	101 +	**2,226** −	**660** + +	− **23** +	+ **1,566** −	+ **1,543**
9. Chem. mfg.	320 +	**2,745** −	90 + +	230 +	**2,383** −	362 +	− 140 +	+ **2,021** −	+ **1,881**
10. Lum. & wood	**1,153** +	1,912 −	**455** −	**698** + +	1,610 −	302 +	− 243 +	+ 1,308 −	+ 1,065
11. Machinery mfg.	218 +	**2,847** −	82 + +	136 +	**2,767** −	80 −	− **54** +	+ **2,687** −	+ **2,633**
12. Mot. veh. mfg.	113 +	**2,952** −	66 + +	47 +	**2,878** − −	74 + +	+ **19** +	+ **2,804** −	+ **2,823**
13. Trans. equip.	132 +	**2,933** −	48 + +	84 +	**2,823** − −	110 + +	− **36** +	+ **2,713** −	+ **2,677**
14. Other mfg.	430 +	**2,635** −	151 + +	279 +	**2,519** −	116 −	128 +	+ **2,403** −	+ **2,275**
15. R.R. trans.	783 +	2,282 −	**346** +	**437** +	1,327 +	**955** −	− **91** +	+ 372 −	+ 281
16. Truck. & whsg.	**1,142** +	1,923 −	**253** −	**889** +	1,083 +	**840** −	− 636 +	+ 243 −	− 393
17. Other trans.	259 +	**2,806** −	81 +	178 +	**2,273** − −	533 + +	− **97** +	+ **1,740** −	+ **1,643**
18. Communication	425 +	**2,640** −	145 +	280 + +	1,562 − −	**1,078** + +	− 135 +	+ 484 −	+ 349
19. Utilities	596 + +	**2,469** − −	**265** + +	331 + +	**2,119** − −	350 + +	− **66** + +	+ **1,769** − −	+ **1,703**
20. Whole. trade	473 +	**2,592** −	122 +	**351** + +	1,596 +	**996** −	− 229 +	+ 600 −	+ 371
21. Food & dairy	527 + +	**2,538** − −	242 + +	285 + +	1,740 − −	**798** + +	− **43** + +	+ 942 − −	+ 899
22. Eat. & drink.	**611** + +	2,454 − −	**319** + +	292 + +	1,776 − −	**678** −	+ **27** + +	+ 1,098 − −	+ 1,125
23. Other retail	581 + +	**2,484** − −	216 + +	**365** + +	1,641 − −	**843** −	− 149 + +	+ 798 − −	+ 649
24. F.I.R.E.	149 +	**2,916** −	84 +	65 +	**2,375** − −	541 + +	+ **19** +	+ **1,834** −	+ **1,853**
25. Personal serv.	523 + +	**2,542** − −	**284** + +	239 + +	1,772 −	**770** −	+ **45** + +	+ 1,002 − −	+ 1,047
26. Bus. & repair	**978** −	2,087 +	194 −	**784** −	684 − −	**1,403** + +	− 590 −	− 719 +	− 1,309
27. Amuse. & rec.	465 +	**2,600** −	191 −	274 +	1,474 − −	**1,126** + +	− **83** +	+ 348 −	+ 265
28. Priv. hsehld.	**791** + +	2,274 − −	**495** + +	296 + +	1,595 +	**679** −	+ **199** + +	+ 916 − −	+ 1,115
29. Prof. serv.	**788** +	2,277 −	**281** +	**507** +	936 +	**1,341** −	− 226 +	− 405 −	− 631
30. Civ. gov.	574 −	**2,491** +	222 + +	**352** −	1,047 +	**1,444** −	− 130 +	− 397 −	− 527
31. Armed forc.	135 +	**2,930** −	26 + +	109 +	**2,887** − −	43 + +	− **83** +	+ **2,844** −	+ **2,761**
Total (1940–70)	18,462 + +	76,553 − −	7,691 +	10,771 + +	58,351 − −	18,202 +	−3,180	+40,149	+36,969
Average	596	2,469	248	347	1,882	587	− 103	+ 1,295	+ 1,193
Percent	19.43	80.56	8.09	11.34	61.41	19.16	3.35	42.26	38.91
Intermediate aggregates (%)[b]									
Total resources (ind. 1–3)	**43.54** +	56.45 −	**20.88** −	**22.66** + +	49.83 −	6.62 −	− 1.78	+ **43.21**	+ **41.42**
Total manufact. (ind. 5–14)	12.01 +	**87.99** −	4.96 + +	7.05 +	**79.86** − −	8.14 + +	− 2.09	+ **71.72**	+ **69.63**
Transaction serv. (ind. 15–20)	**20.00** +	80.00 −	6.59 +	**13.41** +	54.16 −	**25.84** +	− **6.82**	+ 28.32	+ 21.50
Retail trade (ind. 21–23)	18.69 + +	**81.31** − −	**8.45** + +	10.24 + +	56.08 − −	**25.22** −	− 1.79	+ 30.86	+ 29.07
Total services (ind. 24–29)	**20.09** +	79.91 −	**8.31** −	**11.77** +	48.05 −	**31.87** +	− **3.46**	+ 16.18	+ 12.72

Notes: Boldface numbers indicate cell counts that are above the all-sector average. Table II-6 is a table of county frequencies corresponding to the color plates.

[a] Indication of gains or losses in cell frequency between first and last decade of period. Double sign indicates above or below average change; in effect, the sign and rough magnitude of the rate derivative.

[b] Intermediate aggregates expressed as percentage distribution of frequencies to facilitate comparison.

TABLE II-7. Proportion of the net positive and negative competitive shifts in employment accounted for by each of the C-code classes for each industry, 1940–70

	Specialized				Unspecialized				
Industry	Leading gains	Lagging gains	Lagging losses	Leading losses	Leading gains	Lagging gains	Lagging losses	Leading losses	Total (percent)
Agriculture	62.1	6.3	−1.0	−93.8	18.2	13.4	−1.7	−3.5	±100
Forestry & fishing	49.2	3.0	−3.4	−86.5	38.2	9.6	−5.1	−5.0	±100
Mining	45.6	2.1	−2.6	−93.9	39.6	12.7	−1.0	−2.4	±100
Contr. const.	35.4	31.6	−12.5	−54.5	27.4	5.6	−25.0	−8.0	±100
Food manufacturing	27.8	11.8	−12.1	−54.7	44.1	16.3	−26.2	−7.1	±100
Textile	63.5	.4	−.8	−86.1	27.9	8.1	−7.4	−5.7	±100
Apparel	13.8	.7	−17.4	−75.4	68.0	17.5	−3.4	−3.8	±100
Printing & publishing	21.9	13.0	−12.8	−74.0	38.1	27.1	−7.5	−5.7	±100
Chemical manufacturing	23.2	3.1	−31.1	−55.1	54.7	19.0	−7.1	−6.8	±100
Lumber & wood	45.9	1.5	−.8	−74.3	35.5	17.2	−17.8	−7.2	±100
Machine manufacturing	11.7	4.8	−12.7	−77.4	58.7	24.8	−9.2	−.8	±100
Motor vehicle mfg.	31.7	.3	−1.7	−89.0	52.6	15.4	−8.4	−.8	±100
Trans. equip.	22.2	4.1	−21.1	−68.4	57.3	16.4	−9.0	−1.5	±100
Other manufacturing	9.5	6.2	−17.4	−65.3	53.0	31.3	−16.0	−1.4	±100
R. R. trans.	56.3	7.3	−11.2	−52.6	18.5	18.0	−16.2	−19.9	±100
Truck. & whsg.	32.9	9.1	−32.8	−45.1	33.6	24.3	−8.5	−13.6	±100
Other trans.	36.7	6.2	−30.5	−51.5	31.7	25.4	−10.7	−7.3	±100
Communications	26.9	15.1	−30.5	−44.5	37.7	20.3	−9.0	−16.0	±100
Utilities	11.9	28.2	−25.0	−62.7	45.0	14.8	−8.5	−3.9	±100
Wholesale trade	32.0	13.3	−34.7	−40.6	37.0	17.7	−9.4	−15.4	±100
Eat. & drink.	23.6	20.9	−25.3	−60.7	33.5	22.0	−8.4	−5.6	±100
Food & dairy	21.2	30.4	−42.3	−41.8	28.0	20.4	−6.4	−9.5	±100
Other retail	26.0	26.4	−18.8	−64.2	27.9	19.7	−9.7	−7.3	±100
F.I.R.E.	25.7	21.1	−18.4	−70.5	27.2	26.0	−8.7	−2.3	±100
Lodging & per. serv.	31.0	21.8	21.9	−57.7	21.4	25.8	−11.7	−8.8	±100
Bus. & repair	57.6	12.4	−24.2	−31.9	17.9	12.2	−12.2	−31.6	±100
Amusement & rec.	37.6	22.0	−40.5	−31.2	24.7	15.7	−13.9	−14.3	±100
Private household	26.8	16.7	−7.3	−25.3	42.2	14.2	−40.9	−26.6	±100
Prof. services	38.0	19.2	−42.2	−18.8	22.5	20.2	−15.3	−23.7	±100
Civ. gov.	31.3	13.8	−36.4	−31.9	36.0	19.0	−13.7	18.1	±100
Military	16.1	.9	−.2	−87.0	70.1	13.0	−11.7	−1.1	±100
All-industry shifts	28.7	13.3 (42.0)	−21.3	−57.3 (78.6)	38.4	19.6 (58.0)	−12.0	−9.4 (21.4)	±100
All-industry county frequency count[a]	7.1	4.6 (11.5)	−4.6	−33.6 (38.2)	39.2	49.1 (88.3)	−23.3	−39.5 (62.8)	±100

Note: Numbers in parentheses are sums of gains or losses within specialized or unspecialized categories.
[a] See chapter note 5.

from the likelihood of experiencing gains or losses to their dimension, as represented in table II-7, the picture changes in an important way. Taking into account all industry sectors, specialized counties accounted for more than three-fourths of the total losses. So far, this is consistent with the picture given by the frequency count. Since these losses were accounted for by only 11 percent of all county-industry items (panel C in table II-6), we can also see how extremely localized were the areas disadvantaged by the developmental dynamic.

However, the 8 percent of all county-industry items that were specialized (and that nonetheless recorded competitive gains) accounted for 42 percent of all competitive gains. Clearly the specialized counties that continued to do well did very well. These were most heavily concentrated in certain manufacturing and transaction-service categories. All of this suggests two different aspects of the developmental changes at work during the study period. There was clearly a general tendency for the experience of activity specialization to be spread progressively to formerly unspecialized counties. At the same time, an important part of the dynamic was a rearrangement of activities between already specialized areas.

There is a bit of support in these records for the old basic–nonbasic hypothesis. The leading gain category (C1 + C5) displays both above-average frequency counts and proportional shifts associated with resource and manufacturing sectors. Above-average frequencies for weak gains and losses are more apt to be associated with urban-service sectors. Thus, there is something to the notion that the so-called basic activities tend to lead, while urban-servicing activities follow. However, in an advanced urban society such as ours, this venerable generalization is so riddled with exceptions as to raise serious questions about its utility. Every industry sector (save one) served to lead the gains of more than 10 percent of all U.S. counties. The leading gain items account for less than 50 percent of the total competitive gain for only one industry sector. This includes the urban-service sectors. Furthermore, the major rearrangement in transaction networks that occurred during this era made many localized urban services the most likely source of leading losses: In any given geographic field and over any given period, any industry sector may turn out to be basic in the sense that its development is for a time a leading source of localized growth and development (or decline).

So much for the overview. In chapters 4 and 5 we examine additional perspectives provided by our newly found developmental code.

Notes

1. This perspective was introduced in chaper 15 in volume I, which employed synthetic B code regions. There it served to summarize the work of part three and to anticipate volume II.
2. Employing the aggregating scheme outlined in map 8 in volume 1.
3. Capitalization of U.S. regions in this book does not follow conventional rules.
4. Regional Economic Analysis Division, Bureau of Economic Analysis, U.S. Department of Commerce.
5. In table II-6, the county frequency count for each industry is identical; hence, interindustry comparisons can be made without complication. The actual employment shifts underlying table II-7 are not dimensionally commensurable in the same way. They are expressed as percentages of the net positive and negative total shift for each industry sector. The bottom line of table II-7 reproduces the total frequency line from table II-6 converted to commensurable percentage terms.

4

Some Systemic Characteristics of Industry-Sector Shifts

Chapter 13 of volume I developed the urban-system characteristics of the shift-share technique with respect to the summary line shifts corresponding to the differential code (B). In this chapter something similar is undertaken with respect to the whole array of industry sectors by employing developmental code categories (that is, C codes) that focus attention on competitive shifts.

We begin by aggregating all county units in accordance with their familiar trade-center and household-transaction-field characteristics. Then for each aggregated set, competitive shifts are arrayed to identify each industry as a leading (countertrend) or lagging gainer, and conversely a leading (countertrend) or lagging loser. For the period 1940–70 the results are depicted in the tables in this chapter. This echoes the procedure followed for twelve geographical regions in table II-4.

This representation is supplemented by frequency patterns formed by tabulating industry-by-county developmental code descriptors corresponding to these synthetic regions. The complete frequency tabulations for 1940–70 are found on microfiche in appendix II-L. Percentage distributions for a variety of C code combinations are in appendix II-M. Additional derived tables are in appendixes II-J and II-K.[1]

Trade-Center Shift Patterns

The competitive shifts experienced by trade-center categories are provided in table II-8. The summary, all-sector competitive shifts correspond to those in the last column of panel B in table 34, in volume I (p. 158). Thus, table II-8 provides an "industry-sector explosion" of the overall patterns previously considered. We are reminded again that most of the total competitive shifts were restricted to the highest order trade centers (plus complete shopping centers). The large metropolitan centers accounted for virtually all of the net competitive losses, while large wholesale-retail, complete shopping, and small metropolitan centers (in that order) accounted for the bulk of the gains. In net terms, the small wholesale-retail centers and the lowest order trade centers accounted for little.

But this overall view hides a revealing part of the story. Take the case of the large metropolitan centers. Although these centers accounted for virtually all of the net total competitive losses, eight industry sectors displayed, on balance, substantial countertrend competitive gains. Three of these were resource sectors (a seeming anomaly we will consider shortly). Three (railroads, trucking and warehousing, and wholesale trade) are major urban-linkage services, while two (business and professional services) are the principal emerging information-processing activities. The proportions of their respective sector gains are impressive. Such centers, for example, accounted for three-quarters of all of the net total system gains in business services.

Competitive losses of the large metropolitan centers were dominated by manufacturing and retail sectors, while the aggregate of all service sectors broke even. It is interesting that the manufacturing losses were lagging rather than leading the transformation, contrary to what the media suggested. Household-oriented retail and personal service activities lead the relative declines. During the study period large metropolitan centers shifted their urban-service functions from household, final-demand-oriented functions to business-and-intermediate-activity-oriented support functions. In this connection it is also well to note that the net competitive losses experienced by two urban-linkage, information-servicing sectors (civil government and communications) lagged substantially behind all-sector losses. This suggests that they, too, retained a measure of metropolitan center strength. All of this suggests that the relative dominance of large

TABLE II-8. Leading and lagging industry-sector competitive shifts in employment for trade-center classification regions, 1940–70

Metropolitan, large		
Industry rank	S or U	Percent shift[a]
Countertrend		
Bus. & rep.	S	+72.7
R.R. trans.	S	+56.2
Agriculture	U	+53.7
Mining	U	+48.5
Truck. & whsg.	S	+39.0
Wholesale trade	S	+23.9
Prof. services	S	+12.2
For. & fish.	U	+9.2
Lagging decliners		
Total services		−0.2
Civ. gov.	S	−33.2
Lum. & wood	U	−39.4
Textile mfg.	U	−55.8
Other mfg.	S	−69.9
Communic.	S	−75.2
Armed for.	S	−76.4
Amuse. & rec.	S	−80.1
Mach. mfg.	S	−85.8
Chem. mfg.	S	−91.8
Total mfg.		−96.6
Food & dairy	S	−96.8
Contr. const.	S	−97.6
Food mfg.	S	−97.8
Mot. veh. mfg.	S	−98.9
All-sector line R_{ij}		−98.9
Leading decliners		
Total retail		−99.3
Priv. hsehld.	S	−99.4
Trans. equip.	S	−99.6
Apparel mfg.	S	−99.7
Other retail	S	−99.9
Lodg. & pers.	S	−100.0
F.I.R.E.	S	−100.0
Eat. & drink.	S	−100.0
Utilities	S	−100.0
Other trans.	S	−100.0
Print. & pub.	S	−100.0

Metropolitan, small		
Industry rank	S or U	Percent shift[a]
Leading gainers		
R.R. trans.	S	+23.1
Mining	S	+22.0
Civ. gov.	U	+21.2
Whol. trade	S	+19.8
Trans. equip.	U	+18.9
Other retail	S	+18.4
Total serv.		+17.6
Prof. serv.	S	+16.0
All-sector line R_{ij}		+12.9
Lagging gainers		
Priv. hsehld.	S	+11.1
Food & dairy	S	+10.5
Total retail		+9.7
Truck. & whsg.	S	+9.2
F.I.R.E.	S	+8.9
Other mfg.	U	+8.7
Utilities	S	+8.7
Contr. const.	S	+8.5
Lodg. & pers.	S	+8.0
Communic.	S	+7.8
Amuse. & rec.	S	+6.6
Other trans.	S	+5.9
Bus. & repair	S	+5.9
Eat. & drink.	S	+5.6
Apparel mfg.	U	+4.3
Total mfg.		+4.0
Print. & pub.	S	+3.4
Agriculture	U	+2.0
Chem. mfg.	U	+1.7
Countertrend		
Textile mfg.	U	−0.2
Mot. Veh. mfg.	S	−0.3
Armed for.	S	−0.5
Mach. mfg.	U	−1.4
For. & fish.	S	−1.7
Food mfg.	S	−2.0
Lum. & wood	S	−20.2

Wholesale-retail, large		
Industry rank	S or U	Percent shift[a]
Leading gainers		
Amuse. & rec.	U	+87.4
For. & fish.	U	+80.3
Total services		+78.4
Communications	U	+77.0
Prof. serv.	S	+68.9
Other retail	S	+65.5
Food & dairy	S	+64.4
Civ. gov.	U	+64.3
Total retail		+61.8
Lum. & wood	U	+60.5
Contr. const.	S	+60.1
Eat. & drink.	U	+55.3
Lodg. & pers.	U	+54.6
Print. & pub.	U	+52.0
Whol. trade	U	+52.0
F.I.R.E.	U	+51.4
All-sector line R_{ij}		+47.8
Lagging gainers		
Chem. mfg.	S	+47.0
Agriculture	U	+42.6
Truck. & whsg.	U	+41.3
Mot. veh. mfg.	U	+33.5
Bus. & repair	U	+20.9
Priv. hsehld.	S	+19.5
Armed For.	S	+17.1
Trans. equip.	S	+15.9
Other trans.	U	+10.7
Food mfg.	S	+9.9
Utilities	S	+9.0
R.R. trans.	S	+8.2
Apparel mfg.	U	+5.7
Countertrend		
Total mfg.		−3.6
Mach. mfg.	S	−12.9
Other mfg.	S	−30.3
Textile mfg.	S	−41.0
Mining	S	−46.6

Notes: S = specialized; U = unspecialized, 1940. F.I.R.E. = Finance, insurance, and real estate.

[a] $\frac{\text{Regional competitive shift}}{\text{Gross competitive shift}}$ (that is, for the summary line and each industry line)

metropolitan centers declined with respect to the more localized, population-oriented activities while the relative dominance of such centers increased in fields formed by interregional, intermediate, business-oriented transaction networks.

Given this scenario, it may seem inconsistent that four of the urban-linkage and information-processing sectors were prominent leading decliners in these large centers. However, each was responsive to uniquely changing linkage factors. For example, finance, insurance, and real estate activities provided facilitating transaction services to a transaction network that was becoming more extensive and more finely articulated. Public utilities provided direct distribution and collection services serving a spreading manufacturing-based network. Printing and publishing was dominated by newspaper publishing and

TABLE II-8. Leading and lagging industry-sector competitive shifts in employment for trade-center classification regions, 1940–70 *(Continued)*

Wholesale-retail, small

Industry rank	S or U	Percent shift[a]
Leading gainers		
Mining	S	+17.0
Priv. hsehld.	S	+6.3
Civ. gov.	U	+4.2
Communic.	U	+4.0
For. & fish.	U	+3.8
R.R. trans.	S	+3.0
Other retail	U	+2.6
Total retail		+2.4
Eat. & drink.	U	+2.4
Trans. equip.	U	+2.3
Food & dairy	S	+2.3
Other mfg.	U	+2.2
F.I.R.E.	U	+2.2
Contr. const.	U	+2.0
Food mfg.	S	+2.0
Lodg. & pers.	S	+2.0
Chem. mfg.	U	+1.8
Amuse. & rec.	U	+1.6
Summary line R_{ij}		+1.5
Lagging gainers		
Total service		+1.5
Print. & pub.	U	+1.3
Prof. serv.	S	+1.0
Utilities	S	+0.9
Mach. mfg.	U	+0.7
Total mfg.		+0.6
Apparel mfg.	U	+0.2
Countertrend		
Agriculture	S	−0.6
Truck. & whsg.	S	−0.6
Mot. veh. mfg.	U	−0.8
Bus. & repair	U	−1.0
Other trans.	U	−2.1
Textile mfg.	U	−3.0
Armed for.	S	−4.6
Whol. trade	S	−5.3
Lum. & wood	S	−18.2

Wholesale-retail, outside

Industry rank	S or U	Percent shift[a]
Leading gainers		
Lum. & wood	S	+29.9
For. & fish.	U	+16.6
Textile mfg.	S	+11.3
Mot. veh. mfg.	U	+10.2
Truck. & whsg.	U	+9.9
R.R. trans.	S	+9.7
Mach. mfg.	S	+9.3
Other trans.	U	+8.4
Eat. & drink.	U	+8.4
Other retail	U	+7.9
Total retail		+7.4
Summary line R_{ij}		+7.3
Lagging gainers		
Armed for.	U	+7.0
Communic.	U	+6.7
Food & dairy	U	+6.7
F.I.R.E.	U	+6.6
Print. & pub.	U	+6.4
Total mfg.		+5.3
Food mfg.	S	+4.8
Utilities	S	+4.6
Mining	U	+4.5
Contr. const.	U	+4.4
Civ. gov.	U	+3.6
Lodg. & pers.	U	+3.2
Agriculture	U	+2.6
Amuse. & rec.	U	+2.4
Priv. hsehld.	S	+2.1
Other mfg.	S	+1.6
Whol. trade	U	+0.7
Prof. serv.	U	+0.6
Total services		+0.4
Countertrend		
Trans. equip.	U	−0.4
Apparel mfg.	S	−0.7
Bus. & repair	U	−2.8
Chem. mfg.	S	−8.2

Complete shopping

Industry rank	S or U	Percent shift[a]
Leading gainers		
Armed for.	U	+68.5
Mach. mfg.	U	+58.8
Textile mfg.	S	+52.5
Total mfg.		+50.8
Other mfg.	U	+46.3
Food mfg.	U	+45.6
Apparel mfg.	U	+40.3
Other trans.	U	+38.5
Utilities	U	+36.5
Mot. veh. mfg.	U	+35.2
Trans. equip.	U	+34.5
Priv. hsehld.	S	+34.0
Print. & pub.	U	+29.6
Summary line R_{ij}		+28.9
Lagging gainers		
Chem. mfg.	U	+26.0
Eat. & drink.	U	+24.3
F.I.R.E.	U	+20.6
Lodg. & pers.	U	+18.9
Contr. const.	U	+16.9
Total retail		+16.6
Food & dairy	U	+14.1
For. & fish.	S	+10.3
Other retail	U	+3.1
Lum. & wood	S	+2.6
Communic.	U	+0.5
Countertrend		
Amuse. & rec.	U	−6.2
Civ. gov.	U	−17.4
Prof. serv.	U	−26.6
Agriculture	S	−31.6
Total services		−32.4
Mining	S	−42.2
Truck. & whsg	U	−45.9
Bus. & repair	U	−52.5
Whol. trade	U	−60.4
R.R. trans.	U	−83.3

Notes: S = specialized; U = unspecialized, 1940. F.I.R.E. = Finance, insurance, and real estate.

[a] $\frac{\text{Regional competitive shift}}{\text{Gross competitive shift}}$ (that is, for the summary line and each industry line)

commercial printing, both responsive to a shifting clientele. In large metropolitan areas "other transportation" was dominated by water transportation and mass transit. Thus, an important part of the competitive loss of this sector was a subsector mix effect reflecting the major relative decline of water transport and the effect on mass transit of the automobile. If we separate air transport from the aggregate, we find it becomes a countertrend gainer. This is a further reflection of the changing role of large metropolitan areas.

In contrast, the large wholesale-retail centers experienced competitive employment gains equal to almost half of the metropolitan centers' total net losses. It appears that a leveling out of the structural differences between

TABLE II-8. Leading and lagging industry-sector competitive shifts in employment for trade-center classification regions, 1940–70 (*Continued*)

Partial shopping

Industry rank	S or U	Percent shift[a]
Leading gainers		
Other mfg.	U	+22.8
Food mfg.	U	+21.3
Apparel mfg.	U	+21.2
Total mfg.		+20.8
Utilities	U	+20.0
Textile mfg.	U	+18.5
Mach. mfg.	U	+18.1
Armed for.	U	+17.9
Chem. mfg.	U	+14.1
Trans. equip.	U	+14.0
Mot. veh. mfg.	U	+13.7
Priv. hsehld.	U	+12.9
Other trans.	U	+10.9
Print. & pub.	U	+5.3
F.I.R.E.	U	+4.1
Lodg. & pers.	U	+3.5
All-sector line R_{ij}		+1.5
Lagging gainers		
Other retail	U	+0.3
Countertrend		
Eat. & drink.	U	−0.4
Total retail		−1.6
Food & dairy	U	−2.7
Contr. const.	U	−4.3
Amuse. & rec.	U	−8.0
R.R. trans.	U	−10.1
Mining	S	−10.6
Lum. & wood	S	−12.6
Communic.	U	−12.7
Whol. trade	U	−20.2
Bus. & repair	U	−22.7
Truck. & whsg	U	−25.2
Civ. gov.	U	−26.1
Agriculture	S	−28.7
Total services		−33.5
Prof. serv.	U	−35.1
For. & fish.	S	−36.3

Full convenience

Industry rank	S or U	Percent shift[a]
Countertrend		
Apparel mfg.	U	+15.4
Utilities	U	+10.7
Other mfg.	U	+10.1
Food mfg.	U	+9.9
Total mfg.		+9.6
Other trans.	U	+8.8
Mining	S	+8.6
Trans. equip.	U	+8.3
Priv. hsehld.	U	+7.8
Armed for.	U	+7.6
Mach. mfg.	U	+7.1
Chem. mfg.	U	+6.0
Textile mfg.	U	+4.8
Mot. veh. mfg.	U	+4.4
Contr. const.	U	+2.2
Lodg. & pers.	U	+1.7
F.I.R.E.	U	+1.6
Print. & pub.	U	+1.3
Eat. & drink.	U	+0.4
All-sector line R_{ij}		−0.9
Leading decliners		
Total retail		−1.1
Food & dairy	U	−1.8
Other retail	U	−2.1
R.R. trans.	U	−2.9
Amuse. & rec.	U	−6.7
For. & fish.	S	−7.9
Whol. trade	U	−10.6
Communic.	U	−11.8
Lum. & wood	S	−12.5
Bus. & repair	U	−12.9
Agriculture	S	−15.4
Truck. & whsg	U	−16.6
Civ. gov.	U	−19.5
Total services		−21.0
Prof. serv.	U	−22.3

Hamlet & minimum convenience

Industry rank	S or U	Percent shift[a]
Countertrend		
Textile mfg.	U	+12.9
Apparel mfg.	U	+12.5
Other trans.	U	+10.6
Utilities	U	+8.7
Total mfg.		+8.7
Other mfg.	U	+8.0
Priv. hsehld.	U	+7.0
Food mfg.	U	+6.7
Trans. equip.	U	+6.1
Mach. mfg.	U	+5.9
Contr. const.	U	+4.0
Lum. & wood	S	+4.0
Lodg. & pers.	U	+3.9
Chem. mfg.	U	+3.3
Mot. veh. mfg.	U	+2.9
F.I.R.E.	U	+2.6
Eat. & drink.	U	+1.5
Print. & pub.	U	+0.4
Other retail	U	+0.2
Total retail		+0.1
Mining	S	0.0
All-sector line R_{ij}		−0.2
Leading decliners		
Armed for.	U	−0.5
Food & dairy	U	−0.7
Amuse. & rec.	U	−1.1
R.R. trans.	U	−3.6
Communic.	U	−4.3
Whol. trade	U	−5.5
Bus. & repair	U	−8.5
Civ. gov.	U	−10.6
Truck. & whsg.	U	−12.3
Total services		−14.9
Prof. serv.	U	−17.3
Agriculture	S	−22.9
For. & fish.	S	−33.8

Notes: S = specialized; U = unspecialized, 1940. F.I.R.E. = Finance, insurance, and real estate.

[a] $\frac{\text{Regional competitive shift}}{\text{Gross competitive shift}}$ (that is, for the summary line and each industry line)

the large metropolitan and wholesale-retail centers may have been underway, especially if one examines the sectoral array of competitive shifts. At the outset, the metropolitan centers tended to be much more specialized in most retail trade and service activities. Although these sectors led the competitive losses of the metropolitan centers, they were prominent among the leading gains of the wholesale-retail centers. (Only in the business-and-information services did the large metropolitan centers continue to show superior strength.) In contrast, at the outset, the large wholesale-retail centers tended to be much more specialized in manufacturing activities. Although large metropolitan centers experienced relative manufacturing losses, they were lagging losses. In contrast, the wholesale-retail centers experienced leading losses in manufacturing activity. Such differences in the developmental dynamics of the two kinds of centers substantially narrowed the structural differences between them. (This also had the effect of weakening the utility of the trade-center typology.) This convergence is shown by the 73 percent decline in the difference between the indexes of regional specialization of these two dominant forms of urban organization (see panel B in table 13 in volume I, p. 107).

Small metropolitan centers were the only other higher order centers with substantial net competitive gains. Here the leading gains were among the service sectors—specifically many of the same urban-linkage, information-processing activities that represented the large metropolitan regions' earlier source of strength. This was true even though small metropolitan centers cannot match the large centers' strength in business-oriented services. Relative losses were predominant among the resource sectors as well as the primary resource-processing sectors (except in mining because of the clustering of small metropolitan regions in the Southwest, such as Lubbock and Odessa; see map 8 in volume I, p. 90).

Small wholesale-retail centers did not account for much of the gross shift, but they, too, underwent significant structural transformation. While the larger, higher order centers recorded the strongest relative gains in service activities, retail trades were the principal gainers in these smaller core-centers. This tends to reflect the transport changes that improved the access of these regions to the household markets of subordinate, non-core trade centers. At the same time, relative losses in wholesaling, trucking, and business services suggest ways that these small centers were coming under the spreading transaction-field dominance of even higher order centers.

There are a few centers, classified wholesale-retail by Berry, that do not perform core-sector functions. These are mostly southeastern manufacturing towns (like Danville, Virginia; Valdosta, Georgia; and Dothan, Alabama) that attracted enough manufacturer's-agent-wholesaling status to rise out of the complete shopping center classification, but without achieving urban-core status. They also experienced variations in their shift profiles, reflecting the difference in their position in the total transaction network. Specifically, the service functions displayed the largest losses, reflecting their nodal function deficiencies. They displayed the strongest relative gains in manufacturing activities among the higher order centers. This reflects their kinship with those lower order complete shopping centers, which also occupy hinterland fields.

The four lower order trade centers showed a remarkable similarity in their overall response to network transformations. Manufacturing sectors were the principal leading or countertrend gainers. These gains were most marked among the nondurable manufacturing categories—although machinery, motor vehicle, and other transportation equipment manufacturing clearly made strong relative gains in these hinterland centers. The public utility infrastructure required by an expanding manufacturing sector was also a strong gainer. Other transportation was an important linkage activity that ran counter to the increasing dominance of higher order centers in carrying out urban-linkage functions. This was primarily a consequence of the relative increase of the intercity and school bus services that came into prominence for the first time in this era. While service activities were shifting to higher order trade centers, there were exceptions among personal service activities (household employment, lodging and personal services, eating and drinking). The lower order centers experienced significant competitive gains in these activities. Finally, one cannot fail to emphasize the major contribution made by armed forces employment to the leading gains of these lower order centers.

The most notable distinction between these lower order trade-center classes was the remarkable net gain in competitive share experienced by complete shopping centers. Almost 30 percent of the national all-sector gains came to rest here. Complete-shopping-center counties accounted for more than half of all manufacturing sector gains. They demonstrated their predominant urban-serviced position among the lower order categories by displaying net gains in other transportation, utilities, and printing and publishing activities that are more than twice as large as the remaining lower order centers combined. It is of special interest that complete shopping centers captured more than two-thirds of the net competitive gains in armed forces employment.

Supplementing this is a perspective provided by the developmental code (C) frequency counts. From panel A in appendix II-J, we make an important contrasting discovery. While the large metropolitan center counties dominate the net competitive losses, more than 70 percent of industry × trade center cells displayed competitive gains. (This was above average for all counties.) Thus, the large metropolitan center competitive losses indicated in table II-8 were highly concentrated in fewer than one-third of the larger metropolitan counties.

Panel D in appendix II-J depicts the net difference in the percentage frequencies formed by the leading gain and leading loss items in each cell. There is a good deal of correspondence between these sector profiles and those identified by the net shifts of table II-8. There are also differences. For example, agriculture, forestry, and fisheries experienced net competitive gains (table II-8), although in disproportionately few counties. As we see from table II-3, these were among the most locally concentrated of all industry sectors. Conversely, retail

TABLE II-9. Leading and lagging industry-sector competitive shifts in employment for transaction fields, 1940–70

Urban core, large		
Industry rank	S or U	Percent shift[a]
Countertrend		
Bus. & repair	S	+67.7
Mining	U	+43.9
Agriculture	U	+42.3
R.R. trans.	U	+16.0
Truck. & whsg.	S	+7.3
Lagging decliners		
Whol. trade	S	−1.6
Prof. Serv.	S	−2.8
Total services		−8.6
For. & fish.	U	−10.6
Lum. & wood	U	−15.8
Textile mfg.	U	−26.0
Civ. gov.	S	−45.3
Mach. mfg.	S	−51.1
Other mfg.	S	−61.9
Armed for.	S	−71.9
Communic.	S	−73.1
Amuse. & rec.	S	−73.1
Other trans.	S	−78.7
Other retail	S	−78.8
Chem. mfg.	S	−81.3
Total mfg.		−83.8
Food & dairy	S	−84.9
Contr. const.	S	−85.9
Total retail		−89.4
All-sector line R_{ij}		−90.0
Leading decliners		
Apparel mfg.	S	−93.0
Priv. hsehld.	S	−94.9
Food mfg.	S	−96.8
Trans. equip.	S	−99.7
Lodg. & pers.	S	−100.0
F.I.R.E.	S	−100.0
Eat. & drink.	S	−100.0
Utilities	S	−100.0
Mot. veh. mfg.	S	−100.0
Print & pub.	S	−100.0

Urban core, medium		
Industry rank	S or U	Percent shift[a]
Leading gainers		
Whol. trade	S	+75.4
Total services		+61.9
Prof. serv.	S	+60.8
Truck. & whsg.	S	+60.1
Other retail	S	+57.0
Civ. gov.	S	+53.1
R.R. trans.	S	+50.0
Amuse. & rec.	U	+50.0
Food & dairy	S	+46.5
Total retail		+45.8
Communic.	S	+42.3
Contr. const.	S	+42.1
Print. & pub.	S	+39.9
Eat. & drink.	S	+39.3
F.I.R.E.	S	+37.6
All-sector line R_{ij}		+36.6
Lagging gainers		
Agriculture	U	+34.2
For. & fish.	U	+33.3
Trans. equip.	S	+33.3
Lodg. & pers.	S	+33.3
Mining	U	+31.9
Bus. & repair	S	+30.3
Priv. hsehld.	S	+16.1
Utilities	S	+15.2
Mot. veh. mfg.	S	+12.4
Chem. mfg.	S	+8.7
Lum. & wood	U	+6.7
Countertrend		
Armed for.	S	−0.7
Food mfg.	S	−3.0
Apparel mfg.	U	−7.4
Other trans.	U	−8.1
Total mfg.		−12.8
Other mfg.	S	−25.9
Textile mfg.	S	−32.0
Mach. mfg.	S	−35.9

Urban core, small		
Industry rank	S or U	Percent shift[a]
Leading gainers		
Communic.	U	+41.8
Amuse. & rec.	U	+41.6
Prof. serv.	S	+38.0
Total services		+36.4
Lodg. & pers.	S	+33.6
Armed for.	S	+32.4
Civ. gov.	U	+32.1
R.R. trans.	S	+28.9
For. & fish.	U	+28.6
Food & dairy	S	+26.9
F.I.R.E.	U	+25.4
Total retail		+25.3
All-sector line R_{ij}		+25.0
Lagging gainers		
Eat. & drink.	U	+24.0
Chem. mfg.	U	+22.4
Contr. const.	S	+21.6
Truck. & whsg.	U	+21.1
Other retail	S	+20.6
Mot. veh. mfg.	U	+19.3
Agriculture	U	+19.1
Mining	U	+18.0
Whol. trade	S	+17.8
Priv. hsehld.	S	+16.3
Print. & pub.	U	+14.2
Utilities	S	+8.4
Food mfg.	S	+6.5
Apparel mfg.	U	+6.3
Trans. equip.	U	+3.5
Bus. & repair	U	+1.5
Countertrend		
Total mfg.		−3.6
Other mfg.	S	−12.5
Mach. mfg.	S	−13.0
Lum. & wood	S	−16.8
Other trans.	U	−21.1
Textile mfg.	S	−26.4

Notes: S = specialized; U = unspecialized, 1940. F.I.R.E. = Finance, insurance, and real estate.

[a] $\frac{\text{Region competitive shift}}{\text{Gross competitive shift}}$ (that is, for the summary line and each industry line)

trade sectors were disproportionately frequent as leading gainers while accounting for an important part of the overall competitive losses for large urban centers. It is not surprising that these were among the least localized of the industry sectors. Thus, one can see that the shift measurements and the frequency counts based on the developmental code classifications tell related but different stories.

Transaction-Field Shift Patterns

Table II-9 represents the share of the total competitive shift (plus or minus) experienced by each composite transaction field for each industry. (Recall that Berry's labor force field classification is the basis for the typology—see p. 60 in volume I.) Consider, first, the summarizing, all-industry shifts (boldface in table II-9 and

TABLE II-9. Leading and lagging industry-sector competitive shifts in employment for transaction fields 1940–70 (*Continued*)

Primary labor field, large

Industry rank	S or U	Percent shift[a]
Leading gainers		
Other trans.	U	+32.1
Chem. mfg.	U	+26.8
Print. & pub.	U	+16.5
Mach. mfg.	U	+16.0
Mot. veh. mfg.	U	+14.1
Contr. const.	U	+11.2
Communic.	U	+10.9
Civ. gov.	U	+9.5
Trans. equip.	U	+9.1
Total mfg.		+8.5
F.I.R.E.	U	+6.8
Truck. & whsg.	U	+6.6
Eat. & drink.	U	+6.2
Apparel mfg.	S	+5.9
Food mfg.	U	+5.6
Lum. & wood	U	+5.4
Utilities	U	+5.2
All-sector line R_{ij}		+4.9
Lagging gainers		
Total retail		+4.8
Food & dairy	U	+4.5
Other mfg.	S	+2.4
Amuse. & rec.	U	+2.4
Other retail	S	+2.2
Whol. trade	U	+1.8
Countertrend		
Lodg. & pers.	U	−0.4
Agriculture	S	−2.0
Priv. hsehld.	U	−4.4
Bus. & repair	U	−4.6
Prof. serv.	U	−5.6
Total services		−5.7
Armed for.	U	−9.4
Textile mfg.	S	−15.6
R.R. trans.	S	−31.1
For. & fish.	S	−32.8
Mining	S	−37.7

Primary labor field, medium

Industry rank	S or U	Percent shift[a]
Leading gainers		
Trans. equip.	U	+20.5
Mach. mfg.	U	+17.8
Mot. veh. mfg.	U	+17.7
Other trans.	U	+16.5
Lum. & wood	S	+16.5
Total mfg.		+14.4
Print. & pub.	U	+13.2
Chem. mfg.	U	+12.8
Other mfg.	U	+11.8
Food mfg.	U	+10.2
All-sector line R_{ij}		+10.1
Lagging gainers		
Contr. const.	U	+10.0
Eat. & drink.	U	+9.1
Lodg. & pers.	U	+8.2
Utilities	U	+8.1
Other retail	U	+8.0
Priv. hsehld.	U	+8.0
Total retail		+7.9
Food & dairy	U	+7.2
F.I.R.E.	U	+6.7
Textile mfg.	S	+5.8
Truck. & whsg.	U	+4.3
Amuse. & rec.	U	+3.5
Armed for.	U	+3.5
Apparel mfg.	U	+3.3
Whol. trade	U	+2.3
R.R. trans.	U	+1.8
Civ. gov.	U	+0.9
Communic.	U	+0.8
Countertrend		
Mining	U	−2.0
Total services		−2.3
Prof. serv.	U	−2.6
Bus. & repair	U	−8.3
Agriculture	S	−11.3
For. & fish.	S	−17.4

Primary labor field, small

Industry rank	S or U	Percent shift[a]
Leading gainers		
Lum. & wood	S	+68.9
Textile mfg.	S	+37.4
Other mfg.	U	+31.0
Total mfg.		+27.0
Chem. mfg.	U	+24.0
Apparel mfg.	U	+22.4
Mach. mfg.	U	+21.2
Armed for.	U	+20.6
Food mfg.	U	+18.9
Priv. hsehld.	U	+17.0
Utilities	U	+16.0
All-sector line R_{ij}		+15.0
Lagging gainers		
Other trans.	U	+13.8
Mot. veh. mfg.	U	+12.9
Lodg. & pers.	U	+11.0
Contr. const.	U	+9.6
Food & dairy	U	+8.0
Other retail	U	+7.9
F.I.R.E.	U	+7.8
Total retail		+7.7
Eat. & drink.	U	+7.0
For. & fish.	U	+5.8
Print. & pub.	U	+4.6
Trans. equip.	U	+3.3
Amuse. & rec.	U	+0.6
Whol. trade	U	+0.1
Countertrend		
Communic.	U	−0.4
Civ. gov.	U	−0.8
R.R. trans.	U	−2.1
Truck. & whsg.	U	−4.6
Total services		−9.3
Mining	S	−9.8
Prof. serv.	U	−11.6
Bus. & repair	U	−13.5
Agriculture	S	−29.1

corresponding to the last column of panel B in table 33, in volume I, p. 157). It is clear that the largest minus-to-plus, all-sector competitive gains were largely restricted to the urban cores and their associated primary transaction fields (called primary labor force fields in the Berry classification). The largest urban cores dominated the losses. The medium and smaller cores and all primary transaction fields dominated the gains. Two-thirds of the all-sector losses of the large core centers were captured as all-sector gains by medium and small core centers. This is consistent with the pattern for the trade center classification in the previous section, where the highest order trade centers dominated the total shift.

Again the overall view hides important variations in industry-sector experience. The net losing, large urban cores (containing many counties from both large metropolitan and wholesale-retail categories) displayed a rank order of sector shifts resembling that of the large metropolitan counties, albeit with some dimensional differences. The medium and small urban cores captured all

TABLE II-9. Leading and lagging industry-sector competitive shifts in employment for transaction fields, 1940–70 (*Continued*)

Secondary labor field, large		
Industry rank	S or U	Percent shift[a]
Leading gainers		
Mach. mfg.	U	+9.7
Food mfg.	U	+7.8
Other trans.	U	+7.6
Print. & pub.	U	+5.9
Agriculture	S	+5.6
For. & fish.	S	+5.4
Other mfg.	U	+5.4
Total mfg.		+5.0
Apparel mfg.	U	+4.0
Eat. & drink.	U	+3.9
Utilities	U	+3.0
F.I.R.E.	U	+3.0
Mot. veh. mfg.	U	+2.3
Priv. hsehld.	U	+2.3
Other retail	U	+2.2
Total retail		+1.9
All-sector line R_{ij}		+1.7
Lagging Gainers		
Lodg. & pers.	U	+1.6
Contr. const.	U	+1.0
Food & dairy	U	+0.7
Textile mfg.	S	+0.1
Amuse. & rec.	U	0.0
Countertrend		
Trans. equip.	U	−0.2
Civ. gov.	U	−0.3
Armed for.	U	−0.6
Chem. mfg.	U	−1.0
Communic.	U	−1.1
R.R. trans.	U	−3.3
Prof. serv.	U	−4.1
Total services		−4.8
Truck. & whsg.	U	−6.0
Bus. & repair	U	−7.5
Whol. trade	U	−8.9
Mining	S	−18.8
Lum. & wood	S	−19.1

Secondary labor field, medium		
Industry rank	S or U	Percent shift[a]
Leading gainers		
Priv. hsehld.	U	+14.1
Other mfg.	U	+13.6
Apparel mfg.	U	+11.6
Total mfg.		+10.5
Other trans.	U	+10.3
Trans. equip.	U	+10.1
Utilities	U	+9.6
Armed for.	U	+9.5
Mach. mfg.	U	+9.2
Food mfg.	U	+7.9
Eat. & drink.	U	+7.0
Mining	S	+6.8
Mot. veh. mfg.	U	+6.6
Textile mfg.	U	+6.5
Lodg. & pers.	U	+6.3
All-sector line R_{ij}		+5.9
Lagging gainers		
Chem. mfg.	U	+5.3
Total retail		+4.9
Food & dairy	U	+4.6
F.I.R.E.	U	+4.3
R.R. trans.	U	+3.4
Print. & pub.	U	+2.9
Contr. const.	U	+2.7
Other retail	U	+0.6
Countertrend		
Civ. gov.	U	−0.5
Communic.	U	−1.0
Amuse. & rec.	U	−1.9
Total services		−4.5
Prof. serv.	U	−6.0
Agriculture	S	−6.1
Bus. & repair	U	−7.5
Truck. & whsg.	U	−12.0
Whol. trade	U	−17.4
Lum. & wood	S	−20.0
For. & fish.	S	−24.1

Secondary labor field, small		
Industry rank	S or U	Percent shift[a]
Leading gainers		
Textile mfg.	S	+39.6
Armed for.	U	+37.3
Apparel mfg.	U	+20.7
Food mfg.	U	+18.5
Total mfg.		+17.2
Other mfg.	U	+16.4
Utilities	U	+12.0
Priv. hsehld.	U	+11.2
Mach. mfg.	U	+9.0
Mot. veh. mfg.	U	+7.6
Trans. equip.	U	+6.4
Other trans.	U	+2.2
F.I.R.E.	U	+1.4
Print. & pub.	U	+1.1
All-sector line R_{ij}		+0.5
Lagging gainers		
For. & fish.	S	+0.4
Countertrend		
Chem. mfg.	U	−1.5
Eat. & drink.	U	−1.9
Lodg. & pers.	U	−2.5
Total retail		−4.9
Contr. const.	U	−5.0
Other retail	U	−5.7
Communic.	U	−5.9
Food & dairy	U	−6.3
Amuse. & rec.	U	−7.9
R.R. trans.	U	−10.6
Civ. gov.	U	−11.1
Lum. & wood	S	−13.9
Bus. & repair	U	−18.7
Mining	S	−18.8
Whol. trade	U	−20.5
Total services		−23.3
Prof. serv.	U	−24.6
Truck. & whsg.	U	−25.0
Agriculture	S	−33.9

Outside		
Industry rank	S or U	Percent shift[a]
Countertrend		
For. & fish.	S	+41.
Apparel mfg.	U	+25.
Food mfg.	U	+24.
Utilities	U	+21.
Other mfg.	U	+19.
Total mfg.		+17.
Mach. mfg.	U	+17.
Priv. hsehld.	U	+15.
Armed for.	U	+14.
Trans. equip.	U	+13.
Textile mfg.	U	+10.
Other trans.	U	+9.
Mot. veh. mfg.	U	+7.
F.I.R.E.	U	+5.
Lodg. & pers.	U	+2.
Eat. & drink.	U	+1.
Print. & pub.	U	+1.
Lagging decliners		
Total retail		−7.
All-sector line R_{ij}		−10.
Leading decliners		
Food & dairy	U	−10.
Contr. const.	U	−10.
Mining	S	−12.
Chem. mfg.	U	−16.
Agriculture	S	−16.
Lum. & wood	S	−16.
Other retail	U	−16.
Amuse. & rec.	U	−19.
Communic.	U	−22.
Bus. & repair	U	−40.
Total services		−43.
Prof. serv.	U	−43.
Civ. gov.	U	−46.
R.R. trans.	S	−52.
Truck. & whsg.	U	−53.
Whol. trade	U	−54.

Notes: S = specialized; U = unspecialized, 1940. F.I.R.E. = Finance, insurance, and real estate.

[a] $\frac{\text{Region competitive shift}}{\text{Gross competitive shift}}$ (that is, for the summary line and each industry line)

of the net competitive gains in total service activities (linkage and information-processing were especially prominent). These cores also captured two-thirds of the net competitive gains in retail employment. Net losses were restricted largely to manufacturing employment. At 16 percent, these losses are the complement of the 84 percent net losses experienced by the large urban cores.

One-third of large-core employment losses (overall) were transmuted into gains in the primary transaction or labor force fields. Significantly, the proportion of the overall gain increases as one progresses from the primary transaction field associated with the largest cores to those associated with the smallest, and this progression was largely accounted for by shifts in manufacturing employment. On balance, primary fields experienced net losses in the service sectors while the urban cores continued to dominate in this realm. Moving from the largest to the smallest primary transaction fields, the increasing progression of net gains in manufacturing was also associated with a change in the profile of manufacturing sectors experiencing these gains. Machinery, motor vehicle, transportation equipment, chemical, and printing and publishing employment assumed lower ranks among the competitive gains as one moved from the large-core to the small-core transaction fields. In contrast, textile, apparel, wood products, and other manufacturing tended to assume higher rank among the competitive gains as one made the same progression.

Apart from relative declines in resource activities, the principal losses in these core-associated primary fields were in the linkage and information-processing services increasingly dominated by the core centers—railroads, trucking, communication, wholesale trade, business services, professional services, and civilian government employment.

The profiles of the gains and losses in secondary transaction fields were roughly similar to those reported for the primary fields, although the net gains appear to have been much less strong. It is interesting to note that two-thirds of the net losses in service activities were generated by outside counties (that is, outside any core-associated transaction field), and including the secondary labor force fields of the smallest cores. These more remote fields were also the only ones outside the large urban cores to experience net losses in retail employment. In contrast, they accounted for 35 percent of the net gains in manufacturing. The utility sector that provided infrastructural services supporting the expanding manufacturing activities matched those gains.[2]

The reader should note that the tables that have appeared throughout part one will also serve as important references for the more detailed presentations in part two. In addition, they will be helpful to the reader wishing to pursue special interests.

Within-Group Variations

We have seen that it is instructive to examine variations in the shift patterns formed by differences in spatial and functional categories. However, one should remember that all complete shopping centers or other trade-center categories are not homogeneous entities. This was pointed out in volume I when we examined the imprecise nature of the classification scheme. This potential for exhibiting structural differences is further amplified by the fact that (1) for the lower order trade centers, the statistical units are not trade centers, but counties classified according to their highest order, component trade centers; and (2) we are examining the changing structure of the full range of employment sectors and not just those activities employed in the trade-center classification exercise. As a consequence, there must be variations in the all-sector employment profile between different trade centers of the same class, although there are no easy means to check this.

For the moment, however, we are more concerned with the fact that the same kind of trade center differently situated in the transaction network of an urban system may be subject to different growth and developmental effects. Such centers may display quite different profiles of change, even though they begin with similar structural forms. We can represent these differences quite well within the framework of our scheme.

The relevant table, appendix II-I, is derived from a shift-share computation in which the lower order trade centers (complete shopping, partial shopping, and so forth) were further differentiated according to the transaction fields (primary labor force [PLF]—large, small, and so forth) in which they are located. The higher order trade centers and core-center counties were then aggregated. In this format, three-quarters of the negative competitive shifts were generated by the aggregate of higher order functions.[3] It is of interest that in this classification, all of the competitive gains, and one-quarter of the competitive losses, were linked to the lower order trade centers. Two-thirds of the competitive gains were located in primary labor force fields. Three-quarters of the gains were accounted for by complete shopping centers.

There are two aspects of the within-group variation revealed by appendix II-I. The summary line reveals significant overall variations and the industry sector profiles reveal structural variations in the relative gains. The first perspective is summarized in table II-10. There are several things worth noting. Complete shopping centers located in primary labor force fields were particularly favored with competitive gains; those in secondary fields less so (column 2). Those located outside core-center transaction fields actually experienced competitive losses on balance. Similar variations were characteristic of the other trade center types, except that they also tended to experience competitive losses in medium and small secondary fields.[4]

Taking 1940 employment as a scalar base (column 3), additional within-group variations appear. Relative to this base, complete shopping centers displayed the largest gains in all transaction fields except the medium-to-large primary labor force fields. In this domain, partial shopping centers displayed more strength relative to their own bases. This may be an echo in another form of the shadowing phenomenon portrayed in part two of volume I (there expressed in terms of trade-center frequencies and sizes). It could be that the primary fields of the larger urban regions were more congenial to partial shopping centers, even though the complete shopping centers

TABLE II-10. Comparison of the performance of lower order trade-center categories located in different transaction fields, 1940–70

Transaction-field category	Trade-center category	Competitive gains & losses (1)	Percent of $/\Sigma R_{ij}/$ / 2 (2)	R_{ij} / 1940 employment (3)
Core & higher order trade center aggregate		−941,192	−72.7	−.0312
PLF, large	Complete shopping	+158,775	+12.4	+.2519
	Partial shopping	+57,747	+4.5	+.3644
	Full convenience	+33,345	+2.6	+.3457
	Hamlet & minimum convenience	+16,920	+1.3	+.1915
PLF, medium	Complete shopping	+186,342	+14.5	+.1929
	Partial shopping	+56,477	+4.4	+.2423
	Full convenience	+6,489	+0.5	+.0640
	Hamlet & minimum convenience	+12,423	+1.0	+.1353
PLF, small	Complete shopping	+242,994	+18.9	+.1650
	Partial shopping	+58,045	+4.5	+.1137
	Full convenience	+533	0.0	+.0024
	Hamlet & minimum convenience	+31,704	+2.5	+.1593
SLF, large	Complete shopping	+45,414	+3.5	+.0728
	Partial shopping	+9,339	+0.7	+.0627
	Full convenience	−189	0.0	−.0017
	Hamlet & minimum convenience	+1,607	+0.1	+.0423
SLF, medium	Complete shopping	+239,768	+18.7	+.2207
	Partial shopping	−13,303	−1.0	−.0415
	Full convenience	−9,607	−0.7	−.0510
	Hamlet & minimum convenience	−1,560	−0.1	−.0152
SLF, small	Complete shopping	+49,540	+3.9	+.0318
	Partial shopping	−24,923	−1.9	−.0408
	Full convenience	+1,009	+0.1	+.0038
	Hamlet & minimum convenience	−3,708	−0.3	−.0158
Outside LFF	Complete shopping	−76,613	−5.9	−.0289
	Partial shopping	−95,007	−7.3	−.0866
	Full convenience	−63,032	−5.0	−.0894
	Hamlet & minimum convenience	−64,968	−5.0	−.1186

Notes: PLF = primary labor field, SLF = secondary labor field. R_{ij} = the competitive shift component of the shift-share methodology.

displayed dramatic overall gains in these fields. In these same-base comparisons, full convenience centers were the poorest performers in most fields. This may be another reflection of the way full convenience centers appear to have been most disadvantaged by changes in the transaction network. Recall the Hodge study, as reported in chapter 7 of volume I of this study, p. 92.

The second aspect of within-group variations has to do with structural differences in competitive shifts. Employing appendix II-I, contrast the set of complete shopping centers located in the primary transaction field of large urban cores with those located outside the secondary transaction fields of any significant size core. Those within the more highly articulated networks associated with the large-core, primary fields demonstrate much greater competitive strength in transaction linkage, retail, and service activities than the same class of centers outside. In contrast, complete shopping centers in the more remote fields display greater relative gains in manufacturing activities (plus utilities, households, and armed forces). Appendix II-I can be employed to draw other contrasts between similar trade center categories situated in different transaction fields.[5]

The Hodge study also provides indirect evidence suggesting that, over time, some transformation of one trade center category into another is likely—particularly among the lower order categories. It seems quite possible that some of the 1960 complete shopping centers located in the primary transaction fields recently achieved that status by emerging from lower order categories under the impact of network pattern changes at work during the study period. Likewise, it would not be surprising if

TABLE II-11. Average deviations measured across 31-sector percentage competitive shifts, 1940–70, for each of twelve geographical regions, nine trade-center categories, and ten transaction-field synthetic regions

Geographical region		Trade-center category		Transaction-field category	
Upper New England	1.6	Metropolitan, large	45.5	Urban-core, large	42.2
Middle Atlantic	18.1	Metropolitan, small	8.4	Urban-core, medium	22.4
Upper Appalachia	3.2	Wholesale-retail, large	27.3	Urban-core, small	14.6
Lower Appalachia	4.9	Wholesale-retail, small	2.9	Primary labor field, large	10.1
Midwest-Great Lakes	15.4	Wholesale-retail, outside	4.7	Primary labor field, medium	7.0
Southeast	17.0	Complete shopping	30.7	Primary labor field, small	13.6
Peninsular Florida	7.8	Partial shopping	15.4	Secondary labor field, large	4.5
Southern Plains	8.3	Full convenience	8.5	Secondary labor field, medium	7.1
Northern Plains	10.7	Hamlet-minimum convenience	7.2	Secondary labor field, small	12.9
Northern Mountains and Pacific Northwest	8.1			Outside	23.0
Southern Mountains	4.9				
Metropolitan California	12.0				
Total average deviation across 31 sectors	9.3		16.7		15.7

Source: Derived from tables II-4, II-8, and II-9.

some of the complete shopping centers lying outside urban-core transaction fields did not regress to lower order status under the impact of changing transaction network patterns. Much more could be revealed if a larger study along the lines set out by Hodge were undertaken.

Structural Consequences of Developmental Change

In tables II-4, II-8, and II-9, the range of percentage competitive shifts varies considerably from one trade center, one transaction field, and one geographical region to another. It seems a safe inference that those categories that experienced very large average deviations (measured across thirty-one industry sectors) were the fields within which the developmental factors subsumed in competitive shifts were bringing about the greatest structural reorganizations. Table II-11 records the total average deviations for each of the synthetic regions. Table II-12 records the average deviations and relative deviations for each of the thirty-one industry sectors taken separately.

An examination of this record supports several interesting generalizations about the effect of developmental factors on total urban-system structure. First, the effect of developmental changes has been far greater on the systemic properties (that is, the generalized access characteristics) of the urban-system network than upon the system's broad geographical structure. The average deviation of the trade-center synthetic regions is 80 percent greater than that displayed by the twelve geographic regions, and that of the transaction fields is 70 percent greater. Thus, it is a salient feature of the study epoch that it changed the abstract, transaction topology of the system far more than its topography. The key characteristic of the study period was the degree to which developmental changes transformed the "topo-logic" (if I may be allowed to coin a phrase) of urban-system organization.

From the trade-center perspective, the greatest structural transformations were experienced by the large metropolitan centers. Complete shopping centers came next. In volume I we noted that the latter emerged as the dominant urban-system workhorse in those fields outside urban-region cores. Table II-12 testifies that this corresponded with a major change in the functional roles that complete shopping centers play. The large wholesale-retail centers record the third largest average deviation. In contrast, the small wholesale-retail centers appear to have experienced only minor structural changes. The hierarchical structure of all trade centers appears to have been substantially reorganized.

From the transaction-field perspective, the large and medium urban cores and the most remote transaction fields outside the household transaction fields of all urban-region cores underwent the greatest structural changes. From the perspective of the twelve geographical regions, the Middle Atlantic corridor, the Southeast, the Great Lakes and Upper Midwest, Metropolitan California, and the Northern Plains all experienced larger than average structural reorganizations. Upper New England and the Appalachian regions experienced the least.

In terms of the broad categories of activity, it is no surprise that the resource sectors were the most radically restructured. They experienced relative deviations more than twice the thirty-one sector average. Given the extraordinary developments in agricultural technology, plus the substitution of fossil fuels, that attended the

TABLE II-12. Average and relative deviations of percentage competitive shifts for each industry sector and six intermediate aggregates, 1940–70, measured across twelve geographical regions, nine trade-center categories, and ten transaction fields

Industrial sector	Average deviation % R_{ij}s across geographical regions (1)	Average deviation % R_{ij}s across trade-center categories (2)	Average deviation % R_{ij}s across transaction fields (3)	Geographical regions, relative deviation (4)	Trade-center categories, relative deviation (5)	Transaction fields, relative deviation (6)
Six intermediate sums:						
Total resources	21.2	35.6	26.7	2.28	2.12	1.70
Total manufacturing	5.3	14.0	15.7	0.57	0.83	1.00
Total retail trade	2.7	3.8	2.9	0.29	0.23	0.18
Total linkage	3.0	6.5	5.1	0.32	0.39	0.32
Total personal services	4.2	4.1	5.2	0.45	0.24	0.33
Total informational services	7.2	30.4	25.9	0.77	1.81	1.65
Thirty-one sectors:						
Agriculture	24.9	33.6	26.9	2.68	2.00	1.71
Forestry & fisheries	20.9	28.9	24.6	2.25	1.72	1.57
Mining	13.3	40.2	26.8	1.43	2.39	1.71
Contract construction	5.2	5.3	3.5	0.56	0.32	0.22
Food manufacturing	7.1	11.9	13.1	0.76	0.71	0.83
Textile manufacturing	16.9	23.6	29.3	1.82	1.40	1.87
Apparel manufacturing	11.2	13.4	14.4	1.20	0.80	0.92
Printing & publishing	4.1	2.9	5.8	0.44	0.17	0.33
Chemical manufacturing	8.4	6.8	8.4	0.90	0.40	0.54
Lumber & wood	13.3	22.6	27.4	1.43	1.35	1.74
Machinery manufacturing	8.4	16.8	22.1	0.90	1.00	1.46
Motor vehicle manufacturing	16.4	6.6	8.4	1.76	0.39	0.54
Trans. equip. manufacturing	13.3	9.0	9.7	1.43	0.54	0.62
Miscellaneous manufacturing	4.6	19.5	20.5	0.49	1.16	1.31
Railroad transportation	10.7	28.2	21.6	1.15	1.68	1.38
Trucking & warehousing	7.5	18.7	18.4	0.81	1.11	1.17
Other transportation	3.2	7.5	13.8	0.34	0.45	0.88
Communications	6.7	9.8	8.1	0.72	0.58	0.52
Public utilities	3.6	7.6	7.9	0.39	0.45	0.50
Wholesale trade	10.5	22.7	21.7	1.12	1.35	1.38
Eating & drinking	7.2	3.0	4.2	0.77	0.18	0.27
Food & dairy	2.1	4.8	3.7	0.23	0.29	0.24
Other retail trade	2.5	6.1	6.7	0.27	0.36	0.43
F.I.R.E.	3.7	2.2	3.6	0.40	0.13	0.23
Lodging & personal services	5.6	4.0	4.9	0.60	0.24	0.31
Business & repair services	13.9	38.2	31.6	1.49	2.27	2.01
Amusement & recreation	7.6	13.5	9.7	0.82	0.80	0.62
Private households	3.9	8.1	9.3	0.42	0.48	0.59
Professional services	7.4	30.3	25.1	0.80	1.80	1.60
Civ. government	7.5	22.2	15.4	0.81	1.32	0.98
Armed forces	12.3	15.9	15.6	1.32	0.95	0.99
Total average deviation	9.3	16.8	15.7	1.00	1.00	1.00

Note: F.I.R.E. = Finance, insurance, and real estate.

development of the internal combustion engine, this is not surprising. Nor is it surprising that the principal reorganization effect was on the geographical distribution of these activities rather than on their urban-system structure—in contrast to the all-sector tendency. What may seem surprising though is the fact that developments in the domain of information-processing services were not far behind in effecting a structural reorganization.

I suspect that most economists would believe that changes in manufacturing would have displayed the greatest reorganizational effects, when, in fact, the manufacturing sector comes in a distant third, a little below the all-sector averge deviation. The sector also affected the urban-system organization more than it did the geographical distribution. It seems logical that its reorganizational consequences were greatest for transaction-field rather than trade-center categories. Retailing, personal services, and linkage sectors seem to have played a more restricted role in urban-system reorganization. However, as we shall see later, the linkage-sector transformations were indirectly responsible for many of the more dramatic changes observed.

Revisiting the Growth Track Concept—A Technical Addendum

Recall that in volume I (part one, chapter 4) we extrapolated from the literature to formalize a growth sequence model implicitly based on the ontogenetic analogy. This "growth track" had two principal characteristics. One dynamic element was hypothesized to represent a progression up the hierarchy of final demand-oriented trade centers. Thus, a hamlet, as it grows in scale, would tend to take on the trade-center form of a convenience center, even when the structural profile of what we call hamlets and convenience centers remains unaltered. Given sufficient *scalar change* in population and activities, each of the trade-center types would, in turn, progress to higher order structures. In its growth-model form, the second element views urban-center growth as a progression up a ladder of industrial sectors as well. Thus, lower order centers, which are more apt to be associated with resource activity specializations, would, under the effect of scalar growth, become progressively more specialized in material processing, then intermediate manufacturing, then intermediate services, and so forth.

In the earlier discussions I opined that progressions along such a growth track could never be clearly identified because developmental change keeps shifting the track while the process goes on. I further suggested that the developmental process is so dominant, and the growth process so dependent upon it, that it does not matter much anyway. Such growth pattern transformations would tend to be washed out in the process. It was indicated that an empirical demonstration of this proposition would be taken up later. The time is now at hand to see how the data might relate to this issue.

One can examine the way each industrial sector has shared in the competitive shifts across trade-center and transaction-field boundaries (tables II-8 and II-9). There is very little in these arrays that can be interpreted as a reflection of sector sequences that the growth track hypothesis would suggest. Yet, if these tendencies operate at all, they must be embodied in the competitive shift component (R_{ij}) under consideration here. Recall that chapters 9 and 14 of volume I made this clear in the process of explaining why the mix and growth components could not be assumed to have captured all of the scalar effects. Is there some way that the growth track element of this component could be separated for examination? Not really. But this is another of those places where it is enlightening to play a little data game.

Suppose we take the 1940 cross-sectional employment structures for each of the lower order trade center classes, plus the small, medium, and large urban cores.[6] Assume that over some period of time each of the classes grew in scale to match the size of the class of the next higher order—assuming, in the process, the 1940 structural form of the next class in hierarchical order. In this way, for the initial 1940 employment distribution of each hierarchical class we can construct a hypothetical terminal (19??) employment distribution *that would result if all change were a consequence of a process of scalar growth without any developmental changes in urban structure*. Employing the shift-share technique, we can then compute the competitive shift that would result from such a transformation process.

One might then jump to the conclusion that we could take the hypothetical growth track R_{ij} and subtract it from the actual historical R_{ij} of tables II-8 and II-9 to get a residual R_{ij} representing pure development. Alas, we cannot. A number of logical reasons were set forth in volume I that make such a separation indefensibly artificial. Furthermore, the numbers game is too crude. The two computed R_{ij} vectors are incommensurable in their cardinal dimensions for several reasons. However, the hypothetical and historical R_{ij} vectors are ordinally commensurable. If we arrange our growth track competitive shifts in an array from the largest plus to the largest minus, we acquire the ranking numbers of column A of table II-13.

Before adding anything further to the data game, let us see whether the growth track sequences implicit in these structural vectors are consistent with the conceptual model. The answer is: "Yes, quite." With a few minor exceptions all resource activities have low ranks, indicating that these activities experience progressive competitive losses reflecting their declining importance in the employment arrays of higher order centers. In contrast, we find that the top halves of these arrays are dominated by the typical urban transaction-servicing activities (transportation, public utilities, communication, trade, service, plus printing and publishing). The progression up the trade-center growth track is clearly associated with increasingly important roles for these activities, as the growth track hypothesis would suggest. The growth track implies steady gains in professional services as one progresses up the ladder. This is also true of wholesale trade with the interesting twist that large relative gains in wholesale trade would be especially characteristic of the thresholds between the hamlet and full convenience levels as well as between the complete shopping centers and small urban cores (under 1940 structural conditions).

TABLE II-13. Rank order comparisons of hypothetical competitive shifts based on the simple scalar growth track, with the actual competitive shifts for corresponding trade- and urban-core center categories

	Hamlet shift comparisons			Full convenience shift comparisons			Partial shopping shift comparisons		
Industrial sector	Growth track hamlet → full convenience (A)	R_{ij} hamlet (B)	Rank difference (C)	Growth track full convenience → partial shopping (A)	R_{ij} full convenience (B)	Rank difference (C)	Growth track partial shopping → complete shopping + wholesale-retail, outside (A)	R_{ij} partial shopping (B)	Rank difference (C)
Agriculture	31	30	+1	31	28	+3	31	29	+2
For. & fish.	29	31	−2	19	23	−5	28	31	−2
Mining	28	19	+9	1	6	−5	30	22	+8
Contr. const.	24	11	+14	7	14	−8	16	19	−3
Food mfg.	11	7	+4	7	4	+3	9	2	+7
Textile	2	1	+1	30	12	+18	2	5	−3
Apparel mfg.	26	2	+24	10	1	+9	11	3	+8
Print. & pub.	25	17	−8	17	17	−0.5	14	13	+1
Chemicals	30	13	+17	4	11	−8	29	8	+21
Lum. & wood	17	11	+6	21	26	−6	19	23	−5
Mach. mfg.	9	9	—	28	10	+18	6	6	—
Mot. veh. mfg.	22	14	+8	21	13	+8	22	10	+12
Transp. equip. mfg.	21	8	+13	26	7	+19	22	9	+13
Other mfg.	4	5	−1	4	3	+0.5	1	1	—
R.R. trans.	13	23	−10	8	21	−13	8	21	−13
Truck & whsg.	14	28	−14	25	29	−4	27	27	—
Other trans.	23	3	+20	17	5	+12	25	12	+13
Communic.	15	24	−9	23	25	−3	25	24	+0.5
Utilities	17	4	−13	14	2	+12	17	4	+13
Whole. trade	7	25	−18	12	24	−12	13	25	−12
Eat. & drink.	8	16	−8	11	18	−7	10	17	−7
Food & dairy	5	21	−16	13	19	−6	15	18	−3
Other retail	1	18	−17	5	20	−15	3	16	−13
F.I.R.E.	10	15	−5	15	16	−1	12	14	−2
Lodging	6	12	−6	9	15	−6	7	15	−8
Bus. & rep.	12	26	−14	23	27	−5	23	26	−3
Amuse. & rec.	19	22	−4	19	22	−4	26	20	+6
Pvt. hsehld.	19	6	+13	2	8	−6	5	11	−6
Prof. serv.	3	29	−26	24	31	−7	4	30	−26
Civ. gov.	26	27	−1	27	30	−3	20	28	−8
Armed for.	21	20	+0.5	29	9	+20	19	7	+12

TABLE II-13. Rank order comparisons of hypothetical competitive shifts based on the simple scalar growth track, with the actual competitive shifts for corresponding trade- and urban-core center categories (*Continued*)

	Combined complete shopping and wholesale-retail outside shift comparisons			Small urban core shift comparisons			Medium urban core shift comparisons		
	Growth track complete shopping + urban wholesale-retail − outside → urban core, small (A)	R_{ij} complete shopping + wholesale-retail, outside (B)	Rank difference (C)	Growth track urban core, small → urban core, medium (A)	R_{ij} urban core, small (B)	Rank difference (C)	Growth track urban core, medium → urban core, large (A)	R_{ij} urban core, medium (B)	Rank difference (C)
Agriculture	31	26	+5	31	17	+14	31	14	+17
For. & fish.	28	16	+12	24	8	+16	22	16	+6
Mining	30	28	+2	29	18	+11	26	18	+8
Contr. constr.	14	18	−4	14	13	+1	21	10	+11
Food mfg.	7	4	+3	25	23	+2	13	26	−14
Textile	6	2	+4	30	31	−1	29	30	−1
Apparel	27	9	+18	6	24	−18	2	27	−25
Print. & pub.	26	20	+6	11	21	−11	20	11	+9
Chemicals	29	14	+15	28	12	+16	25	23	+2
Lum. & wood	18	11	+7	9	29	−21	5	24	−20
Mach. mfg.	2	3	−1	3	28	−25	27	31	−4
Mot. veh. mfg.	12	7	+5	5	16	−11	6	22	−16
Transp.	24	12	+12	13	25	−12	8	16	−8
Other mfg.	1	5	−4	1	27	−26	30	29	+1
R.R. trans.	15	31	−16	23	7	+16	28	7	+22
Truck & whsg.	26	27	−2	21	14	+7	20	3	16.5
Other trans.	19	6	+13	18	30	−12	3	28	−25
Communic.	21	22	−1	17	1	+16	17	9	+ 8
Utilities	20	8	+12	22	22	—	18	21	−3
Whole. trade	6	30	−25	7	19	−12	16	1	+15
Eat. & drink.	16	21	−5	16	11	+5	15	12	+3
Food & dairy	17	13	+4	15	9	+6	5	8	−4
Other retail	3	19	−16	4	15	−11	9	4	+5
F.I.R.E.	4	15	−11	2	10	−8	1	13	−12
Lodging	8	17	−9	12	4	+8	10	16	−6
Bus. & rep.	23	29	−7	19	26	−7	14	19	−5
Amuse. & rec.	23	23	−0.5	20	2	+18	13	7	+6
Pvt. hsehld.	11	10	+0.5	27	20	+7	24	20	+4
Prof. serv.	11	25	−15	11	3	+8	11	2	+9
Civ. gov.	9	24	−15	9	6	+3	7	5	+2
Armed for.	13	1	+12	26	5	+21	23	25	−2

Railroading would become increasingly important up to, but not including, the urban cores. All retail trade centers would advance, with the "other retail trade" category being especially sensitive to increasing levels of urban agglomeration.

A number of manufacturing sectors appear in the top half of each array, but they do not seem to reflect as systematic a hierarchical progression as is characteristic of the more obvious urban-center-forming transaction linkage structures. Complex sectors such as the manufacture of motor vehicles and other transportation equipment do not come into the growth track progression in any significant way until the level of the urban core centers is reached. The basic material-processing sectors (such as the manufacture of lumber and wood and the materials-processing components of "other manufacturing") emerge early in the growth track progression. (The higher level appearances of these same sectors are associated with their more complex furniture- and instrument-manufacturing components.) Like the "other manufacturing" category, food manufacturing is a heterogeneous class that finds resource-oriented processing activities emerging in the lower order sequences transmuting into final demand-oriented processes as one moves up the growth ladder. In short, the evidence suggests a rough consistency with the primary–secondary–tertiary component of the growth track hypothesis.[7]

Now add the final step to the data game. In the B columns of table II-13 we record the industry-sector rank orders of the *actual* 1940–70 competitive shifts taken from tables II-8 and II-9. Thus, ordinally the actual shift patterns of hamlets can be compared with the hypothetical shift pattern that hamlets would exhibit if they were to grow up to full convenience status. This is true in a similar fashion for other trade centers. Since the two rank vectors are ordinally commensurate, we can make a crude comparison by employing the rank differences presented in the C columns of table II-13. It is clear that the differences are substantial.[8] It is also clear why the growth track effects cannot be detected in the profiles of tables II-8 and II-9. The positive deviations indicated competitive gains greater than those implied by the growth track scenario; the negative gains indicate the reverse. In either case the dynamic forces of the historical process are at variance with the growth track scenario—dramatically and systematically so for more than three-quarters of the sectors.

Thus, developmental changes have altered the structure of the urban transaction network in such a way that the higher order centers have achieved gains in urban-service functions (as railroads, trucking, communications, wholesale trade, professional services, and entertainment) far greater than a growth scenario would account for. Conversely, the lower order centers displayed gains in the same categories that were substantially less than the growth scenario would indicate. The lower order centers experienced disproportionate gains in the remaining kinds of urban-service activities, principally utilities and other transportation services (busing). Retail trade activities consistently registered competitive shortfalls relative to the growth scenario. The lower order centers experienced manufacturing gains far greater than expected, while the larger urban core centers experienced prominent scenario-falsifying competitive losses.

This little exercise puts the final stamp on a major theme of this study. In the final analysis, scalar growth effects are dependent on and derive from the evolutionary developmental changes in the behavioral-structural logic of a society. To this theoretical conclusion we add the evidence of this little data game. The intersectoral-interregional shifts in activity characteristic of a scalar growth ladder are lost in the historical record for all of the reasons indicated. All considerations suggest that the fascination with formal growth models reflected in the literature may be sadly misplaced.

Notes

1. These appendixes are not called out in the sequential tradition of editorial practice. The reason is given in the introduction to part two.

2. As before, appendix II-K (panels A through D) makes a similar presentation in terms of the code C frequency counts. These relative frequency patterns tell a similar story with modifications accounted for by differences in the degree of industrial localization characteristic of the different sectors. These modifications are similar to those noted in the previous section and the reader is left to pursue the related images further.

3. You will recall that under a different aggregation format (tables 33 and 34 of volume I) it is only the largest metropolitan trade centers and urban cores that contribute negative competitive differentials.

4. The disproportionately large gains of complete shopping centers located in the secondary fields of medium cores must be telling us something, but I am not sure what. It is not attributable to differences in county frequencies. These centers are not disproportionately grouped in any geographical subfield so this does not appear to be the result of unique regional circumstances. This anomaly is worth further investigation.

5. The reader will encounter difficulty if he attempts to match the algebraic sum of all complete shopping centers across all transaction fields in appendix II-I with the shift profile presented in table II-8. There is no direct match because every time we change the structure of the computational matrix (or, metaphorically, when we cast a different boundary net over the universe of observations), the resulting frequency patterns and proportions are changed. The sequence and extent of the balancing of negatives against positives is altered.

6. The small, medium, and large urban cores are chosen over the various sized metropolitan and wholesale retail centers to reduce the

number of categories. Furthermore, the higher order trade centers were not as unambiguously defined by Borchert (1967) and Berry (1977), as were the lower order centers (chapter 5 in volume I).

7. This is not surprising, of course. The computations forming the growth track rankings in table II-11 are tautological. We have made the hypothetical system grow in the way the growth track hypothesis says it would grow. This is defensible because the object is to show how these depart from the rankings based on historical shift patterns.

8. If the historical process conformed to the growth track scenario, the index of rank differences would be zero. In reality the index varies between 50 and 75 percent of the maximum rank deviation that would result from a complete reversal of rank orders. Even if we throw away all rank differences of less than five orders, more than two-thirds of the cells remain.

5

Developmental Sequence Patterns

In this chapter, the developmental (C) code is employed as another bridge to the perspective that is emerging in this volume. Representations of industry-line transformations are generated for each county for each of three decennial periods. They are presented as a three-way cross tabulation in table II-14. This is our resource for discerning the *patterns of change in the change patterns* that we know as the developmental code. This is done in a manner analogous to the early examination of differential (B) code sequence patterns in chapter 12 of volume I.

Hypothetical Sequence Patterns

As before, there are reasons to expect certain sequence patterns to occur more frequently than others. The hypothesized sequences are presented schematically in figure II-1. The dynamic nadir occurs when a leading competitive loss is experienced by a locally unspecialized activity, code C8.[1] Traditional economic theory suggests that such an employment loss may reflect in part the process of adjusting to competitive disadvantage.[2] Economic theory also suggests that, as these losses bring sector employment in line with the region's competitive strength, they will decline and eventually disappear. Thus, a leading loss (relative to the all-industry employment shift) at C8 may translate into a lagging loss over time. It always remains possible, of course, for growth or development to enlarge the comparative advantage of the industry in its localized area. Depending on the strength and timing of such a stimulus, the sector may begin to experience lagging, if not leading, employment gains.

Each notch in the advancing sequence is probably more difficult to reach. First, to advance beyond C7 requires the active intervention of some growth or developmental stimulus, one which may not be accessible to an industry sector in all urban localities. Second, to advance beyond C5 requires the gain to be strong enough, and to be sustained long enough, for a sector's employment to become large enough to change its specialization status.

Those industry sectors that negotiate this phase shift arrive at the zenith of the transformation cycle. In addition to strong leading competitive gains, the specialized status suggests that a locality has a better chance of capturing growth and mix gains as well. But there is another side to this dynamic coin. In the absence of additional developments, such employment gains must use up the growth potential inherent in the comparative advantage. In the process, a leading gain will gradually become a lagging gain. Earlier employment shortfalls may be transmuted into employment excesses, if new developmental changes act to diminish comparative advantage. This hypothesis,

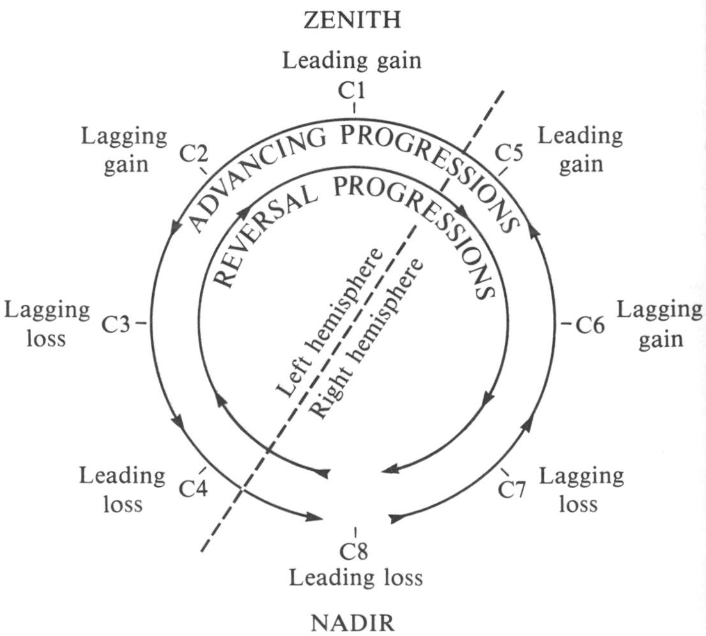

FIGURE II-1. Hypothesized sequence channels for the industry-line developmental code

TABLE II-14. Tabulation of county developmental (C) code for all industry sectors combined, 1940–50, 1950–60, 1960–70

		1960–70 Code C								
1940–50	1950–60	C1	C2	C3	C4	C5	C6	C7	C8	Total
C1	C1	1,082	207	64	819	3	—	—	1	2,176
C1	C2	220	151	28	231	15	15	4	3	667
C1	C3	76	13	43	139	3	—	4	1	279
C1	C4	753	211	133	1,165	148	67	56	126	2,659
C1	C5	2	1	3	2	5	2	—	1	16
C1	C6	—	—	—	1	3	2	—	—	6
C1	C7	—	—	—	1	—	2	3	—	6
C1	C8	—	—	—	—	2	1	1	—	4
Total		2,133	583	271	2,358	179	89	68	132	5,813
C2	C1	265	116	29	322	2	1	—	—	735
C2	C2	171	195	43	213	53	82	18	23	798
C2	C3	22	5	18	53	2	1	—	2	103
C2	C4	174	96	39	284	133	102	49	134	1,011
C2	C5	17	21	5	35	13	20	7	12	130
C2	C6	8	12	5	15	42	75	11	20	188
C2	C7	1	—	2	3	7	8	6	6	33
C2	C8	—	—	—	2	25	19	5	15	66
Total		658	445	141	927	277	308	96	212	3,064
C3	C1	86	18	35	131	—	—	—	—	270
C3	C2	15	11	6	24	2	2	1	1	62
C3	C3	21	3	82	63	2	—	15	5	191
C3	C4	84	10	59	171	69	22	32	56	503
C3	C5	6	5	3	15	6	—	—	4	39
C3	C6	2	1	1	2	1	1	1	4	13
C3	C7	4	1	6	—	11	—	42	4	68
C3	C8	—	—	—	—	13	5	5	4	27
Total		218	49	192	406	104	30	96	78	1,173
C4	C1	456	117	65	711	—	1	—	—	1,350
C4	C2	155	128	22	236	20	30	5	24	620
C4	C3	87	15	85	210	6	3	19	13	438
C4	C4	547	180	165	1,403	299	158	116	324	3,192
C4	C5	133	67	35	350	88	59	35	89	856
C4	C6	29	24	8	89	129	206	49	133	667
C4	C7	14	4	20	35	109	33	74	83	372
C4	C8	3	2	6	22	321	192	115	256	917
Total		1,424	537	406	3,056	972	682	413	922	8,412
C5	C1	597	206	53	700	1	2	1	—	1,560
C5	C2	174	139	27	271	31	38	4	24	708
C5	C3	85	27	49	157	5	4	10	9	346
C5	C4	389	169	67	525	555	304	141	404	2,554
C5	C5	829	380	107	1,270	2,899	1,625	552	1,347	9,009
C5	C6	91	92	17	145	2,054	2,694	190	772	6,055
C5	C7	55	25	30	99	951	330	361	382	2,233
C5	C8	25	14	7	42	1,901	1,101	341	819	4,250
Total		2,245	1,052	357	3,209	8,397	6,098	1,600	3,757	26,715
C6	C1	56	37	10	84	—	—	—	—	187
C6	C2	24	57	6	88	18	35	1	13	242
C6	C3	10	3	1	23	—	—	—	—	37
C6	C4	28	21	14	49	92	65	31	84	384
C6	C5	574	388	94	1,172	2,834	2,623	407	1,624	9,716
C6	C6	71	141	29	188	4,394	9,111	400	1,595	15,929
C6	C7	19	7	9	46	525	300	149	211	1,266
C6	C8	7	10	6	12	1,626	1,358	187	600	3,806
Total		789	664	169	1,662	9,489	13,492	1,175	4,127	31,567

TABLE II-14. Tabulation of county developmental (C) code for all industry sectors combined, 1940–50, 1950–60, 1960–70 (*Continued*)

		1960–70 Code C								
1940–50	1950–60	C1	C2	C3	C4	C5	C6	C7	C8	Total
C7	C1	18	4	8	36	—	—	—	—	66
C7	C2	6	3	2	9	—	2	1	2	25
C7	C3	7	3	5	26	1	—	2	—	44
C7	C4	15	16	10	34	27	11	16	36	165
C7	C5	108	65	37	282	594	256	286	464	2,092
C7	C6	14	13	7	17	237	272	83	192	835
C7	C7	27	8	25	55	444	115	337	224	1,235
C7	C8	2	2	5	8	536	212	180	225	1,170
Total		197	114	99	467	1,839	868	905	1,143	5,632
C8	C1	3	4	1	12	—	—	—	—	20
C8	C2	1	2	—	4	—	1	—	—	8
C8	C3	1	1	1	4	—	—	—	—	7
C8	C4	4	4	3	8	13	7	4	16	59
C8	C5	246	150	71	709	1,064	704	389	1,262	4,595
C8	C6	18	26	12	89	912	1,240	207	984	3,488
C8	C7	9	13	11	43	507	204	272	329	1,388
C8	C8	5	5	3	20	1,175	837	280	749	3,074
Total		287	205	102	889	3,671	2,993	1,152	3,340	12,639
Total all sectors		7,951	3,649	1,737	12,974	24,928	24,560	5,505	13,711	95,015

then, suggests an advancing progression of C-code shift patterns around the circle to C4. Here we come to a second hump marked by the transition from specialized to unspecialized status. If the losses are strong enough and go on long enough, the local sector will lose its specialized status and the transition back to the right hemicycle will be complete.

Because the C7→C6 and the C2→C3 transformations require advantageously timed growth and developmental effects that increase or decrease local comparative advantages, and because the C5→C1 and C4→C8 transformations require comparative advantages and disadvantages to be repeatedly reinforced for a period sufficient to change specialization status, the path of advancing progressions just marked out is not likely to sustain an orderly, uninterrupted passage. We should observe a tendency for developmental code transformations to move along this track, but we should not be surprised if they stay in place for two or more time periods, or even reverse themselves after a localized stimulus has at least temporarily spent itself. Reversal sequences are also possible because growth and developmental effects can be either advantageous or disadvantageous depending on where an activity is situated in the transformation cycle or in the urban transaction field.[3]

This, then, is a sequence hypothesis consistent with the concepts of the sources and sequences of change elaborated in part one of volume I, as well as with the operation of traditional economic system equilibrating tendencies. Consider next how well the image matches the record.

The Sequence Record

Our hypothesis suggests that the competitive change pattern experienced by an urban locality in one period may repeat in the next, or move along the specified channel in either an advancing or reversal direction. Implicit in the hypothesis is the presupposition that cross-cycle transformation pairs would not occur. This would suggest that many cells in table II-14 would either be empty or sparsely settled. Are these hypothesized patterns consistent with the record?

Initial evidence gives strong support. Forty-four percent of all cells in the table are either empty or contain no more than .01 percent of the total frequency. Conversely, 4 percent of all cells contain 50 percent of the total frequency. Clearly a limited set of paths dominates the change pattern sequences.

But the real test comes when we consider point-to-point sequences along the hypothesized path. We do this with the help of table II-15, which is organized in the order depicted by the transformation wheel. First, we consider the dynamic (C code) orientation of each industry sector for each county during the middle decade.

TABLE II-15. Where 1950–60 developmental (C) codes came from in 1940–50 and went to in 1960–70
(percentage of total 1950–60 frequencies for each C code)

Developmental codes	C8	C7	C6	C5	C1	C2	C3	C4	Total
1950–60 C8s									
Came from in 1940–50	**23.1**	**8.8**	28.6	**31.9**	—	0.5	0.2	6.9	100.0
Went to in 1960–70	**20.0**	**8.4**	**28.0**	**42.1**	0.3	0.2	0.2	0.8	100.0
1950–60 C7s									
Came from in 1940–50	**21.0**	**18.7**	19.2	**33.8**	0.1	0.5	1.0	5.6	100.0
Went to in 1960–70	**18.8**	**18.8**	15.0	**38.7**	2.0	0.9	1.6	4.3	100.0
1950–60 C6s									
Came from in 1940–50	12.8	3.1	**58.6**	22.3	—	0.7	—	2.5	100.0
Went to in 1960–70	13.6	3.5	**50.0**	**28.6**	0.9	1.1	0.3	2.0	100.0
1950–60 C5s									
Came from in 1940–50	**17.4**	**7.9**	**36.7**	**34.1**	—	0.5	0.1	3.2	100.0
Went to in 1960–70	**18.2**	**6.3**	20.0	**28.4**	7.2	**4.1**	1.3	**14.5**	100.0
1950–60 C1s									
Came from in 1940–50	0.3	1.0	2.9	24.5	**34.2**	**11.5**	**4.2**	**21.1**	100.0
Went to in 1960–70	—	—	—	—	**40.3**	**11.1**	**4.2**	**44.2**	100.0
1950–60 C2s									
Came from in 1940–50	0.3	0.8	7.7	22.6	**21.3**	**25.5**	**2.0**	**19.8**	100.0
Went to in 1960–70	2.9	1.1	6.5	4.4	**24.5**	**21.9**	**4.3**	**34.4**	100.0
1950–60 C3s									
Came from in 1940–50	0.5	3.0	2.6	23.9	**19.3**	**7.1**	**13.2**	**30.3**	100.0
Went to in 1960–70	2.1	3.5	0.6	1.3	**21.4**	**4.8**	**19.6**	**46.7**	100.0
1950–60 C4s									
Came from in 1940–50	0.6	1.6	3.6	24.3	**25.3**	**9.6**	**4.8**	**30.3**	100.0
Went to in 1960–70	11.2	4.2	7.0	12.7	**18.9**	**6.7**	**4.7**	**34.6**	100.0

Notes: Boldface numbers indicate disproportionately large frequencies relative to that percentage of total frequency for the corresponding time period.
Source: Derived from table II-14.

Then we ask how the 1950–60 change pattern compares with the same counties' industry sectors in the preceding and following decades.

Of the 1950–60 C8s (unspecialized leading losses at the nadir of the transformation channel) about one-fourth were persistent leading decliners carried over from the previous decade. Almost two-thirds were reversal shifts displayed by C5 and C6 change patterns (unspecialized, leading and lagging gainers). During the middle decade these C5 and C6 counties tended to use up (through scalar growth) the comparative advantages leading to first decade gains in employment share. They may also have been affected by developmental changes that tended to erode their competitive bases. The few 1950–60 C8s that *came from* 1940–50 C7s (unspecialized lagging losses) probably experienced a turnaround in comparative advantage also induced by total system change. The 1950–60 C8s tended to *go to* the C5s, C6s, and C7s in that order. These county-industry sectors likely used up (through growth) a preexisting competitive disadvantage as well as receiving a lift from developmental changes that improved their comparative position. A significant number of 1950–60 C8s *came from* 1940–50 C4s (specialized, leading losses) when adjustments to an adverse competitive position likely brought about a loss in specialized status. This is a natural progression from the left to right hemicycle. Movements from right to left hemicycles initiated from the nadir do not, in contrast, fit the sequence hypothesis and are very sparse in the record.

It is already necessary to make a refinement in the sequence hypothesis. The dynamic sequences displayed by individual industry sectors appear to be much more volatile than those displayed by the region-summarizing differential employment shifts (code B) of chapter 12 in volume I. Industry-sector developmental code progressions along the hypothesized sequence channel do *not tend* to make the step-by-step progressions observable in the all-sector differentials. Clearly, developmental sources of change (and their attendant differential growth effects) can alter a region's competitive position for a specified activity sector more markedly and quickly than they change its all-sector position. Countertrend improvements in competitive positions can convert leading losers into leading gainers within comparatively short spans of time (and vice versa). Thus, the largest portion of mid-decade C8s came from and went to C5s. It is likely that following the sequence over a shorter time span would reveal the step-by-step progression along the hypothesized channel, but the decennial period picks up only the origin and the terminus of the progression.[4] With this skip-step character of developmental sequence patterns accounted for, the C8 progressions appear to be remarkably consistent with the hypothesis.

In their own way the change patterns represented by each of the developmental codes tend to confirm the expected progressions. Allowing for the reversal progressions to C8, C7s behaved much like C8s. C6 sequence patterns are also consistent and are remarkable principally because of the prominence of repetitive sequences. This seems to reflect the large numbers of trade and service sectors pulled along as lagging gainers in regions experiencing persistent employment growth under the effect of more dynamic sectors.

C5 sequence patterns are crucial to the hypothesis because they are at the point of advance out of the unspecialized hemicycle. This is the first of the unspecialized classifications of change in each sector for which reversal sequences were more prominent than advancing sequences. This seems to reflect the resistance one would expect in the transformation from unspecialized to specialized status. Still, as is consistent with C5's threshold status, industry sectors did cross over to specialized status in significant numbers.

1950–60 C1s, C2s, C3s, and C4s *came from* 1940–50 C5s in about equal proportions, but the advancing progressions displayed by these categories were disproportionately restricted to the specialized hemicycle. Just as advancing industry sectors in the unspecialized hemicycle showed a tendency to skip ahead to C5, advancing sectors in the specialized hemicycle tended to skip ahead to C4. As sectors advanced beyond C1, they displayed a marked tendency to experience reversal progressions, indicating the likelihood of development-induced reversals of competitive advantage.

Being, like C5s, at the threshold of the advancing progression from one hemicycle to another, C4s likewise displayed a cross-over progression in significant numbers. It is especially significant for the support of our sequence hypothesis that C1s and C8s displayed virtually no cross-hemicycle reversal sequences.

In contrast, there are some sequence patterns in tables II-14 and II-15 that are less easy to reconcile with the advancing and reversal progressions of the sequence hypotheses. They turn out to be relatively few in number, however. Those sequences that represent a crossover from one hemicycle to another and that simultaneously represent a transition gain to a loss (or vice versa) are the most difficult ones to reconcile. All such sequences represent less than 7 percent of the total. Some of these might still be demonstrated to be advancing or reversal sequences that progressed around the track quite rapidly within the time frame of the decennial base lines. Others may be explained as computational anomalies of three types: (1) often localized industry sectors may experience a change in specialization status not because of developmental-growth effects manifest as a localized dynamic, but because their C code classification is *redefined* by changes in the national industrial structure employed as a base in the specialization-localization index computations;[5] (2) a localized industry sector might have its C code classification redefined by changes in the all-sector competitive shift generated by the altered dynamics of other industry sectors in the region;[6] (3) as we have previously acknowledged, the share component employed in developing the C code does not correspond perfectly with the economist's concept of competitive gains and losses. For example, changes in the industry mix of subordinate levels of aggregation might generate share changes with no correspondence to changes in comparative advantage. This is another reason to expect some anomalous sequences in the record.

Nevertheless, there appears to be a remarkable correspondence between the historical record of individual localized industry sequences and the expectation of our sequence hypothesis. That hypothesis, in turn, emerged from combining our concept of developmental change with the short-term equilibrating notion of conventional economic theory. Industry-sector sequences do seem to move along a path like that represented by figure II-1. How far along this path, and for how long, depends on the growth and developmental potential implicit in the sector's localized resource base, its position in the urbanized transaction network of the large system, and its developmental history. It is part of a dynamically evolving complex and may be conceived of as moving along the sequential path in an advancing or reversal direction in accordance with the degree to which changes in its transaction network prove to be advantageous or disadvantageous. Relatively few county-industry sectors seem likely to sustain lengthy progressions around the track. The more common experience is one of ebb and flow or sequence oscillation.[7]

There is a final observation of considerable importance. The generalized sequence pattern summarized here for all industry sectors is duplicated by the data for each sector. The cell percentages displayed by industry-sector tables corresponding to table II-15 are different. Trade and service sectors, for example, appear to be more volatile than manufacturing sectors. Some industries display more left hemicycle (specialized) counties than others. But, even though the frequency patterns of different industry sectors may load differently upon different segments of the transformation wheel, the *transformation patterns* they depict are essentially the same, in terms of their correspondence to the sequence hypothesis.

The Evolutionary Insight

This sequence analysis reinforces and expands the evolutionary insight initiated in part one of volume I. The oscillating ebb and flow of change-pattern sequences suggests an evolutionary process in which a set of behavioral adaptations of one era separately and collectively leads to a new set of adaptive problems in the next. The pattern is consistent with an iterative series of both equilibrating (growth) and disequilibrating (developmental) adaptations to a changing operating environment. The mutual interactions of all establishments form the operating environment for each. Hence, the collective impact of the individual adaptations transforms the operating transactions network in ways that feed back on each behavioral entity. The systemic effects define a new problem-solving context requiring additional adaptations. There is, thus, a continuous progression of both favorable and unfavorable social-activity-wrought changes in localized transaction networks and geographical fields.

This insight into the evolutionary nature of urban-system change calls into question popular organismic analogies. We have already seen how such views lead one to characterize urban change in terms of scalar growth, or something akin to ontogenetic development. Individual social establishments, as well as local or regional subfields of the urban-transaction network, are often treated as reified entities progressing through a life cycle to "maturity" and ultimately "decline." Such a conceptual model of change inclines one to view scalar decline and behavioral regression as pathological conditions to be delayed, repaired, or reversed through external interventions of a clinical sort. This study, my earlier work (Dunn, 1971), and a paper by Kaniss (n.d.) cast this process in a different light.

The evolutionary metaphor suggests that decline or behavioral regression need not be a pathological signal of systemic death or extinction. Rather, decline is often an adaptive strategy by which a living system (biological or social) escapes from obsolete specializations. It is partly through a process of disinvestment or behavioral "forgetting" that urban systems change adaptive directions. The decline of micro-components of a hierarchical urban system may be a form of benign adaptation for both the total system and its transforming establishments, activity sectors, and localized subfields. The pathology lies not in the transformation of the system or its components, but in the destabilizing or limiting problems that such dynamic systems encounter. Behavioral change, possibly attended by the decline of some establishments, sectors, and localized subfields, is an essential part of problem-solving adaptations. The evolutionary insight sees system change as an historical process of system reorganization rather than an unfolding of a "genetic template."

There is a corollary insight. New activities or social structures will tend to seek out, and further articulate, transaction subfields that are less cluttered by obsolete specializations. These need not always be virgin subfields at some extensive margin. Older transaction subfields or urban localities that have progressed through a phase of disinvestment may have cleared urban-service "docking sites" sufficiently to accommodate emerging behavioral specializations more in tune with the remaining transaction networks and with the different problems of an emerging era. Such an explanation must lie behind many of the left hemicycle reversal progressions displayed in table 32 in volume I, and table II-15 of this volume. These conceptual and representational insights carry important implications for normative policy issues that will be discussed in part three.

Notes

1. Because such a sector will not even generate off-setting summary line mix effects—except in the few cases where the total industry growth effect is negative.

2. I recognize that the dimension and direction of the share component may reflect computational characteristics of the shift-share technique not associated with changes in competitive advantage as formally defined by economists. Still, it seems likely that the principal sources of recorded changes in the competitive component are underlying changes in comparative advantage.

3. It should be apparent that the "advancing" and "reversal" terminology simply designates the direction of sequence transformations and carries no value connotation. However, advancing progressions in the unspecialized hemicycle and reversal progressions in the specialized hemicycle are popularly conceived of as at least short-run advantages from a chamber-of-commerce perspective.

4. This is not surprising. It is not unusual for an urban locality to experience positive share gains for all of its constituent activities simultaneously. Although growth and developmental effects might cause an *individual industry* sector to skip from the nadir to the zenith of the transaction wheel within a short time, it is but a single element in the overall regional dynamic. Other industry sectors in the same region may be exercising simultaneous reversal progressions in off-setting losses and lagging gains so that the dynamic characteristics of total employment transformations are dampened. Thus, the aggregate displayed in chapter 12 of volume I moves with a more measured step.

5. Evidence of this factor at work is found when we examine industry sector detail. Of the C7s and 8s that shifted to C4 and the C1s and C2s that shifted to C5, the overwhelming portion occurred in seven retail trade and service categories. These are also the sectors with the smallest deviations from the weighted index of specialization so that a small

change in the weighted index can very easily cause a redefinition of specialization status in these sectors.

6. Once again, however, such reclassifications are likely to occur only for those sectors close to a reclassification boundary.

7. It is interesting to note that advancing progressions outnumber reversal progressions two to one, reflecting the dramatic way in which total system sources of growth and development were shared by most localities and most industry sectors during the study period. About one-third of the sequences involved oscillations between advancing and reversal phases. It is not likely that such an experience can be generalized to the record of every historical epoch.

Part Two

CHANGE PATTERNS IN INDUSTRIAL SECTORS: DESCRIPTION AND EXPLANATION

In chapter 14 of volume I, which recognized the need to move beyond the preliminary and proximal explanations embodied in the shift-share model, some of the developmental factors lying behind the mix effect were examined. We recognized the need to shift attention from the industrial characteristics of interregional shifts in total employment to the geographical characteristics of the interregional shifts in employment of each industry sector. The tables and bridging descriptions in part one of this volume have prepared us for the new perspective. In part two the description of each major industrial sector will serve as a beginning point for a consideration of developmental explanations.

As we peel the onion layer by layer, we will not be following the conventional order established by the standard industrial classification and reflected in the table formats or map sequences of this study. We will be guided by our need to look behind the settlement pattern and employment shifts to consider the changing structure of underlying transaction networks and their higher order explanations. Consequently, the order in which the reader's attention is called to the tables, maps, and color plates will not always follow conventional sequence. The table of contents does, however, list the tables, maps, and color plates in sequential order.

6

Transportation: A Linkage Sector

According to the view emphasized in this study, spatially differentiated changes in settlement and activity patterns are primarily a reflection of changes in the transaction network structure of the urban system (recall part one in volume I). Such changes in turn, are a reflection of developmental changes in all industrial sectors that involve both transferring and transforming activities (recall the volume I distinction). But activities that are directly involved in carrying out the transfer or linkage functions of an urban society occupy a uniquely central place in this process. They have a more direct effect on the structure of urbanized transaction networks and, hence, a more direct effect on the spatial redistribution of other activities.

So it is that we begin with a discussion of the linkage sectors rather than with the so-called "basic" sectors. (Linkage sectors are here taken to include all transportation, communication, public utility wholesale trade, finance, and printing and publishing activities.) The geographical changes in the employment patterns of these sectors do not, of course, directly represent changes in the underlying transaction networks. They do, however, more directly reflect changes in access networks than the changing patterns of the other sectors.

The Historical Problem-Solving Sequence of Access Networks

One of the basic themes of this study is the view that the fundamental explanations of social change are found in the problem-solving sequences of the adaptive, historical social process. In any given era, the problems encountered evoke developmental responses (new ways of doing things, new things to do, and new ways of valuing things). In contrast to scalar-growth-educed managerial adaptations, these developmental responses transform the logic of social processes and the topological structure of transaction networks. Retrieving an expression coined earlier, one might say that developmental adaptations alter the "topo-logic" of the systems they change. Moreover, these attempted solutions to one era's problems do more than transform the structure of social processes, they also alter the nature of problems experienced in subsequent periods.

It follows that changes in transaction networks reflected in the shift patterns of any period are a developmental response to the access problems perceived to be the most critical at the time. But, since there are time lags between perceived problems, creative design developments, and social applications, the adaptations of any era are to some degree responses to problems encountered in an earlier experience. The change patterns revealed by our tables and maps mean more when viewed against such an explanatory backdrop. Consider for a moment the developmental antecedents of study period linkage structures.

To bring order to this historical record it is helpful to distinguish the interurban transaction networks that define the skeletal structure of the total urban system from the intraurban networks characteristic of the semiclosed circuit networks of specific urban centers. During the earliest part of U.S. urban history, it was the interurban or large-scale access problems that dominated developmental concerns.

Until the middle of the nineteenth century, a period embracing the epochs of mercantilism and transmontane spread, the network structure of the total system was quite simple. It evolved in response to a single, overriding problem—how to gain effective access to the resource-rich interior of a vast new continent.

The appropriate adaptive techniques were extentions of already developed "old country" responses. Growth adaptations rather than developmental adaptations ruled the day. Coastal and riverine waterways were the channels; the boat and barge were the primary instruments. Nonnavigable reaches were breached by applying established canal-building techniques. The resulting transaction network was linear. The tidal growth of social activities and population settlements formed a transaction network heavily determined by the natural topography of the nation.

As this system grew into place, the most obtrusive access problems took on a special character. Because of the very scale of the distances involved, the spreading network could only proceed so far on the basis of old-world adaptive strategies. The canal could extend and integrate the river systems, as in the old country. But in England the water systems were short, and they mostly linked natural estuary systems. In America, large river stretches were effectively one-way streets because of rapid flow. In England, hinterland spaces were not excessively landlocked because a manageable cart or wagon trip could reach some water system. In the United States, vast reaches of the continent were inaccessible to the transport technology of that time. Access problems became a much more prominent and persistent aspect of the American experience. This is why the United States soon surpassed England and the continent in inventive, developmental transport technology.

During the period from 1840 to 1870, steam power emerged as the solution to transportation problems. Two dramatic developments were in response to the two major perceived access problems. For the first time, the steamboat transformed the river thoroughfares into effective two-way streets and the "iron horse," riding on iron rails, reinforced the waterway system by extending the rivers' territorial penetration of the interior. This was the era that witnessed the emergence of a genuinely national transportation system. These developments paved the way for the urban structure that was implicit in the commercial-mercantile thrust of U.S. historical growth to come to full realization. For the first time, the national transaction system became a differentiated, articulated and fully interrelated activity network. This was also the first time an urban hierarchy clearly appeared in the nation's settlement patterns.

As before, these very changes further altered society's perception of access problems, so that the fourth epoch (roughly 1870 to 1910) experienced different changes in urban structure.

The developmental thrust continued along familiar lines, representing an outgrowth of the limitations of prior adaptations. The low-pressure steam boilers of the early locomotives (along with structural weakness of their iron rails) were not adequate to generate effective competition for long-distance waterway transport. Although the riverine network of an earlier time had become a more completely articulated transport system, the waterways regime had not been substantially altered. The technological developments leading to the steel rail and the efficient, high-pressure steam engine constituted the developmental response. For the first time, a truly continental transport system emerged; and, for the first time, a land-based transport system became dominant.

The railway did more than extend the fields of urbanized activity to the new west, it initiated an epoch of radical urban-system reorganization. Vastly increased transport efficiency enlarged effective market areas. (During this time rail transport costs alone decreased by two-thirds). This made it possible to satisfy broad regional (and, increasingly, national) demands for goods from a more limited number of centers than before. The larger centers tended to be the first to achieve threshold economies of scale that opened up developmental options and multiplied agglomeration effects. In addition the more complex articulation of the transport net, and the relative decline in the access advantages of the riverine centers, scrambled the order of the earlier urban center hierarchy. Many centers emerged *de novo,* or gained unexpected prominance: among them were Dallas, San Antonio, Houston, Austin, El Paso, Oklahoma City, Tulsa, Denver, Salt Lake City, Springfield, Des Moines, Duluth, Green Bay, Bay City, Madison, Rockford, Jacksonville, Tampa, Butte, Spokane, Seattle, Portland, and Los Angeles. There were relative declines as well. Borchert (1967) describes it thus:

> The largest group comprised the towns along the Ohio, Mississippi, Missouri, and principal tributaries. Smaller centers such as Dubuque and Quincy (Illinois) dropped out of the "metropolitan" ranks; St. Louis, Louisville, and Wheeling fell in the hierarchy, never to recover the relative positions that they had held during the epoch of the steam packet and iron horse (p. 320).

It is clear that the advent of a continental railway system changed the nodality and access characteristics of the network in ways detrimental to the prominent riverine cities of an earlier period. In addition, the five largest urban centers increased their share of the national population more rapidly than in any other period. The total number of fourth- and fifth-order cities registered its greatest growth during this epoch. Finally, urban core populations grew sharply.

Beginning in the epoch of the steamboat and iron horse, and accelerating in the continental railroad era, two additional changes in urban structure emerged. Their explanation, however, is not rooted in the changing access problems and transport technologies that dominated the developmental process to this point. It is rooted in production problems whose solutions fundamentally altered the nature of the economic transactions requiring the services of transport. This came about initially because the solution to the nation's access problems generated a derived change in the nation's production economy.

Let me explain. The advent of the railroad modified the level of demand for iron and steel products so radically that purely scalar changes in the application of existing technology were inadequate. The expanding requirements induced a series of developmental responses in the technology of iron and steel manufacture. These induced the progressive integration of ore and coal mining, iron making, wrought iron and steel manufacturing, and finishing mill operations. The scale of efficient operations also increased dramatically, yielding a highly concentrated industry serving national markets. Because national markets were concentrated in the northeastern quadrant of the nation, and because the largest and most accessible ore and coal reserves were also concentrated in this region, the fourth epoch laid down a northeastern industrial belt that has persisted to this day. This was further reinforced by the manufacture of locomotives and rolling stock, and by the manufacture of the industrial machinery induced by developmental processes.

The resulting change in the production base of the economy brought about major changes in the transaction flows requiring transport. First, the nested hierarchical patterns of the extensive, commerce-based, land-resource-serving, central-place functions of the earlier epoch became overlayed by a substantial set of emerging, industrial-process tree networks. Second, a major part of the large-scale urban structure came to be erected on a resource base distinct from agriculture.

There were dramatic scalar consequences as well. The increasing returns to scale accompanying the exploitation of a rich, empty resource territory, and the increased productivity accompanying the emerging industrial technology, combined to increase the absolute size of the nation's urbanized economy. A dramatic increase in the proportion of the population occupying developing urban centers occurred at the same time that the range of enterprise activities deriving an advantage from urban center locations increased. The most critical access problem came to center on the tasks of reorganizing the expanding, fine-scale, intra-urban networks, rather than on the tasks associated with the reorganization of the large-scale interregional networks of a continental system. Thus it developed that, during the latter part of the nineteenth century and the first part of the twentieth, a different set of dominant access problems emerged that required still another kind of developmental response.

During the nation's entire history prior to the advent of the railway, the *internal structures of individual urban centers* changed very little. Nor, on a modern-day scale, did they change much in geographical extent. Essentially, fine-scale urban organization took the form of a pedestrian city. As one consequence of the large-scale urban reorganization induced by the steamboat and the railway, the largest centers began to experience untenable population densities. These pressures were exacerbated because the new transport technology reinforced the locational advantages of the urban cores for both household and intermediate activities.

The earliest intraregional developments involved adapting the large-scale access technology to the transport problems of cities. Such initiatives achieved limited results. One of the earliest innovations put the horse-drawn trolley on rails. This initiated the phenomenon of suburbanization and the separation of income classes. Later in the century an effort was made to replace the horse with the steam engine, but steam power proved to be much too cumbersome and dangerous to be successfully applied to mass transport. The most important early development resulted from exploiting the new interregional railway trunk lines for commuter service. This did not so much lead to suburbanization in the form we know it today, as to a leapfrogging dispersion of populations into displaced centers that current parlance would characterize as "exurbs." This permitted the wealthy to relocate, but contributed little to solving the access problems of the bulk of the urban population. Terminals sited in the urban cores added to the problems of the crowded city centers.

No further resolution of this problem was possible without the inventive development of newer and more flexible sources of transport power. The system did, in fact, respond with the development of two new power sources in sequence. The first was electric power, making possible first the streetcar—the electrified horsecar—and then the mass transit systems. (In 1890, 70 percent of the street railways used animal power; by 1902, 97 percent were electrified.) The size of the areas served increased exponentially, and local population pressures were substantially reduced.

This degree of reorganization still left the urban region with a rigid, linear transport structure, predominantly radial in configuration. Two pressing problems remained. First, transit in the interstitial spaces between transit lines still depended on the horse and buggy or on "shanks mare." Second, the urban rail systems were mostly people movers. Movement of goods within a city still depended on horsepower drayage. The core center's strangling hold on goods production and distribution remained.

A further adaptive response required the second new source of transport power—the internal combustion engine based on petroleum. The story of twentieth century urban-system reorganization has become, thus, the story of the impact of the gasoline engine on transaction networks. The earliest and most important consequence was the substitution of a personalized form of transport for public transport. A kind of time-and-route flexibility was introduced that was literally unimaginable in an earlier time. The subsequent emergence of truck drayage at urban-region scale did for goods transport what the earlier development had done for people transport.

We are brought, thus, to the threshold of the study period in a position to consider the development of each transport mode against the backdrop of the developmental record it has traced. The empirical record initially considered is a representation of the geographical shift patterns of employment in the linkage sectors. These linkage sectors make a restricted direct contribution to explaining all-sector employments shifts. Together they account for only one-sixth of total employment, and their contribution to the gross interregional shifts is about in proportion. It is significant, however, that employment growth in the linkage sectors was disproportionately larger than in other sectors, that is, relative to the initial year employment base (see appendix II-B, panel A). This is more suggestive of the prominent role these sectors have played in the process or urban reorganization. Nevertheless, these data do point us in the direction of underlying developmental explanations. We now turn to an examination of each transport sector.

The Personal Automobile

The advent of the personal automobile was the most important of these developments, yet it finds no explicit place in our empirical record. The reason is that the automobile is household owned and operated and therefore does not enter into the commercial transaction record. Nevertheless, the human energy directly absorbed is phenomenal. It is estimated that, the average person drives 6,000 work-related miles each year and, if all drivers of personal automobiles were to charge for their services, it would add $500 billion to the gross national product (*The Wall Street Journal,* 1979). By the end of the study epoch, 84 percent of the nation's total transportation budget was absorbed by road transport, only 16 percent by all other modes. Ninety percent of all intercity passenger-miles were accounted for by the automobile.

The automobile's effect on transportation networks extends beyond the way in which it has redefined transport options. It has massively redefined the structure of interindustry and interregional transactions by changing the nature of the economy's nontransport activity mix. The upsurge of automobile production directly stimulated the output of oil, steel, rubber, and many other commodities. It generated massive infrastructural investments in roads, bridges, service stations, automobile dealers, and repair shops. In 1979, about 17 percent of the work force of the nation was absorbed in automobile transport-related activities, and about half of total U.S. assets (more than $2 trillion) owed their existence to the automobile (*The Wall Street Journal,* 1979). These indirect effects have further altered the transaction logic of the system.[1] This single development and its ramifications have done more to transform the topology of the urban structure than any other development in history. Both the intraregional and interregional transaction networks have been redefined. However, the initial effect of the automobile was on the internal structure of the urban region. It was, after all, the access problems of the dense urban cores that stimulated its development. As is always the case, the innovative development of motor transport lagged behind its invention, and the development of the supportive infrastructure (such as public roads) lagged still further. Few people seem to realize that the major effect of the motor vehicle was not realized until late in the 1940–70 period.

A few facts about the development of the highway system will suggest why. At the beginning of the epoch of intra-urban reorganization (1910–40), only about 2 percent of the total U.S. road and street mileage was hard surfaced and almost 90 percent had no surfacing at all. National attention was first drawn to the state of U.S. roads by the railway bottleneck that occurred during World War I, but it was 1921 before the Federal Aid to Highways Act became law. As late as 1940 well over half of the total mileage was still unsurfaced and only 16 percent had a hard bituminous or cement surface. During that epoch most of the attention was devoted to extending and upgrading local urban roads and localized farm-to-market roads, the latter being still largely unsurfaced or gravel roads.

It follows that the initial effect of the automobile was largely on the internal structure of the urban region. The interstitial spaces between the radial trunk roads were filled in, and the population density gradient of the cities flattened. The emergence of the post-automobile city began. But the motor vehicle's principal effect on inter-urban transaction structures was yet to be realized.

It was during our study period that the phenomenal upgrading of the U.S. road system took place and, correspondingly, it was during this developmental epoch that another major reorganization of the nation's urban structure occurred. Prior to 1920, road, street, and highway construction was essentially trivial in modern terms. Of the total real expenditure (that is, corrected for price changes) for public roads between 1920 and 1970, about 30 percent was put in place during the 1920s and 1930s. A phenomenal two-thirds of the total was expended after the World War II construction hiatus. The number of hard-surfaced roads tripled, the number of secondary surfaced roads doubled, and unsurfaced roads declined by 60 percent. By 1970 less than 18 percent of the entire road system lacked an improved surface.

Of particular note was the development of the freeway, or limited-access road, topped by the construction of the 42,500 mile interstate and defense highway system. Although amounting to only .01 percent of the total highway mileage, the interstate system may well be the most important development of all. These highway developments substantially altered the structure of the intra-urban transport network and, for the first time since the advent of the railroad began to redefine the access characteristics of the interurban network.

Relative to any previous experience, the effect of these factors reached almost explosive proportions during the study period. The initial suburbanization surge that occurred before World War II was largely restricted to filling up the radial interstices with residences along with a modest extensive spread. The intra-urban, industrial-commercial structure was not yet radically altered. Jobs were still predominantly core-city oriented and most trips retained a core-city origin or destination. The period since World War II not only changed the extensive and intensive scale of things, it brought about a profound change in topographical structure.

First, the postwar suburbs spread out at an accelerating rate and the modern-day exurb appeared. Farmhouses, formerly emptied to decay as a result of farm consolidation, were snapped up by urban commuters. By 1970, those people living more than 20 miles from their place of work (one way) accounted for almost one-third of total commuting trip miles and those living more than 10 miles away accounted for more than two-thirds (U.S. Department of Transportation, 1977).[2] Map II-1 gives another perspective on the amount of change within a single decade. It displays dramatic changes in the commuting boundaries around major metropolitan areas between 1960 and 1970.[3] Between 1950 and 1975 the percentage increase in the land area associated with suburbanization in the nation's large urban centers ranged between two and five times the relative increase in their populations. This amounted to an expansion of 270,000 square miles, or more than enough territory to contain both Japan and the United Kingdom (U.S. Department of Transportation, 1977). Accompanying this spatial extension of the localized domain of urban access has been a universal flattening of the population density gradients of all large pre-automobile cities.[4]

But the most significant thing about the postwar development has been the radical changes in the topological structure of the urban region. The dominant urban-core, hub-and-spoke logic of the traditional city is in the process of being redefined. There is no longer a single "downtown" for most intra-urban activities. The volume of intra-urban traffic that carries people to and from the old urban cores, relative to the volume of traffic to and from other origin and destination points within the urban region, has declined sharply. By 1970, more than half of the metropolitan area jobs (of the forty-three largest SMSAs) were outside the central city core, and the volume of central-business-district retail sales was only 6 percent of the total (after a decline of 40 percent in a decade) (U.S. Department of Transportation, 1977). Not only have work-related origins and destinations moved outside the old downtown, but they have decreased as a proportion of total trips. The share of shopping, recreation, and social trips has increased.

In addition to the spread in activity densities, urban organization has become increasingly multinodal. A distinctive part of this urban reorganization has been the appearance of the regional shopping center. As recently as 1960 there were still fewer than 1,000 of these in the United States, but by the late 1970s there were almost 20,000. The "trade-center" and "urban-region" language that we employ is becoming increasingly ambiguous. Even relatively small urbanized areas now display several "downtowns." These often form configurations of roughly equal functional order rather than the classical hierarchical order, as noted in volume I. Significantly, the same household or enterprise is often tied functionally to a number of metaphorical "downtowns." Still more significantly, the household is sometimes linked to a whole set of functional destinations that cannot be clearly identified with any localized, bounded, urban entity (characterized by even a semiclosed transaction network).

In short, the motor vehicle-based spreading of the urban region's well-articulated transaction fields has been accompanied by a significant decline in the proportion of trips with a central-business-district origin or destination. It is clear that the changing structure involves more than a flattening of urban density gradients. It seems safe to infer that the linkage network of the urban region has become less linear and polar in structure. At the same time, its nodal form has become less hierarchical, and the localized urban networks display less functional closure. Further graphic evidence of this tendency is presented in map II-2. Clearly the urban fields where polar orientations have declined in a single decade are extensive.

This has also led to a greater interpenetration of transactions between urban-region subsystems. Traditional urban boundaries are becoming increasingly arbitrary, ambiguous, and temporally unstable as the degrees of functional closure they signify are declining. This is true not only for those increasingly differentiated and multinodal trading areas within cities, but also for the 171 urban regions of the kind identified in volume I. You will recall that color plate 1 in volume I documents the extensive interpenetration of the transaction fields of these regions in 1960. No fewer than 36 major urban

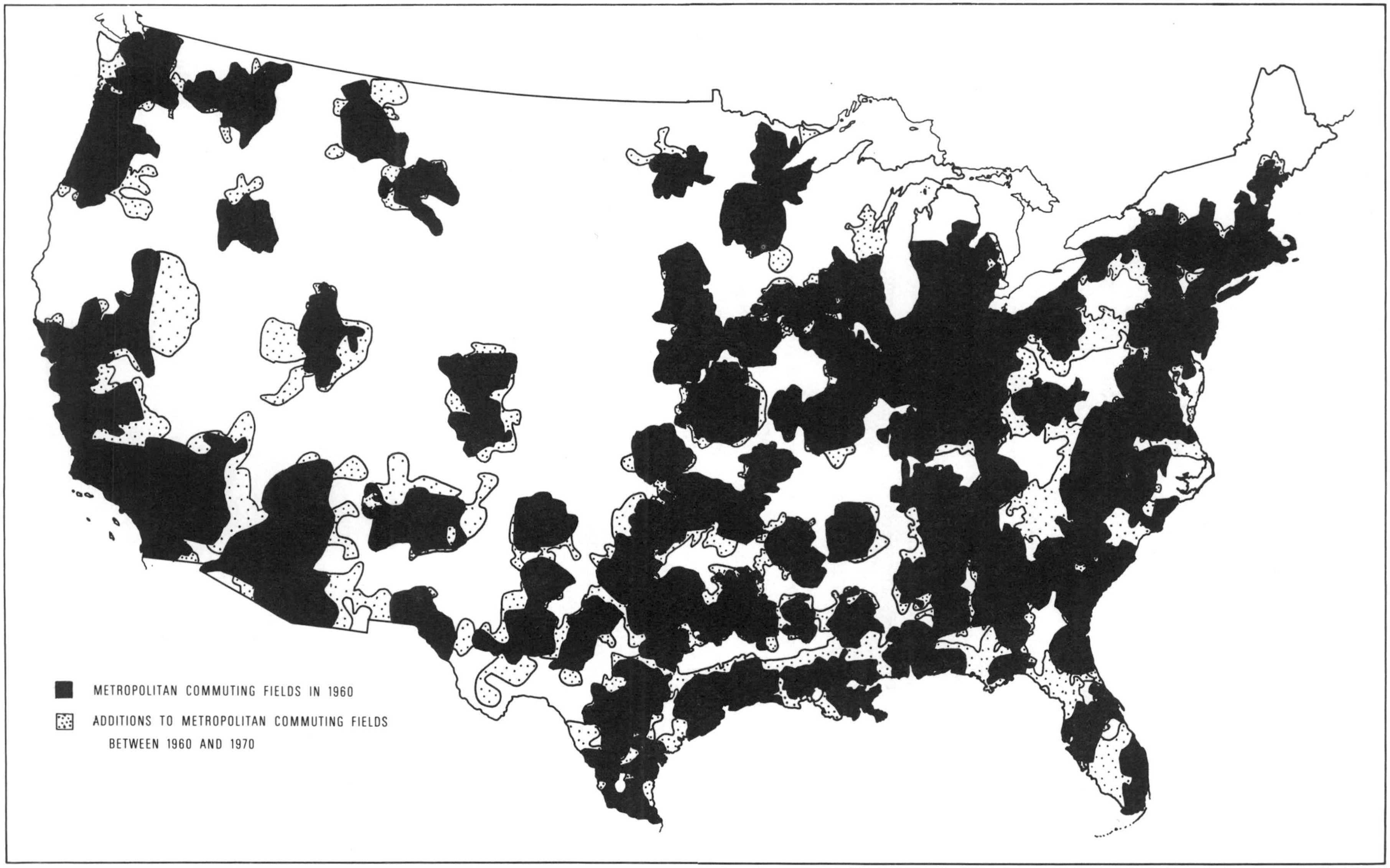

MAP II-1. Additions to Metropolitan Commuting Fields Between 1960 and 1970.
Source: reprinted with permission from Brian J. L. Berry and Quentin Gillard, *The Changing Shape of Metropolitan America: Commuting Patterns, Urban Fields and Decentralization Processes, 1960–1970,* copyright 1977, Ballinger Publishing Company, Cambridge, Mass., pp. 100–101.

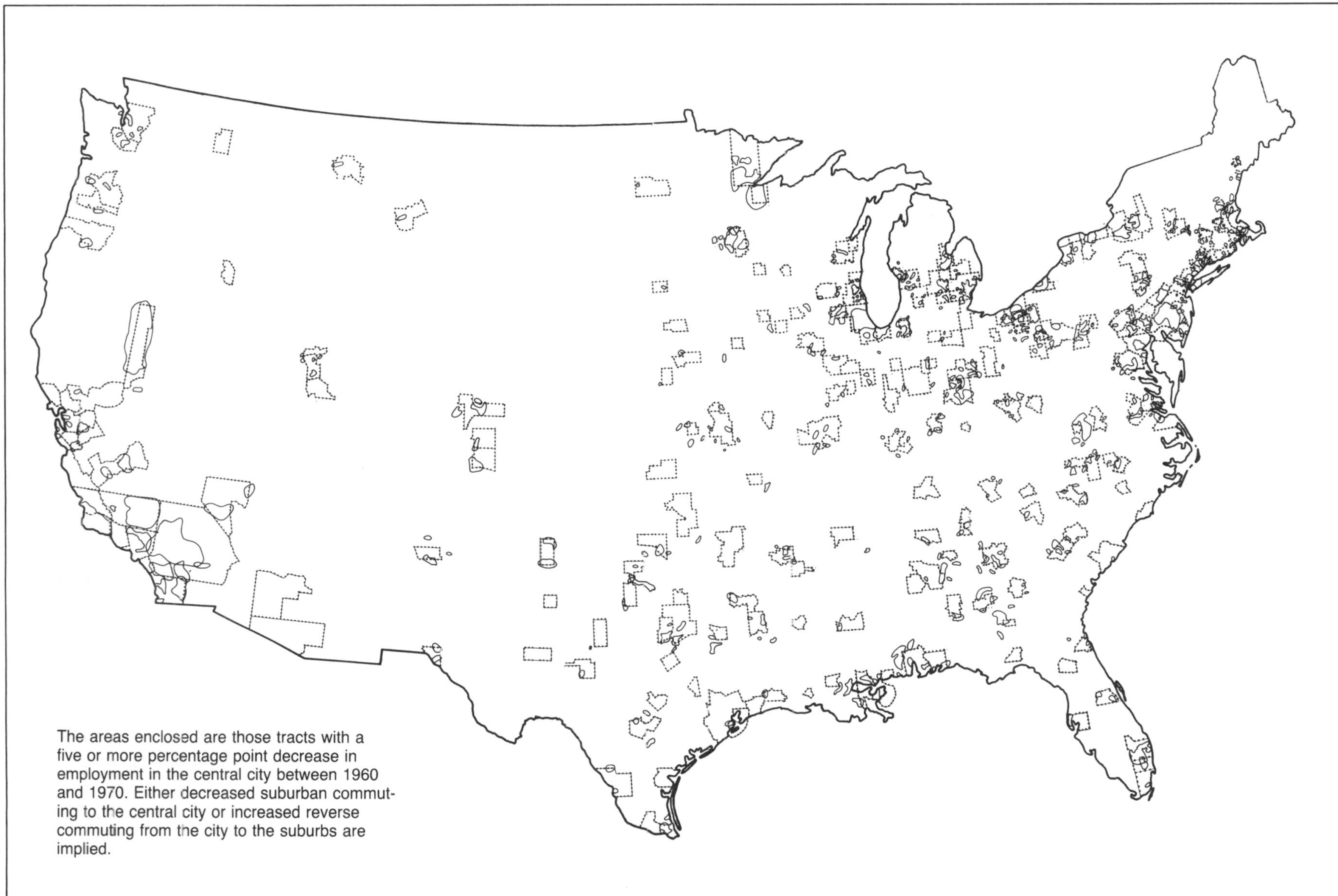

The areas enclosed are those tracts with a five or more percentage point decrease in employment in the central city between 1960 and 1970. Either decreased suburban commuting to the central city or increased reverse commuting from the city to the suburbs are implied.

MAP II-2. Area of Decreasing Dependence on Central City Employment.
Source: reprinted with permission from Brian J. L. Berry and Quentin Gillard, *The Changing Shape of Metropolitan America: Commuting Patterns, Urban Fields and Decentralization Processes, 1960–1970,* copyright 1977, Ballinger Publishing Company, Cambridge, Mass., pp. 76–77.

regions were open to substantial cross-boundary household transactions at the level of primary commuting marketing fields. The number is tripled if we include secondary fields. That this penetration further increased in the 1960s is documented by map II-1.

A part of this is the penetration of household market transaction networks into the boundary zones of densely populated urban regions. An increasingly important part is a new form of industrial commuting involving farmers and small town dwellers. An anecdote helps explain. Five times a week Sam Gaines of Mcleanboro, Indiana, climbs into the driver's seat of an old bus and heads for his job 50 miles away across the Wabash River in southern Indiana. Along the way, in towns like Enfield, Carmi, and Crossville, he stops and picks up more workers, like him destined for the Babcock and Wilcox plant in Mt. Vernon. As he steps down from the bus, he transfers the keys to Phillips Payne who has just finished a different shift. Payne, with a load of thirty workers, makes the trip back over that route dropping passengers in the same localities. Notice that this mininetwork substantially interpenetrates two urban regions, St. Louis (114) and Evansville (55) but lies entirely outside the traditionally defined functional cores of each (for a list of urban regions, see the front endpaper in volume I). Notice also that this development coincided with the completion of three new interstate highways in this area. It is difficult to come by the data to measure this emerging phenomenon satisfactorily, but one set of figures is highly suggestive. In 1960, about one in seven workers living in nonmetropolitan counties commuted to work in a different county. By 1970, that proportion had increased to one in five, an increase of 40 percent.

Another indication of the decline in functional closure of urban regions is the phenomenal increase in the volume of personal interurban transport. It is true that by 1940 the railroad had already been largely displaced as a means of personal interurban transportation. The personal automobile already accounted for about 90 percent of all interurban passenger miles. The great significance of the developments discussed above has been the phenomenal absolute and relative increase in *volume*. While the total population increased by less than half (from 1944 to 1970), the volume of intercity passenger-miles traveled increased by 600 percent. This amounted to a fivefold increase in the volume of intercity travel per person. If the personal automobile made only marginal competitive inroads vis-à-vis other transport modes during the study period, it still radically changed the coefficient of interurban access experienced by the average person. (Map II-3, which is discussed later in this chapter, suggests how radical the change has been.) Indeed, it has been a quantitative and qualitative change of such proportion as to fundamentally alter the character of American life.

On both an interurban and intra-urban scale, the transaction tentacles of the American household have increased in functional complexity and geographical reach. The terminus of each tentacle is no longer easily identified with localized systemic urban entities. The terminus of each tentacle also tends to be much less loyal in its attachments and subject to more frequent realignments. Transaction density gradients (formed by the spatial coincidence of these transactions, and exhibiting some degree of functional closure facilitating the identification of an urban "something") are more ambiguously bounded. The geographical and functional configurations of the transaction networks are in a constant state of transformation and realignment.

The Truck

The development of the truck and its effects upon urban structure lagged behind the personal automobile. Truck registrations were minuscule compared to the motorcar until well into the 1920s. The early truck was developed as a solution to the earliest, second-order sequence of problems to emerge from the impact of the automobile. As urban households spread into interstitial and suburban territories, the problem of household deliveries (newspapers, milk, and the like) and retail outlet deliveries grew apace. The truck was the emergent technological solution.[5] It was also seized upon to help solve another vexing transport problem of the time—moving farm products to local urban markets. But the early trucks were crude and clumsy; they rode on solid tires, which had a deleterious effect on the vehicle, their loads, and the road surface. Trucks were much more handicapped by poor roads than the automobile. It was near the end of the 1920s that the pneumatic tire won general acceptance as a partial solution.

One can readily understand why the early thrust of road improvements was localized. It was the local problem that the motor vehicle was first designed to solve. When I was growing up in the 1920s and 1930s local politics was heavily absorbed with the development of urban streets. State politics was dominated by the rhetoric and passions of "farm-to-market" roads. As recently as 1950 the average truck trip was still only 17 miles.

While the early motor vehicle and road developments were directed to easing localized transport problems, the same kind of problem was being scaled up to the interurban level. World War II revealed once more the nation's critical dependence on the railroad in times of national emergency. The growth of the total economy had made apparent the inefficiency and inflexibility of the railroad for shipments involving bulk-breaks and in serving transport needs under 200 miles. Trailer trucks were almost unknown until after World War II. By 1960 more than a million were in operation. Other advances such as refrigeration and air differential systems (that facilitated the carrying of bulk loads such as cement) emerged. Dieselization took place as well as advances in durability and sustained speeds. With a short span of less than fifteen years the long-distance trailer truck went from next to nothing to accounting for 75 percent of the ton miles by truck (although still accounting for only 40 percent of total road mileage). These developments were part and parcel of the symbiotic, circular cause and effect of the postwar, highspeed highway development already reported.

In the broadest terms it becomes clear that the 1920s, 1930s, and 1940s witnessed a major intra-urban reorganization as the motor vehicle solved major access problems. The 1950s and 1960s witnessed the motor vehicle's belated effect on the interurban organization of the total system.[6] The truly dramatic character of the interurban network reorganization has been slow to emerge in public consciousness. It has been extraordinary in scale. Furthermore, the transforming effect of the long-distance truck has been exceedingly swift. This is graphically portrayed in map II-3.

Map II-3 is based on material derived from the work of Olsen and Westley (1974, 1975). The base data consist of a set of synthetic measures of truck operating times between the core centers of the 171 urban regions in this study for each of three decennial years, 1950, 1960, and 1970. The measures take into account changes in sustained truck operating speeds resulting from technological improvements and from the development of the interstate highway system and other high-speed roadways. These data implement a truncated gravity model measuring the total population to which each urban region has access through the use of overnight trucking (8.3 hours). From these data, roughly interpolated lines of equipotential were drawn as presented in map II-3.[7] These contours represent the rough topography of the interurban access characteristics for those activities that relied heavily on truck transport and were oriented to household final demand.

Panel A of map II-3 represents the 1950 access topography. The heavily inscribed contours indicate those areas from within which an enterprise could gain access to the household final demand of 20 million people. It is interesting to note that well after World War II there were two distinct access mountains. One formed a massif, or ridge, embracing the New York–Washington, Middle Atlantic axis at the eastern end of the Manufacturing Belt. At the western end of the belt, a single-peak mountain was centered on Indianapolis, with Chicago, Toledo, Cleveland, Louisville, and Evansville on its lower slopes. The 10-million-person-access-contour embraced the Michigan peninsula, swinging out into Iowa between Des Moines and Omaha, pulling back to St. Louis, sweeping down to embrace Birmingham, Atlanta, and the Piedmont South, then coming back to the East Coast between Richmond and Norfolk. Upper New England was excluded.

By 1970 (panel B) the change was truly outstanding. The 20-million-person contour line that had delineated two localized mountains only twenty years before had spread to embrace the eastern half of the country, excluding the Gulf and South Atlantic coastal regions. Minneapolis, Kansas City, and Dallas were all approximately on this contour. The east–west saddle mountain of 1950 had merged into a single ridge with the high end located in the Harrisburg–Pittsburgh area. It is important that Upper New England, along with a large section of the Central Plains and the South, were brought into the fold as relatively high access locations, and this in an extraordinarily short time.

Although these spreading contours suggest that large sections of the country may have been passing critical thresholds of access to larger markets, when read for elevation, another aspect of the change becomes apparent. The mountain has grown higher as well as broader in spatial extent. The scale of the total transformation was amazing. When we aggregate the 8.3 hour population access of every urban region to form an aggregated access coefficient, we discover that the total access measure tripled (from 1,824 million in 1950 to 5,454 million in 1970). It is equally amazing that three-fourths of the total change in access occurred in a single decade, the 1960s. This is consistent with the timing of the principal development of the interstate highway system, the beltway, and other high-speed arterial highways.[8]

Of course the effect of changing transport options is different for different intermediate requirements. Many activities are oriented to intermediate suppliers rather than to household final demand. Map II-4 illustrates the difference this makes if we compute overnight trucking access to employment in apparel manufacturing (see Olsen, Bray, and Westley, 1974). Thus, one can see that equally radical changes in access topography were occurring on the supply side as well as the demand side of economic processes.[9]

This gravity model is a useful illustrative tool, but it does not reveal the extent to which the transport of goods, particularly intermediate goods, tends to follow rather linear flow channels. This is illustrated by map II-5, which displays several striking things. Most prominent is the northeast–southwest orientation of the flow. Data are not available to duplicate this map for earlier periods, but from what we know from historical materials this represents a substantial reorientation in the grain of the nation's transaction system. The older pattern displayed more of an east–west orientation with the heaviest flows restricted to the Midwest and Northeast. This has clearly been heavily influenced by the switch from coal

Panel A 1950

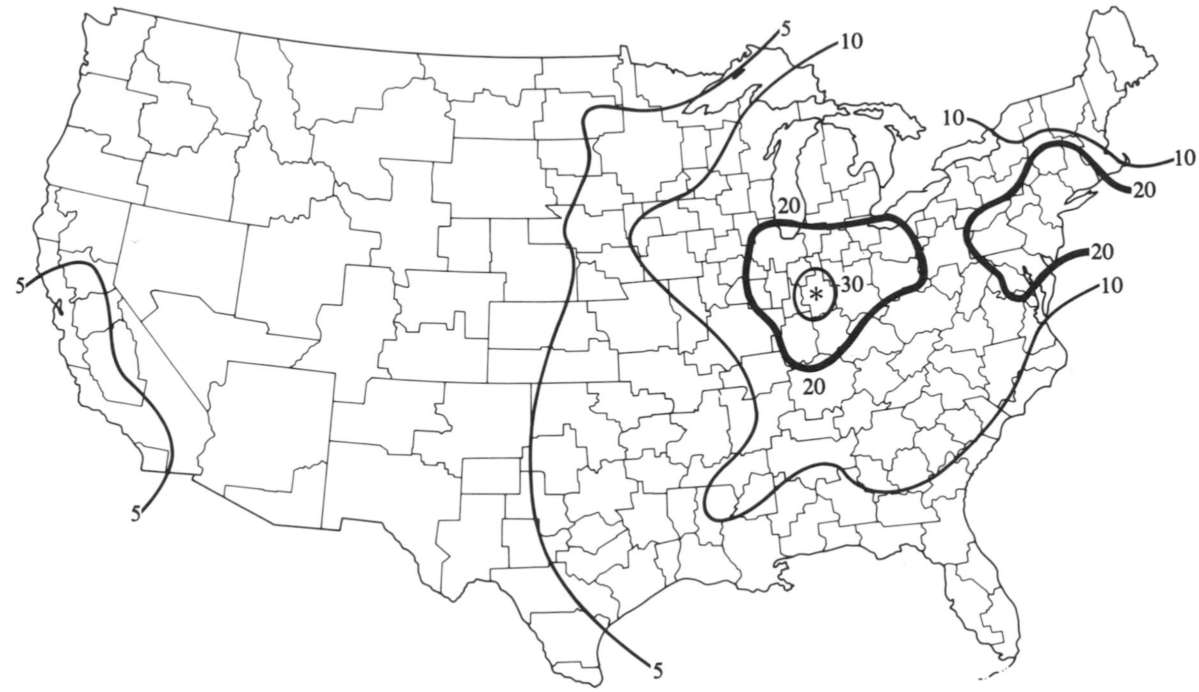

Panel B 1970

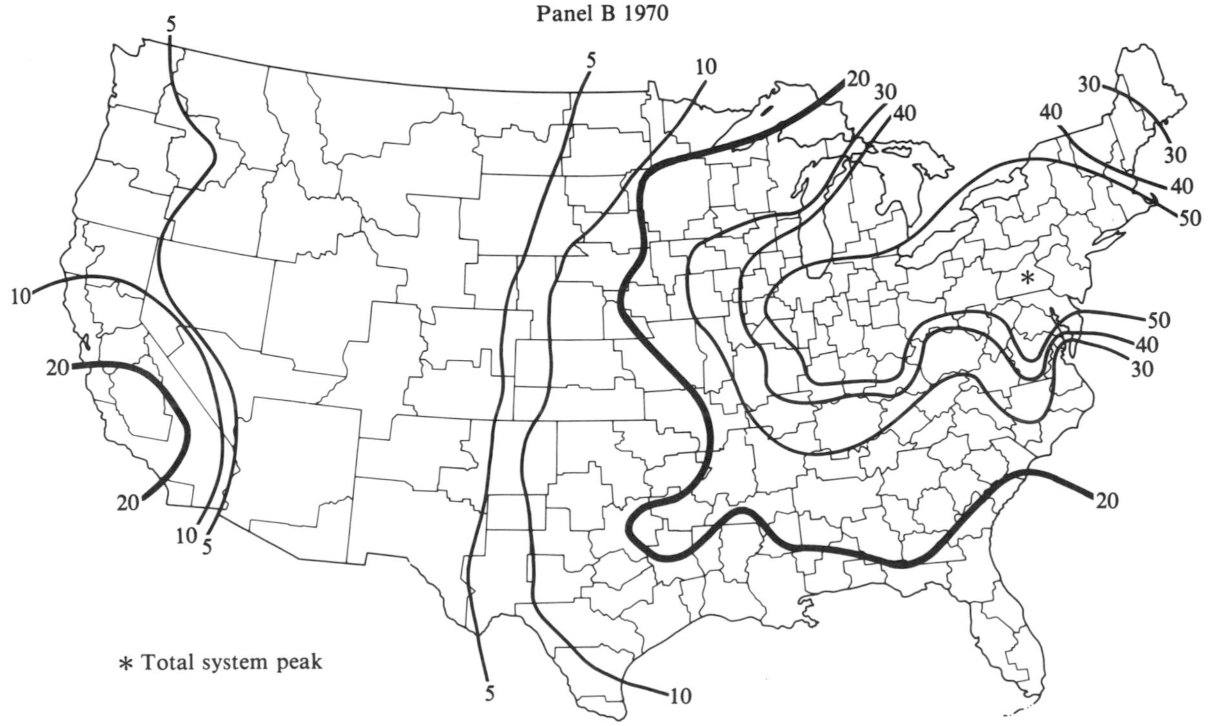

MAP II-3. Interregional Population Access with Overnight Trucking.
Source: based on Richard J. Olsen and G. W. Westley, "Regional Differences in the Growth of Overnight Truck Transport Markets," *The Review of Regional Studies* vol. 4 (1974); and on Richard J. Olsen and G. W. Westley, *Synthetic Measures of Truck Operating Times Between the Metropolitan Centers of BEA Economic Areas: 1950, 1960, and 1970, with Projections* (Oak Ridge, Tenn., Oak Ridge National Laboratory, 1975).

Panel A 1950

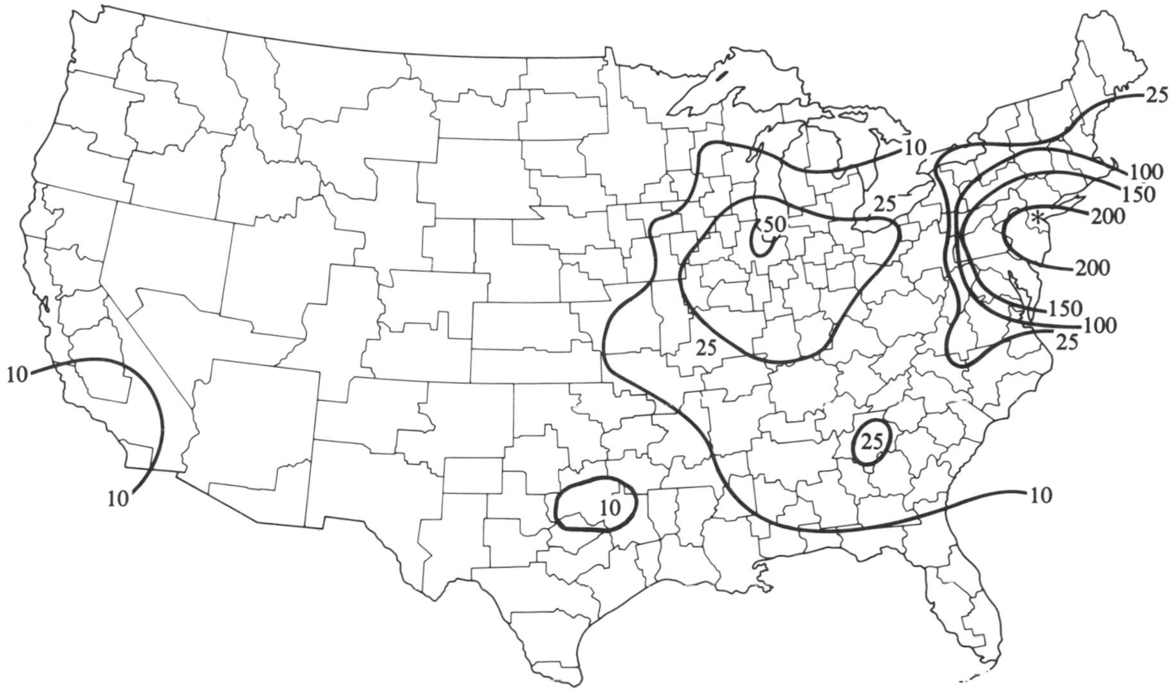

Panel B 1970

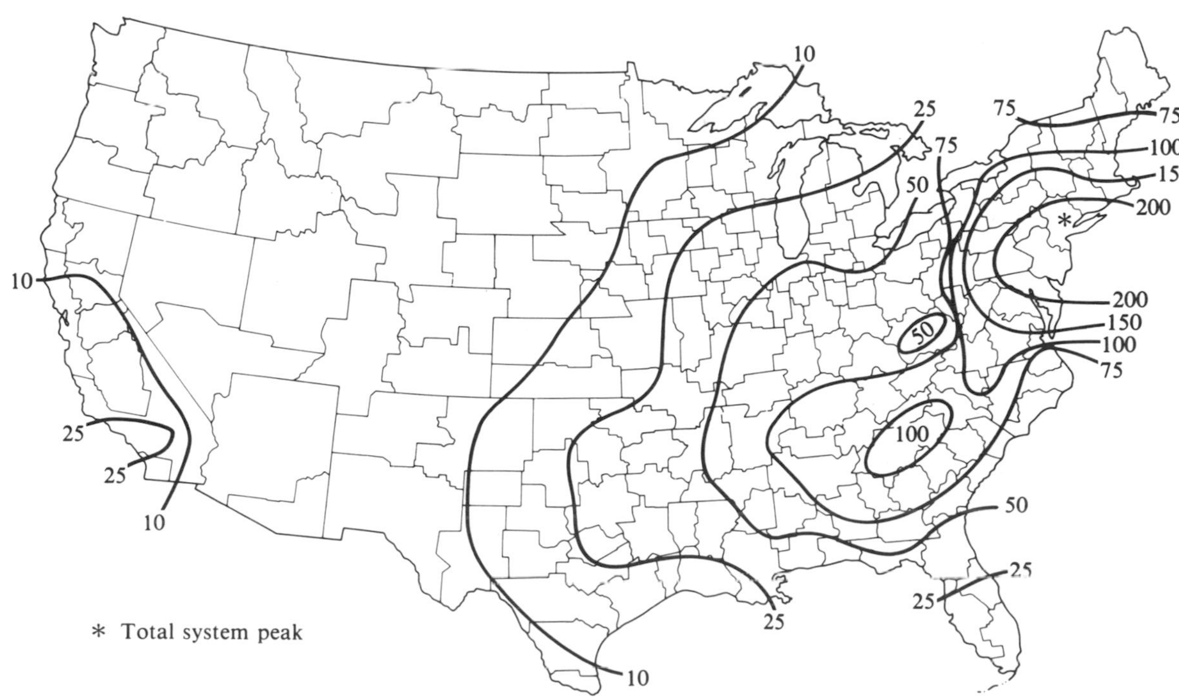

MAP II-4. Interregional Access to Apparel Employment by Overnight Trucking.
Source: based on data from Richard J. Olsen, L. G. Bray, and G. W. Westley, "The Location of Manufacturing Employment in BEA Economic Areas" (Oak Ridge, Tenn., Oak Ridge National Laboratory, 1974).

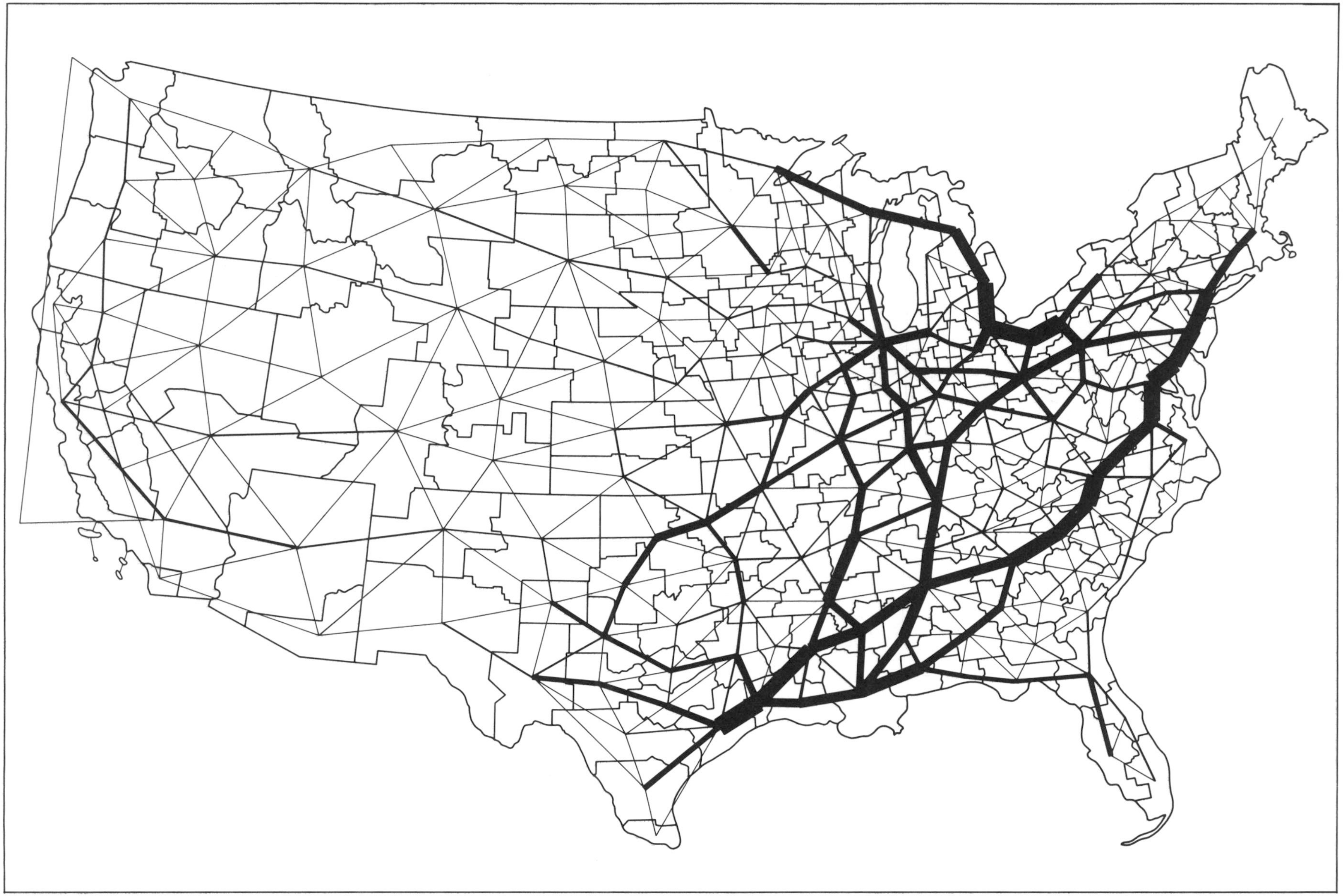

MAP II-5. Total Commodity Flows Between Urban Regions, 1975.
Source: U.S. Department of Transportation, *National Transportation Trends and Choices* (Washington, D.C., U.S. Government Printing Office, 1977).

to oil as the dominant energy base. This illustrates further how the motor vehicle has modified the transaction structure, not only by improving the nature of transfer relations, but also by altering the input–output relationships that reflect the underlying production structure of the economy. We can be certain that the major effect of the flow-network modification came during the study period that claims our attention.[10]

We can begin to see the significance of this if we turn to a consideration of employment in the trucking sector. Map II-6 provides a bridge to the changing perspective. The shaded areas represent those urban regions for which trucking employment represented a leading (or countertrend) employment gain for the period 1940–70, the period 1960–70, or both. Once again the prominent thing about this display is the northeast–southwest grain of the configuration. It is clear that the reorientation of the commodity flow network gave a special impetus to the gains in trucking employment that were favorably situated with respect to this emerging net. It is also clear that most of these urban regions are inside the expanded 20 million equipotential access line in panel B of map II-3.

Now let us shift attention from the historical and explanatory materials pertaining to highway and motor vehicle development to consider the direct consequences of these developments for trucking employment. The developmental code (C) patterns are displayed in color plate II-19.[11] The most striking thing is the pattern formed by the counties that experienced leading or countertrend losses in trucking employment (dark red). First, they are prominent in number. Almost half of all counties experienced leading losses (appendix II-M), and they were mostly counties that specialized in trucking employment in 1940 and accounted for more than three-quarters of all specialized counties (those shaded). Second, the regional concentration of these counties is striking. They are heavily clustered in the North Central and Central Plains regions, reaching as far east as the Lima and Lansing urban regions, as far north and south as the Minneapolis and Springfield, Missouri, urban regions, and as far west as the Grand Island urban region. There is also a secondary cluster in west Texas and a liberal scattering in the western mountains.

It is clear that these counties were predominantly rural and agricultural at the beginning of the period. There is an explanation for that. Recall that as late as 1940 trucking was still in its infancy and its principal use, apart from local urban deliveries, was in the service of short-haul, farm-to-market transport. This accounts for the heavy concentration of trucking employment specializations in rural counties. Recall also that after the war the development of trucking employment was largely associated with the emergence of the trailer truck, the high-speed highway, and long-distance transport. Thus, the early relative competitive advantage enjoyed by specialized, local-region, farm commodity transport was lost during the period relative to the newly developing truck transport functions. The 1940 agricultural counties, most poorly situated with respect to the emergent functions, tended to display leading declines.[12]

Contrast this pattern with that displayed by the counties experiencing leading or countertrend gains (dark blue). We are dealing here with far fewer counties, only 19 percent of the total (appendix II-M). It is not surprising that more than three-quarters of these did not display 1940 trucking employment specializations. The regional patterns are also strikingly different. The limited number of specialized counties that experienced leading gains is clearly associated with prominent urban-region core counties. The rest display a decided linear form, as maps II-5 and II-6 would lead one to expect and a northeast–southeast grain, reflecting the emerging commodity flow patterns already noted. They also tend to be most heavily concentrated in the Southeast, reflecting the region's dramatically increasing access coefficients.

But there is another striking aspect of the pattern of leading-gain counties. If we superimpose the interstate highway system overlay (inserted among the color plates following page 144) on plate II-23, it is clear that the development of the interstate highway system helps to explain the emerging pattern—and this in spite of the fact that the interstate highway system only began to affect developments in the last third of the study period. A frequency count of those leading-gain counties directly served by the interstate system is most revealing. Eighty-five percent of the specialized leading-gain counties were on the interstate system, and well over half were served by two or more interstate highways. Sixty-eight percent of the unspecialized leading-gain counties were located on interstate highways, about equally divided between those at an interstate intersection and those served by a single interstate. Of those not directly served by an interstate, some were served by other prominent high-speed highways (for example, Tulare County in the California valley on U.S. route 99), some were related to specialized trucking developments (citrus and truck cropping counties in Florida, the movement of grain to barge ports by truck, the use of the logging truck in the Pacific Northwest and the Southeast), and some were newly emerging southeastern manufacturing counties next to, but not directly served by, the interstate system.[13]

Given this developmental history it is not surprising that there were major variations in experience depending on the trade-center and transaction-field characteristics of the counties. Stick with the frequency count. Ninety-two percent of all leading-loss counties (1,318 in number) carried lower order trade-center classifications (complete shopping and below, see panel B in appendix II-L). About

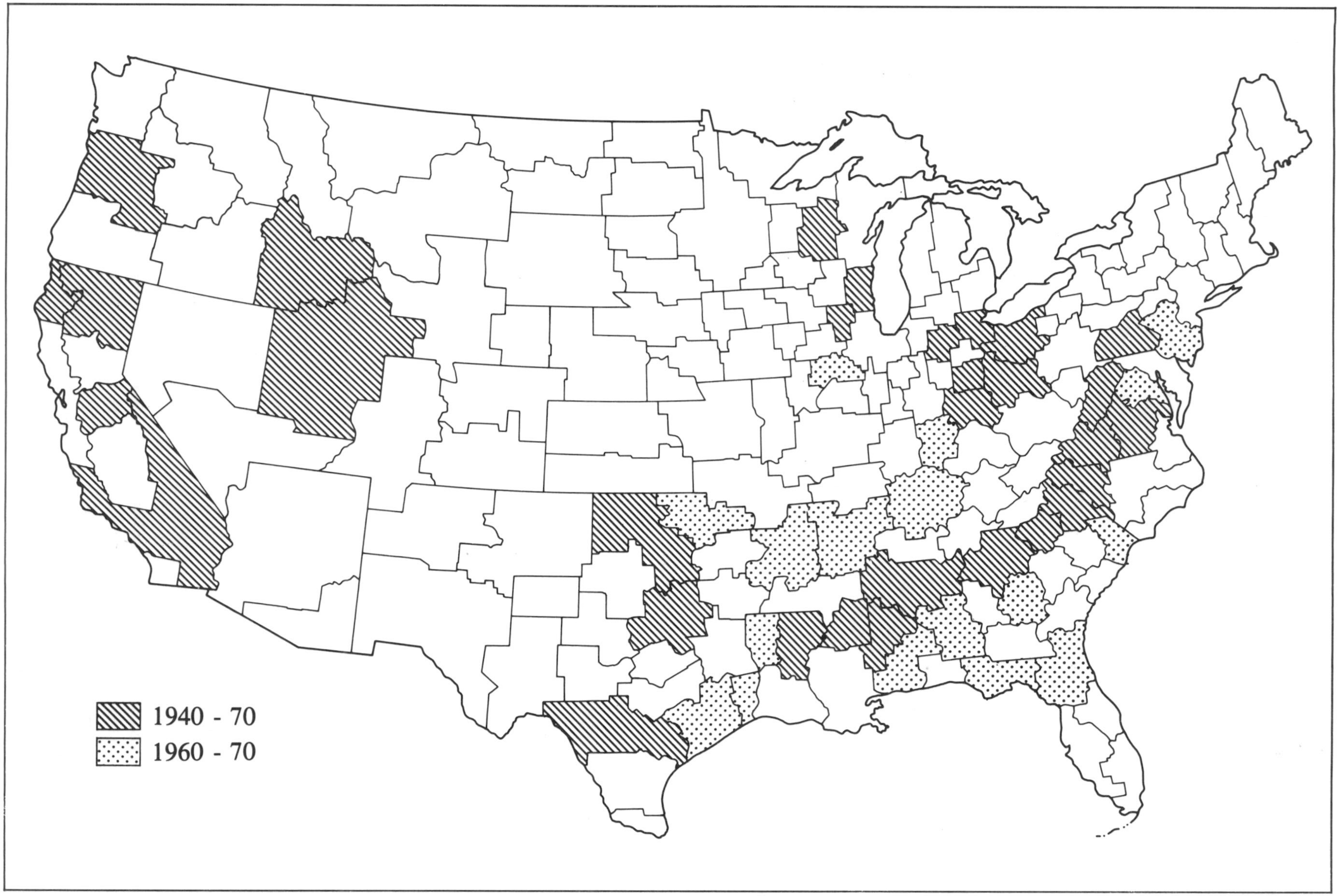

MAP II-6. Urban Regions Experiencing Leading Competitive Gains in Trucking Employment, 1940–70, 1960–70.

TABLE II-16. Summary perspective on competitive trucking employment shifts: trade-center, transaction-field, and broad geographic region classifications, 1940–70

Classification	Specialized or unspecialized 1940 (1)	Code C description (2)	Percent total interclass ± shift (3)	Class percentage point deviation from total employment shift (4)	Percentage point deviation as percent of 31 sector average deviation (5)	Percent counties in class displaying leading gains (6)
Panel A. Trade-center characteristics						
Metropolitan, large	S	Countertrend gain	+39.0	+137.9	+303	43
Metropolitan, small	S	Lagging gain	+9.2	−3.7	−44	28
Wholesale-retail, large	U	Lagging gain	+41.3	−6.5	−24	31
Wholesale-retail, small	S	Countertrend loss	−0.6	−2.1	−72	23
Wholesale-retail, outside	U	Leading gain	+9.9	+2.6	+55	34
Complete shopping	U	Countertrend loss	−45.9	−74.8	−55	18
Partial shopping	U	Countertrend loss	−25.2	−26.7	−173	16
Full convenience	U	Leading loss	−16.6	−15.5	−186	14
Hamlet & min. convenience	U	Leading loss	−12.3	−12.2	−168	12
Panel B. Transaction-field characteristics						
Urban core, large	S	Countertrend gain	+7.3	+97.3	+231	36
Urban core, medium	S	Leading gain	+60.1	+23.5	+105	41
Urban core, small	U	Lagging gain	+21.1	+3.9	+27	32
Primary field, large	U	Leading gain	+6.6	+1.7	+17	27
Primary field, medium	U	Lagging gain	+4.3	−5.8	−83	29
Primary field, small	U	Countertrend loss	−4.6	−19.6	−76	21
Secondary field, large	U	Countertrend loss	−6.0	−7.7	−96	15
Secondary field, medium	U	Countertrend loss	−12.0	−17.9	−86	14
Secondary field, small	U	Countertrend loss	−25.0	−25.5	−198	15
Outside field	U	Leading loss	−53.0	−42.8	−186	13
Panel C. Broad geographic regions						
Upper New England	U	Leading loss	−3.4	1.7	−106	—
Middle Atlantic	S	Lagging loss	−43.0	+9.1	+50	—
Upper Appalachia	S	Lagging loss	−2.9	+1.5	+47	—
Lower Appalachia	U	Leading loss	−3.2	−2.6	−53	—
Midwest-Great Lakes	S	Lagging loss	−16.9	+19.1	+124	—
Southeast	U	Leading gain	+31.9	+8.1	+48	—
Peninsular Florida	U	Leading gain	+16.4	+0.7	+9	—
Southern Plains	S	Lagging gain	+1.5	−10.2	−123	—
Northern Plains	S	Leading loss	−31.1	−26.2	−245	—
No. Mts.-Pacific NW	S	Lagging gain	+1.4	−2.4	−33	—
Southern Mountains	S	Lagging gain	+10.2	−2.7	−55	—
Metropolitan California	S	Leading gain	+38.1	+6.1	+51	—

Sources: Columns 1–3—trade-center characteristics, panel B of appendix II-C; transaction-field characteristics, table II-9 and panel B of appendix II-D; geographical regions, table II-4. Columns 4–5—computations based on sources for columns 1–3. Column 6—trade-center characteristics, panel B of appendix II-J; transaction-field characteristics, panel B of appendix II-K.

three-fourths were located in secondary labor force fields or outside all urban-region transaction fields (panel A in appendix II-L). It may seem paradoxical, but two-thirds of all leading-gain counties (388 in number) carried lower order trade center signatures as well, thus suggesting that the average lower order leading gainers must have been better situated than the lower order leading losers. This is confirmed by appendix II-I, which shows that the aggregate of lower order trade centers located in large, urban-core, primary-transaction fields shows competitive gains in trucking employment, whereas the aggregate of the same trade-center categories located in more remote transaction fields displays competitive losses.

A summary perspective is provided by table II-16, which is compiled from several sources.[14] When we turn our attention from the county frequency distribution to interregional competitive shifts, trucking's role in the reorganization of the urban system is still more dramatically revealed. Eighty-one percent of the net competitive gains were accounted for by the large metropolitan and wholesale-retail counties (panel A). The large metropolitan counties experienced a countertrend gain in spite of a competitive loss in all-sector employment. (The countertrend positive deviation was a strong three times the average deviation of all sectors.) For this to happen in the face of major competitive losses in many other activity sectors is a dramatic indication that the developmental factors at work are giving the large metropolitan centers a much more prominent position in those linkage functions served by trucking. The large wholesale-retail counties accounted for a still larger portion of the total gain. This registered as a lagging gain, but the negative deviation was a weak one-fourth of the average deviation. Here trucking is clearly responding strongly in serving the needs of a field of transactions experiencing strong gains across many sectors. The lower order shopping centers accounted for the bulk of the competitive losses in trucking employment, with complete shopping centers alone accounting for almost half.[15]

The wholesale-retail counties outside of urban-region cores are somewhat anomalous. They were the only counties outside the large metropolitan centers that were, on balance, leading gainers in trucking employment. As we saw in volume I, this is a small group of counties heavily concentrated in the Piedmont areas of the Southeast and largely specialized in nondurable goods manufacturing. Manufacturing and total employments have grown in these areas in part because of the improved access coefficients that were wrought by truck transport developments. It is no surprise, therefore, to find competitive gains in trucking employment playing such a prominent role.

In terms of the transaction fields (panel B), it is significant that the preeminent beneficiary of the gains in trucking employment were the medium-sized urban-core counties (60 percent of the total). These fields dominated the trucking share gains relative to all the rest, but their gains in trucking employment also ranked high among all employment sectors. The large urban cores, like the large metropolitan trade centers, experienced countertrend gains in trucking employment. Though small in comparison, these were notable by being positive deviations of more than twice the all-sector average. Small urban-core counties captured one-fifth of the gains, but, in context, these proved to be lagging gains seemingly pulled along in the service of other expanding activities. Panel B also reveals that more than half of the competitive losses were experienced by counties outside identified transaction fields. The two most remote transaction fields accounted for 88 percent of the competitive losses and displayed the largest negative deviations. (Here recall note 12.)[16]

In closing, a summary statement about the geographical distribution of the shift patterns is in panel C of table II-16. Of the total competitive trucking losses, about two-thirds were in the Middle Atlantic plus the Great Lakes–Midwest regions—the eastern and western ends of the old manufacturing belt. Most of the rest was in the Northern Plains. Trucking employment was a leading loser in the plains because of shifts in trucking employment away from earlier agricultural roots. In this connection, both the Northern and Southern Plains regions experienced substantial negative relative deviations. In contrast the Middle Atlantic and Great Lakes regions experienced lagging losses (that is, positive deviations), suggesting that the role of trucking was sufficiently important in these fields to resist declines originating in other sectors. Florida and the Southeast on one hand, and California and the Southwest on the other, just about split the relative competitive gains. Except for the Southern Mountain region, trucking was, overall, a leading gainer, indicating its dynamic role in the development of these clusters of urban regions.

Other Transportation

Apart from railway transport, the data classification employed here lumps the rest of transport in an "other" category. This category includes all local and suburban people transport (street railway, taxi, and bus), intercity bus transport, as well as air, water, and pipeline transport. It includes the movement of both people and goods by both labor-intensive and capital-intensive transport modes subject to great differences in developmental factors. It is clearly a heterogeneous grouping that requires some sorting out in exposition.

Commodity Movers

The goods movers in the group, water and pipeline transport, made very little contribution in the aggregate to *changes* in other transportation employment. Employment stayed about level, with slight declines, in spite of the fact that the combined ton-mileage more than doubled. The gains in labor productivity were partly technological. The development of large-diameter, high-strength pipe and automated pumping stations with large power units permitted reductions in employment per ton-mile. Increases in tanker size and efficiency had similar effects in the water transport sector. However, an important part of the change was substitutional, as the movement of crude petroleum became the dominant function. Great Lakes grain and ore traffic actually declined, while Mississippi River traffic quadrupled. The latter reflected a shift of grain movement from rail to barge with the truck serving as the intermediary link. The Gulf and Atlantic coastal waterways experienced a phenomenal increase in traffic but resulting in only marginal changes in employment. This was also the period in which the bulk of the pipeline capacity came into being, and by the end, one-fourth of total U.S. freight tonnage was carried by pipeline.

In short, beneath the aggregate, developmental changes were once again playing their role in redesigning the transaction network. The fundamental shift in energy resources from coal to oil prompted by the internal combustion engine shifted the locus of energy resource extraction from the Northeast to the Southwest and South Central regions. Thus, the developmental solution to the twentieth century people-moving problems created secondary commodity movement problems. The oil pipeline and tanker emerged as a subsequent-round developmental solution. The principal axis of the nation's commodity flow network tilted to the Southwest. In terms of total other-transportation employment, the stable aggregate was consistent with substantial competitive gains at the emerging transport nodes in the Gulf regions and at key Atlantic terminals relative to the rest of the Northeast.

Bus Transport

A still heterogeneous street-railway and bus category accounted for 20 percent of the gains in other transportation employment during the study period. Since an important part of bus transportation substituted for street railway transport, bus transport played an even more significant part of the employment gains than indicated.

Once again bus transport was largely a secondary developmental adaptation to access problems that emerged as a consequence of the automobile's response to twentieth century people-moving problems. The automobile facilitated the emergence of the interstitial suburbs, but these were not as readily provided public transport by the rigid, linear street railway. The route flexibility of the bus permitted it to largely replace rail mass transit. The spreading of low-density residential areas made the access to public schools more difficult. This, combined with the consolidation of rural schools, also made the study period the heyday of the school bus. In addition, the emerging transport technology opened up an expansive niche in the intercity movement of people. A much more flexible and finely articulated network of intercity people movement became feasible. The consequence of this for shifting employment patterns will be examined shortly.

Air Transport

Almost the whole development of air transportation occurred during the study period. It is responsible for fully two-thirds of the total gains in other transportation employment, as it has grown from practically nothing to a major industry. It has had an effect on the urban transaction networks second only to the motor vehicle. There was a highly articulated route structure of commercial airlines in 1976 in contrast to the early route structure devoted largely to carrying airmail. The 1926 configuration was served by 100-mile-an-hour open cockpit planes that took 30 hours and six pilot changes to cross the country. Trans World Airlines began the first transcontinental commercial services from coast to coast in 1930, but it took 36 hours and an overnight stop in Kansas City. It was not until the advent of the superconstellation (DC-7) in 1953 (twenty-three years later and thirteen years into our study period) that nonstop, coast-to-coast passenger service was introduced. The 1940s added 4 million passengers to air travel; the 1950s added 50 million, and the 1960s exploded with a 115 million passenger increase. The 1960s leap reflected the introduction of jet travel with the B-707 and the DC-8 in 1959. It was clearly not until the 1950s and 1960s that air transport had a major effect on the nation's transaction system.

The advent of air transport radically changed the character of transactions involving moving people in groups. It created a phenomenal convergence of space–time that virtually nullified the old inverse relationship between distance and travel volumes on a gross scale. It generated a novel set of interregional transaction networks that are still evolving and changing the access characteristics of the economy.

I am indebted to Filani (1972) for a summary image of these air transport networks and their changes over the study period. He combines graph-theoretic and multivariate statistical techniques to assemble an intriguing picture. He shapes the network pattern in two ways. The first portrays the system as a nodal hierarchy. The second portrays the network in terms of the transaction patterns characteristic of broad transport regions.

The first perspective emphasizes the "pecking order" of urban center dominance as revealed by a graph-theoretic analysis of traffic flows. In 1970, there were some 660 commercial air traffic centers. The largest 100 accounted for 90 percent of all traffic; 23 accounted for 75 percent.[17]

Going back to 1950, New York was the dominant center in an eastern system hierarchy containing 24 subordinate centers. Among these were 5 subordinate regional centers. Chicago dominated 19 cities that included 2 third-order, collecting subsystems at Louisville and St. Louis, while Louisville dominated a fourth-order collecting center at Memphis. Atlanta was another system secondary to New York. It, in turn, dominated 10 cities in the Southeast. Pittsburgh was a secondary subsystem dominating Philadelphia and Harrisburg, in turn. Miami dominated Jacksonville, Orlando, and Tampa. Washington dominated Norfolk. Outside the East, Dallas, Los

Angeles, and Seattle formed more or less independent spheres of dominance. Dallas dominated secondary collecting centers at Houston and Oklahoma City. Los Angeles dominated Denver, and San Francisco dominated Salt Lake City.

This early pecking order pattern underwent substantial transformation as a result of the jet and the ensuing traffic explosion. By 1960, New York, Dallas, and Los Angeles had increased the number of their direct satellite cities (in the case of New York, from 24 to 44). Chicago, San Francisco, and Atlanta lost some of theirs. By 1970 half of the largest 100 centers sent their largest passenger flow to New York. All of the satellite cities formerly subordinate to Miami and Pittsburgh were by then directly linked in the hierarchy with New York. Following 1950, New York, Los Angeles, and Dallas successfully increased their areas of dominance, while the remaining hubs lost importance in the hierarchical order of traffic flows. The increased direct connection between the large centers and medium cities progressively reduced the number of levels in the nation's air passenger hierarchy over time.

Filani's second perspective involved grouping the places in such a way that their within-group interaction was greater than the between-group interaction (without regard to the pecking order role that each city plays in a graphic network). This is an instance of employing relational networks to derive taxonomic boundary networks in the fashion discussed in chapter 2 of volume I. It suggests the way in which the total air transport system tends to form semiclosed interactive subsystems.

Viewed in this way, the 1950 air travel system can be seen as four major interactive subsystems. The largest was the New York–Chicago region. The nation's air traffic has been dominated by this region from 1950 on (internalizing almost two-thirds of the interactive variance and 40 of the top 100 cities). The second major interactive region was the Los Angeles–San Francisco–Seattle region (internalizing one-quarter of the interactive variance and 15 cities). The Dallas region accounted for 10 percent of the total interaction and 20 cities. The Atlanta region accounted for only 4 percent of the interaction but served to integrate the flows of 27 cities in the Southeast. By 1970 these four semiclosed interaction systems had merged into 2. The New York–Chicago–Washington–Atlanta–Miami region accounted for 80 percent of the total system interaction and contained two-thirds of the top 100 cities. The Los Angeles–San Francisco–Dallas–Seattle system accounted for the rest. The remnants of the older interaction regions and dominant nodal regions were transformed into collecting and dispersing subsystems.

Thus, Filani has demonstrated that the nation's air transport linkages have been progressively articulated and integrated to the point that in 1970 it appeared only a matter of time before the entire nation would merge into a single, closed interactive system with a limited, almost flat, hierarchical structure. It is possible that full merging may have already taken place.

All of this, of course, has been depicted by employing the top 100 cities in the commercial aviation net. The same developmental forces leading to the progressive integration and closure of a scheduled air carrier transport system have given rise to a large and growing "underground" in the air transport system—one that extends the public system and gives it still greater articulation and flexibility. Furthermore this "general aviation" component of the total system is beginning to take on many of the aspects of the air carrier system. But the bulk of this development has occurred in the period since 1970. We will return to this later.

The Upshot

The effects of these access network developments on the location of other activities will figure in our discussion repeatedly as we proceed. The direct effect on population settlements that was brought about by competitive shifts in other transportation employment is portrayed in plate II-20. Because this is a heterogeneous sector in which the components sometimes offset each other, the resulting pattern is not as revealing as in other cases.

Other transportation activities are not readily subject to regional specialization. Only 8.5 percent of all counties specialized in other transportation at the beginning of the period (at urban-region scale, 24 of 171 regions). The specialized counties were heavily concentrated in core metropolitan centers (40 percent of all large and half of all small metropolitan center counties were specialized). The 24 specialized urban regions are, with a single exception, on the Great Lakes or the coastal waterways, reflecting the historical importance of water transportation in this category. The few specialized counties that were not on the coast were characteristically single counties at interior hubs like Dallas, Memphis, Kansas City, or they were the points of origin of major pipelines like Lubbock, Odessa, and Abilene.

The other transportation developments of the period have changed this picture substantially. Water-transport-oriented urban regions (like Boston, Philadelphia, Jacksonville, Tampa, Pensacola, New Orleans, and Duluth), which were not in a position to capture offsetting air transport gains, lost their specialized status. At the same time, interior regions that developed as air transport hubs, or were functionally air transport dependent (Las Vegas, Atlanta, Minneapolis, Kansas City, Dallas, Denver) became specialized for the first time. They were joined by Tulsa and Lake Charles, largely on the strength of pipeline development.

The few counties with 1940 other transport specializations experienced competitive losses in the proportion of two to one. In contrast, the unspecialized counties experienced competitive gains of four to one. The latter accounts for the overwhelming blue cast of plate II-20. Those specialized counties that experienced leading gains were overwhelmingly concentrated in large metropolitan core counties, reflecting the presence of major air terminals. There were, however, a disproportionate number of these in complete shopping centers. These, in turn, were concentrated mostly in large primary labor force fields or outside conventional transaction fields. The former represents the outlying location of some metropolitan airports. The latter seem to be tied to oil pipeline development or the more nodal functions of outlying complete shopping centers.

The unspecialized counties that experienced competitive gains were most heavily concentrated in lower order trade centers and in the more sparse secondary and outside transaction fields. These counties predominantly reflected the gain in intercity bus and school bus employments.

From this frequency perspective, the geographical spread of the other transportation employment competitive gains was almost universal. But from a share-of-total-shift perspective (of the kind displayed in table II-16), the shopping centers (particularly complete shopping) and the primary labor force fields (particularly of the largest centers) accounted for the bulk of the competitive gains. The large metropolitan trade centers and the urban cores accounted for the bulk of the loss. In regional terms, the Southeast and Pacific regions accounted for the bulk of the gain while the Mid-Atlantic and Great Lake regions accounted for the bulk of the competitive losses.

Railway Transport

The story of the railway was left until the end for a compelling reason. The experience of the railway during our study period was almost totally a result of the competitive effect of the transport developments already discussed. At the end of the 1920s, the railroad was still a full-line transport carrier of people and all types of goods. The access logic of the iron rail, which had dictated the topography and topology of the nation's goods transaction network for more than half a century, was still largely operative. The railway still carried 75 percent of all freight ton-miles, and water carriers accounted for the bulk of the rest. The railroad's former dominance in passenger traffic had already been lost to the automobile and bus, but railways still accounted for more than a third of all passenger-miles traveled.

Barely ten years later (1940) the railway's share of freight ton-miles was down to 43 percent. Interestingly enough, the bulk of that decline was a result of the phenomenal growth of barge and coastal waterway movements, with a major assist from pipelines. Between 1950 and 1970, the railway suffered another 15 percent decline in share of traffic (to roughly a third of all traffic). This was mainly a joint result of the competition of the trailer truck and the oil pipeline. It is worth noting, however, that this aggressive pair had an even greater effect on water transport's share of traffic, which was reduced by half.

Over the same period, the railway was almost eliminated from the passenger traffic business. The passenger-mile share dropped to barely 1 percent by 1970 and has continued to decline. At this late stage, however, the competitive culprit was no longer the motor vehicle. It was the burgeoning air carrier business that knocked out railway passenger transport and bloodied the intercity bus business. Further increases in intercity automobile travel were largely self-generated and had little additional substitution effect.[18]

By the end of the study period, the railway had been transformed into a specialized cog in a highly variegated and integrated national transport system. It was left with a trace role in passenger movement, and a highly encumbered role in break-bulk and high-value-added goods transport. Ninety percent of all ton-miles carried by rail are currently accounted for by fifteen goods sectors that are all either mining categories (coal, iron ore, and the like) or bulk process material categories (lumber; agriculture; chemicals; paper; stone, clay, and glass; iron and steel; petroleum products).[19] These adjustments to a new role resulted in an absolute decline in railroad employment of over 400,000 workers. The number of operating railroads declined from 574 to 351, and the roadbed in operation declined by almost 50,000 miles after reaching a peak in 1931.

These changes are reflected in the shift pattern portrayed in plate II-18.[20] Several aspects of the changing role of the railroad are revealed. First, in contrast to the northeast–southwest tilt of overall commodity flows and their pipeline, waterway, and truck carriers, the retained competitive strength of the railways displayed a distinctly east–west grain reminiscent of an earlier period. The patterns of competitive gain traced the three main cross-continent rail routes—the northern, through Minneapolis, Minot, Spokane, and Seattle; the midline, through St. Louis and Kansas City (or through Chicago and Omaha) on through Denver and Salt Lake City to San Francisco; and the southern, through Wichita, Amarillo, and Albuquerque (or Houston, San Antonio, and El Paso).

Second, this pattern of retained strength was more than a reflection of mainline strength. It was a reflection of the fact that these lines best served the more specialized new-era railway niche—that is, its role as a primary and secondary resource materials carrier. The western half of the nation (past the Minneapolis–Omaha–Kansas City–Dallas population density escarpment) continued as a major resource materials generator. Furthermore, it generated those materials (lumber, grain, and other bulk agricultural commodities, coal ores and processed metals) in those places where the railroad tended to retain a substantial comparative advantage as a carrier.

Third, in the domain of commodity movements the railway was still a vital and competitive channel linking the Pacific Coast semi-nation to the still dominant eastern portion of the urban system. The emerging emphasis on the railway's east–west network is reflected in the fact that the West Coast, Mountain, and Northern Plains regions accounted for virtually all of the net competitive gains when computed on a broad region basis. The Mid-Atlantic and Upper Appalachian regions suffered the dominant competitive losses.

Fourth, we also find the railway's role substantially altered in terms of the fine-scale structure of urban regions. More than half of the net competitive losses in railroad employment occurred in those transaction fields outside core-area labor markets, while almost all of the net competitive gains were captured by metropolitan urban cores (tables II-8 and II-9). In part this reflects the fact that volumes of traffic generated by hinterland rail terminals were quite low relative to capital costs. This made the railway particularly susceptible to the competition from the truck in these areas. In part it reflects the capacity of higher order railheads to service a larger area in cooperation with the truck. In part it reflects an increasing centralization of railway employment in repairs, traffic control, and management (which in turn, reflects changes in technology as well as the railway's changing role). It is interesting to note that the complete shopping centers experienced 83 percent of the net competitive losses. In an earlier period this class of center appears to have been the optimum hinterland railway terminus in terms of size and function.

It is also interesting to note that, on a transaction-field basis, about a third of the net competitive losses occurred in the primary fields of the largest urban cores. These are the only transaction fields outside the urban cores to have developed an earlier railway specialization (save for the resource counties located beyond an urban center's core-function reach). In the nation's larger, older urban regions (New York, Philadelphia, Chicago, for example) the earliest out-of-core dispersals of manufacturing and shipping functions were railway supported. For example, at an early stage, Chicago developed a belt railway that was a functional harbinger of the belt highways of the present era. This is the domain of railway service that stood right in the pathway of truck transport's emerging strength, so the railway was fated to experience strong competitive losses in these areas.

Finally, although the eastern half of the nation did not display the prominent competitive strength of the West in its shifting patterns of railway employment, the specialized role of the railways highlighted those associated commodity specialities that existed in the East. For example, the coal industry's continued dependence on the railway made railway employment a leading or countervailing gainer in the Roanoke, Huntington, Clarksburg, and Baltimore urban regions. Its role in transporting mining and agricultural commodities of the strongly developing Florida urban regions is another case; a similar case is its role in transporting forest and agricultural commodities in Bangor. Finally, the competitive gains of manufacturing in the Southern Piedmont regions helped cushion the railway's decline there.

Notes

1. For a general reference on the effect of the motor vehicle, see Rae (1971).

2. Unfortunately data are not available to make an historical comparison, but it is clear to anyone with a sufficiently long participatory memory that this is a radical change from prewar patterns.

3. This is, in effect, a representation of the change in plate 1, volume I over the decade. This map is taken from Berry and Gillard, 1977.

4. It is interesting that the amount of time the average American spends traveling to and from work is about one hour. It is doubly interesting that that time has not changed much since the pedestrian city of 200 years ago. What has changed is the distance that can be covered in that time and the greater flexibility and mobility that more finely articulated road networks permit.

5. In one midwestern city fourteen motor driven vans replaced fifty horse teams in delivering newspapers. This experience was typical.

6. Both change patterns overlapped substantially, of course—both in time and, as we shall shortly observe, in space. But the distinction is an important one.

7. Since there are only 171 plotting points these interpolated lines are obviously not capable of reflecting the topographic detail that could be shown if, say, county units were employed. However, the graphic changes between panels A and C tell the dramatic and essential story.

8. Taking the United States as a whole, 80 percent of the total change was accounted for by trucks and highway developments, while 20 percent represented a redistribution of population. There were regional variations, however. Population redistribution accounted for only 10 percent of the change in New England, but 40 percent of the change in the Pacific region. See Olsen and Westley (1974).

9. Durable goods industries tended to be different from soft goods industries in one respect. The axis of their access mountain tended to shift more to a northeast–southwest orientation pointed toward Oklahoma City, Dallas, and Houston.

10. This flow pattern, of course, reflects commodity movements by all modes of transport. Interestingly enough, the pattern is not substantially altered if we take out movements by oil pipelines. If we take out rail and water movements, the south–north central commodity flow is emphasized, but the northeast–southwest grain persists strongly.

11. We might observe in passing that these competitive, or devel-

opmental, shifts in trucking employment are more than twice as important as the mix effect in determining the overall, interregional differential shifts in trucking employment.

12. There appears to be a classificational anomaly at work here as well. During the depression years there was a proliferating number of small independent trucking operators serving this need because of the people who lost jobs and put a little capital into a truck as a way of making some money. Much of this washed out of the trucking employment statistics during the study period. It was largely replaced by trucks that were operated and owned as personal or private proprietor vehicles in nontrucking businesses. This tends to exaggerate the measured shifts.

13. This may be a good place to note that Bohm and Patterson (1972) claim to have demonstrated that the interstate highway exerted considerable influence on county population changes from 1960 to 1970.

14. The table is included here to suggest a procedure that will be repeated as we continue. It intends to illustrate how information pertaining to a particular sector is drawn from the perspectives provided by a number of summary tables already provided in the text or included in the appendixes. I will not be repeating such a table in the text every time I collate similar material in discussing the remaining industry sectors.

15. However, the share losses experienced by complete shopping counties amounted to only half of the average deviation of all sectors. In contrast, the partial shopping, full convenience, hamlet and minimum convenience counties, all experienced losses closer to twice the average deviation from all-sector employment changes. In short, these share losses would tend to effect a larger structural change for these lowest order centers than for the complete shopping centers. This seems to be consistent with the complete shopping centers' more important nodal, urban-servicing characteristics.

16. Those who wish to carry these perspectives back to the differential code (B) of volume I can do so by referring to panel B of appendix II-B and to appendix II-H. It is not surprising that 93 percent of the competitive gains in trucking employment were accounted for by codes B1 and B3 ($-k_{ij}$, $+R_{ij}$) categories (with code B1 accounting for the bulk), and with trucking a leading gainer in each case. It is less expected that the B5 ($+k_{ij}$, $-R_{ij}$) counties account for the bulk of the competitive losses even though the losses in trucking employment lagged substantially behind all-sector losses.

17. The largest in order were New York, Chicago, Los Angeles, Washington, San Francisco, Miami, Boston, Detroit, Philadelphia, Dallas, and Atlanta.

18. Much of the data for this discussion can be found in table V.1 in U.S. Department of Transportation, *National Transportation Trends and Choices*, 1977.

19. Ibid, table VII.3

20. Bear in mind that the regions that experienced competitive gains in railroad employment most often did so by experiencing more limited declines than other regions. On an urban-region basis, only Boise, Las Vegas, and Fresno were exempt from absolute declines.

7

Other Linkage Sectors

Transportation activities involve the movement of physical things. When energy and information are carried by conventional transport, they have to be embedded in either materials or animals (including people) that serve as carriers. As the urban system evolved, serious problems emerged that were directly associated with these physical encumbrances. Their solution led to the emergence of additional linkage sectors. Consider the case of communications first.

Communications

In early history the exchange of information was on a person-to-person basis. It involved the transport of people in space and the coincident timing of their encounters. This necessarily created enormous constraints on the organization of human enterprise, constraints that were aggravated mercilessly as soon as an evolving technology generated a degree of specialization that fostered a nonfamilial mode of social organization.

Another Problem-Solving Sequence

Solving this problem required codifying information in languages that could be recorded in artifact memories. Thus, a specialized communications function emerged that facilitated information storage and spatial transfers. Once codified in physical form, information could ride "piggy-back" on all developed and developing modes of transport. As urgent problems in social organization and control emerged, the transfer of information split off from routine goods transfers to form specialized stagecoach or pony express transfer services. This, by and large, was the technology of information transfer in the emergent stages of the U.S. urban system.

When called upon to operate in the context of a far-flung, continental developmental process, this historical communication system proved to be especially constraining. A system of social transactions requiring anything close to real-time information feedback for its effective regulation was restricted to highly localized spans of control. The urban structure of the nation was based on extended markets, both in the vast interior and abroad via ocean trade. Even the traditional transport technologies were stretched over distances not so routinely experienced in Europe. This bred newer and more efficient transport means, as we have seen, but this only served to stretch the necessary spans of social system control still further. The result was a grossly inefficient system. We all know the stories of battles that were fought after the war was over (for example, the Battle of New Orleans), purchases that were consummated after the need ceased to exist, sales that were completed after the supplies were exhausted, and firemen who arrived after the building was leveled, all for want of timely communication.

No solution to this problem existed as long as communication technology depended on information that was recorded on a material base. A more versatile solution would encode information into an energy medium. Then the transmission of energy could serve as the carrier of messages. This understanding of both the problem and its potential solution was not new. Repeater systems based on semaphores (light-wave encoded) and drums (sound-wave encoded) had long been used to reduce time lags in social control loops. (How often we still come across high knolls named "telegraph," "signal" or "beacon hill.") But these were still largely localized communication techniques, and they suffered from high costs and severe limits on the volume of information that could be effectively transmitted. It took a new technology based on a new understanding of the electromagnetic spectrum of energy transfer.

It is no accident that the earliest form of the new technology emerged during the third developmental epoch (1840–70) alluded to earlier. This was the time of an emerging national urban system. F. B. Morse's experimental telegraphic system between Baltimore and Washington was tried in 1844. Innovative applications of the telegraph followed rapidly, indicating the strength of the accumulated pressures of unresolved information transfer problems. The earliest of these were local, linking police precincts, military command headquarters, and local business houses. Public messenger services began. But as soon as the new system proved its value locally, it went national. The telegraph followed the new railway rights-of-way and served to bring that far-flung transport system into a system of integrated control; it enabled the government to establish effective regulatory links with the Mountain and Pacific Coast states; and, I am told, the Civil War would have been quite a different logistic enterprise without the telegraph. Typically, the railway is given all the credit for creating the first truly integrated national transaction system. A strong case can be made that it could not have accomplished this without the telegraph as an effective information transfer partner.

However, the telegraph was only a partial solution to existing and emerging communication problems. The volume of information transfer was still limited and, for many years, its use required the intervention of many human encoders and decoders. The goal of direct voice transmission was responded to when Bell invented the telephone in 1870. It took only two years to install the first exchange in New Haven with twenty-one subscribers. By 1880, there were 138 local exchanges with 30,000 subscribers. Once again, in response to insistent communication pressures, the system development proceeded at an unusually fast pace.

Although the telephone has been an indispensible part of the urban transaction process for one hundred years, its effect on urban organization was almost exclusively local until the recent period here subjected to study. The reason had to do with the central technological characteristic of the new system. Providing random access to a large number of telephones over an integrated network presents astronomical switching problems. For decades the best technology was a hierarchical ordering of hand-operated switchboards—a very slow and labor-intensive process. (Today half of the entire female population between the ages of twenty and forty would be insufficient to work the switchboards, if today's volume of traffic had to be handled with the old technology.) As a consequence, as late as the 1920s (more than forty years later), it still took 14 minutes and eight operators to effect a transcontinental phone call at a cost of $16.50 (or $32.00 in 1970 prices). It was actually well into the 1920s before American Telephone and Telegraph completed a national toll network. There was not even a nationwide plan for good random access service until 1925 and then it took thirty years to implement. The important point is this. It was only after World War II—almost seventy-five years after Bell's invention and well into our study period—that long distance service became available at a speed, reliability, and price encouraging widespread toll calling.

Nevertheless, the availability of effective telephone service clearly was a necessary, if not sufficient, condition for the intraregion urban reorganizations we have been discussing. Under the increasing pressures of core-city growth that attended the development of the railroad, some decentralization of the nineteenth century cities was underway before the telephone arrived. In fact this was one of the developments that so exacerbated the problem of communication in that era that it contributed to the development of the telephone. However in a study of Boston at that time, Meyer (1977) demonstrated that new suburban residential construction did not occur until after the early telephone exchanges were interconnected. Just as in the nineteenth century national railway development could not evolve as an integrated system without the telegraph, the twentieth century automobile-based suburbs would never have taken their present form without the telephone.

The post–World War II developments in the telephone system finally made it an important factor in shaping the more recent interurban transaction network. Direct distance dialing began in the 1960s. The first transatlantic cable permitting consistent, high quality service came in 1956. The first communication satellite, in 1965, vastly increased the number of nations that could be reached by telephone. Routine, economical long distance telephony became a reality. It now became possible for a large corporation to have a production plant in one city, regional warehouses elsewhere, a sales office in another location, and its national headquarters in still another place. Telecommunications as carriers of encoded information and the airplanes as carriers of information in people-packages have made it possible to disperse the operations of business and government on the scale of the national transaction network without loss of effective control. During the study period these developments had not much reduced the location advantage of the core counties of urban regions, but they had expanded substantially the location choices between urban regions. A corollary is that the relative advantages of the information-rich locations, such as New York City, are declining. The symbiotic partnership of the telephone and motor vehicle has redefined the logic of the national urban transaction system during our study period.[1]

The story of the development of the radio is heavily tied to the development of marine communications. After Maxwell elaborated the theory of electromagnetic waves in 1864, it was not long until fertile minds envisaged ways of solving the problem of communications at sea. This application spread rapidly after the first wireless demonstration in 1902. Nevertheless, the broadcast use of radio did not really come into its own until the late 1920s and the 1930s. Television, of course, is totally a story of the recent era. During our study period it has served largely as a pure broadcast medium. This, however, is changing rapidly in the present emerging era as we shall come to observe.

Direct Consequences for Employment

The changing access characteristics of the nation's information network have modified the transaction connections of all activities, of course. For the moment, however, we will concentrate on the changing patterns of employment in the communications sector.

In the data record employed here, the several components of the sector—telegraph, telephone, radio, and television—are indistinguishable, but the exhibited employment patterns are primarily a reflection of telephone developments. More than four-fifths of communication employment is in the telephone sector. In spite of the fact that automatic switching substantially reduced the labor-intensive character of telephone technology, telephone employment almost tripled in the study period. Telegraph employment declined (by 20 percent) as that technology shifted into the narrow specialization of data transmission. Radio and television employment quadrupled. The television component was erected on the old foundation of network radio, while the radio shifted to the hinterland as an ever-expanding local service function. Both the large-scale and small-scale reorganizations of the communications network are reflected in the resulting employment shifts.

About three-fourths of the net relative losses in competitive share were experienced by the large, metropolitan, urban-core counties (tables II-8 and II-9, the B panels of appendixes II-C and II-D). These were precisely the areas where communications employment was concentrated at the beginning of the period. Other trade-center categories would naturally display larger relative gains as the new technology spread the communication network more evenly across the land. The core counties are also the locations that came to absorb the greatest decline in switchboard operator employment as automatic switching was introduced. Still, these competitive share declines lagged substantially behind the relative declines in all-sector R_{ij} shares in these areas. The growth of television employment was an important part of the offset, but it is also important to note that the greatest strength of the larger centers still resides in their linkage activities. Their relative decline in competitive share disguises a stubborn hold on such activities. In the case of New York City, for example, the positive mix gains stemming from its strength in communications were substantially greater than the communication sector's competitive losses. Thus, even the competitive losses are consistent with a positive relative deviation.

Most remaining competitive share losses were concentrated in the lower order trade centers outside the major transaction fields. (See also, appendix II-I.) This seems partly a reflection of the fact that the newer automatic switching and servicing technologies permitted telephone service in the more remote areas without building up the volumes of employment that would have been necessary at an earlier time. Another part of this has to do with the interesting fact that the number of rural telephones actually declined in the 1930s and 1940s as the early farmer-owned mutual systems gradually deteriorated. Bell Telephone found it unprofitable to take over such service, as it had the earlier local urban exchanges, and it was 1950 before Congress authorized the Rural Electrification Administration to provide rural phone service. Notwithstanding, that assistance came too late to offset the competitive share losses experienced in the Central and Northern Plains regions where absolute population declines were taking place (see plate II-21).

If the large metropolitan counties experienced most of these share losses, the large wholesale-retail centers experienced most of the share gains. In transaction-field terms, these were mostly medium and small urban-core counties (table II-8 and II-9 again). Communication employment continued to be predominantly a higher order trade-center and urban-region core-county activity, but the gain in importance and the more complete articulation of the long-lines service spread this activity into the higher order trade centers in smaller urban regions. It also enabled cities that were formerly predominantly manufacturing-based to improve their position in the provision of urban-system linkage functions.

Apart from this, and quite naturally, the major net gains in competitive share came in those broad regions of the nation where the competitive gains in all-sector employment were occurring (see table II-4 and plate II-21). The Southeast captured about half. These were leading gains, because this was the region that had benefited least from earlier communication developments. Here, the new technology was riding a "catching-up" wave. Most of the balance of the share gains were in Metropolitan California. These were leading gains as well, reflecting the coast's strategic involvement in overseas communications and in providing the essential and growing linkages with the East Coast parent region. Not surprisingly, the greatest relative declines were in the Middle Atlantic and Northern Plains regions. However, apart from metropolitan California, all of the positive relative deviations were in the East. (That is, the negative competitive shifts in the East lagged behind the negative total employment shifts—a demonstration of relative strength.)

The reorganization of the communications system at a more localized urban-region scale is also manifest. Although the large urban-region core counties experienced competitive share losses, their primary transaction fields experienced substantial gains (table II-9). Furthermore, of the urban-region core counties that experienced leading competitive gains in communications employment, more than three-fourths had previously been unspecialized in this activity, suggesting that core-region counties outside the old central business districts were experiencing gains in comparative advantage in providing communications services.[2]

Wholesale Trade

A major part of the transaction network implicit in both linkage and production technologies shows up in the structure of wholesale trade. Transactions that require anything more than localized transfers involve an extension of activities in time and space and are not well served by the management processes of production specialists and local market traders. It is a function that begs for specialized attention, so the merchant trader has been an important figure in the social fabric for hundreds of years. Wholesale trade has come to play a special role in shaping the urban-system network.

Role in Shaping the Urban System

For some curious reason wholesale trade has received very little attention from urban and regional scholars, yet it is clear that it has played a prominent role in the development and growth of the U.S. urban system. James Vance (1970) is almost alone in his treatment of this matter. The classical wholesaler was and is the merchant trader. He accumulates the demand of final or intermediate users over space and time and he matches it with an accumulation of supplies from resource and intermediate producers. Historically this has required the accumulation of commodities in a buffering stock necessary to negotiate a break in bulk and necessary to match commodity flows in time. In addition, the effective creation and management of this specialized function requires the assembly of information about the conditions of demand and supply at a distance and through time. There is a natural melding of communication and transport functions. In short, the wholesaler functions as the integrating node of a set of lines of transfer (the vertex of a set of graph-theoretic network edges). *Indeed, the basic role of the wholesaler can be viewed as the creation of graph-theoretic nodes that effectively integrate (theoretically optimize) a transaction network.* He is the specialized controller of a complete transfer system.

This is the classical urban-servicing function and it served as the seed-core of the early American city. As Vance said, ". . . wholesaling and cities came to America on the Mayflower and were just as much the tools of pioneering as the axe and hoe" (pp. 10–11). The Yankee trader was a dominant figure in early Americana. The colonial cities began as the mercantile outposts of a developed European parent region. They were trading cities assembling hinterland resources and exchanging them for supplies manufactured in the parent region. The siting of these wholesaling nodes was an important factor in the siting of the early American city. The nature and volumes of the goods transferred, combined with the technology of transport and the distribution of buyers and suppliers, determined the possible points in the network where the unraveling of commodity distributions and the accumulation of assembled commodities might be effectively carried out.

From the point of view of the European parent region, the colonies were an investment in trade. They were the creation of the world's first modern wholesale structure. The first Atlantic Coast "urban hinge" cities were established under the authority of trading companies. The first line included Boston, Newport, Hartford, New Haven, New York, Philadelphia, Baltimore, and Charleston. They were traders' towns built at the unraveling point of trade. As the trade grew progressively in volume and spread inward along the rivers and lakes, the transforming network called forth new transaction nodes at Pittsburgh, Cincinnati, St. Louis, Buffalo, Cleveland, Detroit, and Chicago. The subsequent reach westward established Minneapolis, Sioux Falls, Sioux City, Omaha, St. Joseph, and Kansas City. In the meantime New Orleans and the Pacific Coast entrepôt coastal cities appeared in response to the shifts in the emerging network connections that were sustained by sea; the inside–outside, "urban hinge" function shifted as well. The consistent and obvious characteristic of this opening-up of the continent was its mercantile base. But as changes took place in the volume of trade, in its geographic reach, in the technology of transport and communications, and in the degree of network articulation, accompanying changes in network logic altered commodity flows and the hierarchical order of urban-system nodes. Recall the beginning of chapter 6.

The essential point is this: As the transaction network of the nation's urban system became transformed by a historical, evolutionary, problem-solving process, the network patterns formed by the network's quintessential urban-servicing function, wholesale trade, also changed; as the trading patterns shifted, the relative order of urban centers and the linkages that connect them also shifted. That carries right into our study period and forms the basis for any explanation of change.

Direct Consequences for Employment

At the outset we need to recognize that the evolution of the U.S. urban system has brought a change in the structure of wholesaling itself. As we have seen, until the emergence of a truly national integrated transport system and the manufacturing-based economy of the nineteenth century, wholesaling was conducted largely by the classical merchant wholesaler. The increasing complexity of the system led to increased specialization of the wholesale function. With the growth in resource commodities some wholesalers became specialized assemblers of farm products and other commodities. A later version of this same phenomenon was the twentieth century emergence of the petroleum bulk plant. The development of a prominent manufacturing base led to the development of specialized manufacturer's sales branches as well as merchandise agents and brokers. These various specializations assumed different degrees of importance in different segments of the overall transaction network.

So, by 1940, wholesale merchants, once the sum of all wholesaling, accounted for only 40 percent of total wholesale sales. About half of the remainder was contributed by agents (including factors, brokers, and manufacturer's sales agents without stock) who had no direct contact with the storage and transfer of goods. In short, a substantial part of the information-processing component of wholesaling became functionally and locationally split from the common stem. This was greatly facilitated by the development of modern communications. As was pointed out in part one of volume I, the topo-logic of information transaction networks is different from goods transaction networks. This meant that, as the conventional, goods-handling, merchant-wholesaling function progressively followed a spreading and growing economy to its unraveling points, an increasing portion of its former activities was left behind in older, higher order centers.

In the meantime, another 30 percent of the 1940 wholesale sales had split into primary and intermediate commodity specializations. These specialized wholesalers were also taking advantage of a differentiated topo-logic. The grain assembler, for example, tended to form a hierarchy of nodes reaching westward from the eastern edge of the plains, each order creating the image of a topographic "escarpment" in functional terms. Grand Rapids, Michigan, and High Point, North Carolina, developed elaborate furniture wholesaling functions based, not on traditional goods distribution functions, but on large volumes of local manufacturing distributed through manufacturers' sales branches and sales agents. So a part of wholesaling became further differentiated by the transaction logic of restricted, intermediate-product networks and regional specializations.[3]

This pattern changed still further during the 1940–70 study period under the impact of continuing problem-solving activities. We are well past the time when wholesaling played such a creative role in locating the urban centers of this nation, but the networks hung on these nodal structures are still being rewoven.

These changes are reflected in the patterns of employment that are the empirical base of this work. When we shift attention to employment, we should first note that merchant wholesaling, though accounting for only about 40 percent of sales in 1940, accounted for about 60 percent of wholesaling employment. (One would expect this more conventional, goods-handling form of wholesaling to be more labor intensive.) Thus, the pattern changes observed are still dominated by the experience of merchant wholesaling. Consider the record.

The urban-system characteristics of tables II-8 and II-9 are a good starting point. Note that all of the *net* competitive gains in wholesale employment share are restricted to the metropolitan and large wholesale-retail centers. However, these were most heavily concentrated in the medium-sized urban cores (75 percent). Virtually all of the share losses are concentrated in the lower order centers—especially those outside urban-core-dominated transaction zones. Metropolitan centers are shown to be adding to an already formidable specialization in these activities. It is especially interesting that the large metropolitan centers that dominated the losses in all-sector competitive share claimed significant countertrend gains in the competitive share of wholesaling employment (and the positive relative deviations were prominent). But the most dramatic competitive gains (over half) were experienced by the large wholesale-retail centers. It is also noteworthy that almost two-thirds of the net share losses were experienced by complete shopping centers. The frequency distributions of county developmental (C) codes (in table II-6 and appendixes II-J, II-K, II-L, and II-M) tell a roughly consistent story.

What we see here is primarily a reflection of dramatic network changes wrought by the motor vehicle and modern communications. During the study period, there was an accelerated differentiation of the information-processing functions of wholesaling. For example, "manufacturers' sales branches-without-stock" was a rapid growth sector while employment in "manufacturers' sales branches-with-stock" actually declined. As a consequence, the volume of sales per person for manufacturers' sales branches more than doubled. This phenomenon represented more than a shift to information-processing specializations; there was also growth in the proportion of traditional goods-handling specializations devoted to information processing. Salesmen increasingly made their rounds with established customers by telephone. Sophisticated computer-based inventory-handling systems and linear programming transport optimization systems began to come on line toward the end of the period. Within the spectrum of wholesale specializations, the role of resource and agricultural commodity assemblers declined (both relatively and absolutely). All these tendencies reinforced the competitive position of the higher order centers.

The truck and automobile had a dramatic effect. Along with the telephone, the automobile gave the salesman a much more extended and flexible access to hinterland buyers. Similarly, the truck expanded the areas accessible to goods distributors, particularly those not previously well served by water and rail. Perhaps the most dramatic effect on these developments was to increase greatly the flexibility with which goods supplies and demand could be matched in time. Many of the time lags that had characteristically plagued wholesaling demand accumulations were drastically reduced. The truck, telephone, and, increasingly, the computer also made it easier to break bulk and assemble differentiated orders in combinations formerly out of the question. The consequence of this was that the wholesaler could operate with substantially smaller inventories. Wholesaling establishments came less and less to resemble goods storehouses waiting for intermittent buyers and came more to resemble pumping stations speeding a steady flow of goods through a highly articulated network of distribution channels. The factors altered the topo-logic of information transfer as well as the topo-logic of goods transfer, thus further enhancing the tendency of wholesale trade activities to move back up the trade center hierarchy.

In this connection, the two-thirds share of competitive decline experienced by complete shopping centers is instructive. In an earlier period the complete shopping centers appeared to enjoy a strategic position on the brow of one of the topological escarpments of the wholesale trade network. It is clear that the developmental changes of this epoch caused the natural unraveling point of the trade function attended by these centers to back up to more centralized locations. In consequence, complete shopping centers seem to have borne the brunt of the change. There is another contributing factor. In volume I, we observed that complete shopping centers played a prominent role in the agricultural plains regions. During the study period, many of these were also experiencing absolute declines in their hinterland rural and lower order trade center populations. It might even be that some of the complete shopping centers that were so designated in 1960 regressed to lower order trade center status during the 1960s.

However, at the same time that wholesale trade employment was climbing back up the ladder of the trade center hierarchy, its transaction fields were becoming less concentrated at the top. It is the medium-sized rather than the largest urban core centers that profit the most. And these are heavily laced with the larger wholesale-retail centers. You will recall that the latter (somewhat ambiguously named in the Borchert-Berry exercise) were primarily manufacturing specialists most heavily concentrated in the Northeastern Manufacturing Belt. We observe that the change in the transaction network improved the relative position of these centers with respect to an activity formerly considered to be preeminently metropolitan in character. Though initially unspecialized as wholesaling centers, they were the preeminent leading gainers.

Now turn to the geographical patterns represented in plate II-23 and table II-4. Apart from the generalized changes taking place in the urban system's topo-logic, a broad interregional redistribution took place. In the broadest terms the most apparent pattern is formed by a concentration of mostly specialized leading losses (code C4s and some C8s) in the Central Plains and mostly unspecialized leading gains (C5s) in the Southeast and Gulf Coast urban regions. The Plains region experienced early specializations based on commodity-assembling wholesaling, and, more locally, merchant wholesaling activities oriented to the rural hinterland. Complete shopping centers were the last and lowest escarpment. Both the declining importance of commodity wholesaling (in employment terms) and the absolute declines in regional populations (independent of the forces directly affecting wholesaling employment) caused wholesale trade to lose relative competitive strength in this broad region. It is not surprising, therefore, that on an urban-region basis (see appendix table E, in volume I) such regions as Duluth, Scottsbluff, Grand Island, Sioux City, Fort Dodge, Waterloo, and Oklahoma City not only suffered leading declines, but, by 1970, had lost their status as wholesale trade specialists as well.

In contrast, southeastern urban regions had earlier been largely wholesale-trade-deficit regions with a later developing and flatter hierarchy of trade centers than experienced in the Northeast and Midwest. The development of trucking in the study era changed this radically in two ways. First, it seems to have brought large segments of the Southeast past thresholds of access to final demand (recall map II-3 and the attending discussion). Second, this improved access helped foster a substantial growth in manufacturing employment. The employment mix shifted away from its traditional agricultural base, and per capita incomes rose at a rate that narrowed the gap vis-à-vis other sectors of the nation. All of this fostered a more rapid growth in all trade, including wholesaling. In addition, nondurable goods manufacturing tends to make especially heavy use of the manufacturers'-sales-branch form of wholesaling. This directly supported wholesale trade increased in the Piedmont area. It is not surprising to find that urban regions like Richmond, Charlotte, and Atlanta not only experienced leading competitive gains but also became wholesaling specialists by 1970.

In net terms, Florida and the Southeast captured 56 percent of the competitive gains; metropolitan California accounted for the bulk of the rest, but in the latter case the situation was quite different. The Pacific Coast developed an early specialization in wholesale trade because of its strategic transfer position with regard to foreign trade and its almost independent-nation status relative to the rest of the country (that is, its relatively high degree of system closure). Here the latter-day competitive gains in wholesale trade tended to lag behind and be drawn along by the other sources of growth in resources, manufacturing, and other urban services.

These changes in network structure, together with the interregional tidal flows of the total transaction network, especially favored a small set of well-situated urban regions. Los Angeles, Miami, Atlanta, and Houston accounted for one-fourth of the net gains. Detroit, Dallas, Charlotte, Washington, and Phoenix accounted for another quarter. In contrast, New York and Chicago accounted for one-quarter of the competitive share declines, while Boston, Pittsburgh, Duluth, Minneapolis, Sioux City, St. Louis, Kansas City, and Oklahoma City accounted for another quarter. These were all wholesale trade specialists whose comparative advantages were being dissipated by topological changes in network structure.

Detroit may seem a bit of a surprise in the leading gain category, but it was favored by an important aspect of the changing geographical structure of wholesaling. It was not just the medium-sized cities, but large wholesale-retail trade centers whose competitive positions were improving. It was especially those that were well positioned in the total network vis-à-vis the older established wholesale trade specialists. Detroit, for example, was well positioned in southern Michigan to improve its position vis-à-vis Chicago, Cleveland, and Indianapolis. Memphis—well positioned vis-à-vis St. Louis, Atlanta, New Orleans, Dallas, and Tulsa—is another urban region that became a wholesale trade specialist during the period; as did Billings, Montana—well positioned in the field between Spokane, Salt Lake City, Denver, and Minneapolis.

The importance of the automobile, truck, and highway in changing the network logic of wholesale trade is certainly suggested when we superimpose the interstate highway system on plate II-23. With a single exception, all specialized leading gain counties (C1s) were located on the new interstate system. More than three-quarters of these were served by two or more interstate highways. They were obviously well positioned with respect to the transforming transport network. Seventy percent of the unspecialized leading gain counties (C5s) were also located on the interstate network. Most of the C5s that were not were either adjacent to an interstate highway, were served directly by other high grade arterials that form the national system, or both. A full third were served by two or more interstate highways. Contrast this with the counties that experienced leading losses (C4s and C8s). Almost 60 percent of these were in transaction fields with no direct interstate highway service.

Up to this point we have focused exclusively on the large-scale transaction network. The changing transport and communication base of the wholesale trade function has brought about changes in intra-urban network patterns as well. The logic of this network appears to have been changed in two ways. During the study period, those wholesaling functions that were directly involved in information processing found considerable advantage in the old central-business-district cores. But those engaged in goods handling were largely released from the old center-city locations by the development of the motor vehicle and modern communications. Now that such a large part of the goods come into the city and leave by truck, the best break-bulk, unraveling sites for intra-urban wholesaling have tended to move to beltway and radial highway locations at the edges of the urban cores. In addition, the study period has seen a growth in the share of "pariah-type" wholesaling functions such as bulk plants and waste and scrap dealers. Most of this shift does not show up in statistical classifications because the urban-region core counties cover most of the heavily developed urban-region cores along with the old central business district. They are defined broadly enough to hide most of the small-scale shifts. Still, the primary labor force fields do show moderate competitive gains in wholesale employment. These fields also record above average numbers of counties experiencing competitive gains.

Public Utilities

As long as energy could only be transported when embodied in a solid, material substrate, it was incapable of continuous application to work at any place except those specialized sites where energy conversion took place. Begin with the late nineteenth century context. Energy conversion locations of that time were restricted by the necessity for transporting heavy, bulky materials like wood and coal, and by a rather chunky minimum scale of operation. The latter was dictated by the technology of converting energy to steam, and by the use of belt drives to convert steam power to mechanical applications. Both the location options and applications permitting effective energy utilization were severely constrained. There were few ways that mechanical power could be applied to the work of the house or farm. Much of the work of manufacture still had to rely on human power. Where steam power came to be applied, the factory layout was dictated by the logistics of belt transmission. Power users were limited to sites with direct access to the sources of raw materials like coal, or to heavy-duty rail and water terminals that could distribute them economically. These constraints had much to do with building up heavy localized urban populations in the late nineteenth century.

The invention of steam power had, of course, taken place as a developmental solution to an earlier set of problems. In the eighteenth century there were access and production problems for which there was no solution until some means was developed for the conversion of stored energy in a manner facilitating its direct application to mechanical work. It was precisely the great success of the developmental process in ameliorating these problems that led to the late nineteenth century and its newly obtrusive set of problems. As we have already noted, these problems centered around problems of localized access, in contrast to concerns in the earlier period about interregional access problems. And it was the early success with the mechanical applications of power to production that focused attention on a vast array of work applications that still lay outside the scale limitation of the then-existing technology.

A further developmental solution to this emerging array of problems required some new technique for separating the energy conversion stage from the energy transport and mechanical application stages. Enter the development of electrical power generation and distribution. In direct-current, low-voltage forms, electricity appeared earlier in its applications to the telegraph and telephone. Effective power generation and transmission required the development of high-voltage, alternating-current generators. These were effectively applied only around the turn of the century. Throughout the period of reorganization of intra-urban transport (1910–40), power generation and distribution systems grew apace. The earliest applications were to local transit (beginning with the electric tram) and to household and commercial lighting.[4] But by the end of the period, the electric motor was becoming ubiquitous, bringing changes in plant layout and location as well as vast changes in the variety and scale of work applications. Thus, it turns out that much of the intra-urban reorganization we recognize to have depended so heavily on the motor vehicle and telephone was significantly aided and abetted by the development of electrical power and its effective, instantaneous, continuous transmission to localized points of use in the factory, business, home, and farm. Both the internal combustion engine and electric power vastly increased the work and location options to which mechanical energy could be applied.

Just as the fifth epoch (1910–40) was absorbed with the initial task of infrastructure building to create an effective motor vehicle transport network, so was it heavily devoted to the task of building infrastructure in the power industry. The earliest developments depended on a hydroelectric, firm-power base, with steam generation more commonly employed for peak power. The initial distribution systems were quite naturally developed to serve the larger urban centers, especially those where uses in manufacturing were important. So, by the time the 1940–70 period arrived, the industry was well established.

Once again, however, several critical post–World War II developments altered dramatically the face of the industry and gave rise to the employment shifts identified in our study. These developments were largely aimed at what was conceived to be the most important remaining problem in power generation and distribution—namely, its still largely localized and regionalized concentrations. The large-capacity steam turbine came into application for the first time, and steam power finally came to take over the base-load power generation task. This development, combined with the development of high voltage, long distance power transmission, and the emergence of power interchange systems, made feasible a much more highly articulated power distribution system—one with a more extensive geographical reach. Perhaps of equal importance was an institutional innovation—the Rural Electrification Administration (REA) was established to encourage the extension of power service into sparsely settled areas and to encourage the application of power to farm tasks. The significance of this can be appreciated when we note that in 1940 only three-fifths of all dwellings and less than a third of farm dwellings had electric power service. Fifteen years later these figures stood at 99 and 96 percent, respectively. The power industry story in our study period is one of further articulation and extension of the network to the point where power service became virtually ubiquitous. This was also a time in which the proportion of residential (as opposed to industrial and commercial) usage increased substantially.[5]

The public utility sector of our study contains more than the electric power industry. It includes gas distribution systems (excluding pipelines) and water and sewerage systems as well. (However, the electric utilities accounted for almost two-thirds of total public utility employment.) These other systems have been going through a remarkably similar developmental experience. The technology of sanitary sewerage and water supply also matured around the turn of the century. The period since then has also been devoted to the building up of infrastructure, beginning with the larger centers and their emerging suburbs.

The identified competitive shifts in public utility employment appear to be a faithful reflection of this developmental history. Taking note of tables II-8 and II-9, all of the relative competitive losses are concentrated in the large metropolitan centers and urban-region cores. These are precisely the fields that satisfied their infrastructure requirements earliest. They are also the fields that have suffered the largest relative declines in power demand partly because of the fact that the widespread availability of power encouraged a relative loss in their share of manufacturing, an important power user. In contrast, 75 percent of the gains were experienced by the lower order trade center counties—especially the shopping center categories (57 percent). The largest single gain in share was experienced by those counties outside the shadow of the dominant urban centers. Together with the secondary labor force fields, this category accounted for almost half of the competitive gain. In all of these lower order centers and more remote fields, the competitive gains were leading gains. The primary transaction fields experienced somewhat weaker relative competitive gains, indicating that the servicing requirements of the continuously spreading suburbs remained an element in the picture.

The geographic picture derived from plate II-22 and table II-4 rounds out the story. The relative declines were most heavily concentrated in the Manufacturing Belt regions. Once again these were the areas where infrastructure requirements were fulfilled the earliest and the areas where manufacturing applications of power were most concentrated. The leading gains were most heavily concentrated in the Southeast and Southern Plains. These are the areas with the most concentrated hinterland populations remaining to be served. These were also the areas where the spread of manufacturing activities out of the Northeastern core made the most substantial additions to power demand.

Apart from this, the shift picture reflects certain special regional features. For example, leading gains were especially disproportionate in the Tennessee Valley regions, reflecting the effect of the Tennessee Valley Authority. The Spokane urban region showed the effects of the strong Pacific Northwest power developments. The Beaumont–Port Arthur region reflected the importance of natural gas sources in providing a special regional advantage. Indianapolis profited from both demand- and supply-side developments. The region increased demand relatively by profiting from a redistribution of manufacturing activities in the western end of the Manufacturing Belt. It was also on the receiving end of major new source pipelines.

Now widen the angle of the lens once more. The largest early specializations in electric power occurred in the middle regions of the Manufacturing Belt astride Appalachian coal (Pittsburgh, Youngstown, Cleveland, Columbus Huntington–Ashland, Clarksburg). Although these regions suffered competitive losses in power employment, they tended to lag behind the competitive losses of other sectors. Also, these regions continued to experience differential gains in public utility employment on the strength of strong mix effects that were larger than the competitive losses.

Finance, Insurance, and Real Estate

Finance, insurance, and real estate (hereafter F.I.R.E.) is another heterogeneous sector, but all of the components have one thing in common: they all function as part of the shadow network of information-processing transactions forming the economy's transaction control system. Therefore, we might expect the redistribution of these activities to have been heavily influenced by the redistribution of the generalized transactions they are designed to serve. That this is the case is supported by the fact that, of all the linkage sectors, F.I.R.E. shift patterns deviated from the total employment shifts the least (an average deviation of about 3 percentage points, see table II-13).

Nevertheless, there were systematic pattern deviations that had their roots in the developmental factors at work. Tables II-8 and II-9 reveal that the large metropolitan urban cores accounted for all of the net competitive losses. Historically these have been the prominent centers of the F.I.R.E. employment (accounting for about two-thirds of total F.I.R.E. employment in 1940). Given all of the factors that have loosened up the transaction structure of the nation, it is not surprising that this should be the case, or that all other trade-center categories and transaction fields should be experiencing net competitive gains. There appear to be two quite different thrusts to this reorientation. One thrust favored the slightly less large at the expense of the large centers. The other favored the very small and remote centers.

From the trade-center perspective, the larger wholesale-retail centers captured more than half of the net competitive gains in F.I.R.E. employment. From the transaction-field perspective, the medium and small urban cores similarly experienced leading gains and captured almost two-thirds of the total net competitive gains. The main aspect of the urban-system reorganization experienced by F.I.R.E. employment can be seen as a "ratchet-down-a-notch" in the urban function and size hierarchy. As I have already hinted, this was, to an important degree, a F.I.R.E. *growth* response to urban-system reorganizations fostered by technological *developments* at work in other fields—in other words, a servicing response to shifts in the locus of F.I.R.E. demand. However, the transforming developments in communications have undoubtedly tended to loosen the hold of the largest metropolitan cores on F.I.R.E. services. Institutional and organizational developments likely have played a role as well. For example, an increase in the number and variety of correspondent relationships between banks seems to have reduced the dominance of the old metropolitan core banks.[6]

The second redistributive thrust was not the dominant stream, but one of significance for the story it tells. From the perspective of the trade center classification, the lower order trade centers displayed prominent competitive gains. Complete shopping centers claim a fifth of the total. This prominence is not surprising because we have already come to appreciate the special role that such shopping centers appear to have played as dispersed nodes of a number of urban-servicing activities. The remaining lower order centers combined account for less than half as much gain, but note that these are all leading gains. And, in the case of convenience centers and hamlets, these are countertrend gains that run against the tide of other activity losses. From the transaction-field perspective, the more remote fields display leading and countertrend gains.[7] Finally, more than 90 percent of these remote, lowest order counties did experience competitive gains. One might infer that some developmental factor must have been at work to open these areas up to F.I.R.E. activity to such a degree.

Communication and other information-processing developments (like the computer) have undoubtedly facilitated this reorganizing trend. One suspects that organizational innovation such as the rapid extension of branch and group banking practices played an important role as well. Important developments during the depression rationalized the savings and loan industry and gave greater impetus to this preeminently local financial organization. The industry appears to have geared itself much more successfully to the task of accumulating small-scale savings and making small-scale investments (especially home mortgages). Those more familiar with the industry may perceive other factors at work.

Finally, there has been a broad-scale geographical reorganization of the industry at work, as revealed by such sources as plate II-25, table II-4, and appendix II-N. Once again the shift patterns show a great deal of correspondence with total employment shifts—a situation that might be taken to represent F.I.R.E.'s response to a shifting demand for its services. By and large the leading (rather than following) reorganizational shifts have been associated with the higher order trade center counties (appendix II-C). So the significant effects have more to do with the prominent financial service requirements of commerce and industry. In this connection, it is significant that Miami, Dallas, and Los Angeles account for more than a fourth of the total competitive gains (on a 171-urban-region basis, appendix E in volume I). Tampa, Atlanta, Washington, Houston, Phoenix, and San Francisco account for another quarter. Richmond, Atlanta, Jacksonville, Tampa, Jackson, Oklahoma City, and Phoenix acquired F.I.R.E. specializations by 1970. In an earlier period, only San Francisco, Los Angeles, Denver, Dallas, Houston, and Miami had acquired specialized status. In almost every case, the core counties were displaying leading gains.

Thus, an important part of the leadership role in the world of commerce and industry, and accordingly in the world of finance, moved out of New York to those centers that were strategically placed relative to new industry and resource bases (Dallas, Atlanta, Houston, and Oklahoma City) and developing channels of international commerce (San Francisco, Los Angeles, and Miami). Both new demands for, and new sources of, financial capital have been generated outside of the old northeastern quadrant. (In keeping with its former and continuing preeminence in the industry, New York suffered especially prominent relative competitive losses—60 percent of the total recorded by all 171 urban regions.) To keep perspective, however, one should note that New York gains on mix effect still exceeded its competitive losses so that F.I.R.E. employment continued to expand. The information-processing, communications, and institutional developments that have loosened New York's hold on the industry have clearly favored most those large metropolitan centers strategically located to provide the F.I.R.E. services of a developmentally reorganized resource and manufacturing transaction base.[8]

Printing and Publishing

A broad-brush treatment of the printing and publishing sector should suffice. Like the communication, public utility, and F.I.R.E. sectors, printing and publishing competitive shifts were highly correlated with competitive shifts in total employment. Two-thirds of all U.S. counties experienced either lagging gains or losses. In short, the developmental factors at work in this sector yield relatively mild structural changes that tend to follow, and to be largely explained by, the shifts in all-sector employments. This can be understood if we observe that this employment category is dominated by the printing and publishing of newspapers. This is a function more akin to communication and financial services than to the manufacturing categories where the standard industrial classification places it.

It is not surprising, therefore, to observe some similarities in the change patterns exhibited by the printing and publishing and the communication sectors. As in the case of communication employment, the large metropolitan and urban-core counties dominated the competitive declines. New York and Chicago accounted for 57 percent of the losses; if we add Boston and Philadelphia, the figure goes to 70 percent. The largest beneficiaries of the shift were the large wholesale-retail centers and, in transaction-field terms, the medium urban cores and their primary labor force fields. Thus, a part of the structural change seems to be associated with the way in which large wholesale-retail centers and medium-sized urban cores have been improving their competitive positions in providing urban-servicing linkage functions to the system.

Shopping centers (especially complete shopping) also claimed an important share of the relative gains. But these shopping centers were disproportionately concentrated in the primary and secondary transaction fields of urbanized linkage activities whose network concentration has displayed a general tendency to step down a notch in trade center hierarchy and size and to spread out in transaction space into fields where the network configurations remain highly articulated.

Still there are some significant geographical competitive shifts that are different from the broad shifts in print media markets. If we switch to the perspective of the 171 urban regions, those that display leading gains in printing and publishing employment are largely restricted to the eastern half of the nation. Though sizable, the competitive gains displayed by a number of western urban regions (for example, Los Angeles) have uniformly tended to lag behind all-sector activity shifts.

There are four noticeable aspects of this shift pattern. All seem to be related to a structural change in the location factors affecting standardized large-run printing activities, mostly periodicals and books. The dramatic increase in urban-linkage services and their network articulation, especially in communications, made it possible for a part of this processing component to split from its publishing roots and seek lower labor costs. The major component of the shift was a relatively short geographical shift out of the major concentrations in New York City and Chicago to nearby hinterland urban regions. Thus, in the case of New York it was the nearby Hartford, Wilkes-Barre, and Harrisburg regions that displayed leading gains. In the case of Chicago it was Green Bay, Milwaukee, Champaign–Urbana, Indianapolis, Dayton, and Des Moines. The concentration of North Central region gains was particularly associated with the tendency of periodical printing to find a relatively central location with respect to national market distribution. This was supplemented by the search for lower labor costs.

The second significant pattern of change was the leading gains experienced by the District of Columbia, Baltimore, Staunton, and Richmond. These seem to be heavily associated with the disproportionate increase in the printing and publishing of government documents and to the many private activities that have come to be linked with national government concerns. The third discernible pattern involved a set of Upper South urban regions with leading competitive gains—Bristol, Lexington, Louisville, Nashville, and Memphis. These appear to have benefited primarily from the decentralization of large-run book printing activities. Finally, there were three westward reaching urban regions—Minneapolis, Dallas, and Denver—that appear to indicate a disproportionate printing and publishing gain in urban regions strategically placed to serve broad emerging regional markets.

If we turn our attention to the finer scale of observation involving counties within an urban region, we find a localized reorientation paralleling that described above. One-fourth of the competitive gains in printing and publishing employment were claimed by the primary and secondary labor force fields of the largest urban cores, as the printing activities ancillary to publishing moved out of the core counties, but to locations that retained good access to publication roots. For example, such counties as Suffolk, Westchester, Dutchess, Orange, Passaic, Bergen, and Sussex in the New York region experienced leading gains in printing and publishing employment.

Notes

1. Considering the proliferation of publications about the effect of transport changes on economic organization, very little attention has been paid to the role of communication. The collection of essays published by Ithiel de Sola Pool in 1977 is a somewhat limited exception. Even there, the system consequences of the telephone are poorly developed.

2. The advent of the computer following World War II needs to be considered. At first glance the computer appears to be a transformation machine—one producing information transformations so essential to the production work and the design of an operating system. This is how it was first conceived. But suddenly we discover that it finds equal application in linkage or transfer processes. It is an essential part of the latest communications switching technology, for example, and an increasingly important point of origin and terminus of communication signals. We are finding that the distinction between computation, which is a transformation or production function, and communication, which is a transfer function, becomes too artificial to encompass the reality. This has led some to characterize this emerging field of activity as

"compunications." This extraordinary development is not only beginning to reshape the way we perceive things, it is beginning to have a profound effect on the organization of social activity and its transaction network forms. Because the structure of society has barely begun to absorb this new tool, its effect in the last decade of our study period is still small and impossible to pinpoint in the record. But our understanding of what is taking place, and what may take place, could be severely misled if we do not begin to take acount of this development.

3. I might add that the body of conventional merchant wholesaling also developed further differentiated product specializations, each with further differentiated topo-logics, but treatment in this study must be restricted to a sketch. Generally, the effect of these increasing specializations was to facilitate the retention of wholesaling functions in (or their return to) the higher order centers of the national system.

4. At the beginning, it was local transit that made electric power generation feasible. The initial investments could not have been undertaken on the basis of lighting applications alone—given their highly variable 24-hour cycle of use.

5. For those who recall that the REA came into being as a Depression initiative, it may be well to point out that 98 percent of the power generated by the REA in 1970 was put into place after 1940.

6. In this connection we might note this ratchet-down shift is not a direct result of an intercorrelation with interregional geographic shifts. Such urban regions as Saginaw, Lansing, South Bend, Springfield (Ill.), Madison, Cedar Rapids, and Harrisburg are examples of large wholesale-retail urban regions demonstrating these properties and lying inside the larger Manufacturing Belt region that tended to suffer disproportionate losses.

7. Although the sum of all complete shopping centers shows only lagging losses, the fact is that most complete shopping centers also experienced leading gains. We have seen that complete shopping centers were especially prominent in the agricultural plains and Midwest regions that experienced overall competitive losses as a result of the dramatic reorganization of agriculture. These have pulled the aggregate complete shopping category into a lagging growth posture, in spite of the dramatic total gains.

8. Throughout this discussion of F.I.R.E. activities I have ignored the role of the clearly different component, real estate. This is justified here because, although real estate accounted for about one-third of the total 1940 F.I.R.E. employment, it accounted for only a little over one-tenth of the 1940–70 F.I.R.E. employment gain.

8

Resource Sectors

Resource activities were the first activity sectors to be differentiated in the course of developmental history. They were created because of the need to concentrate the energy supplies that supported human systems. This root-problem of all living systems derives from the second law of thermodynamics which specifies that any closed physical system must experience entropy or run down over time. Living systems, including human societies, have evolved ever more complex (anti-entropic) forms by organizing systems open to energy transfer from external environments. The energy transfer permits such systems to defer the effect of the thermodynamic law by accelerating its effects in the supporting environment. Sooner or later the energy pool drawn upon reaches a limit and the evolved life system is threatened unless some new energy pool can be tapped.

Agriculture

It was precisely just such a crisis in the life of human systems that led to the emergence of modern agriculture. Life was lived in a hunting and gathering Eden for approximately 99 percent of the span of human culture. About 10,000 years ago the pressure of population on the material sources of wild grains and animals brought human societies face-to-face with the reality of the entropy process. Developmental solutions yielded a modern agriculture and horticulture based on the domestication of seed crops and food animals. This had the effect of concentrating the energy available in the human system's operating environment (which in turn resulted from the fixation of solar energy).[1]

Urban systems, as we have known them, are a direct by-product of modern agriculture. Agriculture is the original source of modern activity specializations and their attendant transaction systems. These developments brought humankind to a new realization of the limits of human power in a technologically organized task environment. This stimulated tool-making technologies and the harnessing of work animals. Tool making led, in turn, to the minerals technology and the emergence of mining as a resource sector. The processing of metals, and the ultimate limits to the use of animals as a work-energy concentrator, led to the industrial revolution and the mining of fossil fuels. At each stage, the organization of urban transaction systems became more complex. At each stage, the transfer of energy across life system boundaries was accelerated, as was the entropy process in human society's energy-source environments. It may be that the stage is being set for another critical encounter with the entropy law.

But for now we want to examine the structural changes this process has wrought in urban-system, resource-sector activities so that we can more reasonably interpret the changing employment structures depicted by this study. We begin with agriculture.

The Early Problem-Solving Sequences

In his historical analysis of American agriculture, Willard Cochrane (1979) divides the narrative into developmental epochs similar to those sketched in chapter 4 of volume I and chapter 6 of volume II. These can be grouped into two broad periods. The first was characterized by cheap, abundant land and lasted until the closing of the frontier about 1900. The second was marked by relatively more scarce and expensive agricultural land and extends to the present. The problems of each period were markedly different and called forth different developmental responses.

CHEAP LAND AND EXTENSIVE AGRICULTURE. The first two of Cochrane's epochs extends from the 1607 settlements to the early 1800s and can be characterized as the pioneering period. During this period commercial agriculture was limited (apart from the emerging cotton economy in the South). The basic agricultural problem was increasing agricultural output sufficiently to support the growing population. This problem was resolved by the extensive exploitation of the land. Labor was the scarce factor so production increases were best achieved by bringing more land under cultivation. Between 1775 and 1820, the pursuit of land had drawn settlers out of the seaboard as far as the Mississippi River. The principal production tools were the ax, hoe, sickle, and scythe. There was so little concern for productivity in the modern sense that, relative to European practice, agricultural processes actually regressed. The pioneers were mostly concerned with land clearing and land speculation. They mined the soil through constant cropping and let the animals run loose in the woods. Nevertheless, this process did succeed in opening the transmontaine Old West to settlement and agricultural production.

By the early 1800s, agricultural land was losing its attraction as a source of speculative income in the eastern half of the nation. Attention turned more directly to earning a return from the product of the land beyond the subsistence it had provided the pioneer family. This involved the practice of commercial agriculture and a corresponding shift in developmental objectives. There were two major constraining problems—the scarcity of labor and the lack of effective access to emerging urban markets.

What was needed to transform the pioneer farmer into a commercial farmer was a set of tools that would make "his arm longer and stronger." The response began in the village blacksmith shops and emerged by the 1860s as a budding farm machinery industry. The entire technology fostered the substitution of animal power for human power. Because the farm operation was an integrated system of tasks, once started, the mechanization process could not rest until it created a whole technological system. Development began with soil preparation and resulted in the iron plow and moldboard plow. This created a harvesting bottleneck. Since 3000 B.C., the only harvesting development had been the scythe and cradle. The modern response was the mechanical reaper. This shifted the bottleneck problem to the threshing operation and led to the mechanical thresher. All of this put pressure on the seeding process, leading to the planter. In turn, the expanded horsepower requirements made haymaking the bottleneck, leading to mowers and haymaking equipment. This total system transformation was achieved within a remarkably short time span.

In the Old South the problem of labor scarcity educed a different kind of adaptive response—the introduction of slavery. After the invention of the cotton gin had broken the major off-farm bottleneck, both production and slavery expanded rapidly. This set in motion a regional historic dynamic that only found its resolution in our study period. This is an important explanatory root to which we will return.

Increasing agricultural outputs further exacerbated the already critical market access problem. Dependence on the wagon and cattle drive was a major constraint. We have already touched upon the developmental response in chapter 6 in discussing the development of the railroad between 1820 and 1840.

As is always the case, the developments of the first half of the 1880s redefined the problems requiring attention. The growth of the railway, which had been significantly stimulated by the requirements of commercial agriculture in the Old West, opened up the last frontier in the New West. Horse-powered farm mechanization was almost complete. The further development of gang plows, and the combining of the reaper and thresher into the combine, were marginal developments that quickly exhausted the power potential of the largest horse teams (up to forty draft horses).

The access problems associated with the distribution of farm products were still prominent, lending continued impetus to the development of transport channel infrastructures. However, the distribution problem began to spawn a new set of adaptations. One of these was the cream separator (along with the cream tester) and the pasturization of milk. Farmers in more remote areas were able to develop a new agricultural specialization based on feeding skim milk to stock and shipping butter and cheese economically over longer distances. This led to the migration of dairy farming out of the Corn Belt into Michigan and Wisconsin. This period also witnessed the development of the commercial canning industry and the ice-refrigerated rail car. But most important was the beginning of specialized off-farm food processes that substantially altered the network structure of the distributive transfer channels.

SCARCE LAND AND INTENSIVE AGRICULTURE. Throughout the early period, the nature of the problem-solving responses depended on an abundance of cheap land. It was a period of extensive agriculture. Productivity (in the sense of yield per acre) was not important and increased little during the entire first 300 years of American agriculture. There was always more land available to increase production. Farm mechanization served less to increase yields than to spread labor over more acres. With the closing of the frontier around 1900, the whole problem context shifted. Further increases in output could only be achieved by increasing yields per acre. An appropriate problem-solving response was forthcoming.

The next developmental epoch in agriculture immediately preceded the study period. The old developmental concerns by no means disappeared with the closing of the frontier. But the older focus on the mechanization of labor and access to the market was changed in character as a result of the earlier developmental successes.

For example, the advent of gang plows and harvesting machines was pressing the limits of animal power. Furthermore, millions of acres were required to concentrate the solar energy essential to meet the growing horsepower requirements. What was needed was an efficient source of power to pull the large machines—one preferably based on off-farm sources of energy. Early in the century the farm sector experimented with some 5,000 steam tractors in much the same way that urban transit systems experimented with steam power. Again, this source of power was not the answer. These tractors were heavy and difficult to maneuver. Moreover, providing for large amounts of fuel and water at the work site complicated the logistics of field activities. The development of the internal combustion engine was the essential breakthrough. It took a decade of experimentation, but by 1910 farmers began to adopt tractors on a widespread basis.

As we saw in chapter 6, the nature of the access problem was transformed as well. The earliest access problems had to do with opening up territory and moving staples over long distances. The large-scale transport network claimed most of the developmental attention. By the turn of the century, the emerging system of cities was pretty well in place and effectively linked at gross scale. Attention now shifted to local access problems. Local commodity transport still depended largely on horsepower drayage. Agriculture turned eagerly to the truck and the local farm-to-market road. This phenomenon has already been covered in detail.

The effect of the closing of the frontier was mitigated somewhat by the millions of acres released from the support of horsepower, but it soon became clear that further increases in output would have to come from an increase in acreage yields. The developmental response opened a new age of scientific agriculture. It involved the discovery of new relationships of a physiological, chemical, and biological nature, and the development of new technologies, which were based on these relationships and which could be applied to increasing farm productivity. It was during this period that the knowledge-base of scientific agriculture began to take institutional form. James Wilson's tenure as secretary of agriculture from 1897 to 1913 was a significant turning point. He initiated scientific work in plant breeding, entomology, soil chemistry, and animal diseases. This was also the time when the land-grant university system came of age. It was doubly important that scientific agriculture developed in the context of an extension outreach involving both research and farmer education. From the beginning, this new thrust was oriented to the work-site application of new technology.

The period up to the late 1930s was largely devoted to the development of a major research and education infrastructure and the accumulation of knowledge and technique. The explosive application of these techniques did not occur until the study period, although modest increases in yields were achieved by manuring, liming, and applying commercial fertilizers. The new power mechanization also contributed modestly to yields by increasing the timeliness of farm operations.

The same problems forced a new attention to improving the land. This was the period when irrigation was begun on a substantial scale. This was not only a function of the closing of the frontier, it was related to the fact that the western movement of the frontier brought large amounts of arid and semiarid land into potential use. It is no accident of timing that the Reclamation Act, which provided for water development, was passed in 1902.

Agricultural Development from 1940 to 1970

These adaptations accelerated to almost explosive dimensions in our study period. This was partly because the new technologies spawned by scientific agriculture were delayed in application by the depression. Their adoption commonly required capital outlays that were not then sufficiently available. Beyond this, the agricultural sciences reached maturity during the study period. The war and postwar prosperity and an expanding export market removed the capital constraints and encouraged rapid and intensive applications. The burgeoning variety of the technological developments would require a book to discuss, but a short summary is essential.

New developments in farm power and mechanization. During the study period the tractor went through another major shift in its applications to farm work. In 1940, the tractor was still used almost exclusively as a substitute for horses in pulling farm implements. The development of the power takeoff converted the tractor into a general purpose power source for processing as well. The development of the three-point hitch increased the variety of work implements the tractor could accommodate and placed many of them under direct operator control. Beyond this, there were major improvements in horsepower-to-weight ratios. The average horsepower per tractor tripled and other developments such as the pneumatic tire and power steering increased maneuverability and speed, as well as expanded the range of soil conditions under which machinery could work the fields. During the fifth epoch, the number of tractors went from zero to about a million and a half. By the end of the study period there were close to 5 million.

The new power and work capacities of the tractor spawned further enlargements and modifications of earlier forms of farm machinery as well as a whole set of new machines. The cotton picker first came into use, along with a host of new machines for harvesting celery, tomatoes, nuts, and other crops. The number of trucks used in farm production kept pace with the number of tractors, giving agriculture a new dimension of access flexibility both on and off the farm.

We already learned in chapter 7 how rural electrification first came to the farm in a significant way in the study period. This opened another domain of mechanization in a variety of farm tasks (milking, feed mixing, food cooling and freezing, water pumping). As a consequence of electrification, milking and milk processing were converted into a bulk-flow process from the cow to the processing plant.

Developments that increased yields. Power and mechanization developments during the study period amounted to an acceleration and modification of a sequence of developments under way for one hundred years—with each phase opening up new problems, new opportunities, and new solutions. The distinctive thing about agriculture at this time was the phenomenal process changes and increases in yields spawned by the emerging scientific agriculture. This developmental response to the closing frontier—namely, the building of institutional infrastructures and knowledge technologies—came to the point of full fruition only in the study period. Perhaps the most spectacular of these developments was hybrid seed corn, which tripled corn yields; the most bizarre, the development of the square tomato, which facilitated mechanization. The development of drought- and disease-resistant wheats, winter wheats, and beets resistant to curly-top disease and adaptable to saline soils are all examples of breeding improvements.

Pest and weed control chemicals, often applied by plane, made dramatic contributions. Research in animal nutrition improved meat productivity and opened up new cropping options. For example, the discovery of nutrient supplements, trace minerals, and animo acids provided the link needed to substitute soybeans for milk and fish meal as a source of protein for pigs and poultry.

The introduction of primary plant nutrients—nitrogen, phosphorous and potassium—into the soil through fertilization burgeoned. In 1940, there were seven ammonia factories producing 475,000 tons. In 1966, there were sixty-six producing 11 million tons. The tonnage of commercial fertilizer applied on farms more than quadrupled during the study period—almost seven times the increase from 1900 to 1940.

Agricultural science revolutionized the meat production segment of agriculture as well. The case of poultry is especially dramatic. Except for a limited enclave of specialized poultry production in the Delmarva Peninsula, poultry raising in 1940 was still predominantly a way of generating grocery money for the farm family. Genetic improvements, the nutrition research already mentioned, antibiotics, and vitamin D to eradicate pullurom disease made it possible to increase the size of the flocks from 3,000 to 60,000. The chicken was further bred to the tastes of the market. Processing technology provided equipment for on-line picking, eviscerating, and inspection at a rate of thousands of broilers an hour. The market changed from live to New-York-dressed (head, feet, and guts in) to the present fresh, chilled, or quick-frozen product. The market responded by increasing annual poultry consumption from 16 to 50 pounds per person during the study period. In a similar fashion, cattle feedlots have gone from a few hundred to a few thousand and changed the face of the cattle finishing and packing business.

Developments in water control. Soil improvements through irrigation and drainage were practiced in scattered locations in this country from early in the eighteenth century. But the opening of the last frontier to agriculture in the last half of the nineteenth century depended heavily on irrigation because much of this land was either arid or semiarid. However, until the closing of the frontier brought pressure on the land, irrigation was largely a private enterprise and mostly involved the diversion of local streams or windmill pumping. The closing of the frontier intensified the pressures to involve the federal government in developing large-scale irrigation works. The Reclamation Act of 1902 was the beginning. By 1907, the principle of federal public works was established. By 1911, the damming of the Salt River was underway. There was some mixture of federal and private development on a modest scale before the 1930s, by which time private capital could no longer find many opportunities for development.

So once again it was the study period when the major impact of agricultural developments took place. The Hoover Dam added a million new acres to cultivation in the 1950s, much of which was 250 miles and a 1,617 foot pump-lift away in California. The Coolee Dam in the Columbia Basin was built in the 1950s. The Imperial Dam opened the way for irrigation in the Imperial Valley. Within three decades after the Hoover Dam, the federal government had built 252 storage and 126 diversion dams.

In addition, the new availability of cheap electric power for pumping, and the development of the Zybach center-pivot sprinkler (capable of irrigating 133 acres without expensive canals) opened the way to pumping groundwater for irrigation on a large scale. The recent development of agriculture on the High Plains is based on such developments.

All of these developments also displayed important systemic interrelationships and feed-back effects. For example, the increased crop yields and controlled crop rotations permitted by irrigation expanded the possible applications of expensive farm machinery. Indeed, it made possible the initial development of highly specialized machines for fruit and vegetable cropping and processing.

The new technology opened up opportunities for drainage as well. Southern Florida, the South Atlantic Coast, and the Mississippi Delta are places where substantial acreages of fertile land have been upgraded or brought into production *de novo*.

The upshot: During the half century covering the last stages of the exploitation of the New West frontier until 1940, about 14 million acres of land were placed under irrigation. After 1940, more than twice that amount was added.

THE CHANGING STRUCTURE OF AMERICAN AGRICULTURE. These developmental activities have culminated in an extraordinary transformation in the structure of the agricultural sector. A few indicators tell the story. According to U.S. Department of Agriculture sources, in 1820, one farm worker supplied four people with agricultural products. Although yields per acre stayed roughly constant, horse-drawn machinery had increased this to seven people by 1900. This was further increased to almost eleven people from 1900 to 1940, as the tractor improved worker efficiency and converted roughly 40 million acres formerly used for feeding draft animals to food production. During our study period, the effect of scientific agriculture on yields came into play and the number of people supplied per farm worker went from eleven to forty-seven in 1970 and fifty-nine in 1978. In short, since 1940 the combination of scientific agriculture and the changing power base of farm work increased the productivity of the farm worker eight times as much as mechanization alone had been able to achieve in the prior 120 years!

Although the number of farms stayed roughly constant in the early twentieth century, it declined from 6 million in 1940 to 2.7 million in 1970. Seventy percent of the remaining farms grossed less than $20,000 per year and these so-called farmers generated 80 percent of their income from off-farm jobs. The largest 30 percent of the farms accounted for 90 percent of cash receipts from farming; 6 percent accounted for 53 percent. Only the number of farms larger than 500 acres increased. The farm population was about 30 million in 1940—little changed since the beginning of the century. By 1970 it was down to 9.7 million. Thus, the farm population declined from 23 percent to 4.8 percent of the total population in a single generation.

Equally dramatic have been the changes in the transaction linkages the agricultural sector formed with the rest of the economy. As recently as the mid-1930s, farmers were producing most of their own fuel, power, and fertilizer. By 1967, only 28 percent of the inputs to agriculture were supplied by agriculture (outside the livestock and livestock products sector, only 8 percent). By 1960, industry was furnishing farmers with 6.5 million tons of steel annually—more than that for a year's output of cars; 45 million tons of chemical materials—up five times from 1935; 18 billion gallons of crude petroleum—more than any other industry; 285 million pounds of rubber—enough to make tires for 6 million automobiles; and 22 billion kilowatt hours of electricity—enough to serve Chicago, Detroit, Baltimore, and Houston for a year. While 8 million people worked on the farm in 1960, 7 million off-farm workers produced goods and services purchased by farmers.

At the same time, 11 million people were engaged in off-farm jobs that processed and distributed farm products. Indeed, food processing has come to dominate the food production chain. Of the $112 billion that flowed through the food and fiber system in 1969, 70 percent were generated by those agricultural processing and marketing activities. Eighteen percent were generated by activities supplying agriculture with purchased inputs. The farm sector itself added only 12 percent of the total value. Activities supplying prepared foods such as breakfast cereals, cake mixes, frozen foods, and frozen meals ballooned, as did eating out in restaurants.

In short, agriculture has become an increasingly capital-intensive, high-technology, mass production business. The farmer's role has been completely transformed. In a very real sense he assembles packages of technology. Farm animals and plants are now seen to be merely material and energy conversion machines subject to efficiency improvements like any other process. The farmer, with 3,000 acres in wheat and $3 million in assets, including half a million in machinery, can no longer afford to sit on the machine as an operator. He must coordinate a large operation. He is a manager-applicator of the life sciences, the physical sciences, and the social and business sciences. The agricultural revolution has been a managerial and cultural revolution as well. Agriculture has changed from a way of life to a way of making a living.

The Direct Consequences for Employment

Thus, like all activity sectors, agriculture has gone through a sequence of developmental, problem-solving changes that successively redefined the most important problems. In the process, these developments further altered the network of activities forming the urban system. It is precisely during the study period that the developments in agricultural science and engineering had their greatest effect. In terms of the shift patterns employed here to represent these changes, the obvious starting point is the tremendous 6 million person decline in agricultural employment. More than two-thirds of the 1940 employment disappeared in a generation.

THE TOTAL AGRICULTURE MIX EFFECT. As a direct consequence of this employment decline, the mix effect tells a major part of the story in agriculture. It generated interregional employment shifts of more than 2 million workers.[2] Between 1940 and 1970, 70 percent of agriculture's *gross* differential interregional shift ($\Sigma\ D_{ij}$) across 171 urban regions was directly accounted for by the mix effect (appendix II-A). Given the declining rate of employment, the 49 urban regions that did not specialize in agricultural employment in 1940 actually derived differential gains in agricultural employment. These were almost exclusively in the Manufacturing Belt, on the Pacific Coast, and in Florida. The remaining 122 suffered relative losses in total employment attributable to the negative agricultural mix effect (see appendix E in volume I). The bulk of this was experienced by the south-central urban regions and the western end of the Corn Belt extending from Kansas City to Minneapolis. These shifts accounted for 20 percent of the gross mix effect shifts for all thirty-one employment sectors, almost twice the contribution of all manufacturing sectors combined (table II-1). While these shifts contributed substantially to the summary line differential shift in total employment, this mix component was, of course, directly proportional to the degree of agricultural specialization. It left the percentage distribution of agricultural employment between regions unaltered.

THE TOTAL AGRICULTURE COMPETITIVE SHIFT. An examination of the redistributive differentials at the level of the industry line brings us back to this volume's focus on the competitive shift. Agriculture's contribution to gross, all-sector competitive shifts is only a fraction of its contribution to gross mix shifts (table II-1), but even here it remains one of the most important explanatory factors. There was a competitive interregional shift equivalent to 600,000 workers. In examining the pattern of these shifts, we should bear in mind that a competitive gain in a declining industry can reflect a smaller relative loss in employment than in other regions.

The geographical pattern of this redistributive shift is dramatically presented in plate II-1. About 82 percent of the U.S. counties were agricultural specialists in 1940 (shaded areas). Almost all of these experienced leading (or countertrend) competitive gains or losses—about equally divided in proportion. The leading losses (in red) almost uniformly blanketed the southeast and south central portions of the nation, except Florida. They also included the Michigan Peninsula along with northern Wisconsin and Minnesota. There were a few southern mountain counties centered on Albuquerque. The agricultural counties experiencing leading gains (dark blue) were concentrated in the Northern Plains and mountain regions and the western end of the Corn Belt (plus a finger into the eastern end centered on Peoria, Springfield, Champaign, and Lafayette). The High Plains down through Kansas, Oklahoma, and Texas were also included, as was the Central Valley of California.

At the 171-urban-region scale, the delineated southeastern area of leading losses accounted for 97 percent of the total negative shift. The Atlanta, Birmingham, Montgomery, Memphis, and Greenville urban regions in the Old South displayed the strongest losses. Of the leading gains, the greatest concentrations were found (1) in the Minneapolis, Sioux Falls, Sioux City, Dubuque Corn Belt regions; (2) in the Denver, Lubbock, and Amarillo High Plains regions; (3) in California; (4) in the Columbia and Salt River basins; (5) in south Florida; and (6) in an area around New York City. The latter two call our attention to the fact that three-quarters of the unspecialized counties experienced competitive gains and these tended to be the more highly urbanized counties, contrary to popular impression.

This unexpected quirk of the shift pattern is given added emphasis if we examine the county developmental code frequency tabulation in appendixes II-J and II-K. The above-average competitive gain frequencies were concentrated in those categories identified as either urban field core counties or higher order trade-center counties. This phenomenon is given dimension by the synthetic region computations reported in appendixes II-C and II-D. When computed across ten urban field regions, 94 percent of the competitive gains are in the urban cores; when computed across the nine trade center classes, the higher order centers account for 100 percent of the competitive gains. Correspondingly, the heaviest losses were in the lower order shopping centers and in the hinterland fields of the small urban regions.

The net effect of all these shifts left agriculture's index of industrial concentration little altered. However, on a 171-region basis, 6 urban regions ringing Chicago lost their status as agricultural specialists; as did the Michigan urban regions, seven Southern Piedmont regions, and a series of larger urban regions in other specialized territories (Mobile, New Orleans, Dallas, Kansas City, Lincoln, Minneapolis, Albuquerque, and Las Vegas). In the latter case, and in the case of the region around Chicago, this was perhaps brought about as much by the acquisition of nonagricultural activities as by the loss of agricultural activities. By 1970, the Miami, Tampa, Denver, San Francisco, Eureka, Redding, Portland, and Reno urban regions became agricultural specialists for the first time (appendix II-N).

Agricultural commodity subsector mix effects. The next task is to match these developmental shift patterns to the developmental scenario of the first part of the chapter as a source of explanation. Here we encounter a problem that will return to haunt us more than once. Agriculture is by no means as heterogeneous an activity as many people take it to be. As a consequence, at least a part of the total agriculture competitive pattern (thirty-one sector aggregates) must reside in a subaggregate, or commodity level, mix effect. Furthermore, the competitive shifts displayed by individual agricultural commodities can differ substantially from the all-commodity pattern in plate II-1. And it is at the commodity level that the developmental factors discussed earlier come to bear most directly.

Of very little importance overall, the commodity mix effect[3] does resolve one puzzle in the shift patterns just presented. Why, when we aggregate counties according to their urban-system characteristics, do the higher order trade center and urban-region core fields dominate the competitive gains? Agricultural employment has clearly declined less here than in hinterland regions. It seems to defy common sense to assume that the dense urban regions improved their comparative advantage overall in producing agricultural commodities. The answer appears to be partly attributable to the differences in the mix of commodities produced in the highly urbanized fields and in the differences in their rates of employment decline.

From alternative data sources we can get a fix on differences in the rates of change in farm employment and production by farm commodity.[4] Cotton, food grains, and feed grains appear to be the agricultural sectors experiencing the largest declines in employment. These are the sectors with the largest increases in labor productivity resulting from developments in machine technology and scientific agriculture. The employment declines are a direct developmental response. Regions specializing in these activities clearly experienced commodity mix-effect losses. They were mostly urban-system hinterland regions. Agriculture in urban-region core counties (particularly of the large, higher order centers) displayed a different pattern of specialization. The mix was dominated by vegetable truck farms, fluid milk dairy farms, horticultural commodities (like decorative plants and greenhouse products of all sorts), and the like. These are all much more labor intensive than the rest of agriculture. Here modern agricultural technology has not found the same opportunity for labor savings. The slower rates of employment decline in these commodity sectors yield a positive commodity-level mix effect that shows up as a total agriculture competitive gain in these highly urbanized areas.[5]

Commodity-level competitive effects. We can turn now to the the task of linking the competitive shift patterns in plate II-1 to the explanatory, developmental scenario. We set the stage for this by considering underlying changes on a commodity-by-commodity basis.[6]

Consider how developments in agricultural mechanization and scientific agriculture came to bear upon the geographical redistribution of meat animal production. The pattern changes were dominated by shifts out of the Great Lakes states and Corn Belt into the Northern and Southern Plains. The explanatory factors are multifaceted and complex, the most important being the development of irrigation in the High Plains.

New sources of farm power, deep well pumps, and the Zyback central-pivot sprinkler allowed the successful tapping of the Ogallala aquifer. This, combined with the development of hybrid grain sorghums, radically increased feed grain yields in the region. The climate also favored better feed conversion rates.[7] Coupled with this were mechanical improvements in the handling of silage and nutrition research that resulted in the use of more sorghum in the cattle ration. Both of the latter also contributed to the tremendous growth of the feed lot industry. Feed lots were provided many more location options by the development of the truck at the same time that the cost of shipping livestock by rail was pushing production out of the older, traditional feeding areas. (The rail rate increase of 84 percent was far more than the rate increases on finished meat products.)

What may seem curious is the decline in the meat animal production in the North Central region, particularly in the Corn Belt. This region also increased the production of feed grains dramatically, yet meat production and its associated employment dropped. The answer lies basically in the expansion of regional and foreign exports. This region had an easier and more economical access to external feed grain markets through the Ohio and Mississippi river systems at the same time that the Plains region was experiencing a deterioration in rail service. This reach for the export market was abetted by two factors. First, scientific agriculture generally, and hybrid corn in particular, set up a persistent pressure in the direction of a monoculture. Corn Belt farmers were only too glad to drop multiple-enterprise farming (particularly hay and livestock) for concentrated feed grain production. The region's natural advantage in corn production was thus reinforced. Second, another major railroad rate change occurred during this period that made it cheaper to ship feed grain into the Plains and Southeast.

Finally, meat production increased in the Southeast. This is partly because this region improved its access to extended sources of feed grain for the reasons just indicated, partly because this entire region was a deficit supply region, partly because of the facilitating decentralization of meat packing and feed lot practice, and partly because of a shift from row-cropping to cover-cropping (hay and forage) in the face of developments yet to be told.

The milk production story has both similar and different elements. Milk production declined absolutely in the Corn Belt, and for practically all of the same reasons as meat production. It also declined absolutely in the Plains, both North and South, but for different reasons. First, during the study period, the proportion of milk marketed as fluid increased in comparison with that marketed as processed products. Important developmental factors explain this. On the demand side, oleomargarine became a powerful competitor to butter. On the supply side, the technology of homogenization and the bulk processing and transport of fluid milk from the cow to the consumer helped extend the fields of potential operation, but mostly in areas of deficit supply. Because historically the Plains had been more apt to be in surplus supply, milk went more heavily into processing. The trend to monoculture and competition for the land of the feed grain and meat animal enterprises in these regions were also factors. In the first instance, developmental factors operated directly on the milk production enterprise to alter its competitive position; in the second, developmental factors operated indirectly through competition from meat and feed grain enterprises.

The major increases in milk production came in the Southeast. Although the deficit supply and bulk fluid technologies facilitated this, so also did the same factors that encouraged the expansion of meat production. The more economical access to external sources of feed grain and the shift to cover cropping in the Southeast seem particularly important. Together, the Northeast, Mountain, and Pacific regions picked up about 12 percent of the competitive gains in milk production (and associated farm work) mostly on the strength of the pull of excess demand and the operation of similar developmental factors.

The only superficial puzzle was the increase in milk production in the old Wisconsin heartland of the dairy enterprise—this in spite of the area's heavy specialization in the processed products that were experiencing relative decline. Here the developmental pressure toward a monoculture reinforced the natural production advantages of the Old Dairy Belt. Furthermore, the technological developments in bulk fluid processing and transportation expanded the region's access to extended markets for fluid milk at the same time that its competition from the Corn Belt and Plains region was declining. Another neighboring competitor also began to decline. The Michigan Peninsula plus the northern tier of counties of Michigan, Wisconsin, and Minnesota displayed marked sectoral competitive losses of total agricultural employment (plate II-1). These tended to be marginal production areas that were made submarginal by the large capital costs associated with the new bulk milk technology. They were also left somewhat stranded as the economies of scale at the processing plant end of the distribution channel tended to make the market outlet link more remote. The producer who sold milk in 10-gallon cans by the side of the road got left out. Furthermore, the competition from tourism, recreation, timber production, and (in the southern portion) the urban uses of land tended to crowd out the old agricultural enterprises. This was abetted by land zoning practices in the Upper Peninsula that actually promoted the withdrawal of land from agriculture in the sandy, cutover regions.

Poultry and egg production was one of the most dramatic developmental stories and showed an unambiguous regional shift pattern. Poultry displayed competitive gains in the Southeast and competitive losses almost everywhere else. (That is, on a broad regional basis. At the same time, there were counties in Delmarva and California, for example, that displayed competitive gains in poultry production.) The genetic, nutritional, disease control, and mechanical process developments (discussed earlier) created a highly specialized goods conversion operation more industrial than agricultural in character. The easy availability of surplus food grains from the Corn Belt, the availability of abundant cheap labor, a small-farm culture that was losing its traditional agricultural enterprise, the lower costs of building and heating buildings, the improved access to northern urban markets by truck, the vertical integration of enterprises with the aggressive leadership of the feed grain companies and broiler processors were all factors favoring the greatest development in the Southeast.

Because we have already recounted developments in feed grain production (hybrid sorghum and corn) in connection with the shift of meat production to the Plains regions (North and South), there is no need to repeat the explanation of the dramatic gains in these regions. However, counter-balancing these gains have been equally dramatic feed grain losses in the Southeast. This calls for further explanation. The climate and hilly lands of the Southeast render it marginal for feed crop production. As agricultural monoculture grew apace and Corn Belt grains became cheaper and more accessible, the Southeastern feed grain enterprise could not keep up. The shift from row to cover-cropping was further promoted by the small size of the typical Southeastern farm and the rapid development of off-farm employment opportunities. The latter provided further incentive to move out of labor-intensive production enterprises.

It is natural that, in contrast, hay and forage production displayed competitive gains in the Southeast. This was the cover-cropping alternative to the increasingly non-competitive row crops, and it was coupled with the expanded milk and meat production in the area. The other big competitive gainer in hay and forage crops was the Southern Plains. A part of this was the joint-product linkage of sorghum forage and silage with sorghum grain. Another part was a reinforcement of a monocultural competitive gain (analogous to that experienced by the Corn Belt for corn and the Dairy Belt for milk).

But there is an interesting aspect of this that shows how developmental, problem-solving initiatives can yield unanticipated side effects. The collapse of foreign demand for agricultural exports after World War II, the dramatic productivity increases attending scientific agriculture, and the conversion of millions of acres from the feeding of horses all generated a farm commodity oversupply problem of anguishing proportions. The adaptive response was the governmental feed and food grain programs that encouraged the removal of lands from these enterprises. Thus, large acreages of land reverted to grass. This was abetted by the reversion of marginal production lands opened up during the war. The bulk of this land reconversion took place in the Northern Plains and partly for that reason, this region experienced three-quarters of the total competitive gains in farm work devoted to hay and forage cropping.

The experience with food grain production tended to run parallel with that of the feed grains with some interesting variations. Like the feed grains, food grains tended to gain in the Plains region and lose out in the Southeast, and for essentially similar reasons. In the case of the food grains, the development of rust and drought resistant, winter-hardy wheats with high protein yields—explicitly adapted to the High Plains—was an important developmental factor. Relative to other agricultural enterprises, the food and feed grains gained the greatest advantages from continued improvement in mechanization. One of the pattern variations saw the Corn Belt region display a prominent negative shift in food grains, while gaining in feed grains. This was because of the increasing relative importance of wheat in the food grain category, and of corn in the feed grain category. In addition, the increasing practice of monoculture on large farms tended to sharpen the demarcation of the boundary zones between wheat and corn production. This tended to push the cultivation of wheat further west, and of corn further east.

One also observes modest gains in food grains in the South Central and Delta regions as an exception to the Southeastern pattern of decline. This is totally explained by the relative expansion of rice production in that area. After the abolition of slavery, the very labor-intensive form of early rice production in the United States declined rapidly in the old southeastern coastal areas. The developmental story behind the recent expansion of rice production, is the delayed development of mechanization specifically suited to the harvesting of rice. In portions of Arkansas, the Gulf coastal regions of Louisiana and East Texas, and in California's lower Sacramento Valley, the availability of abundant water, and a subsoil (clay in the Delta) that would dry quickly when drained to support the weight of machinery, fostered a revival of rice production. The four areas mentioned account for almost all of U.S. production, with the Delta supplying three-fourths. The key was the modification of wheat harvesting and threshing technology to accommodate the harvesting of rice. Experimentation began in the 1930s and by 1948, only 7.5 worker hours of labor were required in the United States to match the output of 900 worker hours in Japan. Developments in rice production further illustrate the dramatic aspects of modern technology when applied to agriculture. Furthermore, in no other crop has the role of the airplane been as important. The airplane is the seeder, fertilizer spreader, insecticide applicator, and herbicide dispenser. This is the matching, preharvest-stage technology that helped to bring rice production back to life in this country. Notice, in particular, how the airplane made it possible to bypass the task of developing a matching set of sowing and cultivating machines in order for the harvesting developments to make rice culture competitive once again. It also further illustrates the interrelated and systemic nature of technological development.

In regional terms the story of the production of vegetables, fruits, and nuts is almost all about Florida and the Pacific region (especially California). In both cases, a whole system of technologies came together to create a dramatic realignment of production and associated employments.

Take the case of vegetables first. California dominated the competitive gain in the culture of vegetables. The West (mostly southern Arizona, the Salt River Plain, the Puget Sound area, and California's Central Valley) made a respectable showing, as did southern Florida. Every other region displayed relative declines. Prior to the study period, vegetable production was highly seasonal and required much stoop-labor for planting, cultivating, and harvesting. The seasonal characteristics and the delicate nature of many vegetables and fruits inhibited mechanization. Production was concentrated in general farms and truck farms near urban markets (New Jersey, The Garden State). This type of farm enterprise had enjoyed little of the advantages of farm mechanization. There were areas in Florida and California with the warm climates essential to produce multiple crops, but, given the high perishability of the products and the long transport distances involved, little advantage could be found in this. Further, in the case of Florida, there was too much water and, in California, too little.

There was no single technological fix for this set of problems. The soil preparation problem was resolved by the water control developments earlier discussed: irrigation in the West and land drainage in Florida. Thus, multiple cropping with high yields became feasible. But getting the crops to urban markets required a multiple set of technologies. The modern truck with its attendant highway infrastructure was essential to opening these areas to urban markets. Refrigerated trucks were especially important in opening up South Florida production areas. Air freight came to play an astonishing role in moving highly perishable crops to the northeastern markets. The real open sesame involved major developments in food preparation and distribution. The advent of frozen food technology was central. Thus a highly specialized vegetable monoculture emerged in these highly localized production regions.

This, itself, opened the door to sequential developments. Multiple cropping and sustained yields made it possible to exploit even more traditional canning and other processing technologies more intensively. It became possible to exploit scale economies and production efficiencies in food processing. In California more than 90 percent of all vegetables are processed before distribution. Sustained yields also made it possible to do the research and development and undertake the capital investments necessary to mechanize more of the farm work in the vegetable enterprise. It is interesting and significant that, in these areas, scientific agriculture was forced to become interdisciplinary with a vengence. The plant breeder and the agricultural engineer had to work together from the beginning. In the case of tomatoes, this led to the Hanna-bred tomato plant (designed for machine handling) and to the mechanized tomato harvester that can harvest 10 tons of tomatoes an hour. Specialized lettuce and celery harvesters and other equally specialized machines followed.

A similar set of developments lay behind the Florida gains as well, but its more favorable location relative to urban markets in the Northeast inclined it more to the production of table-fresh, rather than processed, vegetables.

A very similar picture emerges in the case of fruit and nut enterprise, but the performance of Florida and California was reversed. The story was dominated by the development of the citrus industry. Florida claimed about 90 percent of the competitive gains in farm work, with the Mountain and Great Lakes regions accounting for the balance.[8] California actually experienced competitive losses in the citrus industry. It had been the early specializing producer of this commodity when the market was essentially that for fresh table fruit. Much of California's relative decline was merely a mirror image of Florida's relative gain, which was based on truck transport and frozen concentrates. In addition, the California citrus enterprise came under intensive competition from urban land uses. California remains a specialist in table fruit, but has no room for expansion based on the new technology because of competing land uses.

There was a dramatic shift in sugar crop production during the study period. California and the High Plains captured all of the competitive gains. The explanation rests with a single crop—the sugar beet. It is a classic example of survival and change through developmental technology.

The sugar beet is essentially the creature of irrigated agriculture in the West. In addition, this crop is highly resistant to salinity, which makes it particularly adaptable to the arid west. In spite of this, the sugar beet industry struggled to survive in the 1930s and 1940s. The first challenge came from the "curly top" virus disease. In 1934, over 85 percent of the planted acreage had to be abandoned. The developmental solution: plant breeders created a disease-resistant hybrid with superior agronomic qualities. The next challenge was the near collapse of the industry in the face of the World War II labor shortages. The developmental solution was fashioned by the mechanical engineers of the University of California at Davis. First came mechanical beet planters and thinners, then the mechanical harvester. A tremendous resurgence of the beet industry followed, all situated in the irrigated West. Naturally, sugar production from cane in the Southern Delta and from the corn in the Corn Belt experienced the major competitive losses in the face of this new competition.

The story of the shift patterns in cotton production is strikingly similar. The basic shift was out of the Southeast, its traditional home, to the irrigated lands of the High Plains, the Southwest, and California. The story of cotton is a particularly significant one because it largely determined the history of southern agriculture, and the history of southern agriculture heavily conditioned the history of southern manufacturing. No other single commodity has ever come close to determining the flow of human history in the United States the way cotton did.

In the earliest days of the colonial period it was King Cotton in the South—and, indeed, in the nation. Early trade was dominated by cotton; and it was not until the end of the nineteenth century that all other agricultural exports combined matched cotton exports. Although cotton lost its crown in the national economy, it was still king in the South until the 1930s. Our study period witnessed the final collapse of a 200-year-old agricultural, economic, and social culture!

The labor-intensive cotton culture created slavery and the black culture with all of its historic and still current ramifications. With the end of slavery, the cotton economy experienced its first major transformation. With the break-up of the plantation system, the labor-intensive nature of the cotton culture created a small farm culture. The cultivation of a product that was worthless until ginned lent itself to absentee ownership, share cropping, and the merchant banker. Three things doomed the southern cotton culture: irrigation, the cotton picker, and the low wage competition of the Third World countries. Western irrigation opened up optional lands with the climate and nutrient conditions essential for cotton to thrive. But it was the mechanical cotton picker, which only emerged in the 1940s, that did King Cotton in. The cotton picker reduced labor requirements in harvesting by 94 percent (a single machine could replace as many as forty men). As late as 1952, only 18 percent of the cotton was picked by machine, but by 1970 more than 95 percent was machine picked.[9]

Mechanization tipped the balance for several reasons. The cotton picker required even terrain and large land holdings to be economical. The southern farm was small and hilly. Mechanization required a large amount of capital to which the small southern farmer had limited access. The whole economic and cultural structure of the region was ill suited for its adoption. The picker was tailor-made for the irrigated lands of the High Plains, New Mexico, Arizona, and California. It rationalized the production and yield advantages of irrigation.

We come, at the end, to oil crops.[10] The farm-work shifts displayed by this commodity class are, as in the case of the sugar beet, largely a story of a single new product and product substitution—in this case the soybean. The soybean was almost entirely a product of the study period. Although it had been grown for many centuries in Asia, it was not until World War II cut off the importation of important vegetable oils that attention became focused on this crop. The emergence of soybeans as a major U.S. crop reflects the enormous developmental power of the scientific, educational, and managerial infrastructures of agriculture in the United States. From a standing start, the nation now produces half the world's supply of soybeans and exports one-third of the total crop. Hybrids were developed that improved oil and protein content. Close-space drilling and the noncultivated soybean culture increased yields by 50 percent. But, most important, nutrition research worked soybean meal into the food ration of poultry and cattle in a major way. This, along with the development of oleomargarine and the increasing emphasis on vegetable oils in the human diet, provided strong markets.

For our purpose, the most important attribute of the soybean is that the soil and climate conditions that are ideal for the soybean are the same as for corn. Thus, the competitive gains in oil crops (including corn oil, of course) were all focused on the Corn Belt, with some overlap in the Great Lakes states and the Northern Plains. The big competitive declines were heavily concentrated in the Southeast. This region had formerly been the oil crop capital of the nation because of its specialization in peanut and cotton seed oils.

A Return to the Regional Perspective

Return, for a moment, to the perspective of plate 7 in volume I. There we saw that the areas experiencing relative declines in total employment (pink, light blue, gray, and white) were most heavily concentrated in the Southeast, along with the Central and Plains regions of the nation. These are also clearly the areas with historical specializations in agricultural employment. They are, correspondingly, the areas where the agricultural mix effect declines (based on the thirty-one sector array) were concentrated. We have seen that more than three-quarters of the gross differential shift (at the 171 urban region level of aggregation) were accounted for by the total mix effect and that the agricultural mix component accounted for more than a fifth of the all-sector gross mix shifts—almost twice that of any other sector. It follows that the employment shifts resulting from the developmental forces operating on agriculture were the dominant explanatory factors underlying the total employment shifts we examined with some care in volume I.

This chapter opened with an historical sketch of the sequential problem-solving developments experienced by agriculture. The closing of the frontier generated the problem-solving response of a highly mechanized scientific agriculture designed to economize scarce land and labor inputs. That developmental narrative constitutes the fundamental explanation for the dramatic declines in agricultural employment. The adaptive solution worked so well that scarce labor was turned into a billowing surplus. The section on the changing structure of agriculture chronicled the statistical consequences of this transformation. Just in the study period, agriculture went from a fifth of all employment to less than 4 percent.

The regional consequences of the mix effect left the regional competitive shifts unaccounted for. We turned next to the competitive shifts in agricultural employment in plate II-1 of this volume and noted the change patterns represented there. The explanation of those patterns was demonstrated not to lie in a commodity sector, subsystem mix effect except in the case of the highly urbanized counties. We proceeded to examine the competitive shifts characteristic of each agricultural commodity group as a basis for developing explanations for the competitive shifts in agricultural employment. Here we focused on the regionally differentiating, rather than the regionally common, effects of the developmental scenario that opened the chapter. Having completed that explanatory exercise, it remains to return to the regional perspective of plate II-1 to summarize the consequences for the changing patterns of agricultural employment.

Begin with the dramatic leading decline in agricultural employment spreading through the Southeast (extending as far as the beginning of the Edwards Plateau in Texas). This decline resulted from the Southeast losing its relative competitive position in all of the labor-intensive row crops that had been traditional to its culture. Feed and food grains lost out to the scientific, mechanized monocultures of the Corn Belt and Plains (except for rice growing in the Delta). Row crop vegetables lost out to the capital-intensive, integrated agribusinesses of Florida and the Pacific Southwest and their newly developed access to urban markets. The old deciduous tree fruits (like peaches and apples) lost out relatively because citrus fruits became a much more important component of the mix (at a sub-subcommodity system level). The sugar crops suffered from the new competition of the western sugar beet. King Cotton was unceremoniously displaced from a 200-year-old throne. Oil crops suffered from the newly developed competition of the soybean and corn oil. This region did experience modest-to-strong competitive gains in hay and forage and in the animal products, meat, milk, and poultry. But, relative to the old row crop culture (particularly cotton), these agricultural enterprises were not strong enough competitively, or labor intensive enough, to mitigate the overwhelming competitive losses in agricultural employment. These were added to major declines in the total agricultural mix effect.[11] In combination, the negative agricultural mix and competitive effects caused the region to undergo probably the most dramatic and far-reaching economic, political, and cultural reorganization that any similar sized region has ever experienced in so short a time in human history (outside the scourges of war). The developmental factors that explain this experience were chronicled in the previous section.

Consider, next, the western half of the nation—say from roughly the 100th meridian, west. This entire area experienced competitive gains in agricultural employment (plate II-1), with the exception of a handful of counties in the High Colorado Plateau of upper New Mexico and Arizona. These were also mostly leading gainers except for the highly urbanized Southwestern counties where competitive gains in nonagricultural employments tended to be even stronger. With the limited exception of the coastal strip of the Pacific Northwest, this entire area constituted the heartland of the water-short arid and semiarid portions of the nation. In this vast domain, nearly all of the land below 8,000 feet is too dry for unirrigated agriculture.[12] The developmental solution was irrigation. During the study period, the governments of the western states and large metropolitan districts, in cooperation with the federal government (represented by the Bureau of Reclamation), created the big dam era that more than doubled the amount of water delivered to irrigation. Thus abetted, agricultural enterprise made the desert bloom in the man-made oases of the Imperial and Colorado River valleys, the Snake River Plain, the High Plains, and the California Central Valley, among others. It was irrigation that painted plate II-1 blue west of the 100th meridian. Irrigation rolled back the frontier a bit one last time and opened new land to intensive cultivation. Irrigation also created two- and three-crop seasons that, through sustained use, made the development of new exotic forms of agricultural machinery commercially feasible.

Leaving aside the High Plains for a moment, this resource expansion was mostly applied to the production of cotton, sugar beets, fruits and nuts, and vegetables (along with some food and feed grains and fluid milk to ameliorate the region's strong deficit position in these commodities). In so doing, it delivered the coup de grâce to traditional Southeastern agriculture.

The irrigated High Plains, along with the more humid plains to the east (to roughly the 95th meridian), displayed the strongest competitive gains in feed and food grains and meat animals. Two prominent monocultural industries emerged side by side—one in the great wheat basket of the world and one based on the sorghum-fed livestock. (There were also localized regions that shared the cotton and sugar beet gains of the rest of the West.) These developments added insult to injury for the devastated historical agriculture of the South where relative feed and food grain losses were added to the list.

Extending east of the Plains is that great heartland of agricultural specialization divided horizontally into the Dairy Belt and the Corn Belt. Here, too, strong competitive gains pointed a narrowing blue finger as far east as the 85th meridian. As we have seen, in the Corn Belt this represented a strengthening of the region's traditional feed grain advantage through mechanization and scientific agriculture plus a major new specialty in the soybean. In the Dairy Belt west of Lake Michigan it represented a similar reinforcement of the region's traditional feed grain and milk cow advantage.

Throughout the historical agricultural stronghold of the Midwest and Northern Plains, agricultural employment declined substantially because of the negative growth effect and the (thirty-one-sector-based) agricultural mix effect, as we saw from plate 7 in volume I. In contrast to the Southeast, however, these regions enjoyed substantial competitive gains averaging perhaps 40 percent of the negative mix effect. Although the gross differential shifts were negative, they were substantially ameliorated by the competitive gains. In fact, in the Corn Belt heartland of the Peoria, Davenport, and Rockford urban regions, the gross differential was positive, as positive competitive effects outmatched the negative mix effect.

Such positive gross differentials were also characteristic of the urban regions of the southern High Plains, the irrigated southern mountain states, and the Columbia River plateau. Amazingly, in the central valley of California, and in the southern Florida regions of Orlando, Tampa, and Miami, the new water-based technologies and the dramatic expansion of access to urban markets created competitive gains strong enough to overwhelm both negative mix and growth effects and to generate absolute increases in agricultural employment—this in the face of a 75 percent rate of decline in agricultural employment nationally.

In the highly urbanized areas of the Northeast and around Chicago, Detroit, and Cleveland, the deficit position in agricultural employment created positive thirty-one-sector-based agriculture mix effects that combined with the positive competitive effects depicted in plate II-1 to yield positive differential shifts in agricultural employment. The positive (thirty-one-sector-based) agriculture competitive gains were dominated by a positive commodity-level, agricultural mix effect. (These urbanized regions tended to specialize in those subsector agricultural commodities whose employments were declining least.) However, agricultural employment declined absolutely here as well. The relative gains were not sufficient to offset the growth effect losses.

Thus, we have seen how the iterative, systemic, problem-solving sequence sketched in the opening portion of this chapter operated to alter significantly the relative competitive position of the nation's agricultural regions.

Forestry and Fisheries

The forestry and fisheries sector does not warrant as detailed a discussion as agriculture. Both total employment and employment shifts were insignificant—accounting for only two-tenths of one percent of total employment in 1940 and one-tenth in 1970. In table II-2, forestry and fisheries is last in the thirty-one-sector array of mix and competitive effects. Furthermore, both the regional shift patterns and their underlying developmental explanations are far simpler than in agriculture.

While the shift patterns are relatively uncomplicated, their representation in the maps and tables presented here is clouded by a set of peculiar sectoral classifications. As activities, forestry and fisheries have little in common. Conveniently, however, plate II-2, in which the shifts are shown, is fairly revealing because there is no significant fishing employment anywhere except in some coastal counties of the nation plus a few counties on the shores of the Great Lakes and the Mississippi River. Urbanized port locations tend to be the base of most fishing activities, while hinterland sites are more common for forest activities. Many of the specialized, leading loss counties (red) along the Middle Atlantic and Southern New England coasts are attributable to the relative competitive declines of the fisheries there. The same is true of some Great Lakes and Mississippi River counties. The competitive gains (blue) of the port counties in Florida and along the Gulf and Pacific coasts are mostly a reflection of relative competitive gains in fishing activities.

The study period developments in the fishing industry do not, by and large, rest on an earlier epoch sequence of developments that need to be understood. The relative shifts out of the historic and traditional northeastern fishing grounds to the southern waters, east and west, can be largely explained by four factors. First, the menhaden catch came to occupy a much more important position in the fishing product and market mix. Fishing for menhaden takes place exclusively in southeastern waters. The commercial value of this catch derives from fishmeal and oil products rather than its use in the human diet. Here is one of those cases where developments in one activity sector have direct interindustry, linked effects on other activities. The nutrition research of scientific agriculture, just discussed, found an important place for fish meal in the cattle and poultry ration. This was almost entirely responsible for the increase in the menhaden catch.

Second, the discovery of major beds of the giant shrimp around Florida and off the Texas coast expanded the importance and popularity of this shell fish. Third, the fishing industry borrowed the preserving and freezing technologies that had been developed for other foods. This resulted in a decline in the proportion of the catch going to the fresh market. That had been the basis for the Northeast's earlier relative advantage. For example, canning increased the relative importance of the tuna catch in the Southern Pacific because the preservation of the fish allowed it to be sold in a wider market. The developing transport and food preservation technologies also worked heavily in favor of the Gulf region shrimp catch. The final reason for the shift to southern waters was the problem of yield cycles and resource exhaustion. The Great Lakes fisheries succumbed to pollution and the lamprey. The Mississippi fisheries succumbed to pollution and overfishing. The salmon run in the Pacific Northwest and the table-fresh catch of the Middle Atlantic region suffered from what were at least cyclical declines in yields. Maine, on the other hand, experienced a resurgence in the yield of lobster and herring after experiencing earlier declines.[13]

The forestry side of this hybrid sector is more ambiguously represented. True, the confusion with fishing shifts in plate II-2 is minimal outside of the coastal counties with good harbors and the best access to fishing grounds. A problem does arise, however, from the strange choices that were made in creating the intermediate aggregates with which we are forced to work. The forestry category is dominated by forest services (timber cruising, fire fighting, tree nurseries, and the like) and timber tract management. It also includes the gathering of pine gum and other forest products. But it excludes what would seem to be the most natural part of the activity—logging. Logging employment appears in the lumber and wood products component of manufacturing, so the shifts represented in plate II-2 do not tell all of the story. The forestry employment depicted is only one-tenth of the logging and sawmill employment historically associated with forest activities. As a consequence, the change patterns shown in plate II-10 are perhaps a more revealing visual reference than plate II-2. Logging, lumber, and processed wood materials account for two-thirds of the competitive shifts in plate II-10. The one-third contributed by furniture and fixture employment most heavily affected fairly restricted areas in the Piedmont Plateau, the Michigan Peninsula, and the Middle Atlantic region.

Looking at plates II-2 and II-10, consider the major pattern changes that call for explanation. The specialized areas that display leading losses were prominent throughout the Southeast, in the upper Great Lakes region, and in Upper New England and Washington State. These are the general areas, of course, that have dominated forest product activities (95 percent of total production, 90 percent of employment, in 1950). The specialized areas with leading gains were most heavily concentrated in Oregon and northern California. Other specialized leading gain counties were scattered throughout older production regions where leading losses were so prominent (Upper New England, the Upper Great Lakes, and the Southeast). Unspecialized leading gainers were widely spread throughout the Plains region and in the southern portion of the North Central region. Although these counties paint the map liberally blue in these fields, dimensionally they are a trivial part of the picture.

What explains these shifts? One important factor is the regionally differentiating effects of what might be characterized as the crop cycle. Here a brief reference to earlier experience is helpful. The history of forest activity in this country has been remarkably similar to that in the pioneer period in American agriculture, except that the forest activity story has persisted into the study period. Such activities have been almost totally exploitative of forest resources. The great virgin forests were, in effect, mined—and the mining sequence moved from one region to another as the volume of final demand grew, its spatial distribution shifted westward, and as existing stands became cut over. The New England and Middle Atlantic forests were the first to be worked out. Relative declines in the Great Lakes forests set in about 1890, and production began an absolute decline at about the turn of the century. "Timber mining" then progressed to the Pacific Northwest, concentrating first in Washington State. Then between 1900 and 1920 began a prominent shift to the Southeast, a process that continued as the Great Lakes states declined. Between 1900 and 1920, New England came to life again with a return-growth cut, while the South went into relative decline. During the 1920s and 1930s, the South began a second cut renaissance, then went into relative decline during the study period. That Pacific region, with its huge stands and remote location relative to national markets, continued to have strong relative gains through the ensuing period, although experiencing important within-region differences in timing.

Two aspects of this growth pattern sequence are important for understanding the forestry shift patterns of the study period. First, while the frontier closed in the agricultural economy in the 1890s, it did not begin to close in the forest economy until the 1930s. By then, it began to become clear that continuing advances in forest productivity would have to depend on shifting from forest mining to a managed scientific sylviculture. Second, because it takes between thirty and ninety years to replace a forest (depending on species and the purpose of the cut), a wave of production cycles was introduced by the progressive movement through the various regional forests. So a part of what shows up in the study period experience is a production wave-form that was historically determined.

Now turn back to the shift patterns of plates II-2 and II-10. The former, as indicated, primarily depicts shifts in employment in land management and forest services. An important part of the pattern is simply explained. Most of those counties that displayed specialized, strong leading gains (dark blue and shaded) correspond closely to the location of the national forests. The Forest Service was an early leader in the development of forest management practices, and Clawson and Held (1967) set 1950 as the date when the Forest Service shifted from custodial to intensive forest management with a substantial growth in employment and resources devoted to this activity.

I have already indicated that the gains in the Plains regions were dimensionally insignificant. This leaves the principal unspecialized leading gains to be distributed throughout the Appalachian regions (all the way into Maine) and the southeastern and South Central regions inside the Pine Barrens of the southeastern coastal regions. The latter strip displayed an extensive concentration of specialized, leading losses which seem anomalous in the face of the reputation of this region as one of the nation's principal wood baskets. There seem to be two possible explanations for this. Historically, this area, plus the Upper Great Lakes and selected Upper New England counties, were the principal areas engaging in gathering and extracting pine gum and other natural forest products. These activities have not only declined relative to other forest activities, but they have declined absolutely during the study period. Further, naval stores production has increasingly become a by-product of pulp and other mill activities. Because the forestry category contains this segment of collecting activity, almost ancient in form, this appears to be an important part of the explanation. This southern coastal strip is also the area where the large private land holdings necessary for the private practice of progressive land management first came into play. As the timber tracts began to be assembled elsewhere, and as, accordingly, forest management services spread in application, these other, nonspecialized, regions began to display gains relative to those achieved earlier in the Pine Barrens.

Plate II-10, wood products manufacturing, displays a significantly related picture because so much of it is involved in forest-related wood processing activities like logging and sawmills. For example, the plate clearly displays the specialized competitive losses (red and shaded) in Upper New England, the Great Lakes, the Southeast, and the Northern Pacific Coast region. The field of losses in the Southeast is much more extensive than in plate II-2 because forest management and service employment had been gaining here at the same time that logging and wood-processing employments had been experiencing relative declines. (As previously indicated, the record is somewhat ambiguous because of the inclusion of furniture manufacturing employment. Gains in this subsector are clearly behind the ridge of blue counties displayed in the Appalachian region of plate II-10.)

The explanation appears to have two principal roots. Part stems from a projection into the study period of the exploitation-cycle wave form. This is displayed with the least ambiguity in the Pacific Northwest. In this field, the historical wave of exploitation hit the Seattle urban region earliest, reaching its peak in the 1920s and 1930s before going into relative decline. Oregon as a whole reached its peak in the 1950s, but the northernmost counties on the western slopes of the Cascades began to decline (relatively) as the wave-form of exploitation moved southward. These regions show up as specialized leading decliners in plate II-10. Portions of Oregon and northern California experienced continuing leading gains, as did the finger of Idaho in the westernmost Rockies. Portions of the other major production regions appear to have a wave-form element in the explanation as well. For example, lumber production in the Southeast declined substantially from about 1930 into the 1960s. The migration of lumber production to the West Coast that began with the cutover of the Great Lakes region before the end of the century was augmented during this period, adding momentum to the leading gains in the southern portion of that region. However, in the Southeast, the production cycle wave-form was only one of a number of operative factors.

The other explanatory root appears to reside in the problem-solving technological developments of the period. As a response to the working out of virgin stands and the closing of the frontier in the forest domain, scientific sylviculture commenced. Still, it began too late and involved too long a pay-out time to have any significant effect on production practices during the study period. Thus, the developments that concern us were primarily labor-saving improvements rather than improvements in forest yields.

In the realm of logging, there were two major developments. First, the logging truck reduced both the amount of manpower and animal horsepower involved in bringing logs out of the forest. It opened tracts of timber to exploitation that were previously inaccessible to the logging railways because of difficult slopes and unreasonable capital costs. This increased the economically accessible yields of the forest and considerably increased the assembly radius of the forest stands that could be drawn upon by centralizing processing mills. Second, the development of the chain saw substantially reduced the manpower requirements for logging. Thus, logging employment became a slow-growth (or in the South, an absolute declining) component for forest activities.[14]

In the realm of mill processing, the new technology was directed both to saving labor and trying to squeeze more products out of the log. The latter is the problem-solving adaptation intermediate in time to the full application of the yield improvements of emerging scientific sylviculture. One way to increase the product yield is to peel a continuous veneer off the log and fashion it into plywood sheets, a process that was mostly a creation of the study period. (This also had a labor-saving advantage in construction that attends the substitution of plywood for dimension lumber in many operations.) Pulp production was another way of increasing the product yield. Improvements in sawmill technology increased the economies of scale characteristic of this historic and traditional process. Log peeling and debarking machines, automatic mill feeds, kiln drying, and lumber-treating equipment, and the like substantially reduced the amount of labor required. (Sawmill employment declined by almost half during the study period.) The truck and the large-scale mills largely ended the two- or three-man portable sawmill that formerly populated the forest in large numbers.

The net effect of all of this caused most heavily forested counties to lose forest product employment (both relatively and absolutely) at the same time that other counties embedded in the forest field experienced leading gains as they became the locus for more centralized and expanded mill production as well as the headquarters of Forest Service activities. Thus, leading gain counties are liberally sprinkled throughout every one of the major production regions where specialized leading loss counties are so prevalent (plate II-10). The effect of changing technologies was to draw forest activities into more centralized and localized sites within the broader specializing production regions.

Mining

When human beings turned to technology to make the feet faster and the arm longer and stronger, they first employed energy-concentrating modes that relied on renewable sources of energy—the domesticated plant and animal to fix solar energy; the wind, ox, and horse for transport and drive power; the forests for firewood. By the time of the Industrial Revolution, the ability of such technology to increase human productivity had reached its limit. The use of stone, clay, and wood as the material base of the developing technology also proved limiting. In displacing these limits, developmental processes created new categories of resources and expanded the categories of human activities we know as mining beyond the production of stone, clay, and precious metals. Humankind turned to concentrated but depletable geological deposits of energy and structural materials.

There are two points to note. First, this historic transition from reliance on renewable resources to nonrenewable resources was a prominent feature of the fourth and fifth developmental epochs of industrial and urban reorganization. This set the stage for understanding events of the study period. Second, changing patterns of mining activities were determined by the way in which an emerging technology continuously redefined the nature and location of those mineral resources that proved economic.

Thus, in the period from 1870 to 1910, the emerging farm machine and railroad transport technologies vastly increased use of the nation's coal and basic metal ores. The manufacture of iron rails for the spreading rail system absorbed two-thirds of the pig iron production at the beginning of this period. Just the energy requirements of the working steam engine absorbed 15 percent of the total coal production and 10 percent of the annual forest cut (Perloff and coauthors, 1960, p. 195). The emerging iron and steel industry absorbed even more. Michigan, Illinois, and Pennsylvania became the expanded sources of the basic metals, and coal mining in Pennsylvania expanded phenomenally. As the railway spread southward, both metal and coal mines opened in the Southern Appalachians to serve the new iron and steel complex in Birmingham. As the railroad opened up the West, new deposits of the basic metals became available for exploitation. The pressure of the emerging electric power technology on supplies of "lakes copper" and the exhaustion of recoverable lead supplies in the Great Lakes region accelerated the trend. As always, the problem→solutions that drew on materials and energy mineral supplies opened up a new set of problems to be solved. Eric Lampard (Perloff, 1960, p. 206) points out that the mining of minerals under a wider range of geological conditions led to the development of a whole new range of technologies in explosives and in drilling, pumping, hoisting, and handling machinery. It also led to new technologies in the geological and chemical sciences. This technology-induced, anti-entropic reach across social system boundaries for mineral resources increased mining employment steadily until the 1920s. Employment leveled off after that, but, apart from some business cycle variations, stayed at approximately the same level until the end of World War II. This set the stage for the mining developments that appeared during the study period.

TABLE II-17. Employment in mining, 1940, 1970
(number)

Subsector	1940	1970	1970 − 1940	Percent change
Total mining	913,600	604,588	−309,042	−33.8
Coal	528,365	137,130	−391,235	−74.0
Petroleum & natural gas	184,219	271,466	+87,247	+47.4
Metals	119,327	91,990	−27,337	−22.9
Nonmetals	81,689	103,972	+22,283	+27.3

The big story of the study period was the substitution of oil for coal. This began with the automobile in the preceding fifth epoch. Petroleum had no previous commercial use except as crudely distilled lamp oil. There were however, by-products of that distillation (the so-called light-distillation fractions) that were precisely what was needed for the automobile engine. A whole new technology emerged. Ancillary to it was the development of the gigantic petroleum industry. Although the industry began in the Northeast (the first commercial well producing crude oil for lamps was in Titusville, Pennsylvania in 1859), the burgeoning demand led to the exploitation of new fields in the South Central and Southwest regions. That demand was further augmented in the study period as new uses for petroleum came into play (to replace coal in locomotives, to heat homes and commercial buildings, to fuel power plants, and to serve as chemical feedstocks, among others).

It makes a great deal of difference in the amount of manpower needed in the energy sector if energy materials can be pumped out of the ground rather than dug up. Table II-17 shows that three-fourths of the 1940 coal mining employment (almost 400,000 jobs) had disappeared by 1970. During this time, petroleum and natural gas employment increased by half (although production was tripling). But, because petroleum mining is nowhere near as labor intensive as coal mining, this offset only about one-fifth of the decline in coal mining employment. In consequence, total mining employment declined by a third (over 300,000 jobs). Because these losses and gains were concentrated in regionalized coal and oil fields, this effected a massive shift in mining employment.

This is prominently displayed in plate II-3. The specialized, leading-loss counties are clearly heavily concentrated in the Appalachian and Central State coal mining regions. On a 171-urban-region scale, the Appalachian regions accounted for two-thirds of the competitive losses in mining employment—all coal mining regions combined, almost four-fifths. At the same time, the oil producing regions accounted for 70 percent of the all-mining competitive gains. The leading gains were concentrated most heavily in the Gulf, Texas, Oklahoma, Southern California, and the easternmost Mountain states. The fact that the fossil fuel developments dominated the all-mining shifts is not surprising when we realize that almost three-quarters of all mining employment was in fossil fuels and 90 percent of the gross employment changes were accounted for by the fossil fuels (table II-7).

Since coal employment declined and oil employment increased substantially, a major part of these total mining competitive shifts is a reflection of the commodity-level, or subsystem, mix effects. In fact, this subordinate level, mix-effect dominance—along with the shift in other mining activities—largely disguised the commodity-level competitive shifts that took place. For example, during this period, an employment shift took place out of the Pennsylvania fields into West Virginia, eastern Ohio, and Kentucky. This is why in plate II-3 there are a few specialized leading gain counties (blue, shaded) speckled throughout portions of the specialized leading loss field (red, shaded). A part of this is a consequence of the marginal mines being taken out of production first, so that those counties with the deposits that could be mined the easiest lost employment less rapidly than the industry as a whole. But this tendency was heavily reinforced by a set of defensive developmental responses. Faced with the heavy direct and indirect competition from oil in its traditional markets, the industry introduced new techniques. These had the effect of redefining the economic viability of different deposits, thus reinforcing the differential retrenchment phenomenon.[15]

In addition, there were coal mining shifts into western Colorado, the Provo, Utah, area, and the Four Corners region, along with the Ozark region and east Texas. These increases were relatively small on an industry scale and they were predominantly a response to shifts in coal markets as the demand for iron and steel production and for power expanded in these areas. These gains were also largely concentrated in the last decade of the study period. The coal that was produced there was almost exclusively for local regional markets. For example, 94 percent of the coal mined in Colorado in that decade was shipped within the Mountain Division and the balance went to the Pacific Division (U.S. Department of Commerce, various years).

In the oil production subsector, interregional shifts took place, as exploration, discovery, development, and resource depletion proceeded in an advancing wave—particularly so, because the employment created by the discovery and development of an oil field is greater than that maintained by the production process. Thus, the earliest fields in Pennsylvania, Ohio, Kentucky, Michigan, and Illinois—which came on strong with the advent of the twentieth century—began a relative decline as the Oklahoma and East Texas fields gained ascendency in the 1910–20 period. The California field began producing during the 1920–30 period. So by the study period, these earlier fields were experiencing relative declines (within the petroleum subsector). The biggest competitive gains were focused in Louisiana and spread eastward along the Gulf Coast. Wyoming and the Mountain states made important gains, as well.

It is interesting to note that, by the last decade of the study period, the relative declines were reversing themselves in Texas, California, and, amazingly, in the older fields of West Virginia, Ohio, and Michigan. This was partly explained by the increasing importance of natural gas in the energy picture, partly by the beginning of a return to declining wells with second-recovery methods, and partly by the increasing importance of the administrative functions of the oil mining companies—particularly in the Dallas and Houston urban regions.

Taken as a group metal mining activities experienced declining employments. That means that the within-metal mining subsector was negative for those regions that were specialized in metal mining at the beginning of the period. That three-quarters of metal mining activity was concentrated in Michigan, Minnesota, and the Mountain states helps to explain the concentration (see plate II-3) of specialized leading loss counties in these regions. If we move to the commodity level within metal mining, we find that precious metal mining (gold and silver) was experiencing the greatest employment declines. The fact that these activities were heavily concentrated in the Mountain states helps explain the numerous relative declines in Mountain region counties.

In fact, when we make a competitive shift map just for metal mining, it shows a market shift out of the Western Pacific and Mountain regions into the eastern half of the nation, with several notable exceptions. Metal mining declined in Alabama as a consequence of the relative decline of Birmingham in the nation's iron and steel complex. In the West, Arizona experienced strong metal mining competitive gains (more than a quarter of the total). At the commodity level, this was most heavily associated with the shift of copper, lead, and zinc mining out of its early Michigan strongholds into selected counties of the Mountain Southwest. In recent times, prospecting added significantly to the known reserves of copper ore in Arizona, New Mexico, and Utah. Advancing mining technology significantly altered the comparative cost advantage of the open pit mines of Arizona (and New Mexico) relative to the older, partly worked-out, shaft mines in Michigan (and Montana). Selected counties in Utah and California benefited from some growth in iron ore mining as the steel industry developed capacity to serve Western regional markets. Michigan and Minnesota experienced strong gains in iron ore mining employment during the first part of the study period because of the strong demand associated with the war and expansion of the nation's capital stock in the postwar period. However, during the latter half of the period this relative strength was weakened by scientific and technological innovations in the materials field (as well as by growing competition from imports).

This new emphasis upon the exotic metals lies behind a second exception to the Mountain region's relative decline in the metals field. Selected counties in New Mexico, Colorado, Utah, and Wyoming (especially Wyoming) claimed the bulk of the growing employment in uranium mining. The growth in the importance of aluminum led to the expansion of bauxite mining in the Ozarks, and also in Alabama and Georgia. Mostly because of this growth, Arkansas matched Arizona's 25 percent share of total metal mining competitive gains. For the rest, the expansion in the production of a whole array of metals tended to improve the relative position of the eastern half of the nation in metal mining employment (beryllium in Alabama and Georgia; magnesium metals in Georgia; titanium in Georgia, Florida, Virginia, New Jersey, and New York; and zirconium in Florida and Georgia).

We turn, finally, to the nonmetallic minerals. A competitive shift picture constructed at this level would, on a broad regional basis, display the largest competitive losses in the industrial Northeast and East North Central regions with the rest of the nation displaying competitive gains. This is because the picture is dominated by the production of sand, gravel, crushed stone, and cement rock. More than 90 percent of total nonmetallic production is accounted for by these categories. In contrast to most minerals, substantial deposits of these materials are spread throughout the nation. They are mostly used in construction, so demand is widely distributed as well. Since it is uneconomical to transport these commodities much more than 200 miles, they are mined in virtually every state. As a consequence, nonmetallic mining is more widely distributed than any other mining activity, more than agricultural employment and over half of the manufacturing sectors as well. It is not surprising, therefore, that the study-period shift in these activities paralleled shifts in total population and employment. This is also the principal reason that a multitude of unspecialized mining counties (not heavily engaged in fuel or metal mining and displaying competitive gains) painted plate II-3 blue.

Apart from this, there were a number of localized areas that experienced strong gains because of the targeted nature of some of the developmental changes already discussed. These were mostly associated with the expanding importance of the chemical minerals in response to the developments in industrial science and scientific agriculture. For example, scientific agriculture's emphasis on soil preparation has created a dramatic increase in the demand for potash, phosphate, and lime. Lime is widely available and is mined in thirty-nine states. But 90 percent of the nation's potash comes from New Mexico and 90 percent of its phosphate rock from Florida. This is an important explanatory factor behind the strong gains displayed in parts of these states. Salt and sulfur are found in the same geological formations as petroleum so some Texas and Louisiana counties have experienced strong gains in the production of these commodities. Lesser minerals like talc, feldspar, barrite, and mica account for gains in other counties, particularly in the Appalachian regions.

We return to the total mining level for a closing observation. You will recall that we were startled when, upon consulting the urban-system categories in appendix tables II-C and II-D, we discovered that the urban cores dominated the competitive gains in agriculture. We identified the result as an artifact of the commodity-level mix effect at work. When we examine the same tables, we make a similar discovery about mining employment. In both cases we are startled because of our general perception of resources being rural or urban-hinterland-oriented activities. It appears, however, that this perception is not quite accurate in the case of mining. Hoch (1978) reveals that more than half of petroleum and gas mining takes place within Standard Metropolitan Statistical Areas. This was also true for about a third of coal production.[16] Once again, though, there is little direct evidence that the urban-region cores experienced an increasing comparative advantage in mining production over the period. Nor is there anything in the logic of mining system linkages to suggest an explanation. Again, the result seems to be an artifact of the mix effect at work. This follows as a consequence of the fact that petroleum mining is substantially more urban oriented than coal mining, and is becoming increasingly important in the total mining employment mix.

Resource Activities in General

We close with an observation about resource activities in general. It is a conventional image that the urbanized economy is erected on a static resource base. The narrative of this chapter challenges this view. The changes we have observed taking place are not adequately explained by the phenomenon of an urbanized society sending its resource roots deeper and further as it grows in size. The developmental forces at work in a transforming society have not only redefined what constitutes economical access to a given resource base, but have radically redefined that which society considers to be a resource. Within a single century, we have seen the energy taproot of society shift from the forest to the coal mine, to the oil well, to the uranium mine. We have seen worthless bauxite become a significant resource and copper transformed from a craft metal to a basic tonnage metal. We have seen a transformation in the capacity of different localities to support agricultural production. In each case, the transaction structure of an urbanized society, as well as the termini of its resource roots, were mutually redefined. We have seen the spatial and structural patterns of the urban system's activities and settlement patterns completely transformed in the process.

Notes

1. It also marked the beginning of an evolutionary process whereby technology was purposely directed to transforming the operating environments of life systems.

2. We are speaking here of the mix component of the shift in agricultural employment that, together with the other sectors in the thirty-one sector array, helped determine the total, summary line mix effect.

3. The total agricultural mix effect (based on the thirty-one major sectors) was a dominant component of the differential shift in agricultural employment because agricultural employment fell at the same time that most nonagricultural sector employments rose. But all of the subsector agricultural commodities shared the declining rates of employment, and the dispersion of the rates was small compared to that displayed by the thirty-one major employment sectors.

4. From U.S. Department of Agriculture, *Changes in Farm Production and Efficiency, 1977.* These data are not strictly comparable to our employment data for a variety of reasons, but they provide a handle.

5. Since there is little independent evidence to suggest that these urban field specialties were enjoying significant competitive gains vis-à-vis the same activities elsewhere, the prominent, urban core, total agriculture competitive gain is most likely an artifact of the subsystem commodity mix effects. But how does this compare with the earlier assertion that these commodity mix effects were not a major element in establishing the total agriculture shift patterns in plate II-1 (or even in the 171-urban-region patterns summarized in appendix II-N)? The answer is worth spelling out in detail because it calls attention to the extreme care one must exercise in interpreting the results of data games of this type. It is a characteristic of the shift-share formula that the more aggregated the regions on which the computation is based, the larger the proportion of the gross interregional differential shift that is formed by the mix effect. (To understand this, one has merely to realize that at the limit of a single region—for example, the entire United States—the entire regional differential shift is mix effect. See the table on page 192 of volume I.) Consequently, when we compute the shift share on the basis of nine or ten synthetic regions employing the trade center or transaction field characteristics, the mix component is proportionately greater than if we are making a computation for 171 urban regions or 3,065 counties.

The fact that, for the rest of our story, the commodity-level mix effects can be largely ignored can be demonstrated in the following way. The Northern Mountain and Plains and the Western Corn Belt regions are precisely the areas specializing in those agricultural subsectors (food and feed grains) that have experienced the most rapid declines in agricultural employment though they must experience negative subsector commodity mix effects within all agriculture, as indicated in plate II-1. This is direct evidence that, at the 3,065 county scale the subsystem competitive effect dominates the all-agriculture competitive effects. (This is also demonstrated to be true of the 171-urban-region computations summarized in appendix II-N.)

6. I will not burden the text here with a recitation of all the auxiliary sources and computations that underlie this discussion. It would constitute a distraction from the heart of the narrative.

7. One begins to notice that this whole explanatory narrative is so technologically and systemically interrelated that any arbitrary narrative form (that tries to maintain a subsystem, commodity, or regional order) keeps breaking out to linked subsystems during the discussion.

8. In the latter case, displaying competitive strength in deciduous tree fruits. The southern tip of Texas also displayed a bit of strength in the citrus enterprise.

9. Indeed, the picker was the only thing that partially saved commercial cotton in the United States from the competition of cheap-labor foreign sources and from synthetic fibers.

10. We can pass *tobacco production* with a wave of acknowledgment. It is a trivial element in the total picture, and the developments of the epoch only served to reinforce the localized area production advantages of the Southeast.

11. In fact, on a 171-urban-region scale, the southeastern competitive shifts in agricultural employment were twice as great relative to the gross regional differential, as was characteristic of the average of all regions. It is particularly interesting to note that the more highly industrialized urban regions of the Southeast, such as Charlotte, Greenville, Atlanta, Mobile, and New Orleans, experienced competitive losses actually exceeding the very substantial losses in the total agricultural mix effect. It is clear that wherever there were better off-farm employment opportunities, the farm workers left the farm at a much faster rate.

12. Taken as a whole the Mountain states receive only 12 inches of annual rainfall—right on the border of the true desert line of 10 inches. Except for a narrow strip along the coast, Southern California actually receives less than 10 inches of rainfall a year, as does much of the Southern Mountain region.

13. Of course a far more detailed fishing industry story can be told involving the effects of foreign competition, the advent of manufacturing ships, and other factors, but further elaboration is not warranted here.

14. So in plate II-10, leading-decline counties are prominent in part because of an activity-subsector, negative mix effect.

15. In the fifties and sixties conveyor belts replaced coal cars for transport in the mines. In the sixties the convertible battery-cable car was introduced. The Joy Ripper, first introduced in 1948, permitted continuous mining. In the fifties came power-advancing roof supports. Major advances in the earth-moving equipment employed in strip mines also took place.

16. A part of this is a consequence of the coincidence of new petroleum discoveries coming where urban concentrations already existed. A part is the consequence of the fact that mining activities tend to generate urban settlements in a way not matched by agriculture (recall the settlement pattern discussion of chapter 7, volume I).

9

Manufacturing as a Whole

Manufacturing as we know it today is strictly a modern phenomenon. Prior to the last two hundred years only simple crafts and trade enterprises separated consumers from their resource roots, and this, characteristically, for only a portion of their needs. The tremendously complex and roundabout network of intermediate activities of the modern economy is also a phenomenon of quite recent origin. As before, the developments of the study period will be clarified if we examine the historical antecedents.

More About Developmental Sequences

Much has been made here of the historical process as an iterative, sequential, problem-solving progression by means of which human social systems make behavior-changing responses to challenge and how those developmental responses in turn often alter the situation in ways leading to new problems and new responses. With some experience in visualizing the process, it now seems helpful to reexamine this characterization.

There are two reasons that so much attention has been devoted to this view of the matter. First, this developmental dynamic seems essential to understanding and explaining the changes that engage our attention. Second, it is more common to write simple narrative history about specific inventions, their inventors, and the resulting artifacts. Even where an occasional historian like Abbott Usher gives emphasis to the "techno-logic" of the development sequence, the chronology is almost always developed in the context of a specific human task—the plowing of a furrow, the harvesting of a crop, the spinning of a fiber, the sailing of a ship, and the like. When operating in this tradition one "loses sight of the forest for the trees." As we proceed it will be useful to be armed with a more generalized image.

The underlying reason that the problem-solving process takes on an iterative, sequential form should now be emerging clearly. It is because the *perceptions* of problems and the development of adaptive solutions are commonly reductionist in nature—rarely are they system-wide in scope. Consequently, every problem-solving change alters system relationships in ways not intended or expected and some of these results are subsequently perceived as new problems. Even when some problem-solving subsystem of an economy does achieve a satisfactory steady state, it is only a question of time before linked changes in the larger systems within which it is embedded (or in the smaller quasi-autonomous systems of which it is composed) shocks it out of its reverie.

But it is precisely the systemic character of human social relationships that permits us to generalize about the nature of these sequences at some level of abstraction above the specific task. If we move back this step, we can see that problems and their developmental responses can be broadly characterized by their systemic traits. The same kinds of problems can be seen at work in quite different kinds of task situations; and different kinds of problems may be dominant at different times in the same task context.

Where can we turn for a characterization of human social systems that can provide such a typology? We need go no further than chapter 1 of volume I where the reader was introduced to the four levels of social behavior that constitute the four levels of observation (recall figure 1 in volume I). Remember that the first level dealt with the results that system activities generate (that is, the output of physical products or information). This is not the behavioral level at which problems are most apt to be recognized. The reason is simple. The products and services generated by an economy are all inputs to intermediate or terminal (consumption) *processes*. Their limitations are always experienced as limitations in the effectiveness of the processes they serve.

So it is at this second level of system behavior that all developmental problems can be seen to have the same generic roots. These roots trace back to the repeated discovery that people are not strong enough, cannot work fast enough, and cannot reach far enough to satisfy the needs they perceive. These limitations have to do with the technology for applying energy to work. In every concrete instance, the path to a solution involves some change in technology that changes behavior—a change that amplifies the strength and speed of human social activity. That part of the developmental chain that has attracted most attention has been the embodiment of new knowledge in physical artifacts like tools and machines. These externalize and amplify human capabilities by channeling external sources of energy into activities that mimic and amplify aspects of individual human behavior.

It is also at this second level of behavior, the level of physical process technology, that we begin to visualize a problem typology. The problem can be identified as originating in any of three kinds of limitations. Thus, *type-one problems* may involve some defect in the basic process design (including the product design of important artifacts employed as inputs or produced as outputs). That sequence of second-level acts intended to produce a specified first-level result may, in fact, be an inadequate simulation of human activities in a task environment. The conception of the process is in some respect flawed or incomplete. This would require modifying the activity sequence in some constructive way—that is, learning how to do better. It may be that the concept of the simulation is itself adequate, but constrained by a *type-two problem.* The external source of energy or the way that it is harnessed may fail to meet the requirements of the task. The solution may involve harnessing a new energy source. Again, it may turn out that both the activity concept and the energy source are adequate to the task but that the physical materials employed to embody the act and channel the energy have some structural limitations that constrain the effectiveness of the process in some way—a *type-three problem.*

We can now understand more clearly the way developmental initiatives interact. Modifying a process design may uncover unappreciated limitations in the energy source. The attempt to substitute another source may encounter the fact that traditional materials lack the essential properties for full success. Each corrective modification alters the system of relationships that constitutes the total field of activity.

But this problem typology revealed at the lower levels of system behavior does not exhaust all of the constraints one may encounter in the whole system. A *type-four problem* can occur when any set of adaptive changes of the first three types shows up limitations in the cybernetic control or managerial coordination exercised at the third level of behavior (figure 1 in volume I). The solution does not so much involve redesigning a process sequence as learning how to coordinate or manage them better. It does not involve the process that produces the primary result. It involves the superordinate process that maintains the effectiveness and preserves the coherence of that process. The solution to these problems requires the revamping of managerial controls, which may involve changes in organizational and institutional design.

The process of finding solutions to problems of the first four types is not itself a source of problems of other kinds if there already exists a shelf of worked-out solutions that can be mimicked. It is characteristic of the pure growth model (developed in part one of volume I) that, when growth passes scalar thresholds calling forth new modes of behavior in the localized fields of intensive and extensive margins, local system managers can turn to the parent regional system and find stock solutions for all four types of problems. If all solutions could be imitative, our problem typology would be complete. Alas, most serious problems involve the creation of novel products, processes, controls, and material and energy properties.[1] Amplifying the strength, speed, and coordination of human processes involves enlarging the informational content of these processes. This engages the fourth level of system behavior (figure 1 in volume I) that carries out self-reorganizations—the level that reprograms or redesigns all of the subordinate levels of system behavior. Here we often encounter a *type-five problem:* there may not be sufficient learning resources in the system under stress. Throughout most of human history, development has rested on the chance occurrence of a creative individual mind occupying a position of strategic influence in a stressed system. It is only with the recent advent of science that the social process has begun to institutionalize a learning resource occupying the fourth level of behavior. Science has begun to provide the inventive mind with an informational shelf to turn to, but this is a cultural institutional development and it has left unresolved a large set of problems of the fifth kind that are now being encountered by formal organizations and political processes. We will be returning to this point.

The manner in which this subject has been developed could leave the implication that there is a natural problem-solving sequence that runs from type-one problem encounters through type-five, as each projected solution uncovers unsuspected problems of the higher order type. It certainly can and has happened this way. But, in any concrete instance, the event that triggers a sequence can happen anywhere in this seeming hierarchy. It may stop where it starts, or it may evoke sequential problems either up or down the typological scale.[2]

Early Problem-Solving Sequences

The colonial period of U.S. history down to the early nineteenth century displayed two prominent characteristics. First, there was still only a shallow hierarchy of traditional activities separating consumers from their resource roots. Second, as we noted earlier, social change during these formative years was dominated by scalar growth rather than the development of new technologies. When technology was introduced that was novel to the regions, it was characteristically an imitative adaptation of techniques drawn from parent England.

Allan Pred has described the state of affairs: "American manufacturing was characterized predominantly by an emphasis upon consumer rather than capital goods, by handicraft rather than machine techniques, and by rural dispersion rather than concentration in urban centers" (1966, p. 14). Manufacturing did exist in urban centers, but it played a subsidiary role and was largely restricted to those activities that grew naturally out of traditional mercantile activities, that is, such processes as sugar refining, flour milling, wholesaling, and warehousing. Other activities such as printing and coopering were directly linked to commercial activities. There was some manufacture of construction materials like glass, nails, and paint.

It would seem as if this protracted period of scalar growth would have been a perfect setting in which the stage theory concepts of the growth could be realized. However, even this experience did not fit the ontogenetic stage theory concept. The expectation that the emerging urban region would leave the parent region's nest by engaging in extensive input (import) substitutions did not come to pass for two hundred years. America became stuck at that stage where the parent region's reach for resource inputs was matched by the adolescent region's reach back for the essential nourishment of many intermediate and final products. As late as 1820, less than 5 percent of U.S. exports consisted of finished manufactures. At the same time, well over half of U.S. imports were finished manufactures. The balance was mostly coffee and tea, that is, consumer goods rather than industrial raw materials.

The import substitutions leading to the development of American urban manufacturing were delayed by the single minded dynamic of the continental filling-up process—a process that created both labor and capital shortages. Indeed, the coastal entrepôt cities of the colonial Northeast began to take on parental functions vis-à-vis the transmontaine interior before they were themselves weened. You might say that they became teenage parents or parents-by-proxy, as they continued to pass the responsibility for quality end-products and for capital goods manufacturing back to the British parent.[3]

There were only two exceptions to the consumer-handicraft-household orientation of early manufacturing. The early New England ports became the locus of a substantial shipbuilding industry. We have discussed at length the problems associated with continental access, but the most prominent access problem of the colonial period was associated with maintaining ties with parent England. The second exception was the appearance of textile manufacturing toward the end of this early growth period. Samuel Slater broke the English textile manufacturers' machinery monopoly. Household textile manufacturing began to be displaced to some fall line sites in New England.[4]

By the time America began to mechanize by mimicking England's earlier industrial revolution, such imitative developments had already become thoroughly mixed with indigenous creative advances. During the transmontaine spread, problems began to mount that could no longer be resolved by imitating existing ways of doing things. By the Civil War, America had simultaneously shed its growth-cycle adolescence and raced to the front of the technological revolution.

In discussing resource and linkage activities we noted that the universal problems of limited time and energy were especially acute in colonial America in the form of the labor shortage. (Wages were twice as high as in England.) The pressures to increase the productivity of labor through mechanization were acute, but this was delayed by the matching scarcity of capital and the alternative of continuing to suckle parent England. However, by the early nineteenth century, commercial enterprise was beginning to generate more free capital in this country and during the wars of independence and 1812, the teat was withheld. Furthermore, after the conflicts were resolved, this country's negative balance of trade encouraged the import of English capital. Thus stimulated, mechanization began to take root throughout the economic structure.

We earlier told the story of scarce labor and the mechanization of agricultural tasks during this period. The McCormick reaper (1834) was a technological response to the energy problem (the second in our typology of problems) constraining agricultural practice. The reaper solved the problem of hitching a new source of power (the horse) to the human-powered scythe and sickle. In rapid succession, the same generic constraint was resolved for each of the traditional farm tasks in a related system of activities. In the textile industry, the mechanization of the task system (carding → the water frame, spinning → the spinning jenny, weaving → the power loom) also required breaking through the power constraint. Here the new motive source was water power. The textile industry was completely mechanized by 1860.

In chapter 6 we learned that access problems were severe during this period. The power problem was critical in this case as well. Sufficient power had to be harnessed to move a riverboat against the current. There was also the matter of harnessing sufficient power to move heavy loads across land. Emerging transport requirements simply overwhelmed the capabilities of the sail and the draft horse. What was needed here was not a way to simulate human motions, but a way to develop and apply new sources of power to work. In addition, for the second time, the textile industry was running up against the limitations of its initial adaptive solution. Water power proved to limit site selections severely and it placed a constraint upon further machine developments that seemed feasible, were a stronger and more consistent source of power available. These pressures favored development of the steam engine. The new power source was applied first to the riverboat and railway, but began to be experimentally applied as a prime mover in emerging industrial processes as well.[5]

The new machines required structural embodiment in metal. The existing forms of industrial iron were initially adequate. Still, the expanded demands placed strains on the capacity of the small charcoal-based refiners and the hammer forges of the day. As a consequence, the American iron industry adopted three British developments. The rolling mill began to replace the hammer forge, particularly in meeting the expanding demands for flat plate—a first-order, activity sequence, or process, solution. The puddling furnace was adapted as an instrument for further refining pig iron—a minor, third-order materials problem solution. Coal began to replace charcoal as the fuel—a second-order, energy problem solution. Apart from these limited modifications, the fundamental character of the industry did not change significantly.

So, apart from the growth and developmental mechanization of the traditional industries, there was the linked growth and imitative development of the iron industry. New manufacturing industries also emerged. There was the fledgling machinery industry. Most prominent was the agricultural implement specialty, which slowly separated itself from the village blacksmith. The development and manufacture of new machines placed new strains on the techniques for metal shaping. Parts had to be machined to new tolerances, partly because of the necessity to refine and control more complex motions, and partly because evolving assembly practices placed a premium on standardized parts. So the problem sequence became displaced one more step to the need to develop new machine tools to make the new machines. In the production of heavy machine tools the United States again relied largely on the British. Nevertheless, the small arms industry (that served to win the nation's independence, open up the continent, and consolidate the nation) spawned a very advanced small machine tool industry capable of producing standardized components. This was a harbinger of signficant future developments.

Once problem-solving moved down the path of mechanization, it began to run up against problems of the fourth kind: difficulties of coordination and control emerged. Newly differentiated activities of human beings and machines needed to fit into a coordinated process sequence. The various forms of craft organization gave way to the mill, which evolved into the factory. Explicit (though fixed-station) assembly line techniques began to emerge. By the 1850s, all four stages of production in textiles were integrated into a single factory organization. The factory system was also present in the manufacture of farm implements, small arms, clocks and watches, shoes, and wagons.

All of these manufacturing developments began to have a powerful effect. Beginning in the 1830s, manufacturing spread rapidly throughout the eastern United States. During the antebellum period it stretched westward to the Ohio Valley and Chicago. The establishment of the Brady Bend Iron Works in Pennsylvania was a pointing finger. At an accelerating pace, manufacturing employment went from less than 3 percent of total employment to 14 percent. In the single decade from 1850 to 1860, the output of iron products and machinery doubled. By 1860, the United States was second only to Britain in the industrial world. The increasing importance of manufacturing increased the relative importance of the urban centers. At the turn of the century only 5 percent of the total population was in urban centers; by 1860, more than 20 percent. The number of new urban places added during the 1840s, 1850s, and 1860s was five times greater than all of those previously existing.

For all that, this was only the awakening era for manufacturing. Food processing and garment making were little developed and continued in the home until after the Civil War. The crafts and craft shops remained dominant until 1850. Apart from that, it was still the era of the mill rather than the factory. The steam engine was slow to be applied. It had a high initial cost and frequently broke down. As late as the Civil War three-fourths of all power was from animals, and water power was still more important than steam.

So the nation entered the epoch of industrialization and national transport reorganization (the fourth epoch 1870–1910) with the power base for an industrial economy still unresolved. The power constraint remained critical because the most promising line of development, the steam engine, began to encounter material constraints. The efficiency and power of the steam engine could only be improved by building higher pressure machines designed for finer tolerances of fit. The requirements had passed the limits of the maleable wrought irons of the period. Thus, the type-two power constraint became transmuted into a new type-three material problem. The expanding railway system brought this matter to a head, not only because of its need for higher performance and safety than that required of stationary steam engines, but also because iron rails were inadequate to support the stress of high speeds and heavy loads.

Steel was the only answer. High-carbon crucible steel had long been produced in small quantities for such things as cutlery, but no known method existed for meeting such levels of demand. Solutions were not long in coming. William Kelly in the United States and Sir Henry Bessemer in England simultaneously and independently developed the blast furnace. It first operated in 1864. The open hearth furnace followed a few years later. The basic lining (for the removal of phosphorous) came in 1880, the by-product coke oven in 1890, and the electric furnace in 1900. For a single furnace, production went from 7 to 10 tons of steel a day to over 500 tons—and all of this with less coke consumption per unit of output. If textiles, then farm machinery, were the preeminent manufacturing industries of the first half of the century, iron and steel became the queen industry of the second half. And, thanks to steel, steam power had become the dominant source of power by 1890.

It was during this period as well that those industries formerly passed by were successfully mechanized. The first truly national transportation system vastly expanded the size and accessibility of the market, but this had proved of little advantage to the producers of perishable agricultural products. The invention of the tin can replaced the glass jar used for canning in the home, and commercial canning became firmly established by 1880. Ice-refrigerated storage rooms and rail cars opened the way for the large, national meatpackers. By 1890, the slaughterhouse had been mechanized. Flour milling developed roller grinding that could handle the hard wheats of the Plains region, in turn opening the way for producing blends of flour that were standardized in character. These developments emerged in a linked, circular developmental relationship with the new cracker and biscuit bakeries whose success depended on the availability of standardized flours.

The textile industry moved toward greater automaticity with the advent of ring spinning in 1870 (permitting the continuous drawing, spinning, and winding of yarn) and the automatic looms in 1895 (ending the need to shut down for a bobbin change). The mechanization of woolen textiles, which had presented greater technical problems, finally occurred in the period from 1870 to 1910. The invention of the sewing machine in the 1850s finally opened the way to the mechanization of the apparel and shoe industries. The sewing machine was followed by cutting machines in 1870, power driven sewing machines in 1895, and treadle pressing irons at the end of the period. Men's clothing production became fully mechanized under the impetus of the Civil War uniform requirements. Women's coats, hosiery, and underwear followed, although women's dresses remained a craft enterprise throughout this period. As recently as 1860, the shoe industry was still organized as a craft enterprise attached to merchant employers. But by 1914, the industry was fully mechanized. There were machines for stitching, eyeletting, lasting, and heeling, and in 1875, the Goodyear welt process for attaching soles was developed. The reduced demand for skilled labor permitted that part of the industry devoted to the manufacturing of standard work shoes, and the like, to migrate from the historical New England base to Chicago, Milwaukee, Cincinnati, and St. Louis.

But, during the last half of the nineteenth century the problem-solving, problem-generating interactions began appearing so fast they almost tumbled over each other. Steam power, that great redeemer of animal muscle, began to reveal clay feet. Just as the fall-line water power sites had excessively restricted the topography of manufacturing during the first half of the century, steam power (involving the energy conversion of a solid material substrate, coal) excessively restricted manufacturing to nodal sites in the heavy transport net. There was a vast array of work activities in the household, farm, and factory for which muscle power remained supreme, and where opportunities for work relief had been highlighted by previous developments.

The beginning of electric power as a developmental response came near the end of this fourth epoch. Electricity was first exploited for lighting. This proved to be a powerful amplifier of time by removing the daylight hour restraint from a host of work-related and other activities. The additional development of the electric motor offered a power option of vastly greater flexibility and divisibility, but it was still tied to the storage battery. It had to wait for the right power system and infrastructure to give it wings.

The successive ameliorations of the type-two power constraints revealed new opportunities for solving type-one process design problems through mechanization and the reorganization of stages of work. This is too complex an historical record to trace here, but attempted solutions again revealed type-three limitations in the materials employed to realize these evolving processes. The increasing torque, speed, weight, and precision required by the successive revisions of the machine technology quickly proved the original carbon steels to be inadequate. The development of steel alloys followed, and the requirements of electric power converted copper into a major industrial metal. These new requirements brought the open hearth furnace into ascendancy over the blast furnace by 1890, because this process accepted scrap and provided for greater control over the production of alloys. The open hearth technology could also be implemented on a smaller scale, opening up the movement of the industry to expanding regional markets like Birmingham.

The production of machine tools of every size emerged, reducing the earlier dependence on England. 1860 was the take-off point, and by 1900 America was matching the English in every category. By 1910, Cincinnati had become the dominant center in the machine tool industry, an industry that assumed a special significance for other reasons. This whole fertile, creative period uncovered vast limitations in the system's capacity to solve type-five problems. The creative, inventive, self-reorganizing initiatives fueling this vast reprogramming of the social system remained essentially *ad hoc,* disjointed, and tied to the initiatives of localized individuals and establishments. Nevertheless, the evolutionary process began to generate an informal network of creative contacts, without which this accelerating industrial revolution would have taken quite a different course. The machine tool industry became the heart of that network on the design side. People with inventive ideas for process modifications often went there to find a repository of effective design ideas and to seek support in creating prototype machines. Perceived problems of the fifth kind also led to the establishment of the U.S. Patent Office. And it was in the last half of the nineteenth century that scientific societies began to emerge in America—although mostly still on a localized scale.

This may also be the point to recognize that these emerging industrial processes were creating and exacerbating problems of type four. The growing complexity of activity processes within the enterprise (and the growing connectivity of linkages between enterprises, supply sources, and markets) presented new problems of cybernetic control. Such problems led to some of the most distinctive developments of the period. First, this was the epoch when mass production appeared. It was at least partly in the interest of effective managerial control that continuous process and interchangeable parts manufacturing were developed. Second, as the size and complexity of industrial establishments grew, the problems of internal control grew apace. It was no accident that F. A. Taylor, the father of modern industrial management, began his work studies in the 1880s.

Third, the advent of large numbers of modernizing industrial enterprises, competing in a newly emergent national market, created transaction market instabilities of a kind not previously experienced. This led to the famous combination movement between 1880 and 1905. Initially this brought mostly horizontal combinations. A systemization of purchasing, manufacturing, marketing, and financing activities in such industries as distilling, feed manufacture, sugar refining, meat packing, oil refining, and rubber production took place. But the real driving force of industrial combination was the attempt to control the market in the interest of market stability. The second half of the period was dominated by vertical integrations of production stages. This was when U.S. Steel was organized and 3,000 mergers occurred in seven years.[6]

Finally, the multiplication of managerial problems initiated the mechanization of third-level (figure 1, volume 1) information processes as well as second-level material and energy processes. Thus, toward the end of the century a host of business machines began to emerge.[7]

As a consequence of these powerful developments, major changes in economic and demographic structures emerged. This was the period when the economy took on modern characteristics. Labor productivity more than doubled. By 1890, the value of manufacturing output exceeded that of agriculture for the first time. Barely ten years later it was twice as large. By the end of the period, the United States produced one-third of the world's manufacturing output and became the world's leading industrial power. By 1895, the U.S. foreign trade balance became positive for the first time. It was also about this time when finished manufactures became a larger portion of exports than imports. (The largest increase in exports came in iron and steel, machinery, and copper products; the largest import increases were in industrial materials like rubber, tin, hides, and forest products.) The shift to an industrial base accelerated the concentration of population in urban centers. The Census-designated urban population increased from 20 to 51 percent of the total. While the total urban population increased two and half times, centers of population over 100,000 increased three and a half times.

There were broad regional shifts as well. Although virtually every part of the nation enjoyed absolute increases in manufacturing employment, the historically dominant New England and Middle Atlantic regions suffered relative losses. The development of the heavier industries based on iron and steel (agricultural machinery, iron rails, machine tools) were drawn westward to their primary material sources in response to the creation of a new national economy that was, itself, being drawn westward. About a third of the relative competitive gains in manufacturing came at the western end of what we still call the Manufacturing Belt (Illinois, Michigan, Wisconsin, Minnesota). The largest gains elsewhere came on the Pacific Coast because the remote location of that region caused it to develop to some extent as a separate nation.

By the end of the period, this great geographic reorientation was beginning to feed back upon the industrialization process that created it. Large urban populations created public health problems, leading to the development of sewer and water utilities. They created novel problems of access to power, leading to the electric power utilities. They created new transportation problems, leading to transit railways. They created novel communication problems, leading to the telegraph and telephone. The increased need for large public buildings created construction problems, leading to steel frame construction and skyscrapers. All of this fed the ongoing developmental process and expanded further the volume of industrial production.

We are brought, thus, to the era (1910–40) immediately preceding the study period. By the twentieth century, the developmental process had become so complex, and was moving so fast, that the problem → solution → new problem sequence characterization was too simple to describe adequately the reality. Its defects arise from the fact that the concept accommodates our instinctive reach for classical, linear-causal explanations a little too nicely. In complex dynamic systems, developmental sequences become circular; they become both constrained and amplified in ways that defy linear-causal reasoning; indeed, at times, they become counterintuitive in their outcomes. These characteristics have begun to change the nature of the developmental process itself. Despite its limitations, our problem typology becomes an essential descriptive and explanatory crutch.

A major part of the developmental effort involved a continuing response to type-two energy process problems. Each of the previously emergent forms of prime mover (the horse, the water wheel, the steam engine) proved to displace (to a degree and for a time) the constraints on the evolving processes of urbanized transactions systems. We have traced the circumstances that led to the mechanization of agricultural and industrial production and a nationwide transaction system. We have also seen how the urbanization process had reached a limit beyond which it could not proceed without some means of applying power in more fractional and mobile units. The gasoline engine and the electric motor were the responses. The interesting thing to note here is that the developmental process was becoming systemic with a vengeance. The application to work of the electric motor required the development of the electric public utility industry. Both came to fruition in the fifth epoch. The automotive applications of the gasoline engine required the tremendous infrastructure of public roads, as well as trade, service, and repair industries. We have already seen that it was not until late in the study period that the infrastructural requirements were sufficiently satisfied for automotive transport to "take off." In situations like these it is no longer possible to talk about individual problem and solution sequences. Each problem becomes an element in a set of closely related problems. The problem begins to transform itself so that we are increasingly dealing with systems of problems in a form that modern analysts are beginning to call a "*problematique*."

In any case, the automotive transport, farm implement, and power and light developments added sizable new industries to the manufacturing scene during the early twentieth century (the fifth epoch). The development of the electric motor also opened the door for a whole range of type-one process developments. Take the steel industry, for example. The electric motor provided the fractional and flexible power units essential for developing continuous metal-handling-and-shaping processes. This made possible the integration of the stages of steel making in one plant so that the molten metal need not be reheated and so that by-product gases could be used as sources of energy. In this case the solution to a type-two work-energy problem led to the development of new type-one process options that made possible the solution of a quite different set of energy problems.

The electric motor opened up another set of type-one process developments. Previously, available power units only permitted the mechanization of the large-scale work functions of agriculture and industry. The electric motor, however, provided the fractional sources of power that opened up the possibility of mechanizing household processes. It was during this fifth epoch that the appliance industries emerged. The electric washing machine and refrigerator were the prominent developments.

The internal combustion engine also provided a power source sufficiently light and compact (utilizing a fuel that could provide much more power per cubic foot) to make feasible the dream of air transport. The Wright brothers responded with their famous 1903 flight. By World War I military aviation was established, and in the 1920s air mail became a reality and "barnstorming" was the vogue. A new manufacturing industry was spawned.

All of these developments served to uncover additional type-three material constraints. It was under the impetus of military aviation that aluminum ceased to be an exotic metal and moved into the tonnage class. The vastly expanded demand for copper quickly exhausted the high percentage copper ores and revealed the limitations of earlier refining techniques. The Firth flotation process and electrolytic refining methods were developed, bringing new forms of metal processing to the manufacturing sector.

The increasing complexity of these emerging processes exacerbated managerial and creative processes to a degree not previously experienced. Managerial developments showed up on the factory floor in the form of the moving assembly line instituted by Ford in 1908.[8] The new discipline of management took serious root during this period. The first truly professional managers came into prominance (Pierre Du Pont, Alfred Sloan of General Motors, Rosenwald, then Wood, of Sears). The Gilbreths, Mary Parke Follet, and Chester Barnard were building on the work of F. A. Taylor. The Harvard Business School was established. Cybernetic control problems required better communication linkages. The telegraph and telephone, although fourth-epoch inventions, now became major components of the urbanized transaction system. The radio was developed to maintain contact with ships at sea. The growing information-processing requirements brought continuing improvements in the primitive nineteenth century business machines, including the electrification of some.

The continuous unfolding of developmental problems stimulated the growth and success of scientific disciplines. Indeed, industrial science was formed and fed in a manner quite like the developments in agricultural science reported earlier. There was no counterpart to the land-grant college and extension service system, but the period did see the emergence of the engineering college. This is also the period when some businesses began to organize research and development divisions—particularly in the electrical, chemical, and rubber industries in the 1920s.

As a result of these developments, the productivity of workers doubled again. Manufacturing employment reached its highest point (29 percent of total employment in 1930). The export of finished manufactures expanded to two-thirds of all exports (with automobiles, petroleum, iron, steel, and machinery dominant). Imports of finished manufactures dropped to 16 percent, the lowest point before or since. The population became two-thirds urban. Child labor, still 20 percent of the total in 1900, virtually disappeared; the number of women in the work force tripled; labor force participants over 65 years of age declined by a third.

The western end of the Manufacturing Belt consolidated its strength, with almost half of the total competitive gains of the period. The automobile gave Michigan, alone, a quarter of the total. Southeastern gains, tentative in the fourth epoch, became strong on the basis of textile and wood products manufacturing, with North Carolina displaying the third largest competitive gain of any state. This was the period when Californian manufacturing competitive gains began to become impressive—still mostly a manifestation of the semi-independent nation phenomenon. Texas was also strong because of activities based on petroleum.

The Role of Chemistry in the Developmental Process

The narrative just completed is, I believe, unusual in its developmental sequence structure. It is conventional in its emphasis on power-and-mechanics-oriented solutions because the problem of material constraints only recently became a critical element in the developmental sequence. In earlier times technologies depended either on naturally available materials or chemical transformations of natural materials that had been accidentally discovered and that were perpetuated and practiced as crafts. This was true of early metals, mortars, ceramics, glasses, dyes, soaps, mineral acids, pharmaceuticals, and all fermented products.

There was room for the early mechanization and industrialization processes to continue for a while before existing materials proved to be seriously constraining. There were also improvements and substitutions that could be made on a craft basis. By the nineteenth century, it was becoming clear that "amplifying the strength and reach of the arm of man" was running up against material constraints requiring solutions beyond the power of the chemical crafts. It was not until the 1860s that theoretical chemistry emerged and laid the ground for scientifically based materials industries.

Only then could metallurgy become more than an intuitive trial and error process; only then could the new chemical elements be discovered (the rare metals and radioactive elements, the inert gases); only then could electrochemical processes so important to the development of metallic and other inorganic materials be understood; and only then could all of the processes that depend on gas reactions emerge. Only then could organic chemical processes make possible the intelligent study of chemical processes in plants and animals. The way was also opened for the development of aniline dyes; synthetic drugs and perfumes; large-scale production of organic compounds, plastics, synthetic varnishes and paints, silicone products, detergents and wetting agents, and petroleum chemicals, among others.

Had this chemistry-based materials technology not displaced major material constraints, the most dramatic recent developments in agriculture, food, textiles, petroleum, paper, metals, glass, nuclear energy, medicine, and all the subsequent mechanical and electronic technologies would have been impossible. Yet this developmental story is largely untold and lies largely in the background of our consciousness.

Theoretical chemical science developed rapidly during the latter part of the nineteenth century. It became institutionalized during the first part of the twentieth century, and industrial chemistry began to have an important effect on the developmental process. But because of the time lag involving the diffusion of scientific knowledge, the training of a critical body of scientists and engineers, and the accumulation of expensive technological infrastructures in the chemical process industries, the major effect of scientific chemistry on industrial and urban change came during the study period.

Manufacturing Development

So we arrive again at the point of explaining the study-period developments as emergent modifications of these historical sequences. However, because manufacturing as a whole is such a heterogeneous collection of activities, the descriptive and explanatory narrative is best approached on a sector-by-sector basis. This will be accomplished in chapters 10 and 11, following which an overview will be presented. We will be content here to offer an anticipatory observation. We have seen that in the last part of the nineteenth century the sequence paths formed by the five problem types and their attempted first-order solutions began to take on a more variable sequence order and to display more systemic interdependencies. Managerial and developmental problems (types four and five) began to claim more explicit attention than had been characteristic historically. The first part of the twentieth century displayed an intensification and acceleration of these trends. These modifications in dynamic patterns appeared to reach a significant threshold in the study period. First, there were explosive changes in the structure of manufacturing and nonmanufacturing activities alike. Second, there appears to have been a major systemic change in the character of technological evolution. Third, we experienced a phase shift in the kinds of problems that are becoming obtrusive and in the kinds of solutions they require. If the world negotiates an unstable transitional period successfully, the structure of urban society will likely be further altered by these developments. We will want to give content to these generalizations as we proceed.

Direct Consequences for Total Employment

The next task is to form an initial image of the changing geographical patterns of manufacturing taken as a whole. This should prove to be a useful reference pattern when considering the changes exhibited by specific industry sectors as well as when we come to fashion a summary. These aggregated competitive shift patterns are presented in plate II-4 and text maps II-7 and II-8.

The shaded counties of plate II-4, and the corresponding urban regions of map II-8 indicate that, in 1940, the fabled northeastern Manufacturing Belt was still in place—very much so. Table II-18 reveals that 70 percent of the total manufacturing employment was still in the historical manufacturing heartland. Our discussion of the developmental roots of the study period documented the transformation of manufacturing from its original nondurable goods base to a predominantly durable goods enterprise. We noted that for a hundred years this change in structure had given a competitive edge to the western end of the Manufacturing Belt.[9] However, this glacial drift still left 60 percent of total Manufacturing Belt employment in New England and the Middle Atlantic states. By 1940, a minor second belt of manufacturing specialization stretched along the Piedmont hills from Roanoke to Atlanta; and a third minibelt had appeared in the coastal counties of the Pacific Northwest based on wood products manufacturing dominated by logging and sawmill employment. Apart from this, only scattered counties or groups of counties had reached the threshold of manufacturing specialization by 1940.

TABLE II-18. Manufacturing employment in Manufacturing Belt regions, 1940, 1970

Region	1940 Number of employees	1940 Percent	1970 Number of employees	1970 Percent
New England	1,186,827	11	1,509,768	7
Middle Atlantic	3,297,005	31	4,602,798	23
Great Lakes	2,953,850	28	5,255,892	26
Manufacturing Belt	7,437,677	70	11,368,458	57
U.S. total manufacturing	10,739,594	100	20,019,822	100

The structural rearrangement, which became appreciable after the Civil War, accelerated substantially during the study period. Plate II-4 and table II-6 reveal that 85 percent of the U.S. counties experienced competitive gains in manufacturing employment between 1940 and 1970. Because only 12 percent of U.S. counties were manufacturing specialists in 1940, and two-thirds of these experienced competitive losses, an overwhelming 94 percent of the counties that experienced competitive manufacturing gains were initially unspecialized. They paint plate II-4 blue from coast to coast. Of the third of all specialized counties that continued to experience competitive gains, the largest concentration was in the southeastern Piedmont belt. The rest were mostly scattered throughout the old Manufacturing Belt, or represented localized manufacturing specialties in other parts of the country. Almost half of the counties displaying manufacturing gains experienced leading competitive gains. This dark blue portion of plate II-4 blankets most of the United States east of a line running roughly from Minneapolis to Dallas and back to Houston. Throughout the Florida Plains, Mountain, and Pacific regions, and most of the Gulf coastal counties, manufacturing competitive gains tended to lag behind all-sector competitive gains (light blue).

Approximately 60 percent of all specialized manufacturing counties experienced losses and two-thirds of these displayed leading competitive losses. It almost necessarily follows that these were heavily concentrated in the Old Manufacturing Belt—with most in the oldest portion from Pittsburgh eastward. This is the developmental code (C) picture.

But plate II-4 has one representational defect. It is a typological picture without dimension. An accompanying

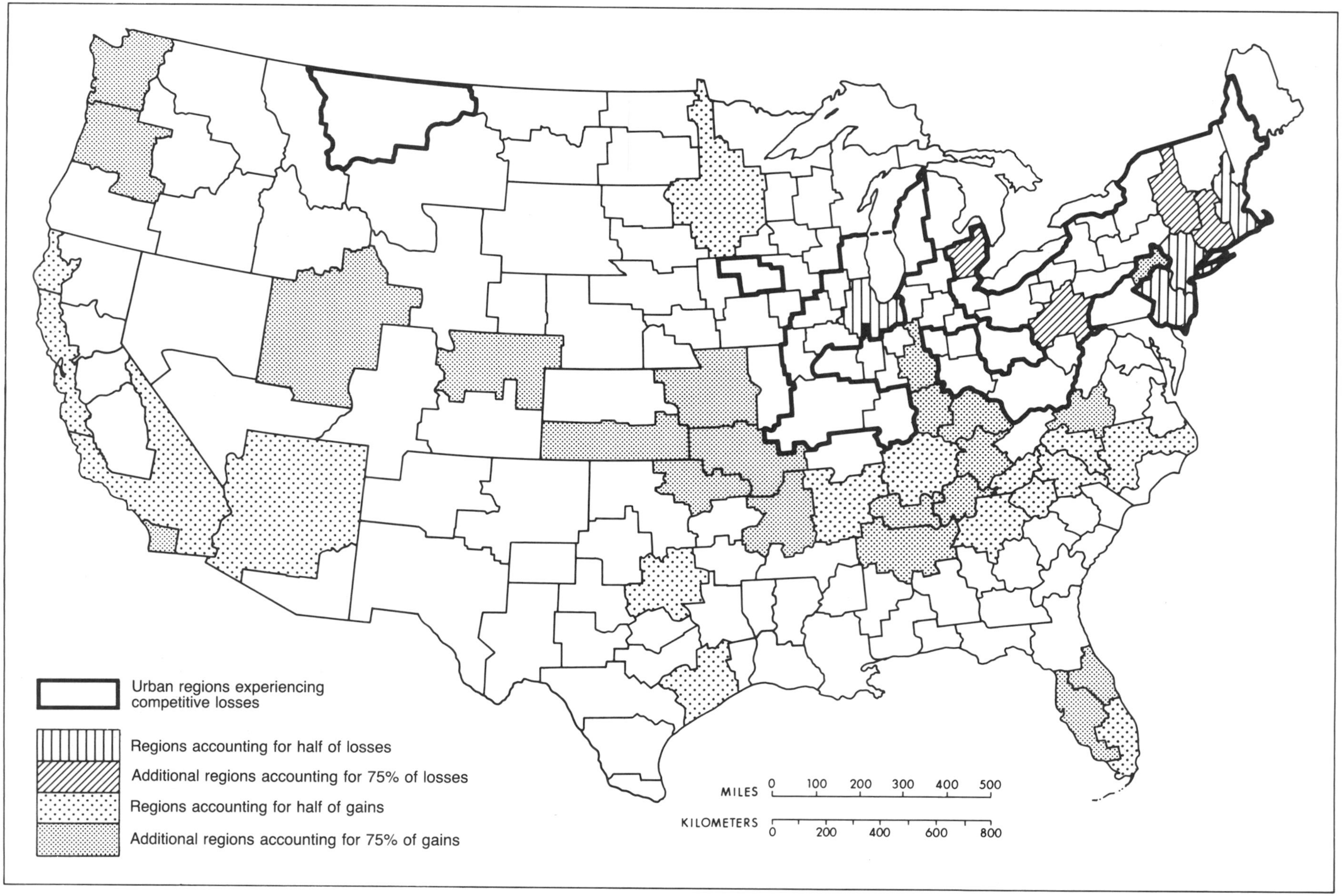

MAP II-7. Competitive Gains and Losses in Manufacturing Employment, 171 Urban Regions, 1940–70.

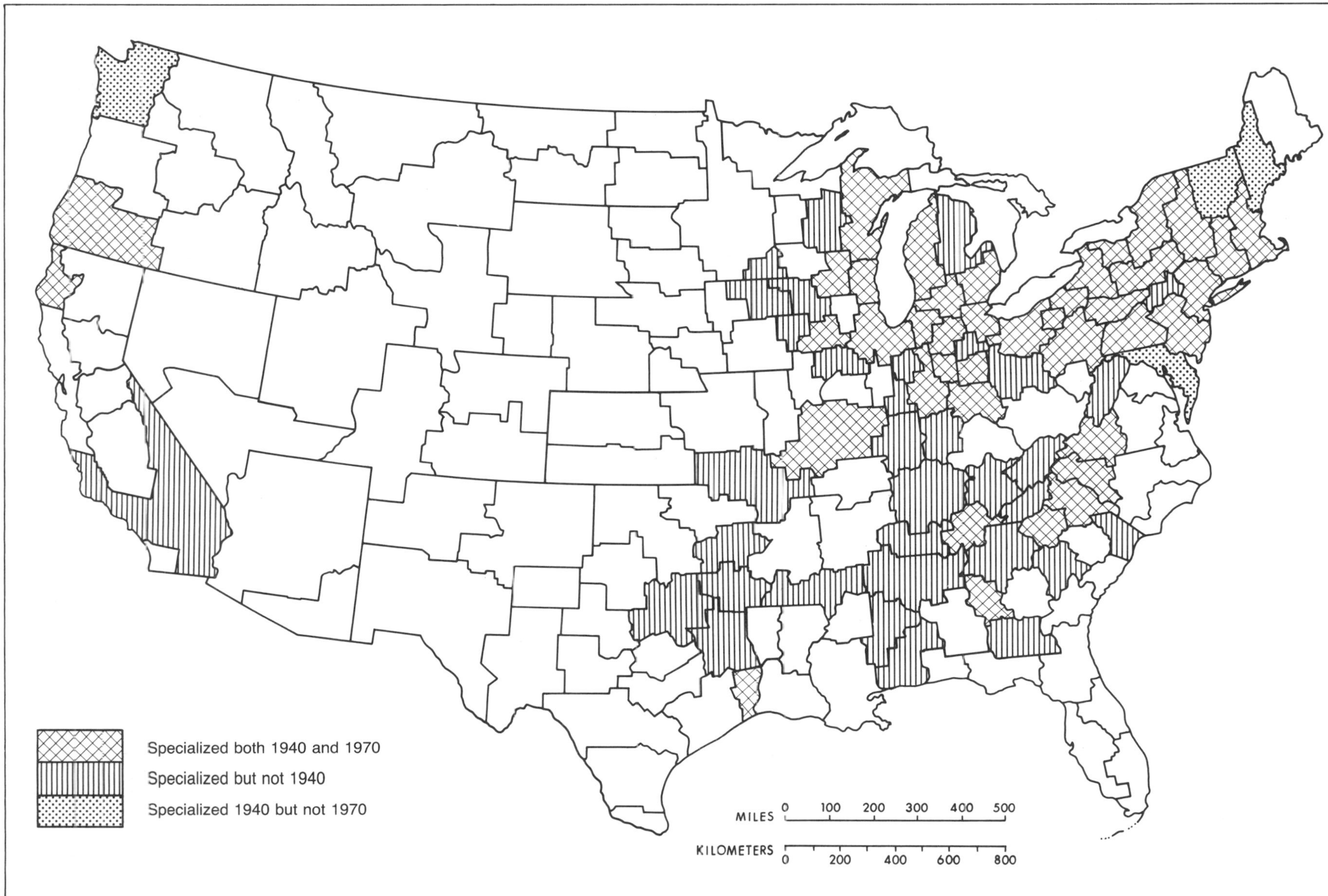

MAP II-8. Urban Regions Specializing in Manufacturing, 1940, 1970.

dimensional picture is summarized roughly by map II-7 and table II-19. It is striking to note that one-fourth of all competitive losses were contributed by the New York urban region. With the addition of Boston, Chicago, and Philadelphia, half of the total is accounted for. The addition of Pittsburgh, Detroit, Hartford, and Albany accounts for 75 percent. Only sixteen urban regions accounted for 90 percent of all competitive losses. As has been noted, the competitive gains were widespread, but the major portion of the gains was much more highly concentrated than plate II-5 would suggest. Most of those blue counties spread across the face of the nation made trivial contributions to overall competitive shifts—even though manufacturing employment was leading the all-sector competitive gains in many of these counties. Most were starting from minuscule bases and many were coun-

TABLE II-19. Ranked manufacturing employment competitive gains and losses for principal urban regions, 1940–70 (an elaboration of map II-7)

Rank	Region number	Region	Competitive shift	Percent	Cumulative percent
		Gaining regions			
1	165	Los Angeles	+555,526	15.16	15.16
2	127	Dallas	+202,552	5.53	20.69
3	26	Charlotte	+140,698	3.84	24.53
4	44	Atlanta	+115,154	3.14	27.67
5	36	Miami	+110,825	3.03	30.70
6	171	San Francisco	+107,166	2.93	33.63
7	25	Greensboro, etc. N.C.	+94,530	2.58	36.21
8	91	Minneapolis	+91,315	2.49	38.70
9	28	Greenville, S.C.	+81,269	2.22	40.92
10	46	Memphis	+79,502	2.17	43.09
11	49	Nashville	+73,291	2.00	45.09
12	141	Houston	+72,705	1.98	47.07
13	162	Phoenix	+70,758	1.93	49.00
14	23	Raleigh	+70,307	1.92	50.92
15	47	Huntsville	+54,316	1.48	52.40
16	148	Denver	+53,927	1.47	53.87
17	54	Louisville	+52,715	1.44	55.31
18	45	Birmingham	+51,126	1.40	56.71
19	20	Roanoke	+48,892	1.33	58.04
20	48	Chattanooga	+48,383	1.32	59.36
21	35	Orlando	+44,646	1.22	60.58
22	164	San Diego	+43,292	1.18	61.76
23	117	Little Rock	+41,782	1.14	62.90
24	50	Knoxville	+38,641	1.05	63.95
25	53	Lexington	+38,447	1.05	65.00
26	157	Portland	+38,173	1.04	66.04
27	37	Tampa	+37,454	1.02	67.06
28	111	Kansas City	+36,615	1.00	68.06
29	119	Tulsa	+35,862	.98	69.04
30	13	Wilkes Barre	+34,505	.94	69.98
31	60	Indianapolis	+30,828	.84	70.82
32	116	Springfield	+30,613	.84	71.66
33	32	Augusta	+29,927	.82	72.48
34	29	Columbia	+29,606	.81	73.29
35	30	Florence	+29,110	.79	74.08
36	110	Wichita	+28,321	.77	74.85
37	151	Salt Lake City	+28,188	.77	75.62
38	155	Seattle	+27,196	.74	76.36
39	64	Columbus	+25,177	.69	77.05
40	27	Asheville	+25,019	.68	77.73
41	51	Bristol	+24,031	.66	78.39
42	130	Tyler, Texas	+23,807	.65	79.04
43	158	Eugene	+23,056	.63	79.67
44	142	San Antonio	+21,969	.60	80.27
45	120	Oklahoma City	+20,457	.56	80.83
46	19	Staunton, Va.	+20,183	.55	81.38
47	167	Stockton, Ca.	+19,868	.54	81.92
48	40	Montgomery	+18,907	.52	82.44
49	41	Albany, Ga.	+18,836	.51	82.95
50	168	Sacramento	+18,320	.50	83.45
51	137	Mobile	+18,055	.49	83.94
52	135	Jackson, Miss.	+16,935	.46	84.40
53	42	Macon, Ga.	+16,736	.46	84.86
54	24	Wilmington	+16,505	.45	85.31
55	34	Jacksonville	+16,049	.44	85.75
56	166	Fresno	+15,573	.43	86.18
57	131	Texarkana	+15,459	.42	86.60
58	138	New Orleans	+15,293	.42	87.02
59	107	Omaha	+14,994	.41	87.43
60	72	Saginaw	+14,984	.41	87.84
61	80	Cedar Rapids	+14,372	.39	88.23
62	43	Columbus, Ga.	+14,353	.39	88.62
63	18	Washington, D.C.	+13,954	.38	89.00
64	134	Greenville, Miss.	+13,693	.37	89.37
65	33	Savannah, Ga.	+13,111	.36	89.73
66	145	El Paso	+12,569	.34	90.07
		Losing regions			
1	14	New York	−862,985	23.51	23.51
2	4	Boston	−375,188	10.22	33.73
3	77	Chicago	−374,463	10.20	43.93
4	15	Philadelphia	−297,123	8.09	52.02
5	66	Pittsburgh	−261,186	7.12	59.14
6	71	Detroit	−239,869	6.53	65.67
7	5	Hartford	−196,219	5.35	71.02
8	6	Albany, etc.	−117,582	3.20	74.22
9	69	Cleveland	−112,467	3.06	77.28
10	9	Buffalo	−102,092	2.78	80.06
11	114	St. Louis	−82,015	2.23	82.29
12	7	Syracuse	−77,724	2.12	84.41
13	17	Baltimore	−73,918	2.01	86.42
14	84	Milwaukee	−67,863	1.85	88.27
15	67	Youngstown	−43,539	1.19	89.36
16	62	Cincinnati	−40,485	1.10	90.46

tertrend shifts. This not to suggest that massive geographical and structural shifts were not underway. No other time or place in history has ever experienced anything like it! Appendix II-A reveals that manufacturing contributed more to the all-sector regional competitive shifts (30 percent) than any other sector. This was five times all resource sectors combined, twice as much as all linkage sectors, two and one-half times all retail trade, and half again as much as all service sectors. Only the information-processing sectors came close to matching the importance of manufacturing changes in accounting for interregional competitive changes in U.S. urban regions during this time.

What map II-7 and table II-19 reveal is that most of these gains were contributed by a relatively few regions. Los Angeles, Dallas, and Charlotte account for 25 percent of the gain. A total of fourteen regions (also including Atlanta, Miami, San Francisco, Greensboro, Minneapolis, Greenville, Memphis, Nashville, Houston, Phoenix, and Raleigh) accounted for half. The pattern of those accounting for half of the gain is revealing. The Piedmont carried its strong, fifth-epoch gain into the study period. Dallas and Los Angeles displayed some strength in the fifth epoch, and also some dramatic gains in the study period. Phoenix, Houston, Miami, Minneapolis, and the Nashville–Memphis concentrations represent developments that were mostly study period events.

When we add the urban regions accounting for 75 percent of the gains, we make a revealing discovery. At urban-region scale, the major concentration of leading gains in manufacturing employment consists of an almost solid belt stretching from the interior south Atlantic coastal regions all the way to Witchita and Oklahoma City. This belt lies immediately below the Old Manufacturing Belt and extends only as far south as northern Georgia and Alabama. A narrower finger points westward. It is almost as if the Old Manufacturing Belt had developed "middle-age spread."

Previous discussions have already suggested approximate explanations for this. The pattern has to be associated in an important way with the changes in market and input access generated by the development of trucking and the high-speed, limited-access highway (recall maps II-3 and II-4). This shifting of regional competitive advantages was also led by the continuing structural changes revealed by the input–output tables. The proportion of those inputs flowing directly from original material and energy sources into manufacturing diminished (this is true of eighteen out of twenty manufacturing sectors).[10] At the same time, the proportion of manufacturing outputs going directly to consumer final demand diminished (also true of eighteen out of twenty manufacturing sectors). This was while seventeen of twenty manufacturing sectors increased their inputs from other manufacturing sectors, and eighteen out of twenty increased the proportion of their inputs coming from urban-service activities. The increased roundaboutness of the transaction linkages, the decreased orientation to terminal supply and demand nodes, and the larger number of options for material and energy substitutions have all certainly added to the loosening up of manufacturing transaction networks brought about by the emerging transport technologies.

Apart from this dramatic emerging belt, it seems clear that the remaining major beneficiaries were more discrete regional concentrations fed by more localized resource base developments (food manufacturing in Florida, petroleum and chemicals in Dallas-Houston, wood products in Eugene) or which more recently achieved internal and external economies of scale yielding a competitive advantage in serving regional markets (Denver, Salt Lake, Minneapolis, Dallas, lower California, and the lower Florida Peninsula).

These study period shifts have been so substantial that they have permanently altered the geographical distribution of American manufacturing. Something of the magnitude of the change is suggested in table II-8. By 1970, the Old Manufacturing Belt's share of U.S. manufacturing employment had dropped from 70 to 57 percent. The rest of the nation was coming up fast on half of the total. The greatest relative declines were in the older Mid Atlantic–New England regions. Map II-8 also adds significantly to the story. The Manufacturing Belt and Piedmont regions that were manufacturing specialists in 1940 remained so to the end (with the exception of Portland [Maine], Burlington, Baltimore, and Seattle). The striking thing is how the domain of manufacturing specialization had spread. Newly specialized regions stretched the Old Manufacturing Belt toward Minneapolis, into upper Michigan, and southward down the Mohawk Valley. By 1970, the Piedmont Belt spread eastward toward the Atlantic Coast, westward across the Cumberland Plateau, northward to join up with the old belt through Nashville and Louisville, further westward across the Ozarks to Dallas, and southward to Mobile. Los Angeles first achieved specialized status during this period.[11]

More detailed descriptions and explanations will emerge as we examine individual manufacturing sectors. However, we might anticipate just a bit. Because the nondurable manufacturing activities led the way out of the historical manufacturing sectors into the Piedmont South, many people have the impression that most of the spread is attributable to nondurable manufacturing. In fact the interregional shifts in durable manufacturing employment were about 40 percent greater than for nondurable manufacturing. And, just as the early durable manufacturing specializations developed west of the Alleghenies, while the nondurable specializations remained mostly in the East, the new durable goods specializations emerged as westward extensions of the Old Manufacturing Belt (and in new concentrations in the East Texas and Ozark regions) while the new nondurable goods specializations represent a spreading of the Piedmont concentrations into the Cumberland Plateau and the Pine Barren regions of the Atlantic and Gulf Coast interior.

This broadly sweeping narrative can be made complete by examining the way manufacturing shifts have been related to urban-system structure. Table II-20 abstracts the picture from tables II-8 and II-9. First observe that manufacturing employment shifts have contributed more to the reorganization of the urban-system characteristics of the U.S. economy than to its geographical restructuring. Table II-12, for example, reveals that the relative deviations formed by transaction-field manufacturing shifts are almost twice as great as that characteristic of broad geographical region shifts.

On balance, it is the urban core counties that experienced competitive losses, and, among these, it is specifically the large metropolitan and wholesale-retail centers that experienced the losses, with the large metropolitan centers dominating. It is the lower order trade centers and the regions outside urban cores that experienced the competitive manufacturing gains. The shopping centers accounted for more than 70 percent of the gain, while the topographically strategic complete shopping centers claimed more than half. In transaction-field terms, the primary labor force fields accounted for half of the gains and the small urban-region, non-core counties 40 percent of the gains. In short, manufacturing employment tended to shift downward to the smaller urban regions, while tending to stay within the most accessible commuting range of these smaller urban cores. Relative to each other, the durable goods sectors tended to favor the primary labor force fields and the nondurable sectors, the secondary labor force fields. Durable goods sectors also tended to favor the large and medium regions disproportionately, while nondurable goods favored small urban regions and those fields outside urban core commuting radii. The county frequency patterns of appendix tables II-J and II-K tell a story consistent with the above.

TABLE II-20. Proportion of manufacturing employment competitive gains and losses ($\pm R_{ij}$) by trade-center and transaction-field categories 1940–70

Category	Code C description	Percentage shift
Trade-center class		
Metropolitan		
Large	Lagging loss	−96.6
Small	Lagging gain	+4.0
Wholesale-retail		
Large	Countertrend loss	−3.6
Small	Lagging gain	+0.6
Outside	Lagging gain	+5.3
Complete shopping	Leading gain	+50.8
Partial shopping	Leading gain	+20.8
Full convenience	Countertrend gain	+9.6
Minimum convenience/hamlet	Countertrend gain	+8.7
Transaction-field class		
Urban core		
Large	Lagging loss	−83.8
Medium	Countertrend loss	−12.8
Small	Countertrend loss	−3.6
Primary labor field		
Large	Leading gain	+8.5
Medium	Leading gain	+14.4
Small	Leading gain	+27.0
Secondary labor field		
Large	Leading gain	+5.0
Medium	Leading gain	+10.5
Small	Leading gain	+17.2
Outside core-oriented fields	Countertrend gain	+17.3

The Developmental Signature

We have seen that the problem-solving sequences of urban-system development have given to each epoch a special signature. In each period, the obtrusive problems and innovational responses have fashioned a reorganization of the urban system typical of that time. Thus, the colonial period was most heavily absorbed with access problems that called forth imitative growth responses. The pre–Civil War period was dominated by the development of farm machinery, the river steamboat, and the early iron horse. The post–Civil War period was dominated by steel, the national railway system, the steam engine as universal prime mover; the initiation of food, apparel, and machine tool industries; and the beginnings of scientific management. The pre–World War II period was dominated by the development of the automobile, petroleum, electric power, telephone (and radio) communications, and the increasing prominence of agricultural and industrial science.

All of part two constructs the developmental profile of the study period, so a final characterization of this epoch's signature is properly deferred until this task is complete. However, it is useful here to acquire a preliminary image of the period's change patterns in manufacturing. It will help us to order the course of inquiry in the two chapters to come.

Such a preliminary image is given by the list of rapidly growing products and industrial sectors. The product picture is revealed by a pair of articles that cover the first two decades of the study period.[12] An analysis of these lists yields a startling insight. About three-fourths of the products listed in the rapid-gainer category were processed materials. Most of these were chemical products: primary chemicals, like benzine; further processed chemical materials, like synthetic fibers and plastics; and drugs. Also on the list were nonferrous primary metals and a long list of other materials like plywood, glass, cement, paper, and the like. The next longest list was household appliances: such items as freezers, dryers, air conditioners, disposals, dishwashers, washing machines, televisions, phonographs, and home power tools. Also significant were products in the transportation equipment field (aircraft, truck trailers, tractors, and diesel locomotives—a defensive adaptation); construction, mining and industrial machinery; and electric power turbines. One can detect the beginnings of the currently exploding electronics field.

All the same, lists of products give no weighting in terms of output or employment. If we turn to the three-digit manufacturing industries in the Standard Industrial Classification and examine the most rapidly growing sectors (in terms of employment) the materials- and household-oriented industries show up plainly once more. Although the materials product list was far longer than the household appliance list, employment in these two broad categories was about equal. But we encounter another important aspect of the developmental profile not so apparent in the product lists. (In part this is because the lists do not include the last decade of the study period.) Prominent among the rapidly growing industry sectors were those manufacturing activities best characterized as serving information processes. These include office machinery; communications equipment; professional, scientific and control equipment; and aircraft.

Thus, the developmental signature of the study period within manufacturing was marked by proliferating materials products, the mechanization of households tasks, the production of information-processing artifacts and materials, and the continued expansion of transportation equipment manufacture. The stage is now set to examine individual manufacturing sectors so that the developmental factors modifying patterns of change can be selectively elaborated. We will begin with the material-processing sectors.

Notes

1. You will recall that this differentiation between imitative innovations and creative developments is strained in most operating contexts. One may indeed encounter adaptations that are "pure" copies, but most require at least some creative modifications when taken out of one operating environment and applied in another. In any realistic instance, we encounter a mixture of imitative and creative adaptation and the proportions may cover the entire spectrum from pure mimicry to pure invention. Still, the development of concepts requires us to be clear about this distinction.

2. For example, although responding to a different stimulus, an improvement in management processes might reveal an unsuspected opportunity for improving the production process subject to its control. (It should be understood that opportunities are merely chances to carry problem solutions to an unanticipated level.)

The reason any type of problem may be the initial point of problem perception within an enterprise system rests on the fact that intersystem relationships commonly exist between that system and others (external to it) at every level of system behavior. Consequently, changes in the behavior of externally linked systems can be the source of problem stimuli, and such stimuli can have an effect at any level of behavior. This is why there is no hope of developing a successful stage theory of social change outside of the growth model. True, development may involve adaptations of a limited number of general types, but their evolutionary sequences cannot be determined in advance.

3. One can advance a number of reasons for this extended adolescence. Normal lag factors in the spread of parent-region technologies undoubtedly played some role. American populations were much more dispersed in space than in England, so that market concentrations representing essential thresholds of scale economies were less common. The English textile manufacturers maintained a machinery monopoly for a number of years. But the evidence suggests that the most important reason had to do with the U.S. shortages of labor and capital. The difficulties inherent in changing the ways of doing things were not willingly addressed when there remained abundant opportunities for gain through simple growth. Households expended their capital-accumulating energies by claiming virgin land through settlement. Colonial enterprises had ample opportunities to reinvest their capital through the expansion of traditional mercantile functions. Canal and turnpike investments claimed priority in a commercially oriented economy.

4. It is interesting to notice an important reason New England proved to be the locus of this earliest form of modern manufacturing. These early establishments were started by the Boston commercial interests because their more limited access to the transmontaine region left them with less profitable outlets for their accumulated capital than the Middle Atlantic merchants had.

5. A more complete historical narrative could point to other developmental initiatives as well. For example, it was during this period that the shipbuilding industry developed the famous clipper ship that cut three months off the trip to California around the Horn. However, this was a development within the traditional technology of the sail and enjoyed an amazingly brief success before the British developed the machine screw application of steam power to ocean ships. It turned out that this false turn, so to speak, was one factor that caused the United States to lose permanently its early prominent position as a commercial maritime power.

6. The usual historical accounts of this experience emphasize the problem associated with monopoly and industrial power (remember the trusts and "robber barons"?). But one can see that this was a logical adaptation to a compelling set of type-four management problems. The subsequent trust-busting era was directed at higher order, social control problems that only emerged as a consequence of successful problem-solving efforts to control unstable markets.

7. The Burroughs adding machine in 1894, the Underwood typewriter in 1895, the first dictating machine in 1887, the A. B. Dick mimeograph in 1887, the cash register in 1884, the first time-registers in 1892, the first coin counter in 1902.

8. This cut the time for assembling an automobile from 12 hours to an hour and a half. By 1920 the method had spread to the appliance, electrical equipment, food-processing, and cigarette industries.

9. The abbreviated description of the historical shifts presented in this chapter can be elaborated further by consulting Lampard's work in part II of Perloff and coauthors (1960).

10. See Carter, 1970.

11. A gentle reminder is worth repeating. We are concentrating here on the competitive shift component (R_{ij}). Were we to construct a map like map II-6 that represented the total differential shift (D_{ij}) (where the mix effect (K_{ij}) and competitive effect (R_{ij}) are netted), the picture would be quite different. The Ohio and Michigan urban regions, which show up as negative shifts in map II-7, would show up as net positive shifts. That extended midlatitude belt of gains in the South would disappear (under the impact of negative mix effects), save for the Piedmont and Cumberland concentrations.

12. Paradiso and Hirt (1953), Hirt (1961).

10

The Materials Industries

Given the urban system's transaction structure, the ideal order of discussion would follow process chains from raw materials to final uses. However, the Standard Industrial Classification was never formed to represent process or network relationships. As a consequence, when viewed from the perspective of this study, many of the manufacturing categories are heterogeneous in the extreme. Material-processing industries are often lumped in the same classifications with fabricating industries, for example.[1]

Still it is helpful to trace transaction networks to the extent possible. Consider, first, the material-processing activities that tend to be only one or two process stages removed from their primary resource roots. A rough characterization of the materials sectors includes food, textiles (except knitting mill products), lumber and wood, chemicals, paper, petroleum refining, glass, cement, and primary metals. During the study period, these sectors accounted for just over one-third of all manufacturing employment, with fabricated manufactures just under two-thirds. In spite of the spectacular growth of some materials during this time (paper, cement, nonferrous metals, synthetic fibers, drugs), the material-processing share of total manufacturing employment decreased relative to fabricating-processing employment. This appears to reflect the fact that the developing materials-processing technologies were more labor saving than the developing fabricating technologies.

Food Products

The food industry is, of course, the foremost material-processing industry, both in terms of its primacy in history and in the life process. It is precisely here that society first encountered problems requiring technology and social organization for solution. The fundamental nature of food sector problems has not changed from the earliest time to the present; namely, (1) how to render food suitable for digestion and palatable to human taste, and (2) how to preserve inherently perishable commodities so that they can be stored in time and transported in space. Without the latter, the time and space arbitrage essential for an urbanized organization of society is impossible.

Like all chemical processes, the preservation and preparation of foods were strictly empirical crafts prior to the nineteenth century. Animals were butchered. Grains were ground into flour and meal. To preserve them, foods were cooked, dried, salted, fermented, pickled, or cooled. Most of these processes were carried out on the farm or in the household; and, as late as the beginning of the twentieth century, the farm and household were still coincident entities for close to two-thirds of the population.

Food processing as a distinct industry was slow to develop. As the nineteenth century brought an increasingly industrialized and urbanized society, the farm household became either an urban household or an urbanized one. The transaction paths linking farms to household final demand multiplied. We have seen how the development of ice refrigeration and low-pressure, low-temperature canning made possible the mid-century development of the meat packing and canning industries. The end of the nineteenth century and the beginning of the twentieth brought the development of the first ready-to-eat breakfast cereals, commercial baking, artificial ice making, and pasteurization—processes making it possible to increase the temporal and spatial span of urbanized food transactions. Food processing began to move off the farm and out of the household.

Three characteristics marked the twentieth century developments. First, agricultural and industrial specialization created an almost totally urbanized economy. Food necessarily entered a more extended transaction chain. Second, scientific chemistry provided the knowledge base for vastly improving techniques of food preservation and for preparing food in new forms. Third, chemistry was part of the technological base for freeing household labor, as it had previously been for the worker in the field and factory. The differentiated food industry came into its own. Much has been made in this volume of the access problems that were displaced by transport and communication developments. These developments could never have brought about such dramatic urban reorganizations without the food preservation developments of scientific chemistry and the industrialization of food processing. Just two generations ago people ate mostly unprocessed or lightly processed foods, and they ate at home. Now more than 50 percent of the national diet consists of foods prepared outside the home.

The food-processing developments of the study period were a continuation of these trends. A major limitation of earlier food preservation techniques was the fact that they changed the taste and texture of foods. High-pressure and high-temperature canning in the early 1900s helped this, but it was not until the study period that the major science-based changes emerged. There was the development of aseptic canning in 1949. There were a host of new drying techniques—vacuum drying, freeze drying, and spray drying. Frozen foods, still experimental in the 1930s, came to full development. Tenderizing and aging agents inhibited the biochemical process of rigor mortis in meats. Methods for refining, extracting, and hydrogenating vegetable oils emerged. There were a host of chemical additives such as modified starches, emulsifiers, antioxidants, perservatives, flavors, colors, and vitamins. Vast improvements were made in the shelf life of foods, in their transportability, and in the retention of natural flavors. There were years during the study period when as many as 5,000 new food products were put on the market (although, on the average, only 10 percent survived).

This developmental history can be read into the empirical shift record being presented. If we examine the nine three-digit subsectors of food manufacturing, "canning and preserving" was the runaway leader in the rapid-growth category.[2] It was followed by the miscellaneous foods category (itself heavily weighted with canned and frozen seafoods, and a host of specialty foods like coffee, gelatin, peanut butter, potato chips, and the like). We can see the regionally differentiating effects of these developments most clearly if we examine each subsector in turn.

Explaining Shift Patterns

Meat packing was the largest of food products industries in terms of employment. It received three-fourths of its inputs from agriculture and contributed 90 percent of its output to final demand. Thus, access to both suppliers and markets would appear to be important. This was reflected in the historic pattern of the industry laid down when meat packing began to serve national markets following the Civil War. The industry concentrated in Chicago and St. Louis, with a later development in Kansas City. These were intermediate, rail-based, nodal positions between the largest market concentrations in the East and the prominent stock raising activities in the Plains and North Central regions. This historical pattern was still largely in place in 1940.

This distribution was radically altered during the study period by above-average shifts relative to the sector's 1940 employment base. Roughly 80 percent of the competitive losses in meat processing were in the North Central urban regions, while close to 90 percent of the gains were in the Southeast and South Central regions.

This is partly explained by the changes in the agricultural process technologies that shifted the geographic distribution of meat animal agriculture, as already discussed in chapter 8. There we saw that developments in feed grain culture in the Plains, and the conversion of Southeastern farms from row to cover cropping, increased the relative supply of meat animals in these areas. In the Southeast this was dramatically augmented by the newly differentiated poultry and egg production activities. The development of dispersed commercial feedlots provided larger quantities of process-ready animals in regionally distributed fields. The shift away from multiple-enterprise farming in the North Central regions further reduced the relative supply of animals nearest to the historical meat packing centers.

At the same time that the regional distribution of meat supplies was shifting, the final market was changing shape. We have already documented the southern and western trends on a national scale; both market and meat supply factors proved to work in the same direction. We have also noted the increased relative importance of medium-sized and spatially distributed core centers, along with the growing significance of hinterland, complete shopping, trade centers. This more diffused articulation of important market channels also served to weaken the advantage of the historical meat packing centers.

Of course, the automobile and truck redefined transport networks in a way coincident with these market shifts, but the truck also served to change the effective supply and distribution networks of the packing industry. The highly concentrated nodal production sites corresponding to the "topo-logic" of the rail network were no longer mandated by a more highly connected network. A larger number of regionally distributed nodal options became available. The relative demise of the older centers was hastened by a change in the transport rate ratio between feed grains and livestock favoring the feed grains.

Finally, all of this took place at a time when the Chicago and St. Louis plants were not only becoming obsolescent, but were wearing out as well. It took place at a time when the changing economic base of these large metropolitan centers was generating large external diseconomies for the packers. It no longer made sense to have cattle yards in the middle of a metropolitan center. (During the initial period of regional dispersal, there was also some chasing of cheaper wages, but the wage differential was rapidly nullified.)

Relative to other sectors, the processing of dairy products experienced only moderate interregional competitive shifts. On a broad regional basis the shifts corresponded pretty much to the shifts in dairy farm outputs discussed in chapter 8, and for essentially the same reasons. There were minor variations. The Great Lakes dairy farming region increased its relative position in processed dairy products more than in farm-based fluid milk production because of its more efficient reach for external butter and cheese markets. Also, the Mountain region made disproportionate gains in dairy processing relative to the Pacific Coast regions because the region became a processed-product specialist vis-à-vis the Pacific Coast markets in a similar manner. New England and the Middle Atlantic regions experienced relative declines, largely by virtue of their declining shares of final demand.

The canning and preserving subsector of the food industry made spectacular gains in employment. When combined with "miscellaneous food products," it experienced interregional shifts approximately three times as great (relative to the initial-period employment base) as all other food-processing subsectors. Since canning is primarily associated with vegetable and fruit agriculture, this is not surprising. We have already seen how radically agricultural production of these commodities has shifted. As one would expect, more than half of the relative gains came in the Pacific and Mountain urban regions in association with the expansion of their irrigated vegetable culture. A good part of the balance was in Florida. New England and the Middle Atlantic urban regions along with the Old South experienced the greatest competitive losses.

On a broad regional basis, the North Central urban regions just about held their own, but three clusters appeared to make strong competitive gains: (1) Sioux City, Sioux Falls, Fort Dodge, and Lincoln; (2) Davenport, Dubuque, Rockford, and Madison; and (3) Grand Rapids and Lansing. In the case of the first two this involved canning such things as sweet corn, snap beans, peas, and vegetable- and meat-based soups. These are vegetable crops that find the California and Southern climates too hot. They do well in many of the valleys of smaller rivers tributary to the Mississippi and Missouri rivers. In the case of the east coast of Lake Michigan, fruit canning is the main activity. This is clearly associated with the moderating effect of the lake on the climate.

These three clusters of urban regions (plus a few near neighbors) also appear to represent a movement of traditional North Central canning activities away from the old rail centers (Minneapolis, Des Moines, Kansas City, St. Louis, Chicago, and Indianapolis) under the influence of an access network that has been redefined by truck transport. In addition, a substantial amount of vertical integration of vegetable and fruit agriculture with canning and preserving has taken place. Food-processor-owned farms, and contract growing for the canning firms, created a new symbiosis between processor and agricultural producer that fostered the regional specialization of both.

The reorientation of miscellaneous food product manufacturing was much like shifts in canning and preserving because a very large part of that category consists of the canning of fish products. Naturally Florida and the Pacific Coast had the greatest competitive gains, and the North Atlantic coastal centers experienced the greatest relative losses (recall the discussion in chapter 8 of fishing employment shifts).

In terms of employment, the grain mill products subsector was among the smallest of the food industries. In broad regional terms, its spatial distribution was relatively stable with below-average relative shifts. The competitive shifts are largely explained by two factors. The East North Central urban regions captured most of the competitive gains, and these were largely attributable to the increasing importance of wet-corn milling that produces the important corn starches, sugars, and oils. The other significant trend was the increased consumption orientation of the feed mills that serve livestock and poultry producers, which improved the competitive position of prepared food products in the Plains and West Central urban regions (both north and south).

Chemical and engineering advances in the refining and hydrogenation of vegetable oils dramatically increased the importance of the oil products subsector of food manufacturing, with the East North Central urban regions getting the bulk of the gain (because of the soybean and corn oil developments) and California getting most of the balance (because of the big relative gains in cottonseed production previously noted). It is not too surprising that the old peanut and cottonseed producing areas in the Southeast suffered the greatest relative declines.

The remaining food manufacturing sectors—bakery, confectionary, and beverage products—are notoriously oriented to final demand. (Add to this some categories of miscellaneous food products like potato chips, manufactured ice, and the like.) The shifts in food manufacturing in these areas tended to correspond closely to the interregional shifts in population. In broad regional terms, the New England, Middle Atlantic, and North Central urban regions tended to experience competitive losses while the South and West experienced gains.

Summary of Regional Shifts

Begin with the shift profile of plate II-5. The first impression is of the widespread character of competitive gains in food manufacturing employment, as was the case with manufacturing employment generally. About three-fourths of all counties displayed competitive gains (table II-6). Ninety percent of these had been previously unspecialized. These were divided almost equally between those representing leading (or countertrend) gains and those registering lagging gains. However, the 42 percent of all counties that experienced leading gains accounted for almost three-fourths of the all-region competitive gains (table II-7). Of the one-fourth of all counties experiencing losses, two-thirds recorded strong losses. Both leading and lagging losses contributed proportionately to the all-region negative shifts.

The number of counties specialized in food manufacturing was greater than all other manufacturing categories except wood products; and about three times as many of these experienced competitive gains as was true for total manufacturing. So, although food products manufacturing experienced a widespread redistribution of activities, traditional production areas retained more competitive strength than most other manufacturing categories.

It is clear that the competitive loss counties were disproportionately located in the New England, Middle Atlantic, and North Central regions. There was also a concentration running down the eastern edge of the Plains. Another set ran along the Gulf Coast from Mobile to Houston. Apart from scattered counties, competitive gains prevailed everywhere else. Nevertheless, those counties experiencing leading gains (and accounting for three-fourths of total gains) were more restricted in their distribution. The largest cluster was in the new southern Manufacturing Belt (identified in chapter 9) except for the eastern portion dominated by textiles. Interestingly enough, prominent gaining counties were scattered throughout the Old Manufacturing Belt, with two principal clusters—in the area between Minneapolis and Kansas City, and in the area between Chicago and Minneapolis and along the eastern edge of Lake Michigan. California, central Florida, and the Salt and Columbia river basins also had identifiable concentrations.[3]

Plate II-5 provides pattern but no dimension. Table II-21 gives a clear picture of where these gains and losses were concentrated at 171-urban-region scale.[4] Twelve regions accounted for 75 percent of the total negative shifts. New York, Chicago, Boston, and St. Louis accounted for half. Though the gains were more widely distributed, thirty urban regions accounted for two-thirds of the gains while thirty-nine accounted for three-fourths.

TABLE II-21. Ranked food manufacturing employment competitive gains and losses for principal urban regions, 1940–70

Rank	Region number	Region	Competitive shift	Percent	Cumulative percent
		Gaining regions			
1	165	Los Angeles	+14,212	6.54	6.54
2	44	Atlanta	+13,045	6.00	12.54
3	167	Stockton	+10,495	4.83	17.37
4	152	Idaho Falls	+6,883	3.17	20.54
5	32	Tampa	+6,791	2.90	23.44
6	46	Memphis	+5,968	2.75	26.19
7	36	Miami	+5,586	2.57	28.76
8	23	Raleigh, N.C.	+5,561	2.56	31.32
9	119	Tulsa, Okla.	+5,520	2.54	33.86
10	45	Birmingham, Ala.	+5,191	2.39	36.25
11	117	Little Rock, Ark.	+4,387	2.02	38.27
12	25	Greensboro, etc. N.C.	+4,370	2.01	40.28
13	148	Denver	+4,185	1.93	42.21
14	171	San Francisco	+3,981	1.83	44.04
15	159	Boise City, Idaho	+3,972	1.83	45.87
16	16	Harrisburg, Penn.	+3,918	1.80	47.67
17	135	Jackson, Miss.	+3,276	1.51	49.18
18	26	Charlotte, N.C.	+3,266	1.50	50.68
19	127	Dallas	+3,142	1.45	52.13
20	19	Staunton, Va.	+3,097	1.43	53.56
21	35	Orlando, Florida	+3,070	1.41	54.97
22	79	Davenport, Iowa	+2,999	1.38	56.35
23	131	Texarkana, Tex.-Ark.	+2,975	1.37	57.72
24	81	Dubuque, Iowa	+2,955	1.36	59.08
25	47	Huntsville, Ala.	+2,932	1.35	60.43
26	142	San Antonio, Texas	+2,694	1.24	61.67
27	34	Jacksonville, Fla.	+2,652	1.22	62.99
28	1	Bangor, Maine	+2,522	1.16	64.15
29	48	Chattanooga, Tenn.	+2,498	1.15	65.30
30	118	Fort Smith, Ark.-Okla.	+2,410	1.11	66.41
31	162	Phoenix	2,366	1.09	67.50
32	156	Yakima, Wash.	+2,301	1.06	68.56
33	141	Houston	+2,297	1.06	69.62
34	83	Madison, Wisc.	+2,292	1.06	70.68
35	168	Sacramento, Calif.	+2,264	1.04	71.72
36	130	Tyler, Texas	+1,978	.91	72.63
37	116	Springfield, Mo.	+1,968	.91	73.54
38	99	Sioux Falls, S.D.	+1,956	.90	74.44
39	144	Brownsville, Texas	+1,797	.83	75.27

TABLE II-21. Ranked food manufacturing employment competitive gains and losses for principal urban regions, 1940–70 (*Continued*)

Rank	Region number	Region	Competitive shift	Percent	Cumulative percent
		Losing regions			
1	14	New York	–43,508	20.03	20.03
2	77	Chicago	–34,070	15.68	35.71
3	4	Boston	–18,711	8.61	44.32
4	114	St. Louis	–10,717	4.93	49.25
5	66	Pittsburgh	–10,566	4.86	54.11
6	111	Kansas City	–10,201	4.70	58.81
7	71	Detroit	–8,008	3.69	62.50
8	9	Buffalo, N.Y.	–6,824	3.14	65.64
9	15	Philadelphia	–5,498	2.53	68.17
10	68	Cleveland	–5,034	2.32	70.49
11	60	Indianapolis	–5,009	2.31	72.80
12	138	New Orleans	–4,179	1.95	74.75

There were four notable clusters. The most important was a group of urban regions at about thirty-five degrees south latitude extending from Raleigh in the East through Atlanta, Birmingham-Huntsville, Memphis, Little Rock, Tulsa, and Dallas; the second was a set of California regions extending from San Francisco through Phoenix; the third comprised the four urban regions of peninsular Florida; the fourth was a set of regions in the Snake River Valley extending from Idaho Falls to Portland. There were a few others: Denver was prominent within the Mountain States; Houston and San Antonio in southern Texas; and Bangor in Maine.

There were also four smaller clusters that show up in the Old Manufacturing Belt. They only accounted for 17 percent of the competitive gains (at 171-urban-region scale) in a broad area that also accounted for 90 percent of the competitive losses. However, they illustrate changes taking place in the logic of the transactions network. Much of the earlier production had been attached to highly nodal railway cities. The competitive strength of the gaining clusters seems clearly linked to the access advantages of truck transport. The first cluster embraces the Sioux City, Sioux Falls, Fort Dodge, and Lincoln urban regions just west of the older Minneapolis, Des Moines, Kansas City concentrations; the second involves Davenport, Rockford, Madison, Wausau, and Rochester between the older Chicago–Milwaukee and Minneapolis concentrations (this was by far the strongest competitive cluster in the Old Manufacturing Belt); the third includes Grand Rapids, Lansing, Fort Wayne, Lima, and South Bend between old Detroit, Cleveland, and Chicago concentrations; the fourth embraces the Harrisburg, Staunton, and Baltimore urban regions between the old Pittsburgh and New York–Philadelphia concentrations. In short, while the Old Manufacturing Belt was accounting for most of the competitive losses overall, the old metropolitan centers that had dominated production historically were double losers as production within the region was shifting to adjacent hinterland areas.

This aspect of the story can be enlarged upon by examining the urban-system characteristics of the shift patterns revealed by appendixes II-C and II-D. Given the nature of the network changes discussed, it is not surprising that counties identified with metropolitan centers accounted for all of the competitive losses in food manufacturing. Wholesale-retail centers accounted for one-sixth of the gain, but the bulk came outside higher order centers. Shopping center counties accounted for two-thirds of the gain, with complete shopping centers alone claiming half. The largest urban cores accounted for 90 percent of the competitive losses. Two-thirds of the gains came in the external transaction fields of the smallest urban regions or in fields outside core-center transaction fields. Still, there was stubborn strength in the urban cores. The medium and small urban cores retained more strength in food manufacturing than in manufacturing as a whole. Core centers of the wholesale-retail classification made significant gains in food manufacturing in the face of losses for total manufacturing. It was clearly the very large metropolitan centers that were the most disadvantaged by developments. This is also shown by the list of competitive losers in table II-21.

A good deal of this movement was associated with the decentralization and articulation of the total transaction network. (In a survey by the National Trucking Association in 1963, food processors put access to good highways and markets ahead of access to resources in selecting a location.) But an important part has to do with changes in the subsector mix of food production. For example, in the beverage sector, soft drinks gained substantially relative to beer and ale, and they tend to be produced and bottled in smaller, more localized markets. Again prepared feeds became a more important part of grain mill product manufacture, and those processes tended to be located in smaller centers than activities engaged in the preparation of food grains. Poultry dressing became a much larger proportion of meat processing and tended to be located in smaller centers than the national meat packers. The canning and freezing of fruits and vegetables was the big gainer, and these activities also tended to be located in smaller centers. Similarly, within the "confectionary and sugar" category, sugar refining was the rapid gainer. This activity favored locations remote from the big city confectionary concentrations.[5] Thus, subsector changes in mix contributed to the observed process of urban-system reorganization.

Now consider the combined regional effects of these food manufacturing subsector shifts. New England experienced a competitive loss in food manufacturing overall. Virtually every food product subsector contributed, although not dramatically. The big exception was the canning and preservation of fish, which displayed a marked countertrend gain. Still, relative declines in food manufacturing lagged behind declines in both total manufacturing and total employment. The Middle Atlantic regions accounted for 43 percent of the competitive losses. Every food manufacturing subsector contributed, although meat products, miscellaneous food products, and the bakery-beverage-confectionary products categories displayed quite modest declines. Again the food product losses lagged behind both manufacturing and total employment losses.

The North Central region accounted for 53 percent of the total losses, and there the losses led the declines in both total manufacturing and total employment. This was the region where the bulk of the food manufacturing specializations were located at the beginning of the period, and, clearly, it experienced a major restructuring under the effect of developments. Still, the picture was decidedly a mixed one, as five of the nine food product subsectors actually experienced competitive gains. The losses were dominated by two categories. This historical center of the meat-packing industry experienced 82 percent of the meat product competitive declines for the nation. The region also recorded 81 percent of the miscellaneous food product declines. The latter largely involved such things as leavening compounds; cocoa, coffee and tea products; condiments; and a variety of products made from purchased materials intermediate to the resource product stage. The losses recorded by these two sectors were three times as great as the combined gains of the five sectors that improved their competitive positions. The reasons should be clear from the commodity-level discussions.

In contrast, the nation's North Central food basket accounted for all of the competitive gains in grain mill products. Almost four-fifths of that gain was in the Corn Belt heartland of the East North Central region and was heavily linked to the growing importance of wet-corn milling. Another significant factor was the growing importance of prepared breakfast cereals. The region claimed almost a fifth of the competitive gains in dairy products—a testament to the staying power of the Old Dairy Belt. It also claimed more than a fifth of the competitive gains in canning and preserving. Some of this was associated with the fruit processing in western Michigan, but the largest portion appears to have been mixed vegetable and soup canning heavily concentrated in the urban-region cluster between Chicago and Minneapolis.

We might take note of an additional explanatory factor. The competitive declines in food manufacturing employment experienced by all of the Old Manufacturing Belt regions thus far discussed were undoubtedly exaggerated by a negative subsector mix effect. With the exception of beverages, all of the food processing activities oriented to the urban market were also the slow growth activities of the period. Historically, these were largely concentrated in the urban Northeast, hence the negative subsector mix effect.

Almost two-thirds of the competitive gains in food manufacturing came in the South—from the Atlantic coast to the Southern Plains. Leading the parade was meat processing with 93 percent of nationwide competitive gains. The market-oriented dairy, bakery, beverage, confectionary, and miscellaneous food activities followed with lesser shares of the total gain. In contrast, grain mill and oil products were countertrend decliners for supply-side reasons explained earlier. Canning and preserving also declined in the Old South but not in Florida or the South Central portions. Indeed, Florida experienced marked competitive gains—again, for obvious reasons. Food manufacturing tended to lead total manufacturing and total employment gains in the Southeast, although not in the Southern Plains.

California and the Mountain States accounted for about one-third of food manufacturing competitive gains—although these tended to lag behind gains in total manufacturing employment and total employment. Three-fourths of the competitive gains in California were associated with urban-market-oriented food products. The balance was in canning and preserving activities oriented to agricultural production in the San Joaquin and Imperial valleys. There were relative declines in meat, dairy, and grain mill products. The Mountain region displayed a different configuration. It also experienced important gains in canning and preserving tied to irrigated fruit and vegetable crops in the Colorado, Snake, Columbia, and Willamette valleys. However, the refining of beet sugar was a major factor, and the region recorded almost one-fourth of the nationwide competitive gains in dairy products manufacture. (We earlier noted that vis-à-vis the coast, it was emerging as a dairy supply region.)

All of these food manufacturing developments brought about major changes in the industry's spatial distribution. At the beginning of the period, twenty-seven specialized urban regions in the North Central region dominated manufactured food production. (The five principal specialists were Chicago, Kansas City, Minneapolis, St. Louis, and Milwaukee.) In contrast, there were only five specialized regions in the eastern end of the Old Manufacturing Belt, five in the Southeast (all Gulf Coast except Dallas) and seven on the Pacific Coast. By the end of the period, twenty-three previously unspecialized urban regions had become new food manufacturing specialists in the South, as had four more in the Mountain regions. However, the old North Central food basket still predominated. Although three regions lost their specialized status during the period (Indianapolis, Muncie, and Columbus), eleven new ones were added. Most of the regions that lost food manufacturing specializations during the period were elsewhere (Norfolk, Mobile, Dallas, San Diego, Sacramento, and Seattle).

In sum, the shifts in food manufacturing employment resulted from a mixed set of developmental factors. Part of the interregional shift stemmed from underlying shifts in agricultural resource inputs. We saw that shifts in the availability of meat animals, oil crops, fruits, and vegetables were particularly important. There were significant shifts in urban settlement patterns that carried along urban-market-oriented food processes. These increased the significance of small- and medium-sized urban regions, their secondary transaction fields, and the shopping trade centers spread throughout the field of the urban system. A substantial increase in the urban population accentuated the importance of food processing in the transaction net of manufactured commodities. This was largely a result of the change in transport access that attended the development of the automobile, truck, and highway. The more articulated access network also facilitated the redistribution of food-processing activities generated by the changing settlement patterns and agricultural base.

Critical to the whole process was the development of canning and preserving, which probably contributed as much to liberating transport and transaction constraints in the total economy as the transport improvements themselves. Indeed, the shifts in settlement patterns conventionally attributed to motor vehicle transport would have been nowhere near as great were it not for the tremendous access-improving characteristics of modern food-processing developments.

Finally, there were important shifts of activities off of the farm (like the processing of dairy, poultry, and egg products) and out of the household (like the preparation of baked goods, beverages, breakfast cereals, and sandwich materials) that had a definite effect on the redistribution of food processing. All of these developments both inside and outside food manufacturing were at work. The effects were combinatorial. They were symbiotic, mutually causative, and multiplicative in nature, rather than linear and additive.

Textiles

The textile story is a much simpler one to tell. The interregional shift of the textile industry was almost totally a shift from the historical New England and Middle Atlantic concentrations into the Southeast. It began in the nineteenth century, but only became substantial in the first part of twentieth. At the beginning of the study period, 55 percent of textile employment was still in the industry's historical stronghold. But by the end of the period, 70 percent was in the Southeast, with the greatest concentration in the Piedmont region.

Explaining Shift Patterns

The explanatory factors are correspondingly simple because the component subsectors were much less heterogeneous. Since the largest single input to textiles came from cotton agriculture, which was predominantly southeastern when the shift got underway, there was much early talk about textiles moving to cotton. Miernyk (1952) conclusively established that this was not the case and that textile manufacturing initially moved to the cheap labor associated with the South's peculiar version of the English enclosure movement. As late as 1954, 53 percent of textile manufacturing costs were labor costs, the highest of any manufacturing sector. In my own work (Perloff and coauthors, 1960), these tendencies were summarized as follows:

> Baled cotton has a very high value per unit of weight and undergoes little weight-loss in processing. Thus, interregional differences in transfer costs on both inputs and products are very small compared to the interregional differences in labor costs. The dramatic shift in location is, therefore, a result of a change in each region's access to labor inputs. Over the years New England has grown into a relatively advanced industrial region. Accompanying this have been increased demands upon the labor force, increased needs for special labor skills, and widespread unionization. All of these things tended to raise the level of wages. Over most of the period, the labor-intensive cotton-tobacco economy in the Southeast built up a large population. As this agricultural system broke down, a large supply of "low-wage," relatively immobile labor was created. Since the interregional wage differences were sizable, and labor costs are important in the textile industry, the resulting movement into the Southeast is not surprising (p. 419).

Thus, the differential in labor costs was the main explanation for the movement of cotton textiles into the South. Yet, more than half of the employment was still in the older centers in 1940. This was partly a consequence of a natural time lag, further extended by the depression experience. The industry had had insufficient time to respond fully to differential advantages. But there were large segments of the industry that still clung to northeastern locations for more substantive reasons.

Three reasons appear to have been predominant. First, New England held onto the woolen mills largely because most wool is imported and Boston was established early as the nation's principal wool market. Add to this fact that 60 percent of the weight of greasy wool is lost in scouring, that New England mills experienced fewer climatic moisture differentials (important for keeping threads from breaking in the loom), and that fabrics went through frequent pattern changes in response to the demands of the nearby New York apparel centers. Second, knitted textiles tended to remain where they were partly because of a greater association with woolen fibers and partly because knitting technology had not yet lent itself as readily to the use of unskilled labor. Third, during the first part of the century, the freight rate structure still favored the movement of raw materials into the old industrial areas and the movement of finished products out to national markets. During the study period, the factors that held these components in the Northeast largely disappeared with the consequence that the industry became even more localized in the Piedmont South. (Table II-3 indicates that, in the face of a 33 percent decrease in the weighted index of industrial localization, textile manufacturing experienced a 10 percent increase in its index.)

As we move into the study period, the large wage rate differential between the Northeast and the Southeast narrowed substantially. (I have been told by industry sources that there are now places in the textile South where the wage rates are actually higher.) Rising relative wage rates, combined with the competition from foreign textiles, force the leading firms into major labor-saving developments (for example, water and air-jet shuttles). The success of these labor productivity adaptations is reflected in the fact that the labor coefficient for the textile industry was halved between 1939 and 1961 (Carter, 1970). Total employment in the textile industry actually declined 12 percent at a time when output more than doubled. Curiously, this tended to strengthen the industry's position in the South. The new technology required plants of substantially greater scale for which the traditional production centers of the North were poorly suited.

Another explanatory factor was even more important. Humidity and temperature conditions had always been an important factor associated with shutdowns occasioned by breaking threads and yarn. The advent of air conditioning substantially improved productivity on this score and reduced the relative disadvantage of the South. There was a set of changes that mitigated the earlier access advantages of the major northeastern centers. The development of rapid truck transport and the articulated highway system substantially diminished the market location advantages of the Middle Atlantic States. Combine this with the fact that the market itself experienced major shifts to the South and West. Communications developments and the automation of pattern controls further reduced the advantage of the traditional centers. Communications plus commercial and general aviation made it possible to coordinate production, management, and manufacturing functions in different locations.

Perhaps the major change in the industry came as a result of modern scientific chemistry. All of the synthetic fibers except rayon emerged during the study period. In addition, the advent of new dyes and other finishing treatments has created fabrics that are washable, permanently creased, wrinkle resistant, waterproof, soil resistant, and flame retardant. These qualitative changes in durability, comfort, texture, style, and maintenance constituted the first major product changes since the advent of the industry. These developments also tended to reinforce Southeastern location of the industry in several ways. The new synthetics (for example, nylon, acrylan, Orlon, Dynel, and Dacron) were largely derived from petroleum-based chemical intermediates (in contrast to rayon, which was based on wood cellulose). The production of these intermediates tended to favor raw material sites in the Texas–Gulf Coast region, but the production of synthetic fibers themselves tended to be oriented more to the fiber-market regions.[6] This brought into the region what has become the major source of the industry's material inputs. Second, this innovative process was best carried out in what was then becoming the new textile heartland where management, technicians, and specialized industry services were readily available. Third, these developments created additional stages of textile processing (for example, the new finishing operations) so that the subsector, intra-industry transfers increased measurably (in an amount equivalent to approximately one-fourth of the changes in input–output coefficients experienced by the industry in the first two decades). Finally, the producers of textile machinery began to search out southern locations. In short, a set of regionally localized, external-scale economies emerged during the study period. Symbiotic, multistage transaction linkages came to share a common field of operations in the Piedmont.

Summary of Regional Shifts

The revealed shift patterns were correspondingly unambiguous. The changes were overwhelmingly associated with those counties in plate II-6 that were already specialized in textile manufacturing. One hundred and sixty-one specialized counties, mostly in the Piedmont, experienced leading competitive gains. This handful of counties accounted for two-thirds of all competitive gains. At the same time, 172 specialized counties, mostly in the New England and Middle Atlantic regions, experienced leading competitive losses. This small group accounted for 86 percent of all competitive losses. There was a group of specialized textile counties, mostly in the Nashville, Huntsville, Birmingham, and Atlanta urban regions, that experienced leading losses as well. This reflects the fact that the textile industry actually increased its localization within the Southeast itself. This is a manifestation of the substantial scale economies of the large mills and of the obsolescence of many of the smaller mills that were first established in the South.

Most of the blue counties representing competitive gains (89 percent of all counties) make only a trivial quantitative contribution to the total shift. At urban-region scale, four regions accounted for half of all competitive gains (Charlotte, Greensboro, Greenville, and Chattanooga). Six more (Raleigh, Roanoke, Florence, Ashville, Augusta, and Atlanta) brought the proportion above 75 percent. The Southeast as a whole accounted for more than 95 percent of the gains. The only urban region outside the South that claimed more than half of one percent of the total shift was Los Angeles. This appears to be a reflection of (1) southern California's ready access to local cotton agriculture, (2) the availability of cheap Mexican labor, and (3) the West Coast's semi-independent nation status. All of these shifts left the geographical configuration formed by textile specialization little altered.

A few closing comments about the urban-system characteristics of these shifts are in order. The higher order trade centers in the core counties accounted for all of the competitive losses. (These were countertrend losses for the wholesale-retail centers and lagging losses for the large metropolitan centers.) Small wholesale-retail and shopping centers outside urban cores accounted for 82 percent of the competitive gains and were heavily concentrated in the primary and secondary transaction fields of the smallest urban cores. The strategic complete shopping centers accounted for more than half of the gains (see appendixes II-C, II-D, II-I, II-J, and II-K and text tables II-8 and II-9). This change in urban-system patterns was partly a reflection of the older urban location patterns in the Northeast giving way to the newer patterns of the Southeast.

Lumber and Wood Products

The lumber and wood products industries are an important and traditional materials sector. For detailed discussion of the shifts exhibited by this industry, the reader is referred to the resource sectors in chapter 9.

Chemicals

The chemical industries are as heterogeneous and complex in nature as agriculture and the food industries, and they experienced as dynamic a period of structural change. If told in detail, the story would be incredibly complex. Even when the industry is subdivided into subsectors (like organic, inorganic, drugs, cleaning compounds, plastics, fertilizers, and so forth), we are still dealing with complex and heterogeneous bundles of processes and commodities. Take the case of synthetic fibers. There are today seventeen man-made fibers, but within each of the seventeen main types there are up to several thousand variations. The 3-M Company, a firm specializing in chemical coating and adhesive products, makes 45,000 products. Process linkages can be extraordinarily diverse and systemic in nature. A single inorganic chemical intermediate like calcium fluoride is used in the production of such diverse products as aluminum, refrigerant gases, aerosol propellants, dentifrice additives, and atomic reactor fuels. A single organic chemical may be absorbed into a variety of agricultural chemicals, paints, pharmaceuticals, plastic intermediates, synthetic fibers, and synthetic rubber. The degree to which transaction linkages like these have been changed by scientific chemistry is astounding, and the rates of change phenomenal. For example, of the major synthetic plastics, only rayon and synthetic rubber were in commercial production at the beginning of our study period, and these were still in their infancy.

The employment shifts in the chemical process industries are dimensional manifestations of these changing product and process relationships and can be satisfactorily explained only in these terms. Since we are dealing with a heterogeneous set of explanatory factors, perhaps we should try to sort some of these out before we turn to the total industry shift patterns. Given the structural and dynamic complexity of the experience, we are limited to assessing the most prominent changes with no assurance that something of critical importance might not have been overlooked.

Explaining Subsector Shift Patterns

Consider, first, the behavior of the component chemical sectors for the United States as a whole. Total chemical industry employment more than doubled during the study period (+135.7 percent), an ample reflection of the growing relative importance of chemical materials. The rate of gain would have been greater still except for the fact that the new science of chemical engineering generated enormous increases in labor productivity. (Increases in the value of the industry's output at constant prices were ten times larger than increases in employment.) The rapidly growing component sectors were plastics, detergents, agricultural chemicals, and drugs, in that order. The slow-growth sectors were the organic and inorganic chemical intermediates, paints, and miscellaneous chemical products.

More than a third of chemical industry employment was contributed by the subsector producing industrial organic chemicals (excluding plastic materials). This sector produces hundreds of organic chemical intermediates from wood, coal, and petroleum feedstocks. At the beginning of the period employment was most concentrated in the upper Appalachian coalfields and the petroleum-rich Gulf Coast region of Texas and Louisiana, with the greatest specializations being along the Gulf. Although a highly complex industry, the major effect of the changes is fairly clear. It had to do with the development of petrochemicals—to the point that close to 90 percent of organic chemicals are now produced from petroleum feedstocks. The production of industry-feeding organic intermediates proved to be most economical near the resource base. This is partly because the outputs form a tree network with branching paths (see chapter 2 in volume I) and partly because joint product relationships make vertical process combinations common. As a consequence, the Gulf Coast regions dominated the relative gains, and the old plants oriented to coal and the early northeastern oil and gas fields have accounted for most of the relative losses.

The plastics industry was spawned by organic chemicals but has come to be treated as a separate category. This sector has a split personality. Part of the activity is devoted to the production of the chemical intermediates that go into the production of plastic materials. They are predominantly based on petrochemicals and are, accordingly, added to the relative gains of the Gulf Coast region in inorganic chemicals.[7] In contrast, the production of synthetic textile fibers has tended to be oriented toward markets in the textile South.

Industrial inorganic chemical and fertilizer manufacture need to be discussed together. Because fertilizer production is oriented to agricultural markets, the specialized regions were in the Southeast and the Plains at the beginning of the period.[8] With its earlier reliance on intensive row cropping, the Southeast alone accounted for more than half of the total employment in the fertilizer industry.

Recalling the shifts in agricultural production and employment described in chapter 8, it is easy to anticipate the shifts in fertilizer production. About two-thirds of the competitive gains went to the Plains—about equally distributed north and south. A few Pacific and Mountain regions accounted for a quarter of the gain. The South accounted for roughly two-thirds of the loss. About a quarter of the loss was accounted for by the Corn Belt regions. This appears to be largely a result of the tremendous growth of soybean cropping—soybeans being legumes, which fix nitrogen in the soil, and thus reduce the relative demand for nitrogen fertilizers in that region.

The production of industrial inorganic chemicals is second only to industrial organics in importance. Here we are talking mainly about the mineral acids, alkalies, and salts (save for the industrial gases, which were a relatively small part of the total).

Superficially one might expect these industries to be oriented to their mineral industry sources. This is certainly true of alumina production. There is a large weight loss (two tons of bauxite yields one ton of alumina) so the expanding alumina production came along the Gulf Coast which had ready access to imported bauxite and the Mississippi River network of inland waterways. The impression of resource orientation is further strengthened when we observe that the regions that specialize in inorganic chemicals are in the South and West, presumably good sources of mineral materials.

However, superficial impressions can be misleading. Major industrial chemicals such as sulfuric acid, chlorine, and caustic soda tend, in fact, to be market oriented. The manufacture of sulfuric acid involves a weight-gaining process. It is produced in industrial quantities in forty-two of the continental states. The acid equivalent of crude sulfur is only about one-third of the weight of sulfuric acid. Both chlorine and caustic soda are produced by the electrolysis of salt solutions. With them there is no weight gain, but higher transport costs prevail on the finished product than in the case of salt.

But, bear in mind, the markets served are all intermediate industrial markets. Forty percent of the output of sulfuric acid goes to phosphate fertilizers and an additional 10 percent is used in producing ammonium sulfate, another fertilizer intermediate. Ten percent goes into petroleum refining processes. The balance goes into a wide variety of chemical and metal process industries. Chlorine and caustic soda are used in petrochemicals as well, but are also major inputs into the paper, textile, and food industries. Further, bear in mind that developments in chemical engineering have increased the scale of processing plants so that establishments for some commodities tend not to be as widely distributed in their intermediate market fields as at the beginning of the period.

Given these factors, it is not surprising that the Gulf Coast regions displayed competitive gains in inorganic chemicals. These not only represented expanding markets in petrochemicals, petroleum refining, and fertilizer production, but also a major source of sulfur and salt. Similarly, the Tampa and Miami regions in Florida represented a coincidence of growing fertilizer demand and phosphate mining. For similar reasons, the Gulf regions also displayed strong competitive gains in chlorine and caustic soda production.

Industrial inorganics also tended to register relative gains along the Ohio River Valley from Paducah to Louisville, an intermediate location with good access to both mineral sources and markets. The Middle Atlantic region—especially Philadelphia—strengthened its share of inorganic chemicals. These gains appear to have been dominated by industrial gases, inorganic dyes, and otherwise unclassified inorganics. It is likely of some relevance that, although this was the earliest and most prominent region of chemical manufacturing specialization, it was, at the beginning of the period, in a substantial deficit supply position with respect to inorganic chemicals. Localized gains in California and the Northern Mountains involved fertilizer and inorganic chemical gains.

Competitive losses in the inorganic sphere were prominent in the South Atlantic region (except Florida) as a result of the shifts in fertilizer production. The heaviest early concentration of inorganic production was in the East-North-Central regions, and this region tended to experience relative losses because of the other factors discussed. However, a part of this was an interregional shift, as the lower Ohio valley regions gained enough to partially offset the larger region's relative loss.

Lump the four remaining categories together (drugs, soap and detergents, paints, and miscellaneous chemicals). At the beginning of the period, the Old Manufacturing Belt plus California were the regions specializing in all of these chemical commodities. The production of detergents and paints is a mixing operation that tends to orient to markets. This also appears to be true of drugs and miscellaneous chemicals as a group, although drugs have shown a tendency to agglomerate along the Mid-Atlantic Coast where major medical and research centers abound. It is not surprising that these sectors were responsive to the market shifts southward and westward. The South has been a competitive gainer for all of these commodity groups. The West has gained in detergents and paints. The Great Lakes regions gained in miscellaneous chemicals (as the East's early dominance was weakened) because it still served a mixed industrial market near the nation's center of gravity.

A narrative explanation of this sort no more than scratches the surface of the dynamic changes in the chemical industries. Still, by emphasizing the sectors that dominated production (in terms of value, tonnage, and employment), some success has been achieved in pointing up the major factors. Now we must translate this into a suggestive account of the observed shifts.

Summary of Regional Shifts

Begin with color plate II-9. Widespread competitive gains continued to be characteristic (80 percent of all counties). Even so, only a little more than a third of all counties displayed leading gains, far less than most other manufacturing sectors. One-third accounted for substantially more than half of all competitive gains. Characteristically, 72 percent of the specialized counties experienced competitive losses and 87 percent of the unspecialized counties experienced competitive gains. Counties that were specialized at the beginning of the period were most heavily concentrated in the eastern end of the Old Manufacturing Belt, in the coal regions of Appalachia, and along the Deep South sandy plain. The strongest specializations were in the New York and Philadelphia urban regions, and in the Cincinnati, Huntington, Roanoke, Bristol, and Asheville regions of the Appalachian coal country. There were also metropolitan concentrations in Chicago, Cleveland, and St. Louis.

It develops that, at urban-region scale, only twenty-five urban regions (15 percent of the total) account for 80 percent of all competitive gains, and twenty-two urban regions account for 80 percent of the losses.

It is not surprising that the largest portion of the competitive gains (30 percent) came in the Gulf Coast urban regions, extending from Houston to Pensacola. Houston alone accounted for 15 percent, and New Orleans and Beaumont joined it in the top five regions. This experience was clearly dominated by organic industrial petrochemicals and salt-and-sulfur-based inorganic chemicals. The region was favored by both expanding markets and raw materials sources. In drugs, soaps and detergents, paint, and miscellaneous chemicals, it made moderate gains, as these sectors responded to market shifts. But the big gainer was organic petrochemicals. The corresponding census region accounted for roughly 90 percent of all competitive gains in organics during the study period, as well as a major portion of the plastic intermediates.

The second largest clump of competitive gains consisted of two southeastern clusters centered in the Piedmont and Cumberland regions and separated by the Appalachian spine. To the east of the ridge the cluster consisted of Charlotte, Greenville, Columbia, and Augusta, and to the west, Knoxville, Chattanooga, and Huntsville. These seven urban regions accounted for almost one-fourth of all chemical industry competitive gains. Knoxville was second only to Houston in this department. All seven were in the nation's top twelve regions. Probably as much as 80 percent of the gains in synthetic fibers came in this cluster (disclosure rules and changes in classification make it difficult to be precise). Knoxville and Augusta also recorded major gains in uranium-based inorganic chemicals because of their ties to the atomic program. The Southeast as a region captured between 30 and 70 percent of the competitive gains in drugs, detergents, paints, and miscellaneous chemicals, but these were more widely distributed and were often more than offset in localized regions by declining fertilizer and inorganic chemical shares.

The third largest geographical clump of competitive gains lay in the western end of the Old Manufacturing Belt. It consisted of three urban regions along the lower Ohio Valley (Paducah, Evansville, and Louisville) and extended northward in a narrow finger through Indianapolis, Lafayette, South Bend, Lansing, and Grand Rapids. Together these regions accounted for about 10 percent of all chemical manufacturing competitive gains. The underlying factors appear complex and less easy to discern without further detailed study. The Ohio River region appears to have gained in industrial chemicals and plastics on the strength of a well-located intermediate position between Gulf Coast supply areas and a highly diversified, intermediate manufacturing market in the old belt. This region, plus the northward extending finger, also appeared to be sharing a reorganizational experience with other manufacturing activities in the broad North Central region. The urban regions listed are all located in the crack between the dominant early metropolitan centers, Cleveland, Detroit, Chicago, and St. Louis. This also reflects a movement down the trade-center hierarchy that has been so characteristic of many manufacturing activities during this time. Although the North Central region as a whole experienced competitive losses in chemical employment, this clump of regions benefited from a degree of intraregional reorganization that favored smaller, well-located wholesale-retail centers.

The fourth largest competitive gain was centered in the Los Angeles urban region (third in rank). This appears to be another manifestation of the Pacific Coast's tendency to grow like a semiautonomous nation. Apart from industrial inorganic chemicals, the region registered competitive gains in every chemical category. Fertilizer was a natural large gainer. However, about 72 percent of the region's chemical industry gains came from the urban-oriented chemicals like drugs, detergents, paints, and miscellaneous chemicals.

In the Middle Atlantic region the tendency for overall competitive losses was resisted by the Philadelphia urban region. This is probably the Du Pont phenomenon combined with the region's strategic position with respect to markets and imported petroleum. Finally, there is a cluster of competitive leading-gain counties in the Plains (bunched in the Kansas City, Omaha, Des Moines, Davenport areas) and another in the Salt River Valley. These gains were dominated by fertilizer production and a small amount of industrial inorganics. None was very important dimensionally.

The flip side of all this is the story of those regions experiencing competitive losses. There were three major concentrations that, together, accounted for more than four-fifths of the total. The first consisted of a strip of Appalachian urban regions stretching from Buffalo to Atlanta. These accounted for 28 percent of the total, with Buffalo, Pittsburgh, and Huntington dominating. The explanation appears to lie mostly with the region's failure to maintain its early strength in the production of industrial chemicals—both organic and inorganic. The decreased relative importance of coal as a feedstock was the obvious major cause.

The second consists of the Atlantic coastal urban regions from Boston through Norfolk (with the exception of Philadelphia and Hartford). This strip accounted for another 28 percent of the total competitive loss (New York and Boston dominated with 23 percent). Every subsector shared in the relative loss except industrial inorganic chemicals, in which the region appears to have started out in a short supply position. The losses were most striking in paint and varnishes and the miscellaneous chemical categories. This strip accounted for between 85 and 90 percent of the national share losses for these commodities. This was simply a matter of the expanding markets elsewhere having captured most of the incremental gains in products oriented to final demand. However, this region that produced more than half of the nation's drugs did not yield much of its preeminence in this field. Its rate of employment growth, in what was a rapidly growing sector, almost matched that of the nation.

The third area of concentrated relative loss stretched from Charleston, Savannah, and Jacksonville in the east to Texarkana in the west. This strip included all of the urban regions just inside the Gulf Coast strip (that, in contrast, displayed such strong competitive gains on a petroleum, sulfur, and salt base). The interior strip accounted for 12 percent of the total competitive losses. Here the explanation rests with the previously discussed shift in the production of fertilizer and inorganic chemicals associated with the underlying changes in agricultural production. These relative losses were widespread throughout the entire South, of course. But in the textile and petroleum production regions, employment associated with chemical industry gains more than offset these agricultural chemical losses.

Finally, four metropolitan North Central regions (Cleveland, Detroit, Chicago, and St. Louis) accounted for 10 percent of the total loss. These relative losses were again dominated by the industrial chemicals, although drugs and soaps were significant contributors. Interestingly, though, miscellaneous chemicals, paints, and varnishes did well, reflecting the strategic position of the North Central region vis-à-vis national markets.

Consider in closing, the urban-system characteristics of the shifts in chemical manufacturing. The notable thing is that this sector did not move as far down the trade center hierarchy, or push out from the urban cores to the degree characteristic of manufacturing as a whole. The large metropolitan centers and urban cores fared just as poorly. But the medium and small urban cores accounted for almost one-third of the relative gain and the large wholesale-retail centers (that experienced relative losses for manufacturing overall) actually captured almost half of the total competitive gains within the trade center aggregation (see appendixes II-C and II-D). From a transaction-field perspective it is the primary labor force or commuting fields that experienced the greatest relative gains (two-thirds of the total). The reasons are not hard to fathom. Industrial and agricultural chemicals are tonnage materials. An American Trucking Association study (1963) reveals that three-fourths of the chemical plants were oriented to rail sidings and only the petroleum, lumber, and paper industries moved less of their physical throughput by truck. Between 1955 and 1960, more than three-quarters of the firms that reported moves, and that were initially city-based, sought out either new city or suburban locations, rather than rural locations. As a consequence, table II-13 reveals that the broad geographical reorganization of chemical manufacturing activity was substantial while its urban-system reorganization was relatively limited.

Other and Miscellaneous Manufacturing: The Material Sectors

The industry category, "other and miscellaneous manufacturing," is a horror of heterogeneity. This classification was forced on us by the problem of matching categories over a period of thirty years. Almost half of the 1940 employment was in the material-processing sectors—paper; petroleum refining; all stone, clay, and glass materials; and all primary metals. The other half included the production of rubber, leather, plastic, glass and clay products (that is, all stages beyond the material process); fabricated metals; professional and scientific equipment; and miscellaneous manufacturing. It is an impossibly complex task to relate the components of this hybrid to the shift patterns collectively fashioned. As a consequence, we concentrate here on five material-processing subsectors.[9]

Paper

Ever since paper became the basic material substrate for the communication and storage of information, the industry has struggled with a recurrent developmental problem: the growing demand for paper products frequently outstripped the availability of basic raw material supplies. At the outset this was limited to straw, rags, and wastepaper. The first major innovation involved the chemical bleaching of colored rags to increase the available material base. By the nineteenth century, the pressures were so strong it became evident that new sources of cellulose fibers were required. Scientific chemistry responded with the sulfite pulping process for converting wood fibers to use as paper stock. This occurred in the second half of the century. Although papermaking is not classified as a chemical process industry, this is essentially what it has become.

Historically, papermaking had been oriented to urban centers because this was the predominant source of both markets and raw materials. Since the chemical pulping of wood fibers requires 2 tons of wood to yield 1 ton of pulp, and pulping and papermaking can often be profitably integrated, new plants went into the forests. But this meant the forests of the Middle Atlantic urban regions closest to the industry's historical base and urban markets. New England and the western end of the Manufacturing Belt also shared in the development.

But the old developmental problem persisted: the sulfite process did not work with resinous woods. The forests of the Northeast and Great Lakes regions were already under heavy pressure because of the demand for dimension lumber. Because the industry's investors and managers continued to show a strong preference for the traditional sites of paper production, they continued to construct new capacity in these regions for a decade after wood supplies began to grow scarce (see Hunter 1955). Faced with overcapacity and material shortages, the industry needed a process that would make resinous wood available for pulping. The sulfate process permits this. Although developed in Germany about the turn of the century, the first U.S. sulfate plant was built in 1929. However, the further introduction of the process was retarded for twenty years by the depression and World War II. Furthermore, since the industry is heavily capital intensive, the industry's managers were reluctant to walk away from existing capacity. They absorbed the rising cost of pulp as long as marginal costs were covered; they imported foreign pulp; and they converted their equipment to the production of higher grades of paper.

As a consequence, in 1940 about three-fourths of paper manufacturing employment was still in the Great Lakes and Northeast regions.[10] However, during the study period, the sulfate process made progress, and, by 1970, accounted for 70 percent of all production. By then, a third of the nation's total timber production was going into pulp. This could only be achieved by exploiting additional timber resource regions. The sulfate process made the resinous pines of the South a feasible raw material.

A profile of the resulting shifts (from 1950 to 1970 only) is offered in color plate II-14. It is clear that most of the counties experiencing competitive losses (red on plate II-14) were concentrated in the historical production regions of the Northeast and Great Lakes regions. However, the earliest production regions in the Southeast and Northeast also displayed significant competitive losses. The competitive gains (blue) covered the bulk of the nation, with lagging gains the more frequent occurrence.[11]

Consider the quantitative dimensions in broad terms. Roughly two-thirds of the competitive losses taking place during the study period were experienced by the Northeastern historical core of the industry. Another one-fourth occurred at the western end of the Old Manufacturing Belt. All of those red counties in the Southeast accounted for less than 10 percent of the competitive losses (when county data are aggregated to urban-region scale). In contrast, more than half of the competitive gains occurred in the Southeast. (The Atlanta, Jacksonville, Memphis, Charlotte, Dallas, Little Rock, and Mobile urban regions were most prominent.) More than two-thirds of this was concentrated in the New Manufacturing Belt of the Upper South. The balance of the competitive gains were evenly split between selected urban regions in the old production regions (whose experience ran counter to the generalized relative losses experienced by the broader production region). These countertrend shifts were registered by Cedar Rapids, Des Moines, Omaha, Huntington, Columbus, Dayton, Detroit, Saginaw, Wilkes-Barre, Harrisburg, Baltimore, and Los Angeles.

Although the grounds for the fundamental shift out of the traditional production centers into the Southeast was basically the introduction of the sulfate process, at least two other factors accelerated the trend. Much of the southern forest was coming into second growth during this period. The fact that the pine reaches pulping size in a much shorter time than when it is destined for saw timber provided a short-cycle option for a commercial harvest. Indeed, large tracts are now settling into a scientifically managed silviculture based on the pulpwood crop cycle. This was also the time when the burgeoning demand for paperboard outran its traditional wastepaper base. Southern forest virgin kraft fibers were much in demand for this purpose.

All of which brings us to a second set of developments. If any one thing characterized the study period, it is the materials explosion that took place under the impetus of scientific chemistry. Papermaking came to share in this transformation. This is the period during which paper ceased to be primarily an information-processing substrate and became predominantly a material-processing component. The revolution in food and chemical processes, the development of supermarket retailing and modern advertising, and the articulation and fractionation of transport distribution processes all created new problems in the packaging field that were best resolved with paper products. Employment in the box and container segment of the industry almost tripled, the biggest gain of any paper industry component.[12] The new chemistry opened the way for a whole range of converted papers that satisfied a multitude of needs, some new, some traditional. Special coated and glazed papers showed up in gummed, carboned, waxed, tarred, oiled, enamelled, cloth-lined forms that found special uses in packaging, photography, office supplies, home supplies, and so forth. The study period witnessed the advent of the disposable sanitary paper products. Kleenex became as much a symbol of the time as any other single product. There were also the new pressed and molded pulp goods that form common utensils. Finally, paper moved into production in a big way as roofing paper, sheathing paper, fiberboard, insulation material, and as the bind-matrix for the ubiquitous "dry wall" that has made plaster obsolete. Since all of these conversion stages of the industry, as well as the basic pulping process, were created by modern chemistry, it is no surprise that the direct input of chemicals to the industry has grown to 10 percent of the total.

What is relevant here is the fact that these changes in use and process engineering lie behind two other major shifts in the orientation of paper manufacturing. One of these is largely a scale phenomenon. Examine plate II-14 once more. If you look at the earliest production areas in the Northeast and Great Lakes regions, as well as in the Southeast, you can see that the specialized counties that experienced competitive losses were interlarded with a smaller number of counties that displayed leading gains—even though some of them were initially specialized. Here we witness a phenomenon rather like that we saw in the lumber and wood sector. The new additions of capital took the form of increasingly larger and more integrated mills that, with the advent of the truck, drew their logs from a substantially larger supply field. So, even the older southern production regions that experienced substantial net losses displayed numerous instances of localized gain.

The other location factor of significance is related to the growing importance of converted paper products including boxes and packaging materials. These conversion processes do not need to be carried out at the production site of the basic paper stock. They add value, and often bulk, in ways that favor a market orientation. This certainly lies behind the prominent gains in the California urban regions, for a relatively minor amount of pulping takes place in the West, and that largely in the Pacific Northwest. This has also been a factor augmenting the southern expansion because of the expanding markets there. It also helps explain why, in the South, the largest urban regions (like Dallas, Atlanta, Jacksonville, Memphis, and Charlotte) dominate the gains in an industry otherwise known to be heavily resource oriented. Finally, this explains the metropolitan counties in a region like New York and Philadelphia that registered specialized leading gains in the face of major regional losses.

In this connection, it is also interesting to note that the Binghamton, Wilkes-Barre, Harrisburg, and Baltimore urban regions recorded leading competitive gains. They form a ring around the older metropolitan production centers, thus constituting well located, lower order centers for paper-finishing activities wanting to escape the agglomeration diseconomies of the older centers. This also seems to be the rationale for the Columbus–Dayton,

Detroit–Saginaw gains. Finally, the Cedar Rapids–Des Moines–Omaha relative gains seem to be linked to the region's emerging specialization in magazine publications, an industry that makes heavy use of specially treated and coated papers.

Primary Metal Manufacturing

The advent of scientific chemistry has had as large an effect on primary metal manufacturing as on any other. For example, in 1900 there were only fourteen metals in common use. Since then, more than thirty new ones have emerged as important industrial materials. Such metals as aluminum, magnesium, and titanium are among the best known. In addition, literally thousands of alloys with special characteristics have become available. All of these metallurgical developments were addressed to the multitude of problems raised by the new machine technologies—problems associated with temperature extremes, corrosive environments, the newly found significance of centrifugal strength, and so forth. How has all of this changed the face of the industry? Consider each subsector in turn.

IRON AND STEEL. At the beginning of the period the ferrous metals accounted for two-thirds of the total employment in primary metal manufacturing. The story behind this industry's shifting patterns of production and employment has been well documented.[13] In the days before the Civil War, metallurgy was still a chemical craft. It took 5 tons of coal and 2 tons of ore to produce a ton of steel. The rule of thumb concerning location was "iron moves to coal." The steel industry became centered in the Pittsburgh–Youngstown area on top of the nation's richest deposits of good coking coal.

But with scientific chemistry, grounded in the principles of thermodynamics, oxygen-lacing substantially increased productivity. The coal content of a ton of finished steel was reduced to less than two tons. Add to this the fact that transport rates for finished steel were higher than for raw materials, and the fact that it also became feasible to use scrap in the charge, and it is easy to see that the market became the dominant factor in the location orientation of the industry.

So, during the first part of the twentieth century the industry was already beginning to move. New capacity was first established in Chicago, Cleveland, Buffalo, and Baltimore. More recent developments came in the Los Angeles, Salt Lake, and Dallas urban regions. However, because of the natural inertia of capital-intensive industries, the traditional iron and steel heartland (Pennsylvania, Ohio, and West Virginia) still produced 57 percent of the industry's output at the beginning of the study period. That this may have represented a lag in adjustment is suggested by the fact that the same states absorbed only 30 percent of the output.

The center of gravity of the intermediate markets served by the industry has been progressively shifting westward and southward at the same time that industry was trying to catch up with the changing "techno-logic" of its location matrix. The shifts in the study period reflect this. The World War II period saw the establishment of the integrated Kaiser mill in southern California and an additional plant at Geneva, Utah. Then came the Armco plant at Kansas City and the new tube and pipe mills in Texas.

The period also witnessed the beginning of an important new development—the electric arc "minimill." Although a large integrated steel works may produce 2 million tons a year, a minimill can function economically at a rated capacity of only 50,000 tons. These are specialized mills that operate almost exclusively on market-generated scrap. They concentrate on a few products, like concrete reinforcing rods and a limited set of construction shapes. They began to emerge in the seams between the markets of the major mills. Such places as Atlanta, Tampa, Denver, several West Coast cities, Phoenix, Boston, Roanoke, Binghamton, Evansville, and Columbus acquired such facilities. This trend continued into the 1970s with new mills in the Carolinas (Georgetown in the Florence urban region, for example), in Nebraska, and more in Texas. While these developments have given the industry a more widespread presence than could have been envisaged a short time ago, the bulk of the capacity and employment is still in the Old Manufacturing Belt.

ALUMINUM. The great development in the nonferrous metals came largely during the study period and transformed the scene in the primary metals. By the end of the study period, employment in the ferrous metals had declined from 62 to 43 percent of all primary metals, so it is apparent that the relative position of the old and the new metals almost exactly reversed in the thirty years. Although the nonferrous metal story is too multifaceted to develop fully here, this subsector was dominated by the development of the aluminum industry, and aluminum's basic location story can be told briefly.

The production of aluminum is not a highly integrated process like that of iron and steel. The transformation of bauxite ores into alumina is a chemical process largely independent of the primary reduction stage. That story has already been told. The production of pig aluminum also began as an input-oriented process. Although it takes 2 tons of alumina to make a ton of aluminum, the industry has never sought juxtaposition with alumina plants. The early orientation of the industry was to economical electric power. Being a voracious power consumer, a price difference of one mill changed the cost of pig aluminum by $18.00 per ton (in 1950 prices).

The successive installations of new capacity traced out the industry's quest for cheap power. The first plant in the United States was at Niagara Falls in 1903. The next additions came fifteen years later at Alcoa and Baden, North Carolina. These were all waterpower sites and represented the total capacity of the industry at the beginning of the study period. Since then more than thirty new plants have been established. In the early 1940s these were, with a single exception, all still waterpower oriented. They were established at the emerging public power sites in the Tennessee Valley and Washington State. In the meantime, intermediate markets were expanding in the Texas–South Central regions (where substantial alumina capacity was also located; so the 1950s brought a half-dozen new mills in Arkansas, Texas, and Louisiana based primarily on cheap natural gas as a power-generating feedstock. In the 1960s, however, the pattern began to change again. Interregional differences in the cost of power began to narrow considerably, and the low-cost power sites began to use up their earlier excess capacity. A few new plants were established at water sites in Oregon, Washington, and Alabama, and several new gas-based plants emerged in the oil country, but a new path of orientation emerged.

While the industry had been choosing cheap power sites, the continuing concentration of fabricators in the Old Manufacturing Belt drew attention to that region's shortfall in production capacity. Thus, in the late 1950s and 1960s the Ohio Valley became the locus for substantial capacity based on more efficient coal-based generating plants (Ravenswood, West Virginia; Clayton and Hannibal, Ohio; Evansville, Indiana; Sebree and Hollinville, Kentucky). The valley sites were favored because of access by barge to alumina from the Gulf Coast facilities. Some of the plants established, for the first time, a semi-integrated posture vis-à-vis casting, rolling, drawing, and extruding operations by shipping molten metal in special rail cars directly to nearby processors. The importance of access to intermediate markets came to assert itself as the availability of cheap power declined.[14]

While there is much more to the metals story, this narrative is sufficient to explain much of what we see in the employment shift record. Color plate II-15 is the opening point of reference. It is immediately clear that most of the competitive losses were associated with the historical centers of the iron and steel industry. The Pittsburgh, Youngstown, Cleveland, and Buffalo urban regions have a markedly reddish hue. On a 171-urban-region basis, this heartland of the modern iron and steel industry accounted for 70 percent of the competitive losses. For the rest, there are clusters of competitive-loss counties in the Syracuse and Detroit urban regions, in all of the Atlantic Coast urban regions from Hartford through Baltimore, in the Birmingham region, and in scattered counties elsewhere, particularly through the mountain regions.

There is an additional reason for the association with the traditional iron and steel centers. The ferrous subsector of primary metals experienced a slight decline in employment during the period because of the substitution effect of the new metals as well as the labor-saving effect of the new metallurgy and continuous-flow processes. In contrast, the new metals more than doubled employment in spite of substantial productivity increases. Thus a part of the relative decline in the older iron and steel centers was the result of a subsector mix effect.

But there is a seeming anomoly. A good 12 percent of the competitive loss came in the Middle Atlantic Coast region that was one of the intermediate market concentrations that the literature identifies as gaining in market-oriented capacity. However, most of that shift came in the preceding, or fifth, epoch. More important, and a harbinger of more recent developments, we see here the emergence of the East Coast's vulnerability to foreign competition, as the study period came to a close.

The pattern of competitive gains is again widespread on the color plate, although the leading gains were especially numerous in the North and South Central regions. In quantitative terms, the bulk of the competitive gains were much more concentrated (ninety-one urban regions registered less than one-third of one percent of the total competitive gains or losses). First, a substantial concentration of gain came in the western end of the Old Manufacturing Belt. Save for Detroit, all of the urban regions from Toledo southward to Indianapolis and Terre Haute, westward to Peoria and northward to Green Bay experienced competitive gains that, collectively, amounted to 25 percent of the total—this in spite of the individual counties in regions like Chicago and Rockford that displayed leading competitive losses. This is clearly a reflection of the westward component of the market shift. The gains experienced by Grand Rapids, South Bend, Fort Wayne, Milwaukee, and Peoria were particularly notable. As we shall see shortly, this was significantly associated with the growth of the farm machinery industry on the western edge of the belt.

It is also significant that the Columbus, Huntington, Roanoke, and Richmond urban regions displayed significant gains (about a fifth of the total). These were on the southern border of the old production region heartland. They constituted some compromise between the expanding southern markets and the still significant production advantages of coal-region sites. Collectively, the rest of the South accounted for about 40 percent of the competitive gains, split about evenly between the Texas–Louisiana–Arkansas energy belt and the rest of the Southeast. In the oil country, Houston, Dallas, Tyler, New Orleans, and Little Rock accounted for the bulk of the gains. In the rest of the South, Evansville, Nashville, and Huntington were the leaders. Atlanta and southern Florida displayed gains as a result of new iron and steel minimills.

Aluminum production played no role in the gains at the western end of the Manufacturing Belt, but were significant in the southeastern story. The Evansville region acquired two aluminum plants and was flanked by two more in the Paducah and Louisville regions. The Columbus and Huntington regions acquired three new plants. The Huntsville urban region acquired two, and the Texas–Louisiana–Arkansas grouping acquired eight more.

The remaining fifth of the gains were concentrated on the Pacific Coast, with Los Angeles alone accounting for almost 11 percent of the national total. The Pacific Northwest accounted for about 5 percent. The latter was heavily based on aluminum production, with ten plants being established during the study period. The southern California gains were based on iron and steel. No aluminum reduction plants located there. However, an important part of the play came from (1) nonferrous casting, rolling, drawing, and extruding activities that were stimulated by the tremendous West Coast growth in intermediate markets; (2) gains in miscellaneous primary metal products (such as heat-treated products, metal powders, and pastes); (3) the recovery of metals associated with nonmetallic mining activities; and (4) the production of nails, tacks, and staples. The Pacific region, for example, accounted for more than one-fourth of the gain in miscellaneous primary metal activities.

One may wonder how so many counties in plate II-15 can be painted blue when they cannot be the site of even minimills. The answer lies with the significance of these third-stage nonferrous and miscellaneous processing activities. Many of these processes are carried out on a small scale in many different places. Gains in these third-stage processes were particularly strong throughout the Southeast.

Petroleum Refining

In 1950 there were seven regional concentrations of production and employment in petroleum refining: (1) the New York and Philadelphia urban regions; (2) a Buffalo–Erie–Pittsburgh strip astride the early Northeastern oil fields; (3) Chicago, Toledo–Lima, and Indianapolis in the western end of the Old Manufacturing Belt; (4) the Gulf Coast stretch from Corpus-Christi through New Orleans (plus Tyler, Shreveport, and Greenville, Mississippi); (5) the Texas–Oklahoma interior stretching from El Paso–Odessa through Amarillo–Wichita Falls, on through Oklahoma City, Tulsa, and Springfield to St. Louis (plus Wichita and Kansas City on the northwestern edge); (6) Cheyenne atop the Wyoming field; and (7) Los Angeles–San Francisco–Fresno on the Pacific Coast. It is not surprising to find that most of the competitive shifts between 1950 and 1970 involved changes in the relative positions of these traditional production regions.

The competitive shift patterns depicted by color plate II-16 obscure major elements of the story. It only takes 12 urban regions (out of 171) to account for 75 percent of the competitive gains. One hundred and five urban regions experienced competitive shifts that amounted to less than one-third of 1 percent of the total. The broad expanse of blue counties in plate II-16 was rarely involved in any petroleum refining at all. There was a scattering of small-batch distillation refineries, but most of the counties were involved in such things as the mixing of asphalt paving or roofing compounds (a category also included in petroleum refining), or included nonproduction employees of refining companies. Still, plate II-16 provides some small-area detail of interest after the major outline has been established.

There has been little in the literature on the location factors at work in the oil refining industry in the United States. Lindsay (1956) published a paper early in the study period seeking to anticipate production trends. He examined the technology and comparative costs of twenty different prototype refineries, along with the assembly and distribution costs of their input–output flows. He showed that refiners serving the East Coast sites achieved their greatest economics operating at Gulf Coast sites. Naturally, these sites were superior in serving southeastern and south-central markets as well. In contrast, Lindsay determined that refineries serving the Great Lakes regions would find it advantageous to locate near the market and import crude from the South. For consuming areas in the Mountain and Pacific Coast regions, the market pull was alleged to be even more pronounced.

Lindsay made his location comparisons in broad regional terms, and in these terms, his anticipations were partially borne out by the experience of the study period. Between them, the Middle Atlantic Seaboard and the Buffalo–Pittsburgh regions accounted for more than half of the total competitive losses. The Great Lakes regions experienced about one-fourth of the gains. The Gulf Coast oil belt accounted for another fourth and the Texas–Oklahoma interior registered about 15 percent. But the Mountain regions only a little more than broke even, and the Southern California region actually experienced losses. Furthermore, in each of the production regions there were shift anomalies that could not be anticipated on the basis of a study like Lindsay's. Most of these were accounted for by changes in the transport net serving markets and assembling resource materials.

The nature of these shift patterns at urban-region scale is portrayed in map II-9. The first anomaly relative to the Lindsay scenario shows up in the Philadelphia region. While the Northeast as a whole contributed half of the competitive losses, Philadelphia accounted for over 7 percent of the competitive gains. This came fairly late in the period and was associated with the increase in use of imported crude oils.

The second anomaly was in the Great Lakes region. Although this broad region met the expectation of the Lindsay scenario, it did so in an unanticipated way. One would have expected the gains to be captured by the traditional midwestern refining centers like Chicago, Indianapolis, Toledo–Lima, and St. Louis. Actually, Chicago, Indianapolis, and Lima did experience competitive gains, but they were quite modest. The big gains came in the Saginaw–Bay City urban region and in Minneapolis. In fact, Saginaw displayed the leading competitive gain for the nation with almost 18 percent of the national total. Minneapolis displayed the fifth largest gain. Yet both of these regions were on the northern margin of the market region and furthest away from the South-Central oil fields.

There appear to be two major components to the explanation. First, during the period, a crude oil pipeline was completed from the Canadian field in Alberta. It came across the Upper Michigan Peninsula to Ontario with a spur to Minneapolis. The second reason is of particular interest because it shows how public policy can significantly alter the comparative advantages of regions in unintended ways.

In 1959 the voluntary oil import control program, which had been in effect for five years, was made mandatory. Shortly after, a so-called hemisphere preference was put into effect that exempted imports from Canada and Mexico. This exaggerated the advantage to the "northern tier" refiners initially established by the pipeline. Furthermore, when the mandatory quota program started, these refineries had received import quotas with respect to Canadian oil. When the Canadian imports were exempt, the initial quotas were not rescinded. The refineries continued to receive quota tickets which they could exchange at a profit for domestic oil. Thus, the economic advantage of these refineries was further augmented.[15]

The Gulf Coast region also registered about one-fourth of the total gain. However, the distribution was most uneven. The Houston–Beaumont area dominated the gains. In contrast, New Orleans weighed in with a significant competitive loss. The interior urban regions of the East Texas field—San Antonio, Tyler, Shreveport, and Greenville—also displayed competitive losses (this shows up markedly in plate II-16, as well). Several factors appear to have been at work.

What we see is partly a result of changes in transport networks, partly a change in the locus of supply sources, and partly a change in production technology; and these exhibited tight interdependencies. First, there was a relative shift in supply sources in favor of off-shore wells and imported crude. This augmented the advantage of coastal sites, particularly Galveston Bay. The supertanker, along with the development of crude oil pipelines from the interior fields, changed the access network further in favor of the Gulf Coast. Finally, there was an interplay between changes in production technology and depletion of wells. During the early history of petroleum refining, firms tended to locate plants near proven reserves. Each new field led to a rapid increase in small-batch distillation plants with a typical capacity of 7,000 barrels per day. As production declined, these were shut down. Refinery shutdowns reached their peak in 1948. Coincident with the latter tendency, the technological merger of distillation and conversion into large, continuous-flow plants took place. Because of the changing circumstances, such plants tended to gravitate to the coast.

The interior refinery belt, stretching from Odessa to St. Louis, also displayed a mixed pattern. The Tulsa, Oklahoma City, and Odessa urban regions registered about 15 percent of the total competitive gains. Tulsa was dominant with almost two-thirds of that amount. St. Louis and Springfield on the northeastern end displayed significant losses. (Again plate II-16 elaborates the county detail.) The same general set of change factors was at work here. With respect to the more remote interior counties in this field, the decline of the small-batch refineries and the advent of the modern integrated refinery favored a nodal center like Tulsa–Oklahoma City. The advent of new pipelines was significant, not only in assembling the crude of these centers, but in distributing products to northeastern markets. The product pipelines appear to have been a particularly important developmental factor in this case—undoubtedly contributing to the decline of the St. Louis–Springfield urban regions.[16]

When we compare the coastal refinery belt with the interior, the degree to which competitive gains were offset by competitive losses was much greater. It turns out that, net of the off-setting losses, the Gulf Coast gains were about four times as great as those recorded by the refineries in the interior belt. If we compare the oil belt regions as a whole with the Great Lakes region, the net competitive gains were greater in the Great Lakes region (the northern tier refineries phenomenon).

The Mountain region remained relatively stable except for some local redistribution of activity. The oldest production region at Cheyenne experienced relative losses, but competitive gains in surrounding areas like Billings, Salt Lake City, and Grand Junction were about equal. The region maintained its earlier self-sufficiency in refinery products.

The Pacific Coast also experienced some differences from Lindsay-scenario expectations. Los Angeles and Fresno recorded almost 10 percent of the total nationwide

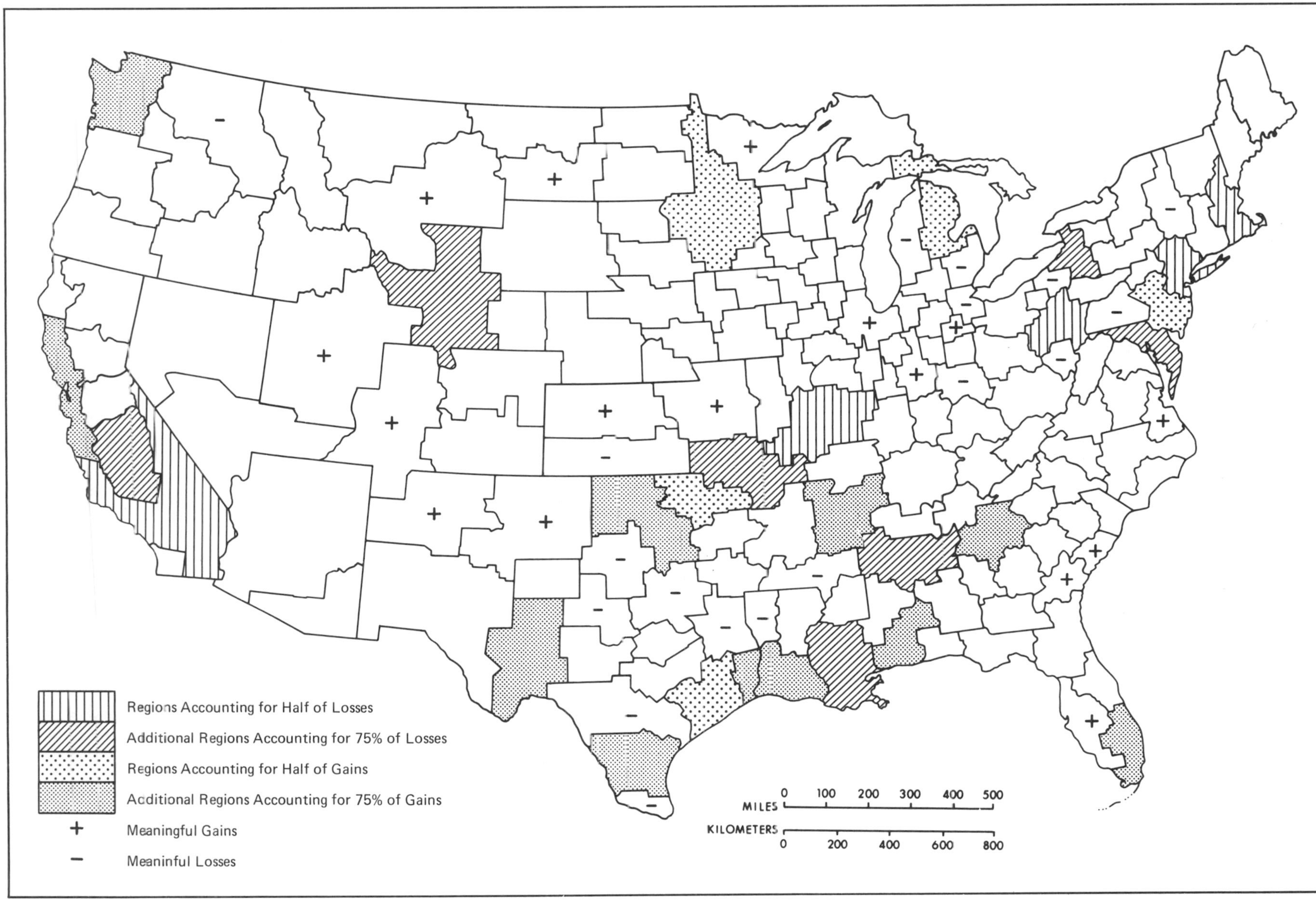

MAP II-9. Competitive Gains and Losses in Petroleum Refining Employment, 171 Urban Regions, 1950–70.

competitive losses. A part of the change in relative position seems related to the fact that this was one of the earliest developed fields, so relative depletion and small-refinery obsolescence was important. Moreover, the West Coast was not in as favorable a position with respect to the expanding foreign crude sources. Finally, a product pipeline from the Texas region ate into the market advantage of the coastal refineries.

There were other minor developments, such as the crossing of two petroleum pipelines in the Memphis region (altering its access characteristics relative to Birmingham) and the development of asphalt plants in the Southeast. However, the main lines of the story are in place. The tremendous increase in pipeline capacity, the advent of new pipelines, the shifts in the locus of supply sources, and the changes in refinery technology all modified the transaction network in ways consistent with the shift patterns described.

Stone, Clay, and Glass Materials

We have had some success in breaking down the heterogeneity of the shift pattern displayed by the "other manufacturing" category (of the basic thirty-one sector classification) by considering the period after 1950. We are now down to the residual "miscellaneous manufacturing" category. Only a brief reference to appendix A in volume I is necessary to establish that a mixed bag of categories remains. The residual still includes tobacco manufacturing; rubber and plastic products; leather and footwear; all of the items generally subsumed under the "stone, clay, and glass" category; fabricated metals; professional and scientific equipment; and other "not specified" manufacturing activities. The only materials activities left are flat glass, cement, abrasives, structural clay, and concrete products. These material categories accounted for only 11 percent of the total employment in this residual. We will be content with one major generalization.

The stone, clay and glass materials are overwhelmingly associated with the construction industry. In employment terms, the manufacture of cement, ready-mix concrete, concrete blocks, bricks, and tile dominate the sector. These activities also displayed spectacular growth, almost tripling in scale, although the growth of bricks, tile, and other structural clay products was dampened by the technological developments in concrete construction technology. We have already established that most of these products cannot be economically shipped for more than 200 miles (see chapter 8) and that their nonmetallic mineral base is widely distributed. It naturally follows that production and employment shifts followed the general westward- and southward-oriented differential gains in total employment characteristic of the study period.[17]

There you have it. Changes in material process technologies, changes in the nature of materials, changes in transport nets and transport modes, changes in the spatial distribution of intermediate and final markets, and changes in the locus of resource supplies have all operated in multifaceted ways to bring about major changes in the orientation of the manufacture of major economic materials, and in the localization of associated employment.

Notes

1. We have already seen that the wood products category includes logging (a resource activity), lumber and mill products (material-processing activities), and furniture (a fabricating activity). "Other manufacturing" includes material processes (like primary metals, petroleum refining, and paper, glass, and cement manufacturing) and fabricating processes (like fabricated metals and instruments).

2. The reader should be reminded that the descriptive explanation in part two frequently draws on three- and four-digit industry detail from the same basic data sources. This is often necessary to penetrate the confusing heterogeneity of some two-digit aggregates and to make the analysis more meaningful. However, these data are not reproduced in this study because (1) the detail is too voluminous and (2) disclosure suppressions often make shift computations dimensionally inaccurate, even though often ordinally sufficient to support explanation.

3. Though in California and Florida major gains in some counties showed up as C-code lagging gains because of even more prominent gains in other manufacturing trade and service activities.

4. Derived from appendix E in volume I.

5. A report giving the urban size location tendencies of four-digit manufacturing categories was published by Duncan (1959).

6. See Airov (1959). Nylon salts (a chemical intermediate) can also be produced economically in integrated fiber plants in the Textile region.

7. The production of nylon salts demonstrates greater locational flexibility and contributed to relative gains in the Textile South.

8. For a detailed explanation see Perloff, and coauthors, 1960, p. 439.

9. It should be noted that the shift patterns cover only the period from 1950 to 1970. Because these computations were undertaken after all of the main study had been completed, we also lack the supporting information generated by the urban-system tabulations and other routines.

10. All of the New England and Middle Atlantic regions (except Binghamton and Wilkes-Barre) were paper manufacturing specialists (on 171-urban-region scale). There were three specialized clusters in the Great Lakes Region: (1) the Cincinnati–Columbus–Dayton–Toledo urban regions, (2) the Chicago–South Bend–Lansing–Grand Rapids urban regions, and (3) the Green Bay–Wausau–Eau Claire–Duluth urban regions. In the Southeast, most of the specialized activity stretched from Savannah and Jacksonville along the Gulf Coast to New Orleans and Monroe. There were additional concentrations in Florence, Ashe-

ville, and the Roanoke–Richmond regions. On the Pacific Coast, the Seattle and Portland urban regions were also specializers.

11. As before, the levels of production and employment were much more heavily concentrated than this pattern profile indicates. The combined counties in each of seventy-four urban regions accounted for less than one-third of one percent of the total shift in competitive shares.

12. Associated with this was the corresponding decline in the wood container industry noted earlier.

13. See Hartshorne (1928), Isard (1948), Rodgers (1952), and Craig (1957).

14. Continuing through the 1970s, still another trend is emerging. The expanding Southeastern markets are being chased. But new capacity is not moving back to TVA power; it is going to places outside the area like Buckstown, Maryland, and Holly, South Carolina. A mixture of coal and nuclear generating power provides the base. As I write this, plans have been revealed for a new plant in North Carolina.

15. A regulation to end these quotas was published, but it ran into a political snag. Those quota tickets provided the only market for 12,000 barrels of oil a day from North Dakota. These wells were not connected to the refineries by pipeline. Without the quota subsidy, the oil was too expensive to be pumped. Thus, regional political support kept the subsidy in force. See Bohi and Russell (1978) for a fascinating study of the oil import program.

16. You will recall that, in chapter 7, the development of the large-diameter seamless pipe and expanding pumping capacities were identified as factors that changed the logic of the access network.

17. This shift has been all the more pronounced because the industry has not always been so market oriented. For example, in 1900, 70 percent of the cement came from the Lehigh Valley in Pennsylvania, which had excellent limestone deposits and cheap coal. Technological changes that permitted the economical use of fuels other than coal and lower grades of raw materials have destroyed the earlier resource-base advantage.

11

The Fabricating Industries

The fabricating industries are the next step down the transaction trail to final demand. These sectors dominated the manufacturing industries, accounting for roughly two-thirds of manufacturing employment during the study period. This is natural because, except for food and textile manufacturing, material processes tended to be more capital intensive and fabricating processes more labor intensive. The fabricating sectors tended to experience rapid growth in employment relative to the material processes, and their share of total manufacturing increased.

Apparel

There is a tendency for one to think of textiles and apparel together. Both are labor intensive. They represent juxtaposed vertical stages in the materials processing and fabricating chains of activities. Nonetheless, their location histories, their patterns of localization, and their study-period shift patterns were quite different.

Consider the distribution of the industry at the beginning of the period. Eighty percent of apparel manufacturing employment was in the Old Manufacturing Belt (versus only about half for textiles). Roughly 60 percent was in the highly specialized New York and Philadelphia urban regions (versus 3 percent for textiles).

This reflected differences in their developmental histories. The textile industry was established while garment making was still largely a household activity. The former emerged in Boston and its environs because (1) it was initially attached to water power; (2) New England merchants did not have the same opportunities for investments in the continental interior as did those of New York and Philadelphia; and (3) New England had previously become established as the important center for the importation of woolen products and raw wool. The apparel industry was initially developed by retail and wholesale dealers as an extension of their entrepôt function. Because they were primarily located in the larger cities, so also was the new industry. But New York City soon came to dominate for reasons sketched by a New York metropolitan region study. New York's dominance

> . . . was insured by a historic coincidence: The women's ready-to-wear industry was emerging fast in the nation at the same time that large scale Jewish immigration from eastern Europe was taking place. The production of . . . apparel is primarily labor oriented, and immigration brought New York a pool of cheap labor as well as a skilled labor supply. . . . Once the immigrant had helped make New York the capital of production, it also became the chief market, and it could build on its position as a cultural center to take complete charge of the artistic design of garments. As a result . . . many other industries and services ancillary to production and marketing gathered around and became, in turn, sources of economies. . . . (Helfgott, Gustafson, and Hund, 1959, p. 113).

Still, before the study period, this initial concentration was beginning to break up under the impact of new forces. As the relatively new industry matured, competition became keen and fostered the separation of production from marketing and design. Much of the actual sewing was done in contract shops, a specialization of function that brought a degree of flexibility to an uncertain business. This, combined with the advent of the motor vehicle, made it possible to maintain a showroom and design shop in the garment district and a production shop in the hinterland where the wages were lower. The high cost of loft space and other agglomeration diseconomies also contributed.

Thus, the production component began to diffuse: first, from Manhattan to Brooklyn, next to the outlying counties of the urban region, then to neighboring regions like Wilkes-Barre where the wives of unemployed coal miners were found in abundance, finally outward to New England (related to the decline of the textile industry there) and into the South (in part to escape the wage effects of unionism). These developments brought apparel specialization to the Boston, Hartford, Albany, Rochester,

Wilkes-Barre, Harrisburg, and Baltimore urban regions—all within the broader New York regional environment. In the South a band of urban regions including Atlanta, Chattanooga, Nashville, and Paducah, plus Roanoke, had established modest specializations, with Chattanooga showing the largest relative concentration. No other apparel manufacturing specializations were apparent in the nation except for a modest concentration in Chicago.

So, we are brought to the perspective of the study period. Consider first the distribution of the specialized counties in plate II-7. From the discussion thus far, we are prepared to see the concentration in the Mid-Atlantic and Southeast, but we are not prepared for the dispersed scatter of specialized counties throughout the western end of the Old Manufacturing Belt. The degrees of specialization were weak, and, save for Chicago, they netted-out at urban-region scale. All of the specialized counties in the Southeast and North Central region had a common characteristic. They were production regions that specialized heavily in those segments of the industry where style and labor force skills were least important, and where mechanization and the division of labor were most important (for example, in the making of underwear, shirts, trousers, and work clothing). These were also the products that could be marketed in national and broad regional markets through more conventional channels of distribution.

Consider the shift patterns. Most of the specialized counties in the industry's Middle Atlantic birthplace and in the western end of the Old Manufacturing Belt experienced losses, primarily leading losses. However, in the Southeast most of the counties that had achieved specialized status at the beginning of the period experienced leading gains. Here the pre-1940 tendencies were reinforced. Throughout the New Manufacturing Belt, and in the West North Central region southward from Minneapolis to Kansas City, most counties experienced leading gains. In the balance of the nation, most gains were lagging behind the economic performance of other activities. In dimensional terms, the specialized counties combined accounted for 93 percent of all competitive losses and 75 percent of the leading losses. The unspecialized counties accounted for 85 percent of total gains and 68 percent of leading gains. (In contrast, the textile industry was still engaged in a shift from one preexisting regional concentration to another.)

The dimensional picture can be summarized at 171-urban-region scale. The coastal urban regions of the Middle Atlantic accounted for 75 percent of all competitive losses, while those at the western end of the Old Manufacturing Belt accounted for 21 percent. The New York urban region, alone, accounted for 57 percent of the loss. At the same time, the interior Middle Atlantic urban regions (Williamsport, Binghamton, Wilkes-Barre, Harrisburg, Staunton, and Pittsburgh) accounted for 9 percent of the competitive gains. These were the regions heavily engaged in contract sewing for the New York firms. Thus, a part of the parent region's relative decline represented a broader intraregional redistribution. This reflected a continuation of the forces at work at the beginning of the period. Roughly 60 percent of the competitive gains were registered by the urban regions comprising the New Manufacturing Belt in the South. Elsewhere, the Los Angeles, Dallas, and Miami urban regions recorded impressive competitive gains (Los Angeles ranked second and Miami fifth).

As a consequence of these shifts, three urban regions in the Northeast (Hartford, Albany, and Rochester) and two in the Midwest (Chicago and Gary) ceased to be apparel manufacturing specialists by the end of the period. At the same time, thirty-eight urban regions spread throughout the South registered apparel manufacturing specializations for the first time. These competitive shifts were not trivial. Only three of this study's thirty-one industry sectors experienced competitive shifts that were larger (as a percentage of the 1940 employment of the sector). Still, apparel manufacturing remained twice as concentrated as total employment.

Apparel manufacturing moved down the trade center hierarchy to lower order centers and out of the dense transaction fields of the urban cores into the non-core fields of the smallest urban regions, and even into the fields lying outside the influence of urban-region cores. This was an experience common to many manufacturing sectors, but more marked in the case of apparel manufacturing.

Now return to the realm of explanation. Moving into the study period, factors already at work became intensified. Their effects on shift patterns were of two sorts. The first had to do with subsectors of the industry engaged in providing nonstyle goods. These were the sectors most sensitive to labor cost differentials and least concerned with the designing and marketing functions of the old garment center. The earlier shift of these activities into the western end of the Old Manufacturing Belt was aborted during the study period. This appears to have been a consequence of a rapidly narrowing labor cost differential. This was the time when these same areas were making competitive gains in a range of manufacturing activities that were traditionally higher wage industries than was apparel manufacturing. During the study period some of that production moved on into the West North Central regions at the extreme western edge of the Old Manufacturing Belt.

But the bulk of the relative shift was an accentuation of the older shifts into the South. These fanned out into the entire field, especially that defined by the New Manufacturing Belt. Here the effect of labor cost differentials appeared to be sustained for a longer period than in the Great Lakes regions. In addition, we have seen that the Southeast improved its relative access to vital markets more than any other region. Within the southern regions there were further differences in shift patterns. For example, the Piedmont region where the textile industry had come to an earlier dominance was not the locus of the greatest southern gains. Apparel manufacturing gains were concentrated further west in the Nashville, Memphis, Huntsville, Birmingham, and Atlanta urban regions. This was an apparent effort to avoid competing excessively for the same labor pools. Furthermore, urban regions like El Paso, Phoenix, and San Diego experienced strong competitive gains based on Mexican labor.

The second set of effects on shift patterns had to do with such activities as the production of men's suits, female outerwear, hats, women's foundation garments, fur goods, and miscellaneous apparel (like ties, robes, and the like). New York and its immediate hinterland region had maintained a stubborn hold on the bulk of this activity right down to the study period (claiming more than two-thirds of the employment in those sectors in 1940). Some contract production had already migrated to nearby hinterland regions, although design and marketing functions were still dominated by the Garment Center. These trends continued, as we have seen.

But a new set of factors assumed a growing importance. A new pattern of American life led to a more casual pattern of "separates," dungarees, slacks, shorts, and sports garments. This substantially reduced the relative importance of more formal dresses, coats, and suits. Furthermore, within women's dresses, the production of high-style, unit priced dresses declined substantially relative to priced-by-the-dozen dresses. Since the high-style formal attire had been the specialization of the New York region, these developments began to undermine what had been a persistent advantage. The cheaper, more utilitarian attire did not require the design and marketing services, or the highly skilled production workers, that had formed that advantage. Furthermore, the study period saw the rise of the new synthetic fabrics. Helfgott, Gustafson, and Hund (1959) point this up:

> New York manufacturers [were] not as free as others to switch to less expensive fabrics because such action would require them to lower their price in order to remain competitive. Once in the lower-priced field, however, they could not match the wage costs prevailing in competing areas outside New York. . . . Shifts in fabrics [also] . . . enabled producers located elsewhere to produce garments formerly in the price domain of producers [inside] New York (p. 79).

This emphasis on more casual style also opened the way for competing style and marketing centers of significant size to emerge outside the New York region. These were the forces behind the prominent competitive gains registered by Los Angeles, Miami, and Dallas.

The Hidden Sectors

There are several major manufacturing sectors (accounting for almost 10 percent of 1940 total manufacturing employment) that are hidden in the aggregates employed in this study. Although we cannot give them a corresponding empirical representation, a few general observations about the experience of each will help round out the study.

Furniture

Remember that the manufacture of furniture and fixtures was lumped with lumber and wood products in plate II-10. Because their location and developmental factors were quite different, the resulting picture is ambiguous. However, some of the forces at work can be suggested.

First, observe that furniture making adds considerable bulk to the fabricated product. Only the quality grades can carry the cost of long distance transport. At the same time, moderate-sized plants can realize competitive efficiency. Hence, production is substantially oriented to the market. Indeed, the distribution of furniture manufacturing is more closely associated with population distribution than any other manufacturing category.[1] Still, the influence of styling factors, resource factors, and the history of the industry resulted in some differential concentrations. The most notable was in the Great Lakes region. A quotation from earlier work sets the stage for the study period:

> The Great Lakes states (and their best-known furniture city—Grand Rapids) represent the region-of-origin in the United States for the production of furniture using factory methods. During the last century this area was a leading lumbering area and the furniture industry was an outgrowth of lumbering. At the outset it concentrated on factory-produced cheap furniture (referred to by the trade as "borax"). As factory organization for furniture production became more widely established, the region moved gradually into furniture styling and quality production in order to retain its position in the face of competitive producers oriented more to markets. The chief regional competition . . . came from the Southeast. Even before the turn of the century, the Southeast was producing wood furniture aimed at the local market. With decades of experience, it has evolved an industry that has some of the largest and most advanced plants in the country. It has moved into quality furniture and has become an important style center with permanent exhibitions at High Point, North Carolina (Perloff and coauthors, 1960, p. 428).

Thus, by 1940 the two principal concentrations in a widespread industry were in the Great Lakes region (most notably the Grand Rapids, Lansing, Fort Wayne urban regions) and in the Southeast (most notably Roanoke, Greensboro, and Charlotte urban regions).

The historical trend continued into the study period. About two-thirds of the relative losses were concentrated in the Great Lakes region and about two-thirds of the gains in the Southeast. The historical concentrations in the Great Lakes region proved to be overdeveloped with respect to total access to inputs and markets—particularly as they continued to shift southward and westward and as synthetic materials came increasingly into play. The Southeast appears to have been the most underdeveloped relative to these factors. The South also benefited from labor cost differentials, the emergence of "industrial-complex" economies, and, with the advent of the truck, the improvement of access to the large northeastern markets.

With respect to this last point, note the string of specialized leading-gain counties in the Southern Piedmont that stretch in a line through the Staunton and Roanoke urban regions, then fan out into a cluster in the Greensboro, Charlotte, Asheville, and Bristol urban regions. The interesting aspect is that, at the northern end, the string stretches along interstate highway 81 pointed at the densely populated Northeast. At the southern end it spreads out into a cluster richly served by interstate highways 81, 85, 40, 77, and 26. The changing access patterns wrought by the truck and highway broke the traditional northern metropolitan hold on high-styled and upholstered furniture (with the historical markets in Chicago and New York) and allowed the High Point market to assume major importance. The Southeast claimed about 90 percent of the competitive gains in the household furniture subsector. Los Angeles also became a minor market center for "fashion" furniture, reflecting the influence of the movie industry and the modern American architecture spawned on the coast.

But there is a buried component of this picture that behaved quite differently. Although the manufacture of household furniture absorbed roughly 70 percent of the industry's employment, by far the most rapidly increasing sectors of furniture manufacturing were the nonhousehold furniture sectors, and they marched to a different drum. The most rapidly growing sector involved the production of store and factory furniture (like partitions, shelving, lockers, display cases, counters, work benches, cabinets, and the like). It is interesting to note that the Great Lakes region, which suffered such marked competitive losses overall, captured almost a third of the competitive gains for this subsector. For this activity, the Pacific Coast and the South Central regions also overshadowed the Southeast. Clearly the shifts in industrial supply sources and intermediate markets were paramount here. This was further accentuated because metal plays a more prominent role in the production of these items.

The production of office furniture was another major rapid-growth sector. It is fascinating to note that almost half of the subsector gains were in the Middle Atlantic region. It is certainly more than a coincidence that this region strengthened its posture as the office capital of the nation during the study period. In contrast, the Great Lakes region experienced 100 percent of the subsector competitive losses. It had become the major subsector specialist in the earlier period when wooden office furniture was standard.

The remaining hidden sectors are buried in the "other and miscellaneous manufacturing" category that has plagued us. They include the manufacture of tobacco, rubber, plastic, and leather products.

Tobacco

Tobacco manufacturing is actually more of a material-processing activity, like the production of food. The study period changes are a classic illustration of the reorienting effects of major technological developments. In this case, it was Mr. Duke's cigarette machine, and his intensive, centralized, marketing innovations that wrought the changes. These developments induced widespread tobacco addiction of a sort unknown when the cigar and pipe prevailed. The increase in enterprise scale fostered by both the machine and marketing developments increased the relative concentration of the industry in its Southeastern heartland (principally Richmond and Raleigh–Durham), while causing both absolute and relative declines in twenty-seven cigar-manufacturing states.

Rubber and Plastic Products

Historically the rubber industry was also concentrated in the industrial Northeast, although the greatest concentration was in the Great Lakes region, specifically Ohio, even more specifically, Akron. As was the case with so much of the early location of American industry, the initial concentrations were to some extent sited by accident. Akron became the rubber capital because in the late nineteenth century a young, traveling entrepreneur, B. F. Goodrich, obtained local financial backing for a business. Water needed for the manufacture of rubber was available in quantity. The early location was further reinforced as the automobile industry very conveniently emerged in nearby Detroit and as a skilled labor force and industrial infrastructure emerged with the industry. But, as the industry matured and mechanization reduced the significance of labor skills, distribution economies became more important, and a noticeable decentralization of the industry ensued. This was particularly marked in the case of the tire-making subsector. New plants emerged in Iowa, Kansas, Colorado, Oklahoma, Texas, California, Alabama, Mississippi, North Carolina, South Carolina, and Tennessee.

An explanatory statement I wrote in 1960 is still substantially correct:

> Two factors are in effect here: (1) the growing importance of market access. Because of market rivalry there is a service advantage in being closer to markets, and there are usually transport savings on the final product because the production process adds considerable value and bulk. (2) The fact that there have been important interregional shifts in the market stemming from (a) the westward shift in population and (b) a marked regional decentralization in automobile assembly. We might add that the presence of the textile, carbon black, and synthetic rubber industries in the Southeast and Southwest meant that changing market advantage could be exploited without incurring significant penalty in the assembly of inputs. Further, natural rubber, which is imported, can be delivered at many points at approximately the same cost (Perloff and coauthors, 1960, pp. 442–443).

The balance of the rubber industry is engaged in producing thousands of molded, pressed, laminated, foamed, and extruded products. Even when grouped, they form a list of over 100 categories in the Standard Industrial Classification. This segment of the industry, being historically older than the tire industry, had its roots in southern New England and the Middle Atlantic regions. It experienced a similar erosion of its relative position.

Thus, all of the competitive loss in the rubber industry was visited on the Old Manufacturing Belt. The Great Lakes region accounted for well over half, with Ohio bearing the brunt. New England accounted for more than one-fifth. The Middle Atlantic region lost as well, but the losses lagged behind other manufacturing sectors and bespoke the region's substantial strength in miscellaneous rubber products. The South captured about half of the gain, with miscellaneous rubber products being more important in the South Atlantic portion and tire products relatively more important in the South Central portion. The Pacific region accounted for most of the rest with the greatest relative strength displayed by miscellaneous rubber products.

The Standard Industrial Classification has placed the new plastics industry in this sector, but its performance traced quite a different pattern. We cannot compute a shift pattern for this subsector because the industry is so new there was no meaningful baseline. However, we can determine where the subsector displayed especially heavy concentrations at the end of the period relative to, say, all-manufacturing employment. Here is the surprise. The Old Manufacturing Belt contained two-thirds of the employment in this new industry in 1970 versus slightly more than half of all-manufacturing employment. The Middle Atlantic states captured an especially disproportionate share. Elsewhere, only California came close to capturing a proportional share of the new plastic products industry.

This phenomenon suggests a speculative explanation of some importance. In spite of the fact that most of the final markets were now located out of the region, in spite of the fact that the major feedstocks came from the South, and in the face of a relative shift of manufacturing activity out of the Old Manufacturing Belt (including the older plastics, rubber), this region went against the grain of the shift patterns and captured a disproportionate share of the new activity. This suggests that during the study period the Old Manufacturing Belt still enjoyed some advantages in initiating a new product and process technology. Such things as chemical process research centers, a diversified and skilled labor force, an entrepreneurial tradition, and so forth, must still have been at work where developmental problems outweighed the problems of performance management. Furthermore, since the new plastics industry shared many process similarities with the older rubber industry, that industry's decline may have left an underutilized infrastructure of particular relevance to the newer enterprise.

Shoes and Leather

First a word about the historical setting. Like textiles, the shoe industry developed early in New England under the guidance of the region's entrepôt merchants. It was a handicraft industry heavily agglomerated by the requirements of skilled labor. There were three problems facing the industry at the end of the nineteenth century: (1) the restrictive costs and scarcity of skilled labor, (2) the shift of the major sources of hides to the Great Lakes region at the same time that organic tanning methods kept the tanning industry tied to the bark supplies of eastern forests,[2] and (3) the center of gravity of consumer markets was moving steadily westward and away from the core of the industry.

Two major technological developments began to release the industry from its historical bond during the first part of the twentieth century. First, the development of shoe machinery and the segmentation of tasks significantly reduced the binding force of skilled labor. Furthermore, the practice of leasing shoe machinery wiped out interregional differentials in capital costs. Second, scientific chemistry developed concentrated tanning fluids and inorganic tanning methods that diminished the need for transporting bark. These developments freed the industry to respond to shifting market and supply sources. The industry's base was extended from New England to the Middle Atlantic region, and then to the Great Lakes—particularly Cincinnati, Detroit, Chicago, and Milwaukee. This broader distribution formed the setting for the beginning of the study period.

After 1940, New England continued to experience competitive losses amounting to about one-third of the total. More significant, the earlier shift to the Great Lakes region was dramatically reversed, with the region accounting for almost 60 percent of the competitive losses. Two factors were at work. (1) As the Midwest became the most heavily specialized manufacturing region in the nation, the shoe and leather industry experienced the dislocating pressures of increasing labor costs, as had the apparel industry. (2) The great relative decline of meat packing in the Great Lakes region (for reasons already detailed) reduced the relative supply of hides. The supply sources were moving out into the plains regions and, interestingly enough, back to the Middle Atlantic seaboard where imported hides assumed new significance.

The production of shoes slipped further to the south and west. The St. Louis urban region became the prominent center and it provided the organizing hub for a series of satellite production regions in Evansville, Paducah, Nashville, Memphis, Little Rock, and Springfield. This region had the advantage of being nearer to shifting markets and having better access to relatively cheap labor in the South Central region, while still providing agglomeration economies of a sort. This South Central organization captured more than two-thirds of the competitive gains.

Two smaller variations in the shift patterns are worth note. The Middle Atlantic region, although historically important in the industry, experienced only modest competitive losses (in fact, experienced a gain during the early part of the study period). This was accounted for by two factors. First, imported hides dampened its losses in tanning and the production of cut stock. (Cut-stock activities—unassembled soles, heels, and uppers—tend to be located near leather sources because of the weight loss involved.) Second, for reasons similar to those operating in the apparel industry, the Middle Atlantic region retained considerable strength in the production of style shoes, gloves, handbags, and miscellaneous leather products. The Plains region experienced moderate gains (with emphasis on tanning and the production of cut stock) as it became a larger source of hides.

Fabricated Metals

This is one of the two-digit manufacturing classes partially buried in the "other and miscellaneous manufacturing" category. It is substantial in scale (6 percent of total manufacturing employment in 1940, 12 percent in 1970) and was exceeded in employment growth only by those sectors producing electrical and business machinery, aircraft, and professional equipment. We can get at this sector by breaking out the 1950–70 shift patterns, as we did with the primary metals. However, the descriptive and explanatory task is still complicated by the fact that this category is heterogeneous in the extreme. There are nine three-digit subsectors that vary as widely in character as the difference between the production of metal cans and the fabrication of bridge or ship sections; as the difference between the production of knives and steam boilers. The standard classification forms a list of more than 1,000 product groupings articulating the four-digit classification, and each of these encompasses myriad product variations. To adequately assess the structure and dynamics of this polyglot sector is well beyond the capacity of this study. This is a painful restriction because of the vital role these activities play in the linkage structures of all manufacturing, and because of the major transformations that have been taking place. The fog of aggregation and heterogeneity will be penetrated as much as limits will allow.

Begin with the five major areas of specialization in 1940 revealed in plate II-17. The first was the Eastern Seaboard concentration extending from outside Boston to Baltimore. Hartford displayed the greatest relative concentration of any region except Chicago. (Philadelphia displayed the fifth greatest concentration.)

There were differences in subsector composition, however. Hartford displayed the greatest relative concentrations of general hardware and screw machine products production. The historical reasons seem clear. The production of cutlery, hand tools, and general hardware constituted the beginning of the fabricated metal industry in colonial New England. Serving final markets as well as intermediate, having established distribution channels, relying on a highly skilled work force, and being least influenced by the process developments leading to large-scale capital-intensive establishments, this subsector held most tenaciously to its place of origin. In contrast, the Philadelphia end of the seaboard belt concentrated more on the production of (1) structural metal products serving regional construction and shipbuilding activities, (2) cans serving the food processors oriented to the New Jersey and Delmarva farming regions, and (3) forgings and stampings serving regional intermediate metal processors.

The second region of concentration shows up as a cluster of counties stretched along the shore of Lake Erie from Buffalo to Cleveland, a third stretched across southern Michigan; a fourth emerged in the Columbia, Cincinnati, Muncie, and Indianapolis urban regions; and a fifth in the Chicago, Milwaukee, Davenport, and Rockport urban regions. Beyond this, there were small clusters in the St. Louis and Chattanooga urban regions plus a scattering of individual counties in the Houston, Los Angeles, San Francisco, and Minneapolis regions.

In terms of subsector specializations, the Great Lakes region (taken as a whole) formed a contrast to the Eastern Seaboard. The greatest relative specializations were in the forging, stamping, and screw machine products that fed the production of motor vehicles, agricultural machinery, appliances, and other assembly-oriented intermediate industrial processes. The western end of the Old Manufacturing Belt was, and is, the heartland of these industrial processes. There were variations in the intensity of specialization within this generalized picture. For example, with its close ties to the automobile industry, southern Michigan displayed specialization in the production of forgings and stampings three times the national average. The Ohio and Indiana concentrations were especially marked in the production of plumbing and those parts of miscellaneous fabricated metals engaged in the production of pipes, valves, and fittings. Southern Michigan was also the only production region outside Hartford to display at least a weak specialization in the production of cutlery and general hardware. Outside these major historical production clusters, the more widespread, localized concentrations were most heavily devoted either to the production of structural metal products, or cans, or both for the obvious reason that their markets in construction and agricultural production were more widespread.

Now turn to the patterns formed by competitive shifts during the study period. First, it is clear that with localized exceptions, the broad regions of historical specialization in the Old Manufacturing Belt experienced competitive losses. At urban-region scale, 43 percent of the total loss was concentrated in the Atlantic Seaboard, with the balance in the Great Lakes region. However, the loss relative to initial-year employment was much more severe in the East. The Great Lakes heartland position in the industry yielded mostly lagging losses. It is noteworthy that, in the face of these region-scale losses, there were large clusters of counties in central and northern Michigan, in northern Indiana, and in north central Illinois that displayed competitive gains.

As was true of manufacturing generally, the balance of the nation was experiencing competitive gains. However (again as was true of manufacturing generally), a small number of localized urban regions were the principal beneficiaries. The Los Angeles, San Francisco, and San Diego urban regions captured a quarter of the gain (with Los Angeles over 17 percent). While the southeastern part of the nation captured about half of the gains, one-third of all gains were concentrated in two clusters—one centered on Memphis, Huntsville, and Birmingham, but reaching northward through Nashville and Louisville to Evansville; the second centered on Houston, Tyler, Shreveport, Texarkana, and Dallas. There were modest concentrations of gains in the familiar Piedmont region and a heavy concentration (given its almost nonexistent historical base) in peninsular Florida. In fact, Orlando claimed the largest share of the gain of any urban region except Los Angeles. Another minor cluster of gain centered on Minneapolis, plus Waterloo, Des Moines, and Omaha.

What were the subsector manifestations of these shifts and how are they explained? Take the commodity cut first. In the production of cans, the Middle Atlantic region, first, and the North Central region, second, were the competitive losers while the rest of the nation experienced competitive gains. The major gains were in the Pacific, Mountain, and Florida urban regions that displayed the dramatic gains in fruit and vegetable cropping noted earlier. A second subsector, fabricated structural metal products, displayed shift patterns with an equally unambiguous explanation. This subsector had the largest correlation with total population (over .9) and it provides direct inputs for the construction of residential, commercial, industrial, and governmental structures. Because the latter had shifted to the South and West in response to the thoroughly described shift in settlement patterns, it is not surprising to find the production of structural metal products following in their wake. The South (from the Atlantic Coast through Texas and Oklahoma) was the principal gainer; the West experienced more moderate gains.

The production of heating and plumbing equipment also serves construction processes and is more widely distributed than fabricated metals generally. However, it does tend to be more concentrated than structural metal products because of more complex processes and greater scale and skilled labor requirements. By 1940, only the Chattanooga and Memphis urban regions had recorded specializations outside the Great Lakes region (although at county scale, several counties in the Houston, Shreveport, Los Angeles, and San Francisco urban regions did so). The West South Central, Pacific, and South Atlantic regions (in that order) captured the study-period competitive gains.

All of the remaining fabricated metal subsectors supply inputs for other intermediate metal processing industries that produce machinery, transportation equipment, appliances, and so forth. Historically these have been most concentrated in the Old Manufacturing Belt. For example, although that belt claimed only half of all employment in 1940 and two-thirds of all manufacturing employment, it claimed 98 percent of all motor vehicle employment and 87 percent of all machinery employment. The latter were particularly important intermediate consumers of fabricated metal products. It is not surprising, therefore,

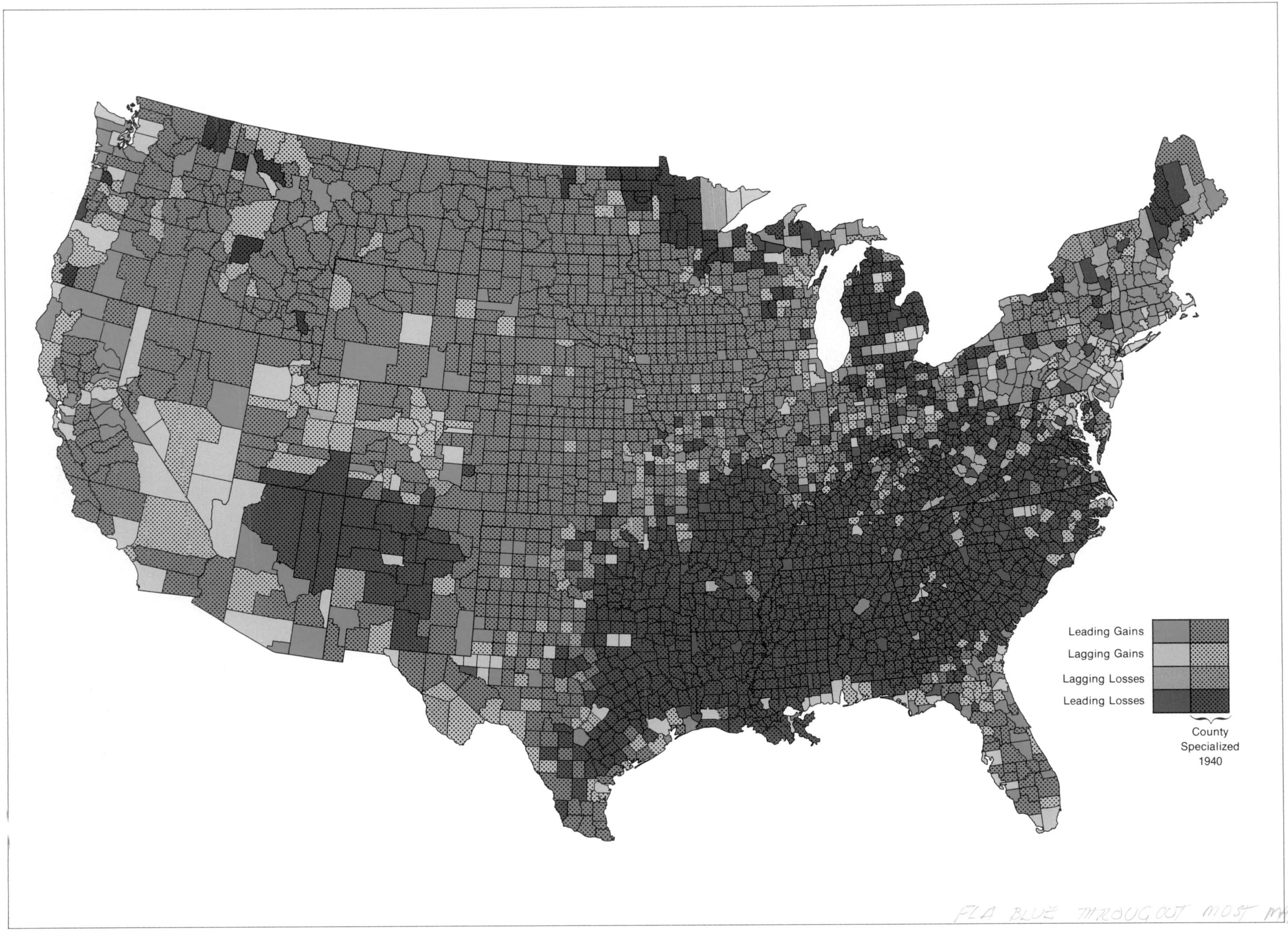

PLATE II-1. Agriculture, 1940–70: Leading and Lagging Competitive Shifts

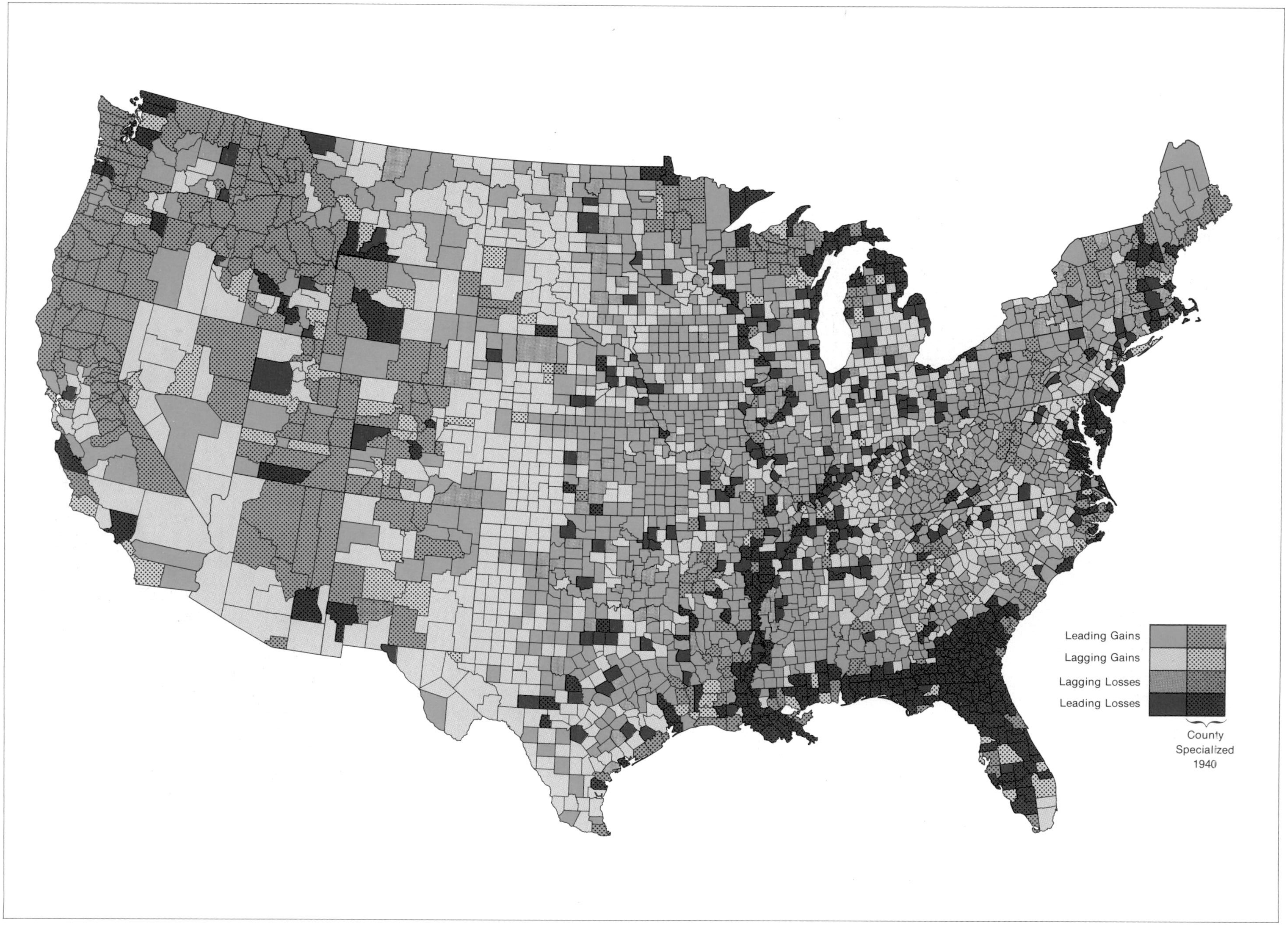

PLATE II-2. Forestry and Fisheries, 1940–70: Leading and Lagging Competitive Shifts

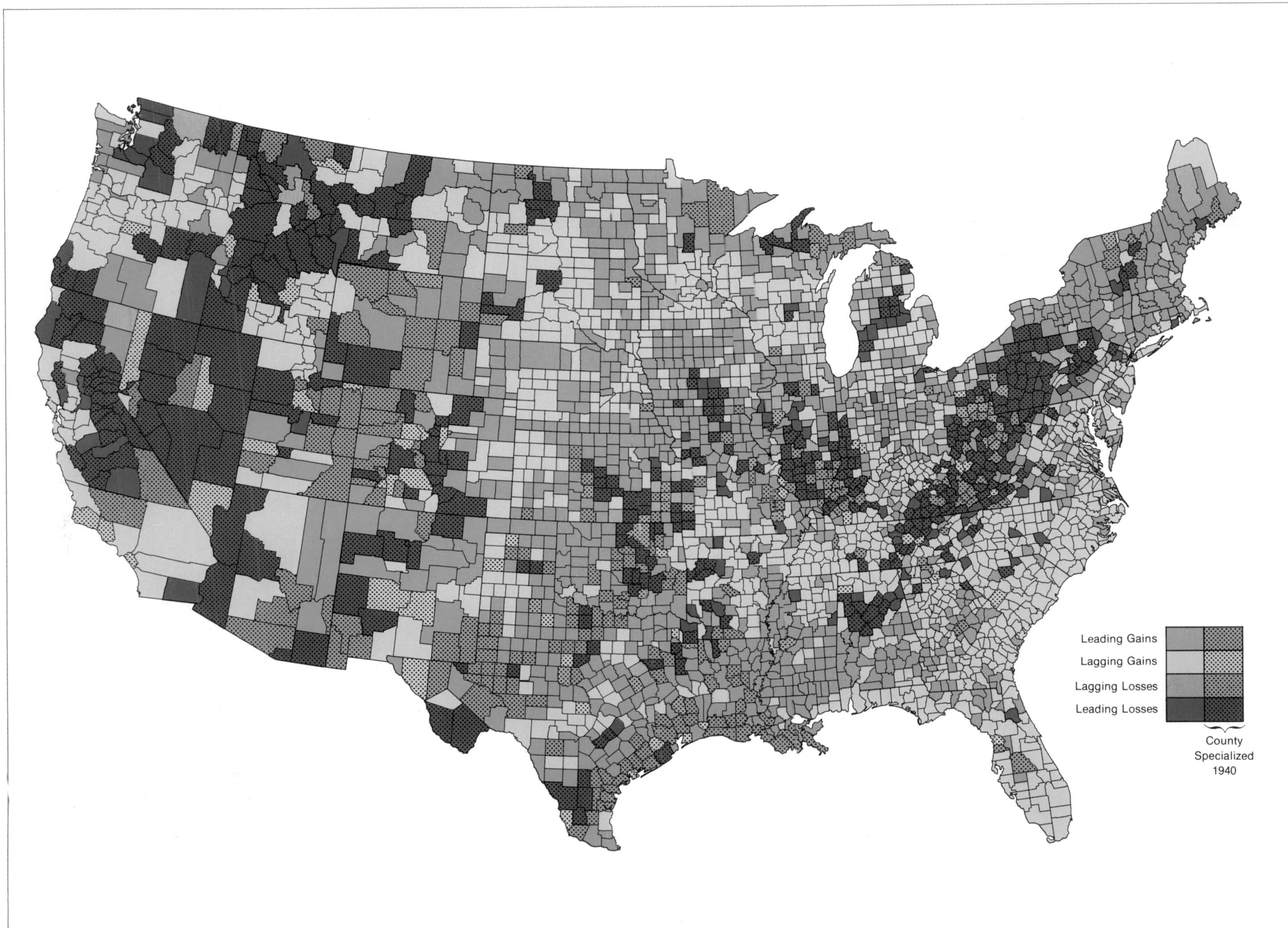

PLATE II-3. Mining, 1940–70: Leading and Lagging Competitive Shifts

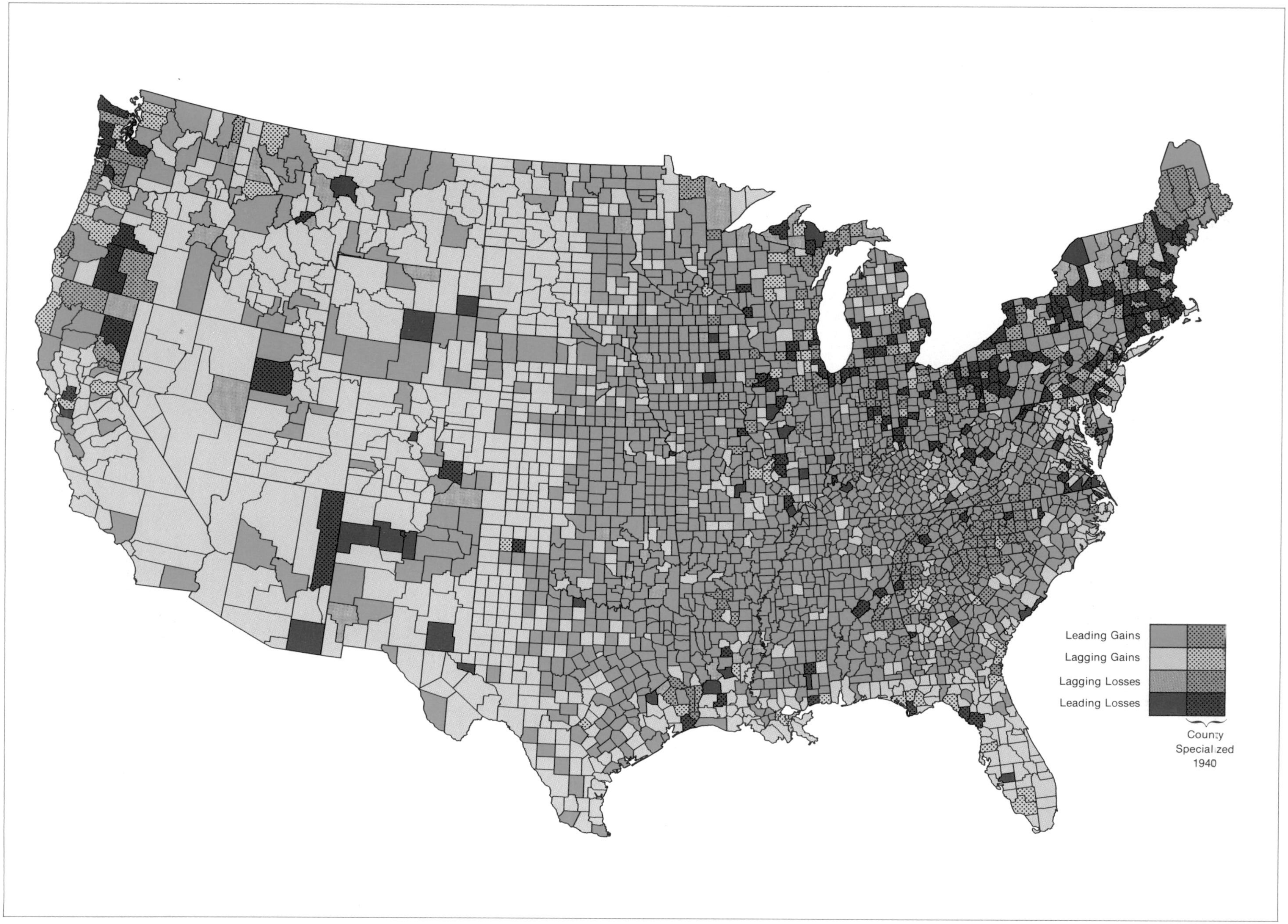

PLATE II-4. Total Manufacturing, 1940–70: Leading and Lagging Competitive Shifts

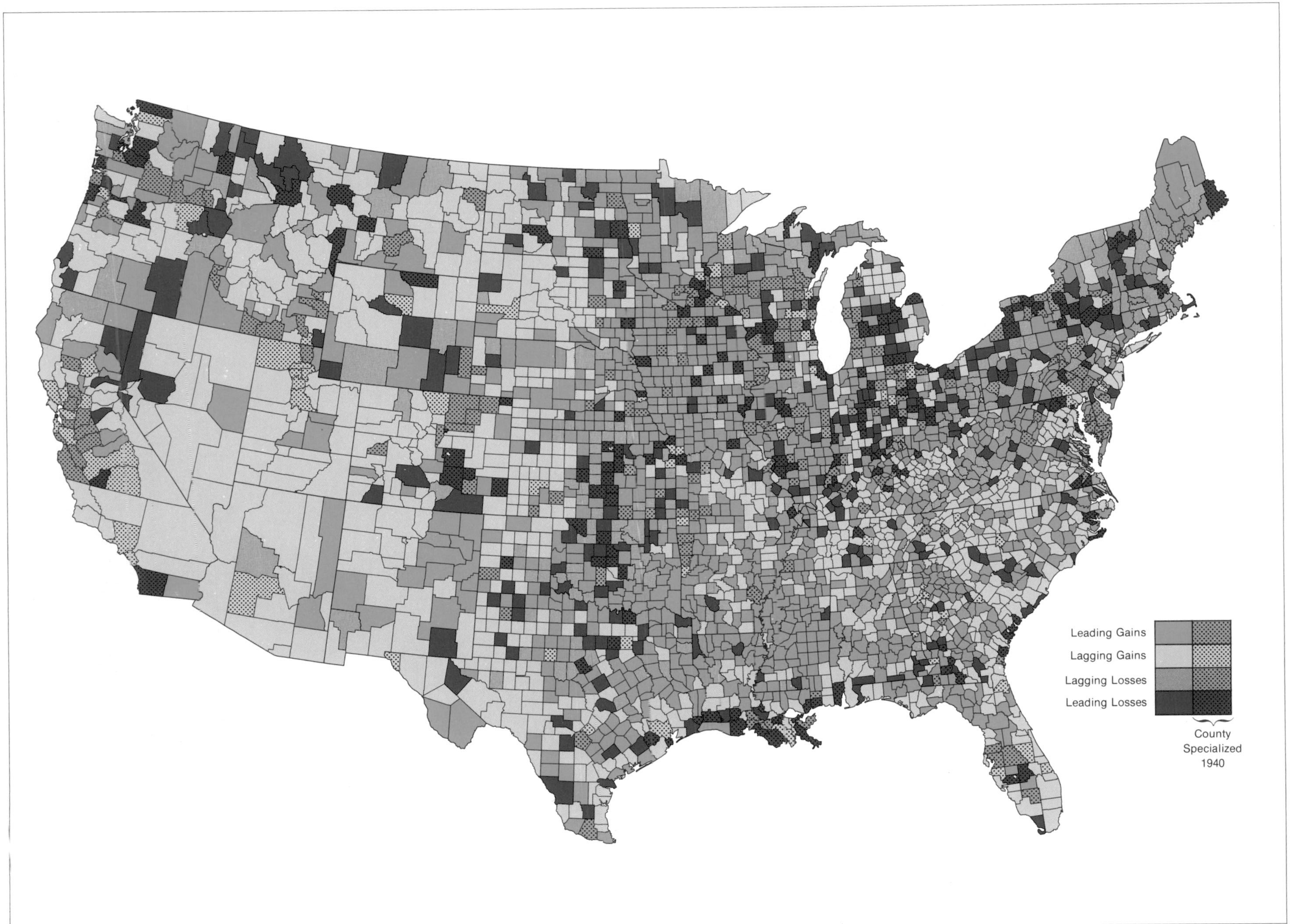

PLATE II-5. Food and Kindred Products, 1940–70: Leading and Lagging Competitive Shifts

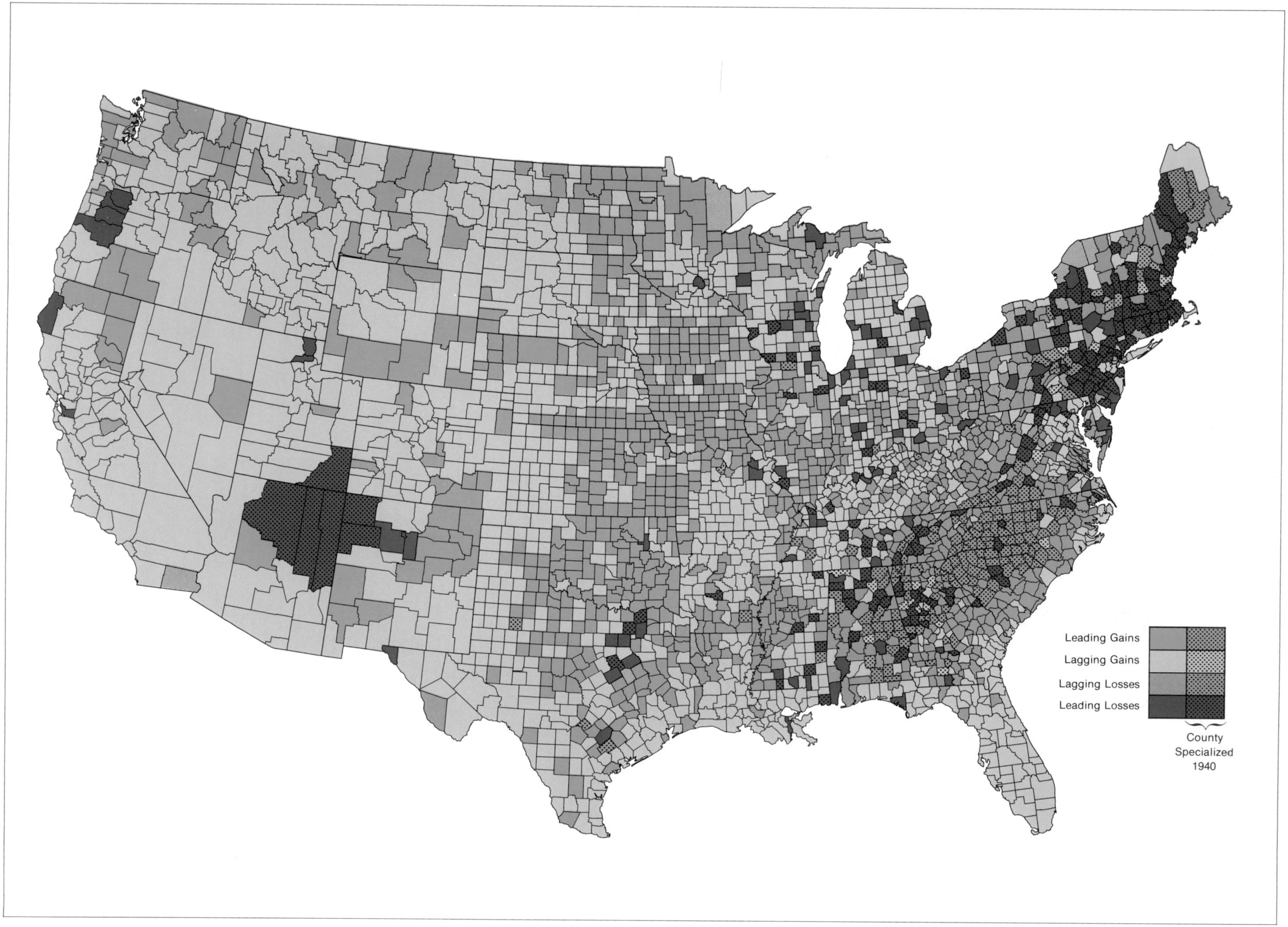

PLATE II-6. Textile Mill Products, 1940–70: Leading and Lagging Competitive Shifts

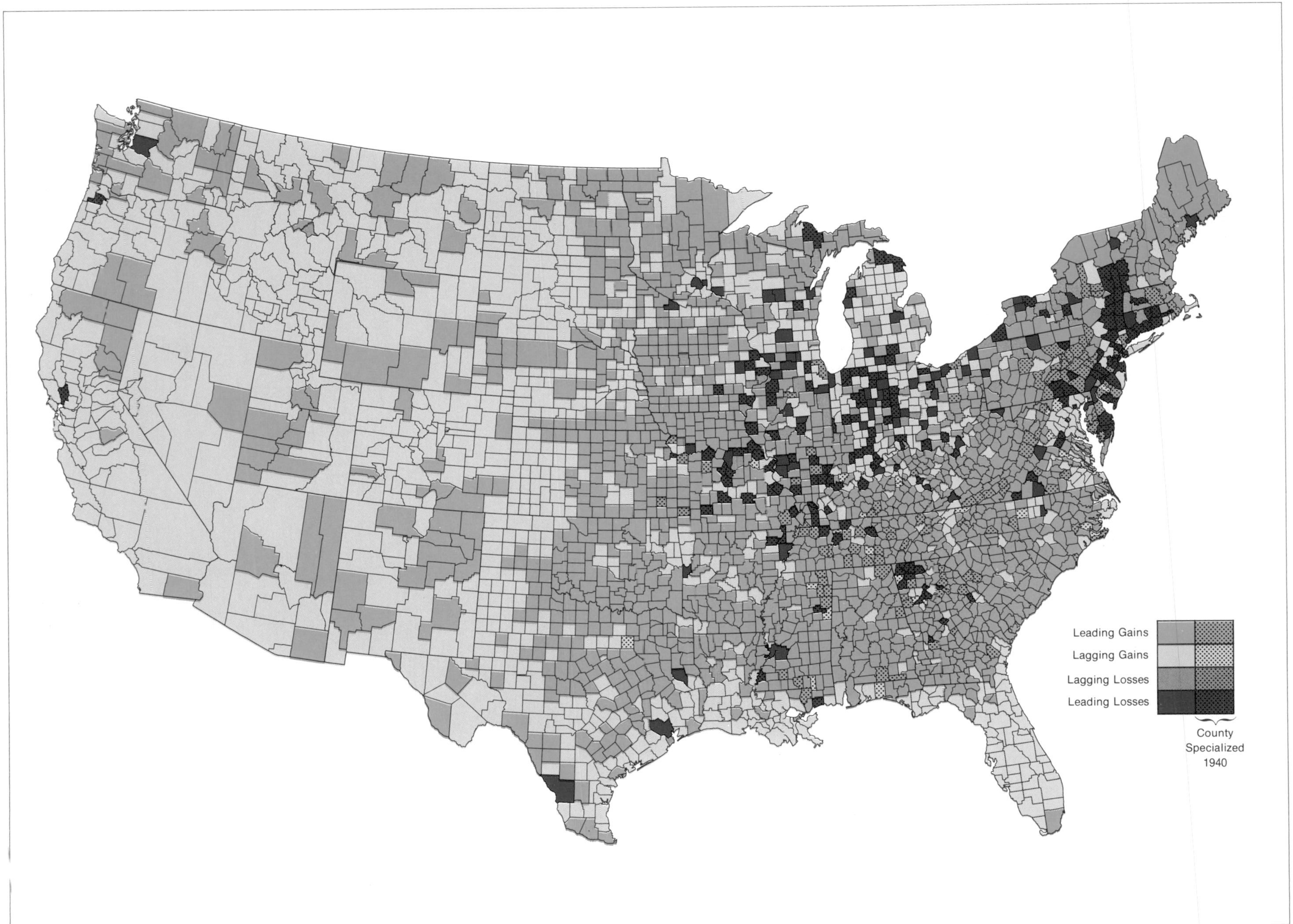

PLATE II-7. Apparel, 1940–70: Leading and Lagging Competitive Shifts

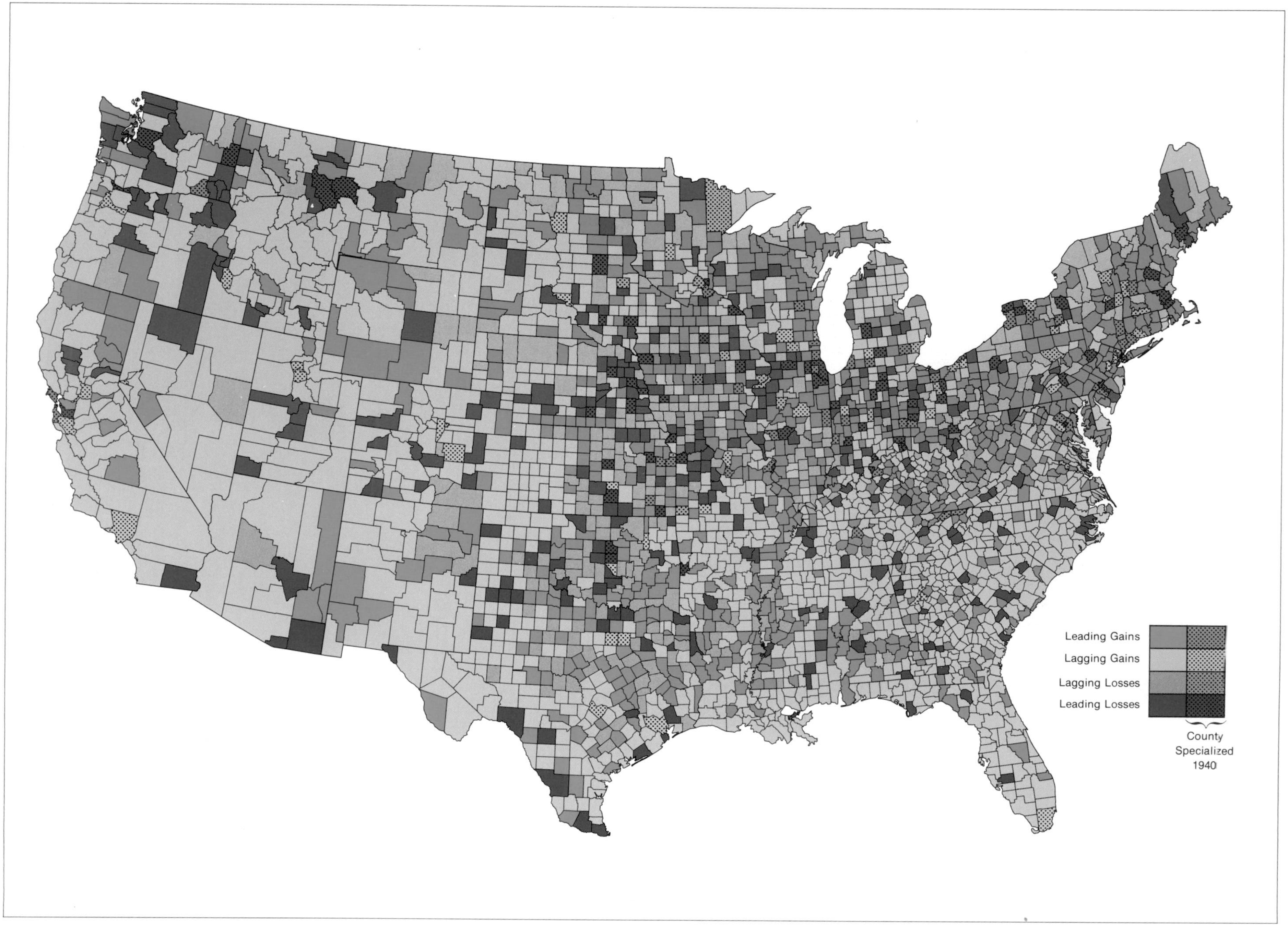

PLATE II-8. Printing and Allied Products, 1940–70: Leading and Lagging Competitive Shifts

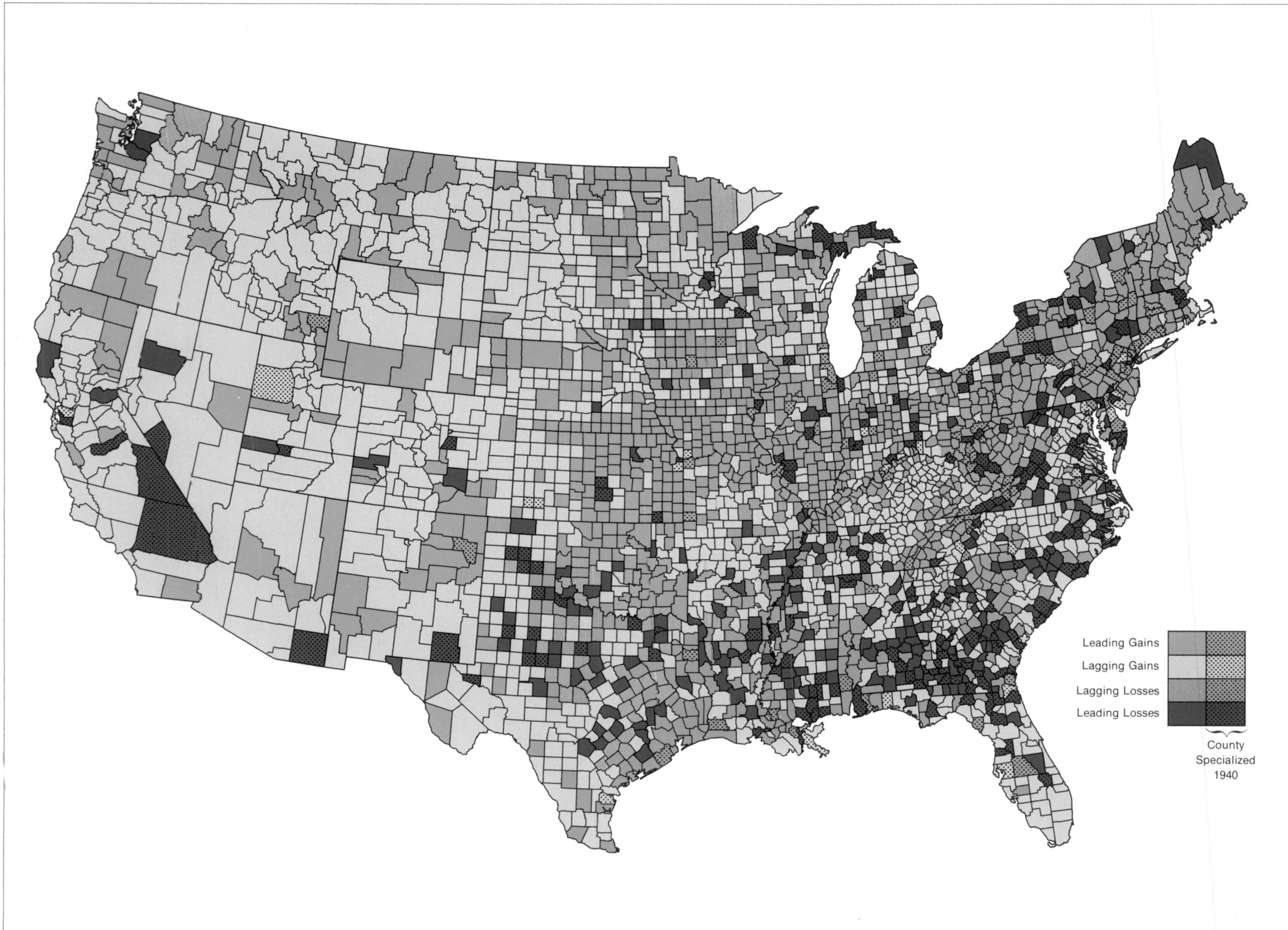

PLATE II-9. Chemicals and Allied Products, 1940–70: Leading and Lagging Competitive Shifts

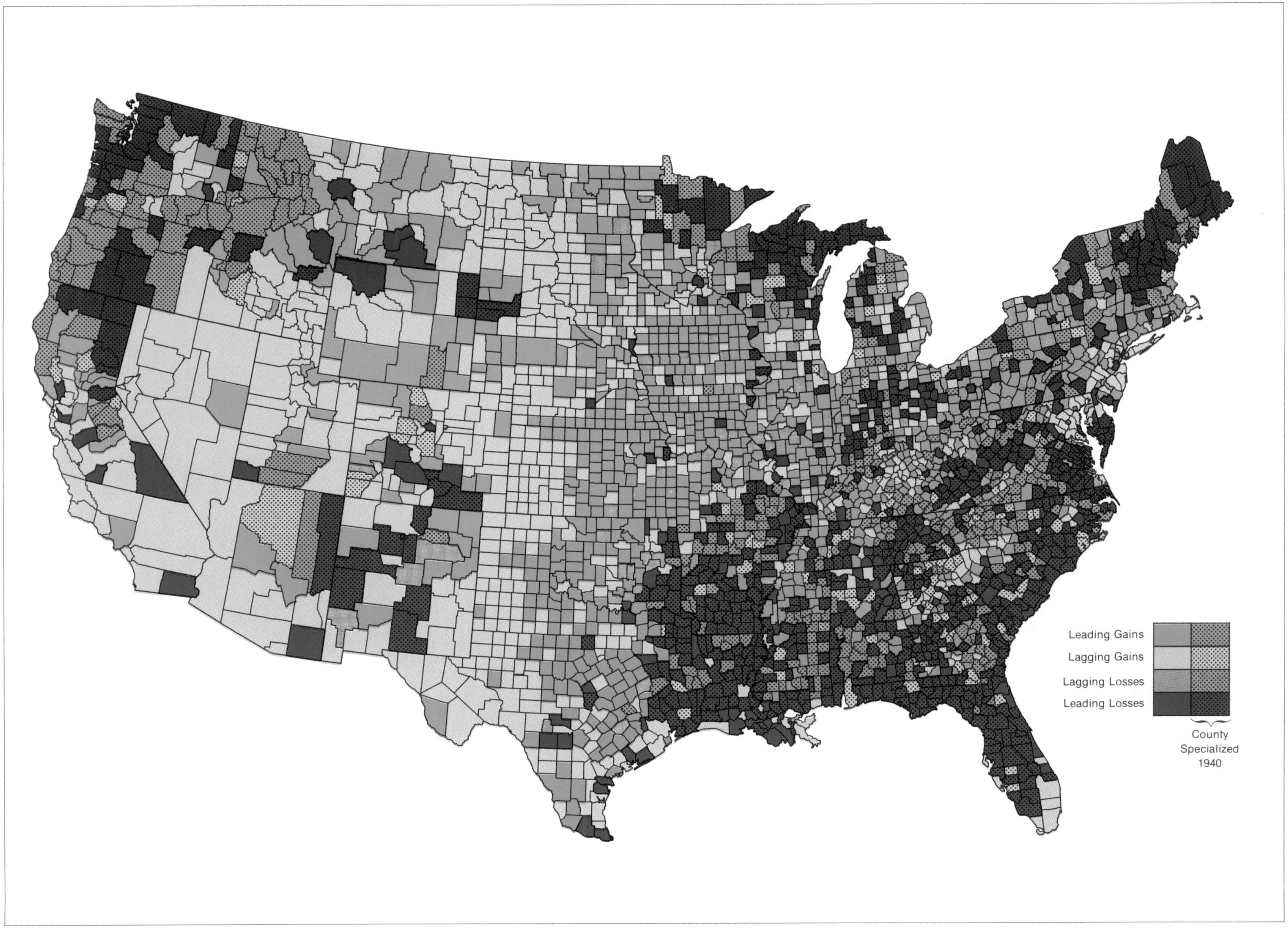

PLATE II-10. Wood Products and Furniture, 1940–70: Leading and Lagging Competitive Shifts

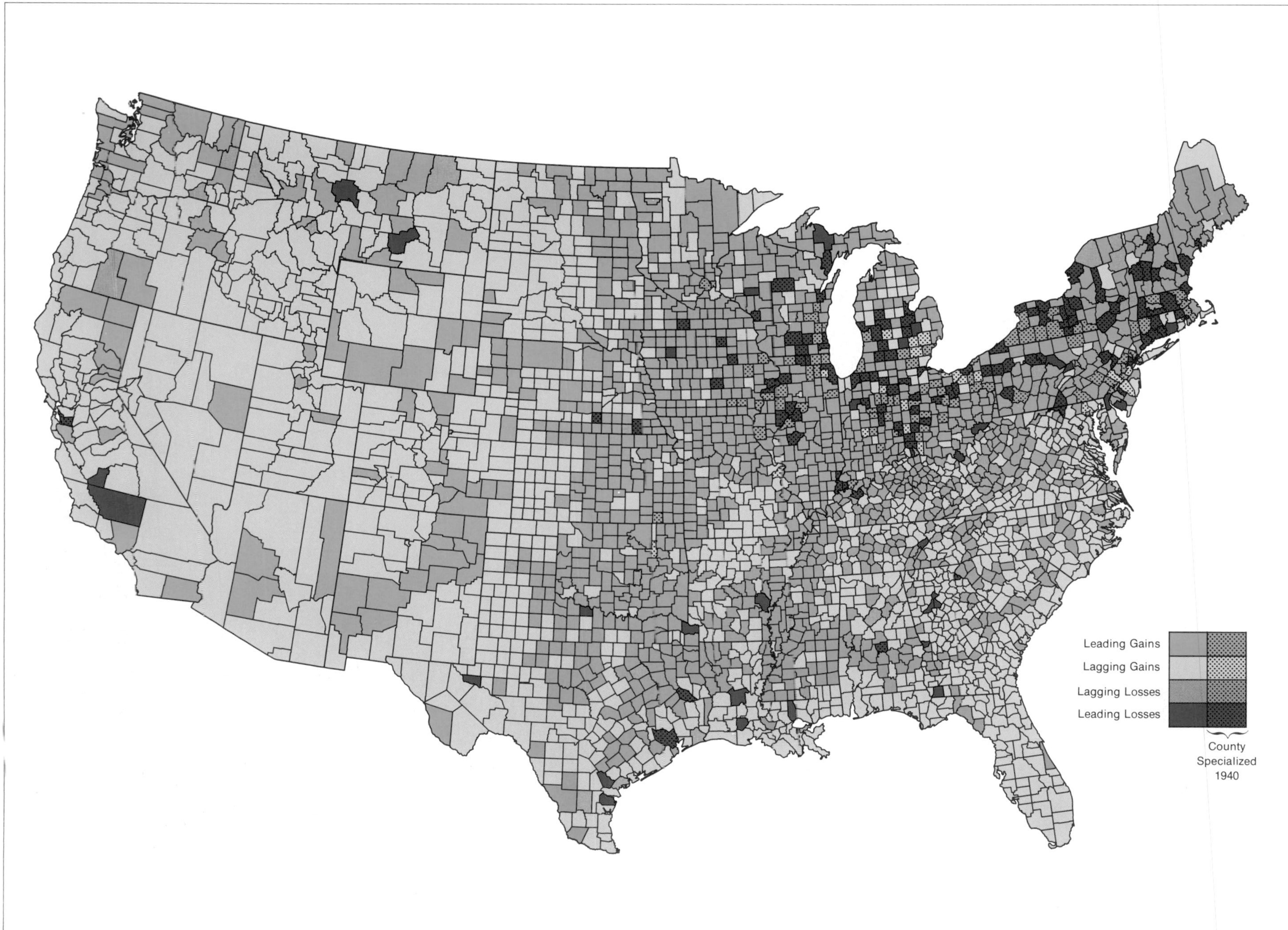

PLATE II-11. Total Machinery, 1940–70: Leading and Lagging Competitive Shifts

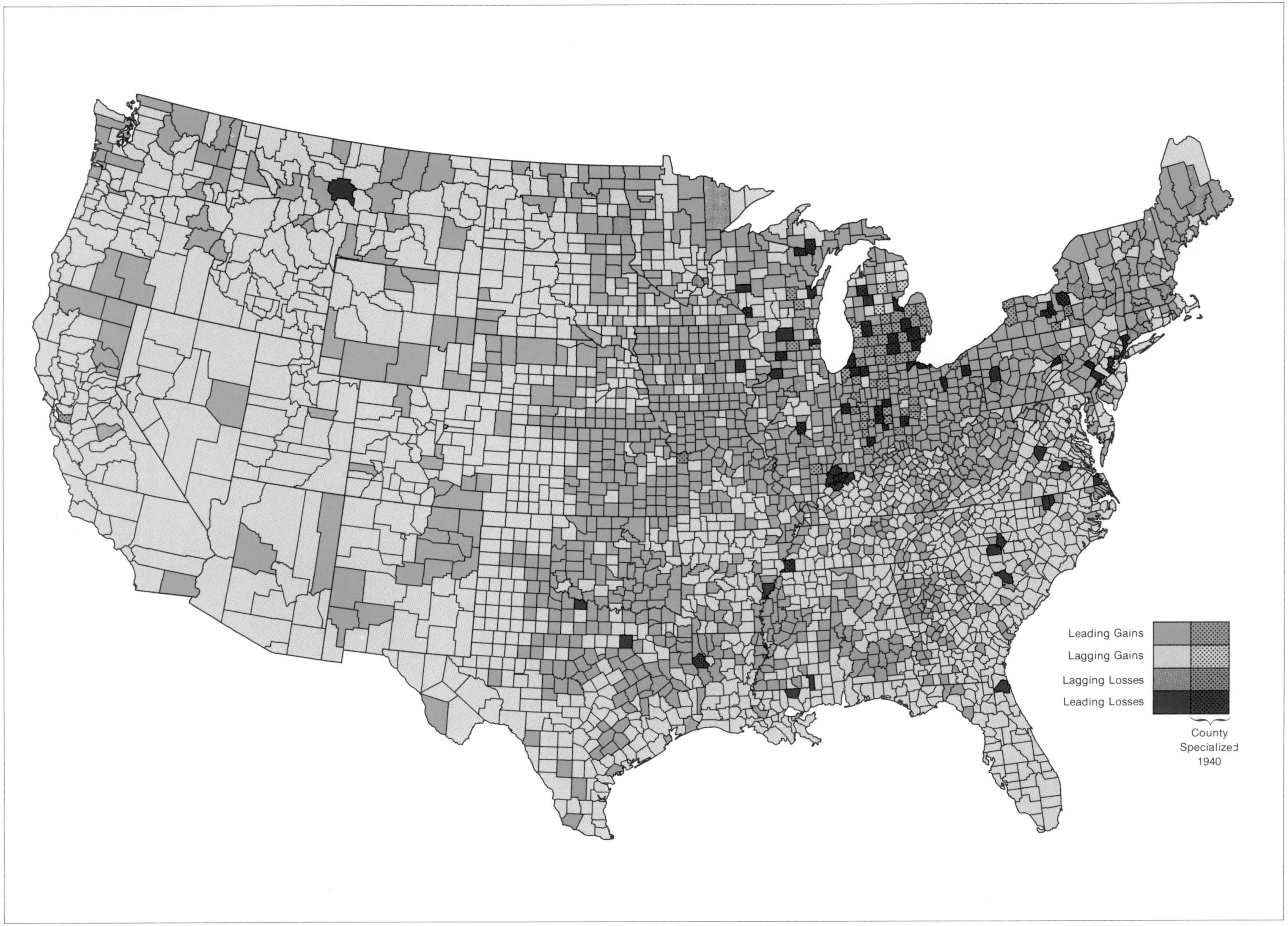

PLATE II-12. Motor Vehicles and Equipment, 1940–70: Leading and Lagging Competitive Shifts

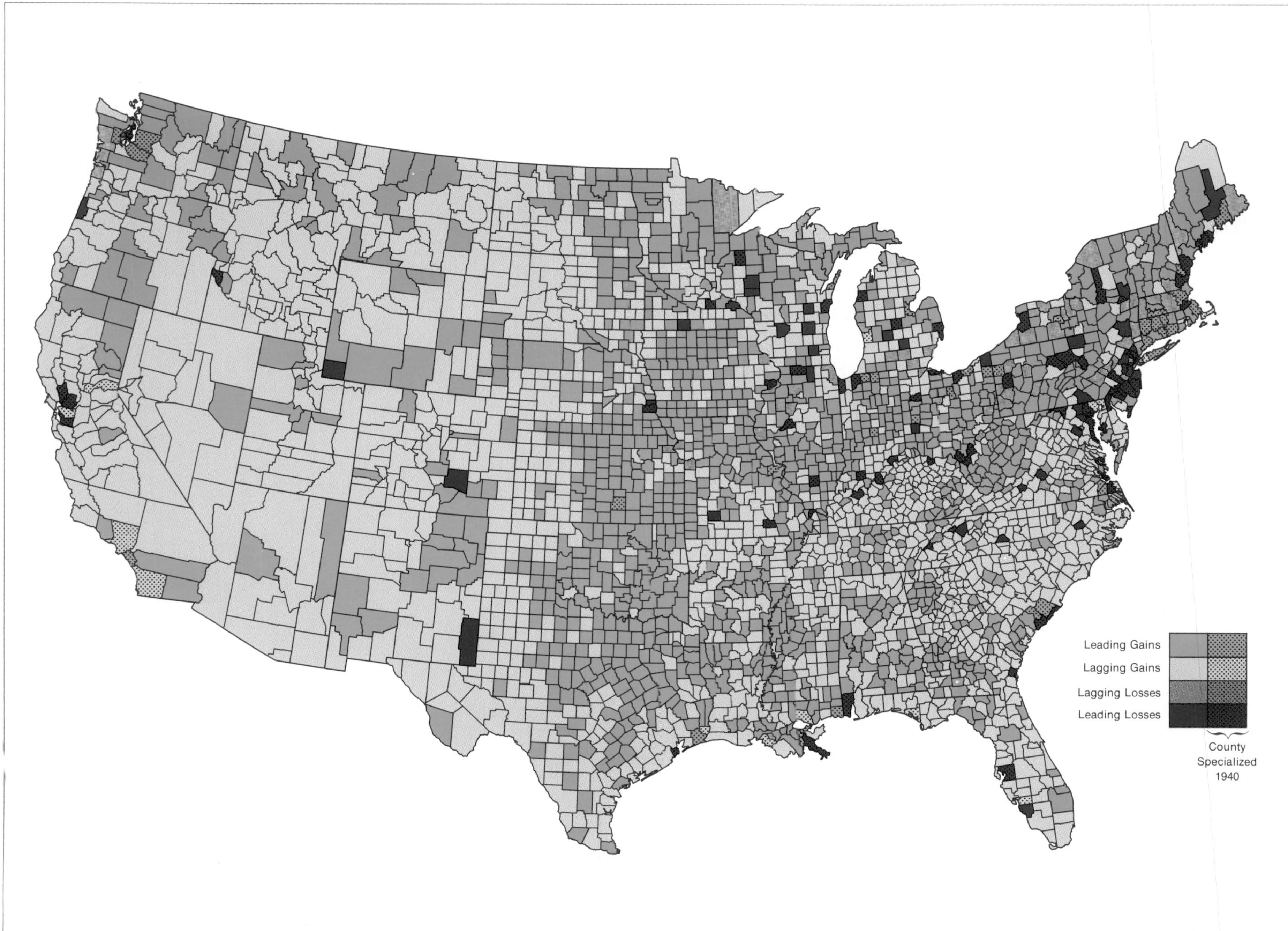

PLATE II-13. Other Transportation Equipment, 1940–70: Leading and Lagging Competitive Shifts

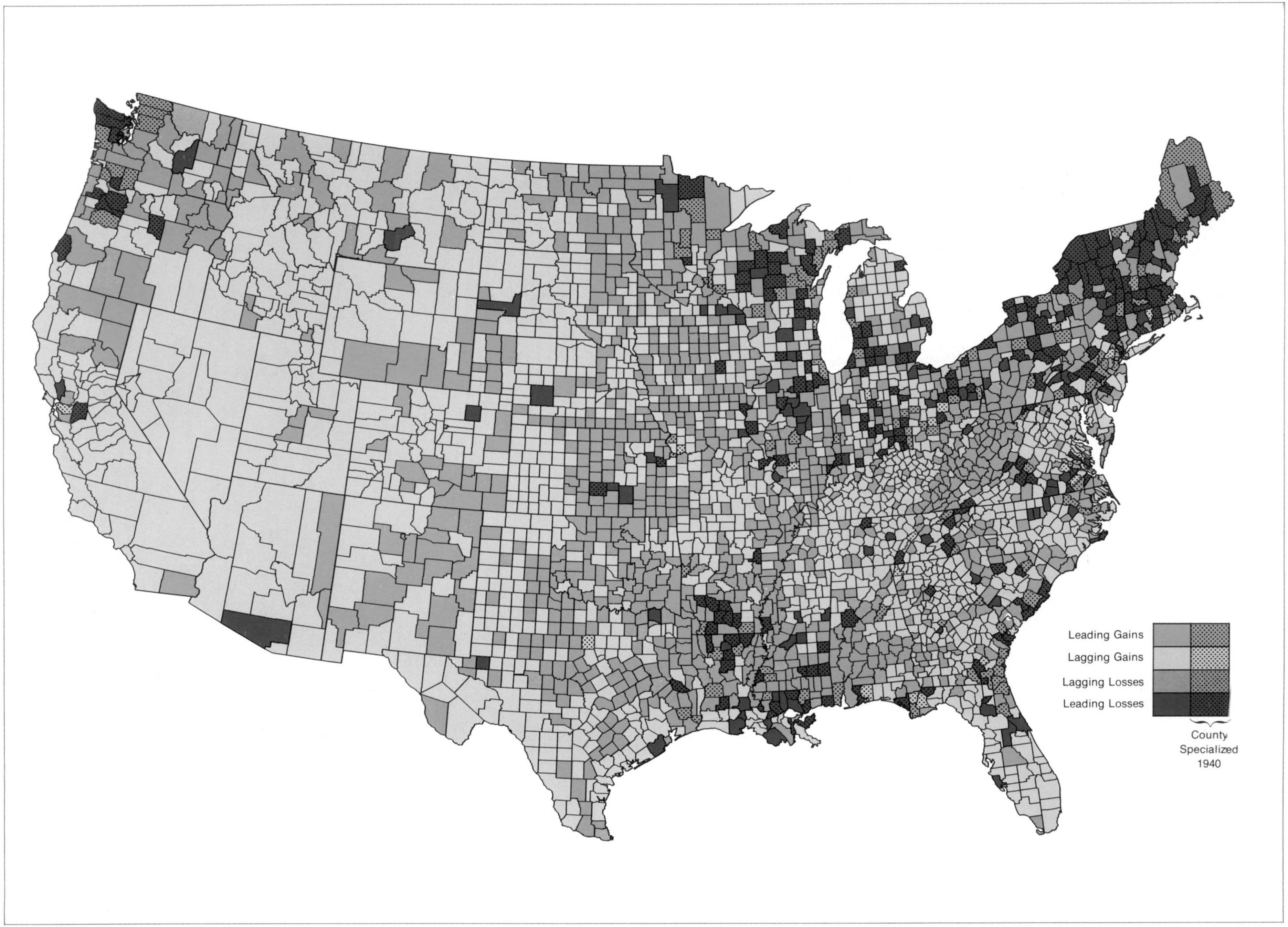

PLATE II-14. Paper, 1950–70: Leading and Lagging Competitive Shifts

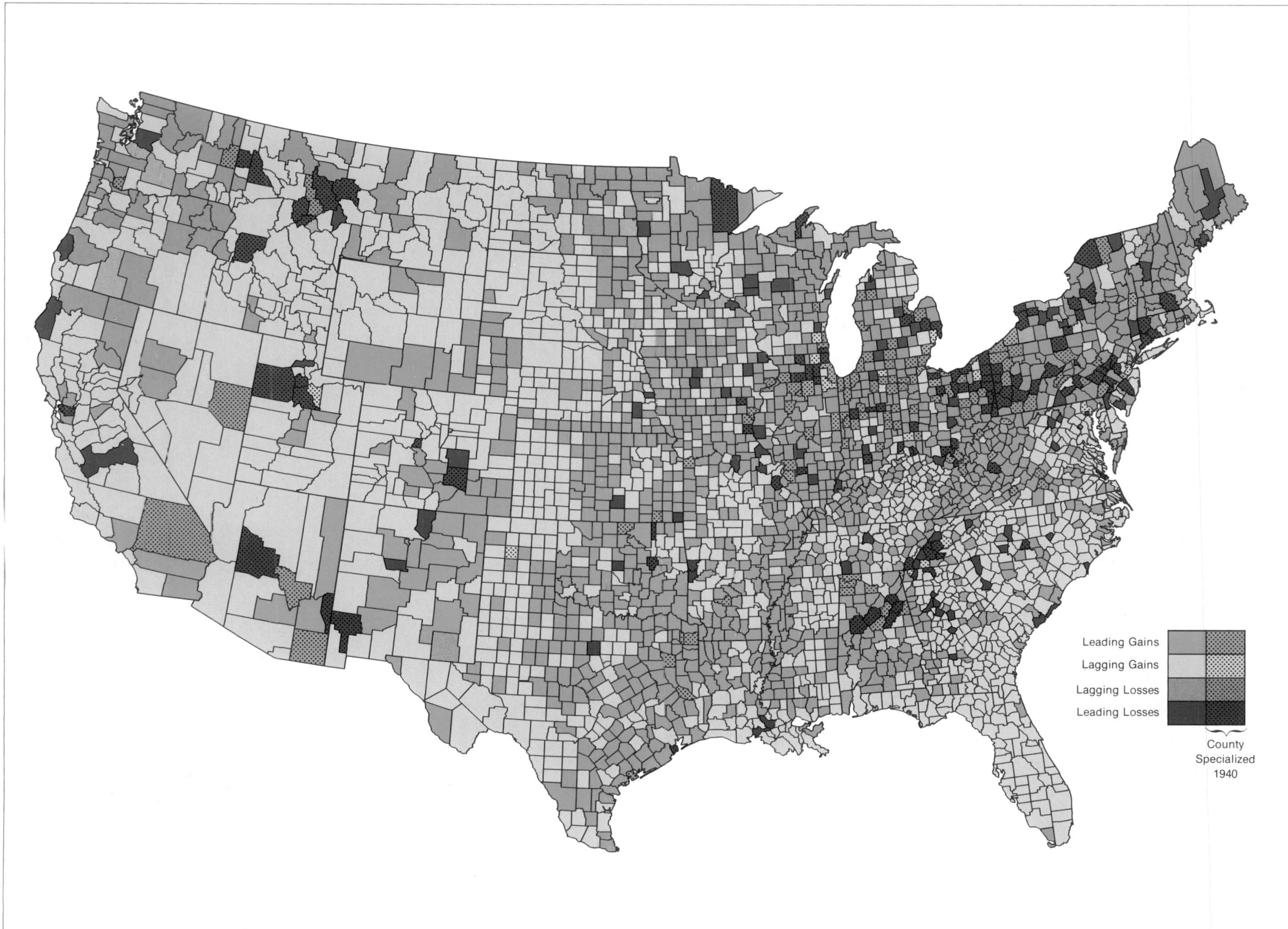

PLATE II-15. Primary Metals, 1950–70: Leading and Lagging Competitive Shifts

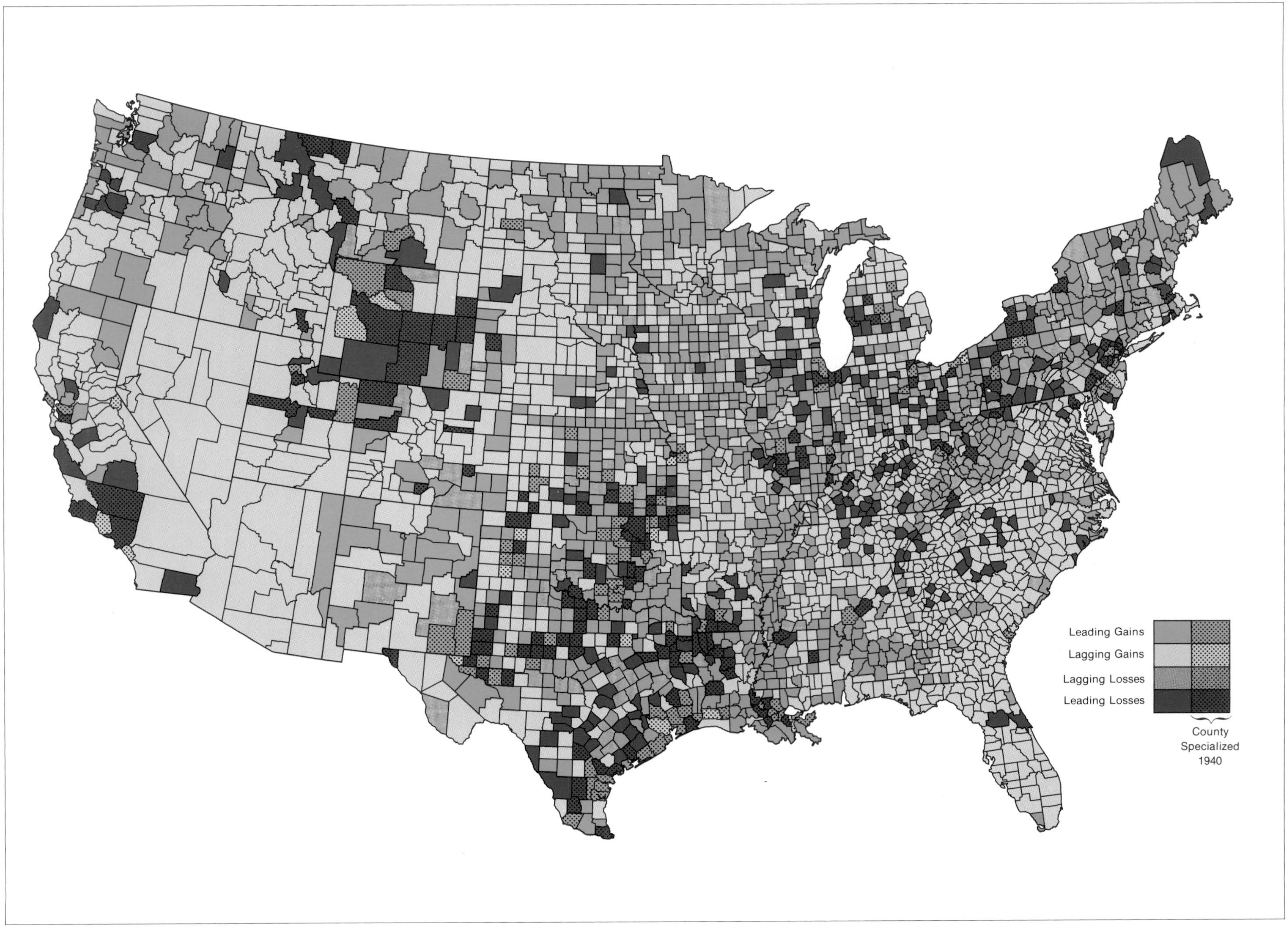

PLATE II-16. Petroleum Refining, 1950–70: Leading and Lagging Competitive Shifts

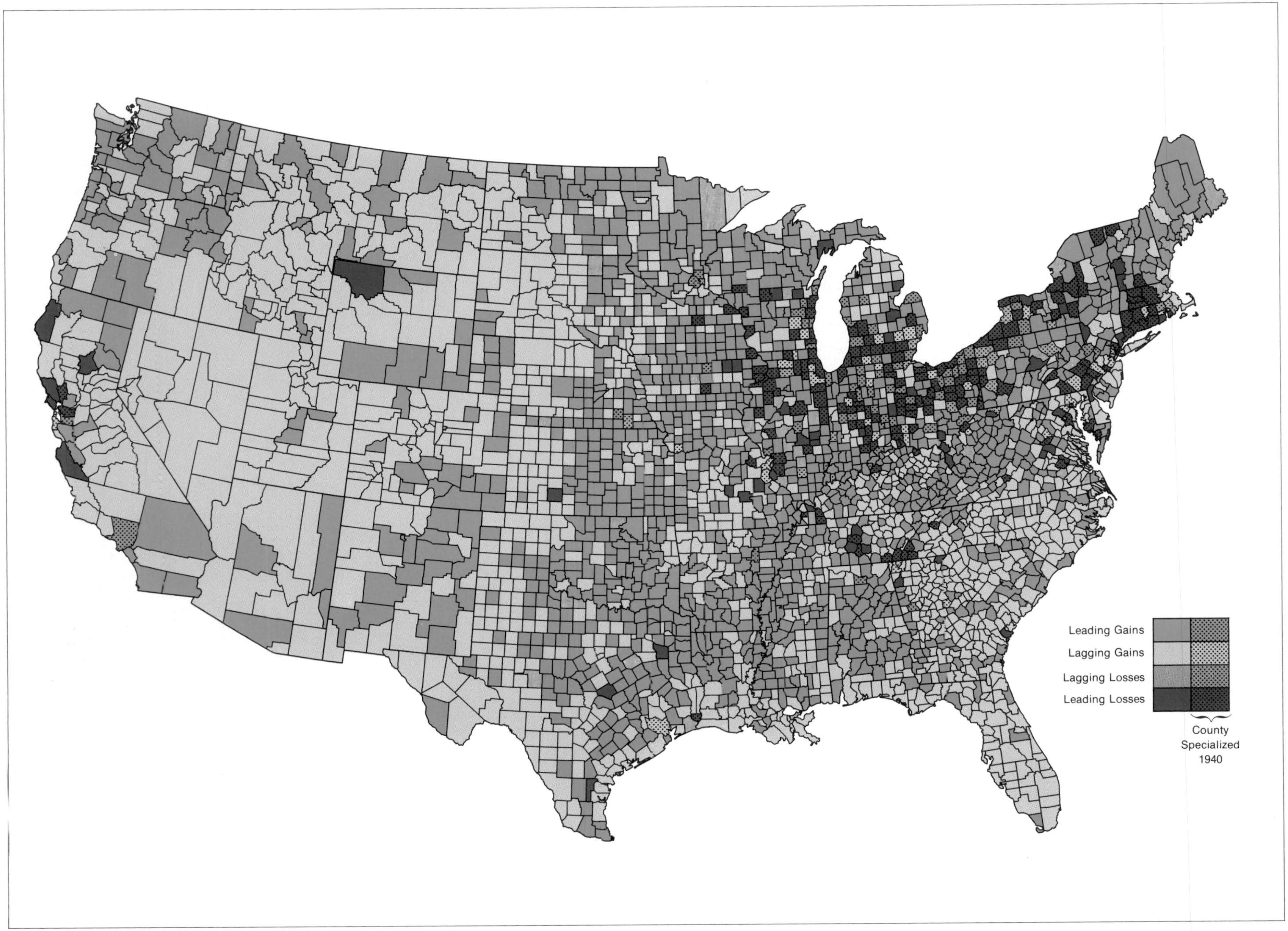

PLATE II-17. Fabricated Metals, 1950–70: Leading and Lagging Competitive Shifts

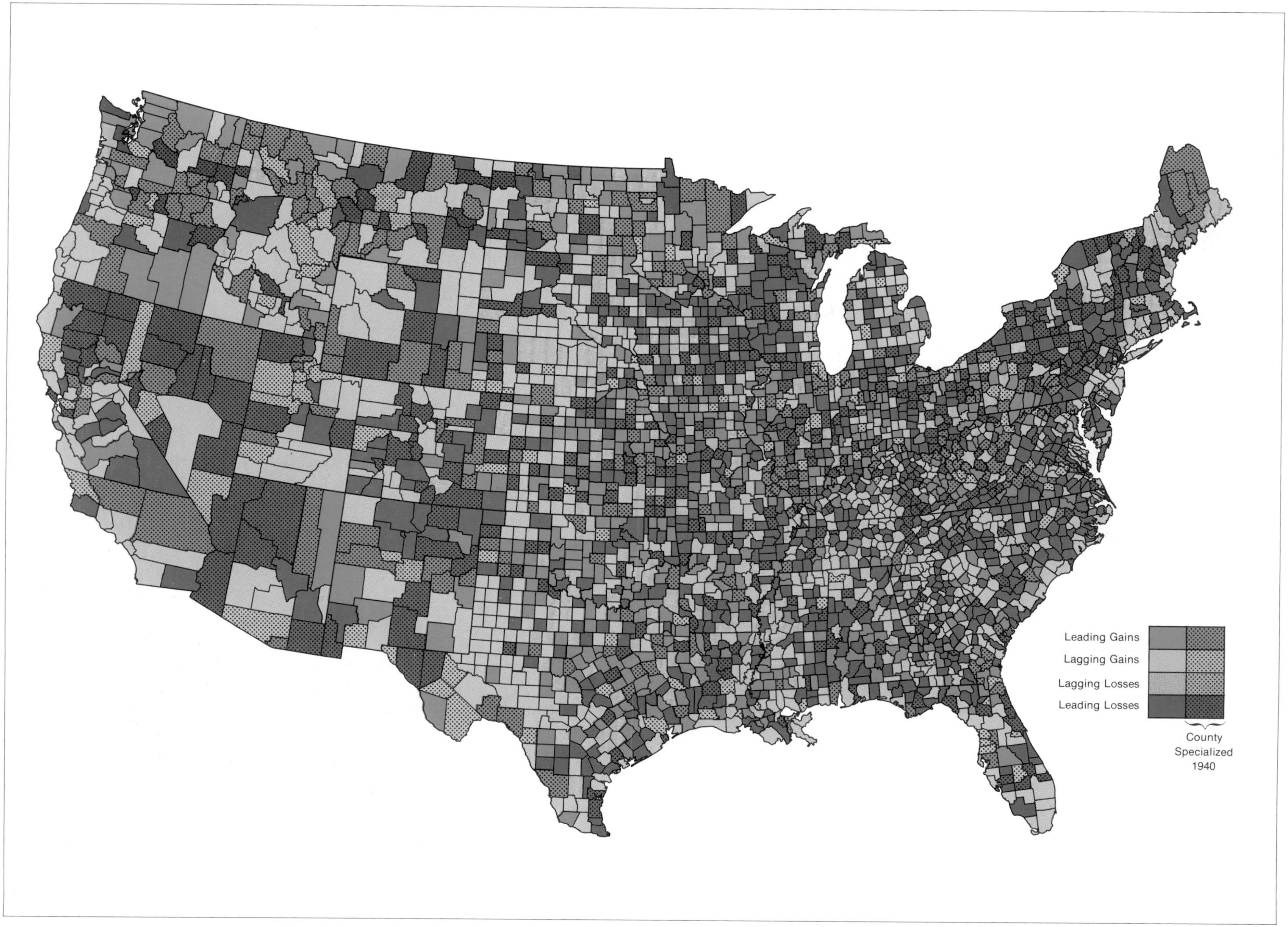

PLATE II-18. Railroad Transportation, 1940–70: Leading and Lagging Competitive Shifts

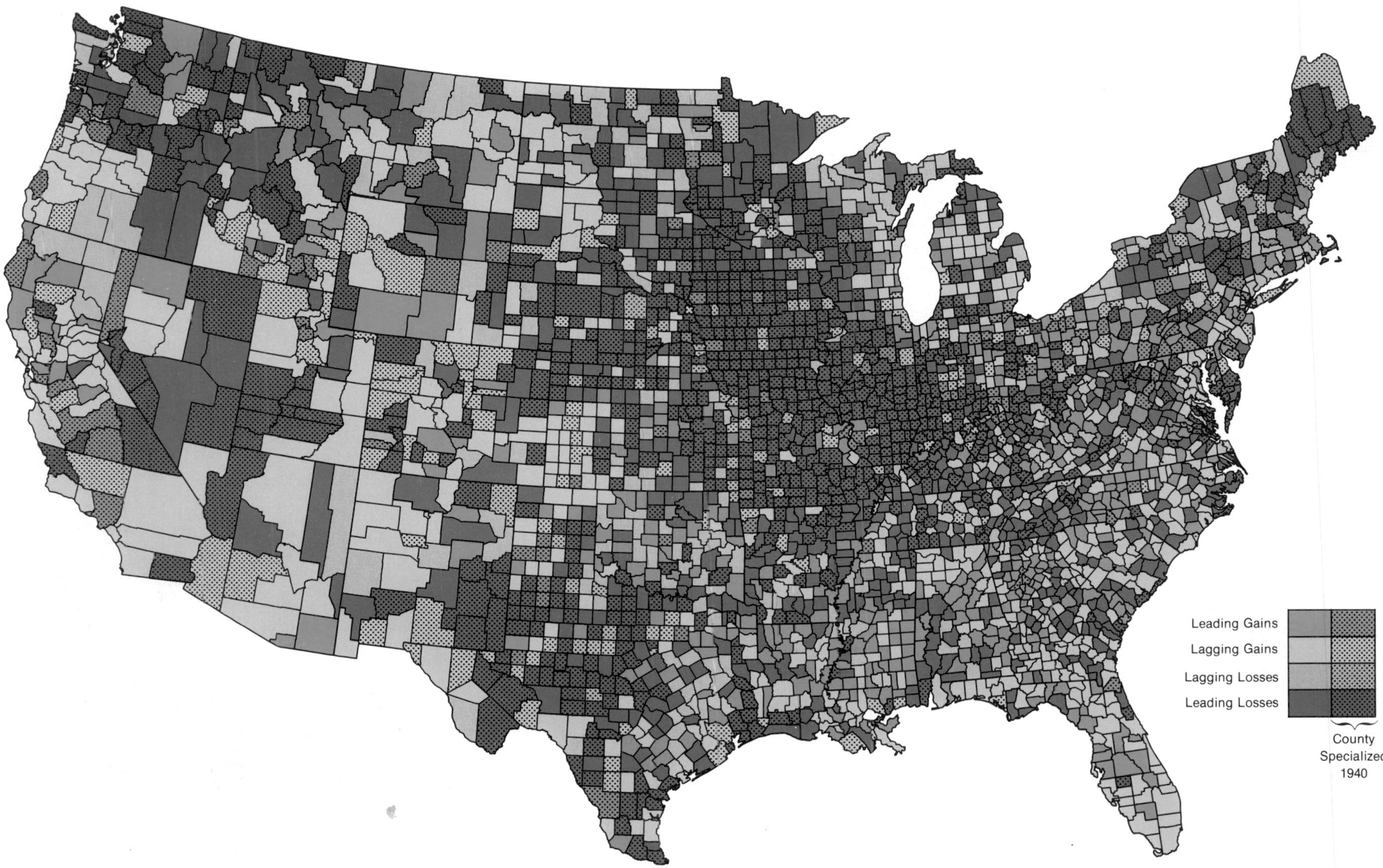

PLATE II-19. Trucking and Warehousing, 1940–70: Leading and Lagging Competitive Shifts

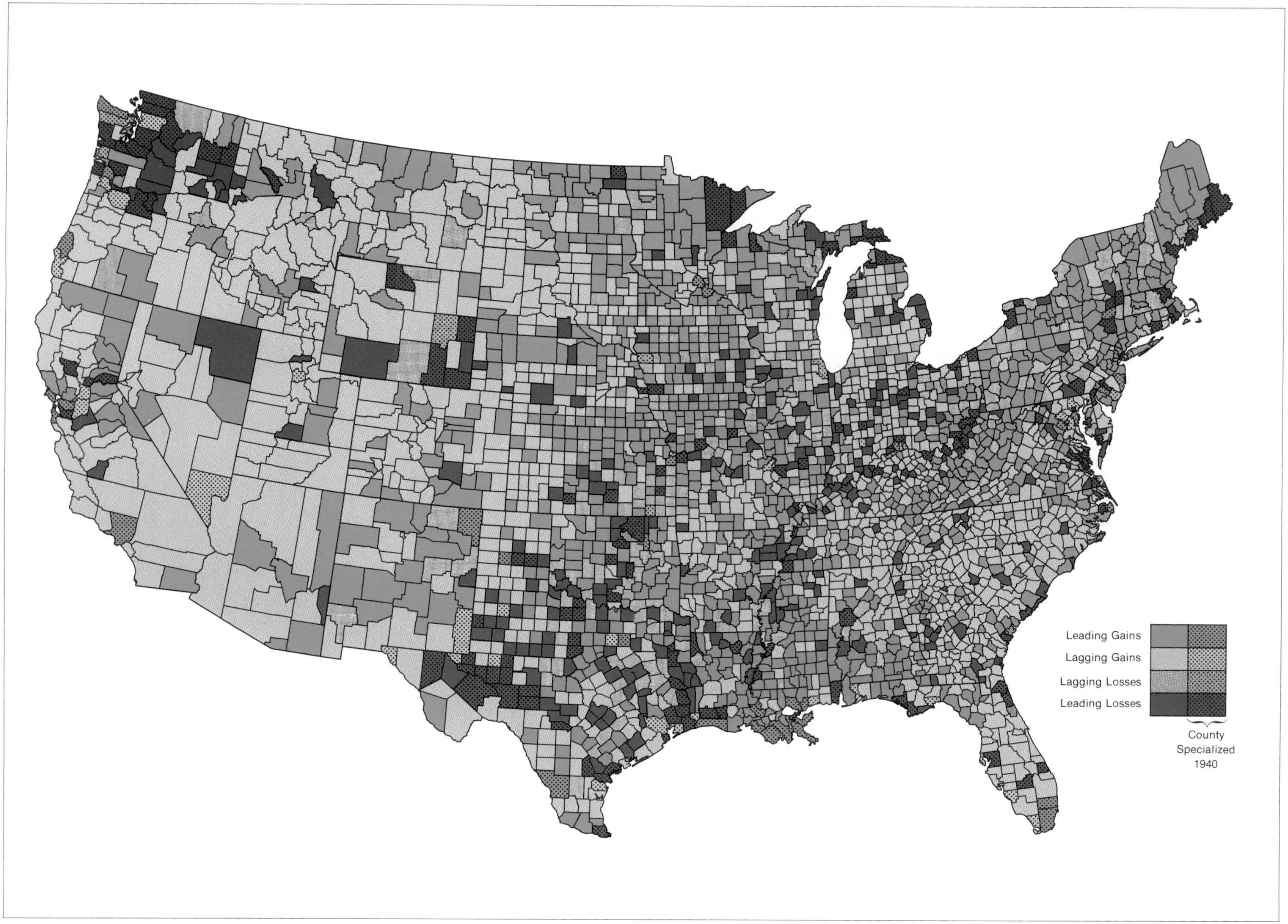

PLATE II-20. Other Transportation Services, 1940–70: Leading and Lagging Competitive Shifts

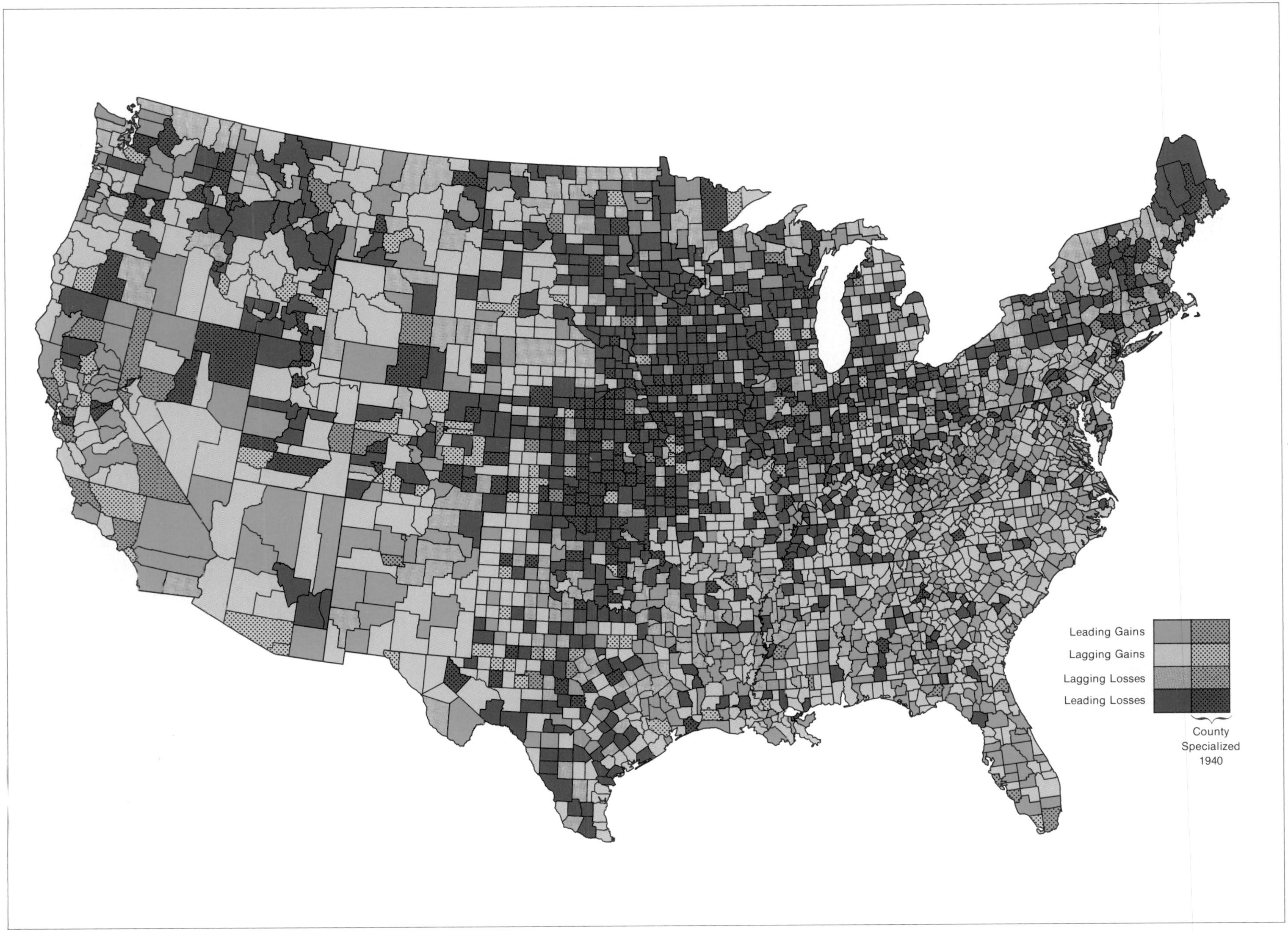

PLATE II-21. Communications, 1940–70: Leading and Lagging Competitive Shifts

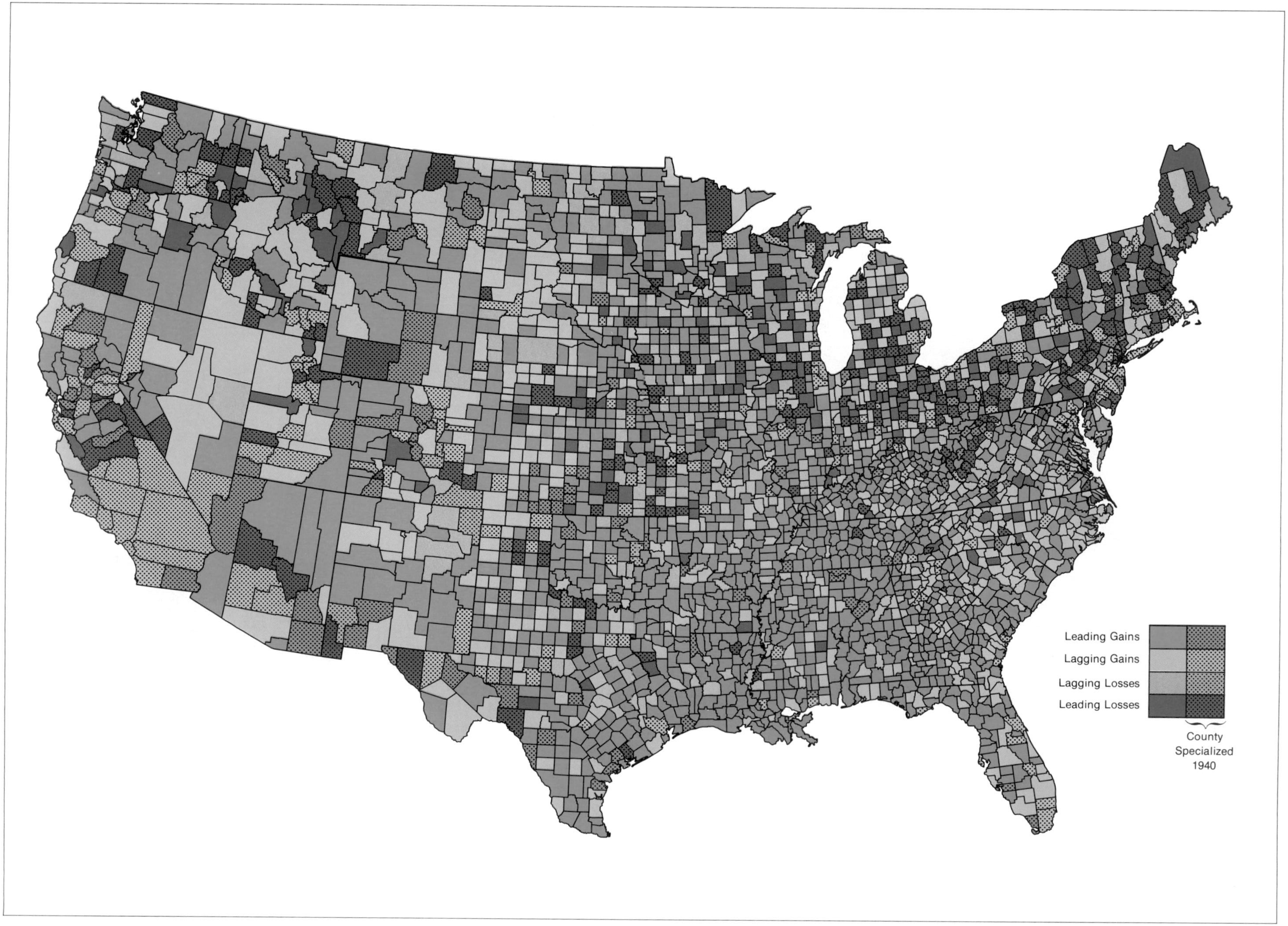

PLATE II-22. Public Utilities, 1940–70: Leading and Lagging Competitive Shifts

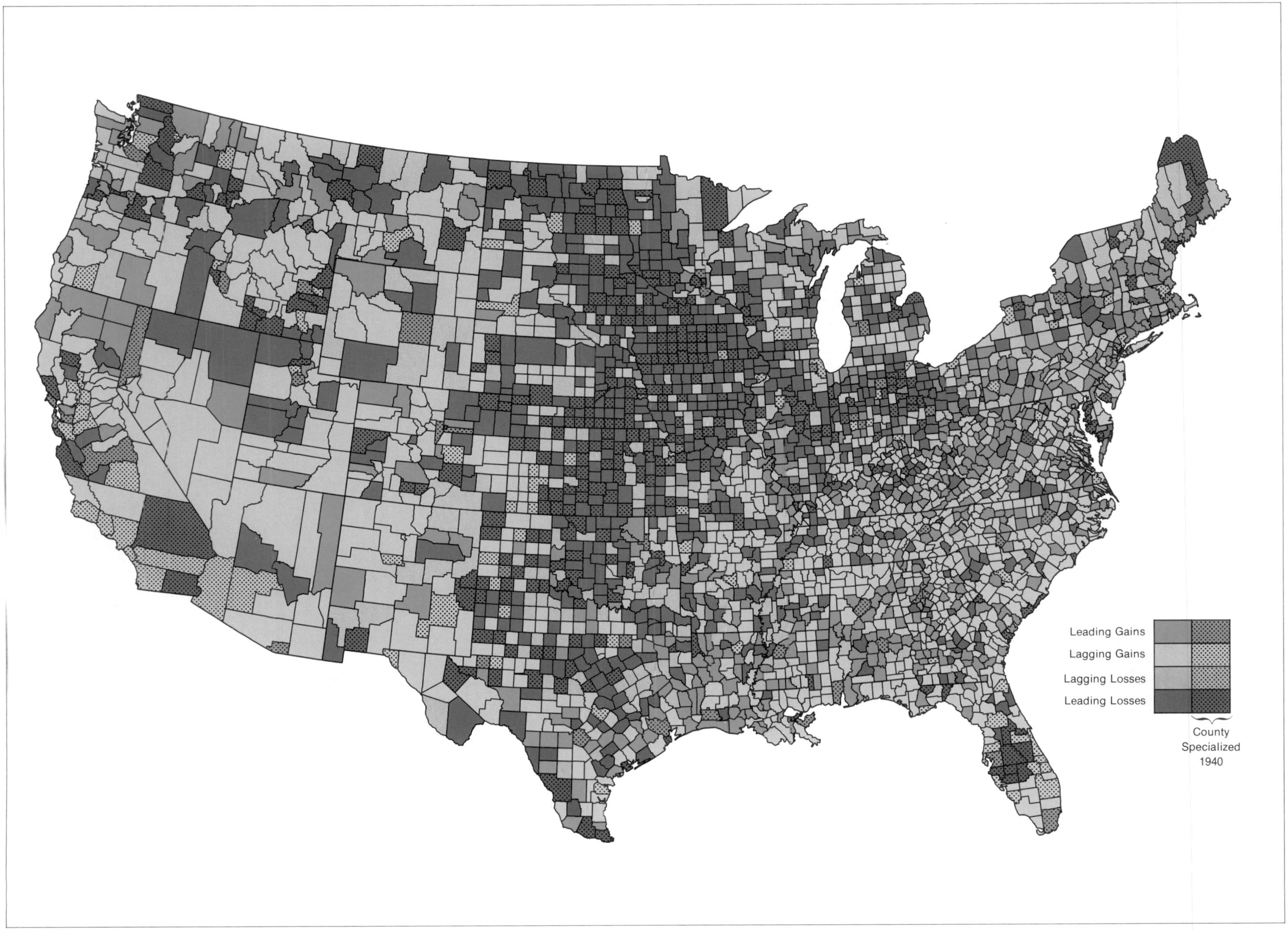

PLATE II-23. Wholesale Trade, 1940–70: Leading and Lagging Competitive Shifts

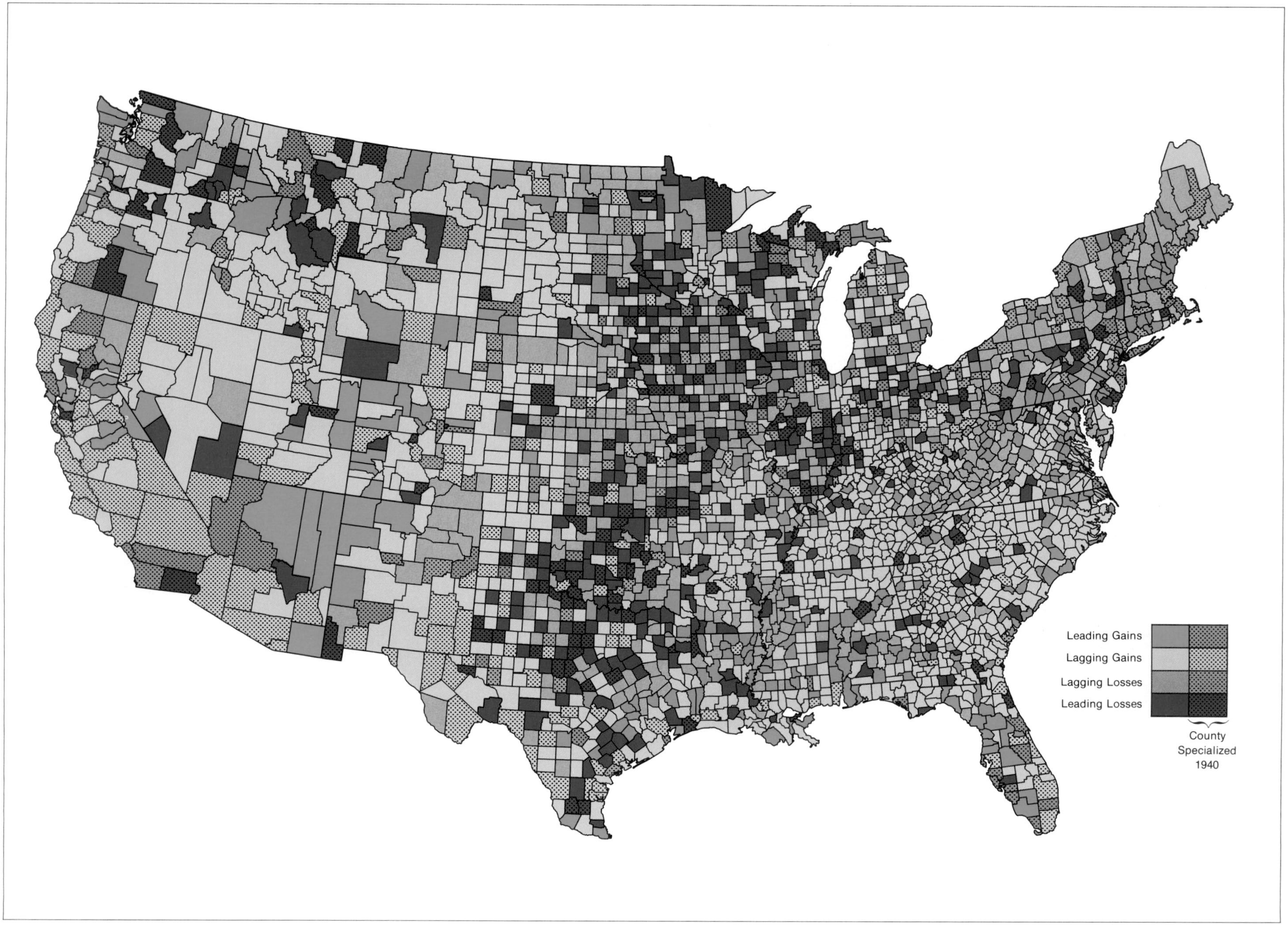

PLATE II-24. Retail Trade, Total 1940–70: Leading and Lagging Competitive Shifts

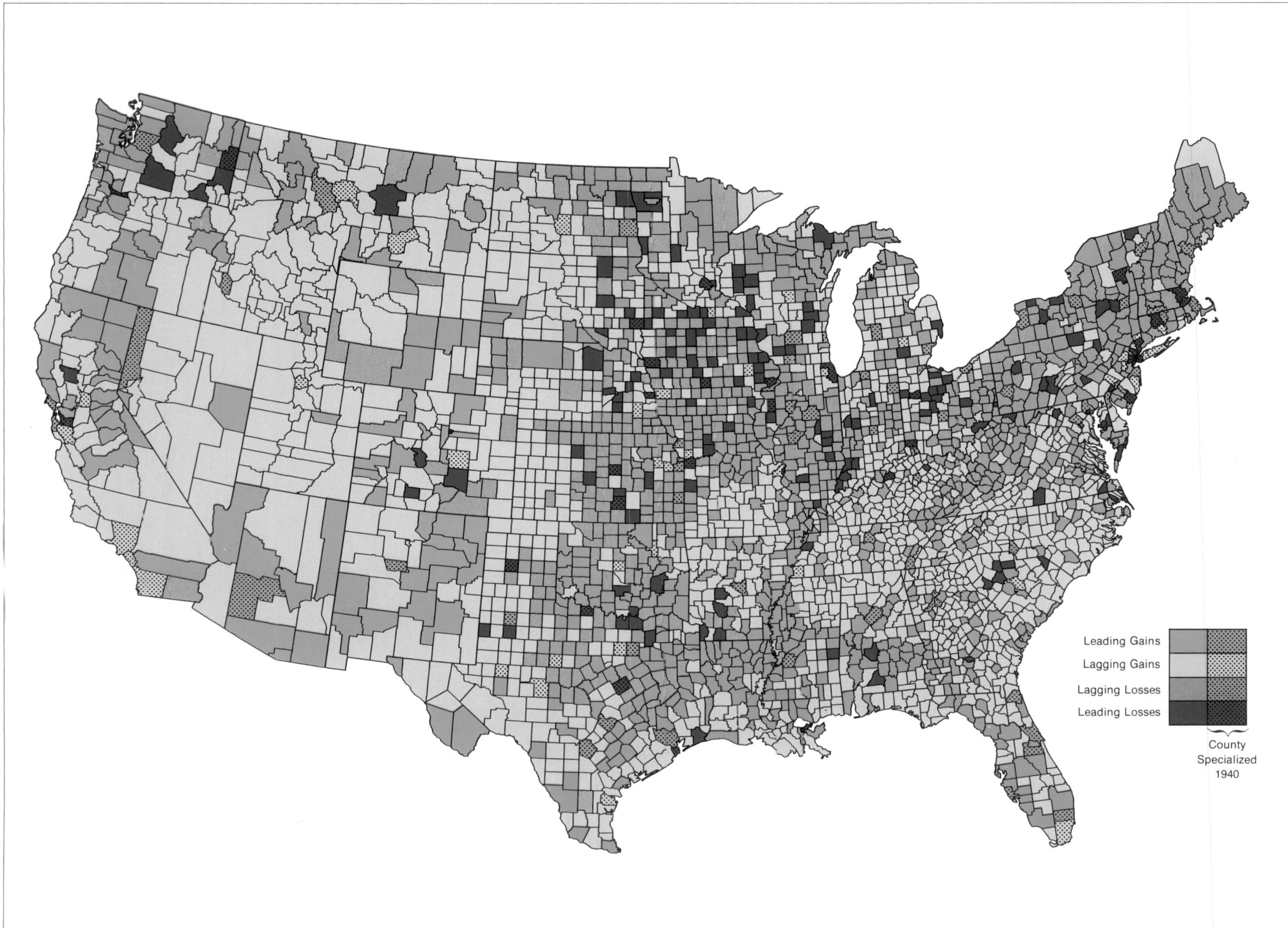

PLATE II-25. Finance, Insurance, and Real Estate, 1940–70: Leading and Lagging Competitive Shifts

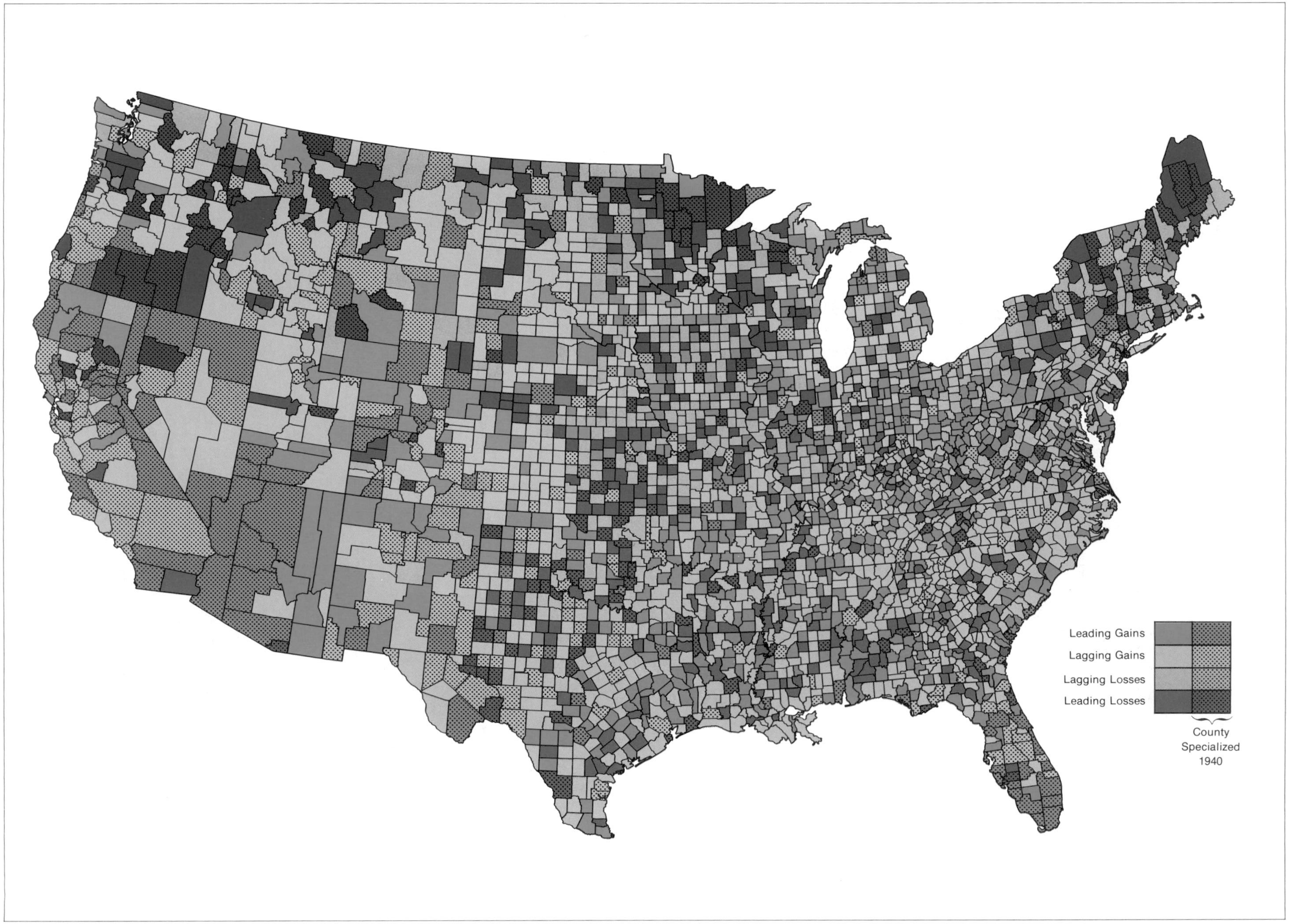

PLATE II-26. Lodging and Personal Services, 1940–70: Leading and Lagging Competitive Shifts

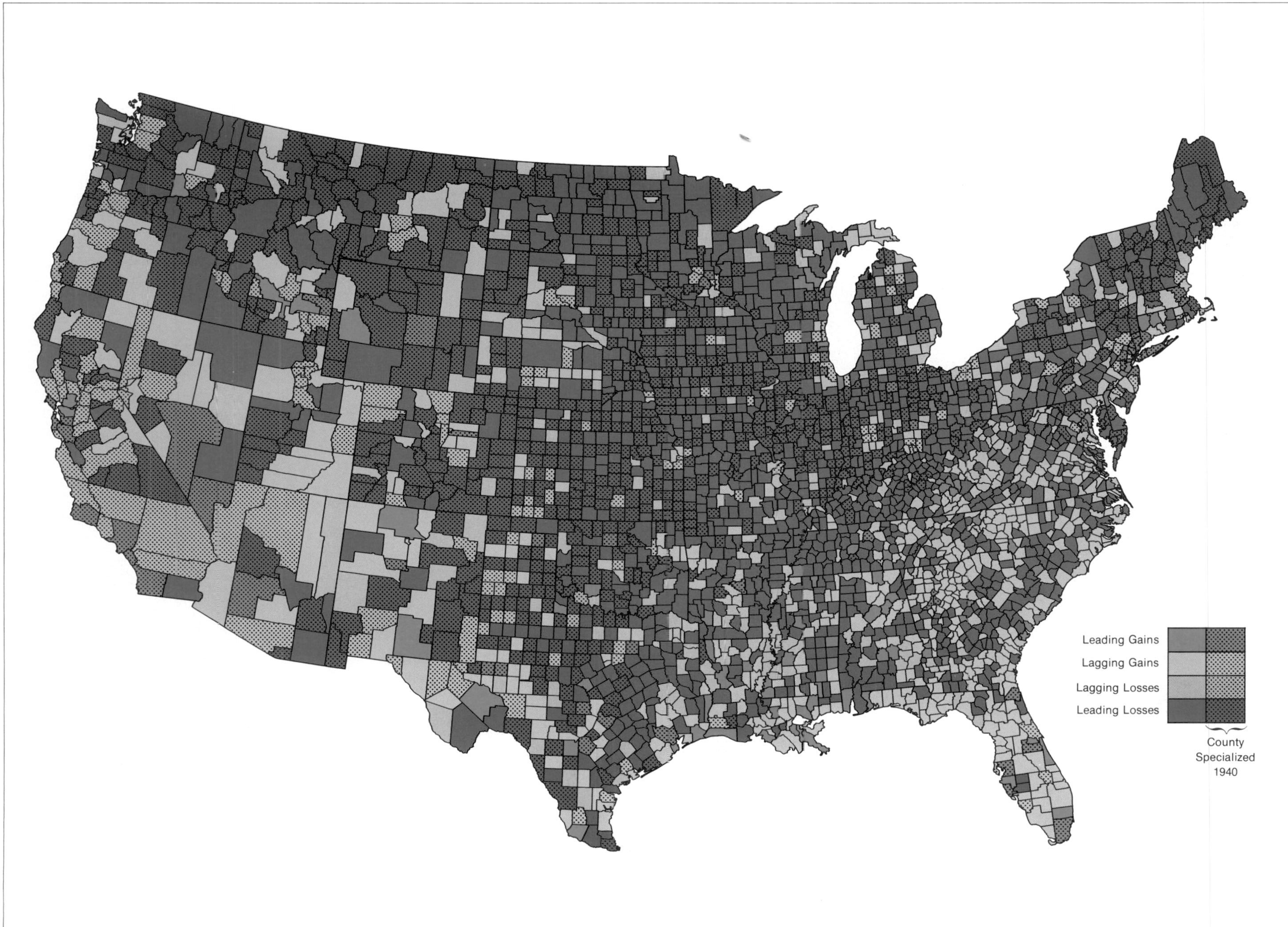

PLATE II-27. Business and Repair Services, 1940–70: Leading and Lagging Competitive Shifts

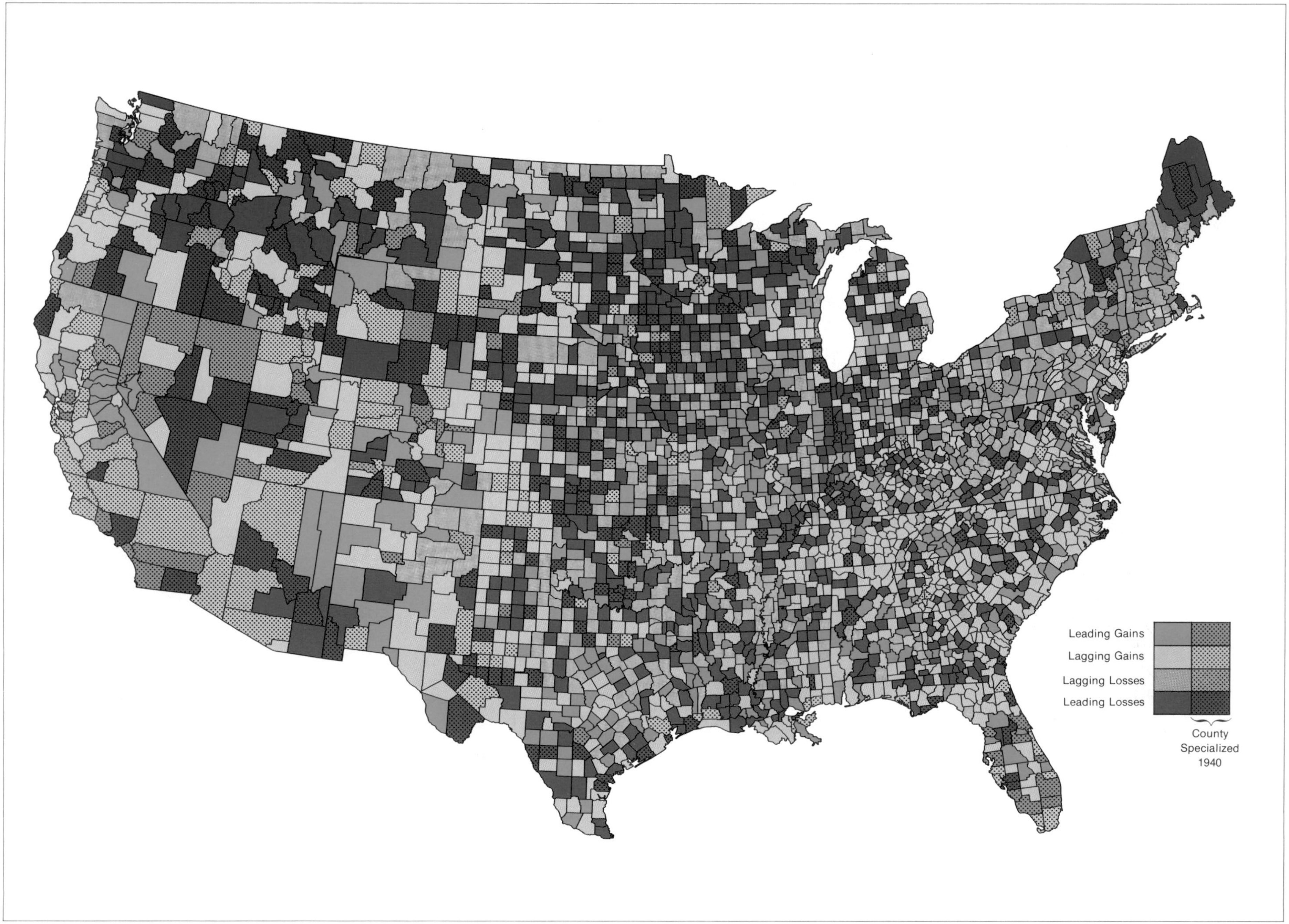

PLATE II-28. Amusement and Recreation, 1940–70: Leading and Lagging Competitive Shifts

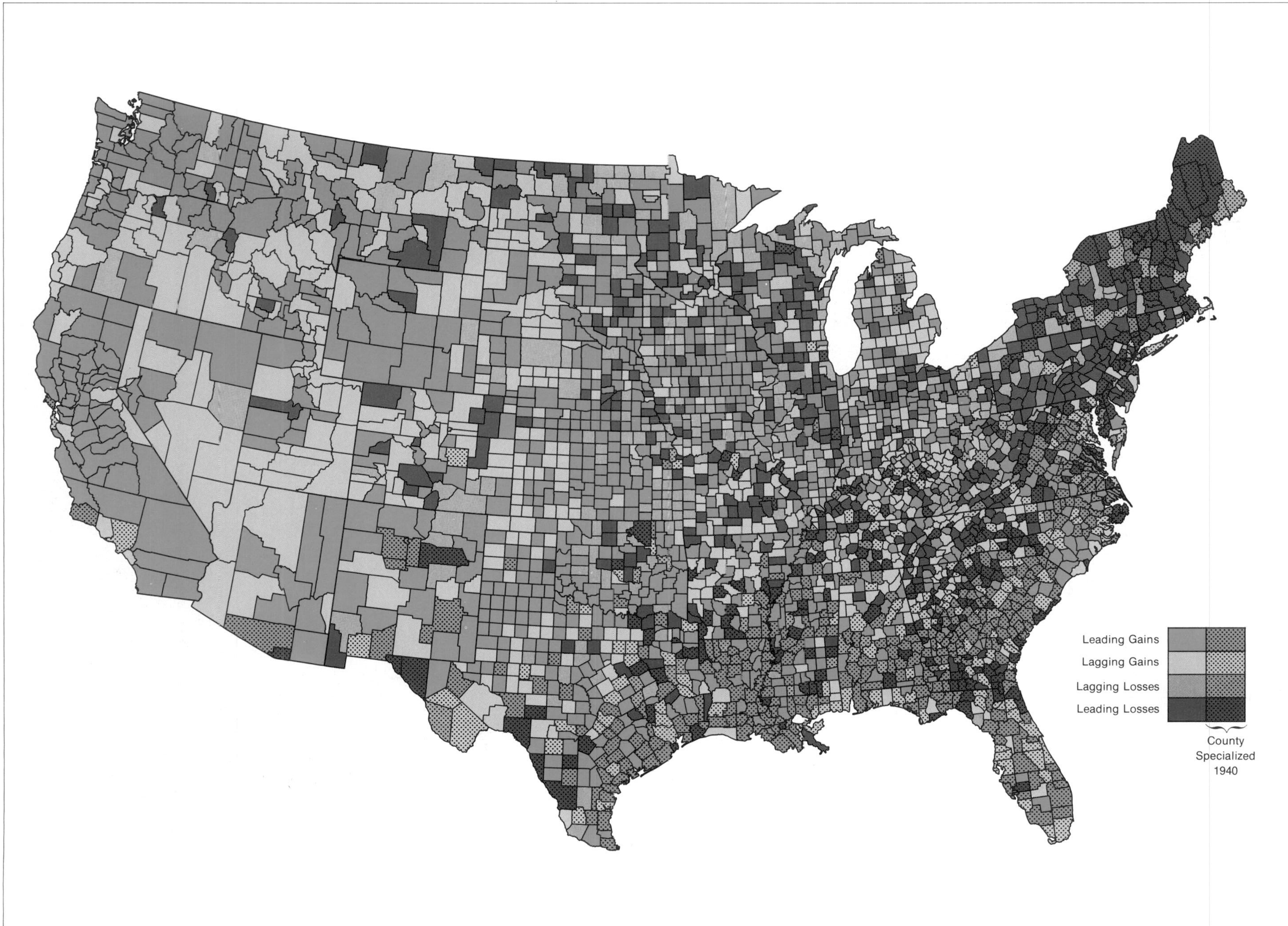

PLATE II-29. Private Households, 1940–70: Leading and Lagging Competitive Shifts

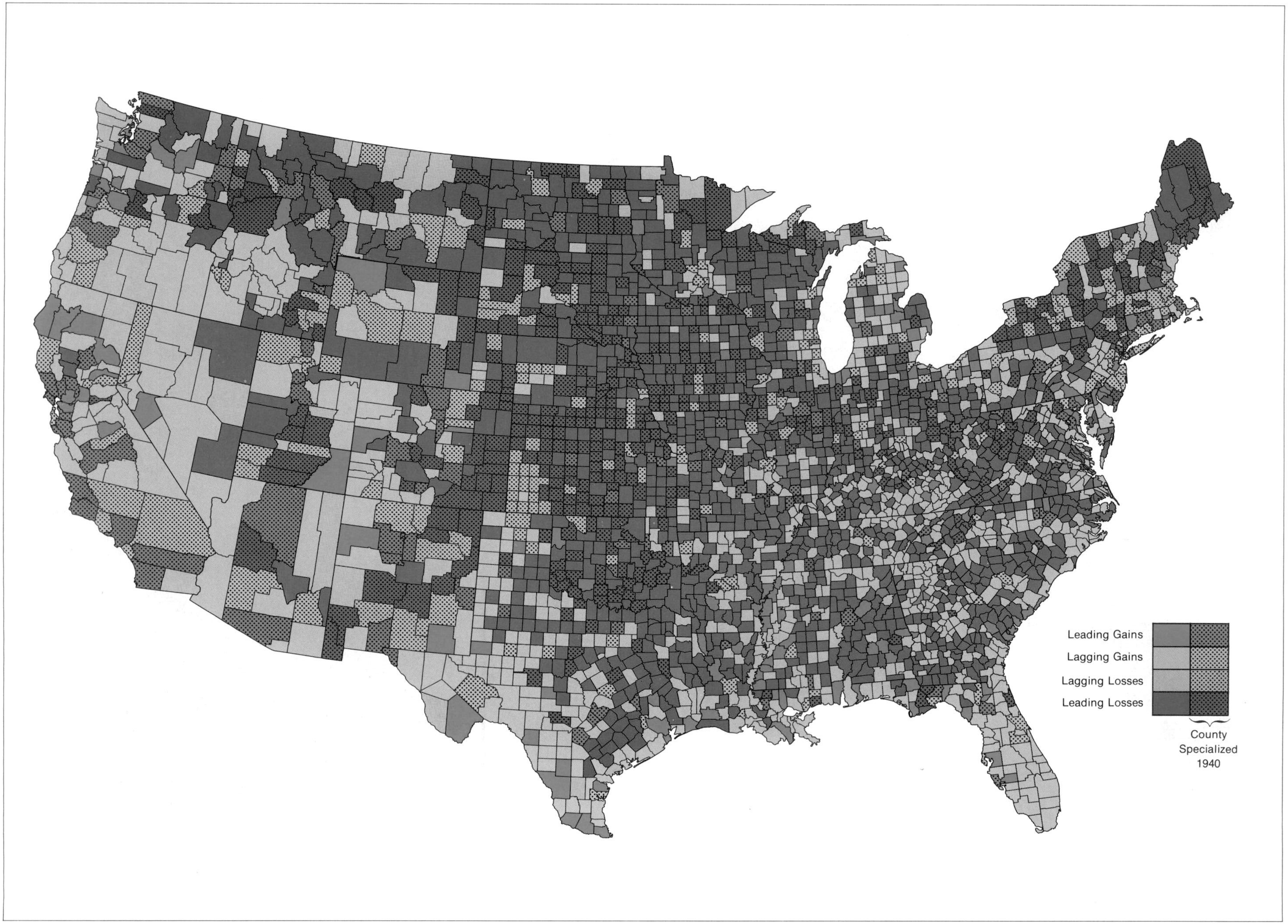

PLATE II-30 Professional Services, 1940–70: Leading and Lagging Competitive Shifts

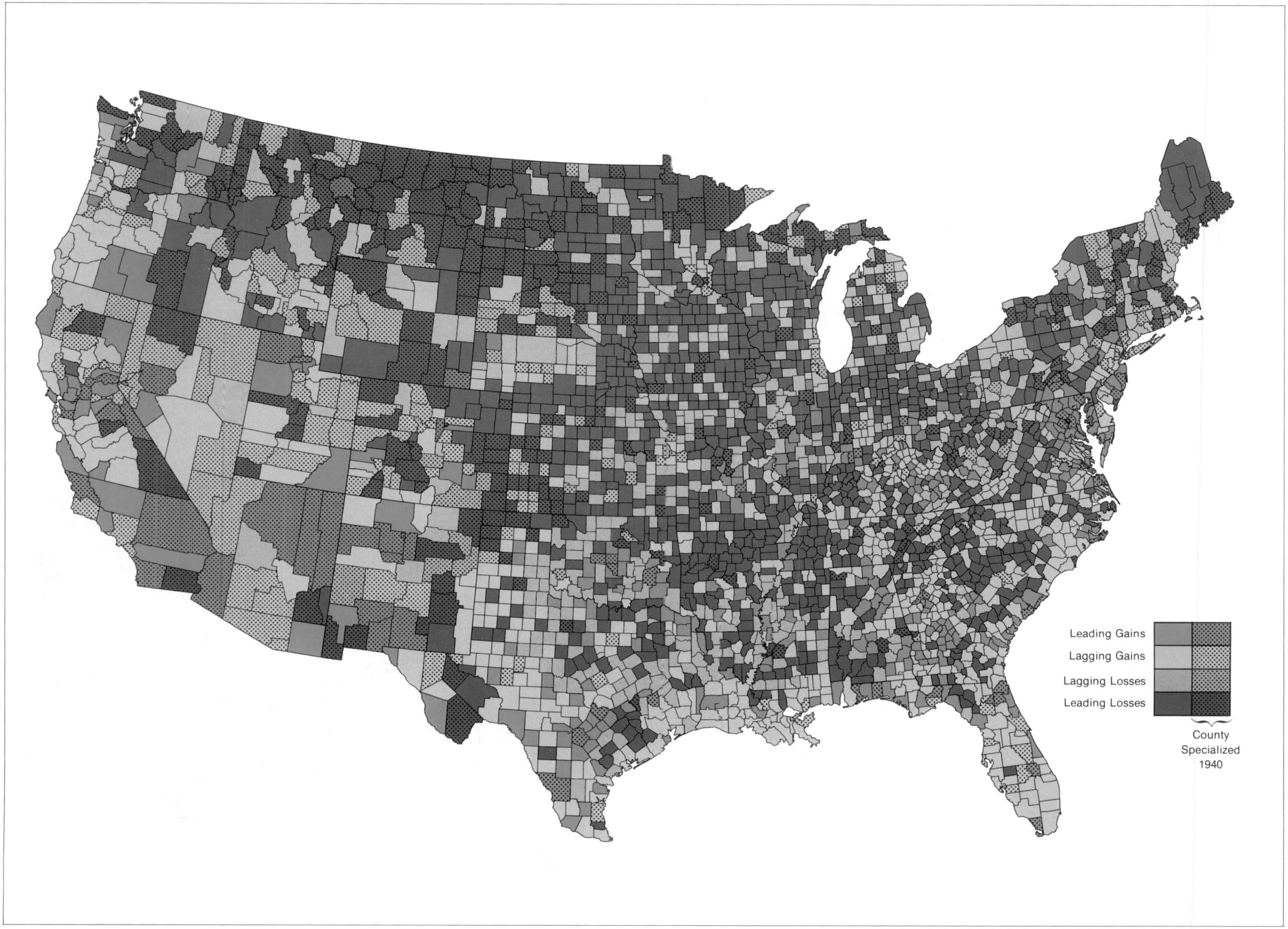

PLATE II-31. Civilian Government, 1940–70: Leading and Lagging Competitive Shifts

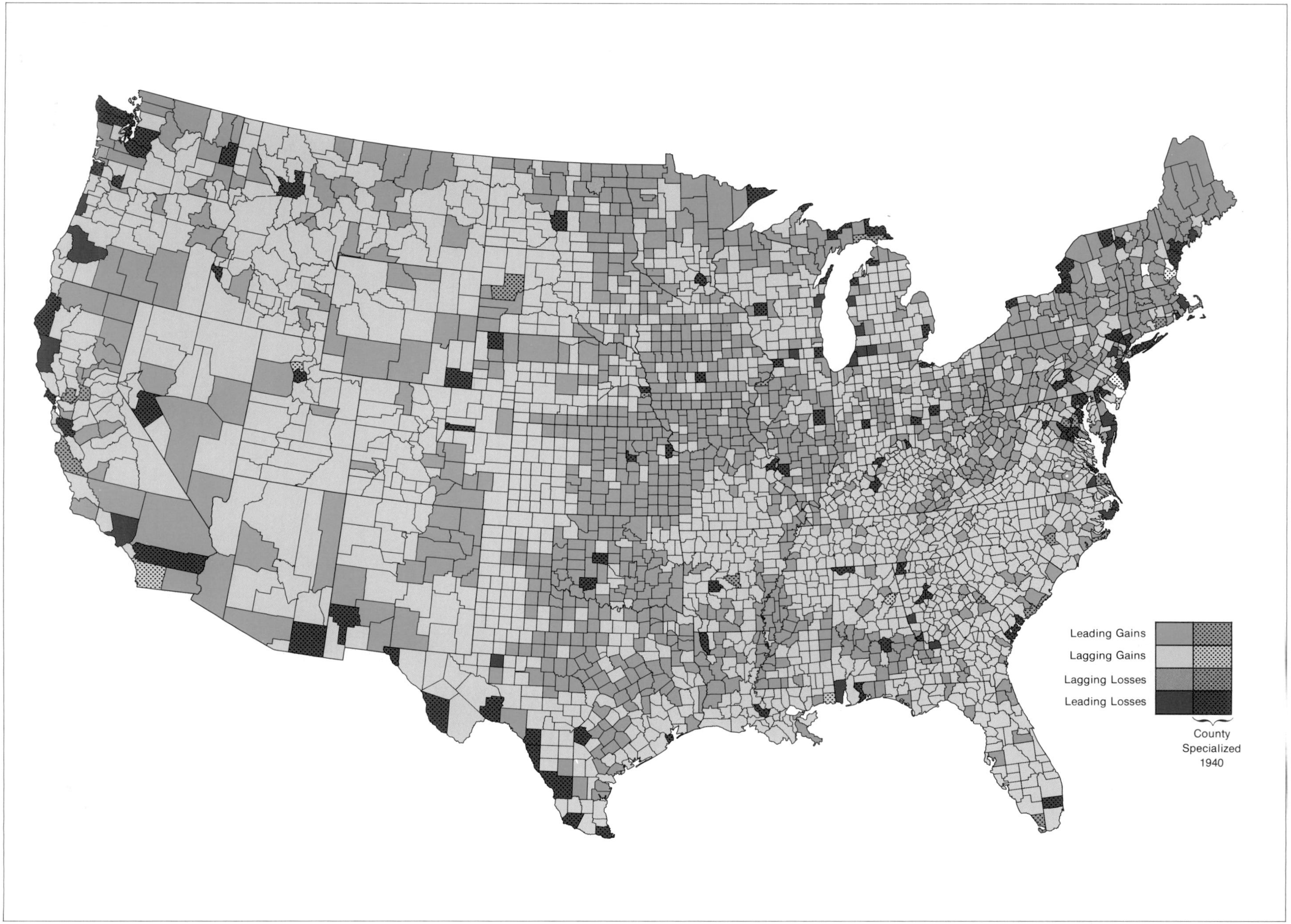

PLATE II-32. Armed Forces, 1940–70: Leading and Lagging Competitive Shifts

to find close to 90 percent of employment in the production of forgings, stampings, screw machine products, and general hardware located there (plus three-quarters of the electroplating and miscellaneous hardware products).

As a consequence, the observed shifts in the remaining fabricated metal activities largely constituted a response to shifts in the intermediate processing activities they served. New England and the Middle Atlantic urban regions led in the competitive losses in general hardware, screw machine products, metal forgings and stampings, electroplating, and miscellaneous fabricated metals. This seems to have been a continuing lagging adaptation to the progressive relative shift of the metal process industries to the western end of the Old Manufacturing Belt, then on to the South and to the West Coast. We have already seen that the Great Lakes region played a more prominent role in the competitive losses of canning, plumbing, and structural metal product activities. It added the relative decline in the production of general hardware and in the miscellaneous products category producing industrial pipes and fittings. But, dramatically, the Great Lakes region proved to be a strong gainer in the production of metal forgings and stampings, and a more moderate gainer in the electroplating and the production of screw machine products—this at the same time that the region was almost matching the East Coast in overall losses. This was a period of phenomenal growth for the automobile and farm machinery industries in the western end of the Old Manufacturing Belt, which made the intermediate products that formed the markets for just these fabricated components.[3]

For all remaining sectors, the dominant competitive gains went outside of the industrial Northeast. The Southeast picked up much of the relative share of general hardware lost by New England, as well as the forging and stamping losses so prominent in the Middle Atlantic regions. These relative gains were most prominent in the East South Central regions dominated by Memphis, Huntsville, and Birmingham. The most dramatic gains in miscellaneous fabricated metal products came in the West South Central region dominated by Houston, Dallas, Texarkana, Shreveport, and Tyler. This is no surprise because the dominant subsector of this category is the production of fabricated pipe, fittings, and valves for industrial use (in contrast to plumbing for construction use already considered). Of course, this is precisely the region where industrial petroleum and chemical flow processes have come into prominence during the study period. The other subsector of the miscellaneous category is the production of wire products in heavy demand by both construction and agriculture, both of which were also expanding markets in this area for reasons already discussed.

The Pacific Coast shared in the gains of most fabricated metal products but was not characteristically a front rank gainer for most subsectors. The major exception was the production of screw machine products. It seems that there is no industrial activity that makes as intensive use of metal fasteners as the aerospace industry, which enjoyed phenomenal gains on the West Coast during the study period.

Nothing has yet been said about the Florida gains because they are not prominent in the overall picture. Nevertheless, they were pretty substantial, given the region's almost nonexistent production base in 1940. Two fabricating subsectors tell the whole story—cans, oriented to a burgeoning citrus and truck crop agriculture, and structural metal products, responding to the construction boom attending the state's dramatic gains in population settlements.

Machinery

Machinery manufacturing is one of the most important activity sectors. Employment almost tripled during the study period making it the fourth most rapidly gaining sector (matched by transportation equipment, exceeded only by professional services and the armed forces—see table 37 in volume I). By the end of the study period, employment was almost twice as great as in any other manufacturing sector (in the thirty-one-sector typology of this study). It is not surprising, therefore, that the sector made a prominent contribution to the thirty-one-sector gross shifts depicted in table II-1. Its contribution to the gross mix shift was second only to agriculture and accounted for a third of the total manufacturing contribution. It made the third largest contribution to the gross competitive shift and accounted for one-fourth of the total manufacturing contribution. But perhaps the greatest indication of the tremendous dynamism of this sector is the fact that both the mix and competitive components of the machinery sector shifts were roughly equal to the sector's total 1940 employment. In the thirty-one-sector array this was matched only by transportation equipment and the armed forces.

Machinery manufacturing activities were not only prominent in scale, but they experienced a remarkable geographical and structural transformation during the study period. This is not surprising considering the important role that machinery played in all of the major problem-solving initiatives of the epoch. The shift of the energy base to petroleum required the development of new forms of mining machinery. The great revolution in scientific chemistry required the complex machinery of continuous-flow petroleum refining and petrochemical processes. The integration of steel processes required new forms of material-handling and metal-forming machinery. The production of the airplane required the development of new engines, and the evolution of the motor vehicle required the massive development of new machine tools. Scientific agriculture required new forms of farm machinery. The new pipelines required new pumps, and machines to produce seamless pipes. The communications-electronics revolution, born of the explosion of information-processing functions, generated new machine production activities. To top it all off, the machine finally invaded the household in the form of appliances, radio, and television. In short, the machinery-producing activities were necessarily, and dramatically, influenced by the innovative, problem-solving activities of the period.

Once again, however, we are confronted with difficulty in representing the shift patterns. The machinery manufacturing sector is even more heterogeneous than fabricated metals, and it is fraught with systemic interdependencies. It is engaged in the production of diverse products from huge steam turbines to power driven hand tools, and from large power transformers to typewriters. Its initial focus on mechanical machinery has been overwhelmed by an entirely new complex of electrical machinery and electromechanical hybrids that confuse the product-based taxonomies of traditional classifications. We can only describe and explain the industry's shift patterns at a superficial level, but I hope it is one sufficient to serve the study's developmental theme.

In 1940 the machinery industry was still heavily concentrated in the Old Manufacturing Belt. Although that broad region contained almost half of all employment and two-thirds of manufacturing employment, it claimed 86 percent of machinery manufacturing. The concentrations were even higher in some categories (98 percent of lighting and wiring equipment; 96 percent of printing machinery; 95 percent of appliances, office and computing equipment, and metal-working machinery; 92 percent of engines and turbines, textile machinery, paper machinery, and communications equipment; and 90 percent of all electrical transmission equipment). Farm, mining, construction, food preparation, and wood-processing machinery were least concentrated. This was natural given the more widespread geographical distribution of the resource and intermediate industries to which they are linked. There were also differences in the more localized concentrations of these activities within the Belt.

New England began the period with two-thirds of the employment in textile machinery and disproportionate shares of office and computing machinery, metal-working machinery, and other special industrial machinery. Thus, although New England did enjoy an advantage in some electrical industrial equipment, it was primarily a specialist in mechanical machinery, as befits its historical position as the parent region of the industry.

The Middle Atlantic region was the early specialist in electrical machinery with heavy concentrations of those activities producing transmission equipment (37 percent of U.S. employment), communication equipment (41 percent), appliances (51 percent), and radio and television (45 percent) (although in the mechanical realm it claimed half of the nation's employment in the production of printing machinery and a third of that producing paper and industrial service machinery). The East North Central or Great Lakes region claimed half of all machinery manufacturing employment by 1940 to become the dominant seat of the industry. This region accounted for three-fourths of the employment in lighting and wiring equipment (recall that Michigan was the early seat of copper mining and refining in the nation), two-thirds of the employment in farm machinery (its competitive market position relative to the East is obvious), 60 percent in engines and turbines, and 57 percent of metal-working and industrial service machinery. This region was clearly the production center of heavy industrial machinery. Nothing like these concentrations existed elsewhere, but the West North Central, or Northern Plains region, was, not surprisingly, a specialist in agricultural, food, and mining machinery. The Southeast was a relative specialist in specific types of industrial machinery like those serving food, paper, textiles, and wood products processes. It also began the period as the one broad region outside the Middle Atlantic to display relative concentrations of appliance, radio, communication, and miscellaneous electronics activities. The Texas–West South Central regions claimed a not-surprising 54 percent of the production in mining and construction machinery. The Pacific Coast's relative strength was in the production of food-processing machinery, reflecting its already revealed prominence as a food processor.

In accordance with the now well-established game plan, the central focus turns to the way these historical patterns were modified by the developmental processes at work during the study period. The beginning image is provided by plate II-11. Several observations are pertinent. First, notice the distribution of the specialized counties (black dots). It appears that there were only 218 of them (only the production of transportation equipment was concentrated in fewer counties). All but nine of these were inside the Old Manufacturing Belt. Thus, even within the specialized Manufacturing Belt region, a relative handful of counties serves as production loci in a densely concentrated industry. It turns out that the distribution of competitive losses (shaded red) is strongly associated with these specialized counties. Only 216 counties displayed competitive losses. One hundred and thirty-six of these were initially specialized and they accounted for 90 percent of all competitive losses. All but two-tenths of 1 percent were located in the Old

Manufacturing Belt. Plate II-11 reveals the bulk of the losing counties to be located in the New England and Middle Atlantic regions. One thing is clear from this pattern. Although the specialized counties of the Old Manufacturing Belt accounted for virtually all of the competitive losses, the picture was not all bad for this heartland of the machine industry. Eighty-two specialized counties, mostly in the Great Lakes portion of the Old Belt, accounted for 17 percent of the total competitive gains experienced by the industry (tables II-6 and II-7). Further, the remaining 83 percent of all counties that experienced competitive gains were well represented among the unspecialized counties in the Old Manufacturing Belt.

That undifferentiated expanse of blue indicates that the bulk of the competitive gains in the industry were spread throughout the nation. Still, at urban-region scale almost one-fourth of the competitive gains were captured by regions within the Old Belt. Overall, only twenty-five urban regions accounted for 75 percent of the gains (appendix E in volume I). Los Angeles and San Francisco were the largest gainers and, together with Phoenix and San Diego, accounted for 30 percent of the total. The third largest gaining region was Dallas and the fourth, Minneapolis. There were three clusters in the Southeast. One extended from Indianapolis down through Louisville, Lexington, Nashville, Huntington, and Memphis. Another set formed a belt from Baltimore down the Piedmont to Atlanta. The third consisted of Orlando, Tampa, and Miami. A few other urban regions like Portland, Denver, Kansas City, Cedar Rapids, and Columbus, Ohio, were among the top twenty-five. As for competitive losses, only twelve urban regions, all in the Old Manufacturing Belt, accounted for 75 percent of the losses. Chicago, New York, Hartford, Cleveland, and Albany accounted for half.

In the case of machinery manufacturing, this developmental, competitive rearrangement of the industry was substantially tempered by the differential impact of the thirty-one-sector mix effect. Since the machinery sector was a very large and rapidly growing one, and heavily localized as well, one would expect the mix effect to be significant. Indeed, for the machinery sector, the mix effect was larger than its own gross competitive shift and second in importance only to the agricultural sector mix effect (appendix II-A). Consequently, these Old Manufacturing Belt urban regions that specialized in machinery manufacturing experienced mix-effect gains that countervailed in varying degrees the competitive losses they experienced. In the case of the great machinery manufacturing heartland stretching from Cleveland and Columbus westward to Quincy, Cedar Rapids, and Dubuque, the combined shifts yielded total differential gains ($+ D_{ij}$). This was also true for a string of northern Appalachian regions stretching from Syracuse and Rochester through Williamsport, Binghamton, and Harrisburg. However, on balance the offset was not strong enough to yield net differential gains in the eastern portion of the Old Belt. For the rest of the nation outside the Manufacturing Belt, the components of the total differential shift presented a contrasting picture. There, negative thirty-one-sector mix effects tended to offset the competitive gains, yielding total differential shift losses. There were only a few exceptions—the four Pacific Southwest urban regions, plus Denver, Dallas, Houston, Huntsville, Greensboro, Greenville (South Carolina), and southern Florida.[4]

But in this study, explanation is concerned with the developmental dynamics more clearly reflected by the competitive shifts. Our image is sharpened to the extent that we can differentiate the performance of the subordinate sectors of machinery manufacturing.

First observe that the electrical machinery component of machinery manufacturing took all of the growth honors (see the thirty-one-sector array of table 37, in volume I). The electronic stamp of study-period developments is emphasized by the fact that the most rapidly growing machinery subsector was that engaged in the production of electronic components—the generic fabricated parts of most electrical artifacts. The household, that last refuge from the mechanization of work, finally succumbed under an eightfold expansion of the activities producing household appliances. The remaining rapid-growth subsectors in order were radio and television, electrical industrial apparatus, miscellaneous electrical machinery (batteries, controls, X-ray machines, and the like), materials-handling machinery (for construction, mining, and manufacturing), office and computing machinery, lighting and wiring apparatus, and communication equipment.

Notice several things. First, these are all electrical machinery subsectors, except one. It is interesting that the exception involves materials-handling machinery.[5] The increasing complexity of material and industrial processes has placed strains on older transfer and transaction technologies. The adaptive response was to develop an array of lifts, hoists, conveyers, and industrial trucks. Furthermore, the huge infrastructures required by the new transportation developments involving large construction projects have called forth larger and more sophisticated earth-moving machines.

All of the electrical machinery subsectors reveal one of two characteristics, or both. First, except for household appliances, they were all involved in producing the technological artifacts required by the burgeoning information processes that characterized the epoch. Second, household appliances, industrial apparatus, light and wire, and the miscellaneous subsectors were also engaged in applying electric power to work. Electric motors provided the fractionally flexible sources of power so essential to the new technology.

How do these developments help explain the geographical shifts that took place? Our best clues reside in the subsector competitive shifts.[6]

Although we have noted competitive shifts in machinery manufacturing employment out of the Old Manufacturing Belt and into the rest of the nation (notably the South and Pacific Coast), there was considerable variation in the contributions made to the fortunes of each region by the different component sectors. Since the Great Lakes and New England sectors began the period as the great specialists in mechanical machinery, it is not surprising that they were the greatest competitive losers in this category (with the Great Lakes region taking the lead). Conversely, the Middle Atlantic region was the initial specialist in electrical machinery and experienced the leading competitive losses in that activity. (Correspondingly, the Middle Atlantic suffered relatively mild declines in mechanical machinery and New England in electrical machinery.) Furthermore, all of these traditional production regions experienced countertrend movements that partially offset the general tendencies already noted.

By and large, the mechanical machinery activities have shifted in response to changes in the locus of the intermediate process activities that they serve most directly. Thus, the East North Central region that claimed two-thirds of all farm machinery employment in 1940 found its share reduced to 39 percent by the end of the period. Fifty-five percent of the competitive gains went to the Northern Plains and the West North Central regions. Forty percent was claimed by the Southeast with the East South Central claiming the bulk. Minneapolis, Rochester, Omaha, and Kansas City figured prominently. Recalling the story of the interregional shifts in agricultural production favoring the Plains region, this can come as no surprise. However, as farm machinery manufacturing shifted from its old base, it resisted stretching too far. Most of the shifts represented a westward spread of the Old North Central production region. The South captured part of the gain because of its deficit supply status and favorable access to intermediate inputs. This was concentrated in the southward extension of the North Central production base. The Mountain and Pacific regions experienced only modest competitive gains, in spite of major competitive gains in agricultural activities and in spite of the well-publicized creative efforts of the agricultural engineers at the University of California at Davis. Clearly a deficiency of intermediate supply links, and perhaps agglomeration economies, served to constrain a development so far removed from the traditional industrial core.

In the case of mining, construction, and materials-handling machinery, it was mining machinery that dominated the interregional shifts. The major competitive loser was the Middle Atlantic region and the principal gainer, the Texas–West South Central region. This was a direct reflection of the shift from coal to oil. The Pacific and Mountain regions joined in the competitive decline, as one might have expected from the record in chapter 8.

Because New England was the region where the production of metal-working machinery originated, it still claimed a disproportionate share of the sector's employment in 1940. However, the intermediate processes employing this equipment have for many years been moving on with the nation's development. So, by 1940 the West North Central region had captured 57 percent of the sector's employment. New England's lagging adjustment to the changing location matrix continued into the study period. It weighed in with the dominant competitive losses. The East North Central region's losses were second in importance, although, relative to its employment base, its losses were only one-sixth as strong. The South Central region and the Pacific Coast were the principal gainers.

The manufacture of special industrial machinery was especially prone to chase prior movements in the intermediate processes that it serves. Food machinery employment experienced its greatest relative losses in the Middle Atlantic region, followed by losses in the nation's North Central food basket.[7] Most of the competitive gains came in the South and Pacific regions in response to the tremendous gains in canning and freezing activities reported in chapter 10, which, in turn, were a response to the shifts in agricultural production reported in chapter 8.

Similarly, it is not surprising that 96 percent of the competitive losses in the manufacture of textile machinery came in New England and 100 percent of the competitive gains in the South Atlantic Piedmont. During the study period, the traditional New England production base eroded by 75 percent, while the tentative South Atlantic base went from 5 to 45 percent of the industry's employment. In a similar way, the production of paper machinery and wood-processing machinery shifted out of the Old Manufacturing Belt into the South, although much less dramatically. New England and the Middle Atlantic regions were the principal losers, respectively.

There is a mixed bag of mechanical machinery manufacturing activities that supply general industrial equipment useful to many different kinds of industrial processors—things like pumps, compressors, roller bearings, ovens, transmissions, pistons, valves, merchandising machines, laundry equipment, and refrigeration equipment. These activities tended to follow the general, continental spread of the broad manufacturing, trade, and service sectors. The East North Central region claimed more than half of the competitive losses, with the Middle

Atlantic regions and New England following in order (although New England's loss was greatest relative to its industrial base). The Pacific Coast and the Texas–West South Central regions captured about two-thirds of the gain, split evenly. The South Atlantic regions tagged along.

In the case of electrical machinery, disclosure and classificational problems prevent a satisfactory subsector shift analysis. This is precisely because this has been the dynamic, innovative, volatile component of the machinery industry. Electrical machinery employment grew six times as fast as mechanical machinery and the gross interregional shifts were three times as large (relative to the 1940 employment base). The gross competitive shift was equivalent to a shift of 60 percent of 1940 employment across major census region boundaries. The Middle Atlantic region experienced the greatest relative losses, as befits its status as the earliest electrical machinery specialist. The East North Central and New England regions followed. The South captured 60 percent of the relative gains (with the South Atlantic region most prominent) and the Pacific Coast 30 percent.

There are two other sectors outside the electrical machinery classification (S.I.C. 36) that have also become largely electronics industries. The first is office and computing machinery (S.I.C. 357, recall note 5) and scientific measuring and controlling instruments (S.I.C. 38). (The latter is buried in the miscellaneous and other manufacturing category.) For these activities, the Pacific Coast (including Phoenix) claimed 61 percent of the competitive gains (just the reverse of S.I.C. 36 as a whole).

Although the data preclude a more detailed shift analysis, there are other descriptive sources that tell a story of major importance.[8] The performance of this sector is one more manifestation of the tremendous developmental and reorganizational effect of modern academic and industrial science. Just as agricultural science revolutionized agriculture, just as chemical science revolutionized the food and materials-processing industries, electronic science began the revolution of the fabricating industries (by transforming the way energy is applied to work) and all information-processing activities. The effect of this developmental process on the urban-system structure of the electrical machinery and instruments industry is worth special comment.

This was a classical demonstration of the big city as a breeding ground of new products and enterprises. The historical locus of these emerging activities was the Middle Atlantic region (more than half of 1940 employment) more specifically, the New York metropolitan region. The advantage New York brought to the early development of this industry can be appreciated when measured against the location factors considered most important by industry executives (developed by Speigelman in 1961). The first was personal factors, a consideration we will return to shortly. The second was the availability of professional staff. In the 1930s, when communication and consumer electronics were beginning, the New York region was unmatched in this regard. As recently as 1954, 43 percent of all the engineers graduated in the nation came from New York and New Jersey. New York also represented the largest pool of technical process skills at that time. The third item listed was proximity to educational, testing, and research facilities. New York was in the center of an array of great technical universities in New York, New Jersey, and eastern Pennsylvania. There were numerous industrial research labs like the Bell Laboratories and those of International Business Machines (IBM), International Telephone and Telegraph, The Radio Corporation of America, United Aircraft, General Electric, and so forth. Much of the work of inventors like Edison and De Forest was carried on in the New York urban region. Much of the early developmental work in aviation and defense technology was also centered there.

The fourth location factor was the need to be close to suppliers and markets. But this was not a concern with the traditional material access issues of Weberian location economics. The overwhelming consideration was information liaison. The process of design and testing in a rapidly developing field placed a premium on primary producers being in close and creative communication with component subcontracts and research and design facilities. Horizontal information exchanges within professional communities also became important. In the case of radio and television, market access was also important in more conventional terms. The first radio station in the nation (WDKA) and the first television station emerged here. This was where the first sources of programing developed. So this is where the first market for these appliances developed. However, that market rapidly dispersed during the study period.

For all of these reasons, the New York urban region and its near neighbors spawned the radio electronics of the 1930s, the military and scientific electronics of the 1940s, and, to a lesser degree, the television and electrical appliance developments of the 1950s. But it is often the fate of entrepreneurial loci to find their grip on production weakened as the new processes mature. Other more prosaic location factors begin to take command. The subsequent shift patterns took three distinct forms. The first had to do with appliances and consumer electronics. These activities were, by nature, essentially assembly operations that rapidly settled down to produce highly standardized products in large-scale enterprises engaged in long production runs. The products were much larger and bulkier than the components from which they were assembled. A location nearer the center of emerging national markets became the most important consideration. These consumer product activities tended to shift primarily to the western end of the Old Manufacturing Belt.

The enterprises engaged in producing the components for these and other electronic applications made a different kind of emergent adaptation. As component manufacture became more standardized and engaged in long production runs, the same opportunities for leaving the developmental womb emerged. However, the path was different. Transportation costs have never seemed to be important here. The industry is notorious for extensive cross-hauls spanning the entire nation. Labor costs proved to be much more important. Because the enterprises providing electronic components were also much smaller in scale than those providing finished products, and because they did not serve nationwide markets through commercial channels, they were freer to seek the most significant cost savings available to them. The subsequent shifts of electronic component manufacture were, first, into smaller towns and rural areas near the New York urban region; second, into New England where the decline of the textile industry offered a good quality labor supply at differential wages; and, third, into the South. General Electric, for example, opened a components plant at Anniston, Alabama.

A third adaptive shift pattern took place that is in many ways the most interesting. A significant part of the industry stayed in a developmental, creative posture, engaged in the design and production of new technologies and new products. This included such things as computers, other communication and information-processing devices, military electronics, aviation and space-related electronics, industrial controls, scientific and research implements, engineering and testing equipment, and medical equipment. The location of these activities remained governed by the overriding concerns of the entrepreneur absorbed with the development of new products and new enterprises—such things as the availability of professional staff; access to educational, testing, and research facilities; close liaison with buyers, suppliers, and designers; and so forth. This is another of those segments of a modern economy in the process of institutionalization. But this case involved providing coherence and continuity to developmental processes, as distinct from managerial or performance processes. One would presume that the Middle Atlantic region would continue to be the natural locus of these activities. And so it was for a substantial period after its share of consumer and components electronics began to decline (see Hall, 1959).

In any event, other developmental factors caused the Middle Atlantic region to lose its early monopoly of creative and entrepreneurial functions. New developmental seedbeds were emerging. Major university and research complexes of international standing were emerging elsewhere, and the New York region rapidly lost its dominance in supplying engineering and technical education. Massachusetts Institute of Technology (MIT), California Institute of Technology, Illinois Institute of Technology, and Stanford emerged as stars in the scientific and engineering firmament. Route 128, the Boston beltway, emerged earliest as the site of many high-technology companies linked with professional staffs at Harvard and MIT. Many were particularly heavily involved in military electronics. A southern California concentration grew out of the seed of Cal-Tech and the state's rapid expansion of military and aerospace industries. In mid-period, 75 percent of the electronics industry in Southern California was dependent on defense procurement. A Chicago concentration crystalized around Illinois-Tech with greater attention devoted to the measurement and control problems of industry. The space program at Cape Canaveral stimulated a concentration in the Orlando urban region.

But perhaps the most interesting and spectacular development emerged from the Stanford seed in Santa Clara County. This burgeoning locus of the high-technology electronics industry has been dubbed Silicon Valley. By the early 1970s, there were 800 pioneering technology companies built around a powerful base of 4,000 PhDs plus countless engineers and other technicians. While all of these emerging entrepreneurial centers increasingly fulfilled the four locational requirements listed, perhaps none illustrates so well the first—personal considerations.

There appear to have been two operative aspects of this. One was the considerable importance to highly trained professional people of the amenities of climate, educational resources, urbanized cultural and entertainment infrastructure, and each other. The second is the sometimes critical importance of individual, creative, scientific, and entrepreneurial initiatives. What seems extraordinary here is the critical role played by one man, Frederick Terman, an electrical engineering professor at Stanford University (see Bylinski, 1974).

There had been a locus of creative activity in the area for many years. De Forest and his colleagues perfected the vacuum tube as a sound amplifier in Palo Alto in 1912, only to move to New York to carry out the commercial exploitation. The Federal Telegraph Company of Palo Alto developed the loudspeaker and spawned both Magnavox and Charles Litton of Litton Industries. But there was not yet a critical mass. The drain of brains and entrepreneurial talent to the East was common. Terman deliberately set out to change this and encouraged some of his students to start enterprises near the university. Among the first were William Hewlett and David Packard. Professor William Hansen and the Varian brothers developed the klystrom tube that formed the basis for radar and for microwave communications. After

World War II, Terman, then dean of engineering, opened an active exchange with industrial scientists and established the Stanford Industrial Park. There was an explicit plan to create a center of high technology. Silicon Valley became the world center of the semiconductor and laser industries. New technologies (such as magnetic tape recording and the magnetic disc storing device) emerged in profusion. By the end of the period, older electronics companies such as General Electric, IBM, Sylvania, General Precision, and Lockheed had moved significant research and development operations into the area.

One characteristic of this component of the industry deserves further emphasis—its extreme localization. Spiegelman (1961) revealed that more than half of the plants in the instruments component of the industry (S.I.C. 38) were located in just nineteen highly urbanized counties (out of 3,061). Furthermore, although the industry expanded dramatically between 1949 and 1957, and the number of new plants increased by 65 percent, the same nineteen counties continued to dominate the industry and in roughly the same degree. The interregional shifts that we have observed primarily constituted a shift between already established and highly localized clusters of creative science and entrepreneurship. This was also characteristic of the other scientific, military, and industrial electronic centers.

I have taken the space to indulge in this vignette because it is a powerful illustration of two important changes in urban-system dynamics beginning to take place. First, in the science-based, high-technology sectors of manufacturing, it is the logistics of information processing, rather than the logistics of material and energy processing that has become most prominent. Under these conditions, the network structure of enterprise transactions is significantly changed (recall chapter 2 in volume I). Second, under these circumstances, the personal values and preferences of the new entrepreneurs (as well as their much more professionally autonomous employees) can play a much more prominent role in siting the emergent nodes of activity. The fortuitous locus of these creative and entrepreneurial drives is an important influence in the siting of emerging fields of industrial activity.

Motor Vehicles

If the fabricated metal and machinery sectors were complex and heterogeneous, the motor vehicle manufacturing story is the essence of homogeneity and simplicity. In 1940, 82 percent of motor vehicle manufacturing employment was concentrated in eighteen specialized urban regions centered on Detroit. Detroit itself contained 55 percent of the nation's motor vehicle employment. With minor exceptions these regions were (1) on the Michigan Peninsula, (2) formed a narrow southward band embracing Indianapolis and Dayton, or (3) represented a turn around the corner of Lake Erie to Cleveland. As plate II-12 indicates, the degree of geographical concentration was even greater at county scale. There were only 113 counties that specialized in motor vehicle employment in 1940, the smallest number of any sector. The principal cluster involved 33 counties spread across southern Michigan from Detroit, through Lansing to Lake Michigan, as far north as Bay City and as far south as Toledo. There was a twin cluster to the south in the Fort Wayne and South Bend regions, and another further south in Indianapolis, Muncie, and Dayton. Beyond this, there were only scattered counties.

The shift pattern was correspondingly uncomplicated. Eighty-eight percent of the competitive losses during the study period were experienced by the Detroit urban region. Most of the balance was contributed by South Bend and was directly associated with the demise of the Studebaker automobile company. At county scale, more than 90 percent of the losses were concentrated in 47 specialized counties. There was a sufficient development of small-scale operations (producing everything from specialized accessories to custom truck bodies) to yield competitive gains in 96 percent of all U.S. counties and in 147 of 171 urban regions, but the scale of employment in the bulk of these was trivial. Most of the competitive gains were associated with two different locational rearrangements.

A little more than half of the competitive gains came in the thirteen urban regions that made up the highly specialized industry core at the beginning of the period. Thus, Lafayette, Indianapolis, Muncie, Toledo, Cleveland, Saginaw, Grand Rapids, Lansing, and Fort Wayne all experienced specialized leading gains. Although not initially specialized in motor vehicle manufacturing, Champagne, Cincinnati, Columbus, Lima, Youngstown, and Chicago experienced significant competitive gains. All were directly on the fringe of the older specialized core. In Lima and Youngstown, the gains were sufficient to make them industry specialists by the end of the period. At county scale, this meant that sixty-six specialized counties claimed a third of the total U.S. competitive gains. It is also clear from plate II-12 that the bulk of these were in the historical heartland of the industry.

Eighty percent of the balance of the competitive gains were claimed by a relative handful of urban regions (and characteristically, only within a single county or two in each region) widely distributed throughout the United States in strategic nodal positions—Buffalo, Harrisburg–Baltimore, Louisville–Nashville, Atlanta, St. Louis, Kansas City, Oklahoma City–Dallas, Los Angeles, and San

Francisco. St. Louis, San Francisco, and Atlanta displayed the major competitive gains.

The explanatory factors behind these shifts were also not particularly complicated. By the study period, motor vehicle manufacturing was becoming a mature industry. It was still growing rapidly but only 10 percent faster than total employment. The early multitude of producers had largely settled down to the three big full-line companies. The organizational and process patterns were pretty well worked out. Increasing demand, production, and employment accompanied the still-expanding role of the automobile and truck. With 55 percent of the national motor vehicle employment in a single urban region, and the total growing at a compounded rate of 3 percent a year, urban agglomeration diseconomies were making the industry's parent region less competitive. At the same time, under the influence of shifting population and the phenomenal articulation of the highway infrastructure, the industry's market was becoming markedly redistributed.

The Detroit diseconomies mostly had the effect of pushing the production of such things as assembly components, trucks, and special purpose vehicles out into the closely neighboring urban regions that formed the industry's heartland. The movement had already progressed far enough by 1940 to have generated the cluster of specialized regions previously noted. It continued and accelerated throughout the study period as this industry, like all manufacturing industries, found new opportunities for separating research and management from the production of material components and final assemblies—opportunities born of the developing effectiveness of the linkage services. Production and employment shifted out of the large, metropolitan parent region, but only next door, both geographically and in terms of urban-transaction fields.

The remaining shifts to the centers of broad regions (Baltimore, Atlanta, Dallas, and San Francisco) reflected the decentralization of the final assembly function. Labor force savings could be realized at first, particularly with respect to fringe benefit costs. Cheaper sites and other urban-system economies could be realized. Transport costs were cheaper for components than for the assembled vehicle. However, the economies of scale dictated by process technologies limited these outpost sites to a few urban regions that could serve large hinterland market fields.

Other Transportation Equipment

The "other transportation equipment" sector is also heterogeneous. It includes the manufacture of aircraft and parts, ships and boats, railway equipment, motorcycles and bicycles, missiles and space vehicles, and a miscellaneous category (including such things as travel trailers, snowmobiles, golf carts, and the like). In 1940, two-thirds of the specialization differential was concentrated in a line of urban regions spreading down the Atlantic Coast from Portland, Maine, to Norfolk, Virginia, with New York and Philadelphia representing the dominant core. The second major concentration was in the Los Angeles, San Diego, San Francisco, and Seattle urban regions. For the rest, only a few scattered regions proved to specialize (Charleston, Tampa, Mobile, and Beaumont in the South; Buffalo, Lima, and South Bend in the Great Lakes area). Plate II-13 displays the 1940 specializations at the county level. It also shows a fair number of widely scattered counties at the western end of the Manufacturing Belt that become washed-out at urban-region scale.

The Northern and Middle Atlantic Seaboard became heavily specialized as the center of both the shipbuilding and railroad equipment industries. Furthermore, the early development of the aircraft industry concentrated in the Middle Atlantic coastal urban regions. Most of the other 1940 specialists were coastal oriented and predominantly attached to shipbuilding. During the study period, the aerospace and miscellaneous transportation equipment sectors were the rapidly growing ones. Shipbuilding and railroad equipment manufacturing were the slow-growth sectors. The Atlantic Coast's overbearing specialization, therefore, was in the slow-growth activities. Being the parent region of these sectors, it stood to lose relative shares of transportation equipment employment because of both negative subsector mix and competitive effects. It is no surprise, therefore, that 80 percent of the nation's competitive losses in transportation equipment manufacture were experienced by this region. The Buffalo–Pittsburgh–Cleveland area and the Chicago–Milwaukee area contributed most of the remaining competitive losses.

The competitive gains were, again, highly concentrated in a relatively few urban regions, the major ones being associated with the emerging loci of the largely new aerospace industries. Dallas was the strongest gainer. Along with a cluster of neighboring urban regions, it claimed one-fourth of the total. Los Angeles was second and, along with San Diego, Phoenix, and Seattle, it accounted for another fifth. Two other areas brought the accumulated gains to about two-thirds of the total. (1) In the St. Louis–Wichita–Denver area, St. Louis entered the aircraft industry quite early and Wichita became the center for the manufacture of smaller aircraft serving personal and general aviation users. (2) Atlanta, Birmingham, Huntsville, and Memphis became important in aerospace as well.

The aerospace industry went to the South, the Plains, and the Pacific Coast partly because it grew so rapidly that the highly agglomerated urban regions of the Old Manufacturing Belt could not easily accommodate its growth. The manufacture of airframes required large amounts of space and even larger amounts of relatively uncongested airspace for testing. Industry sources also indicate that the climate on the West Coast placed fewer restraints on testing programs than in the East. Furthermore, modern industrial science and its creative, developmental thrust found heavy application in these industries. This tied in strongly with the development of the electronics industries that for many of the same reasons found the West Coast a congenial place for such an emergent culture. A new industry engaged in establishing its industrial base is much less constrained by history. Finally, these industries were a major part of an emerging military-industrial complex. As such, the emerging locations were much more susceptible to political influences. The nature of this influence is well illustrated by the seedbed effects of the space centers in Huntsville and Dallas.

Several additional descriptive observations are worthwhile. If we aggregate to roughly census region scale, the Middle Atlantic and New England regions account for 100 percent of the losses. The Great Lakes region turns out to be a light competitive gainer in the manufacture of all transportation equipment. This is because the space between the Pittsburgh and the Chicago–Milwaukee spheres of competitive loss captured about 10 percent of the total competitive gains. This area included the Michigan Peninsula (excluding Detroit) and extended down through Indiana to embrace Indianapolis and eastward through Dayton, Cincinnati, and Columbus. Quite a variety of activities fueled these gains. With the shift to diesel locomotives, the production of railroad equipment shifted from Philadelphia to the Great Lakes region. Although shipbuilding was a slow-growth component, the manufacture of pleasure boats burgeoned. The Great Lakes region captured a healthy part of this expansion. The area seems to have improved its competitive position in the manufacture of motorcycles and bicycles and certainly did so in the production of miscellaneous transportation equipment. Outside Southern California, no other region displayed competitive increases in such a wide array of transportation equipment manufacturing.

We can observe that the monolithic and massive competitive declines on the Atlantic Coast were interrupted by a significant gain in the Hartford urban region. Indeed, Hartford enjoyed the sixth largest competitive gain at urban-region scale. Two factors seem to have been at work. Most important, this was the home of the Electric Boat Company and the birthplace of the nation's submarine fleet. Beyond this, Hartford was the beneficiary of a phenomenon repeatedly observed. As the share of aircraft, bicycle, and miscellaneous transportation equipment manufacture declined in the New York and Boston urban regions, a part of the shift was into neighboring urban regions. Hartford was ideally positioned to be the beneficiary.

The competitive shifts of shipbuilding out of the Northeast went primarily to the Gulf Coast (Mobile, Biloxi, New Orleans, Port Arthur) and to Southern California and Seattle. These regions gained a major foothold in this activity during the burgeoning World War II shipbuilding push and remained because of advantages of climate, labor, and land costs, and proximity of a shifting marine market engaged in transporting oil. Florida's significant competitive gains were a combination of aerospace manufacturing and pleasure boat building.

Notes

1. Except printing and publishing, which was earlier removed from manufacturing and treated as an information-processing activity. See Perloff and coauthors (1960, p. 427).

2. In the early days, the weight of the bark was five times that of the product and two and one-half times the weight of the hides. Thus, even though hides lose substantial weight in the tanning operation, the old technology required them to be shipped to the East (see Hoover, 1937, pp. 137–155).

3. Although, as we shall shortly see, the automobile industry did decentralize out of Detroit during this period, most of the shift was into neighboring Great Lakes urban regions. Furthermore, the regional assembly plants that invaded the rest of the nation still drew their parts from supply sectors in the home region.

4. We might observe that the total mix effect was attenuated over time. During the decade of the 1940s, the gross mix effect was three times the size of the gross competitive effect. In the 1950s, they were almost equal. By the 1960s, the mix effect was 50 percent smaller. See appendix II-A. Thus, the mix effect appears to be losing its power to mask the competitive dynamics.

5. Although office and computing machinery is also still classified as mechanical by the Standard Industrial Classification. This is clearly a classificational anachronism going back to the fact that the early typewriters, adding machines, and the like were mechanically operated. Today these artifacts are almost totally electronic.

6. The gross subsector mix effect appeared to be only about 10 percent of the gross subsector competitive shifts. Thus, the subsector mix effect was relatively unimportant in explaining the total machine manufacturing competitive shifts.

7. This was partly a result of a subsector mix effect, as these were the areas that specialized most in the baking, confectionary, beverage, meat, and dairy products equipment serving the slow-growth components of the food industry.

8. Two sources of particular interest are: Hall (1959), and Spiegelman (1961).

12

Retail Trade, Services, and Special Cases

The remaining activity sectors are ones that the conventional wisdom of economic-base concepts says we can ignore. The levels of trade and service activities in a region are often thought to be dependent on the "basic" activities of the region (that is, the resource and intermediate processing sectors). Thus, one would expect the interregional shifts of trade and service activities to be highly correlated with the interregional shifts in total employment and population as settlements and their services respond to developmental forces at work in the basic activities. As a consequence, much less attention has been paid to these activities in the literature.[1]

There is, in fact, some truth in this view. Table II-12 reveals that the trade and service categories recorded the smallest deviations from the total employment shifts in the study's thirty-one activity sectors. There is no disguising, for example, the rough pattern correspondence of color plate II-24 depicting the shifts in retail trade with plates 7 and 11 of volume I, which depict the shifts in population and employment. However, this generalization was much more likely to be empirically valid in earlier times. During the study period, many urban regions and localities experienced trade and service employment shifts that deviated substantially from shifts in total employment. In specific times and places it has become common for such sectors to act as the so-called "basic" sectors are alleged to act. Conversely, in chapters 10 and 11 we observed some intermediate activity subsectors that, in fact, tended to follow rather closely shifts in final demand. We are forced to recognize that there are important developmental factors at work in this domain that alter the spatial and functional structure of urban systems in ways that must be accounted for. Trade and service activities can no longer be relied on to "follow the leader." Indeed, the implicit linear-causal logic of the base-theory concept is becoming increasingly untenable.The fact is that any activity (whether characterized as primary, intermediate, or tertiary) can be "basic" in one time and historical situation and dependent in another; it depends on the context formed by the linkage structure and patterns of change of the transaction system to which it is directly linked.

Retail Trade

Consider the case of retail trade. We can build directly upon the earlier discussion of urban settlement patterns in chapters 6 and 7 in volume I to assemble an image of the sources of structural change affecting trade centers.

Sources of Structural Change

It is useful to recall the 1966 study by Hodge (reported in chapter 7 in volume 1, p. 92). It demonstrated how, for a large province in Canada, the spatial distribution of the trade centers, as well as the relative prominence of different trade center types, was markedly altered between 1940 and 1960. There was an absolute decline in the number of trade centers, with convenience centers experiencing the greatest relative losses in number and with shopping and wholesale-retail centers experiencing the greatest relative gains. Hamlets were also revealed to be well sustained in number, although their geographical location was substantially altered. The total urban system experienced a geographical reorganization with lower order trade centers further apart and higher order ones closer together. There were major changes in the functional characteristics of individual trade centers as well. An astonishing 57 percent changed their trade-center classification. Although the transformation patterns of other geographical fields were undoubtedly different in detail, this study makes tangible and evident the reality of trading center reorganization during the study period.

The volume 1 discussion also suggests some of the developmental explanations that lay behind this structural reorganization. As is commonly the case, problem-solving developments in external, but linked, activity sectors had as much to do with the observed changes as those endogenous to the trading activities themselves.

There seems little doubt that the most dramatic source of the changing structure of trade centers was the development of the motor vehicle. It substantially extended the effective shopping radius of the household (or, conversely, the market field accessible to trading center enterprises). Moreover, it did so differentially for different classes of commodities. The market reach of durable goods and style goods was extended more than that of consumption staples. The articulation of the road network that accompanied the motor vehicle further modified the access characteristics of the household and trade-center enterprise.

The development of a mechanized and science-based agriculture, and the increases in off-farm sources of employment, led to extensive urbanization and a reduction in the density of rural populations. This had the effect of reducing the number and increasing the spacing of lower order trade centers servicing such hinterland fields. Developmental changes in the organization of retailing itself contributed to this reorganization. The innovation of self-service retailing, especially in the form of the modern supermarket, also tended to increase the population scale of viable trading fields because these managerial techniques trade on volume to create a competitive advantage for higher order trade centers.

But something more has been taking place than the spatial reorganization of trade centers of a given type in response to changes in the localization of the populations they serve, and to changes in the transfer networks that link them. The developmental changes taking place have altered the functional nature of trading centers in ways that are likely undermining the Borchert typology employed in this study.

Changes in the topology of networks may be having such effects. In volume 1, for example, we took note of evidence suggesting an increase in the phenomenon of multinodal transaction fields. It is likely becoming increasingly difficult to typify the functional character of an urban center (of a given size and occupying a similar environmental field) because of the interpenetrating and multiple-option nature of the new modes of transportation and communication. This reflects in part the growing ambiguity (if not obsolescence) of the trade-center classification itself. Trading transactions may be more appropriately thought of as taking place in fields of connectivity where trading activities can interpenetrate (can cross-haul and cross-communicate) with little economic penalty. The way in which the micro-nodes represented by enterprises form agglomerative nodal groupings in space within a field of given functional order may be increasingly a function of differences in the historical dynamic and the situational context of the field.

Another important factor altering the functional nature of trading centers was the radical change in the commodity content of retail transactions. These were almost all directly related to the developmental factors revealed throughout the previous chapters. Among the distinguishing marks of the study period were the mechanization and capitalization of the work, travel, communication, and entertainment activities of the household. The development of the motor vehicle was explicitly undertaken to solve the problem of personalized transport. Thus, for the first time, a large and growing portion of transport was distributed to the public through retail trade channels in the form of automobile dealers, service stations, and auto supply stores—all activities of recent origin. The whole range of household work appliances and home entertainment devices required new and expanded retail trade channels. Changes in income and in the male–female composition of the labor force led to significant increases in the proportion of eating and drinking done in commercial establishments. The substantial growth of real incomes that attended developmentally induced productivity gains increased the role of specialty shops (sporting, music, camera, jewelry, flower, and gift stores) in the retail trade mix.

Developments during the study period also increased the role of retail trade in the linkage networks of enterprise organizations rather than households. Businesses also found advantage in the use of the motor vehicle for transport and began to make extensive use of the associated retail trade infrastructure. This was the epoch when information processes began to occupy a much larger proportion of enterprise activity. Although an enterprise's traditional material and energy throughputs rarely engaged retail trade channels, the growing demand for office machinery and supplies commonly did. Almost every industrial sector identified in the traditional input–output tables increased the proportion of its inputs acquired through the mediation of the trade sectors.

As a consequence of the changing content of the retail trade function, the number of motor vehicle dealerships, service stations, appliance stores, specialty shops, and eating and drinking establishments increased substantially (as much as two to five times for many categories). In contrast (except for women's and children's specialty clothing stores), the number of clothing and dry goods stores declined. Most of the declines, however, had to do with food and dairy retailing. Even general food stores declined in number as the supermarket drove many of the traditional independents out of business. In addition, the consolidation of many food retailing functions in the supermarket led to major declines in the number of food specialty stores (dairy, fish, meat, vegetable, candy, tobacco, and delicatessen shops).

The Empirical Record

But what have been the consequences of such major changes in retailing for the spatial arrangement of urban-system structures? Consider the record.

First, while total employment increased by 75 percent (table 37 in volume I), total retail trade employment increased by 93 percent—and that in spite of the major labor-saving innovations that transformed the industry. This is a powerful confirmation of the increased importance of retail trade in the urban-servicing processes of the nation. However, employment in food retailing increased only half that amount while that in eating and drinking places grew by 123 percent and in "other retailing" by 105 percent. Within this heterogeneous grouping, motor vehicle, appliance, general merchandise, specialty, drug, and hardware stores more than doubled employment. If we change perspective to the absolute increase in retail trade employment (more than 6 million during the period), two-thirds of the increase (4 million) was accounted for by these other retailing categories. Eating and drinking places (23 percent) and food retailing (10 percent) accounted for the balance of the employment gain.

One would not expect such an increment (equivalent in size to the entire 1940 employment in retail trade) to be governed by the same structural logic that characterized retail trade at the beginning of the period. We would therefore like to know how these developmental processes modified the structure of the urban system. The questions can be put to the data in three ways. First, how have these developments altered urban-system structure at microscale? Here we focus attention on the internal structure of the dense settlement agglomerations we identify as trade centers. The data base being employed in this study does not reveal much about this level of urban organization, so the first question will be largely passed. Second, how have these developments altered urban-system structure at middle scale where one focuses on the internal structure of an urban region embracing a nodal core and a hinterland hierarchy of lower order trade centers? Third, how have these developments altered urban structure at macroscale? Here we are concerned with the way in which relationships between urban regions of different hierarchical order (as reflected by the trade center characteristics of their respective core centers) have been altered. The data base that forms our present exercise can be shaped to respond to the last two questions—albeit imperfectly.

In table II-22, the interregional shifts in retailing employment (column 1) are recorded for the synthetic regions formed by aggregating all counties according to their trade-center classifications (panel A), their urban transaction-field characteristics (panel B), and by broad geographical region (panel C). These are then expressed as percentage point deviations from the corresponding total (thirty-one sector) employment shifts for the same synthetic regions (column 2). These are further transformed into relative deviations by dividing the percentage point deviations by the total employment shifts (column 3). The average percentage point and relative deviations are provided for each trade sector for each set of synthetic regions.

The average relative deviations (in the third columns of table II-22) introduce the first guiding generalizations. If we look at total retailing, the relative deviations from total employment shifts are admittedly small (on the order of 16 percent), but not trivial. The degree of urban trade system reorganization this might reflect is about the same for the trade-center, transaction-field, and geographical region categories. But this aggregate hides significant subsector variations. It is not surprising that food retailing exhibited the smallest deviations from total employment shifts. We have already seen that the changes in food retailing employment were also the smallest, so this portion of retailing cannot be looked to for the major part of the explanation. Other retailing and the eating and drinking trades displayed much more marked deviations and also showed greater disparity in the extent to which their developmental forces modified trade-center and transaction-field structures. So we will need to pay special attention to these more dynamic and variable components.

Consider the differentiating potential of the developments already discussed. Historically, a major part of the eating and drinking trade was associated with the flow of transients in the urban-system network. The transient flow in 1940 was still mostly associated with business transactions, and was mostly heavily concentrated in the metropolitan core centers. Hence, disproportionate concentrations of this trade were located in these centers. However, we have seen many manufacturing and urban linkage functions spread down the trade center hierarchy and outward to more remote transaction fields, so we would expect the restaurant and bar trade to spread with it. Furthermore, changing incomes, lifestyles, and personalized transport have increased tourism and recreation-oriented travel, all of which favored relative increases in the more remote fields of the urban system. Finally, the higher incomes and female labor force participation rates that favor commercial eating places have spread out of the major metropolitan centers where they were first concentrated.

It is just these developments that make intelligible the eating and drinking trade deviation patterns. The whole-

Categories and regions	Total retail: Percent shift[a] (1)	Total retail: Deviation (percentage point)[b] (2)	Total retail: Relative deviation[c] (3)	Eating and drinking: Percent shift[a] (1)	Eating and drinking: Deviation (percentage point)[b] (2)	Eating and drinking: Relative deviation[c] (3)	Food and dairy: Percent shift[a] (1)	Food and dairy: Deviation (percentage point)[b] (2)	Food and dairy: Relative deviation[c] (3)	Other retail: Percent shift[a] (1)	Other retail: Deviation (percentage point)[b] (2)	Other retail: Relative deviation[c] (3)
Panel A												
Metroplitan, large	−99.3	− 0.4	0.00	−100.0	− 1.1	−0.01	−96.8	+ 2.1	+ 0.02	−99.9	− 1.0	− 0.01
Metropolitan, small	+ 9.7	− 3.2	− 0.25	+ 5.6	**− 7.3**	−0.57	+10.5	− 2.4	− 0.19	+18.4	+ 5.5	+ 0.43
Wholesale-retail, large	+61.8	**+14.0**	+ 0.29	+ 55.3	**+ 7.5**	+0.16	+64.4	**+16.6**	− 0.35	+65.5	**+17.7**	+ 0.37
Wholesale-retail, small	+ 2.4	+ 0.9	+ 0.60	+ 2.4	+ 0.9	+0.60	+ 2.3	+ 0.8	+ 0.53	+ 2.6	+ 1.1	+ 0.73
Wholesale-retail, outside	+ 7.4	+ 0.1	+ 0.01	+ 8.4	+ 1.1	+0.16	+ 6.7	− 0.6	− 0.08	+ 7.9	+ 0.6	+ 0.08
Complete shopping	+16.6	**−12.3**	− 0.43	+ 24.3	**− 4.6**	−0.16	+14.1	**−14.8**	− 0.51	+ 3.1	**−25.8**	− 0.90
Partial shopping	− 1.6	− 3.1	− 2.07	− 0.4	− 1.9	−1.27	− 2.7	− 4.2	− 2.80	+ 0.3	− 1.2	− 0.80
Full convenience	− 1.1	− 0.2	− 0.22	+ 0.4	+ 1.3	+1.44	− 1.8	− 0.9	− 1.00	− 2.1	− 1.2	− 1.33
Hamlet or min. convenience	+ 0.1	+ 0.3	+ 1.50	+ 1.5	+ 1.7	+8.50	− 0.7	− 0.5	− 2.50	+ 0.2	+ 0.4	+ 2.00
Average deviation		±3.8	±0.17		±3.0	±0.14		±4.8	±0.08		±6.1	±0.27
Panel B												
Urban core, large	−89.4	+ 0.6	+ 0.01	−100.0	**−10.0**	−0.11	−84.9	**+ 5.1**	+ 0.06	−78.8	**+11.4**	+ 0.13
Urban core, medium	+45.8	**+ 9.2**	+ 0.25	+ 39.3	+ 2.7	+0.07	+46.5	**+ 9.9**	+ 0.27	+57.0	**+20.4**	+ 0.56
Urban core, small	+25.3	+ 0.3	+ 0.01	+ 24.0	− 1.0	−0.04	+26.9	+ 1.9	+ 0.08	+20.6	− 4.4	− 0.18
Primary labor field, large	+ 4.8	− 0.1	− 0.02	+ 6.2	+ 1.3	+0.27	+ 4.5	− 0.4	− 0.08	+ 2.2	− 2.7	− 0.55
Primary labor field, medium	+ 7.9	− 2.2	− 0.22	+ 9.1	− 1.0	−0.10	+ 7.2	− 2.9	− 0.29	+ 8.0	− 2.1	− 0.21
Primary labor field, small	+ 7.7	**− 7.3**	− 0.49	+ 7.0	**− 8.0**	−0.53	+ 8.0	**− 7.0**	− 0.47	+ 7.9	**− 7.1**	− 0.47
Secondary labor field, large	+ 1.9	+ 0.2	+ 0.12	+ 3.9	+ 2.2	+1.29	+ 0.7	− 1.0	− 0.59	+ 2.2	+ 0.5	+ 0.29
Secondary labor field, medium	+ 4.9	− 1.0	− 0.17	+ 7.0	+ 1.1	+0.19	+ 4.6	− 1.3	− 0.22	+ 0.6	− 5.3	− 0.90
Secondary labor field, small	− 4.9	**− 5.4**	−10.80	− 1.9	− 2.4	−4.80	− 6.3	**− 6.8**	−13.60	− 5.7	− 6.2	−12.40
Outside field	− 7.5	+ 2.7	+ 0.26	+ 1.7	**+11.9**	+1.16	−10.5	− 0.3	− 0.03	−16.9	**− 6.7**	− 0.66
Average deviation		±2.9	±0.15		±4.2	±0.21		±3.7	±0.19		±6.7	±0.34
Panel C												
Upper New England	− 1.0	+ 0.7	+ 0.41	+ 0.5	+ 2.2	+1.29	− 1.3	+ 0.4	+ 0.24	− 1.3	+ 0.4	+ 0.24
Mid-Atlantic	−55.5	**− 3.4**	− 0.07	− 70.8	**−18.7**	−0.36	−49.4	**+ 2.7**	+ 0.05	−60.4	**− 8.3**	− 0.16
Upper Appalachians	− 3.6	+ 0.8	+ 0.19	− 0.8	+ 3.6	+0.81	− 4.3	+ 0.1	+ 0.02	− 4.3	+ 0.1	+ 0.02
Lower Appalachians	− 0.6	+ 0.2	+ 0.25	− 1.2	− 0.4	−0.50	− 0.8	0.0	0.00	+ 0.6	+ 1.4	+ 1.75
Midwest-Great Lakes	−30.3	**+ 5.7**	+ 0.16	− 20.2	**+15.8**	+0.44	−33.9	**+ 2.1**	+ 0.06	−28.1	**+ 7.9**	+ 0.22
Southeast	+20.0	**− 3.8**	− 0.16	+ 12.9	**−10.9**	−0.46	+21.3	**− 2.5**	− 0.11	+23.2	− 0.6	− 0.03
Peninsular Florida	+20.7	**+ 5.0**	+ 0.32	+ 19.3	+ 3.6	+0.23	+21.2	**+ 5.5**	+ 0.35	+20.3	**+ 4.6**	+ 0.66
Southern Plains	+ 6.6	**− 5.1**	− 0.44	+ 1.1	**−11.6**	−0.99	+ 8.0	**− 3.7**	− 0.32	+ 7.9	**− 3.8**	− 0.32
Northern Plains	− 9.9	**− 5.0**	− 1.02	− 8.7	− 3.8	−0.78	−11.1	**− 6.2**	− 1.27	− 6.4	− 1.5	− 0.31
Mts. & Pacific NW	+ 3.7	− 0.1	− 0.03	+ 7.2	+ 3.4	+0.89	+ 2.7	− 1.1	− 0.29	+ 3.6	− 0.2	− 0.05
Southern Mountains	+14.9	+ 2.0	+ 0.16	+ 21.2	**+ 8.3**	+0.64	+13.5	+ 0.6	+ 0.05	+12.6	− 0.3	− 0.02
Metropolitan Calif.	+33.0	+ 1.0	+ 0.03	+ 36.2	+ 4.2	+0.13	+32.4	+ 0.4	+ 0.01	+31.3	− 0.7	− 0.02
Average deviation		±2.7	±0.16		±7.2	±0.43		±2.1	±0.13		±2.5	±0.15

Note: Boldface numbers = deviations greater than the average deviation.
[a] Percentage shift figures are taken from text tables II-8, II-9 and II-4.
[b] Percentage point deviations record plus or minus deviation from the all-employment percentage shifts.
[c] The relative deviation is found by dividing the percentage point deviations by the all-employment shifts for each synthetic region to eliminate the scale effect (although introducing an element of base-bias where the total employment shift is very small).

sale-retail centers forming medium-sized urban-region cores have tended to experience positive deviations with the small wholesale-retail cores being most favored. It is not surprising that in such a reordering process the functionally adjacent smaller metropolitan regions should experience the greatest negative deviations. This macroscale reorganization appears to have been predominantly associated with the changing patterns of business-oriented travel.

But at the middle scale of urban-region structure these developments altered urban organization differently. There were two notable shifts. First, the smallest convenience and hamlet trade centers, and the urban fields outside the reach of core dominance, experienced quite strong positive deviations in eating and drinking trade employment. This was clearly a manifestation of the vacation and tourism phenomenon. This is further underscored when we note in panel C that the Upper New England and Great Lakes regions, plus Florida and the Mountain and Coastal West, were the geographical regions displaying positive deviations. In this connection, it adds to our story if we note that the average relative deviations of the trade across the broad geographical regions were twice as large as across the urban-system classifications. In short, the restaurant and bar trade contributed more to the geographical redistribution of activities than to the reorganization of the middle-scale structure of the urban transaction system.

Second, outside the urban cores, the more remote labor force fields of the large and medium urban regions, as well as the primary labor force fields of the large cores, experienced positive deviations. We can speculate that the relative strength recorded by the secondary fields represents a shift of the day trip, eating-out experience to the increasingly accessible portions of the urban region most associated with the enjoyment of outdoor amenities. In contrast, the primary labor field deviations of the largest regions probably reflect the bedroom community concentration of higher incomes and higher female labor force participation rates.

The "other retailing" category was the dominant source of the changing patterns of urban trade. Here we have to cope with the heterogeneity of component sectors. The increasing numbers of specialty shops, household appliance and furniture dealers, motor vehicle sales agencies, office equipment and supply stores, farm equipment and supply dealers, and hardware and building supply dealers are all activities that were more easily displaced toward higher order trade centers and urban cores than those that supply staples. Conversely, the great expansion in service stations and tourist-oriented souvenir and gift shops might be expected to augment the trading options of lower order centers and more remote locations after the fashion of eating and drinking places.

The record of the "other retail trade" employment deviations in table II-22 is consistent with such a bifurcated dynamic. Both the large and medium urban cores displayed positive deviations, with the medium cores most prominent. In trade-center terms, the largest metropolitan centers stayed almost in balance relative to total employment shifts. The small metropolitan and all wholesale-retail centers displayed positive deviations. The small wholesale-retail centers appeared to experience the largest changes in urban trade structure. Such urban regions (that were intermediate in size and functional order, and that were distributed throughout the nation in the interstitial spaces between the historically dominant metropolitan centers) likely experienced a reorganization of their urban trade structures for two reasons: (1) Because they captured an increasing share of the linkage and so-called basic functions, they grew much more rapidly than other regions. Such increases in scale probably pushed them past the threshold for acquiring some of the higher order trade activities. (2) These regions were more advantageously placed to benefit from the macro- and middle-scale transaction system reorganizations that accompanied the new transport and the increased importance of household capital goods in the mix of goods traded.

It was the lower order trade centers not serving as urban-region cores that experienced the most marked negative deviations. They were led by full convenience centers. In contrast, the hamlet and minimum convenience centers at the bottom of the array experienced positive deviations, as they had for eating and drinking places. Other trade activities also displayed positive deviations in the secondary labor force fields of the largest urban areas. These fields were far enough removed from the dominant cores to be less influenced by the core's functional shadow than the primary field, while still serving relatively high population densities and the reverse-flow trade of weekend and evening shoppers and diners.

In sum, at macroscale it was the wholesale-retail centers, especially the small ones, that augmented their role as trading centers. This was partly a scalar growth effect that accompanied their increasing strategic importance as both production sites and transaction centers for intermediate activities of all sorts. It was in part because these centers were in the best position within the urban trade hierarchy to benefit the most from the middle-scale reorganization of trading functions (born of the developmental changes in transport as well as the altered commodity content of the trading enterprise). This middle-scale reorganization most markedly diminished the relative importance of partial shopping, complete shopping, and full convenience centers (in that order), along with the primary and secondary transaction fields of the small and medium urban regions.

TABLE II-23. Relative retail trade sector percentage shifts and percentage point deviations for lower order trade centers situated in different urban transaction fields, 1940–70

Trade sector-trade center designations	Primary labor field			Secondary labor field			Outside labor field
	Large	Medium	Small	Large	Medium	Small	
Complete shopping	(+12.32)	(+14.46)	(+18.55)	(+3.52)	(+18.60)	(+ 3.84)	(− 5.94)
Eating & drinking	− 0.11	+ 3.87	− 8.36	+5.07	+ 0.47	− 4.78	+16.19
Food & dairy	+ 2.62	+ 0.95	− 7.52	+1.97	+ 2.54	−13.36	− 6.20
Other retail	+ 8.20	− 4.07	−16.16	+3.52	− 9.70	−13.35	−28.25
Total retail	+ 3.00	+ 2.20	− 8.31	+3.58	+ 1.34	−10.79	− 1.07
Partial shopping	(+ 4.48)	(+ 4.38)	(+ 4.50)	(+0.72)	(− 1.01)	(− 1.93)	(− 7.37)
Eating & drinking	− 2.15	+ 0.31	− 2.09	−0.79	+ 0.21	− 2.77	+ 2.65
Food & dairy	+ 0.55	+ 0.27	− 1.92	−0.88	− 0.56	− 6.61	− 4.40
Other retail	+ 1.47	+ 5.01	+ 2.08	−0.10	− 2.91	− 3.65	− 3.62
Total retail	− 0.10	+ 1.08	− 1.38	−0.76	− 0.63	− 5.24	− 1.66
Full convenience	(+ 2.59)	(+ 0.50)	(+ 0.04)	(−0.01)	(− 0.75)	(+ 0.09)	(− 4.89)
Eating & drinking	− 1.22	− 0.08	− 0.32	−0.03	+ 1.72	+ 0.43	+ 3.52
Food & dairy	+ 2.28	− 0.28	+ 0.11	−1.47	− 0.29	− 0.54	− 4.43
Other retail	+ 3.52	− 1.69	+ 1.44	+0.71	+ 0.89	+ 1.23	− 9.10
Total retail	+ 1.36	− 0.36	+ 0.68	−0.73	+ 0.55	+ 0.10	− 2.33
Hamlet & min. convenience	(+ 1.31)	(+ 0.96)	(+ 2.46)	(+0.12)	(− 0.12)	(− 0.29)	(− 5.04)
Eating & drinking	+ 0.07	+ 0.21	− 0.37	+0.72	+ 0.70	+ 0.19	+ 3.86
Food & dairy	+ 1.22	− 0.07	+ 0.51	−0.06	+ 0.29	− 1.16	− 2.86
Other retail	+ 2.04	+ 1.48	+ 2.56	+1.39	− 0.36	− 1.10	− 4.04
Total retail	+ 1.01	+ 0.26	+ 0.57	+0.41	+ 0.26	− 0.77	− 0.88

Note: This table is derived from appendix II-I. Each entry represents the percentage point deviation of each trade sector-trade center-transaction field. (That is, each cell is represented by the cross between the trade sector, trade center, and transaction field.) The reader is cautioned against trying to match these deviations directly with the column 2 deviations of table II-22. The cross-tabulation changes the level of aggregation of the program, hence the dimensionality of the results. The numbers in parentheses are the percentage shifts in total employment for each cell from which the positive and negative deviations are computed.

Although this generalized empirical portrait is valid at a certain level of aggregation, it fails to disclose just how differentiated the trade system reorganization turned out to be. There were major within-class variations. It is worth taking a moment to expand on this middle-scale reorganization. For this purpose, we turn to table II-23. Here we are able to differentiate between the percentage-point deviations (that is, deviations of trade sector employment shifts from total employment shifts) for those lower order trade centers of a given type (such as complete shopping) that are located in large or small urban regions, or in primary or secondary transaction fields. Here we make additional discoveries.

First, notice that, though complete shopping centers experienced significant negative retail trade deviations overall (table II-21), these were largely restricted to those complete shopping centers located in the primary and secondary labor force fields of the smallest urban regions, particularly in the secondary fields. In sharp contrast, complete shopping centers located in the transaction fields of the large and medium-sized regions recorded positive retail trade deviations. It is clear that the way complete shopping centers were affected by the reorganization of the urban trading sytem depended heavily on where they were located within the larger urbanized transaction field.

The data lead us to speculate about the sources of these differences. For one thing, the smallest urban regions were most often headed by small wholesale-retail trading centers, that is, those closest in functional order to the complete shopping centers. These were also the regions with the most shallow and sparse complement of lower order trade centers. Hence, as the core extended its transaction reach under the effect of the developmental changes in access and commodity mix, the shopping centers in closest functional competition were likely to suffer the largest regressive functional reorganizations. If we were to conduct a Hodge-type study of these small, secondary fields, we would likely discover such initial-period shopping centers regressing to lower order types.

In contrast, complete shopping centers located in the transaction fields of larger urban regions (more typically headed by metropolitan or large wholesale-retail centers) were, although often closer geographically, further removed from the core in functional order. Furthermore, they might well be performing specialized dormitory functions for urban-core-oriented populations, thus augmenting their share of some trading functions. (But the fact that the complete shopping centers located in the large secondary fields displayed larger positive deviations than in the primary fields suggests that the urban core shadow was still shading the closer shopping centers more than the remote.) Notice that there are subsector variations as well. Positive eating and drinking trade deviations were more prominent in secondary labor fields and smaller sized regions, probably for the reasons already suggested. Positive deviations in other retail trade tended to be more concentrated in complete shopping centers embedded in the largest urban regions. Perhaps this is because the greater population densities made the complete shopping centers so situated a more attractive habitat for specialty shops and appliance dealers.

It is interesting to note that the adjacent-order partial shopping centers did not exhibit this split personality. They experienced negative deviations in every field. This is clearly the reason that the negative relative deviations recorded in table II-22 mark the partial shopping centers as the champion negative deviators. I would speculate that, in the small urban regions, the partial shopping center shared all of the "genetic" weaknesses of its "sibling" complete shopping center in the face of a changing trading environment. But, in the larger urban regions the reorganizational favors enjoyed by the complete shopping center did not reach to the partial shopping center because it was the weak partner in the "sibling rivalry." At the other end of the trade center array, the hamlets and convenience centers did not fare too badly in the face of trade system reorganization. Within the core-oriented transaction fields, they tended (with minor exceptions) to display positive deviations.

All of these pattern changes may be related to a characteristic of the settlement patterns discussed in volume I. Recall that in chapter 7 in volume I (p. 89), we encountered what appeared to be compensating holes and bulges in the frequency distribution of trade-center types that were adjacent to each other in functional order within a given transaction field. We hypothesized there that when, for whatever historical reasons, a bulge or hole occurs in the frequency distribution of trade-center types, the field variations in functional dominance or shading tend to create offsetting bulges or holes in the numbers of the most closely competing trade-center types. I would suggest that we may be seeing a similar kind of influence at work in the change pattern variations. In the small urban regions, the reorganizational reach of the urban cores appears to have extended to the partial shopping centers, while the lowest order centers appear to find a modestly expanded niche in the changing transaction field. In the larger urban regions, the reorganizational fortunes of the complete shopping centers may not have been shared by the partial shopping centers because of the close functional adjacency of the two orders. At the same time, the lowest order centers were sufficiently removed in functional order to ride the upswing of some functional harmonic in the reorganizational pattern.

The effect of these offsetting tendencies may also be seen as a reflection in the macroscale changes. For example, in panel C of table II-22 the Plains and Southeast regions were the broad areas where substantial negative deviations in retail trade occurred. These were precisely the geographical fields where the smallest urban-region cores were found in greatest number and where the transaction fields most often escaped the gravitational effect of the core region's daily urban field. These, in turn, are the fields just revealed to be most extensively reorganized by developments during the study period.

These are speculations, of course, but they are consistent with a carefully constructed conceptual system and with bits and pieces of evidence of various origins. There remains the possibility that some of this pattern may represent an artifact of the aggregation process so that other explanatory factors remain hidden. For example, we have conducted the discussion thus far as if all of these pattern changes were the direct result of changes in the functional logic of a trading system serving community settlement patterns. But the effect of this changing logic may have been moderated, and perhaps occasionally offset, by the effect of regional differences in intermediate, resource, or household activity changes that simultaneously altered the context of trade system reorganization. And could it be that there are dynamic lead and lag effects at work that affect different parts of the transaction field differently?

Take the case of eating and drinking establishments. A significant part of that emergent trade was oriented to outdoor recreation and tourism in a way that had no systematic correspondence with the changing logic of core-oriented, household-serving, commuting retail trade networks. Thus, Upper New England, Upper Appalachia, the Upper Great Lakes, Peninsular Florida, and the Mountain and Pacific West regions attracted a disproportionate share of this rapidly expanding component, and the deviations recorded were without exception different from those recorded by the more traditional trading sectors (panel B in table II-22 and plate II-24). In short, certain geographical regions and more remote urban fields experienced gains in eating and drinking employment not directed to the service of local trade center populations. They emerged to serve a new class of interregional transactions.

A structurally analogous discrepancy shows up in other retailing because motor vehicle service stations load heavily in those parts of the transfer networks heavily utilized by interregional transients. It does not show up as clearly at this gross geographical scale because other retailing is such a heterogeneous category. If we move down to urban-region scale, it becomes apparent that the urban regions that displayed leading or countertrend competitive gains in other retailing were of two sorts.

First, there were those that, like eating and drinking, served the interregional transients drawn to such places as the Upper Great Lakes, coastal resort, and mountain regions. The second set may have to do with a change in retailing unique to the epoch—the emergence of the truck stop (taken as a symbol of all truck-transport-related retail trade activities). Recall the string of urban regions that formed an arc from the Middle Atlantic regions through the Southeast to Houston and Dallas and displayed leading gains in trucking employment (map II-6). Many of these same urban regions also displayed leading competitive gains in other retailing. The point of emphasis in all this is the fact that retailing has acquired new linkage functions that extend substantially beyond its conventional image as a localized, central-place network providing supplies for settled households.

The thrust of the entire discussion in this section is that the retail trade activities have not been spared from major spatial and functional reorganizations by their reputation as passive adaptors of stable form. From an economic-base-theory perspective they can often be seen to be leading basic manufacturing instead of following. But, more important, this study is another part of the accumulating record that says we must view change as systemic in a way that the simpler, conventional notions of causality are inadequate to explain.

Services

The service categories are so diverse in nature that the aggregate of all services is not very useful. Accordingly, we will concentrate exclusively on the components. Private household employment will be treated as a special case elsewhere. The remainder will be considered in two groupings, each widely different in its systemic and geographical orientation and in the change factors experienced. The first group consists of the service trades: lodging, personal services, and recreation. The second group embraces the information-processing, business, professional, and governmental services.

The Service Trades

Lodging, personal, and recreation services were not a very important part of the dynamic picture, together accounting for only 5.5 percent of the service employment increases during the study period. The systemic and geographical orientation of these sectors has been much more like that of retail trade, especially the eating and drinking trades, than like the information-processing services.

In urban-system terms, the competitive losses represented by the service trades were concentrated in the largest urban cores, mostly of metropolitan order. This was a manifestation of the role of the automobile in generating a boom in outdoor recreation, especially in the form of recreational travel. The major urban fields displaying positive deviations from total employment shifts were the medium and small urban cores headed by medium or small wholesale-retail centers. This is consistent with what appears to have been the most prominent aspect of urban reorganization in the study period—the increasing assumption of what were formerly metropolitan, urban-servicing functions by middle level urban-region cores. The automobile shifted a larger portion of the transaction traffic to those more dispersed nodes with attendant effects on lodging services. At the same time, the most widely dispersed form of entertainment, the movie house, was losing its initial-period status under the impact of television, professional sports, amusement parks, public golf courses, and recreation clubs. The provision of these entertainment services was more capital intensive and required much larger service hinterlands.

Still, the trade centers below complete shopping order, and especially those outside the daily urban systems of the region cores, displayed positive deviations in lodging employment. This was clearly related to (1) the automobile-based emergence of recreational travel and (2) the development of the motel, which permitted lower order centers to service commercial and household transients along well-worn channels. This "tail-of-the-dog" effect was not shared by recreation employment in the aggregate because much of what recreational travel seeks access to cannot be commercialized, save for lodging places and gasoline stations.

The geographical picture is consistent with this. Consider color plates II-26 and II-28. The initial-period specializations already displayed the influence of these localizing tendencies. The heaviest concentrations of specialized counties were in the Upper New England, Upper Great Lakes, Mountain, and Pacific regions, plus Florida. Apart from this, there was a dispersed set of nodal counties in urban-region cores.

The subsequent shift pattern is related. Concentrate on those county configurations formed by the leading gains (dark blue) and lagging losses (pink). These are the areas that experienced positive deviations from total employment shifts. These counties were most heavily concentrated in New England (except upper Maine), Upstate New York and the Appalachians generally, the Atlantic Coast of New Jersey and Delaware, and the upper Michigan and Wisconsin counties. All of these represent the scenic and sporting areas most accessible to the great cities of the Northeast. Beyond this, there were concentrations in Florida, the Rockies, and the Reno, Las Vegas, and Phoenix regions. There were also large clusters in the Midwest and Plains regions. The latter seem curious because we do not think of these areas being great sources of outdoor amenities. The answer may lie mostly elsewhere. These areas were the most heavily supplied with lagging declining counties. They were also heavily supplied with the medium-to-small urban regions allotted a larger relative share of transient travel by the motor vehicle. Thus, the agriculture-based employment and population declines in these regions were partially offset by the functional reorganization of the urban system with respect to the service trades.

When we switch from these generalized patterns to consider dimensional shifts, the developmental forces at work are further underscored. The urban regions displaying the greatest competitive gains in recreation employment were Miami, Reno, and Las Vegas—clearly because of their heavy specialization in the kinds of tourism attracted to commercialized establishments and gambling. Tampa, Orlando, and Phoenix showed greater relative strength in lodging as these areas appealed more to the part-year resident and retiree, along with the outdoor tourist. Apart from these regions where gains were fueled by tourism, emerging macroregional nodes like Washington, D.C.; Charlotte, N.C.; Atlanta; Memphis; Dallas; Houston; Denver; and Los Angeles were prominent gainers. Such centers captured disproportionate shares of transient travel and provided the most specialized recreation services (movie making, theater, and the like).

Information Processing

The shifts in business, professional, and governmental services loomed quite large in the gross 1940–70 competitive shifts generated by all thirty-one industry sectors. Professional services made the largest contribution of all subsectors (over 12 percent, see table II-1). Together, the three information-processing subsectors accounted for more than a fifth of the total. All underwent substantial reorganization, their competitive shifts amounting to between 40 and 45 percent of initial-period employment. Together they accounted for 95 percent of the absolute employment gains in all service sectors (excluding household employment) and more than one-third of total (all-sector) employment gains. Table II-12 indicates that these changes were more important in altering the urban-system structure than in reordering the geographical distribution of these information-processing services. In general, this redistribution amounted to an increasing concentration of these activities in the urban cores and those of highest functional order. We can pursue the details on a sector-by-sector basis.

The business and repair services sector is a heterogeneous composite of exclusively business-oriented services mixed with automobile and miscellaneous repairs. However, the information-processing business services accounted for 80 percent of the sector's employment increases. This was one of the most dynamic growth sectors in the nation during the study period. (Employment increased fivefold and only the air transport component of transportation, the radio and television component of communications, and the armed forces displayed more dramatic increases.)

Business and repair services also displayed the greatest changes in functional urban organization of any of the thirty-one industries (table II-12). Just how radical this structural change was can be seen in the B panels of appendixes II-C and II-D. Although the large metropolitan regions accounted for almost all of the competitive losses in total (all-sector) employment, they simultaneously accounted for three-quarters of the competitive gains in business and repair service employment. (The transaction-field data portray a similar picture.) This was partly a subsector mix phenomenon because the largest urban cores tended to be more prominent specialists in rapid-growth business services than in repair services, but there is no question that during that period the new information-processing technologies also strongly favored the most centralized centers of business activity. Perhaps the most convincing testimony to this effect was the experience of the New York urban region. Although the New York region accounted for almost one-third of the nation's competitive losses in total employment (three times second place Chicago), it actually experienced a countervailing gain in business service employment. At county scale, 58 percent of all business and repair service competitive gains for the nation were accounted for by fifty-six metropolitan counties that were already specialized in business services at the beginning of the period, and for which this sector was the leading gainer.

It remains to say a word about the still important geographical shifts. Though 70 percent of the sector's competitive gains came in a few specialized counties, 56 percent of the competitive losses also came in other specialized counties. Clearly some urban counties in one part of the nation were gaining at the relative expense of others differently situated. Except for the New York urban region, the latter were mostly in the older sections of the nation—Boston, Hartford, Philadelphia, Pittsburgh, Chicago, and St. Louis. Even here the losses tended to lag substantially behind total employment losses. At urban-region scale, Los Angeles, San Francisco, Washington, D.C., and Miami accounted for more than half of the competitive gains. Washington became the natural locus for the increasingly important services that mediated government and business linkages. The other three regions were not only in the most rapidly growing sectors of the nation, they were coming to play an increasingly prominent role in mediating foreign trade linkages as the patterns of trade were shifting to nations in the South and West.

Perhaps the best way to picture this is to concentrate first on the geographical profiles generated by 269 counties (less than 10 percent of all counties) that displayed leading gains (dark blue) and lagging losses (pink) in plate II-27. Most of these were clustered in urban-region core centers. Leading (or countertrend) gain counties were most prominently associated with Boston, New York, Philadelphia, Baltimore, Washington, Richmond, Norfolk, Atlanta, Charlotte, Jacksonville, Orlando, Tampa, Miami, Birmingham, New Orleans, Dallas, Houston, Chicago, Detroit, Pittsburgh, Minneapolis, Denver, Phoenix, Los Angeles–San Diego, San Francisco–Portland, and so forth. There were, however, a number of recognizable clusters of leading gain and lagging loss counties that did not correspond with nodal urban centers. These can be seen in the Appalachian coal regions, the mining regions of the Upper Michigan Peninsula, the Lower Mississippi cotton-growing lands, the Louisiana and Texas oil country, and in some oil and mining counties of the Mountain States. Dimensionally, the proportion of the total shift represented by these counties was small, but an explanation is in order. These clusters of positive-deviating counties in what appear to be prominent resource fields have benefited from concentrations of highly specialized business services that rent and lease oil rigs and other mining equipment, that perform brokerage and marketing services, that provide inspection services for cotton and other commodities, that perform field warehousing services, that do commercial testing, and that repair specialized mining and farm machinery.

In contrast, 86 percent of all U.S. counties experienced leading losses or the negative-deviating, lagging gains. They blanket the nation, with the leading losses most prominent in the Midwest, the Plains, and Northern Mountain regions. Some of this was a consequence of a negative subsector mix effect. These predominantly rural regions tended to specialize more in those agricultural repair and brokerage services that were the slow-growth subsectors of the business and repair service category. But the competitive decline of agriculture in some of these regions, and the growing service independence of the larger agribusiness complexes, generated genuine competitive losses in the resource-oriented business services in these areas. Beyond that, the motor vehicle and miscellaneous repair services that penetrated small-town America were slow-growth activities compared with the burgeoning information-processing services.

Summing up, the previously discussed developmental factors that increased the importance of such information-processing activities, and that consequently favored the large centers forming the major administrative and communication nodes, generated a major change in urban-system structure—one that ran directly counter to that being generated by developments in material- and energy-processing.

Professional activities contributed more by far to the functional and geographical shifts in urbanized activities than did any other activity sector. This single sector accounted for more of the study-period gain in total employment (one-fourth) than all ten manufacturing sectors combined. It displayed the largest growth rate (outside of the armed forces which started from a minuscule base, see table 37 in volume 1), recorded the largest gross competitive shifts (table II-1), and accounted for two-thirds of the gains in total service employment. Eighty-two percent of the gains in professional service employment were directly attributable to the growth of educational and medical services. However, the sector also included such rapidly growing activities as museums, legal services, business and trade associations, professional membership organizations, labor unions, and other social and religious organizations.

Nowhere else did the emerging information society have such a sizable impact on urban structure. The systemic effects were very much like those of the business services. Appendixes II-C and II-D reveal that, in the aggregate, positively deviating competitive shifts were restricted to urban-region cores of higher order trade centers. Medium-sized urban regions headed by large wholesale-retail centers captured about two-thirds of the competitive gains, although the largest urban regions with large metropolitan cores displayed the greatest positive deviations relative to total employment shifts. The shopping centers displayed the greatest negative deviations overall. The transaction fields of the smallest urban regions, and those altogether outside core-oriented fields, recorded the largest negative shifts and the largest negative deviations.

These patterns are explained by the developmental history of the period. Take the case of medical services. This was the time when truly spectacular developments in medical technology took place. They were based on all of the scientific advances in biology, biochemistry, physical chemistry, and electronics. As a consequence, the information content of medical practice, and the technological artifacts employed, grew exponentially. This led to both professional and institutional specialization. Specialty medical services, like specialty trade stores, require a larger population base and trading hinterland. Research and testing laboratories become much more important, further leading to the agglomeration of medical services in larger centers.

Technological developments increased the information content of all social processes so dramatically that phenomenally larger investments in human capital were required, with the consequence that education services burgeoned. In public education, the most rapidly increasing employment came in the colleges, universities, and professional schools explicitly designed to raise the technological level of the learning experience. Again, these activities naturally sought more centralized and urbanized locations than the elementary and secondary forms of education that dominated an earlier time. The most rapidly growing sector of educational employment came in the private sector in the form of correspondence, data-processing, business, secretarial, and vocational schools directed to the upgrading of a specialized labor force. These activities also favored the urban cores.

Finally, included in professional service employment is a category of miscellaneous services closely akin to the business services already considered. These included legal, engineering, and architectural services along with noncommercial educational, scientific, and research organizations. Although these activities accounted for only one-tenth of professional service employment, they were rapid-growth sectors and added measurably to the tendency of the study-period increments to seek urban core locations.

The geographical shift patterns in color plate II-30 are quite similar in general orientation to those exhibited by the shift in business services. This was also true of the dimensional shifts recorded in appendix D in volume I. When significant differences in pattern occurred, they tended to be associated with the presence in the region of a major college town or state capital. Thus Oklahoma City, Tallahassee, Austin, Lansing, Madison, and Sacramento showed up prominently because these regions contained both state capitals and major universities.

Problems that arose in connection with the coordination and regulation of increasing social complexity also fostered the emerging information society. A considerable expansion took place in the services of civilian government (considered separately from public education). In keeping with the changing character of governmental and political problem solving, it was federal public administration that recorded the greatest growth rates.[2] It was only natural that this would accentuate the role of governmental activity situated in the urban cores and in the higher order trade-center fields (see appendix tables II-C and II-D). The consequences for urban-system reorganization were quite similar to those exhibited by the other information-processing services. In dimensional terms, however, there were urban regions that made especially prominent gains. As with professional employment, disproportionate gains in government employment were associated with many state capitals, particularly in parts of the nation where development was forcing a larger role for public administration than required in simpler times. Thus, Tallahassee, Oklahoma City, Austin, Salt Lake, Reno, Albuquerque, and Sacramento revealed prominent leading competitive gains. In addition, such regions as Burlington, Boston, Albany, Hartford, and Cheyenne, all encompassing state capitals, experienced positive-deviating lagging losses. Interestingly enough, the seat of the federal government, Washington, D.C., displayed lagging gains in governmental employment. The regions flanking it, Baltimore and Richmond, benefited strikingly from growth in both state and federal government.

But the regions displaying the most marked positive deviations in government employment were areas where there was a particularly marked increase in civilian military employment. Such regions as Norfolk, Charleston, Savannah, Pensacola, Mobile, Wichita Falls, Corpus Christi, Pueblo, and San Diego were prominent in this respect. The record of these shift patterns is in plate II-31 and in appendix E of volume I.

Special Cases

Three of the thirty-one sectors that form the base of this study are special cases in the sense that the change factors at work were unique. They do not fit into any obvious grouping. They are: private household, construction, and armed forces employment. In addition, a few words need to be said about the urban-system consequences of changes in the nation's foreign trade linkages.

Domestic Employment

Domestic employment in this country has always been a residual employment category occupied mostly by blacks and women from immigrant households. Accordingly, it has been associated with a cultural, racial and economic stigma to be escaped at the first opportunity. Consequently, the fortunes of this employment sector have always tended to reflect changes in the supply of domestics attending the waves of immigration and interregional migration, along with changes in enterprise employment options. The experience during the study period was no different in this regard.

The initial-period specializations in domestic employment can be seen in color plate II-29. They were concentrated in the sandy plains lining the Atlantic and Gulf Coasts—the cotton-tobacco-peanut South with its black slave heritage. Beyond this was a set of counties in the major cities of the Middle Atlantic and New England coasts that represented the ports of call of the European immigrants, and a set of counties on or near the Mexican border that represented the initial locus of Mexican immigration.[3] Outside of these areas one can find only occasional specialized counties or county clusters representing localized phenomena.

This pattern was subject to several interesting modifications during the study period. The most important aspect of the change was the phenomenal overall decline in domestic employment, exceeded only by the rate of decline in agricultural employment. A number of changes acted to reduce the supply of domestic workers. The two-thirds reduction in agricultural production forced large numbers of farm workers into urban areas where enterprise job options were better. At the same time, the extension of core-area commuting fields and the rapid decentralization of manufacturing increased the numbers of such options available elsewhere. The gradual reduction in the barriers of racial and cultural discrimination also played a part. While all of this was happening, the rapid development of household appliances and prepared foods dramatically reduced the demand for domestic labor.

But the effects of these tidal changes were not felt everywhere the same. The sandy pine barrens that stretch along the coastal plains from Richmond all the way to Brownsville at the tip of Texas experienced strong competitive gains simply by losing domestic employment less rapidly than the nation as a whole. The same was true of the Plains regions, North and South. In these fields enterprise job options remained relatively weak. In contrast, the Piedmont, Appalachian, and Cumberland regions of the Upper South experienced strong declines in share. Here the supply of displaced black labor was not as great. This was also where the migration of industry most heavily increased the enterprise job options in the South. The latter was also true of a belt stretching from St. Louis down through the Ozarks to Dallas and Houston.

Two-thirds of the competitive losses were concentrated in the seaboard regions from Boston to Baltimore. Here all of these macro supply and demand factor changes were augmented by a decline in European migration. More than half of the share increases were on the Pacific Coast and in the Southern Mountains. Here an entirely different set of factors was at work. The supply of domestic labor actually increased because of increases in the supply of Mexican labor—and a supply of persons peculiarly conditioned by culture and history to domestic employment. In nineteen of the southwest urban regions the competitive gains were not just a consequence of lower relative declines; absolute increases in domestic employment took place.

It was the lower order trade centers, and those mostly in secondary trading fields or outside core-oriented fields, that experienced either leading gains or lagging losses in domestic employment. But these were the areas where agricultural displacement, the availability of enterprise work options, and the decline in racial discrimination had the least effect.

Construction

It is my belief that much needs to be said about the role of construction in the development of the urban system. It is a largely neglected area of study. Unfortunately, this study cannot redress that neglect. The data base is not appropriate to the task.

Contract construction is unique in two respects: (1) In an industrial society, it is the only significant remaining fabricating activity that is carried out mostly at the site of product use. (2) It is engaged in the production of fixed capital of long life, and in this regard, it is commonly anticipatory and future oriented. As a consequence, construction employment is not only sensitive to changes in the geographical locus of emergent urbanized activities, it is hypersensitive. The famous "acceleration principle" of macroeconomics is at work here. Both the fact that construction is anticipatory in nature and that construction activity is not sustained during the lifetime of the construct give this activity sector a tendency to lead and exaggerate changes in populations and total employment.[4] These characteristics tend to yield exaggerated interregional competitive shifts in construction employment.

The problems and opportunities for study that these characteristics yield are not very important in the thirty-year time span of this study. A lot of the spatial dynamics are washed out. In fact, table II-12 reveals that the average deviations of the construction sector's competitive shifts from those recorded by total employment were among the lowest of all sectors. Yet there were a number of confusing, localized, and regional discrepancies in the construction shift patterns when compared directly with shifts in settlement patterns. Because of the peculiar volatility of construction employment, a part of this may have to do with the accident of the timing of the census, thus yielding exaggeratedly high or low beginning or ending period localized employments. These could become the source of confusing shift patterns. This is further complicated by the fact that the highway, utility, industrial, and general construction components all tend to display a different kind of dynamic pattern.

The upshot is that the construction sector data of this study do not add much to the story of this volume. But there is, I believe, a missed opportunity here for understanding some things about the dynamics of urban-system development. If data were assembled more often than ten years and the different components of construction were sorted out, construction might well be revealed as a "leading indicator" of other activity changes that require these constructs for their implementation. A study of such sequence patterns might yield some useful insights about the developmental process.

Armed Forces Employment

Armed forces employment was the most rapidly growing employment category during the study period—expanding from 300,000 to 12 million then contracting to about 2 million by the end of the period. The national security reasons underlying these dramatic and turbulent changes need not be recited here. However, the interregional shifts in military activities made the fifth largest contribution to the gross competitive shifts (table II-1).

In broad regional terms, the Southeast captured about two-thirds of the competitive gains, and these gains were second only to those it experienced for textile employment. We have already seen how an increase in military activity often has a multiplier association with professional and civilian government employment.

Color plate II-32 reveals how widespread the competitive gains were. But the quantitative effect was much more selective. A relative handful of urban regions (20 percent) accounted for three-fourths of the shifts and, typically, only one or two counties in each region were responsible. Camp LeJeune in the Wilmington region; Fort Hood and the Connally Air Force Base in Waco; the Air Force Academy in Colorado Springs; the Navy in Jacksonville, Mobile, and Philadelphia; Fort Jackson in Columbia, S.C.; a host of military operations in the Los Angeles region (including the Pacific Fleet Base, the Naval Ordnance Station, Camp Pendleton, and Camp Irwin, plus several navy and marine air bases); Fort Gordon and the Savannah River Nuclear Plant in Augusta; Cape Canaveral and the McCoy Air Force Base in Orlando; and the Edwards Air Force Base in the Mojave Desert were all highly localized sites that accounted for the great bulk of the competitive gains in armed services employment. Twelve urban regions accounted for three-fourths of the competitive losses. They were primarily older headquarter and base cities on the East and West coasts or old army bases. In terms of employment shares, their relative importance declined as the large substructure of an active military establishment developed. Thus, Hawaii, New York, San Francisco, Baltimore–Washington, and Seattle–Portland accounted for over half of the competitive losses. Certain old bases like Fort Sam Houston in San Antonio and Fort Benning in Columbus, Georgia, accounted for the bulk of the rest.

New and expanded bases that could provide troop training areas and uncongested air space had to be located in more remote areas. So it is natural to find (in appendixes II-C and II-D) that the bulk of the competitive gains came in the secondary fields of the smallest size urban regions and outside of identified urban-region transaction fields. Most of the gains were concentrated in those parts of these fields served by trade centers of complete shopping order.[5] Although this generalized element of rationality in the shift patterns is clear, there is a widely held view that the reasons that particular local sites were chosen, or why the Southeast should have claimed such a disproportionate share of the gain, lies in the distribution of political power and influence at the time. These are factors clearly beyond the scope of this enterprise to assess.

Quite beyond the interregional shifts in armed forces employment, the associated development of the military industrial complex has played a role in inducing employment shifts in other activity sectors, as was frequently noted in preceding analyses. This is a very difficult thing to estimate, but it has not been for want of trying.[6] This much is clear; the geographic impact of defense purchases shifted primarily because the armed services had to adjust to the new requirements of warfare and developing military technology. This led to changes in weapons, changes in logistic equipment, and to new geographical site requirements. The traditional defense manufacturing industries that were earlier concentrated in the Middle Atlantic and East North Central regions did not possess the equipment, labor force, or developmental capabilities to produce the newer weapons. New England, the South, and the West were able to develop these capabilities unencumbered by a production base that was growing increasingly obsolete. By 1963, for example, a special study of the Census of Manufactures[7] revealed that 57 percent of industry shipments to the Department of Defense came from the new aerospace industries and that 56 percent of that came from the West—particularly California. In my view, no convincing case has been made that military procurement played a significant role in siting these emergent activities. However, in the absence of defense procurement, the change patterns previously observed would certainly have been less marked. To give one striking example of the selective impact of defense procurement, the importance of metal mining in government procurement tripled between 1947 and 1963. This was directly related to uranium mining that was concentrated in the mountain areas. By the end of that period, one-fourth of total labor earnings in the Mountain region were generated by federal government purchases. This was an increase of two-thirds in fifteen years.

International Trade

At least a passing word about the influence of structural changes in international trade is in order. There is a great tendency in regional studies to draw study boundaries and ignore the external connections. Unfortunately for the student, these external connections are becoming more and more important as all transaction systems become more and more open. During the last half of the study period, foreign trade rose at a more rapid rate than both domestic production and the gross national product. The tightening web of economic interdependence among nations has been transforming world trade and, as the industrialization of the Third World proceeds, one country after another has altered its patterns of buying and selling on the world market. These changes have had differential regional effects within the U.S. urban system.

Although a systematic study of these factors is out of the question here, several examples of the influence of changing trade patterns may alert the reader to the significance of these external linkages. For example, the study period marked the beginning of significant increases in steel and petroleum imports. These two products went from 5 percent of total commodity or material imports in 1940 to 60 percent in 1970. The increased importance of imported crude oil helps to explain the shift of petroleum refining from the interior sites of the East Texas field to the Gulf Coast. It also explains the competitive gains in petroleum refining in the Philadelphia region when the rest of the Northeast was experiencing relative losses. The increased importation of steel aggravated the excess capacity of the older steel centers of the Pittsburgh–Youngstown regions, accelerating their competitive decline. It also explains why the early-period competitive gains in steel making in the Middle Atlantic Tidewater reversed so quickly and turned into competitive losses by the end of the study period.

If we examine the commodity side of trade exports, there is a corresponding decline (by half) in the proportion accounted for by steel and petroleum. The important increases were in food exports. Wheat and edible oils were the most important, and these clearly augmented the strong competitive gains in agricultural employment favoring the North Central and Plains regions previously noted. The agricultural competitive gains demonstrated by California and Florida were further strengthened by an increase in the export of fruits and nuts. Apart from food commodities, there was an increase in the importance of coal exports. The effect of this was overwhelmed by the mining employment competitive losses experienced by the Appalachian coalfields, but it played an important role in explaining the relative competitive strength of the Norfolk urban region, Norfolk being the principal port of export.

But the most dramatic changes took place in the role of finished manufactures. Although the finished manufacture-commodity mix of U.S. exports did not change greatly, finished manufactures rose from 16 to 56 percent of total imports over the study period. (U.S. exports of finished manufactures in 1940 were six times larger than imports; by 1960, imports and exports were about in balance.) Not since the early nineteenth century had manufactured imports been so important in the U.S. economy. These increases covered pretty much the gamut of the fabricated products from mechanical and electrical machines of most types to automobiles and other transport equipment, instruments, photographic equipment, and even textiles and clothing. Machinery and automobile imports dominated the increase in import share.

In absolute terms, the United States increased the export of machines and automobiles at the same time its imports of these products were increasing. We know that this can make a contribution to efficiency in a free market, but there can be no doubt that structural changes of this dimension had significant localized effects that influenced the shift patterns we have examined. There are anecdotal illustrations one can recite—such as the relative declines in apparel employment in Gloversdale, N.Y. (the highly specialized site of glove manufacturing) under the impact of foreign competition. But to trace the direct and indirect effects of these changes on employment shifts would obviously be a major undertaking. It seems quite reasonable to suggest, however, that the prominent relative declines in manufacturing employment experienced by New England and the Middle Atlantic regions were likely augmented by the region's premier accessibility to the emerging foreign sources of manufactured products. It is highly likely, for example, that the acceleration of the shift of the textile and apparel industries to the South was at least partly stimulated by the growth of foreign competition.

The growth of foreign trade had differential regional effects in other ways, as well. During the study period, New York City experienced an expanding role as a base for conducting foreign trade and American business abroad. Of roughly 1,700 foreign firms operating in the United States in 1970, three-fourths were in the New York Metropolitan region. The number of foreign banks increased substantially during the study period. The number of international law firms tripled. Of the eight major accounting firms that had international business, six were centered in New York. Clearly the New York region's countervailing gain in business services previously noted owed much to the growing importance of international trade.

Notes

1. For example, my own study in Perloff and coauthors (1960) completely ignored these sectors.

2. Although the absolute gains in state and local public administration were almost the same. It should also be noted that the greatest increase in federal employment was associated with the New Deal initiatives and the growing importance of national security related employment. The greatest effect of these changes came in the 1940s and 1950s. By the last decade of the study period, state and local government employment changes once again became very important, and, contrary to popular impression, have continued to be the most dynamic sector during the ensuing period.

3. The visible Upper New England specializations were more of a short-term reflection of the extremely depressed state of New England in 1940. In addition to the ravages of the depression, Upper New England had earlier been experiencing especially strong competitive declines in agriculture, textiles, wood products, and paper—the very core of its industrial base.

4. For example, there was a period in the mid-1960s when Florida's rate of population increase leveled off. This was associated with an *absolute* decline in construction employment.

5. One need not assume that the sites of military bases necessarily have an affinity for shopping center locations. Since Berry's classification was made on 1960 data, one might as well assume that military bases tend to breed trade centers of shopping center order.

6. For example, see the studies of Bolton (1966) and Polenske (1969).

7. U.S. Department of Commerce (1966).

Part Three

SUMMARY AND IMPLICATIONS

13

Summary of the Study

The author of a recent real estate appraisal text identified the three most important factors in appraising the value of a property as (1) location, (2) location, (3) location. There was no sign that he appreciated what a good Weberian regional scientist he had become. There is a further message in this study. It holds that the three most important factors in understanding an urban transaction system are development, development, and development. The existing topology (relational patterns) and topography (spatial patterns) formed by urbanized activities and their changes over time are the consequence of a problem-solving, developmental history. Indeed, without development there can be no long-term change in the system.[1] This concept of development is identified with technological change in the broadest sense: with individuals, households, and enterprises learning how to do new things, how to do old things differently, and how to value things differently. The scalar changes that conventionally attract scholars' attention can in no way be understood or explained without reference to their developmental sources.

With this concept of development in place, the summary will proceed as follows. (1) The generic forms of problem-solving endeavors will be restated, thus providing a basis for understanding the process of change. (2) The system-wide scalar effects of technological change will be seen to give each epoch a characteristic profile of differentiated scalar growth rates. (3) These largely scalar effects will be shown to be transitory and overshadowed by changes in the patterns of networks connecting behavioral entities (individuals, households, and enterprises). The network changes are of two general types: those that alter the structure of the transfer channels (transport and communications) through which inter-entity transactions must flow, and those that alter the structure of the input–output flows that course through these channels. (4) It will be shown that these network changes alter the locations of the individuals, households, and enterprises whose linked activities comprise the urbanized network. A view of this dynamic can be seen in the changing regional specializations and industrial concentrations that the shift-share technique attempts to represent.

Developmental Problem Solving

Patterns of social behavior change only when individuals, households, or enterprises perceive a problem thought to be ameliorable (or an opportunity thought to be exploitable), *if* things can be done or valued differently. The perception of a problem is often initiated by a changing operating environment. Successful behavioral adaptations often modify, in turn, their operating environments. Then other behavioral entities (co-adapting in a physical and social ecosystem of interdependent relationships) frequently experience these systemic changes as new problems or opportunities, next round. Hence, the developmental process is an evolutionary sequence of problems and attempted solutions.

The variety of technological responses thus spawned by history has been almost without limit. But, if we move back a step, we can see that the encountered problems and developmental responses can be broadly characterized by systemic traits. Even though problems are encountered in specific situations, the same kinds of problems occur in quite different kinds of situations. We can, thus, generalize about developmental processes.[2]

All problems that involve physical processes have certain family characteristics, and those involved in information processes display a different set of characteristics. Physical process problems can be further differentiated by the kinds of limitations experienced. First, a problem may involve some defect in the basic process itself—where a process describes a sequential set of activities designed to modify a set of inputs, or to act upon the operating environment.[3] The process concept may be flawed or incomplete. The solution involves redesigning the activity sequence, that is, learning how to do it better. Second, the process design may be quite adequate but fail because the quantity or kind of energy driving it is the source of some constraint. The solution may involve finding larger energy sources or harnessing new forms of energy. Third, it may be that the activity concept and energy sources are adequate, but the process suffers because the materials available do not satisfactorily embody the function. This may set in motion the search for new materials. Often, of course, a problem may involve more than one of these elements in combination.

Physical processes are the handmaidens of the information processes that activate and coordinate them. They are incoherent in the absence of some form of cybernetic control. So, a fourth class of problems has to do with the perceived inadequacies of managerial processes that regulate the recurrent performances of physical process systems. These problems may arise in situations in which all physical processes are otherwise capable of meeting the expectations of the system. The solution requires revamping managerial controls and may also involve organizational and institutional changes. Finally, there are information processes that are actively engaged in reviewing the purposes of the system and the adequacy of the performance processes that serve them. This is the level of behavior at which problems and opportunities are identified and developmental responses designed—the level where the other four types of problem solutions are mediated. These are the self-reorganizing, reprogramming information processes. It sometimes happens that the critical problem in a system is its inability to make developmental changes.

So, we identify five generic types of problems. But this entire set can be doubled. All five types tend to be systematically different depending on whether the problem has to do with changing the form of an input or moving it from one production node to another within the transaction network.

The Development of the U.S. Urban System

Throughout part two, attention was directed to identifying the problem-solving context of the changes observed. What would otherwise be an impossible summarizing task is made somewhat manageable by the fact that there are these common aspects of developmental change. As the developmental process works its way in history, the problems it encounters in a particular situation may be different in kind from those prominent in another time and context.

Before 1940

Review briefly how the contexts of these problems have changed in each epoch. Take, first, the *colonial period* all the way up to the nineteenth century (that is, including the transmontaine period). This was an unusual period in which developmental activity was subordinated to a binge of scalar growth. The established mercantile and agricultural processes of the parent country were poured into the vessel of an empty continent. It took almost 200 years before attention could be lifted much above the task of transcribing existing technology onto the blank page of this new topographic field. The major problem was gaining access to an expansive continent. Increases in production resulted almost entirely from bringing cheap land under cultivation as fast as possible with existing techniques. It took a long time before the lands accessible to coastal and internal waterways were exploited. Conventional sources of energy (wood and horses) and conventional sources of materials (wood, clay, and stone plus charcoal-smelted bog iron) were used. Employment was mostly agricultural and mercantile and increased spectacularly everywhere.

It was not until the nineteenth century that developmental activities began to alter the economic profile substantially. As the eighteenth century wore on, two kinds of public pressures were building. There was (1) the continuing problem of gaining effective access to the interior and (2) the problem of an acute shortage of labor (born of the ever-present opportunities for mercantile expansion). It became apparent that preexisting access technologies were inadequate to cope with so large a land mass. And preexisting production technologies were too unproductive in their use of labor to accommodate the demands of this novel operating environment. The emergence of commercial agriculture required a genuine national access network and a means of reducing the amount of labor needed. The creative responses to these problems gestated slowly, but they had a substantial effect on the structure of the system during the *pre–Civil War period.*

One developmental response was the mechanization of farm work processes. The traditional cottage-based textile industry was similarly mechanized, and for the same general reasons. Another set of developmental responses revolved around converting the old riverine system into a total transport network. This brought forth the steam engine in its application to the steamboat (converting the rivers into two-way streets for the first time) and the early iron horse on iron rails (permitting the water transport system to extend its reach a short way inland).

The physical production problems in agriculture and textiles evoked type-one innovations in process design.

The task was one of amplifying human work processes so that the productivity of scarce labor could be enhanced. At first round, neither energy (type-two) or material (type-three) problems were pressing. The basic iron metallurgy of the time appeared adequate. Mechanical developments were designed to employ the horse or water wheel, both traditional sources of energy.[4]

In the case of the transport problem, the constraint presented itself in the first instance as an energy problem. The horse, sail, and pole were inadequate to move heavy boats upstream. The horse and wagon could not carry enough things fast enough to effectively penetrate the land-locked interiors. The type-two developmental response was the steam engine. This, in turn, required type-one process design developments. Still, the early low-pressure steam engine and drive systems proceeded reasonably well on the basis of the existing iron technology.

Translated into the developmental profile of sector growth rates, we saw agriculture, farm machinery, textiles, transportation equipment, transport and wholesaling activities stepping forward as the growth industries of the pre–Civil War period.

The post–Civil War period began a new phase. The base problems were still continental access and the high cost of labor. These concerns still drove the developmental engine.[5] But the success of the problem-solving efforts of the previous epoch brought new attention to familiar limits and generated new problems. By the last half of the century, the drive to continental access and labor-saving mechanizations ran smack into an imposing power constraint.

Nowhere was this second-round energy constraint more apparent than in the quest for a truly national transport system. The basic coastal and riverine system had gone as far as it could in opening up the land mass of the continent. There was no way to link the West Coast to the emerging national system without fast and effective overland transport. The iron horse had pointed the way to the interior, but displayed a limited reach. Low-pressure steam engines and brittle iron rails could not carry heavy loads very far or very fast. The railway was strictly ancillary to the waterways. High-carbon iron could not handle the pressures essential to make the steam engine efficient, or the stresses of heavy weight and high speed upon wheel and rail. So the solution to the power problem had run up against a serious material problem. Steel had the potential for resolving these material constraints, but at that time, steel was only used for cutlery and small arms. The new steel-making technology was the developmental response. Its development required a further shift in energy sources from wood to coal.

But the power constraint was not felt in the transport sector alone. Agricultural mechanization was running up against the limits of animal power. Inventors dreamed of type-one machine designs beyond the power of the horse team. Millions of acres of productive farmland were required to fix the solar energy at the base of the animal power train. Mechanization in manufacturing was running up against the extreme geographical localization of waterpower sites at the same time it was finding the early steam engine cumbersome and dangerous. By the end of the century, the developments in steam, steel, and coal had forged the first nationwide land transport system, had built a new power base in industry, and were being used experimentally, but not very successfully, in the steam tractor. The labor-saving mechanization of traditional production processes continued, with the apparel industry becoming prominent. Manufacturing was now more absorbed with producing, not only machinery for the traditional work of humankind, but machinery for producing the machinery.

However, another class of problems loomed. Earlier developments had generated a degree of complexity that raised acute problems of managerial coordination and control. The urbanized transaction network was also becoming more interdependent and complex. Managerial problems gave rise to clerical occupations and an embryonic management movement. The need to communicate rapidly at a distance made this the epoch of the telegraph. The pressures on developmental talent and knowledge sources made this the era when science began to become a quasi-organized enterprise and when the machine tool industry began to give some form to the developmental process.

These problem-solving initiatives became translated into a different profile of sector growth rates. Agriculture, textile machinery, and trade, the stars of the third epoch, were now overshadowed by coal mining, railway construction and operation, the manufacture of steel and apparel, and machinery. Increasing urbanization made a growth industry out of construction and lumber production. In an important harbinger of the future, clerical and information-processing workers began to grow rapidly under the pressure of fourth- and fifth-type managerial and developmental problems. However, these activities were largely hidden because they remained an almost subterranean aspect of all enterprises. Only the rapid growth of printing, publishing, and paper manufacturing directly reflected the stimulating influence of information-processing problems.

This century-long, developmental drive to open the continent and mechanize work succeeded so well that the nation's centennial marked an abrupt change in the set of problems confronting the system. The continent had been integrated into a single urbanized system, and the frontier was closed. This key event changed the nature of the urban system's production and access problems.

Begin with the access problems. Previously the nation's preoccupation had been with access to the continent at gross scale. The resulting linear railway and waterway network established many primary nodes where both local and interregional access was maximized. The emergence of the intermediate manufacturing industries vastly increased the off-farm population at these nodes. By the time the national system had been put in place, it had created cities that had to spread to breathe. But the access technologies that absorbed the nation's developmental energies for so long were ill suited for resolving these now pressing, localized, intraregional access problems.

The railway had been developed as a long-distance carrier of people and commodities. Where it was adapted to serve local commuting needs it did little more than allow the wealthy to move to satellite communities. The application of steam to the horse trolley proved inadequate. New ways of applying energy to transport were required. The electric motor and its application to the streetcar resulted. The central public utility emerged to provide transit power and urban lighting. Concurrently, the population concentrations were creating public health problems. The developmental response was the field of sanitary engineering and the installation of water and sewage utilities. The telegraph was useless as a local communication device except for specialized commercial and governmental applications. Localized communication pressures led to the development of the telephone.

These were all localized access network developments necessary for the emerging city to spread. But the cinch binding the cities was breached by these technologies mostly along selected radial spokes. Until some mode of transport came along that provided for greater flexibility in time and routes, the city would continue to struggle to house the activities and populations of the new industrial economy. The developmental response was the petroleum-based internal combustion engine. The motor vehicle finally ungirded the city.

"Meanwhile back on the farm," the power problem had never been satisfactorily resolved. The steam power technology that came to dominate the fourth epoch was not adaptable to the role of the horse. The gasoline engine resolved this power problem as well. The first third of the century became the epoch of the tractor. This was the final resolution of the set of agricultural problems that dominated the nineteenth century. The closing of the frontier caused a complete reorientation of these problems. Formerly, developmental initiative strained to spread scarce labor over more acres of land. With the closing of the frontier, the productivity of the land, rather than the productivity of labor, became the overriding concern. Accordingly, a new set of developmental initiatives emerged. They were all subsumed under the new scientific agriculture and institutionalized in the research and extension activities of the U.S. Department of Agriculture and the land-grant colleges. The major changes involved more use of irrigation and greatly expanded soil preparation practices. Significant changes in animal husbandry and horticulture were also initiated.

This was not just the epoch of the local access problem and the gasoline engine as prime mover. It became the epoch of the electric motor as well. The steam engine was best suited for gross power applications. It could be adapted to fractional power applications only through a complicated array of drive-shafts and belts. Steam power also imposed on the user the logistically cumbersome requirement of converting energy at the work site. This in turn created network rigidities and density problems in the cities. The electric motor not only allowed fractional units of power to be applied at the work site, but it passed along the problem of energy conversion to the public utility. Furthermore, it cleared the way for applying energy to work in a range of tasks that had previously defied mechanization—the work of the home, farm barn, and small craft shop. With the advent of the electric washing machine, the home appliance industry "stuck its nose under the tent."

In the realm of communications, the telegraph-as-problem-solver displayed severe limitations. Possessing a limited signal capacity, it could carry little information. The telephone was the developmental response, even though well into the twentieth century it was primarily a local technology. Telegraphy also failed to resolve the critical problem of access to ships at sea. The beginnings of long-line telephony and the wireless telegraph (radio) were addressed to each of these problems.

Manufacturing came to be absorbed less with satisfying traditional consumer requirements than with the task of producing the new production and transfer process equipment. The impetus that the emerging machine age gave to manufacturing came to full fruition in the fifth epoch. In 1907 manufacturing employment topped agricultural employment for the first time. The industrial economy had arrived, but it was already being subtly transformed. The emerging problem solutions were changing the technological mix from mechanical to electromechanical processes. The new technology also required a change in material processes. The new metallurgy based on chemical science responded with a variety of new alloys of steel. Aluminum and other new metals with a greater variety of performance characteristics emerged. Copper became a tonnage metal. Agricultural and industrial inorganic chemicals became major activities. Petroleum refining developed.

The largely subterranean information-processing revolution continued to build. Increasingly the compelling problems had to do with the management of complexity. Advances in management technology were made. Professional business schools emerged. Technological advances came about in typewriters and other business machines. The whole developmental problem-solving process (type-five) began to take on organizational and institutional forms. Professional schools of engineering and agriculture were set up. Agricultural, industrial, and academic research laboratories came into existence. Educational activities grew rapidly. The functions of government expanded. All of this still seemed to escape attention for it was conceived to be auxiliary to the "real" business of society—the moving and shaping of physical materials.

The developmental profile generated by all of these activities was correspondingly altered. The prominent growth sectors were the manufacture of motor vehicles, tractors, public utility equipment, and other electrical machinery. The necessity to build up the infrastructure of the cities made a rapid-growth sector of construction. In materials, the manufacture of copper, steel alloys, petroleum products, and agricultural and industrial chemicals became prominent. In mining it was copper, petroleum, and the inorganic, nonmetallic minerals that benefited most. The growing need for information processing was reflected in the rapid growth of finance, professional, and governmental services. From an occupational perspective, it was the white collar and service worker categories that registered the most rapid gains.

In the Study Period

All of this brings us to developments during the study period. The recorded patterns of change can now be visualized in the proper developmental context. As in every epoch, the developmental process is an extension into the current period of the historical dynamic of the system. The successes and failures of previous problem-solving efforts set a modified agenda of problems and opportunities for this latest epoch.

Take the domain of access problems. The nineteenth century laid down the arterial framework of a national transport and communication system. The twentieth century brought an altered emphasis on the articulation of the networks between the arterials. At the beginning of the century it was the local access problem that was most pronounced. The motor vehicle, telephone, and urban utilities were the developmental responses. By the study period, these solutions had succeeded well enough that the obtrusive access problem began to shift back to the level of the national system. An increasingly complex transaction network had been forced into a set of national transport channels still largely linear and arterial in form. The articulation of the national system then became the dominant concern. Paramount among the developmental responses were the long-distance trailer truck, the national highway system, and a nationwide motor vehicle service infrastructure.

There was a major reorientation of the functional character of the access problem as well. Transactions were increasingly mediated by the transfer of information. Prior to the study period, most communications were still carried by a physical-material substrate that piggy-backed on basic transportation. The telegraph tried to reach beyond this, but it was restricted in its information-carrying capacity. The telephone tried to reach beyond this, but it was technologically and economically effective only in local service. The radio tried to reach beyond this, but it had all of the limitations inherent in a broadcast technology. Furthermore, the nature of the communications required by the burgeoning managerial and developmental processes more often required information to travel in people-packages. People transport became more important relative to commodity transport. Air transport and an economical, direct-dial, long-lines telephone system were the major developmental solutions. The expanded use of the automobile was also heavily dedicated to the movement of information in people-packages in the broadest sense. The broadcast of entertainment and educational information by radio and television came to fruition in the period.

Although less broadly systemic in their effects, a number of changes in the production side of the economy presented new access problems for solution. For example, the change in the mix of commodity movements from material to liquid fuels presented new transport problems leading to the pipeline and tanker. The increasing necessity to transport perishable foods to support the newly urbanized and concentrated populations encouraged the development of canning and frozen food technologies.

Next take the domain of production problems. For centuries the dominating problems of society had mostly to do with making its arm longer and stronger and moving its commodities further and faster. Virtually all of the responsive technology involved harnessing energy through the development of mechanical processes. But as the machine technology progressed, it required new forms of energy conversion involving higher temperatures and stresses. Increasingly, industrial processes involved processing fluids and gases as well as solid materials. These changes often required smaller ranges of mechanical motion and tolerance, and frequently encountered corrosive environments. These problems had no traditional mechanical solution. They involved material problems requiring chemical process solutions; they involved fractional applications of power requiring electromechanical process solutions; they involved measurement, timing, and control problems requiring electronic solutions. The management of increasingly scarce renewable resources required biological process solutions. As populations became more densely concentrated, matters of health and survival became more pressing, thus placing additional emphasis on biological processes. In short, the study epoch witnessed the emergence of production and transfer processes strikingly different in character from those characteristic of earlier times. The implications for urban-system structure were enormous.

These access and production problems were illustrative of the five generic kinds of problems. This was the period when the new power developments of the late fourth and the fifth epochs were being scaled down to smaller applications, pushed out to new uses, and carried back to old uses. First the scale-down. Several domains of human work had long resisted the application of power-driven mechanics. These were the small-scale, intermittent, individualized work routines of the home, garden, farm, and craft shop. The fractional power electric motor and public utility power breached this barrier, and the study period became the epoch of the appliance and small power tool. The small gasoline engine and the tractor power take-off extended this process beyond the reach of the power line into the garden, farm, and, in the case of the chain saw, into the forest. The thrust toward novel usage was differently manifested. Prior to the gasoline engine there was no power source with a sufficient concentration of energy-to-weight to realize the dream of flying. There was also a carry-back. Traditional mechanical processes, previously served by steam power, adopted the new power sources. The diesel electric locomotive and the electrification of most manufacturing activities were fifth-epoch initiatives that continued strongly into the study period.

The study period became the epoch of new metals, new alloys of old metals, new construction materials (like cement), new chemical materials (synthetic fibers and plastics, new inorganic materials like the rare metals and inert gases, new drugs, and the like), and even newly introduced biological materials like the soybean, sugar beet, and square tomato. In addition to being the epoch of the appliance, the study period became the epoch of the new material.

Although still little noted, the study period became, *above all else,* the epoch in which the information society arrived. This was a response to a major phase-shift in the kinds of problems commanding the attention of society. The production and transfer processes at work had become more complex in terms of the number and variety of (1) the activity sequences constituting most processes, (2) the inputs requiring transformation and transfer, and (3) the outputs passed on to the larger system. Each behavioral unit was enmeshed in a much more extended and highly articulated network involving a much larger set of transactions. All of this posed a mushrooming set of coordination and control problems requiring managerial information-processing solutions.

Increased complexity gave new prominence to other problems as well. Greater complexity was not restricted to the internal operating fields of enterprises and households. As entities, they became more interdependent and coadaptive in a mutually shared external field.

A higher order set of ecosystemic problems began to assume new prominence. There were social problems and attempted solutions (like poverty and welfare), there were total system stability problems and attempted solutions (like depressions and monetary and fiscal policy), and there emerged new common requirements that could not be mediated by the market (like urban-system utilities, defense, nuclear energy, space exploration, and so forth). As the obtrusive problems were, thus, pushed to higher levels of system organization, the information processes we know as government began to grow.

Increasing complexity altered the nature of developmental as well as managerial processes. First, it became increasingly rare to begin to solve problems at the level of simple process components where the individual inventor and entrepreneur could once function effectively. Problems more often emerged in clusters, or systems of problems, that required joint attention. Second, increasingly these problems had to do with information processes rather than physical processes. Third, the scientific, engineering, and managerial knowledge base adequate to deal with these new problem sets became vastly more complex. Thus, the developmental processes themselves placed new demands on education and research, and both required organizational innovations. The management of developmental processes turned out to be more complex than the management of performance processes. We are still struggling with the information-processing problems this phase-shift has visited upon us.

Finally, the century and a half of developments has generated a phase-shift in human aims and purposes that define our problem agendas and shape their solutions. The new technologies have done more than substitute machines for human energy in traditional physical processes. They have done more than increase the proportion of information-processing work. The new technology has freed humankind from all work to a degree undreamed of a short time ago. It has augmented the material standard of living to the point that developments increasingly have less to do with the quantities of goods than with their qualities. More important, with physical wants more easily satisfied, people are turning increasingly to the consumption of information and to the information processes that entails. Recreation, cultural, and educational activities begin to replace the *things* that once dominated people's desires. Even in work, people increasingly look for qualities of experience that serve deeper needs than placing food on the table. These satisfactions are not only sought in work but in work-play, in crafts and hobbies. These changing values are confronting the managerial and developmental processes of society with a new set of problems for solution.

The Change Profile of the Study Period

These emerging developments are in the process of radically altering the activities to which people direct their energies. This was reflected in the developmental profile laid out in table 37 and chapter 14 in volume I.

There were major activity groupings that displayed especially rapid increases in employment. The most important by long odds was a set of information-processing and communication activities. These included information transfer processes (air transport, telephone, postal services, radio, and television), civilian government at all levels, and business and professional activities. These sectors accounted for fifteen of the eighteen fastest growing employment categories. The second most important group included those activities engaged in manufacturing information-processing equipment (aircraft, electronic and mechanical control systems, office equipment, and photographic and scientific equipment). Third, this was the epoch of the home work-and-entertainment appliance. Fourth, the increased transaction interdependence of enterprises and households channeled a growing portion of the system's energies into maintaining trading linkages. Wholesale trade employment increased dramatically. This was especially true of the activities that engaged in title and financial transactions, as opposed to the handling of goods. In retail trade, general merchandise stores were a rapidly gaining sector. They performed the function of nodalizing a variety of transactions, thus simplifying the transport channels through which an increasingly complex set of transactions was required to flow. Motor vehicle and appliance sales stores were also in the rapid-growth category. The increasing need to move food supplies in interregional channels made a rapid-growth category of the production of cans. Fifth, the new materials were prominent gainers (plastics, the new metals, steel alloys, cement, paper, and drugs).

It is extraordinary. Apart from the belated extension of machine technology to the work of the household, barn, and craft shop, the developmental signature of the study period was totally dominated by the new information-processing activities and the changes in physical processes required to support them. After 300 years as an agrarian society, the United States became an industrial society in 1907. The public consciousness filled with this perception. But, only fifty years later in 1957 the total employment engaged in information-processing activities quietly passed all industrial employment. The information-processing society arrived, but no one noticed. It took twenty years for the perception to begin to sink in, and the emerging implications for urban-system reorganization are still attended to by only a handful of seers.

There is a flip-side of all of this as well. If one examines the activities that experienced employment declines during the period, six additional groupings emerge. First, most of the major resource sectors were involved, led by agriculture and coal mining. The sectors manufacturing traditional materials came second (leather, lumber, textiles, structural clay products, blast furnace steel). The activities engaged in the transport of traditional tonnage commodities (railroads and water transport) were third. Next were the industries manufacturing traditional products (like textiles). Domestic employment came fifth. Finally, there were a few retail sectors tied to the distribution of declining commodities or to trends in retail trade reorganization (independent dairy stores, fuel and ice dealers, and the like).

It is important to mention these trailing activities because they call attention to an important aspect of the developmental process. As new activities emerge in response to new problems, it is natural that they would expand relative to those activities performing the ongoing work of the period. But the relative and absolute declines of many of these traditional employment activities are often directly related to the developmental process as well. The solutions to new problems often visit upon the old sectors new problems to solve. For example, faced with the substitution of oil for coal, the coal industry implemented an extensive series of labor-saving technological advances in an effort to preserve as much of its market as possible. The radical decline in agricultural employment was not just a consequence of losing position relative to a rapidly growing layer of new activities. It was a consequence of the active growth in agricultural productivity under the impact of scientific agriculture. We need to be reminded that the new problems and opportunities that emerge in each epoch involve not only the creation of new things to do and new things to do them with, but also ways of doing old things better. So the developmental profile is often signified as much by changes in established activities that make a declining relative claim on human employment as by those attracting new attention.

These sectoral shifts in employment were reflected in a geographical redistribution of employment. It was the core counties of the urban regions (specializing in the information-processing, manufacturing, trade, and transport activities) that experienced dramatic gains in employment. It was the hinterland counties (specializing in the resource and material commodity activities) that experienced the great losses in employment. Accordingly, 370 counties (out of 3,065) accounted for all of the mix-effect employment gains (table 28 in volume I). These were most heavily concentrated in the largest urban cores, mostly of metropolitan order (tables 22 and 34 in volume I). Two-thirds of these were in the old industrial Northeast. In short, changes in the sectoral growth profile generated by the problem-solving developments of the period tended to reinforce already existing geographical patterns of industrial concentration.

The Effect on Urban-System Networks

This discussion would have brought us to the end of a relatively simple tale, except for the fact that most developmental factors had the simultaneous effect of redefining the "topo-logic" of the relational linkages between the components of the system (individuals, households, and enterprises). These changes in network structure had the effect of altering the loci in space of these components and their activities. Typically they had quite different geographical consequences from the mix effects just described. The developmental factors changed network characteristics in two ways. (1) They altered the network structure of the channels (transport and communication) through which inter-entity transactions must flow. (2) They altered the specific input-to-output linkages forming the flows through these channels.

Changes in Transfer Channels and Transaction Networks

Up through the nineteenth century the nation was largely absorbed with putting in place the railway and waterway system that opened up the continent. By the twentieth century, dominant access concerns turned to the connective articulation of transfer channels. By the study period this developmental response was taking firm hold. The network configuration changed in ways that had no historical precedent.[6] This yielded a phenomenal increase in network density reflecting (a) an increase in the total length of the transfer channels serving a given area, (b) an increase in the number of route segments, (c) an increase in route flexibility (through the addition of cross-arterial channels) and (d) the extensions of the fields served by highly connected urban networks. This increase in connective articulation took place at every network scale: at the microscale of the town or city, at the middle scale of the transaction fields forming an established urban region, and at the macroscale of the broad region or nation system.

Within the context of this study, there is no practical way to represent the resulting increase in system connectivity. However, an idea of the impact can be suggested by roughly dimensionalizing the enlargement of the geographical fields affected. At microscale, the Soil Conservation Service has estimated that the amount of rural land converted to the uses of town and city amounted to 27,000 square miles (17 million acres). At middle scale, the primary commuting fields of the core cities were extended 270,000 square miles, more than enough to contain all of Japan and the United Kingdom put together. We learned from map II-4 that, at macroscale, the portion of the United States accessible to a population of 25 million people within an 8-hour road trip was, in 1950, restricted to two small enclaves along the Middle Atlantic Coast and in the Chicago–St. Louis–Cleveland–Detroit area of the Midwest. By 1970 that field had expanded to cover the entire eastern half of the United States (east of Dallas, Kansas City, and Des Moines). Furthermore, this was the period when air travel and the long-lines telephone networks became a highly articulated, economical way of transferring information. Broad regional changes in population access by highway tripled in twenty years. It is likely that the connectivity of the total urban system increased by at least an order of magnitude. There is little doubt that this was unprecedented in historical experience up to that time and remains unmatched elsewhere in the world.

This kind of change in the connectivity of the transfer channels induced extraordinary changes in network options available to each transaction. The greater freedom of choice took two forms. There were important changes in the transfer channel options. Every transactor could more easily form links with others by employing direct, point-to-point transfers, or at least transfers mediated through fewer intermediate transfer points. A greater variety of transport and communication service modes also became available. The frequency, reliability, speed, and flexibility of the services they offered improved substantially. All of these factors measurably reduced the time and space costs transactions had to bear. Second, there were important changes in nodal options. It is characteristic of an articulating network that an increasing number of channels enlarges the number of intersections that become potential production sites. Between-transfer commodity, energy, and information transformations can be located at a wider array of sites.

It follows that changes in the network structure of transfer channels became translated into changes in the flow-network of the transactions that they carried. But changes in the flow patterns require a different characterization. Several points are worthy of mention.

1. The urban system experienced a reduction in the levels of hierarchy required to organize system transactions. The classical "switchboard" function of the urban center became more evenly distributed throughout the system. This attends the fact that direct point-to-point transfers are more often feasible, and the fact that lower order nodes tend to mediate transfers.[7] Urban cores tend to mediate a smaller share of total transactions. Each enterprise and household tends to be oriented not to a single (metaphorical) "downtown," but to a whole array of downtowns differently situated.

2. Urban transaction systems have become much more open. The percentage of transactions internalized by any bounded transaction field tended to decline relative to cross-boundary transactions originating or terminating in that field. Stated differently, transaction fields which, in 1940, had tended to exhibit a high proportion of exchanges that formed circuit networks within the bounded field tended to experience a substantial increase in the proportion that formed tree networks with nodes external to the field (recall chapter 2 in volume 1). Associated with this is the hypothesis (unverified here) that sets of transactions show a tendency to close into broader subnational network circuits larger than the towns, cities, or urban regions employed in this study.

3. The transaction network became more of a continuous-flow network. Pipelines and power lines came to form a much larger part of the whole transfer system. Even traditional transfer modes began to take on continuous-flow characteristics. Greater transfer options (especially the increased span of communication and control) substantially decreased the amount of time-and-space buffering required of conventional commodity inventories. The entire urbanized network moved closer to operating on a real-time basis over much wider fields of interaction.

4. These changes in network structure facilitated changes in enterprise and household linkages. The extended fields of access and spans of organizational control encouraged enterprises to split along functional lines. Thus, a performance subsystem (such as production, sales, management) could find its most advantageous locus (among a vastly expanded set of nodal options) in the urban-system field. Households became oriented to a wider array of income sources (multiple jobs and nonwork sources of income). Household inputs became less susceptible to agglomeration and closure in single, localized nodes.

Several summary generalizations might be suggested. First, the alteration in network patterns provided new options in pursuing lower input–output costs. Sometimes this resulted from splitting enterprise functions (as suggested in point 4 above). This appears to have been a major factor in facilitating the shift of manufacturing activities into the South. The phenomenon was also clearly at work in the regional decentralization of the automobile industry. Sometimes this resulted in the fact that channel network changes affected an enterprise's access to one or more input sources or output destinations more than others. As a broad generalization, for example, it seems clear that the ease of access to information has increased relative to access to materials. Indeed, this was also a factor contributing to the split in enterprise functions just noted. Again, in general (although there were specific exceptions) the advent of the truck tended to improve enterprise access to markets more than to material inputs.

Changes in Input–Output Linkages

Changes in the structure of transaction-flow networks were not exclusively a result of changes in the network of available transfer channels. Changes in production technologies also played a role by reformulating the input–output linkages that connect all processes. Both sources of network change had a hand in shifting population and activities, and in altering the competitive advantages of different geographical regions.

With respect to input–output linkages only the crudest kind of generalization might be suggested. The problem-solving technologies of the twentieth century have clearly had the effect of increasing the roundaboutness of the production system. Production activities intermediate to resource roots and final demand increased in proportion. Input–output linkages were formed more often with other intermediate processes, in turn increasing the degree of locational freedom from both resource roots and final markets. This appears to have been another factor in the observed reorientation of manufacturing activities.

Beyond this general observation, linkage changes were characteristically identified with specific technological developments. To summarize the detailed discussion of part two, some organizing procedure is necessary. Changes in input–output patterns can be grouped according to the linkage changes experienced. The thirteen categories offered below are not mutually exclusive sets. The same structural change can often be viewed from more than one of these perspectives. However, the device seems to serve its summarizing purpose.

1. Advances in production technologies had the effect of substantially redefining the resource base of the urban system. In this way, the resource tentacles of the transaction network were drawn into new regions and localities. The most dramatic and powerful instance of this was the development of oil as an energy source. The new resource sites stretched the system network to the South-

west and disconnected the Appalachian coal region from many of its traditional markets. The new metals also created broad new resource roots where they did not exist before. Bauxite mining in the Ozarks; uranium mining in Wyoming; and berylium, magnesium, titanium, and zirconium mining in the Southeast are examples. Developments in scientific agriculture made potash deposits in Arizona and phosphate rock in Florida new sites of concentrated mining activity. They also made of menhaden a new fisheries resource, thus augmenting fishing employment along the South Atlantic Coast. Developments in irrigation and drainage technology brought lands into the agricultural resource base, most notably in the Mountains, the High Plains, the Mississippi Delta, and Florida. In the coal industry, the development of surface mining technology brought about a relative shift to western strip mines from Appalachian deep-seam mines. The heavy power requirements of the new aluminum reduction technology limited the sites of this new process to economical hydropower sites, or to regions with cheap natural gas or coal. The development of the sulfate process for making paper brought the resinous southern pines into the nation's resource base.

2. Quite apart from this redefinition of the resource base, the accelerating use of nonrenewable resources and the changing technologies of resource exploration encouraged the development of new sites and the depletion of old. This further altered the geographical distribution of the urban system's resource roots. For example, the costs of recovery in the early Texas-Oklahoma oil fields increased relative to the new Gulf Coast and Mountain fields. New sulfur and salt domes were discovered around the rim of the Gulf of Mexico. New shrimp beds were discovered in the Gulf area. The early Great Lakes copper deposits became exhausted; new ones opened up in the Southern Mountains. Timber mining set a wave-form exploitation-cycle pulsing from one forest region to another, and from one segment of each region to another. Each phase altered the distribution of logging, lumbering, and pulping activities.

3. Intermediate, materials-processing activities were frequently relocated in response to shifting resource roots. For example, the regional shifts of meat animal production in agriculture were an important factor in meat-packing shifts. The shift in cotton production and the development of the soybean brought about a reorientation in the production of food oils. The development of the sugar beet in the High Plains brought a shift in sugar refining. The shifts in fruit and vegetable agriculture reoriented the food-processing industry.

4. Modified production processes frequently altered the scale of production establishments, the structure of their input–output linkages, or both. Consequently, traditional activities became differently connected within the transaction network. For example, in steel production, the progressive reduction of the coal content of the charge, along with the increasing importance of scrap, encouraged a shift of the industry out of its initial Appalachian base closer to Midwestern and Atlantic Coast markets. The subsequent development of the minimill permitted the shift of construction steel production into regional markets outside the Manufacturing Belt. The cigarette-making machine increased the scale of tobacco manufacturing so much that it led to the concentration of the industry in North Carolina and Virginia. The cotton picker played a major role in the shift of cotton agriculture out of the Southeast. In the Southwest, the old wellhead-oriented batch refineries were replaced by the integrated, continuous-flow refineries that shifted the industry to transhipment hinge locations on the Gulf of Mexico Coast. New sawmill and plywood technologies increased efficiency and plant scale so much that the old portable saw mills disappeared from the forests. Production shifted to discrete nodes located near the center of larger forest supply fields. Scientific agriculture changed the production function so substantially that specialized monocultures largely replaced general farming. This facilitated the shift of specialized production systems into localized regions with especially favorable climates and soil conditions. The same production-function alterations radically increased the proportion of agricultural inputs coming from off-farm sources. This helped to pull some supply industries closer to the fields of agricultural production. (For example, specialized components of the fertilizer industry can be seen to move with related monocultures.)

5. Not only did developmental processes alter old production relationships, they established new ones. Each one tied a new subset of linkages into the transaction network. For example, at the materials end of the spectrum, it was the new oil refinery technology and the new internal combustion engine that redefined the fossil fuel resource base. This was undoubtedly the most important single modification of urban-system structure during the twentieth century. The development of nuclear weapons and nuclear energy opened up new resource sites and new materials-processing sites. The development of the new organic chemicals created a whole new petrochemical industry, augmenting the network effects of the new petroleum technologies. There was an associated array of new synthetic materials, plastics, and fibers that formed nodal sites intermediate to industrial chemical sources and fabricating establishments. For example, we earlier noted the emergence of synthetic fiber plants in the Southeastern textile region. We also observed how the availability of synthetic materials enabled apparel manufacturers outside the New York region to produce garments formerly not in their price domain. This facili-

tated the shift of the industry. Within agriculture, the citrus fruit, soybean, sugar beet, and broiler chicken were virtually new products. Their production process linkages played a major role in the reorientation of agriculture. The development of aluminum dotted the Gulf Coast area with alumina plants, the lower power cost regions with reduction plants, and the Old Manufacturing Belt with new aluminum fabricators. The development of converted paper products transformed paper from an information-processing substrate into a major industrial and commercial production material. The development of reinforced concrete technology reduced construction's ties to the manufacture of structural clay products, while creating new linkages to the producers of steel and cement. The development of a whole array of food products and processes intermediate to the farm and household reformulated the food production and distribution network of the nation.

At the fabricating end of the spectrum, the new household work appliances added a new and dynamic component to the machinery manufacturing activities of the western end of the Manufacturing Belt. The new electronics industries in all manifestations—home electronics, information processing, communications, and so forth—gave a new cast to manufacturing. Because these activities had no sunk capital at traditional sites, and because they tended to require lower capital costs for physical plant, they could entertain more location options than established fabricators. They tended to spring up disproportionately in Upper New England, the South, and West outside of the Old Manufacturing Belt.

6. Prior to the study period, there was a climate-control technology for cold environments but not for hot. Air conditioning changed this drastically. It diminished or removed many of the disadvantages of the South as a living and working environment. One can hardly imagine today's Houston without air conditioning. This reinforced the effect of other factors acting to stretch the transaction network away from its old Northeastern pegs.

7. Significant changes took place in the labor resource base (analogous to that considered in 3 above). Scientific agriculture displaced 6 million workers out of agriculture. The substitution of oil for coal displaced 400,000 workers out of coal mining. The truck and other factors displaced 400,000 out of railroading. The household appliance and other factors displaced a million out of domestic employment. The chain saw, truck, and logging machinery displaced many more from the nation's forests. These labor supply adjustments were equal to a fifth of the total 1940 employment. More important, they were overwhelmingly concentrated in the Southeast. These workers offered a potential labor force and market for old and new manufacturing processes. They were also concentrated in the area where the automobile and truck had most dramatically augmented network accessibility. These two factors are the main reasons why the South "rose again."

8. Many intermediate processing activities were drawn into new regions, or network fields, as a consequence of shifts in intermediate markets for their products. For example, the increase in the proportion of steel going into agricultural machinery helped draw primary metal production toward the western end of the Manufacturing Belt. The increased portion going into construction steel gave rise to the minimill at distributed production sites. The production of materials-processing machinery experienced radical shifts in response to the relocation of important markets. Thus, the manufacture of textile, paper, and wood products machinery migrated to the South (mostly out of New England) in pursuit of process markets. The development of major new fields of agricultural production in Florida and on the West Coast drew substantial new concentrations of agricultural machinery production to these regions. Partly because the markets for the shipbuilding industry shifted from passenger and freight services to the shipment of oil, the industry shifted from the North Atlantic seaboard toward Gulf Coast sites.

9. The transaction network changes attending the above naturally altered the structure of those trading activities that mediate transactions. Merchant wholesaling became a progressively smaller part of the wholesaling function, while the new commodity brokers and manufacturers' representatives grew apace. The portion of wholesaling activity engaged in information processing increased substantially relative to the physical transfer of goods. Both factors tended to move wholesaling to higher levels in the trade-center hierarchy. The retail trades selling automobiles, trucks, motor vehicle services, office machinery, and business supplies increasingly mediated enterprise-to-enterprise transactions, with the result that higher order trade centers substantially increased their shares of trading activities.

10. Not only did all of this developmental activity restructure the nation's transaction networks, it modified the system's links with external trading nations. Increased imports of oil tended to augment refinery operations at Philadelphia, along the Gulf Coast (versus the Southwestern Interior), and at Northern Tier sites next to Canada. Increased imports of steel shut off the expansion of steel capacity along the Middle Atlantic Coast. Increased imports of machinery dampened the considerable expansion of machinery production in the Old Manufacturing Belt. The growing export of agricultural products revitalized the old port of New Orleans and shifted the locations of grain-producing monocultures. The increase in the export of coal partially offset the loss of coal markets to petroleum and stimulated the development of

the port of Norfolk. Increasing trade links with the Pacific region were an important factor in the leading gains of Seattle, Portland, San Francisco, and Los Angeles. They replicated the earlier Middle Atlantic European Hinge with respect to the growing Pacific world.

11. The proportion of final demand taking the form of public goods increased dramatically. The armed forces became the fastest growing employment sector. We saw how this had a dramatic effect on selected urban regions—particularly in the South and along the nation's coasts. The development of water resources and the nation's highways was largely in government hands. Government entrepreneurship and investment were essential to the development of the new aerospace and atomic energy processes. All of this had major network consequences suggested in the text.

Less easily identified, but significant nonetheless, was the effect of the regulatory and rule-making activities of government. We saw how the "hemisphere preference" provision exaggerated the production advantage of the Northern Tier oil refiners. We saw how the grain acreage programs had the effect of exaggerating the expansion of hay and forage crops in the Plains regions. The legal structure of water rights in the West radically favored agricultural water uses relative to other industrial and urban uses, perhaps exaggerating the gains in agricultural production in the area. It seems clear that the subsidization and encouragement of private home ownership vastly accelerated the suburbanization process. It also changed the structure of localized urban networks.

12. Changes during the study period were especially marked by this fact: at no other time in human history had such dramatic changes in the economic, social, and cultural situation of individuals and households taken place. The productivity gains attending the flood of nineteenth and twentieth century developments dramatically increased both real incomes and the amount of time free from income-generating work. This not only took the form of a shorter work day and work week, it showed up in earlier retirements. Women entered the work force in large numbers, further increasing real income gains. The kinds of occupations that engaged workers were increasingly information-processing activities. Within the physical-processing occupations, intermediate industrial activities expanded relative to agriculture and other resource activities.

These changes substantially altered the nature of the linkages households formed with the enterprises that supplied them as well as the linkages they formed with the enterprises they supplied with labor. They helped change the structure of urbanized transaction networks. There were two major changes in the transaction flows connecting households to their support systems.

First, there was a major change in the distribution of household expenditures between consumption and capital formation. As long as workers were occupied with the physical processes of enterprises, it was the enterprise that supplied the physical capital supporting the processes. As work increasingly began to involve information processes, the necessary support capital more often took the form of human knowledge and skills. Because this form of capital is a private good exempt from proprietary claims, its development became a common goal requiring the joint participation of households and public initiative. An increasing portion of social activity was devoted to education. Local, regional, and national linkage patterns were altered accordingly. In the localized context, urban and suburban neighborhood sites and networks became increasingly influenced by the need to have access to household education inputs. In part two, we also observed how the localization of colleges and universities generated leading competitive gains.

Beyond education as capital formation, the household had the incomes and the incentives of working wives to make household work more productive through the adoption of home work appliances. A whole new industry and attendant linkages emerged. Home ownership became a real option for the mass of the public during this epoch, and its locus became conditioned by the desire (arising from higher incomes) for a single detached home with a yard. This further changed the face of the localized urban network. People also wished to convert the increased freedom of time and choice into greater freedom of place. This required personal transport. So the household took on the capital requirements of transport in the purchase of an automobile and the payment of road taxes.

These capital investments provided consumption activities with greater flexibility in the use of time and space with the result that the consumption of information exploded. This took the form of education as a form of consumption; of spectator entertainment in the sports and the arts; of participatory entertainment in the sports, arts, and crafts; and of other experiential activities such as vacation travel. And, as the epoch wore on, the capital expenditures of the household increasingly came to take the form of household entertainment appliances, rather than household work tools and appliances.

These changes fed back upon the linkages between households and enterprises in many ways. Although a part of the burgeoning food products industry involved the shifting of some tasks off the farm as general agriculture was phased out, most of it represented a shift of food preparation out of the household. This was especially noticeable in the dramatic growth of the eating and drinking trades. By means of traveling vacations, households became linked with distant services and trades. Because of earlier retirement and other factors, the number of households that could locate free of primary work considerations grew substantially. Whole regions like Florida and Arizona became the locus of households whose consumption patterns were geared to a particular phase of the life cycle. The nonwork activities of working households became much more important in determining their location and the structure of their external linkages. The distribution of the household-serving trades and services was drastically altered as well.

13. Because of the growing locational independence of households, the orientation of many manufacturing, trade, and service activities was drawn into new patterns of settlement and linkage. Out of this interactive symbiosis came the supermarket and the regional shopping center—retail trade's primary contribution to developments during the study period. Favored vacation and retirement sites generated multiplier effects just the reverse of those that classical economic-base theory posits.

In the light of the expectations of traditional economic theory, perhaps the most dramatic development was the way in which some production activities began to choose locations based on worker preferences rather than upon the conventional cost calculus of input assembly and output distributions. In one sense this is what happened when the displaced agricultural and mining workers formed a labor surplus that attracted manufacturing to the South. But the location calculus of those traditional industries was not undertaken to accommodate the situation preferences of the poor southern worker. More dramatically, a different set of location factors began to emerge suggesting a change in the way some enterprises orient their activities. During the study period, the developmental process was itself becoming organized and institutionalized in the science-based industries. These enterprises began to consider their product to be innovation. Their critical input became the services of the scientific, engineering, and managerial professionals. Owners and managers were, themselves, typically professionals. Product offerings frequently changed in response to inventive and innovative initiatives, thus altering within relatively short time spans the nature of the physical inputs and outputs (and their attendant linkages). Further, these physical throughputs were not typically in the tonnage class. The traditional locational calculus became much less important. Siting the production establishment came to be dominated by the situational preferences of the entrepreneurial and creative workers, particularly their need to exchange information. The emergence of Silicon Valley is a classical instance of this new calculus at work. Many others could be cited.

Before closing out this typological summary, final notice should be taken of the interactive and feedback nature of these changes. As we attempted to summarize the study-period changes in the urban-system network, we first discussed the developments that altered the transport and communication options channeling the transaction flows of a working society. Then we identified production-process developments that changed the nature of input and output requirements and, hence, urbanized transaction patterns. It should be clear that these different change processes are interactive and symbiotic.

For example, changes in transfer options may alter input–output relationships and production site choices, even when production technology remains little changed. For example, the production technology of the traditional industries (like textiles and apparel) did not change nearly as much as the newer fabricating industries. Yet the change in the access characteristics of the interregional transaction network opened up the possibility of dramatic shifts of these activities into the South. Conversely, changes in production technology are often sufficient to alter transaction flows even when transfer options remain largely unchanged. For example, the bulk-commodity transport system that assembled the inputs and distributed the outputs of the steel industry did not change substantially during the first half of the twentieth century. Still, a substantial reorientation of the steel industry took place in response to changes in production technology that redefined input–output linkages.

There were other kinds of feedback effects as well. The developing substitution of oil for coal altered the network flows of fossil fuels so dramatically that adaptive transfer channel developments (as opposed to transaction flow developments) were required. New pipeline and tankship technologies and transfer channels were created. Conversely, solving the problems of long distance human transport through the application of airplane technology placed strains on existing production technologies and materials, setting in motion technological developments of a different kind.

However, these typological conventions have been necessary to summarize the sources of change behind the transforming urban transaction system. They intend to convey an image of the way the topography of the network was altered, and how, at the same time, the production-node pegs upon which that network was hung were themselves reordered. They intend to convey some notion of how the problem-solving developments of the epoch powered this transformation. If your image of this process has been formed or sharpened thereby, the use of the typological handle will have been justified, in spite of its inescapable artificiality.[8]

Changes Reflected in Employment Shift Patterns

The summary discussion of this chapter has been tied back to empirical shift patterns at many points. We have observed how the industry-sector growth rates generated by the developmental process introduced mix effects favoring the higher order trade centers and Old Manufacturing Belt. The contrasting differential changes in competitive positions experienced were seen to be more directly the consequence of developmentally induced changes in the structure of the transfer channels and input–output linkages.

The results can be seen in the shifts recorded. It can be seen at the microscale of the urban center in the geographical extensions of population and employment. It can be seen at the middle scale of the urban region in the spread of the transaction fields linked with the urban core. It can be seen at macroscale where the high-density network of intermediate-process transactions linking urban regions (especially their urban cores) was extended to include the entire eastern half of the nation. It can be seen in the employment effects of the extension of these intermediate linkages that integrated the West Coast more tightly with the national economy. It can be seen in the effects of the network extension into international markets.

The effect of network articulation can be seen in the reordered trade-center hierarchy. Except for the dramatic gains in air transport and business services experienced by large metropolitan centers, employment shifts in the linkage and information-processing services tended to favor the medium-sized metropolitan and wholesale-retail centers spread throughout the nation. In contrast, manufacturing activities, which had traditionally found their best locations in the large urban cores of the Manufacturing Belt, spilled out of the traditional sites into lower order trade centers (especially those of complete shopping order) and into the hinterland fields of the urban system (especially the primary commuting and marketing fields). The functional retrogression and progression of specific centers tended to reduce the numbers of convenience centers and increase the numbers of complete shopping and wholesale-retail centers. The lowest order trade centers tended to become more widely spread and the middle-order centers became more closely spaced.

Functional reordering can also be seen in the record. One might expect that those parts of the urban field which were either best or most poorly served by the old networks would be the parts most susceptible to functional reorganization by increasing network articulation. Table II-11 suggests that this might have been the case. The largest urban cores, which had been best connected at the beginning of the period, and the fields outside urban-core dominance, which had been most poorly connected, experienced the largest all-sector average deviations in competitive employment shifts. Another consequence of network articulation appears to be the 33 percent decline in the weighted index of regional specialization (when computed at the middle scale of the urban region—table 12 in volume I) (similarly, for the weighted index of industrial concentration in table 23 in volume I).

Apart from these changes induced by improvements in transfer channel accessibility were developmental changes in production process linkages. These were selectively discussed in the last section. In volume I, the combined effects can be read from plate 7 (highlighted by map 24) and map 19. The areas most favored by these developments were those activity fields in (1) the Michigan to Kentucky midfield of the Old Manufacturing Belt, (2) the western extension of the Old Manufacturing Belt to Minneapolis, (3) the Upper South, (4) Florida, (5) Dallas, San Antonio, and the Gulf Coast, (6) the High Plains of Texas and Oklahoma, (7) the Central and Southern Mountains, and (8) the Pacific Coast. The areas least favored by the study period developments were: (1) New England, (2) the Middle Atlantic region, (3) the Appalachians, (4) the Lower South, (5) the Plains (North and South), and (6) the Northern Mountain regions. With the background formed by this summary chapter, and part two of this volume, the reader should be able to return to the empirical record of volume I and part one of this volume with a vastly enriched explanatory base.

Finally, these developmental factors can be seen at work in the empirical record of the sequences of change experienced by regions (chapter 12 in volume I) and activity sectors (chapter 5 in this volume). The shift pattern sequences observed seem consistent with only one interpretation: the regional and sectoral subfields of the urbanized transaction system are engaged in a dynamic process in which comparative advantages are sequentially gained and lost. An ebb and flow of fortunes takes place as the problem-solving adjustments of these subfields become, first, fully implemented and, then, subsequently subjected to the feedback effects of adjustments of other coadaptive regions and sectors—as different regions and sectors (differently situated in the total transaction field) experience different limits on their developmental potential, and as different sectors and regions are at one time in different phases of an adaptive scenario. We discover that no generalization about sequences or phases can be made to apply consistently to different region-by-sector entities, or consistently to similar region-sectors at different times. The only conceptual system that seems appropriate for theorizing about this process is the evolutionary concept. It is timely for our empirical studies to lead us to this point, because this view of the process has a profound bearing on how we may productively view the future.

Notes

1. Save for the effect of entropy in a closed system limited to passive adaptive responses. This is not the way human social systems work.

2. Though not about developmental sequences, as has been shown earlier (chapters 4 and 12 in volume I and chapter 5 in volume II).

3. Process design is also interpreted to include the adequacy of the product designs of the artifact inputs and components of the process. In this context, it is well to note that all products (except for material commodities like food, fuel, and the like) can be seen to be frozen process subroutines (like the hammer that wants to treat everything as if it were a nail).

4. A part of the solution to the scarce-labor problem was the substitution of slavery for free labor—a drastic mistake that inhibited constructive development in a major section of the nation for generations to come.

5. The relative scarcity and high cost of labor were driving forces that operated in two ways: They (1) stimulated labor-saving technology and (2), in turn, increased productivity translated into higher incomes and increasing demand.

6. I am now speaking of changes in topological structure, or to changes in the graph of the network abstracted from geographical referents.

7. Filani demonstrated this with regard to the evolution of the air transport network. Also, before the advent of electromechanical switching and direct dialing, the telephone network was organized in a rigid hierarchy of telephone operators. The new technology flattened the order of that hierarchy.

8. We do not yet possess an adequate language for describing and analyzing complex systems in any other way. We are still tied to the language of partials.

14

What of the Future?

It takes a future-oriented, problem-solving species to generate the record of change we have examined together. What does all of this imply for the future of the U.S. urban system? Our best guide to an answer is the evolutionary perspective underlying the entire effort. Like all of those that preceded it, the developmental epoch following the study period will experience a reorientation of its urbanized transaction networks fashioned by a set of developmental responses to the emerging problems of the time. It becomes feasible to inquire about emergent possibilities because both the problems and the technologies of an historical period cast a shadow ahead of themselves. It is an exercise that, pursued with care, would easily require a third volume. Be that as it may, a few suggestive speculations about the emerging period grow naturally out of the study thus far.

A Phase-Shift in Problems and Technologies

By 1970 the evidence was beginning to suggest that the future isn't what it used to be. The experience of the 1970s leaves little doubt that a phase-shift is underway. The emerging epoch shows promise of becoming a major transition period. The last such period began early in the nineteenth century when the transition from an agrarian to an industrial economy began. The following century was engaged in working out the implications of industrial technology for urban structures. The close of the twentieth century is facing another major transition period—in this case a transition from an industrial economy to an information society. The effect on urban structure may turn out to be as profound as that generated by the industrial revolution, although it seems unlikely that it will take another century for its realization.

This is not to say that structural changes in the industrial economy will not continue to be important. Indeed, another kind of phase shift appears to be taking place—from nation-scale industrial systems to an international-scale system. Even at nation scale, there are inertial consequences of earlier changes that will continue to appear. But there seems little doubt that an extraordinary change in social function and structure is in the offing.

Harken back to the five types of problems guiding our discourse. We can identify a phase shift taking place at every level. *Take the case of the type-one problems, having to do with process designs.* The material and energy processes that dominated the industrial epochs are losing ground in importance to information processes. Even within the realm of physical work, the mechanical processes that resolved the early problems of the industrial age are giving way to electrical, chemical, and biological processes of a different character.

Up to now, problem solving has been absorbed with improving the productivity of those processes that satisfy material needs. Each advance in physical processes permitted the worker to externalize both physical and information processes. At the stage of tool-and-craft technologies, the worker still embodied both the how-to-do-it information of the process and the energy supply for its activation. By subdividing activities, machines were created that embodied an informed component of a process (for example, the hand loom or spinning wheel) although the worker continued to be the prime mover. The industrial age improved productivity further by multiplying the tasks that could be embodied in a machine and by mechanizing the power source as well. The worker's role was reduced to that of machine tender or an assembler of machine products. From the point of view of the production worker this was a vast simplification. Only a narrow range of tasks was addressed by each because much of the human process-knowledge and skill was hardened into the design of the machine. The amount of human information processing required at each work station was dramatically reduced.

Paradoxically, this had the effect of vastly increasing the need for information processes. The segmentation of production processes created a new set of problems because the various segments needed to be linked in time and space. Business systems emerged linking work stations with conveyances. Urbanized transaction systems arose linking businesses with transportation and communication systems. But for a coherent pattern to emerge, all of the flows required coordination. Information processes were displaced upward from the individual physical work station. The plant foreman ceased to be a master craftsman and became a business school graduate. The urbanized transfers came to depend on a host of transaction specialists more absorbed with information processes than with physical transfers. The new industrial technologies placed great strain on information technologies in two ways. They shortened the time span and extended the space span of real-time control.[1] But information-processing requirements were not boosted by the need to maintain coherent production systems alone. They were expanded by the creative requirements of designing, producing, and installing the new industrial technology. They were further expanded by changing human wants. People began to look beyond physical satisfactions to the psychosocial rewards of exercising their human creative potential. But the sciences, arts, crafts, sports, and religions occupying them in this quest are all predominantly information-processing exercises.

During the study period, productivity gains were primarily constrained by limited information-processing technologies. It was not just design requirements that had grown beyond available techniques. Further advances in physical technologies were increasingly hampered by the fact that process designs were conceivable that were still beyond the technology of real-time control.

So we are poised at the moment in history when problem solving has come to focus on information processes. The technological response is just emerging, and with a startling rapidity. As recently as 1960 (two-thirds of the way through the study period), the still embryonic computer technology had barely progressed beyond electromechanical switching and was still hung up on vacuumn tube switching. While such computers were six times as economical in performing basic mathematical functions as a person, the solid-state devices of 1970 were already more than 3 million times as economical. Today (1980) there are 800,000 computers in the world, half in this country alone. They can do the information-processing work of 5 trillion people. That is the work capacity of a labor force equal to 1,000 times the number of people in the whole world! And the technology of robotics is even beginning to take over the assembly and control functions of the worker at the physical work station.

Now *take the case of the type-two problems, having to do with the applications of energy to work.* Here, too, potentially major changes may be underway. The industrial technologies moved the production system from animal-based energy to renewable fuel sources and, thence, to the realm of nonrenewable fossil fuels. But the recent petroleum-based energy system is the one most susceptible to disruption through resource exhaustion and politically motivated market intervention.

This circumstance has set in motion a furious scramble for problem solutions. There is no shortage of coal reserves for the foreseeable future, but expanded use presents environmental problems. Older fuel sources are being given a new technological content (solar, wind, geothermal, and biomass sources), and exotic new sources are being pursued (hydrogen fuels and nuclear fusion). Such developments could change the urban system's resource base and transaction network structure.

Consider the case of type-three problems, having to do with the adequacy of materials. Up to the present, the developmental process has been absorbed with supplying the engineering materials that embody industrial technologies. The resolution of such problems through the application of tonnage-scale metals, plastics, rubbers, and glasses was prominent in the narrative of this volume. However, in the study period the emerging information, aerospace, and medical technologies were finding the common engineering materials inadequate. As a consequence, a phase-shift is underway in the kinds of problems that the material technologies must help resolve. Aerospace requirements force light-weight materials to work under conditions of stress, heat, and corrosion where they are not intrinsically well suited to perform. The new information-processing technologies give prominence to electrochemical properties not known to exist in materials a short time ago.

Problem-solving responses are moving the material technologies into a new phase. The industrial age witnessed a shift from craft materials and processes to a wider range of materials and processes based on modern chemistry. The new information and space society is fostering a shift of material processes to the level of molecular, atomic, and nuclear processes in both living and nonliving materials. Alloying is becoming a more precise science and is developing new techniques like doping and ion implantation. Such methods widen the properties that can be combined in the same material. Even plastic materials are being alloyed successfully. Amorphous (that is, glassy or noncrystaline) materials offer special mechanical and electrical properties. The discovery of the transition metals (with two free electrons) have opened up the prospect of forming bimetal compounds not seen in nature and exhibiting extraordinary properties. Fiberglass components herald a growing array of component materials with special properties. The potter's art is opening up a whole new range of high-technology processes with super ceramics. Genetic engineering is totally new to the emerging epoch. It is likely to change the way we grow our forests and agricultural crops. Specially designed bacterial enzymes may change the way we control chemical reactions, increase the recovery of materials from low-grade ores, help control pollution, and produce new materials. Such emerging material technologies will open up process options not yet even envisaged.

Shifts are also underway in the way we supply the traditional tonnage materials. Increasing demands on nonrenewable resources are forcing a shift toward recycling materials and toward lower quality sources (like oil shale and tar sands). A new technology of resource discovery is emerging, based on advances in geology and new information-processing technologies.

Consider the type-four problems, having to do with the managerial controls that maintain the coherence of organized transaction systems. Information processing is obviously a field in which many of the operational problems of the time will be encountered. Two phase-shifts appear to be underway. First, this is a time of great advances in information-processing technology; second, the nature of the managerial task is changing.

With respect to the first, managerial processes are the last great frontier for improvements in productivity. The conversion to the electronic office is well underway. But, paradoxically, information technology is opening the way for another round of productivity gains on the shop floor. This is because the people down there are production workers in name only. The shop foreman has long since become primarily a process and sequence coordinator. The worker has become a machine tender who, although engaged in some physical motions, is also primarily a sequence coordinator. These are information-processing functions susceptible to further displacement by robot machines that tend other machines and assemble components into final products.

Most important, the managerial task is changing in complexity. The functions of management are being pushed beyond the traditional domain of the formal organization. The problem of coordinating a system of establishments interacting in a less formal, less tightly controlled, ecosystemic set of transactions has become obtrusive.[2] This extension of the managerial range is not just directed to improving enterprise performance. It is also forced by the fact that the industrial economy has achieved such a scale that new and undesirable feedbacks are occurring both within the fields of social transactions and between social activities and their physical environments. There is no way that such extended-field control problems can be resolved successfully without the aid of emerging information-processing technologies.

Finally, *consider the type-five problems, having to do with the design of new and revised processes and with their implementation.* These are processes aimed at resolving the first four types of problems when they require developmental solutions. The problems associated with the creative tasks of reprograming a complex society are also going through a phase shift. Once again there are at least two dimensions.

First, problems are no longer the same. Reductionistic modes of problem solving are discovering their limits. In the early part of the industrial age, a mechanical process technology of type one could be designed while taking type-two energy sources and type-three materials as given. Developing a new material (for example, steel rather than carbon iron) involved changes in material process technology largely independent of the mechanical applications to which the material would be put. And so it went. In the present context, design problems increasingly involve multiple problems that must be tackled simultaneously. The design of the mechanical process more frequently involves tailor-making a material with the specific properties required, and this may require, in turn, accommodation to the special power requirements of the whole process. Further, the designer of each stage in a larger production system increasingly needs to know how that stage will integrate with the larger system of relationships. In short, problems increasingly come in packages. The developmental designer is faced with a "*problematique.*"

Second, we are coming to evaluate problems in the context of different values and objectives. This is partly because the urbanized system has reached the scale where undesirable feedbacks from both the physical and social operating environments are occurring. This causes us to shift more of our attention from the production of "goods" to the avoidance of "bads." It is also partly because people's time and income are less absorbed with the problems of human physical support. We are increasingly free to pursue human enjoyment and development for its own sake. These changing values alter our perceptions of problems and our technological responses.

All of this suggests that the most persistent and perplexing questions of this emerging transitional epoch, and beyond, will be: How do we develop problem-solving technologies of such sophistication? How do we institutionalize them in a society whose dominant managerial, organizational, and political forms were developed to regulate routine performance processes in a simpler industrial age?

The Potential Effect on Urban-System Networks

We have been impressed with the way the industrial technologies progressively altered the structure of transaction networks. Changes in the emerging problems and technologies can have no less an impact on future urban-system structures. Furthermore, these new technologies will embody a different topo-logic from the old. We proceed by examining the shadow cast on the future by emerging problems and technologies. Following the procedure already established, we will consider potential changes in transaction networks wrought (1) by changes in transfer channel networks and (2) by changes in input–output linkages.

Potential Changes in Transfer Channel Networks

During the study period we observed that developments had vastly increased the connective articulation of the nation's transfer channels, as well as the spatial extension of the high-density net. This was seen to occur at every scale (city, urban region, nation). Associated with this was a substantial decrease in the degree of transaction closure characteristic of almost all conceptually bounded regions. The problem-solving developments of the coming period seem destined to carry this structural rearrangement still further. This is inevitable for three reasons. (1) The transaction network effects of communication channels are different from those of physical transfers. (2) The emerging technology promises to make them even more different. (3) The relative increase in the share of all transactions taking the form of information transfers promises to give this difference increasing importance.

Consider, first, the difference. Modern communications technology eats up time and distance unlike any physical transport technology. For area code-800 and Watts-line calls, distance costs have been effectively leveled. For the balance, spatially differentiated costs are so negligible that many sending and receiving site choices are not at all influenced by transfer costs. This stands traditional Weberian location theory on its head.[3] However, by the end of the study period the network implications of this characteristic of communication nets had been little felt and less understood. This was largely because the telephone had been effective in serving the needs of a relatively limited class of information transactions. Most of those that entailed the transfer of information in people packages (characteristically requiring signal capacities beyond telephone technology) remained unaffected by this potentially qualitative difference in network structures, as did those requiring intermediate operators engaged in processing the information between transfers (characteristically imposing a process discontinuity).

Consider, next, the growing significance of the difference between communication and transport technologies. Already existing and easily anticipated technologies assure that communication channels will soon exist of sufficient capacity to remove most of the limitations of current telephone technology. Thus, future developments promise to amplify the special characteristics of information networks. The nature of this technology is too complex to cover here, but there are three aspects of increasing significance for urban-system structure.

First, the signal capacity of communication channels is currently increasing geometrically. It will continue to do so for the foreseeable future. These work-horse capabilities are being rapidly carried into every corner of the nation. Coaxial cables, fiber optics, and satellite communications will all be playing a role, and their potential is barely scratched. Such technologies open up efficient, low-cost paths for visual and spoken communications as well as large-volume alphanumeric data transmission. The capacity of these channels, and their flexibility in use, is vastly expanded by means of their interface with computers. Computer technology provides for digital switching. This opens the way for software control technologies to optimize communications system management. It expands carrying capacity through the use of "packet switching" techniques. Typewriter keyboards, print devices, television screens, speech recognizers and synthesizers, and print readers will join the telephone in providing an interface with human operators. This means there will be an unlimited range of new applications including two-way, or interactive communications over the full range of channel requirements.

Second, in the domain of information processes, the new technology will wipe out the meaning of a technological distinction as hoary as history. Physical production processes have generally been different in character from those that move goods in space. Historically, this has given a critical importance to break-shipment points. Throughout organized social history, urban transaction networks have always been arranged to minimize the number of exchanges across the production–transport interface.

Once information transfers assumed electronic form, the potential existed for reducing this kind of technological determinism. Electronic technology mechanizes not only the movement of information from one place to another, but a wide range of the information transformation processes as well. Note this key point. In information processing, the transfer (communication) and transformation (production-like computation and word-processing) technologies turn out to involve identical processes. Both cases involve the movement of electronic signals in paths and the switching of these signals from one channel to another. The only difference is the sequence in which the switching operations are performed. The different operational functions are no longer distinguishable by their technological form. Computing requires communications, and communications are governed by computers. Specialists in the field now use the term "compunications."

The network implications are profound. In the realm of information processes there is no longer any *compelling technological reason* for the interface between production and transport to have the same operative significance. Indeed, except for those points where human operators intervene in the process, it is often impossible to tell where one function ends and another commences. Combine this with the decline in space and time costs and the location of information-processing activities acquires a degree of locational freedom never enjoyed (and indeed never to be enjoyed) by physical processes.

Such changes will become reflected in the structure of urban transactions. Consider some of the developments likely to occur. The electronic office (that embraces computers, word processors, electronic files, electronic printing, and electronic mail) is rapidly becoming a reality. This in turn opens the way for a widespread substitution of communications for transportation—particularly where it has been traditional to transport information in people packages and in books and printed documents. Segments of enterprises can be distributed around the nation or the world and still operate as a coherent entity *when it matters*. At local scale, satellite work centers hold the potential for a substantial reduction in commuting and labor turnover. It is only an additional step to install home work stations with the result that something like the old cottage industry system could return to vogue. Information utilities are emerging that will eventually include everything from travel schedules to the full collection of the Library of Congress. People will soon no longer need to travel to document sources or have physical documents transported to them to the same degree. The home entertainment center will change the pattern of household recreation trips. It is only a question of time before the educational function moves increasingly into the home, particularly at the adult level. Home banking and television shopping are technologically feasible. All of these activities will become increasingly less constrained by time and space costs and by the old logic of nodal agglomeration. It promises a continuing articulation and expansion of the urban transaction network at every scale—and that expansion includes the extensive interpenetration of international space.

This may be only a beginning. Present technology suggests the potential for even more radical changes in spatial orientation. Satellite communication practice currently employs two technologies. One uses the satellite to extend the narrow-band channels of the traditional ground-based net. The second uses it as a relay for broadcast transmissions. The technology exists for marrying the two by building antenna farms in space that incorporate modern switching technology. This could open up the possibility of dedicated channel communications with transient and portable ground stations. Wrist-band telephones and directed communications to any spot on earth thus become possible *without hardwiring ground channels* or dedicating narrow-band space channels. One only has to examine the explosive use of citizens band radio in recent years to imagine the great impact such a development might have.

If you have not been in a position to follow these developments closely, this may sound like "pie in the sky."[4] However, much of this has already begun. The Atlantic Richfield Company is creating a multimillion dollar, satellite-based telecommunication system for two-way video conferencing. Up to six managers can face their counterparts in other cities on widescreen color television. The system also provides for electronic mail, facsimile transmission of documents, and computer-to-computer data transfers.

Twenty percent savings on current travel costs are expected immediately, with further gains on the way. Several insurance companies already have teleconference meetings of regional managers daily. In the mid-1970s, a Los Angeles insurance company already operated two satellite offices, each about 25 miles from the central office and each employing fifty or more people. These were linked to the main office by "compunication." Significant cost savings and a reduction of labor turnover were achieved. Other banks and insurance companies have followed suit. Control Data Corporation, Walgreens, McDonalds, the Mountain States Telephone Company, and several banks and insurance companies are putting terminals in the homes of secretaries and clerical employees. It is opening a whole new field of employment for the handicapped and for the homemaker and mother. One computer software firm (F. International Ltd. in Britain) employs 600 people with a home office that contains a computer and little else. Almost all the program writers and system designers work at home, and 95 percent are women. Public information utilities like *The Source* and *Videotex* already offer home-terminal information services (like current stock market reports, *The New York Times* and *The Washington Post* news services, theater and airline reservations and tickets, encyclopedia reference services, among others). Proprietary electronic mail services are already widespread, and public service is, at this writing, only months away. Catalogue marketing is already the most rapidly growing sector in retail trade even before the new technology has been brought fully to bear in this market.

Do not misunderstand what I am suggesting. There is a great deal of inertia in the system. Existing urban infrastructure will not become obsolete overnight. But on the time scale of the development epoch, substantial structural changes should become apparent by the end of the century. Over two such epochs, say by 2025, changes in network structure could rival those that accompanied the railroad in the nineteenth century and the motor vehicle in the twentieth.[5]

In examining these potential changes, the implications of information-processing developments have so far occupied our full attention. This is because the other transfer technologies are now relatively mature; they cannot be expected to breed changes in access on the same scale. In two conventional transport systems, an actual retrenchment in channel capacities is underway, but only in the face of new developments that continue to expand and redefine the net. The decline in the railway net is well known. The effects on transaction network options have, however, been more than offset by the motor vehicle.

Current observers are talking most of a retrenchment of scheduled air carrier service. Airline deregulation is part of the cause. More important, schedule reductions have been underway for some time under the impact of competition from general aviation. By 1977, the U.S. business fleet (more than 50,000 planes) was already flying several times as many hours as all domestic airlines combined. A large "underground" air transport system has emerged that carried more than 50 million passengers (again in 1977) (*Business Week,* 1978). This general aviation development more than offsets the retrenchment in scheduled air service in the articulation of the nation's transaction network. Consider the meaning of this phenomenon. For a major segment of air travel (having to do with the transport of business information in people packages) these developments have added more time and space flexibility in travel scheduling. The airplane is increasingly used, like the automobile before it, to provide custom transportation. This freedom from dedicated channels and shared time schedules adds considerably to the articulation and range of the air transport net.

Another significant development is the rapid growth in air freight. The president of Flying Tiger Air Lines expects that air freight will grow by a multiple of 200 by the year 2000 (*Business Week,* 1974). The industry is rapidly moving to specialized planes, containerized freight, and intermodal service. This is generating a substantial extension and articulation of channel options for freight shippers. They are responding by using air freight to reduce time and inventory costs. Sears Roebuck uses air freight to supply local markets from a central clothing warehouse. Extended transport options also expand production options. One television set manufacturer builds chassis in the United States, airfreights them to Taipai for final assembly, and then air freights them back to the United States for distribution. The Ford Motor Company used air freight to ship Pinto engines to U.S. assembly lines from Ford's British factories.

Other developments may emerge whose future shadow is not yet as distinct. For example, a breakthrough on solar photovoltaic devices might make on-site power generation possible, a development that would free power use from the umbilical of the dedicated power line.

The closing judgment of this section holds that none of the emerging transport channel options seems to hold anywhere near the potential for altering the structure of the urban transaction network as that implicit in the emerging information-processing technologies.

Potential Changes in Input–Output Linkages

Future changes in the pattern of activities and settlements will not be the sole consequence of changes in transfer technologies and channels, of course. As before, transaction networks will also be influenced by the way all change factors alter the input–output (I–O) linkages between transaction nodes. The previous chapter considered the changes in I–O linkages that generated changes in urban structure during the study period. We proceed with an illustrative list of similar changes that carry the seed of possible future developments.

1. *Consider some of the ways developmental processes may be redefining the resource base.* The major developments here may come in the energy field. The resubstitution of coal for oil in conventional usages, and the successful development of synthetic liquid fuels from coal, could reverse the competitive shift away from coal. New technologies for extracting and beneficiating low-grade deposits (such as oil shale and sands and the viscose oil deposits) may shift petroleum mining activities to the Mountain States, to Alberta in Canada and, on the international front, to Venezuela. Within the time frame of the year 2000, potential new technologies in solar, geothermal, and biomass sources do not seem likely to supply more than 10 percent of U.S. energy requirements. Therefore, they are not likely to alter substantially the system's resource base (although the linkages forming localized fields might be altered significantly). However, if one projects into a second generation, say the first third of the twenty-first century, developments in both nuclear fusion and solar energy could conceivably form the basis for a shift away from a nonrenewable resource base. This could bring about major alterations in the nation's and the world's transaction networks.

Outside the energy field, forest and fishing activities are moving away from resource mining to sustained-yield biocultures. These changes do not seem destined to create major shifts soon, but some shifts are possible. Take an extreme example. The Tennessee Valley Authority has successfully developed shrimp beds that thrive in the hot water effluents of their power plants, even in midwinter. Should such a technology prove out at commercial scale, the next round of a similar study might find some very curious shifts in fisheries employment taking place. Over time, American forests will likely become more specialized in the species they grow and in the end-product chains that they serve. This happened earlier in agriculture as mechanization and the practice of scientific agriculture progressed. If current experiments with the cultivation and use of Kenaf (an East Indian hibiscus) as a source of paper pulp work out, we could see the input sources of the paper industry make a more pronounced shift to the South. The chemical industry seems on the threshold of major advances in the production of foods from nonfarm resources (proteins from ocean kelp and krill, the fermentation of petroleum hydrocarbons, growing yeasts on paper wastes, synthesizing foods from fatty acids, and so forth). If and when this new technology should become commercially feasible, traditional transaction linkages in the food sector could be shaken up.

Just as a reminder that curious linkage changes can occur in unexpected ways (remember the case of the menhaden in the study period), consider the fact that the new concern with air pollution, and the attendant technological developments, are causing power plants and smelters to capture the sulfur dioxide emissions from their stacks. Once fully implemented this could generate a by-product yield of 30 million tons of sulfur a year (12 percent of the total 1973 tonnage). The associated linkage structures will certainly be bent in the process, even though not radically restructured.

Here is an especially exotic possibility. The advent of the radial tire has placed a new premium on an old resource, natural rubber. Since all natural rubber is now imported (mostly from Southeast Asia) at a cost of a billion dollars of foreign exchange each year, ample incentive exists to develop a domestic source. Goodyear has opened an experimental farm in Arizona which is planted with a desert shrub called guayule. This plant yields a high grade of natural rubber. If preliminary indications hold true, the end of the century could see hundreds of acres of productive desert land where little else has been grown.

2. *Consider how resource discovery and exhaustion could change future linkage patterns.* Undoubtedly the strongest factor at work here is the gradual exhaustion of the world's petroleum reserves, coupled with the politicization of the oil supplies. This, of course, is the problem context prompting some of the technological probes already noted. Aided by these developments, coal may recapture some of its former prominence. This would mean relative gains for West Virginia, Southern Illinois, and Indiana and for the emerging strip fields in North Dakota, Montana, Wyoming, and Colorado. Because the western coals have a lower sulfur content, as well as a less entrenched labor tradition, relative gains will likely favor the West over the traditional deep-mine fields of Appalachia. In addition, as petroleum mining moves on to more marginal sources in the United States, one can expect a shift in production and employment to the Mountain States along with a resurgence in some of the older fields such as eastern Ohio.

Another important development is the final closing of the western frontier with respect to agricultural land use based on irrigation. Only marginal further gains seem likely (for example, in the High Plains of Nebraska). On most such lands, a relative (and in some cases absolute) decline in agricultural production and employment has already begun and can be expected to grow in importance. In places (the Ogallala aquifer in Texas, Oklahoma, and New Mexico), the reserve has been drawn upon at rates that cannot be sustained. In other regions (the Southwestern Mountains), salt intrusion promises to halt expansion, if not reduce, land use. But apart from the fact that water use cannot continue to grow at the old rates, the increased competition for scarce water from urban and industrial uses promises a decline in agricultural uses in some sections of the West.

Several of these factors may work together to alter other activity patterns, such as crop patterns in agriculture. It is becoming clear that the mining of the Ogallala aquifer in the Southern Plains, combined with the increased energy costs of pumping, is going to force a retrenchment in the meat-animal culture in that area. This may partially regenerate the older patterns of range feeding in the Northern Plains and redirect some food grains to feeding applications in the Old Corn Belt.

In contrast to the growing water shortages in the West, excess drainage in the South Florida Everglades has caused muck fires and biochemical oxidization of the soils. Soil subsidence is proceeding at a rapid rate. Muck soils near Lake Okeechobee, which had been 12 to 14 feet thick in 1921, are down to 4 or 5 feet in depth in 1970 and declining at the rate of a foot every ten years. The abandonment of many Everglades farms by the end of the century seems inevitable (L. Carter, 1974).

One response to the increasing demand on resources has been the practice of recycling materials. This became common in the steel industry early on. The recycling of paper and aluminum began much later and promises to continue to grow. Experimentation is now underway in the recycling of urban garbage for both materials and energy. With 2.5 million tires becoming scrap each year, methods are being developed for burning old rubber to produce energy and carbon black and for hydrogenating rubber to produce oil. Some of the recycling developments will undoubtedly serve to change urban-linkage patterns in the future. In general, their effect will be the same as noted for the production of steel—a further reduction in the relative importance of the nation's resource roots relative to intermediate processes and final markets.

Deep-sea mining is a new technology that is likely to become increasingly important. We have begun to see the changes in linkage patterns that attend off-shore drilling for petroleum. (Much of the mining and petroleum refining activity attributed to the Gulf Coast between New Orleans and Houston is linked to off-shore fields.) As we discover new off-shore reserves and move into the ocean domain for other materials, selected coastal areas will expand production and employment activities essential to give logistic support to off-shore mining. Linked material processes will also be affected.

Resource pressures have emerged so recently as a prominent concern that potential technological responses are just beginning. Some suggest the possibility of a relative shift to both old and novel forms of biomass for energy, food, and materials. It is too early to foresee the dimension or form of such a movement. However, biomass sources are spatially extended relative to the typical nonrenewable resource deposit. This suggests the possibility of a further decrease in highly localized employment concentrations.

This does not mean that new mineral deposit discoveries may not open up mining activities in new fields. For example, commercial-grade uranium ores have recently been identified in the Appalachian Mountain region. If these should come into commercial production, new linkage patterns could emerge.

3. In the study period we observed many *cases of intermediate activities shifting in response to changing resource roots*. This kind of sequential change is bound to reoccur. The classic study-period case, of course, was the shift of organic chemical production and petroleum refining to the new southwestern production fields. There seems little doubt that the Mountain States will experience relative gains in these activities in the next decades. And, if the Atlantic off-shore explorations should open new fields there, one can be sure of a resurgence of East Coast petroleum refining. If the guayule fields in the Southwest should prove commercially feasible, latex extraction plants are on the drawing board. Other developmental linkages of this kind are bound to occur.

4. *Changing production technologies can alter input–output linkages* in untold ways. Some of these will result from the defensive strategies of mature and declining industries. We saw, for example, the mechanization of coal mining that took place under the impact of the competition of oil. As the steel industry moves into a difficult future, it is pressing to adopt many innovations such as continuous casting. The market-scrap-oriented minimills that gained a foothold in the study period will undoubtedly continue to spread. (Industry experts expect they may account for 35 percent of production by the year 2000.) Powder metallurgy is a more novel technology that, for the integrated mills, casts a longer future shadow. It draws upon the injection molding techniques of the plastics industry and holds the promise of eliminating the ingot stage of production along with the rolling mill. Design projections suggest that, once perfected, the technology may produce steel with only one-third of the plant required by conventional methods. The question arises: Where will this redesigned capacity be built? How will its linkages with suppliers and markets emerge? The answers to questions can only be approached through a careful study of the process implications, but we can be sure that such technological responses to the pressures of competition will further alter industrial relationships.

However, the greatest future changes in production activities, and in the transaction linkages they engage, are likely to come with the genuinely novel technological systems. Electronics should take the lead in the near future. A longer time shadow cast by genetic engineering is emerging fuzzily, as is the case for the range of space activities (in science, manufacturing, and communications).

In chapter 13, we gained some sense of the changes in network orientation characteristic of the electronics industry. Such changes seem to be characteristic of the other new science-based technologies as well. Further, as these industries mature, cumulative alterations in network orientation seem to occur. This has been the experience of every industry during its emergent phase. The 1970s have already witnessed the spin-off of manufacturing components from parent firms in Silicon Valley and along Route 128 around Boston. These shifts have involved the establishment of thirty-eight new plants in twenty different communities spread throughout the Mountain States, New England, and the South. As the electronics evolution proceeds, it is likely to split into more differentiated strains. For example, the evolving marriage of electronics and the traditional machine tool industry seems likely to increase the relative strength of these activities in the Old Manufacturing Belt. The continuing alteration of the source and market linkages of these activities will undoubtedly modify the orientation of the urban network.

Further development in the electronics field may well generate some of the greatest changes in urban-system structure during the century's closing decades. Fast coming to perfection are robot machines that can perform the functions of the machine tender and assembly worker. The externalization of human physical production functions is coming toward the end of the trail of possibilities. Having conquered the tasks of externalizing the physical motions and energy contribution of the individual, technology is moving in fast on human information-processing and control functions at the production work station. It raises the prospect of factories containing few of what we now call production workers, attenuating still further the linkages between the household and the workplace.

This raises the prospect of another interesting development. As robot machines and their associated industrial controls improve, the old economic imperative that dictated long production runs begins to erode. Production systems will be able to switch rapidly from one product model to another without the old cost penalties. This opens up the prospect for a substantial increase in made-to-order manufacturing.

5. We have already considered how changing transfer options can change the orientation of all transacting activities. But *production process changes that alter input–output linkages can also alter the orientation of trading and linkage services.* The potential growth of small-batch and made-to-order manufacturing should increase mail-order shopping. The potential for robot technology to substitute the information-processing worker for the production worker will likely increase the chances of substituting communications for transportation. Such developments suggest a relative decline in household commuting and shopping trips and a relative increase in parcel delivery services. This is also a suggestive reminder that, because of the mutual-causal nature of developmental change, each new techno-logic spreads its network consequences far from the initial point of change.

6. *Both the new technologies and the progressive spread of the old technologies to new fields of application will alter the future structure of international trade relationships.* It is clear, for example, that the national urban system will not be exempt from the previously observed decline in the functional closure characteristic of all bounded regions. The proportion of all trade that crosses national boundaries is increasing and an extensive two-way flow of capital and international ownership is underway, particularly between the advanced industrial nations. Increasingly, component supplies for intermediate fabricators come as easily from nondomestic and overseas sources. The extension and articulation of the urban transaction field already reach abroad. This promises to be an expanding trend.

This, in turn, suggests the likelihood of future changes in the locus and linkages of many domestic activities. Quite apart from the dramatic short-term difficulties of the automobile industry, it is the longer term developments that are likely to be most important. Automobile ownership is reaching saturation in the traditional producing nations. Future expansion of demand will come in the Third World. This promises an impressive degree of internationalization of production with the assembly of components from many nations becoming common. It seems likely that the historical regional concentration of the automobile industry in this country will be further altered. The textile industry is already beginning a shake-out in the face of the changes in the international transactions network. The president of a large textile company estimates that one-third of the companies and 6,000 plants will disappear (*Business Week,* 1979). A few large and more efficient companies will markedly expand defensive capital investments. Textile manufacturing will change from a labor-intensive to a capital-intensive business. Similar changes can be expected in the apparel industry. The chemical industry will likely experience significant changes in the face of international competition.

The altered trading patterns and the growing importance of information-processing activities in the international transaction net promise to shift people and activities as well. Examples can already be observed. A dramatic but little-noticed instance has taken place just since the end of the study period. Miami has become the new capital city of Latin America. More than eighty multinational firms operate their Latin American headquarters out of Miami. Ninety percent of the 6 million foreign air passengers served in Miami are destined for or come from a Latin American base. Most of the tourists are Latin American. Eleven major U.S. banks opened Miami branches in the last decade. Cargo shipments to Latin America out of the port of Miami have tripled. Miami is becoming set apart from other southern U.S. cities by the dominance of its Latin culture. Elsewhere New York and San Francisco are expanding international information-processing services.

7. One of the persistent phenomena of the last 100 years has been the way that, in each developmental epoch, large numbers of workers have been displaced from a traditional base of activity. Frequently, as in the case of the displaced agricultural or mining worker in the South, these were sufficiently concentrated so that the surplus labor pool became, itself, a source of attraction for labor-intensive industries. *The emerging epoch seems no more likely to be immune from the experience of labor force displacement.* The forthcoming adjustments in the textile industry just cited are expected to displace 400,000 textile workers (one-third of the 1970 base) in the next decade. The apparel industry seems likely to add to that total. This will probably accentuate once again the labor resources of the South. But here a number of questions arise. To what degree will the pool of labor give a continuing impetus to the shifts of manufacturing to the South? To what degree will higher levels of income and mobility enable these workers to migrate elsewhere? Will there be adequate alternatives? Whatever the balance of such considerations, it seems likely that such developments will have an important effect upon the relative shifts of employment activity in the emergent epoch.

There is a chance that the new technology may generate a new and different kind of labor displacement. It seems quite possible that by 2000, industrial robots will have generated a considerable contraction in the traditional industrial work force. For example, General Electric has already launched an automation program that eventually should eliminate half of its 37,000 assembly workers. Fiat expects to reduce its auto assembly work force by 90 percent by 1990. If these changes are expected within the business planning horizon, what further effects might lie in store by the end of the century? Some automation experts are saying that the new "smart robots" could potentially displace two-thirds to three-fourths of today's factory work force.

This raises additional concerns. The displaced agricultural worker was absorbed by an expanding manufacturing industry. But where will the displaced factory worker go? The logical answer is to some form of information-processing work. But routine information-processing jobs are, themselves, on the threshold of substantial automation. If history is a reliable guide there will be enough new jobs in the activities that produce and maintain this new capital equipment, and in the other information-processing activities, to absorb the displaced labor. Alarmist views about technological unemployment have never been sustained by historical experience beyond the usual short-term displacement effects. But it is possible that the future is not what it used to be. It is just possible that we are approaching the point in a long period of technological externalization of human functions in which the only labor-intensive activities that remain sufficient to absorb human energies will be the pursuit of leisure and human development. If that is the case, future epochs will have to cope with a set of social problems of an entirely different order. However this works out, such developments will undoubtedly introduce a period of substantial structural displacement and localized hardship. It may take a generation for the labor force to adjust to the new set of knowledge and skill requirements.

Whatever the form these social changes take, they are bound to affect urban transaction patterns in important ways. Take a single example. One possible institutional adaptation might take the form of a shorter work week. If this should become widespread practice, it would constitute another factor loosening the location ties of the household and workplace, possibly weakening still further the hold of the old urban cores and metropolitan counties.

8. *Research and development became a growth industry in the study period and is bound to continue.* Scientific, engineering, and managerial information processes engaged in the design and implementation of new technologies are not identified by traditional industrial classifications and are largely overlooked. But such developments are bound to have significant effects on urban structure.

One startling manifestation is taking place in Japan (at this writing, 1981). The Japanese government (The Ministry of International Trade and Industry) is convinced that an agglomeration of research and development expertise will create a better climate for research. To that end it is constructing a "technopolis" where laboratories coexist with houses, shops, and other trappings of urban life. It is Tsutuba City, a new town on the outskirts of Tokyo, where most of the big government laboratories will be situated. It is projected to incorporate 200,000 people. This is a striking demonstration of the potential location effects of growing developmental information-processing activities.

There is nothing directly comparable in this country, although we have seen how research and development activities tend to form clusters. So far the important factors appear to have been (1) access to education and cultural facilities, (2) living amenities, and (3) some critical mass of creative activities that can feed the process with ideas and manpower. Route 128 around Boston and Silicon Valley south of San Francisco are examples. I would guess that, for the balance of the coming epoch, we will see many more agglomerations of developmental activity emerging at places that come to fulfill these seeming requirements. But there is nothing to say that the logic of these developmental information-processing activities might not be substantially altered in the future by changing information utility infrastructures. In any case, the changing structural logic of such developmental activities is bound to have an effect on future urban structures. These activities deserve close attention. However, we cannot monitor them without moving beyond traditional sources of statistical data.

One could go on in this fashion, but there is little point. Be clear that this exercise is not offered as a forecast. It is not even a systematic attempt to examine the future shadows of emerging problems and solutions. It is a speculative exercise designed to illustrate the ways that developmental activities may further alter future urban transactions networks. It reflects the conviction, born of this study, that the explanation for the changes that become manifest in the next period will be found in such factors. It intends to suggest that, if one wishes to anticipate the future of urban-system structures, this is the kind of exercise that should prove most enlightening. All of this lies beyond the scope of the popular quantitative projection techniques.

Ebb and Flow

Thus far the discussion has not accounted for the dynamic fluctuations in employment and settlement patterns set in motion by developmental innovations. We earlier documented the ebb-and-flow nature of urban-system change. When the techno-logic of the transaction system is altered, the new structures implied by new methods are pursued along a time path with the consequence that the settlement and activity patterns in any subfield of the network can be seen to experience an accreting flow (or ebb) of activities if they are favored (or disfavored) by developments.

There are several characteristics of this process. First, the two phenomena (ebb and flow) frequently occur together because one activity's fortune is often another's misfortune.

Second, once set in motion, flow tends to breed flow and ebb tends to breed ebb for a time. There are several reasons. Any change tends to create disjunctures between components of the system that set in motion linked scalar effects (for example, more employees require more schools and homes). Problems and solutions often form technological clusters so that one innovation creates system disjunctures leading to additional developments (for example, the development of the harvester led to a threshing bottleneck, the thresher led to a planting bottleneck, and so forth). Thus, subsequent developments often reinforce the transforming thrust of an earlier technology.

Third, over the period of time essential to work out the change, the adaptive thrust first accelerates, then decelerates, then spends itself, as the techno-logic that drives it is fulfilled. When the thrust is spent, it may just merge into a steady-state process, but it is not uncommon at this stage for flow to turn to ebb, or vice versa. This may be because adaptive momentum carries the adjustment beyond the technologically implied steady state (for example, the overexploitation of a resource base as in the case of the mining of a forest or a groundwater aquifer, or the swing of relative prices back in favor of coal). It may happen because the next round of problems generates solutions which sometimes countermand the effects of earlier changes (for example, the automobile countermanded the core-city logic of the railroad).

Fourth, the time span necessary to work out a given development can vary substantially depending on how fundamental the technological changes turn out to be. The larger the proportion of the total transaction network affected, and the more extensive the indirect effects that have to be worked out through linked systems, the longer the time period involved.

An awareness that these adaptive time paths are coursing through history seems essential if we are to cast an intelligent eye on the future. It should not be impossible to identify some fields of activity where flow or ebb are likely to be sustained for some time and other fields where a switch from ebb to flow (or vice versa) may be imminent. The problem is that traditional theory and method do not lead us to look at the record in this way.

The ebb-and-flow phenomenon is shown in the differential experiences of the subfields of the urban system. How they are perceived, therefore, depends on which classificational structure organizes our attention. Ebb and flow can be recognized (1) in activity sectors (for example, such as defined by the Standard Industrial Classification System), (2) in the localized transaction systems we recognize as towns or cities (for example, such as defined by our trade center classification), and (3) in different geographical regions, however bounded in concept.

Consider the activity sector perspective, but, first, back up a bit. In the early nineteenth century, agricultural activity still dominated. (Trades and crafts accounted for only 10 to 20 percent of total employment.) The paramount problems were scarce and expensive agricultural labor, low labor productivity, and the problems of linking agricultural land with agricultural markets. The technological response was to mechanize agriculture and develop the railway. Farm production increased more rapidly than farm employment and population. New off-farm opportunities in trade, transport, and manufacturing resulted. Relative agricultural employment ebbed while manufacturing and linkage activities flowed. This was such a fundamental change that the agricultural and manufacturing technologies successively uncovered new problems within the same set requiring additional technological solutions. The whole process fed itself for a century. It had several collateral effects. (1) It turned coal and iron mining into flow activities. (2) It moved the nation's activity and population base off the farm into the town and city. This prompted a new set of access problems leading to the motor vehicle, telegraph, and telephone, along with their associated manufacturing and transfer services. This augmented the flow of linkage activities. (3) The increased complexity of social activity created information-processing problems. A clerical army fed the flow stream and a creative search for information technologies began. By the late 1930s, the streams of linkage and information-processing activities had become so strong that manufacturing employment began to join agriculture as an ebbing sector (in relative terms).

The interesting thing is that the techno-logic of older, industrial-age developments achieved its fullest realization during the study period. Agricultural productivity advanced to the point that agricultural employment went into a phase of dramatic absolute decline. Coal, the energy base of the early industrial technology, also went into absolute decline under the competitive impact of petroleum. Manufacturing employment turned into relative decline as linkage and information-processing activities flowed strongly.

These broad sectoral movements appear to be approaching major trend-line phase-shifts. By 1970, the absolute decline in agricultural employment had largely run its course. There is a reasonable expectation that ebb will turn to flow at least for a time. (This likelihood is reinforced by the growing importance of agricultural exports, the growing relative demand for more labor-intensive fruit and vegetable cultures, and the sharply increasing costs of the energy base of current agricultural technology.) Similarly, the adaptive adjustment in coal mining employment largely ran its course during the study period. In the meantime, the increased cost of petroleum is creating a reverse substitution movement likely to turn coal mining from ebb to flow. In forest-based activities, the ebbing adjustments to the chain saw and timber truck technologies are complete. Meanwhile, the new silvicultural processes are beginning an expansion in forest management, and new wood-product technologies are restoring the importance of wood in the nation's material supply base.

While the resource activities appear to be ending an ebb phase and showing some promise of resurgence, manufacturing as a whole appears to be entering a crucial phase of absolute decline. Indeed, in 1970, the last year of the study period, total manufacturing employment declined for the first time. The flow of transport-related employment is also showing signs of weakness. The railroads have been in absolute decline for some time, as noted. Commercial air transport employment, such a vigorous flow performer during the study period, shows signs of share loss. There is at least the possibility that the emerging information technologies, by encouraging the substitution of communication for transportation, may turn this activity from flow to ebb in absolute dimension. This retrenchment in transport had not yet reached a turning point in the study period, but could conceivably do so sometime during the last third of the century.

Now consider the perspective of the urbanized cluster identified as a town or city. Here we conceptualize functional and geographical entities that tend to internalize clusters of activities. The town or city functions as a transaction switching center for household activities, for localized business-serving transactions, and for cross-boundary transactions with other sectors in other regions. This nodal switching function prompts many intermediate process activities to choose urban centers as production sites. Towns may also emerge to serve the transaction requirements of a localized resource activity. The activity mix of an urbanized region defines its position in the transaction net and its dynamic path of growth and development. The ebb-and-flow attributes of that path become translated into the ebbing and flowing fortunes of towns and cities.

The early towns in the Transmontaine West largely performed in entrepreneurial, speculative function. They also performed a quasi-military function in opening a sometimes hostile continental land mass. As these functions were fulfilled, and as developments emphasized an emerging two-way entrepôt function with a commercializing agriculture, most of the early towns began to ebb. Many disappeared altogether. This has been a recurring fate of limited-function towns throughout American history. Indeed, the "ghost town" is celebrated in our literature. Those early towns that were well positioned with respect to the topo-logic and techno-logic of an emerging commercial agriculture became larger centers. Some stabilized for a time as the lower order centers of an emerging urban hierarchy. Others advanced to higher levels of transaction organization.

This hierarchical order of urbanized centers was shaken up once more by the developments of the industrial age. There were two important aspects. First, the railroad radically altered the nodal topology of the nation's transport system. Many centers on the old riverine system went into relative if not absolute decline. Towns that gained a railroad prospered, and towns that became the terminus for more than one railroad boomed, as did those that served as forwarding agents linking the rail and water systems. Second, the new intermediate industries took people and activities out of rural areas and lodged them in towns and cities. Because enterprise economies of scale were often great, relatively few centers were favored. Both developments initiated an era of city building. As many earlier towns and cities went into decline, others experienced phenomenal expansion.

We saw this breed great congestion and access problems at a local level. Responding technologies (the motor vehicle, telephone, public utility power, and the like) ameliorated these problems at the local level and permitted the nineteenth century city system to expand into the early twentieth century. But the technology also sowed the seeds for a further redefinition of the national transaction network. We saw that process at work during the study period. The new technology generated a radical articulation and extension of the transfer channels and transaction networks that carry the nation's business. We saw this strengthen the position of the intermediate-sized cities relative to the large cities, the wholesale-retail centers relative to metropolitan centers, complete shopping centers relative to convenience order trade centers, and so forth. We saw cities pass on their former site advantages in manufacturing to smaller, lower order towns.

Thus, in every epoch emerging developments have altered the way activity sectors come together to form the nodal clusters we recognize as cities and towns. In the process, some centers flow while others ebb, with relative declines often progressing to absolute declines (and vice versa). The study by Hodge made clear that smaller trade centers were by no means immune from extinction as late as the study period. However, the internal connective structures of most cities have now become so complex that they do not die easily. Major activity sectors may decline, or even cease to exist. Some urban switching functions may wither or relocate. Initially linked activities may suffer, exaggerating the decline. However, even in the face of major changes, there commonly remains a cushion of activities. The city still provides access to an infrastructure of transfer channels and transaction services. It serves to organize local transactions and to provide potential linkages with outside activities. In time, the loss of obsolete functions opens up new "docking sites" for other activities. These may emerge out of newer technologies, or out of indirect adaptive responses to other changes.[6]

So, if we wish to look at the future of the urban system, we can be sure that emerging developments are redefining that order, as they have in every epoch. Ebb and flow will come to visit different centers differently situated. But how, in the remainder of the century? Again, a few observations are offered merely to suggest a line of approach that could extend further.

Many of the developments already examined suggest that some study-period changes in urban structure may be reinforced in the closing years of the century. It seems likely that the larger, higher order cities will continue to decline *relative* to other centers. This will likely be true not only when compared with the smaller cities, but also with respect to the lower order trade centers located in hinterland regions. Several things suggest this. (1) Manufacturing employment is beginning a phase of absolute decline, and the bulk of manufacturing is still located in the largest metropolitan areas. (2) The mix of manufacturing activities is shifting away from the traditional metal industries to electrical industries. The former are most heavily concentrated in the old cities and rely heavily on tonnage-capacity transport routes. It appears the latter can operate in smaller centers with little penalty. (One can transport $5 million worth of electronic components in the back of a truck.) This tendency will not be uniformly experienced in every region. Textile and apparel manufacturing, for example, have already spread heavily into smaller centers. Their prospective employment declines will adversely affect smaller centers that exhibit heavy specializations in these activities. (3) We appear to be approaching a resurgence of employment in the resource sectors (agriculture, coal, and forest-based activities). These tend to gain access to the urban network through the intermediation of smaller centers. (4) The new technology is in the process of articulating a low-cost, high-capacity "compunications" network. This seems likely to loosen the grip of the larger centers upon many information-processing activities.

The beginning of these adjustments is already discernible in the study-period record with respect to the large northeastern centers. Although cities like Atlanta, Houston, Dallas, and Los Angeles did not yet appear to share this experience, it does not seem likely that they will escape for the remainder of the century. The newspapers of such cities are already reporting signs that core-city problems are spreading to larger cities everywhere.

There is one development that may tend to countervail this restructuring tendency—the rapidly rising cost of the transport energy base. My guess is that this development may dampen and slow down the tendencies indicated. However, it is not likely to alter the long-run thrust of urban-system reorganization.

Over a time period sufficient for new information technologies to mature, new energy technologies to emerge, and a more complete cultural adaptation take place, we will undoubtedly see more pronounced structural changes emerging. We can yet see them only dimly. The big uncertainty is the role that the cities will play in the twenty-first century information society. This is a speculative exercise that needs to be engaged, but too much to undertake here.

Finally, *consider the perspective of the geographical region*. The delineation of geographical regions is, of course, simply another way of identifying a cluster of activities deemed to be meaningfully associated. As in the case of the urban center, that mix of activities defines the region's functional nature and its dynamic path of growth and development. Thus, regions ebb and flow according to the resultant of the dynamic transformations of their constituent activities and urban centers.

Consider the implications of emerging developments at this scale. Again, the two most important factors, and ones likely to be sustained through the remainder of the century, will be the relative and absolute decline in manufacturing and the burgeoning communications and information-processing activities. As manufacturing employment turns negative overall, the absolute declines will first be concentrated in traditional industries such as food, textiles, and apparel, along with the basic primary and fabricated metals and industrial chemicals. These are also the sectors where automation and foreign competition are likely to have their earliest effect. They are quite unequally distributed between geographical regions so the resulting differential changes will have a lot to say about regional ebbs and flows. The Old Manufacturing Belt, containing the largest concentration of these activities, will continue to suffer relative declines that will turn absolute in localized settings. The Piedmont's heavy concentration in textiles and apparel render it vulnerable to a relative decline in manufacturing employment (again with the prospect of localized absolute losses) and probably a slowing of employment growth overall. The residual South and West are likely to experience countervailing relative gains in manufacturing. However, the manufacturing component of their growth and developmental experience is becoming a progressively smaller part of the total.

Anticipating the strongest relative gains in the information-processing activities (and, to a lesser degree, some linkage activities), we would expect the gains to favor most those regions that were specialists in those activities at the end of the study period. This should favor the major information-processing centers of the Old Northeast, particularly strong headquarter centers like New York and Chicago. We already witnessed strong countervailing gains in such places during the study period. Great faith is being placed in these activities as a means of ameliorating the problems of the older cities. This may ultimately be the case. However, in the current epoch, it does not seem likely to me that these activities will be sufficient to stem the ebb tide experienced by the older, larger centers, particularly those of metropolitan order.

Apart from these salient, ongoing shifts, we should experience some significant ebb-to-flow reversals in several geographical regions based primarily on developments in the resource sectors. First, the agricultural adjustment now seems complete. Some *relative* increase in employment share is likely. This means that the overall employment losses experienced in the Plains during every one of the study-period decades should be reversed. Second, the reversal of the substitution relationship between petroleum and coal in the nation's energy base may bring about a reversal of the employment decline in the Appalachian coal country. The development of the western petroleum deposits along with the western coalfields promises to expand mining activities in the Northern Plains and Central Mountain Regions. These developments, combined with the regional decentralization of all urban-servicing activities, are likely to disguise a reversal of the earlier agricultural gains brought to the Mountain West by irrigation. Third, resource sector, time-path fluctuations may reverse shift patterns in other regions. For example, there are strong signs that New England is entering a phase of its forest exploitation cycle that presages a relative expansion in forest-related activities. Nevertheless, it would be my guess that already-ascertainable, resource-based ebbs and flows will not be sustained over as long a time span as the fundamental developments in manufacturing and information processing. Multi-epoch shifts in resource activities should only become clear after we know more about which of the newer energy technologies prove successful.

The Sunbelt–Versus–Frostbelt Imagery

These prospects imply a continuing reinforcement of the broad regional shift patterns that have been dramatized by the Sunbelt-versus-Frostbelt image. While it is true that a broad reorientation of activity is taking place, I believe that we are ill served by this characterization of experience. It is so aggregated regionally and sectorally as to be misleading in some respects. Its confrontation imagery formulates the problem in a way that provokes a political adversary approach to the solution of problems. It reifys and personalizes the historical situation in a way that obscures observation, understanding, and rational public policy formulation. There are several broad reasons I suggest this view.

First, it fosters the mistaken impression that this experience is something new. In fact, the relative gains of the West and South have been persistently characteristic of almost every development period since colonial times. The access technology of the nineteenth century opened up the West for resource-based activities. When the agricultural land frontier closed at the end of the century the activity frontier remained open for those nonresource-based activities well served by the linear transfer channels and low-capacity communications of the time. What is new about the current situation is the fact that the new linkage, information, and manufacturing technologies are again expanding the western and southern frontier for most nonresource activities. Furthermore, employment declines have turned absolute for localized urban centers in the Old Northeast, thus dramatizing the trend. This, too, has its historical precedents, but not within the memory of the present generation.

Second, when confronted with the undeniable reality of these shift patterns, it is easy to exaggerate the scale of the change. On a 171-urban-region basis, the total interregional differential shifts in employment are running at about 4 percent of initial-period employment over the course of a decade. We should not forget that the shift pattern is taken from this 4 percent shift margin. Except for quite localized core counties of large urban centers, every part of the Old Industrial Northeast continued to expand total employment during the study period. While the relative losses of the Frostbelt may increase in proportion in the coming period, absolute employment declines will likely remain a localized phenomenon in the context of the total region.

Third, this Sunbelt–Frostbelt image hides quite significant differences in the experiences of activity sectors and regions. For example, the study revealed that smaller urban regions between major Frostbelt centers (for example, between Detroit and Chicago, Chicago and Minneapolis, Chicago and St. Louis) experienced significant relative gains. Is it also worth recalling (from table II-12) that the structural reorganization of urban-region subsystems was a far more radical aspect of interregional study-period change than the shifts of activity between broad geographical regions. Similar subregional discrepancies should continue to be apparent in the coming period. Current rhetoric ignores the residual vitality of many parts of the Frostbelt.

Fourth, the current image is insensitive to the fact that ebbing regions may be sowing the seeds of future reversal. It is true that this sometimes takes place on the time scale of the developmental epoch rather than the decade, but this is the relevant scale. Let an anecdote illustrate this point. When I was growing up in the 1920s and 1930s, *the South* was considered to be "The Nation's Number One Economic Problem." It was so designated officially by President Roosevelt. Southern economists and sociologists (most notably at the University of North Carolina) developed the theme. Editorialists in the *Atlanta Tribune* and all over the South belabored the theme. The post–Civil War motto, "the South will rise again," had a hollow ring. In fact the South did rise again, and sooner than most expected. It did so because of changes in transaction networks already inherent in the developmental adaptations of the time. But, what emerged was a different kind of South than anyone envisaged. Except for the localized effects of the Tennessee Valley Authority, the regionally oriented policies of the federal and local governments had little to do with the outcome. Now the tables are reversed and everyone is talking about the Industrial North as the nation's number one economic problem. It does not seem helpful to reify our description of economic and social problems in this way. Regions are not problems, nor do they experience problems. Regions are not behavioral entities. They are only localized fields where individual human and enterprise problems become manifest. The problem agenda is usually more productively defined in different terms.

Come back to the seed-sowing business. The articulation of access networks and the change in the techno-logic of manufacturing is, for the time, making obsolete major portions of the activity fields and urbanized infrastructures of the Northeast. But developmental seeds are being sown that may, in time, convert ebb to flow. Adaptations are already clearing old urban "docking sites" so that new activities can find a more hospitable place. There is reason to believe that the population, skills, infrastructures, and sometimes forgotten amenities of the older parent regions will again prove to be attractive. But you can be sure that the Frostbelt will not be restored to its old manufacturing glory any more than the South was restored to its early "glory." It will come to reflect the techno-logic and topo-logic of the emerging era. It will not look like many of its current advocates and adversaries expect.

On the other side of the coin, the South and West will be using up the competitive advantages that new structures are giving them. The larger cities of the region are already experiencing major problems of urban congestion and the undersupply of urban services. The relative fortunes of irrigated agriculture are already reversing. Over time the petroleum resource base is bound to decline. The terms of trade in gaining access to the services of urbanized infrastructures may begin to turn back in favor of the older sections of the nation. There is a limit to the relative gains the Sunbelt can garner from the continuing shifts of a manufacturing base that is declining in importance. Furthermore, the regional effect of the old logistic growth curve may not always be displaced by new developments.

Do not misunderstand my message. The relative positions of the two broad regions will undoubtedly be permanently altered. As the adjustment proceeds, people and enterprises will experience major and painful dislocations. Nor am I suggesting a dispassionate laissez-faire attitude about such misfortunes. This brings us to a fifth point. The Sunbelt–Frostbelt imagery is thought to be relevant to formulating ameliorative public policies. I would suggest that, even if we assume a productive role for policy in this situation, we are not aided in its formulation by such an image. This point will be given further elaboration in the final chapter.

A Mini Update

We have examined a way of viewing the future that emerges from the conceptual orientation of this study. However, at this writing, we are already ten years into the next period. We could be instructed by what has since taken place. However, the census data required to update this study are not yet available. An update is certainly in order at a later time. In the meantime I have undertaken to examine the period from 1970–77 using Department of Commerce employment estimates.[7] They are not fully comparable with study data, but they reveal several things of interest.

First, the expected phase-shift is beginning to show in the rates of change exhibited by the industry sectors. Five of the ten manufacturing sectors experienced absolute employment declines (food, textiles, apparel, transportation equipment, and other manufacturing). Total manufacturing employment increased slightly. However, this was because of (1) the phenomenal continuing expansion of electronics and electrical machinery manufacturing and (2) an increase in motor vehicle manufacturing employment that is an artifact of the business cycle and the arbitrary beginning and ending points of the period. The full decennial employment figures seem likely to show an absolute decline. Bear in mind that this is before robotics can have had more than a marginal impact. The rapid-growth sectors are dominated by information-processing activities along with wholesale and retail trade. Finally, a turnaround in agricultural and mining employment has already begun.

These changes are also bringing about an expected phase-shift in the regional shift patterns. Most spectacular, the Plains region is experiencing a complete reversal of the relative and absolute total employment declines characteristic of all three study-period decades. This reflects the end of the dampening negative mix effect born of the agricultural adjustment. It is also occurring at a time when the articulation of transaction networks is speading manufacturing and urban-servicing activities into these regions. A competitive resurgence of agricultural employment seems underway in the Cornbelt sectors of the region. Appalachian coal regions are also experiencing a turnaround stimulated by the resurgence of coal and its linked trading-sector responses.

Other characteristics of the more recent shifts underscore the caution about the Sunbelt–Frostbelt characterization. (1) A number of urban regions between Detroit and Chicago are actually experiencing an acceleration of already manifest competitive gains. This is similarly true of Minneapolis and places like Cedar Rapids and Wausau on the western edge of the Old Manufacturing Belt. A ring of urban regions extending southeast between Chicago and St. Louis (Dubuque, Davenport, Peoria, Champaign) actually experienced a reversal of earlier all-sector competitive declines. There is a hint also of the regenerative power of the adaptive process in New England and in upstate New York. These study-period relative losses are decelerating substantially. In the northern tier region of Upper New England, ebb has turned to flow as all-sector relative declines have turned to gains.

Accelerating competitive declines are found in four tightly bunched sets of urban regions. They are dominated by the nation's largest and oldest management and production regions. (1. The New York, Philadelphia, and Baltimore regions; 2. the Detroit, Toledo, Dayton, Cleveland, Youngstown regions; 3. the Chicago-Rockford regions; and 4. St. Louis.) This is precisely where the nation-serving manufacturing and linkage functions of the old industrial technology were most heavily concentrated.

The Sunbelt tends to experience accelerating competitive gains, as the scenario would suggest. But, even here, there are meaningful variations. Take the Southeast. In the Piedmont competitive gains display a marked deceleration, though not yet sufficient to reverse the all-sector pattern. This reflects the region's heavy specialization in textiles. It also reflects the fact that this was the first emergent southern manufacturing belt. The developmental flow is passing on to the rest of the South. Peninsular Florida (except for Tampa) is experiencing decelerating competitive gains. An important part of this is the relative decline in the mining and processing of inorganic chemicals. Accelerating competitive gains along the Atlantic Coast and Gulf flatlands suggest the spreading force of the developmental factors already discussed. Most pronounced of all are the accelerating gains displayed by the Upper South cluster (Lexington, Knoxville, Nashville, Asheville, Memphis, and Little Rock). This appears to be an unusually broad-based development that includes most manufacturing, linkage, trading, and information-processing functions. This must reflect the continuing strategic importance for many activities of not getting too far away from the northeastern parent region.

In the Southwest (Texas to the Pacific Coast) there is an interesting differentiation of the continuing relative competitive gains. Regions like Dallas and the Southern Mountain regions of California and Arizona (that dominated study-period competitive gains) are displaying decelerating gains, while the New Mexico and mid-Mountain regions are displaying accelerating gains. This, too, is consistent with the scenario.

These data are too gross to provide much insight into developments affecting the types and sizes of urban centers. It is clear that the largest of the old northeastern metropolitan centers are experiencing continuing and aggravated competitive losses. It is also becoming clear that the largest Sunbelt cities (Charlotte, Atlanta, Miami, Dallas, Phoenix, Los Angeles, San Diego, San Francisco) are beginning to experience a deceleration of their study-period competitive gains while smaller urban cores (like Nashville, Memphis, Little Rock, Birmingham, New Orleans, Tulsa, Denver, Albuquerque, Salt Lake City, Portland) are benefiting more from accelerating, spreading-wave thrusts. These data are blank on what is happening to the lower order centers. We will need decennial-census county data to clarify this.

However, one bit of evidence is significant. Recent studies of workforce migration in the United States have demonstrated a remarkable phase-shift (Brown, 1980). Since 1975, the flow of migrants from rural to metropolitan areas has made a dramatic turnaround. The new deconcentration movement is not confined to metropolitan sprawl but includes counties remote from urban-region cores. It is affecting almost every geographical region of the nation. This reverses a migratory tide that had gone on for generations. Several factors were at work: (1) the end of the agricultural labor force adjustment, (2) the hinterland articulation of transaction networks, and (3) the decentralization of manufacturing employment. These were all structural changes that cast clearly identifiable future shadows by the end of the study period. The fact that the emerging phase-shift was not anticipated by urban and regional students is testimony to the limitations of traditional quantitative projection techniques.

Careful, imaginative, and periodic updates of this picture are important to the explanatory procedures exemplified by this study. When emphasis is placed on seeing the future as the outcome of a developmental, problem-solving scenario, an essential aspect of the method is to subject the scenario to repeated consistency checks with emerging historical experience. Such projective views of the future as have been suggested in this chapter must be continuously rewritten.

Notes

1. For example, the information-processing technology essential to regulate the process sequences in a continuous-flow petroleum refinery or steel strip mill is quite different from that required in traditional craft shops. The amount and kind of information processing required by a vast trading system is different from that required to maintain a village economy.

2. The entire sequence of performance operations (from resource extracting to benefacting to material processing to product fabrication to distribution to consumption and to the recycling of waste through the physical and social ecosphere) is moving away from an often fragmented, discrete, discontinuous set of processes (for which one relies on money-based market signals to maintain coherence) to an integrated, systemic set of processes that flow in real time (on a much faster time scale, over a much vaster space scale) with minimum buffering and with direct information feedback.

3. This also means that the routing of messages in established channels becomes largely independent of time and distance costs. If line-loads are heavy on calls from New York to Los Angeles, a message can just as easily be sent by Dallas as by Chicago. Thus, carrying capacity comes to be defined for the total system rather than for specific channels. This is partially true of transport nets as well, but nowhere near to the same extent. Communication networks are more commonly designed as integrated systems.

4. It has always been thus. In the early twentieth century a writer in *The New York Times* speculated that the motor vehicle was going to radically change the structure of the American city. He was taken to task roundly by editorial and letter writers.

5. If anyone doubts that there are substantial incentives for these developments, consider the fact that urban traffic jams account for 25 to 40 percent of the cost of motor vehicle operation and half of the cost of bus fleet operations. We can be sure that both the "carrot and the stick" will be at work.

6. Recall an earlier discussion that emphasized the importance of "forgetting" in the process of "learning" new functions.

7. Produced by the Regional Economic Measurement Division of the Bureau of Economic Analysis in the Department of Commerce. Unfortunately this volume cannot be extended to incorporate the tables and maps produced by this exercise.

15

Implications for Policy and Methodology: An Addendum

Much interest has been voiced about the implications of this study for policy. The point is at hand for these concerns to be addressed. There are also data problems and methodological issues that deserve consideration.

Implications for Policy

The policy concerns expressed indicate a predominant interest in the way study results might support or challenge particular regional or urban policy recommendations. Before we deal with regional problems and policies in particular, I need to clarify my view of the policy process in general.

What Is Policy?

''Policy'' is a name given to the problem solutions we introduce into the historical process. Because this study views historical sequence as an iterative series of problem encounters and solutions, its orientation speaks directly to the policy process. Policies are clearly the product of information processes carried out at the third and fourth levels of behavior (or levels of observation) discussed in chapter 1 in volume I. The policy literature employs the term indiscriminantly to refer to programs and activities at both levels. Thus, managerial programs are often referred to as policies. Their implementation involves making preprogrammed cybernetic adjustments to anticipated contingencies. Developmental problems are novel disturbances not previously accounted for by managerial plans. Here a policy is a plan for reprogramming lower order, internalized performance processes, or for extending managerial controls to include a part of the external operating environment. A managerial policy is a design for making cybernetic adjustments to changes in operating parameters. A developmental policy is a design *for changing* a physical or managerial performance process. For the balance of this discussion, ''policy'' will refer exclusively to developmental plans.

Understanding the Problem–Policy Context

This two-volume study has dealt extensively with the problem encounters that marked each historical situation, and with the developmental solutions evoked. Little has been said about the process by means of which these solutions were developed and implemented. But it is clear that the formulation of an effective policy requires the problem solver to understand the historical situation in which the problem becomes manifest. The kinds of policy initiatives that emerge depend on the way those responsible for the policy process perceive the problem and what policy strategies are adopted. The kinds of things it is important to understand are best revealed by posing a series of questions.

First, who has the problem? At the outset it is important to emphasize that only identifiable behavioral entities experience problems. Individuals and families have problems. Organized behavioral systems encounter problems—systems with programmed purposes and goals like enterprises and agencies of government. That is all. This is important because we sometimes reify abstract conceptual entities like regions and talk as if they experience problems. We will return to this.

Second, where does the problem originate? A problem arises when a behavioral entity encounters a mismatch between experience and expectation. The mismatch always originates in activity linkages that form processes.

From the point of view of the policy process it makes a difference where the disturbance originates—whether in the transaction field already internalized by management or in external activities linked to it. It matters whether the mismatch is experienced in physical processes or information processes. It matters whether the problem can be resolved by formally organized, managerial processes or only by political processes. Both the nature of encountered problems and the nature of realistic policy responses depend on the character of the field of disturbance.

Third, how is the problem perceived? There are two aspects of this. It is important, of course, for the field of disturbance to be properly perceived if the problem is to be properly defined and a realistic solution developed. Specifying the problem can obviously be done well or poorly. But there is another aspect that might be better understood if we reformulate the question: How is the act of perception carried out? What is the conceptual model brought to the problem experience? What one sees is heavily conditioned by what one is looking for. The most important distinction is whether one holds a closed-system or an open-system image of the total operating environment. If a closed image prevails, there is a tendency to see environmental change as *the* problem. There is little inclination to trace the change to its external roots. There is a tendency to use partial models to define the problem, with reductionistic, mechanistic methods used to formulate the policy. (Find the defective element and fix it.) If an open image governs, there is a tendency to view a disturbance as a symptom of problem roots yet to be identified and described. There is a tendency to see the situation holistically, systemically, and developmentally. There is a tendency to find opportunities in historical encounters, as well as problems. These differences in orientation to the problem situation lead to pronounced differences in the kinds of policies formulated. Hence:

Fourth, what strategies are chosen? Again there are two aspects. The technologies that are relevant in formulating policies depend, of course, on whether the problems have internal or external roots, whether they involve physical or information processes, and whether they are susceptible to organizational internalization.

The second aspect again derives from the conceptual orientation of the observer. A closed-system model is much more likely to lead to a defensive strategy. If the problem is initiated by external change, dam it up. Construct a privileged enclave where customary activity can proceed undisturbed. Even developmental changes are more apt to be reactive (*ex post*) and limited in scope. An open-system image leads to defensive strategies only as limited adjustments tied to a time-phased development plan (for example, infant industry protection). It is more likely to embrace sets of systemically related problems. It is more apt to be opportunistic and anticipatory—to assess emergent benefits and problems in advance.

It will not have escaped you that this characterization is inspired by the conceptual orientation of this study. If realistic, it is clear that there is a strong policy preference inherent in the nature of the historical process. The impacted system that possesses an open-system image of its place in the transaction field and historical process is apt to develop superior policies. Defensive strategies may protect bounded, parochial interests for a while, but in time they will be swept away by the accumulation of unresolved concerns that require genuine process inventions for their solution. Developmental policies that trace problems to their roots and that appreciate the dynamic of problem solutions are apt to be superior.

Fifth, who formulates policy? The behavioral entity experiencing the problem may not always be the one formulating the policy response. Thus, a great deal of what is possible in policy formulation is restricted by the kinds of behavioral agencies that exist and by their capacity and authority to engage in the policy exercise.

Sixth, who implements policy? Just as the entity experiencing the problem need not be the one formulating a policy response, the one formulating policy need not be the one carrying out the behavioral innovation. Again, the kinds of developmental, problem-solving initiatives that are feasible in any given historical situation depend on whether agencies exist that are able to put them into practice.

Finally, just as problems can only be experienced by identifiable behavioral entities, policy responses can only be formulated and implemented by them. There is often a temptation to invent policy options for which no realistic agency of implementation exists. Thus, a part of the policy design may sometimes involve the creation of a new organization to implement the plan. The realistic limitations and possibilities for doing so are often overlooked.

This understanding can now be applied to the implications of this study for policy issues.

A Historical Phase-Shift in the Nature of Policy Problems

The previous chapter suggested that the urbanized U.S. system is going through a phase-shift in the kinds of problems it encounters. We need to review this story sufficiently to identify the emerging challenges to the policy process.

The source of these changes is rooted in the increasing complexity of urbanized production and transaction systems. The increased specialization attending the development of modern technologies increases the knowledge content of activities, the connectivity of transactions, the variety and spatial extent of the system's resource roots, the variety and range of human wants and aspirations, and the systemic nature of dynamic interactions. This all spells complexity. This complexity has been growing steadily since the inception of the industrial revolution. However, in the current transition period, this cumulative process has reached a threshold where the nature of encountered problems is changing radically. Adaptive strategies that were appropriate in earlier situations are proving inadequate. We are encountering a new set of problems and policy issues characterized here as meta-management problems.

The historical situation is changing in three ways. First, increasingly the dominant problems are becoming information-processing rather than physical-processing problems. The sources of this phase-shift have already been discussed. The development of an earlier industrial technology was a response to the need to increase the ability of people to carry out physical work. Physical artifacts were developed that amplified "the strength and reach of the arm of man." But the relational complexity that emerged created problems of process regulation and transaction coordination that are information-processing problems. These problems form the major current constraints on the expansion of social productivity. They have more to do with the "power, speed, and reach of the mind of man."

It is not surprising that the earliest responses to information-processing problems are taking the form of new physical artifacts—for example, the compunication machines that currently dazzle us. But the problem set is marching very rapidly beyond the need for such hardware to the need for information-processing software. At the core of every information process is a set of rules that governs the way it performs. The technological response to increased managerial complexity will require not only the invention of compunication software, but also the creation of new and improved managerial processes in the broadest sense. The managerial process is itself rule structure. Management is the software of social behavior.

The second phase-shift is closely related to the increasing prominence of information-processing problems. Within the domain of information processes, developmental problems are increasing in importance relative to managerial problems. During historical epochs, each behavioral system tended to settle into something approaching steady-state norms for extended periods of time. Disruptions leading to developmental changes occurred only intermittently in the life of the typical enterprise. Developmental-entrepreneurial processes tended to be *ad hoc* and event oriented. But problem encounters have speeded up so much that developmental responses are becoming a more continuous preoccupation of individuals, enterprises, and governments. More of the managerial, entrepreneurial, and political energy of society is being drawn beyond the regulation of ongoing performance processes.

This speedup is a direct consequence of the increased complexity of the system. When one enterprise makes a developmental change, it alters interdependent linkages in ways that sometimes create developmental problems for another. The iterative, problem→solution→problem sequence is accelerated by increased connectivity. There is also an increasing complexity in the structure of problems because they are more often encountered in interrelated sets. Add to this the effect of the accelerating accumulation of knowledge (that is, technological design software) and the speedup in the effective rate of policy implementation. Thus, the increased complexity of the system has expanded and accelerated the exercise of developmental processes. This has compounded complexity because developmental processes are learning processes. Learning processes are inherently more complex than performance processes.

The third phase-shift has to do with the increasing importance of problems that originate in external fields. During the historical epochs dominated by physical processes, most problems tended to arise out of internal operating environments of formal enterprises. Both managerial and developmental problem-solving activities were predominantly oriented to the internal field of activities. The increasing complexity of the urban system is changing this dramatically. Most private and public agencies are increasingly connected with many others in a complex, ecosystemic, coadaptive field of transactions. For example, the physical environment is increasingly drawn upon for energy and materials and increasingly used as a waste depository. This increases disruptive feedbacks from the host physical environment. Problems are increasingly carried by linkages with external, quasi-autonomous entities not subject to direct control. More and more these disturbances go beyond the fluctuations of interface parameters anticipated by managerial programs. Adaptive responses often require new forms of enterprise behavior.

There is a critical difference between the system characteristics of these external linkages and the more friendly, easier understood, internal operating environments. The internal structure of an organized system is a realization of a planned process design. The relational structure of the external environment is not under the regulatory control of any single management system. This external field forms an ecosystem of mutually coadaptive entities. Whatever attributes of coherence and stability this transaction system demonstrates (when behaving as a roughly steady-state performance system) are a consequence of the fact that it tends to form a self-correcting, negative feedback system. A part of this is mediated by transaction markets, a part by the political process, and a part by cultural processes that reinforce those otherwise autonomous responses that tend to be mutually consistent.

As each entity makes developmental changes, it often prompts others to make behavioral adjustments because of changes in shared linkages. Thus, the effect of each developmental change is transmitted along a time-phased network of critical linkages. Collectively, they define a field of disturbance. But because of the ecosystemic nature of that field, both the problems and feasible policy responses are often different from those emerging from internal fields. These disturbances are more often experienced as control problems than as physical process problems. A favorite policy strategy is to internalize the externality. The enterprise tries to capture some benefits by bringing part of the external field under internal managerial control. The combination movements in American industry resulted from this mode of adaptation.

However, there is an opposite policy option. It may also be possible to increase the rewards of enterprise by externalizing internal problems and costs—the classical "problem of the commons."[1] The internalizing strategy, by selecting for those external disturbances that can be beneficially internalized, indirectly exacerbates the remaining common-problem disturbances. The second choice directly exacerbates them. Intentional environmental pollution is a classical case. The externalization of human capital investments (in contrast to physical capital) and the externalization of unemployment are also examples. The essential point is this: With the accelerating increase in complexity, it is these common ecosystemic problems that are becoming the obtrusive problems of the time. In an earlier time it was the internal physical process and regulatory problems of management that were paramount.

These three phase-shifts in the nature of the fields of disturbance imply a major phase-shift in the nature of the policy processes required. These new kinds of problems all require metamanagerial solutions. Most social process technologies are limited in two ways: They were designed for the formal management of internal operating fields. Existing tools of developmental problem solving are most appropriate for carrying out intermittent, reductionistic problem-solving tasks. The overriding problems of the emerging era have to do with our need to deal with rapidly changing complexity, and, thus, the overriding policy issues have to do with the need to develop new social process technologies.

Consider, first, the matter of the complexity of performance processes. The problem presented by the increasing complexity of organizational functions is on its way to solution. Powerful information-processing machines are vastly increasing the ability of organizations to manage complexity. Widespread experimentation with the "software" technologies of managerial processes is also underway.[2]

But the critical new social process problems have to do with the ways of extending managerial control to embrace external, ecosystemic fields of disturbance—fields that are not amenable to traditional managerial technologies. It has been typical to treat this field as the domain of governmental regulatory control. Thus, we rely on a variation of the old policy strategem, a variation that invokes a higher order organization to internalize the problem.

But the existing managerial technologies of government emerged when ecosystemic complexity was not such a problem. In many cases the problem of the commons was amenable to public utility solutions. Classical management could be made to work by assigning a public or private organization the task of carrying out a typical enterprise production function. For the rest, the problem was primarily one of maintaining the honesty and contractual integrity of the transaction process. In the latter case, governmental management relies on proscriptive rules of justice that specify the limits of acceptable behavior, and on the adversarial processes by means of which violations are regulated. This contrasts with the prescriptive rules of performance management and the authoritative commands by means of which they are implemented.

In earlier epochs, most of this work was carried out at the local level. The community instruments of the states (counties, incorporated towns and cities, special tax districts, and the like) administered most justice and provided for nonmarket-type public services. Most transaction networks tended to close into local fields. The industrial era changed all of this by generating the complex, highly interconnected ecosystemic networks described in the text. Resource supply fields, pollutable reservoirs, and transaction markets now extend far beyond the regulatory jurisdictions of local governments. The fields within which problems are generated are external not only to conventional enterprise organizations, but to organized governments as well. The attempt to manage this burgeoning ecosystemic complexity has vastly enlarged the programmatic activities of government organizations, relative to private, and of state and national government, relative to local.

Still, we have no effective handle on many external-field problems. There is a serious and continuing mismatch between the fields of disturbance and the spans of authority. This is not just a consequence of increased complexity. It has been exacerbated by the temptation to seek defensive solutions to problems. In the name of "local rights" political interest groups barricade themselves in community bunkers in such a way that they internalize benefits and load disruptive costs on society. Local "rights" often turn out to mean the right to protect what you've got that is good, to exclude what is bad, and to export what you've got that you don't want. This use of government structures has become widespread. Such defensive approaches to the solution of problems have fractionated and proliferated units of government.[3] They have also exaggerated the problems emerging from external fields. As a consequence, an unresolved tension exists between open- and closed-system policy strategies. When combined with the mismatch between fields of disturbance and spans of authority, this has generated an unstable oscillation in public policy, vacillating between centralizing and decentralizing strategies. At this writing, the political mood is accentuating the latter. But neither set of options works well because local spans of authority are commonly too small relative to many fields of disturbance, and national levels are frequently too large. (Or also too small. To make matters worse, disturbances that arise outside national systems are becoming more important.)

The political process is not yet ready to deal with the subject of matching the regulatory apparatus of government to the problems characteristic of our complex society. Public policy labors under a degree of hardship unknown to private entities. Within those fields of relationship internalized by organizational control, private systems are largely free to reorganize to match spans of control with fields of disturbance. Public systems commonly must choose between existing agencies to implement policy. Just as commonly, they do not match the requirements of regulatory success.

There is also a serious and continuing mismatch between the managerial technologies of government and the need to resolve common problems. There are only the prescriptive techniques of formal management and the proscriptive techniques of adversarial justice. But there is no way we can model ecosystemic complexity well enough to apply prescriptive rules to the regulation of many common problems. Further, the proscriptive techniques of justice only work well when a rule-violating adversary can be clearly identified by administrative justice. But the social costs that are externalized by some private and public entities do not necessarily affect other public and private entities directly and unambiguously. The problem then becomes systemic. Proscriptive justice has a hard time coming to terms with the problem, and people grumble about "the system." The result has been another oscillation between prescriptive and proscriptive strategies. Neither are rich enough to regulate complex ecosystemic disturbances. The legal remedies that are attempted are often contradictory and self-defeating. Policies often generate counterintuitive results. The tax system has become a vehicle for social engineering more than a fiscal tool of government. There can be no doubt that this class of managerial problems is among the most obtrusive of the emerging epoch. Their address requires metamanagerial solutions. The political process is not yet ready to take on this task.

There is a second class of metamanagerial problems created by the phase-shift in the nature of developmental problems. Organization and management have traditionally been absorbed with the task of regulating performance. Developmental problem solving was characteristically intermittent, *ad hoc,* inspired by personal leadership. It appeared serendipitously when needed. But with the need for self-reorganization becoming a more continuous aspect of social adaptation, and with problem encounters coming increasingly in the form of problem sets, another metamanagement problem emerges. How do we organize for self-reorganization? How can we organize to manage programmatic change as well as steady-state performance? Again, the private sectors are beginning to address these policy issues seriously. A number of science-based industries, for example, now claim that their business is innovation. But, here as well, the political process is not ready to acknowledge a new challenge.

The eventual resolution of these metamanagement problems will require a cultural change. The mind-set that emerged during the industrial era does not yet comprehend system complexity. It is still surprised by the counterintuitive results of policies based on reductionistic, mechanistic concepts. It still thinks of production and productivity exclusively in physical process terms.[4] It may take a massive change in the public understanding of the problem context and the policy process before these matters can be effectively addressed. However, there can be little doubt that the major social problems, and the paramount policy issues, of the coming epochs will involve these metamanagement problems and the way in which they are resolved. This reveals another way in which the future isn't what it used to be.

Regional and Urban Policy Issues

When people expressed an interest in the policy implications of this study, it was not likely they had such a response in mind. Their concern was with the assessment of particular regional and urban policy proposals. The path chosen reflects my conviction that an understanding of these more general policy issues is an essential basis for evaluating any policy proposal. It might illuminate both the meaning of these concepts and regional policy proposals if they are considered together.

If one examines the urban-region policy literature in the context of this study, one is struck by the distressingly parochial orientation of most policy suggestions. They are dominated by a different conceptual tradition. First, the characterization of problem fields tends to be simplistic. We are more comfortable with the arbitrary boundaries we draw around regions than the reality of modern transaction networks would seem to justify. We often fall into the reification trap. We tend to view regions as behavioral entities with "interests" that are threatened or supported. Problems tend to be characterized as "regional conflicts." Thus, we become endlessly absorbed with the conflict of interests between urban and rural regions, between the city core and the suburbs, between the Frostbelt and the Sunbelt, and so on. The identification of problems with abstractly conceived and arbitrarily bounded entities tends to obscure the relational patterns of problem sets and their more fundamental roots. This is also partly a result of the equally arbitrary way we aggregate partial decisions.

Second, the temporal orientation is similarly parochial. The temptation to see change as *the* problem seems irresistible. Problems are defined as conflicts between present behavioral states and emergent transformations. Policy proposals tend to be protective of existing states. Rarely is any understanding of the creative nature of the historical process shown. Rarely is policy required to find some consistency with that process. The exercise of forecasting change is carried out by a denatured process of mapping historical structures onto the future. This reinforces the tendency to see change as the problem, because technique hides explanation.

Third, the functional orientation is correspondingly parochial. Problems tend to be seen as a conflict between the interest of organized systems and their external operating environments. The characterization of problems and solutions tends to be partial and reductionistic. The "tail," "leg," and "trunk" of the problem "elephant" are described in detail without recognizing that the problem is an "elephant."

Where it is recognized that current behavior cannot be successfully barricaded against change, change is largely seen as scalar, not developmental. There is a widespread commitment to the idea of balanced growth: "Growth should not be allowed to play favorites." The fact that such a policy may run counter to the reality of the historical process is not acknowledged.

A few examples should illustrate. Take the perceived conflict between rural and urban interests. It became widely accepted that it was a bad thing for populations to become so concentrated in cities "at the expense of" small towns and rural areas. Public policy was directed to "revitalize the heartland." Presidential commissions were formed to develop a "national growth policy," by which was meant a population redistribution policy.[5]

This led to a concern about the optimum size of a city. It as widely held that cities had grown beyond optimum size. Academic scholars busily set to work to measure this. Here is an example of the irresistible temptation to reify the region. We sought to define the optimum-sized city in terms analogous to the classical "production function" of an economic firm. We can talk of such a function for a firm, which is a coherent behavioral entity. A city is not such an entity. There might be a limited sense in which there are definable scalar efficiencies in the provision of a specific city service, but this misses the point for several reasons. (1) The activities and the population settlements we know as cities are a consequence of the technologically defined, spatial coincidence of transaction-switching functions. These are carried out by coadapting, quasi-autonomous private enterprises that do not collectively constitute a behavioral entity. The city is mostly defined by a transfer function, not a production function. (2) The transaction structure of the city at any time is not the most efficient representation of some logical structure implicit in current technology. It is a compromised and lagged result of an historical process. (3) By the time one could determine what city size might correspond to such an implicit logical structure, if indeed one could, the historical process will have changed it. (4) There is a fundamentally insoluble operational question concerning where the boundaries might appropriately be drawn to internalize the transfer nets that define the city and its transfer functions.

The concern about the distribution of populations also led to specific policy recommendations. One thing you might do is "keep 'em down on the farm." This was an important part of the justification of a generation of American farm policy. It failed miserably. "If you can't keep them on the farm, then keep them out of the big cities by encouraging growth in smaller centers." This was the thrust of the "new cities" movement. It was born of the same set of presuppositions that gave us the optimum city. But cities in Western democracies are not entities that are planned for and put in place by some exercise of entrepreneurship. They happen as a consequence of the dynamic emergence of transaction networks. In any case, what are the realistic policy options? What common-problem agency existed to formulate a new cities policy? Where was the technology for creating whole cities *de novo*? How can they be created in a way that integrates successfully with the larger urban-system network? Even if we presume these are answerable questions, where does an agency of government exist that can implement such a policy? The upshot is that the highly touted new cities like Reston and Columbia were not new cities at all, but large suburban developments "entrepreneured" by private interests. They worked because they filled out the network structures of existing urban regions. They did not provide realistic options for a policy of urban–to–rural population redistribution.

A more sophisticated set of proposals for slowing the rural–to–urban flood also emerged. These were designed to encourage the growth of existing centers spread throughout rural hinterlands. Grants to support urban infrastructure, tax incentives for private firms, and the like, were among the policy options suggested. Because the territories at issue were so vast and the potential recipients so numerous, a sophisticated theory emerged for "targeting" communities. The concepts had to do with "growth poles" and "key industries." One supported hinterland population growth where one had the best chance of achieving "leverage."

The orientation of this study would suggest several problems with this approach as well. The theory is that you identify urban regions with good prospects for growth. This is done by identifying key industries that have good prospects for growth and are good "multipliers." A good multiplier is a key industry whose growth is spread through localized linkages to other activities, thus amplifying the initial stimulus. Leaving aside the formidable problem of identifying the best growth poles and key sectors, these policy proposals again fail to accommodate the reality of urban transaction structures and the historical processes that create them.

First, it is assumed that the urban region chosen to serve as a growth pole is a sufficiently closed transaction net for the initial stimulus to have a significant internal multiplier effect. This may have been effectively true at an earlier stage of the industrial era. The assumption is subject to serious question in a time when the degree of localized network closure is everywhere declining rapidly.[6] Second, judging the growth prospects of key industries presupposes some technique for anticipating the localized network effects of a national developmental process. Such a technique is not supplied by growth-pole theory. The present study of the nature of that process suggests this kind of microforecasting defies standard forecasting techniques. Third, the theory suggests that public infrastructural investments encourage growth. Good local public utility services are necessary for growth, but not necessarily sufficient. It is no easier to anticipate when such investments will generate multiplier effects than it is for key industries. And, if the transaction context is right, how necessary is a subsidy? The provision of transport and communication access channels may offer the best leverage in providing regional development. We certainly have the evidence of the dramatic contribution of highway development on the development of the postwar South. But again, the conditions have to be right, and they were right at that time. One should also remember that the National Highway Program was not conceived as a policy instrument for implementing a growth-pole strategy. Furthermore, how does one target an articulating network? Fourth, the theory suggests that the important sources of local growth are tied to key "basic" industries. We have already seen that regional shifts during the study period had more to do with changes in transfer technologies and household functions than with the redistribution of so-called basic manufacturing activities.

Take as another example the widely perceived conflict between the core city and the suburbs. "Urban sprawl" and the declining city core are sources of stress. It has been an oft-stated goal of urban policy to revitalize the city core. A host of proposals were motivated by this concern. Consider a single example. Many were convinced that the revitalization of urban mass transport was of critical importance. The romance of traditional surface and subway rail systems proved especially strong. This was supposed to revitalize downtown shopping, reduce motor vehicle congestion, move core city workers to jobs in the suburbs, and so on. Once again, these proposals run counter to the historical development process. Mass transit was the technology of the disappearing industrial age. One winds up reemphasizing highly linear hub-and-spoke transport channels at a time when transit requirements demand a highly articulated network providing greater time-and-route flexibility. One ignores the fact that rapid transit is but one of a set of transfer channels in an increasing array of transport and communication options that are becoming increasingly substitutable. This is a classic case of reductionistic problem solving applied to complex systems. Such hardwired transport systems cannot survive over any extended period without heavy subsidies that substantially alter both the urban network and the income distribution process.

Finally, take the widely perceived conflict between broad geographical regions such as the Frostbelt and the Sunbelt. This is also linked with a concern about the alleged decline in the competitive position of the Frostbelt vis-à-vis international markets. This is thought to require a revitalization of the Industrial North. The policy instruments proposed include industrial subsidies and investment tax credits (often targeted to specific industries), laws prohibiting plant closings, government purchase of plants, among others. There is a view that all traditional industry needs is a little help to restore its competitive position, absorb the nation's unemployed, create balanced growth, and so on. There is no acknowledgment of the phase-shift to an information society. Just as the adjustment to a mechanized, scientific agriculture created a 6 million-worker decline in agricultural employment during the study period, the next generation will likely see a major absolute decline in manufacturing employment—particularly in the more traditional industries. And if one chooses to encourage reindustrialization with the application of investment tax credits, for example, one accelerates the historical shift by encouraging the investment in the robot worker and other new information-processing technologies. Thus, what one conceives as a defensive strategy may turn out to have counterintuitive results. Such a program also proves inconsistent with other proposals designed to slow down plant closings. Further, such countervailing proposals are often put forward by the same interests.

One is so easily misunderstood, it is time to introduce two caveats. First, these illustrations do not pretend to be a systematic application of this volume's view of the policy process to the regional and urban literature. They only intend to suggest how easy it is to mischaracterize social problems and public policy solutions if one is not attentive to the reality of the historical situation. When we reify regions, ignore complexity, and reduce the development process to an image of scalar growth, we are frequently led to unrealistic policy formulations. Second, nothing written here implies that the historical process is some deterministic juggernaut lying outside the power of human-social intervention. Quite the contrary. The process has been consistently described as being itself the result of iterative, human, problem-solving interventions. The discussion only seeks to emphasize that, at this point in history, partial theories and mechanical-fix solutions can no longer be successful in addressing our most serious problems. Indeed, the most serious ones we face are metamanagement problems commonly ignored in policy discourse. Metamanagement developments will likely have more to say about the structure of transaction networks and the location of populations over the next two generations than all of the explanatory factors that conventionally claim our attention.

Implications for Methodology

We are brought, at last, to a point of confession. As a quantitative empirical representation, this study stands revealed as a methodological anachronism. This should not surprise you. "Methods and meaning" sections were repeatedly employed in volume I in an effort to make plain the limitations of achievement. The limitation is a consequence of the fact that the empirical methods and data structures we customarily employ are not adequate to represent changing urban structures. This study not only implies an emerging phase-shift in the problems and policy issues but a phase-shift in the methods and data structures required to represent them, as well.

This derives from two aspects of the concepts driving the study. First, an understanding of urban-system structures requires an image of the network of transactions that tie social activities into a coherent performance system. Second, understanding the way in which these urbanized structures change requires one to understand the nature of a developmental, evolutionary, historical process.

Consider the methodological implications of the need to represent transaction networks at the second level of behavior (recall chapter 1 in volume I). This involves observing production and transportation activities and how they are linked to form integrated activity sequences we call *processes*. The resulting network pattern is given by their technological content. These patterns can be represented by abstract descriptions like engineering plans, or by empirical descriptions generated by observing activities at work. Either way, the units of observation and description are *acts*. The methodological tools required to describe and analyze their patterned connections are primarily *relational*.

Therein lies the rub. Most of the data structures of social science are either object data or, at best, they offer state descriptions of activities. They only represent the results of performance.[7] Further, the representational methodologies of social science are largely classificational-statistical, rather than relational. They lack the capacity to represent activity and process relationships directly and unambiguously. We understandably shrink from the unfamiliar, and often formidable, methodological and data collection problems of representing activity systems. We have tinkered mightily with traditional tools so as to fashion empirical images supporting inferences about their underlying nature. We employ clever tricks that are useful and helpful, but plagued with hidden traps. Consider a sample of these devices and their limitations.

The key device is a reliance on object or state data as surrogates for genuine activity data. To make the difference clear, we need to understand what is involved in observing and recording an act. The description of that act contains three elements—descriptors specifying an original state, descriptors indicating the nature of the transforming act, and descriptors specifying a terminal state. For example, at a certain level of aggregation (where we already lump sets of individual acts that form processes), we might describe a productive activity like this: "In 1970 the Youngstown plant of U.S. Steel produced 1 million tons of ingot steel (terminal state) employing the open hearth method to smelt (generalized process description) 5 million tons of ore (original state)."

This is a complex datum describing a specific *activity process* and its linked *relationship* to original input and terminal output states. A common trick is to monitor the physical output of the process at the terminus—that is, the first-level results of performance. The datum then reduces to: "In 1970 the Youngstown plant of U.S. Steel produced 1 million tons of ingot steel." This produces a simple *classified count* stripped of all relational information. We leave it to inference that some unspecified antecedent production activity took place. We assume that the use of the data is unaffected by whether the product was created by an open hearth or Bessemer process, or whether the input was ore or scrap. In fact, there are many uses where one does not need to know these things. There are additional uses where this works because it is understood that those using the data already know what is going on at the process level. Thus, management often knows when it is safe to ignore what is going on at the activity level. They can get away with treating the process level as a "black box" because, for them, it really isn't.

We use another trick to get closer to the activity level. Sometimes we employ classifications that describe, not the products of activities, but the nature of *activity states*. Occupational descriptors are commonly of this sort. Thus, we might say that 750,000 workers were employed as secretaries in New York City in 1980. The description indicates that they were *in the state of being engaged in secretarial work*. "Secretarial work" is taken to be a process description about which all parties may have a sufficient understanding for the datum to serve. Here we are talking more directly about activities, but in a way that allows us to treat them methodologically *as if they were* classified objects. Explicit relational information is still missing. The data are still easily processed using common classificational-statistical tools.

We often discover patterns of descriptive association by applying statistical multivariate techniques to object and state descriptors. For example, we might identify two kinds of manufacturing activity that are commonly located together in the same city. From this we might infer that they are directly connected in a transaction net. That might be correct, but on the strength of this statistical association alone one cannot be sure. They might be spatially associated while completely independent. Juxtaposition might result from their both being functionally connected to localized urban transaction services. Furthermore, two activities in quite different locations might still be related through direct transaction links. Without being measurably associated by statistical tests, we cannot tell with this kind of data. The powerful statistical techniques we employ can give us high levels of "statistical confidence" without giving us much confidence in the meaning of our results. This is particularly true if our problem and interests require that we look inside the black box identified with the activity level of behavior.

The trade-center classifications we have employed in this study were based on just such a spatial association of retail and wholesale trade enterprises in towns and cities. It was disclosed early on how poorly this taxonomy differentiates between one case and another. (For the overlapping of categories, see figure 5 in volume I, p. 63.) The justification for forming such a classification is derived from central place theory, but that theory is a boundary network model fundamentally at variance with transaction network concepts (see pp. 23–24 in volume I). Indeed, this overlapping of categories is very likely a manifestation of the multinodal and interpenetrating nature of urban transaction fields. This is a reality that cannot be represented by state-classification methodologies. We are caught in a trap. We want to identify bounded geographical fields (to be employed as sorting bins for statistical enumerations) that are functionally differentiated in terms of transaction characteristics, but to do so without transaction data. Transactions are activities that form relational nets. When we specify bounded fields with only state-variable classifications as tools, what appear to be homogeneous classes in terms of the state descriptors may prove to be quite heterogeneous in terms of the underlying activity structures. Work in this field proceeds as if we are not even aware what an enormous compromise with cognitive fidelity has been made. Still, this study was faced with the usual problem. When undertaken, the only data game in town was the traditional one.

The inherent limitations of using state variables as surrogates for activity data exposes us to another serious problem. Whatever the degree of representativeness that can be achieved by employing such data turns out to be highly perishable. Yet, the methodology employed imbues these data with a seemingly permanent character. In truth, underlying activity patterns can change radically without so much as rippling the surface of the state-variable descriptor.

Continue with the trade-center classification as an example. Hodge made us aware that over time specific urban centers frequently jump from one categorical bin to another (Hodge, 1965; also volume I, pp. 92–94). This fact flashes a big yellow caution light on inferences we are tempted to draw based on the trade-center data. We were forced to apply the 1960 classification to 1940, 1950, and 1970 data as well. Thus, the 1940 shopping center data sets, and the 1940–70 shifts in behavior they displayed, were characterized *for those centers as classified by 1960 shopping center characteristics*.

There is another perishability problem that even the Hodge study does not reveal. Beyond the fact that the classification net may catch a different collection of "fish" when thrown into the pool on different occasions, there is also the problem that the net may only be constructed to catch the fish that are in the pool at a particular time, while fish that have evolved in a different era may swim right through the net. The collection of trading establishments termed a convenience center in 1940 might be quite different from the set that might sensibly be so named in 1970. Furthermore, the 1940 drugstore whose presence helps identify a convenience center may be a radically different establishment in 1970. The fact that we still call it a drugstore need not make it the same animal. In short, the set of relational connections lying behind the state classifications we employ can change radically without our quantitative data games giving any inkling of what is going on—especially when the problem-solving context necessarily involves underlying activity patterns. One has to be continuously alert to avoid cognitive illusion. Our profession has a pretty lethargic record.

There are several ways we have tried to improve on these tools by inventing state-variable surrogates that move us closer to inferred activities and by generating a small amount of activity data.[8] For example, when we talk about the characteristics of trade centers, we beg the question of what constitutes an urban system. Traditionally, urban centers have been designated by a combination of traits having to do with legal boundaries, spatial contiguity, and population density. In a dense nineteenth century town or city, statistical entities might enable one to infer something about transaction activities directly linked to local households. As the twentieth century centers spread, however, the ambiguity of the state-variable-determined boundaries increases and their utility decreases.

One adaptive response can be seen in the development of commuting data. These are crude activity data that have been employed to make more sophisticated boundary delineations for the Bureau of the Census "metropolitan areas" and also in delineating the urban transaction fields. This leads to an improvement over earlier boundary standards, but we are still left with serious difficulties. For example, the Census now defines a metropolitan area as a core city and the surrounding, closely settled areas that, among other things, send 15 percent or more of their residents to the central city for work. But, as the articulation of the transaction network has proceeded, substantial outlying areas are emerging in which work trips remain internalized or shared between neighboring concentrations in a multinodal field. Indeed there is evidence that spoke-to-hub nodality may be becoming a diminishing aspect of some transaction fields. Substantial urbanized populations may exist and many activities take place in such fields without being captured by such simplistic definitional boundaries. The statistical bins we call Standard Metropolitan Statistical Areas increasingly fail to capture reality, although the use of commuting data does allow for systematic revisions of a sort. The urban regions or transaction fields employed in this study suffer from similar limitations.

There is another important way that we in the profession have tried to get closer to activity data. It turns out that we do have sources of data about the commodity purchases and sales of business establishments. These have been employed to construct input–output accounts. The result is a matrix of commodity transactions that turns out to be one of the few genuine network representations in all of social statistics. These data structures and associated methodologies have generated great excitement and industry. But we get little help from this source in carrying out regional and urban studies. The widely bruited reason is the practical impossibility of developing a full set of genuine *interregional* coefficients. But there are, to my mind, far more important reasons that weaken the utility of the tool for network analysis at any level of spatial and functional aggregation.

The more serious difficulty emerges because input–output techniques were not designed to carry out process-oriented network analysis. To some extent this is an unavoidable consequence of the nature of the Standard Industrial Classification. The S.I.C. descriptors are first-level product classifiers rather than second level activity-process classifiers. But it is linked activities that determine the structure of a transaction network. Linking original and terminal states in an I–O table organizes only two-thirds of an activity datum (connecting process descriptions are omitted). In principle, and at an appropriate level of disaggregation, one might infer the nature of activity connections from the flow of commodities. In practice, this is often impossible, not only because of the establishment and product base of the Standard Industrial Classification (S.I.C.), but also because the I–O accounts were created by scholars who were little interested in either activity representation or in networking problems and methodologies.

The complications are of two sorts. First, underlying process characteristics were not taken into account in organizing data sets into the intermediate classifications commonly used. For example, the steel industry purchases zinc, which is used to galvanize steel. The I–O accounts thus show a network path leading from the zinc industry to the steel industry to all uses of steel. In fact, the steel industry is a bundle of processes. The galvanizing process is applied to only about 10 percent of the output. Thus, the table implies transaction paths that do not exist. Accordingly, if we use the zinc-steel coefficient to estimate the effects of a change in steel usage on the production of zinc, there is an enormous potential for error.[9]

A certain amount of this distortion is an inevitable consequence of the establishment-product-classification base of the S.I.C. The problem is even greater because those who constructed the accounts had only social accounting constructs and econometric modeling in mind. Despite the unique capabilities of the mathematical matrix model for network analysis, the I–O pioneers had little interest in this use. As a consequence, when intermediate aggregates were formed, rather obvious process sequences that could have guided the aggregation were ignored. Thus, even if one wishes to represent only a crude network of transactions between resource sectors, material-processing sectors, fabricating process sectors, and final demand, it is impossible to do so with the existing tables. Too many sectors are heterogeneous classifications in two or more of even these four broad attributes.

Disaggregation is only a limited solution to the problem. True, some improvement could be made if we formed intermediate classifications out of the most detailed codes, and with network analysis initially in mind. However, the problem has a more fundamental source. From the point of view of network analysis, the S.I.C. categories are not only process heterogeneous at every level, they are product heterogeneous as well (data being classified in accordance with the establishment's *primary* product). The most significant relationships are rendered inaccessible by these frozen data structures.

The meaning of linkages is further diminished by forcing the I–O structure into conformity with the national income and product accounts. For this reason, the interindustry transactions forming the core of the matrix are limited to current account transactions. Thus, the bulk of the interindustry transactions of capital good sectors (such as new construction and machinery manufacturing) are netted out to the final demand matrix margin. The structure of the remaining current account transactions of capital goods industries surely displays a markedly different network pattern than would be displayed by the excised capital account transactions.

Finally the I–O table is also seriously plagued with the problems of perishable descriptors. For example, total transportation service input coefficients declined substantially from 1947 to 1967 at the very time that transport services were becoming proportionately much more important. This was largely because with the advent of the motor vehicle, households and businesses took on many of the transport functions formerly provided by public transport enterprises. The transport input coefficients of all intermediate categories were distorted. The activity content of the classification descriptors changed without an adaptive change in the classification. This led to a nonsense representation.

There is a final grievous problem associated with traditional S.I.C. classifications. It arises out of the fixation on object-state descriptors. This creates a puzzle when we discover establishments that do not produce physical products at all (like financial, real estate, legal, and accounting enterprises). Many enterprises engage exclusively in third-or-fourth-level information processes. In these cases, *the process is the product*. The results of performance (that, for physical processes, occupy the first level of behavior) disappear as a concrete, observable manifestation of activity. Process linkages do not involve the intermediation of physical product transforms and transfers. We handle this problem by creating a fiction: We speak of "service products." We treat them as if they were physical products. (This is facilitated by the process of utilizing dollar value measurements rather than enumeration counts.)

This creates a major defect in traditional data structures. We wind up accounting for information-processing activities only where these are carried out by identifiable establishments that do nothing else. Where information processes are conducted inside establishments that produce physical products, it is commonly impossible to differentiate them from physical processes. Thus, the very fundamental conceptual and descriptive distinction between information processes and physical processes is totally confused by existing data structures. Indeed, standardized descriptors do not even accommodate the distinction.

All these representational problems are even worse if we wish to explain how urban networks change over time. You see, the source of all change is rooted in problem-solving responses to historical situations (carried out at the third and fourth levels of behavior—figure 1 in volume I). Every attribute of change can be traced to changes in behavior—to changes in ways of doing things and in ways of valuing things. But human values and technologies are described by activity and process statements not adequately represented by quantitative, object-state data structures. When we restrict ourselves to traditional representations, then we are forced to treat all higher order activities as if they are in a black box.

But the most serious aspect of the methodological limitation is the way it distorts our conceptual models of reality. With our conventional methodology we can only map object-state data structures onto history.[10] As a result, most regional and urban projection models are techniques for mapping empirically scaled growth models onto the future (or past). Such projections prove to be useful for limited managerial purposes if they cover a time span sufficiently short for structural inertia to be prominent. For any period of time running to a decade or more, the results turn out to be largely meaningless. It would be an extreme historical accident for the projected scalars to prove correct, because the model can in no way account for developmental changes. Some might claim a redeeming benefit by saying that the model can be made to serve policy. But in what fashion? The most it can do is say: "Look, this is what will happen if we do not introduce policy changes." But, how often does one need an elaborate, formal, empirical mapping to say this? Such models provide no guidance for determining what needs to be changed, or how to change it. All of these issues take root in the realm of technologies and values. One has no choice but to deal explicitly with the attributes of activities at the higher order levels of behavior.

We can only penetrate this realm by accounting for the historical, problem-solving process. This means we have to get inside the black boxes we have traditionally set aside. To do so means we have to treat activity data and process relations seriously. We must learn to manipulate relational methodologies (in addition to the explicitly classificational and statistical). We will have to work with nominal or qualitative data, as well as quantitative. This is even more difficult because many of us carrry a prejudice that this is not "true science." We erroneously speak of these kinds of data as "anecdotal"—a term with pejorative connotations. History is not considered to be science. There are a number of fundamental as well as phony issues in the philosophy of social science and history at play here, but there is not room for their elaboration. Suffice it to say, we cannot expect to deal successfully with change if we place the behavior fields where change is spawned off-limits to observation. We can no longer assume them to be inaccessible to objective and disciplined inquiry.[11]

Where does the shift-share technique so extensively employed in this volume come in? It stands revealed as a limited analytical scheme (see pp. 118 and 174–175 in volume I for a discussion of methodological limitations). It does use traditional data and methods in a way that moves us closer to the developmental processes we have to tackle. It attempts to portray *the structure of the changes in structure* generated by historical change, as recorded by conventional, object-state data sets. In doing so, it makes a pseudodistinction between the growth elements (mix effects) and developmental elements (competitive effects) involved in change. It generates a novel description of historical change that provides different insights. It moves us into a discussion of developmental factors in an orderly fashion. It provides the discipline of a data framework that assigns some order-of-importance to historical materials. However, it is only a transitional tool used to sweep complexity under the rug until we can obtain a preliminary grasp on the nature of change.[12]

It is the intention of this closing chapter to leave you with this thought: The future is also not the same as it used to be for regional and urban studies. We need to learn new techniques; we need to develop and employ new data sources; we need to open up the black box of activities and the historical process. If we do not, we increasingly run the risk of reifying empirical constructions that are closed to those fields of reality that have most to do with the social problems and social processes that must concern us.

Notes

1. So-called because the overgrazing of the village commons became the metaphor for the genre.

2. "Matrix management," "participatory management," and "intrapreneurship" techniques of great variety are replacing older "command and control" methods. Both the new compunication technologies and the new managerial innovations tend to rely heavily on "distributed information-processing strategies" that employ semiautonomous subsystems where "spans of control" are appropriately matched with the span of subordinate fields of disturbance. In terms of cybernetic theory, it is a means of expanding "requisite variety" to match complexity.

3. For example, over 1,400 government entities exist in the New York metropolitan region alone, each with the capacity to raise and spend money and provide services. Can there be any doubt that the well-publicized difficulties of the region are at least partially rooted in this phenomenon?

4. On the day this page was penned the "op ed" page of *The Washington Post* offered up this gem: "This is the tragedy of modern America. The people who make things have been replaced by the people who shuffle paper and get paid lots of money for producing absolutely nothing."

5. For example, The Urban Growth and New Community Development Act of 1970. See also the work of Sundquist (1975), 1978.

6. This presupposition has been challenged on somewhat similar grounds by Pred (1977).

7. In other words, they either count objects, like people, or count the number of people in the "state" of working. In the latter case, an activity involving a time frame and process signature is treated *as if* it were a stated object. The datum is abstracted from its dynamic and relational referents. Key to the following discussion is the epistomological distinction between "states" and "processes" as distinct cognitive structures.

8. One technique, which will be mentioned only in passing, is exemplified by migration estimates. By counting the population of two or more regions at two points in time, then making an adjustment for estimates of natural increase, we *infer* that the remaining difference must reflect a from→to movement on the part of some people. This still does not count as a record of activity moves because only the net effect of a gross set of moves is estimated. The actual number of moves, and the total moves from one cell to another, remain clouded in the absence of direct observation of second-level activities.

9. I am indebted to Stedman Noble (1981) for this example.

10. Our conceptual models of change turn out to be crude scalar growth models. (The nature and limitations of such models were discussed in chapters 3 and 4 in volume I.) The principal exceptions are stage theory models that have never had much play in the regional and urban fields. These do allow for true development, but they try to establish a sequence of stages through which development must proceed. These theories view history as a deterministic process—as prophecy.

The historical record is full of evidence to challenge such a proposition. The fact that such stages are only discernible at an exceedingly high level of aggregation is, itself, a demonstration of theoretical weakness. This is not to deny that physical and biological process constraints do not help set the historical agenda and limit the policy options available to human-social responses. But historical stage theories are not typically presented as a representation of the range of adaptive possibilities offered by history. The limitations of growth models and the philosophical grounds for challenging historicist models are discussed in Dunn (1971).

11. There are possibilities that social science has not begun to explore. Take one example. The mathematical logic of relations and relational mathematics are both highly developed as formal tools. Relational mathematics can operate on nominal data as well as dimensionalized data. Thus, it is quite possible to form network representations of process technologies and subject them to an analysis of connective patterns without any recourse to quantitative data. Such constructions could then be utilized to trace some of the possible structural changes implicit in a variety of policy proposals. These could be future-mappings with real problem-solving relevance.

12. Some have proposed that shift-share be used as a component of predictive models, but thus applied, the technique does not escape any of the limitations common to all growth models. I do not favor this use.

Appendixes

(Appendixes II-E, II-F, II-G, II-L, II-M, and II-N are on microfiche inside the back cover.)

APPENDIX II-A. Industry-Sector Gross Shift Components, 1940–70, 1940–50, 1950–60, 1960–70
(Each Summed—Without Regard to Sign—Across 173 Urban Regions)#
(1940–70, 1940–50, 1950–60, 1960–70)

Time Period	National Growth Effect G_{ij}	% of Total #2	Total Interregional Differential D_{ij}	% of Total #2	Industry Mix Effect k_{ij}	% of Total #2	Region Share (Compet.) Effect R_{ij}	% of Total #2	D_{ij} as % of Base Empl.	k_{ij} as % of Base Empl.	R_{ij} as % of Base Empl.	R_{ij} as % of k_{ij}
Total Employment 1 (Net summary line shift components summed across 171 regions)												
1940-70	33,931,997		8,679,070		6,907,003		9,473,254		19.1	15.2	20.9	137.2
1940-50	12,099,066		2,331,376		2,173,459		2,410,961		5.1	4.8	5.3	110.9
1950-60	8,897,744		2,988,291		2,166,120		2,984,677		5.2	3.8	5.2	137.8
1960-70	12,935,240		2,830,087		1,352,866		2,911,957		4.3	2.0	4.4	215.2
Total Employment 2 (Gross industry line shift components below summed across 31 industry sectors)												
1940-70	49,546,001	100.0	14,399,947	100.0	10,268,899	100.0	12,688,367	100.0	33.1	22.6	27.9	123.6
1940-50	16,499,491	100.0	4,933,984	100.0	3,607,001	100.0	4,468,177	100.0	10.9	7.9	9.8	123.9
1950-60	16,469,864	100.0	6,013,712	100.0	3,786,355	100.0	4,874,830	100.0	10.5	6.6	8.5	128.7
1960-70	19,240,991	100.0	5,507,041	100.0	2,777,639	100.0	4,679,510	100.0	8.3	4.2	7.1	168.5
1 Agriculture												
1940-70	* 5,795,360	11.7	2,339,952	15.6	2,049,799	20.0	594,955	4.7	27.3	23.9	6.9	29.0
1940-50	* 1,500,445	9.1	749,845	15.2	530,707	14.7	922,122	20.6	8.8	6.2	10.0	173.8
1950-60	* 2,673,958	16.2	1,158,922	19.3	972,008	25.7	397,342	8.2	16.4	13.8	5.6	40.9
1960-70	* 1,620,951	8.4	697,364	12.7	595,178	21.4	232,084	5.0	15.8	13.4	5.2	39.0
2 Forestry and Fisheries												
1940-70	12,754	.0	35,286	.2	7,121	.1	30,922	.2	32.0	6.4	28.0	434.2
1940-50	653	.0	12,977	.3	316	.0	26,110	.6	11.8	.3	23.6	8262.7
1950-60	* 31,052	.2	26,970	.4	15,942	.4	15,388	.3	21.0	12.4	12.0	96.5
1960-70	17,634	.1	14,757	.3	9,851	.4	14,761	.3	14.9	9.9	14.9	149.8
3 Mining												
1940-70	* 291,152	.6	364,485	2.4	172,203	1.7	226,437	1.8	39.3	18.6	24.4	131.5
1940-50	13,465	.1	114,800	2.3	7,963	.2	114,734	2.6	12.4	.9	12.4	1440.8
1950-60	* 270,522	1.6	270,873	4.5	161,827	4.3	153,488	3.1	28.8	17.2	16.3	94.8
1960-70	* 34,093	.2	84,962	1.5	19,596	.7	73,391	1.6	12.7	2.9	11.0	374.5
4 Construction												
1940-70	2,390,388	4.8	561,110	3.7	192,185	1.9	510,479	4.0	26.6	9.1	24.1	265.6
1940-50	1,407,436	8.5	289,049	5.9	113,155	3.1	271,395	6.1	13.7	5.4	12.9	239.8
1950-60	459,257	2.8	220,825	3.7	37,527	1.0	216,129	4.4	6.3	1.1	6.1	575.9
1960-70	523,693	2.7	230,536	4.2	37,353	1.3	221,794	4.7	5.7	.9	5.5	593.7
Total Manufacturing												
1940-70	9,325,903	18.8	2,241,832	14.9	2,727,251	26.6	3,671,137	28.9	20.9	25.4	34.2	134.6
1940-50	4,043,085	24.5	748,846	15.2	1,022,650	28.4	744,791	16.7	7.0	9.5	6.9	72.8
1950-60	3,443,828	20.9	856,039	14.2	921,796	24.3	1,298,045	26.6	5.8	6.2	8.8	140.8
1960-70	1,838,986	9.6	1,116,706	20.3	538,212	19.4	1,371,526	29.3	6.1	3.0	7.5	254.8

APPENDIX II-A (*continued*)

Time Period	G_{ij}	%	D_{ij}	%	k_{ij}	%	R_{ij}	%	D_{ij} % of Base Empl.	k_{ij} % of Base Empl.	R_{ij} % of Base Empl.	R_{ij} % of k_{ij}
5 Food and Kindred Products Manufacturing												
1940-70	360,435	.7	210,489	1.4	61,549	.6	221,526	1.7	18.8	5.5	19.7	359.9
1940-50	311,093	1.9	86,588	1.8	53,120	1.5	67,778	1.5	7.7	4.7	6.0	127.6
1950-60	460,552	2.8	101,659	1.7	77,958	2.1	117,062	2.4	7.1	5.4	8.2	150.2
1960-70	* 415,210	2.2	110,160	2.0	58,258	2.1	105,069	2.2	5.8	3.1	5.5	180.4
6 Textiles Manufacturing												
1940-70	* 143,420	.3	31,718	2.1	80,012	.8	294,154	2.3	26.7	6.9	25.2	367.6
1940-50	88,459	.5	99,833	2.0	49,347	1.4	80,881	1.8	8.6	4.2	6.9	163.9
1950-60	* 271,735	1.6	200,774	3.3	158,969	4.2	141,805	2.9	16.0	12.7	11.3	89.2
1960-70	39,851	.2	124,695	2.3	23,839	.9	116,940	2.5	12.7	2.4	11.9	490.5
7 Apparel Manufacturing												
1940-70	490,585	1.0	366,530	2.4	213,516	2.1	463,376	3.7	45.0	26.2	56.9	217.0
1940-50	264,758	1.6	131,728	2.7	115,230	3.2	98,900	2.2	16.2	14.1	12.1	85.8
1950-60	132,627	.8	151,710	2.5	54,879	1.4	167,436	3.4	14.1	5.1	15.5	305.1
1960-70	93,203	.5	187,573	3.4	36,137	1.3	194,233	4.2	15.5	3.0	16.0	537.5
8 Printing and Allied Products Manufacturing												
1940-70	761,949	1.5	157,293	1.0	167,925	1.6	152,942	1.2	24.5	26.1	23.8	91.1
1940-50	224,469	1.4	50,876	1.0	49,471	1.4	39,087	.9	34.9	7.7	6.1	79.0
1950-60	327,689	2.0	60,325	1.0	65.309	1.7	56,827	1.2	7.0	7.5	6.6	87.0
1960-70	209,776	1.1	59,190	1.1	35,717	1.3	61,967	1.3	4.9	3.0	5.2	173.5
9 Chemicals and Allied Products Manufacturing												
1940-70	606,723	1.2	209,721	1.4	178,343	1.7	194,736	1.5	47.0	39.9	43.6	109.2
1940-50	221,381	1.3	83,910	1.7	64,887	1.8	68,676	1.5	18.8	14.5	15.4	105.8
1950-60	233,472	1.4	96,869	1.6	66,859	1.8	86,795	1.8	14.5	10.0	13.0	128.8
1960-70	151,873	.8	87,050	1.6	45,624	1.6	86,121	1.8	9.7	5.1	9.6	183.8
10 Lumber Products and Furniture Manufacturing												
1940-70	84,994	.2	159,932	1.1	31,757	.3	162,744	1.3	16.8	3.3	17.1	512.5
1940-50	255,773	1.6	137,947	2.8	95,566	2.6	99,508	2.2	14.5	10.0	10.5	104.1
1950-60	* 107,051	.6	120,718	2.0	41,942	1.1	94,353	1.9	10.0	3.5	7.8	225.0
1960-70	* 63,730	.3	82,610	1.5	24,454	.9	74,882	1.6	7.5	2.2	6.8	306.2
11 Total Machinery Manufacturing												
1940-70	3,058,997	6.2	766,584	5.1	1,205,406	11.7	1,003,411	7.9	70.5	110.9	92.3	83.2
1940-50	1,022,283	6.2	360,946	7.3	402,832	11.2	122,492	2.7	33.2	37.1	11.3	30.4
1950-60	1,078,406	6.5	323,414	5.4	401,424	10.6	387,564	8.0	15.3	19.0	18.4	96.5
1960-70	958,313	5.0	327,066	5.9	281,918	10.1	420,047	9.0	10.3	8.9	13.2	149.0
12 Motor Vehicles and Equipment Manufacturing												
1940-70	492,205	1.0	264,313	1.8	330,780	3.2	246,162	1.9	45.5	56.9	42.4	74.4
1940-50	298,547	1.8	179,240	3.6	200,638	5.6	81,474	1.8	30.8	34.5	14.0	40.6
1950-60	* 5,001	.0	113,259	1.9	3,171	.1	111,101	2.3	12.9	.4	12.6	3503.7
1960-70	198,651	1.0	138,884	2.5	119,714	4.3	102,821	2.2	15.9	13.7	11.8	85.9

APPENDIX II-A (*continued*)

Time Period	G_{ij}	%	D_{ij}	%	k_{ij}	%	R_{ij}	%	D_{ij} % of Base Empl.	k_{ij} % of Base Empl.	R_{ij} % of Base Empl.	R_{ij} % of k_{ij}
13 Transportation Equipment, Excluding Motor Vehicle Manufacturing												
1940-70	886,030	1.8	473,964	3.2	437,063	4.3	465,898	3.7	152.2	140.3	149.6	106.6
1940-50	176,553	1.1	117,013	2.4	87,090	2.4	100,970	2.3	37.6	28.0	32.4	115.9
1950-60	530,147	3.2	277,225	4.6	239,913	6.3	189,386	3.9	56.8	49.2	38.8	78.9
1960-70	179,353	.9	152,023	2.8	73,722	2.7	155,885	3.3	15.0	7.3	15.4	211.4
14 Other Manufacturing												
1940-70	2,727,405	5.5	752,962	5.0	841,024	8.2	1,210,431	9.5	20.8	23.3	33.5	143.9
1940-50	1,179,769	7.2	294,958	6.0	363,797	10.1	274,840	6.2	8.2	10.1	7.6	75.5
1950-60	1,060,722	6.4	325,972	5.4	289,063	7.6	481,300	9.9	6.8	6.0	10.0	166.5
1960-70	486,906	2.5	460,369	8.4	105,428	3.8	500,463	10.7	7.9	1.8	8.6	474.7
15 Railroad Transportation												
1940-70	* 476,140	1.0	94,613	.6	88,439	.9	65,987	.5	8.2	7.7	5.7	74.6
1940-50	254,397	1.5	83,485	1.7	47,253	1.3	58,230	1.3	7.3	4.1	5.1	123.2
1950-60	* 428,741	2.6	94,117	1.6	84,882	2.2	48,340	1.0	6.7	6.0	3.4	56.9
1960-70	* 301,805	1.6	68,066	1.2	65,115	2.3	35,042	.7	7.0	6.7	3.6	53.8
16 Trucking and Warehousing												
1940-70	641,628	1.3	137,993	.9	59,033	.6	139,185	1.1	26.9	11.5	27.1	235.7
1940-50	198,980	1.2	44.450	.9	18,304	.5	40,522	.9	8.7	3.6	7.9	221.4
1950-60	236,705	1.4	56,930	.9	21,695	.6	57,744	1.2	8.0	3.0	8.1	266.2
1960-70	205,950	1.1	50,073	.9	19,627	.7	53,194	1.1	5.3	2.1	5.6	271.0
17 Other Transportation and Services												
1940-70	640,879	1.3	247,603	1.7	175,267	1.7	190,260	1.5	45.0	31.9	34.6	108.6
1940-50	324,030	2.0	72,707	1.5	88,619	2.5	62,649	1.4	13.2	16.1	11.4	70.7
1950-60	54,822	.3	78,559	1.3	12,228	.3	71,128	1.5	9.0	1.4	8.1	581.7
1960-70	262,021	1.4	99,159	1.8	63,514	2.3	74,233	1.6	10.7	6.9	8.0	116.9
18 Communications												
1940-70	748,052	1.5	165,430	1.1	114,769	1.1	173,709	1.4	41.4	28.7	43.5	151.4
1940-50	319,382	1.9	47,601	1.0	48,999	1.4	44,944	1.0	11.9	12.3	11.3	91.7
1950-60	135,534	.8	45,783	.8	15,690	.4	49,517	1.0	6.4	2.2	6.9	315.6
1960-70	293,149	1.5	81,283	1.5	26,177	.9	77,129	1.6	9.6	3.1	9.1	294.6
19 Utilities												
1940-70	509,759	1.0	141,399	.9	66,540	.6	178,174	1.4	25.6	12.1	32.3	267.8
1940-50	243,401	1.5	56,017	1.1	31,768	.9	73,386	1.6	10.2	5.8	13.3	231.0
1950-60	138,683	.8	54,386	.9	10,209	.3	54,347	1.1	6.8	1.3	6.8	532.3
1960-70	127,671	.7	51,234	.9	8,524	.3	53,766	1.1	5.5	.1	5.8	630.8
20 Wholesale Trade												
1940-70	1,961,028	4.0	357,357	2.4	273,680	2.7	340,585	2.7	29.2	22.4	27.8	124.4
1940-50	781,809	4.7	129,972	2.6	109,111	3.0	104,868	2.3	10.6	8.9	8.6	96.1
1950-60	301,095	1.8	114,227	1.9	35,091	.9	117,814	2.4	5.7	1.8	5.9	335.7
1960-70	878,126	4.6	174,429	3.2	87,644	3.2	176,957	3.8	7.6	3.8	7.7	201.9

APPENDIX II-A *(continued)*

Time Period	G_{ij}	%	D_{ij}	%	k_{ij}	%	R_{ij}	%	D_{ij} % of Base Empl.	k_{ij} % of Base Empl	R_{ij} % of Base Empl.	R_{ij} % of k_{ij}
Total Retail Trade												
1940-70	5,928,499	12.0	1,357,303	9.0	483,861	4.7	1,368,678	10.8	21.0	7.5	21.2	282.9
1940-50	2,273,929	13.8	398,491	8.1	189,207	5.2	463,569	10.4	6.2	2.9	7.2	245.0
1950-60	1,247,105	7.6	416,401	6.9	53,241	1.4	411,881	8.4	4.8	.6	4.7	773.6
1960-70	2,407,479	12.5	458,708	8.3	76,826	2.8	452,916	9.7	4.6	.8	4.5	589.5
21 Eating and Drinking Places												
1940-70	1,394,726	2.8	327,147	2.2	172,618	1.7	309,419	2.4	28.0	14.8	26.4	179.3
1940-50	579,516	3.5	91,888	1.9	71,723	2.0	97,672	2.2	7.9	6.1	8.3	136.2
1950-60	160,701	1.0	81,652	1.4	13,134	.3	82,348	1.7	4.8	.8	4.8	627.0
1960-70	654,514	3.4	152,950	2.8	42,023	1.5	148,858	3.2	8.2	2.3	8.0	354.2
22 Food and Dairy Stores												
1940-70	558,866	1.1	214,178	1.4	48,740	.5	237,931	1.9	14.4	3.3	16.0	488.2
1940-50	230,370	1.4	91,368	1.9	20,309	.6	105,060	2.4	6.1	1.4	7.1	517.3
1950-60	9,691	.1	81,210	1.4	435	.0	81,368	1.7	4.6	.0	4.6	18705.3
1960-70	318,812	1.7	78,326	1.4	12,921	.5	84,184	1.8	4.4	.7	4.7	651.5
23 Other Retail												
1940-70	3,974,907	8.0	845,723	5.6	282,953	2.8	857,217	6.8	22.3	7.4	22.6	303.0
1940-50	1,464,043	8.9	247,140	5.0	105,449	2.9	271,778	6.1	6.5	2.8	7.2	257.7
1950-60	1,076,713	6.5	278,318	4.6	44,689	1.2	274,336	5.6	5.3	.8	5.2	613.9
1960-70	1,434,153	7.5	260,013	4.7	52,859	1.9	261,442	5.6	4.1	.8	4.1	494.6
24 Finance, Insurance and Real Estate												
1940-70	2,412,515	4.9	508,613	3.4	516,968	5.0	581,367	4.6	34.2	34.7	39.1	112.5
1940-50	452,957	2.7	91,769	1.9	97,059	2.7	115,478	2.6	6.2	6.5	7.8	119.0
1950-60	872,576	5.3	167,164	2.8	149,728	4.0	170,199	3.5	8.6	7.7	8.8	113.7
1960-70	1,086,988	5.6	193,747	3.5	145,697	5.2	156,367	3.3	6.9	5.2	5.6	107.3
Total Services												
1940-70	11,427,505	23.1	2,347,491	15.7	1,040,555	10.0	2,357,493	18.6	26.7	11.8	26.8	226.6
1940-50	1,498,316	9.1	455,748	9.2	231,756	6.4	527,096	11.8	5.2	2.6	6.0	227.4
1950-60	3,868,363	23.5	689,527	11.5	207,668	5.5	637,142	13.1	6.7	2.0	6.2	306.8
1960-70	6,060,863	31.5	810,224	14.7	412,387	14.8	704,880	15.1	5.7	2.9	5.0	170.9
25 Lodging Places and Personal Services												
1940-70	516,355	1.0	297,106	2.0	51,243	.5	292,630	2.3	17.2	3.0	16.9	571.1
1940-50	172,529	1.0	93,004	1.9	17,124	.5	94,250	2.1	5.4	1.0	5.5	550.4
1950-60	137,600	.8	108,473	1.8	10,087	.3	104,726	2.1	5.7	.5	5.5	1038.2
1960-70	206,232	1.1	118,057	2.1	13,541	.5	114,452	2.4	5.7	.7	5.5	845.2
26 Business and Repair Services												
1940-70	1,527,252	3.1	427,660	2.9	147,420	1.4	353,770	2.8	48.5	16.7	40.1	240.0
1940-50	451,492	2.7	59,360	1.2	43,585	1.2	63,695	1.4	6.7	4.9	7.2	146.1
1950-60	350,139	2.1	185,657	3.1	26,140	.7	171,734	3.5	13.9	2.0	12.9	657.0
1960-70	725,629	3.8	173,448	3.1	80,835	2.9	129,432	2.8	10.3	4.8	7.7	160.1

APPENDIX II-A *(continued)*

Time Period	G_{ij}	%	D_{ij}	%	k_{ij}	%	R_{ij}	%	D_{ij} % of Base Empl.	k_{ij} % of Base Empl.	R_{ij} % of Base Empl.	R_{ij} % of k_{ij}
27 Amusement and Recreation Services												
1940-70	228,562	.5	93,664	.6	39,785	.4	81,465	.6	23.1	9.8	20.1	204.8
1940-50	98,646	.6	25,115	.5	17,168	.5	32,660	.7	6.2	4.2	8.0	190.2
1950-60	23,903	.1	35,299	.6	3,133	.1	33,216	.7	7.0	.6	6.6	1060.2
1960-70	106,017	.6	41,165	.7	14,931	.5	35,671	.8	7.7	2.8	6.6	238.9
28 Private Households												
1940-70	* 1,088,226	2.2	211,967	1.4	146,959	1.4	179,059	1.4	8.9	6.2	7.5	121.8
1940-50	* 708,258	4.3	102,481	2.1	95,645	2.7	115,930	2.6	4.3	3.9	4.9	121.2
1950-60	328,621	2.0	150,967	2.5	58,411	1.5	133,230	2.7	9.0	3.5	7.9	228.1
1960-70	* 708,596	3.7	133,268	2.4	129,298	4.7	64,083	1.4	6.5	6.3	3.1	49.6
29 Professional Services												
1940-70	10,243,562	20.7	1,564,508	10.4	795,056	7.7	1,565,389	12.3	46.3	23.5	46.3	196.9
1940-50	1,483,907	9.0	241,759	4.9	115,173	3.2	264,552	5.9	7.2	3.4	7.8	229.7
1950-60	3,028,100	18.4	374,049	6.2	192,083	5.1	326,662	6.7	7.7	4.0	6.7	170.1
1960-70	5,731,581	29.8	539,392	10.0	302,134	10.9	455,277	9.7	6.8	3.8	5.8	150.7
30 Civilian Government												
1940-70	2,831,759	5.7	849,768	5.7	376,074	3.7	669,334	5.3	56.8	25.1	44.7	178.0
1940-50	1,042,550	6.3	323,480	6.6	138,456	3.8	256,294	5.7	21.6	9.2	17.1	185.1
1950-60	791,151	4.8	242,618	4.0	125,889	3.3	186,911	4.0	9.6	5.0	7.4	148.5
1960-70	998,041	5.2	284,401	5.2	148,273	5.3	193,459	4.1	8.7	4.5	5.9	130.5
31 Armed Forces												
1940-70	1,689,488	3.4	940,879	6.3	944,672	9.2	694,713	5.5	308.0	309.2	227.4	73.5
1940-50	728,140	4.4	422,678	8.6	407,137	11.3	297,242	6.7	138.4	133.3	97.3	73.0
1950-60	752,898	4.6	414,788	4.2	396,040	10.5	295,234	6.1	40.4	38.6	28.8	74.5
1960-70	208,469	1.1	250,791	4.6	97,737	3.5	205,506	4.4	14.5	5.6	11.9	210.3

* Industry sectors whose total growth rates are negative.

\# We can only compute the gross shift-share components for each industry sector if we take into account an asymmetry in the output matrix generated by the method. When we add the shift-share components for a region across the thirty-one industry sectors, there is some offsetting of effects but a meaningful and interpretive residual remains. The summary line reveals a total outcome reflecting the influence of all activities. However, when we sum the shift-share components for a single industry across 173 urban regions, the mix and share components add to zero precisely because of the way they are defined. The shifts of employment out of one set of regions has to equal the shift into another set. The solution is to add these two shift components without regard to sign and divide by two.

(shaded) Industry-Sector percentage shift greater than All-Sector percentage shift.

APPENDIX II-B. Shift-Share Computations by Industry Sector for B-Code Category Synthetic Regions

Panel A: Six-Sector Grouping

B-Code	1940 Sector Employment	Col 1 % of Total Empl.	Employment Change $G_{ij}+k_{ij}+R_{ij}$	G_{ij}	k_{ij}	R_{ij}	% Total ± R_{ij}	R_{ij} % of 1940 Empl.	R_{ij} % of k_{ij}	Total Employ. Growth Rate %
All-Sector Employment										
B-1	5,620,224	12.4	+ 14,056,587	+ 4,202,807	+ 1,513,391	+ 8,340,389	+ 56.4	148.4	551.1	+ 250.1
B-2	1,838,807	4.1	+ 2,440,473	+ 1,375,058	+ 734,124	+ 331,291	+ 2.2	18.0	45.1	+ 132.7
B-3	4,015,102	8.9	+ 6,665,440	+ 2,986,126	- 1,148,577	+ 4,827,891	+ 32.6	120.2	420.3	+ 166.0
B-4	3,496,929	7.7	+ 3,314,301	+ 2,615,004	+ 1,491,437	- 792,140	- 5.4	22.7	53.1	+ 94.8
B-5	14,607,008	32.3	+ 4,824,582	+ 10,923,129	+ 5,100,398	- 11,198,945	- 75.6	76.7	219.5	+ 31.0
B-6	5,704,085	12.6	+ 1,926,735	+ 4,255,361	- 3,619,018	+ 1,290,392	+ 8.7	22.6	35.7	+ 33.8
B-7	3,710,883	8.2	+ 721,808	+ 2,774,999	- 374,333	- 1,678,858	- 11.3	45.2	448.5	+ 19.5
B-8	6,228,146	13.8	- 267,937	+ 4,642,743	- 3,776,975	- 1,133,705	- 7.7	18.2	30.1	- 4.3
Total	45,221,184	100.0	+ 33,681,989	+ 33,775,227	± 8,879,127	± 14,796,806	± 100.0	32.7	166.6	+ 74.5
Resource Sectors										
B-1	544,498	6.4	- 131,364	- 750,427	+ 415,494	+ 203,639	+ 41.2	37.4	49.0	- 24.1
B-2	126,130	1.5	- 67,784	- 245,523	+ 166,000	+ 16,739	+ 3.4	13.3	10.1	- 49.8
B-3	1,210,863	2.5	- 564,946	- 533,184	- 237,767	+ 206,005	+ 41.7	17.0	86.6	- 46.7
B-4	161,648	1.9	- 73,141	- 466,919	+ 364,193	+ 29,585	+ 6.0	18.3	8.1	- 45.2
B-5	456,103	5.3	- 235,334	- 1,950,366	+ 1,676,521	+ 38,511	+ 7.8	8.4	2.3	- 51.6
B-6	2,863,864	33.4	- 2,037,413	- 759,810	- 1,111,866	- 165,737	- 34.2	5.8	14.9	- 71.1
B-7	884,300	10.3	- 599,514	- 495,486	+ 18,517	- 122,545	- 25.3	13.9	661.8	- 67.8
B-8	3,314,971	38.7	- 2,303,024	- 828,979	- 1,277,353	- 196,692	- 40.6	5.9	15.4	- 69.5
Total	9,562,377	100.0	- 6,007,520	- 6,030,694	± 2,633,856	± 489,727	± 100.0	5.1	18.6	- 62.8
Total Manufacturing Minus Printing and Publishing										
B-1	1,056,508	10.5	+ 2,852,417	+ 1,054,564	- 52,314	+ 1,850,167	+ 40.4	175.1	3536.7	270.0
B-2	501,509	5.0	+ 461,908	+ 345,028	+ 125,377	- 8,497	- .2	1.7	6.8	+ 92.1
B-3	783,566	7.8	+ 1,536,514	+ 749,275	- 394,173	+ 1,181,412	+ 25.8	150.8	299.7	+ 196.1
B-4	1,050,555	10.4	+ 722,794	+ 656,156	+ 576,924	- 510,286	- 11.1	48.6	88.4	+ 68.8
B-5	4,555,696	45.2	+ 500,161	+ 2,740,821	+ 1,691,385	- 3,932,045	- 85.6	86.3	232.5	+ 11.0
B-6	795,279	7.9	+ 1,433,669	+ 1,067,754	- 812,990	+ 1,178,905	+ 25.7	148.2	145.0	+ 180.3
B-7	809,674	8.0	+ 371,387	+ 696,299	- 183,421	- 141,491	- 3.1	17.5	77.1	+ 45.9
B-8	535,186	5.3	+ 618,197	+ 1,164,953	- 921,452	+ 374,696	+ 8.2	70.0	40.7	+ 115.5
Total	10,087,973	100.0	+ 8,497,047	+ 8,474,850	± 2,379,018	± 4,588,750	± 100.0	45.5	192.9	+ 84.2

APPENDIX II-B Panel A (*continued*)

B-Code	1940 Sector Employment	Col 1 % of Total Empl.	Employment Change $G_{ij}+k_{ij}+R_{ij}$	G_{ij}	k_{ij}	R_{ij}	% Total $\pm R_{ij}$	R_{ij} % of 1940 Empl.	R_{ij} % of k_{ij}	Total Employ. Growth Rate %
Linkage Sectors										
B-1	1,001,171	15.4	+ 2,699,663	+ 907,006	+ 269,767	+ 1,522,890	+ 60.7	152.1	564.5	+ 269.7
B-2	317,132	4.9	+ 440,421	+ 286,935	+ 56,508	+ 96,978	+ 3.9	30.6	171.6	+ 102.8
B-3	428,292	6.6	+ 1,190,283	+ 623,121	- 188,078	+ 755,240	+ 30.1	176.3	401.6	+ 277.9
B-4	630,229	9.7	+ 623,777	+ 545,674	+ 158,160	- 80,057	- 3.2	12.7	50.6	+ 99.0
B-5	2,777,483	42.7	+ 1,190,816	+ 2,279,345	+ 923,322	- 2,011,851	- 79.2	72.4	217.9	+ 42.9
B-6	391,951	6.0	+ 501,724	+ 887,971	- 518,362	+ 132,115	+ 5.3	33.7	25.5	+ 128.0
B-7	476,515	7.3	+ 162,909	+ 579,062	- 165,365	- 250,788	- 9.9	52.6	151.7	+ 34.2
B-8	480,307	7.4	+ 248,477	+ 968,809	- 523,221	- 197,111	- 7.8	41.0	37.7	+ 51.7
Total	6,503,080	100.0	+ 7,058,070	+ 7,077,923	± 1,401,392	± 2,523,515	± 100.0	38.8	180.1	+ 108.5
Total Retail										
B-1	946,160	14.7	+ 2,232,882	+ 743,729	+ 149,173	+ 1,339,980	+ 58.2	141.6	898.3	+ 236.0
B-2	288,107	4.5	+ 373,638	+ 243,332	+ 24,189	+ 106,117	+ 4.6	36.8	438.7	+ 129.7
B-3	505,165	7.8	+ 1,182,499	+ 523,426	- 61,777	+ 715,850	+ 31.1	141.7	1158.8	+ 234.1
B-4	556,779	8.6	+ 512,152	+ 462,752	+ 57,603	- 8,203	- .4	1.5	14.2	+ 92.0
B-5	2,510,320	39.0	+ 503,498	+ 1,932,961	+ 401,349	- 1,830,812	- 78.8	72.9	456.2	+ 20.1
B-6	512,265	8.0	+ 608,644	+ 753,030	- 283,523	+ 139,137	+ 6.0	27.2	49.1	+ 118.8
B-7	508,599	7.9	+ 183,286	+ 491,066	- 23,632	- 279,148	- 12.0	54.9	1181.2	+ 37.0
B-8	614,560	9.5	+ 360,168	+ 821,582	- 255,988	- 205,426	- 8.8	33.4	80.2	+ 58.6
Total	6,441,955	100.0	+ 5,961,767	+ 5,976,878	± 628,617	± 2,312,337	± 100.0	35.9	367.8	+ 92.5
Personal Services										
B-1	672,319	16.4	+ 221,054	- 57,720	- 24,451	+ 303,225	+ 51.2	45.1	1240.1	+ 32.9
B-2	168,633	4.1	+ 6,476	- 18,885	+ 3,132	+ 22,229	+ 3.8	13.2	709.7	+ 3.8
B-3	391,614	9.5	+ 134,816	- 41,010	- 19,395	+ 195,221	+ 33.0	49.9	1006.6	+ 34.4
B-4	337,465	8.2	- 64,493	- 35,914	- 2,067	- 26,512	- 4.4	7.9	1282.6	- 19.1
B-5	1,360,124	33.1	- 541,796	- 150,015	+ 84,028	- 475,809	- 79.0	35.0	566.3	- 39.8
B-6	421,072	10.3	- 17,659	- 58,442	- 30,339	+ 71,122	+ 12.0	16.9	234.4	- 4.2
B-7	319,229	7.8	- 105,758	- 38,111	+ 2,030	- 69,677	- 11.6	21.8	3432.4	- 33.1
B-8	434,269	10.6	- 107,336	- 63,762	- 13,234	- 30,340	- 5.0	7.0	229.3	- 24.7
Total	4,104,725	100.0	- 474,696	- 463,859	± 89,338	± 597,068	± 100.0	14.5	668.3	- 11.6
Information Services										
B-1	951,110	15.3	+ 4,716,820	+ 1,819,121	+ 380,890	+ 2,516,809	+ 65.5	264.6	660.8	+ 495.9
B-2	342,599	5.5	+ 912,936	+ 595,173	+ 64,445	+ 253,318	+ 6.6	73.9	393.1	+ 266.5
B-3	482,828	7.8	+ 2,222,486	+ 1,292,497	- 141,441	+ 1,071,430	+ 27.9	221.9	757.5	+ 460.3
B-4	536,117	8.6	+ 1,273,902	+ 1,131,864	+ 167,334	- 25,296	- .7	4.7	15.1	+ 237.6
B-5	2,216,285	35.7	+ 3,093,176	+ 4,727,907	+ 516,866	- 2,151,597	- 55.4	97.1	416.3	+ 139.6
B-6	509,637	8.2	+ 1,054,034	+ 1,841,867	- 591,846	- 195,987	- 5.0	38.5	33.1	+ 206.8
B-7	545,986	8.8	+ 590,544	+ 1,201,116	+ 89,417	- 699,989	- 18.0	128.2	782.8	+ 108.2
B-8	625,902	10.1	+ 719,661	+ 2,009,538	- 480,423	- 809,454	- 20.8	129.3	168.5	+ 115.0
Total	6,210,464	100.0	+ 14,583,559	+ 14,619,083	± 1,216,331	± 3,861,940	± 100.0	62.2	317.5	+ 234.8

(shaded) Industry sector ratios greater than corresponding ratios for all-sector employment

APPENDIX II-B (*continued*)

Panel B: 31-Sector Grouping

B- Code Category	R_{ij}	% Total $\pm R_{ij}$	R_{ij}	% Total $\pm R_{ij}$	R_{ij}	% Total $\pm R_{ij}$
	All-Sector Employment		Agriculture		Forestry & Fisheries	
B-1	+ 8,340,389	+ 56.4	+ 134,480	+ 38.3	+ 3,484	+ 33.1
B-2	+ 331,291	+ 2.2	+ 15,584	+ 4.4	- 947	- 11.7
B-3	+ 4,827,891	+ 32.6	+ 131,250	+ 37.4	+ 4,368	+ 41.5
B-4	- 792,140	- 5.4	+ 22,465	+ 6.4	+ 577	+ 5.5
B-5	- 11,198,945	- 75.6	+ 41,044	+ 11.7	- 1,936	- 23.9
B-6	+ 1,290,392	+ 8.7	- 192,173	- 55.7	- 3,034	- 37.5
B-7	- 1,678,858	- 11.3	+ 5,991	+ 1.7	+ 2,093	+ 19.9
B-8	- 1,133,705	- 7.7	- 152,552	- 44.3	- 2,173	- 26.9
	Mining		Contract Construction		Total Manufacturing	
B-1	+ 65,675	+ 37.7	+ 361,920	+ 49.4	+ 2,011,288	+ 41.5
B-2	+ 2,102	+ 1.2	+ 13,319	+ 1.8	+ 5,720	+ .1
B-3	+ 70,387	+ 40.4	+ 266,274	+ 36.3	+ 1,254,626	+ 25.9
B-4	+ 6,543	+ 3.8	- 24,038	- 3.2	- 512,563	- 10.6
B-5	- 597	- .3	- 546,377	- 73.7	- 4,176,649	- 86.1
B-6	+ 29,470	+ 16.9	+ 91,280	+ 12.5	+ 1,197,270	+ 24.7
B-7	- 130,629	- 75.4	- 86,545	- 11.7	- 160,666	- 3.3
B-8	- 41,967	- 24.2	- 84,175	- 11.4	+ 373,349	+ 7.7
	Food Manufacturing		Textile Manufacturing		Apparel Manufacturing	
B-1	+ 81,797	+ 27.7	+ 1,372	+ .5	+ 74,796	+ 16.4
B-2	- 4,292	- 1.5	- 9,527	- 3.7	- 4,845	- 1.1
B-3	+ 87,618	+ 29.7	+ 70,595	+ 27.7	+ 65,179	+ 14.3
B-4	- 25,380	- 8.6	- 31,416	- 12.3	- 41,540	- 9.1
B-5	- 245,343	- 83.3	- 155,343	- 60.8	- 411,669	- 89.9
B-6	+ 87,802	+ 29.7	+ 176,147	+ 69.0	+ 195,029	+ 42.8
B-7	- 19,507	- 6.6	- 59,042	- 23.1	+ 41,586	+ 9.1
B-8	+ 38,211	+ 12.9	+ 7,171	+ 2.8	+ 79,005	+ 17.3
	Printing and Publishing		Chemical Manufacturing		Lumber and Wood Products	
B-1	+ 161,121	+ 60.4	+ 105,166	+ 46.7	+ 50,234	+ 38.9
B-2	+ 14,217	+ 5.3	- 3,351	- 1.5	- 6,507	- 5.0
B-3	+ 73,214	+ 27.4	+ 80,327	+ 35.7	+ 62,778	+ 48.6
B-4	- 2,277	- .9	+ 893	+ .4	- 12,114	- 9.3
B-5	- 244,604	- 91.5	- 208,074	- 92.4	- 53,291	- 40.7
B-6	+ 18,365	+ 6.9	+ 38,726	+ 17.2	+ 16,052	+ 12.4
B-7	- 19,175	- 7.2	- 12,947	- 5.8	- 18,876	- 14.4
B-8	- 1,347	- .5	- 787	- .3	- 40,163	- 30.7

APPENDIX II-B Panel B (*continued*)

B-Code Category	R_{ij}	% Total $\pm R_{ij}$	R_{ij}	% Total $\pm R_{ij}$	R_{ij}	% Total $\pm R_{ij}$
	Machinery Manufacturing		Motor Vehicle Manufacturing		Transportation Equipment Mfg.	
B-1	+ 649,142	+ 49.0	+ 90,008	+ 32.3	+ 212,790	+ 50.8
B-2	+ 5,401	+ .4	+ 17,599	+ 6.3	+ 4,731	+ 1.1
B-3	+ 302,310	+ 22.8	+ 65,268	+ 23.5	+ 110,032	+ 26.3
B-4	- 219,248	- 16.5	+ 13,673	+ 4.9	- 111,854	- 26.7
B-5	- 1,106,439	- 83.5	- 278,312	- 100.0	- 306,637	- 73.3
B-6	+ 210,865	+ 15.9	+ 54,824	+ 19.7	+ 62,007	+ 14.8
B-7	+ 47,202	+ 3.6	+ 12,654	+ 4.5	+ 3,706	+ .9
B-8	+ 109,983	+ 8.3	+ 24,244	+ 8.7	+ 25,308	+ 6.0
	Other Manufacturing		Railroad Transportation		Trucking and Warehousing	
B-1	+ 584,862	+ 42.0	+ 43,137	+ 59.5	+ 116,065	+ 58.7
B-2	- 7,706	- .6	+ 2,647	+ 3.6	+ 13,785	+ 7.0
B-3	+ 337,325	+ 24.2	+ 22,457	+ 31.0	+ 66,664	+ 33.7
B-4	- 83,300	- 6.6	- 3,213	- 4.4	+ 1,135	+ .6
B-5	- 1,166,743	- 92.8	- 43,941	- 60.6	- 112,250	- 56.5
B-6	+ 337,453	+ 24.3	+ 4,298	+ 5.9	- 2,283	- 1.1
B-7	- 132,267	- 10.8	- 18,294	- 25.2	- 28,463	- 14.3
B-8	+ 131,724	+ 9.5	- 7,039	- 9.7	- 55,572	- 28.0
	Other Transportation		Communications		Utilities	
B-1	+ 179,389	+ 65.7	+ 137,458	+ 62.5	+ 83,534	+ 39.8
B-2	+ 4,728	+ 1.7	+ 5,354	+ 2.4	- 100	- --
B-3	+ 73,929	+ 27.1	+ 69,558	+ 31.6	+ 66,245	+ 31.6
B-4	- 14,485	- 5.2	- 8,510	- 3.8	- 13,627	- 6.5
B-5	- 234,145	- 83.9	- 158,925	- 70.6	- 178,452	- 84.5
B-6	+ 14,934	+ 5.5	+ 7,680	+ 3.5	+ 41,119	+ 19.6
B-7	- 25,157	- 9.0	- 25,131	- 11.2	- 18,936	- 9.0
B-8	- 5,374	- 1.9	- 32,525	- 14.4	+ 18,729	+ 8.9
	Wholesale Trade		Retail Trade		Eating and Drinking	
B-1	+ 336,260	+ 64.8	+ 1,339,980	+ 58.2	+ 270,408	+ 54.6
B-2	+ 31,279	+ 6.0	+ 106,117	+ 4.6	+ 26,060	+ 5.3
B-3	+ 143,560	+ 27.7	+ 715,850	+ 31.1	+ 156,195	+ 31.5
B-4	+ 7,506	+ 1.4	- 8,203	- .4	+ 9,405	+ 1.9
B-5	- 365,855	- 69.6	- 1,830,822	- 78.8	- 426,448	- 84.7
B-6	- 5,991	- 1.1	+ 139,137	+ 6.0	+ 33,410	+ 6.7
B-7	- 58,904	- 11.2	- 279,148	- 12.0	- 42,907	- 8.5
B-8	- 94,671	- 18.0	- 205,426	- 8.8	- 33,964	- 6.7
	Food and Dairy		Other Retail		Finance, Insurance, Real Estate	
B-1	+ 845,207	+ 58.6	+ 224,365	+ 59.5	+ 465,926	+ 59.4
B-2	+ 65,894	+ 4.6	+ 14,163	+ 3.8	+ 25,068	+ 3.2
B-3	+ 452,481	+ 31.3	+ 107,174	+ 28.4	+ 239,613	+ 30.5
B-4	- 23,032	- 1.6	+ 5,424	+ 1.4	- 46,586	- 5.9
B-5	- 1,114,224	- 76.5	- 290,140	- 76.5	- 673,679	- 84.6
B-6	+ 79,840	+ 5.5	+ 25,887	+ 6.9	+ 53,993	+ 6.9
B-7	- 183,982	- 12.6	- 52,259	- 13.8	- 56,728	- 7.1
B-8	- 134,629	- 9.2	- 36,833	- 9.7	- 119,312	- 2.4

APPENDIX II-B Panel B (*continued*)

B-Code Category	R_{ij}	% Total $\pm R_{ij}$	R_{ij}	% Total $\pm R_{ij}$	R_{ij}	% Total $\pm R_{ij}$
	Total Services		Lodging and Personal		Business and Repair	
B-1	+ 2,233,265	+ 64.9	+ 234,670	+ 56.2	+ 373,357	+ 74.5
B-2	+ 209,474	+ 6.1	+ 14,676	+ 3.5	+ 24,929	+ 5.0
B-3	+ 999,637	+ 29.0	+ 130,980	+ 31.4	+ 90,178	+ 18.0
B-4	- 21,207	- .6	- 7,849	- 1.8	+ 12,500	+ 2.5
B-5	- 2,117,766	- 61.0	- 345,104	- 80.4	- 200,861	- 39.9
B-6	- 97,722	- 2.8	+ 37,264	+ 8.9	- 68,314	- 13.6
B-7	- 526,334	- 15.2	- 46,381	- 10.8	- 85,176	- 16.9
B-8	- 709,141	- 20.4	- 29,813	- 6.9	- 149,022	- 29.6
	Amusement and Recreation		Private Households		Professional Services	
B-1	+ 72,447	+ 60.3	+ 68,555	+ 39.4	+ 1,484,236	+ 64.1
B-2	+ 7,288	+ 6.1	+ 7,553	+ 4.3	+ 155,028	+ 6.7
B-3	+ 38,531	+ 32.1	+ 64,241	+ 36.9	+ 675,707	+ 29.2
B-4	+ 1,323	+ 1.1	- 18,663	- 10.8	- 8,518	- .4
B-5	- 89,580	- 73.5	- 130,705	- 75.5	- 1,351,516	- 58.0
B-6	+ 499	+ .4	+ 33,858	+ 19.4	- 101,029	- 4.3
B-7	- 13,187	- 10.8	- 23,296	- 13.5	- 358,304	- 15.4
B-8	- 19,089	- 15.7	- 527	- .3	- 510,690	- 21.9
	Civilian Government		Armed Forces			
B-1	+ 586,769	+ 63.8	+ 241,759	+ 33.0		
B-2	+ 66,073	+ 7.2	- 168,912	- 26.6		
B-3	+ 267,014	+ 29.0	+ 436,459	+ 59.6		
B-4	- 30,601	- 3.3	- 147,333	- 23.2		
B-5	- 509,640	- 54.1	- 288,965	- 45.6		
B-6	- 27,143	- 2.9	+ 39,557	+ 5.4		
B-7	- 243,322	- 25.8	- 28,675	- 4.5		
B-8	- 130,653	- 13.9	+ 14,797	+ 2.0		

(shaded) Industry sector ratios greater than corresponding ratios for all-sector employment.

* For a few employment sectors (notably Transportation Equipment and Miscellaneous Manufacturing and the Armed Forces) the sum of the pluses and minuses may not appear to balance. The discrepancy is due to an accumulation of rounding errors because all of our synthetic regions are combinations of counties. There is an additional systematic bias resulting from the computational formula in those cases where a very large gain occurred out of a small initial year base. This will be true of the B Panels of Appendixes B, C, and D.

APPENDIX II-C. Shift-Share Computations by Industry Sector For Trade-Center Synthetic Regions

Panel A: Six Sector Grouping

Trade Center Category	1940 Sector Employment	Col 1 % of Total Empl.	Employment Change $G_{ij}+k_{ij}+R_{ij}$	G_{ij}	k_{ij}	R_{ij}	% Total ± R_{ij}	R_{ij} % of 1940 Empl.	R_{ij} % of k_{ij}	Total Employ. Growth Rate %
All-Sector Employment										
Metro-Large	19,791,561	43.8	+ 18,484,473	+ 14,800,141	+ 6,813,300	- 3,128,968	- 99.0	15.8	45.9	+ 93.4
Metro-Small	871,167	1.9	+ 1,208,311	+ 657,436	+ 145,093	+ 405,782	+ 12.9	46.6	279.7	+ 137.4
Whol/Ret Large	7,196,779	15.9	+ 7,643,719	+ 5,381,758	+ 754,420	+ 1,507,541	+ 47.9	20.9	199.8	+ 106.2
Whol/Ret Small	689,548	1.5	+ 528,388	+ 515,645	- 34,519	+ 47,262	+ 1.5	6.9	136.9	+ 76.6
Whol/Ret Out.	1,522,588	3.4	+ 1,245,994	+ 1,138,590	- 123,557	+ 230,961	+ 7.3	15.2	186.9	+ 81.8
Comp. Shop.	9,060,337	20.0	+ 4,215,722	+ 6,767,140	- 3,461,891	+ 910,473	+ 28.9	10.0	26.3	+ 46.5
Part. Shop.	3,090,200	6.8	+ 337,999	+ 2,287,996	- 1,996,249	+ 46,252	+ 1.5	1.5	2.3	+ 10.9
Full Conv.	1,689,323	3.7	+ 57,564	+ 1,263,277	- 1,178,608	- 27,105	- .9	1.6	2.3	+ 3.4
Min Con/Ham.	1,301,681	2.9	- 40,178	+ 963,239	- 997,534	- 5,883	- .2	.5	.6	- 3.1
Total	45,221,184	100.0	+ 33,681,992	+ 33,775,222	± 7,752,586	± 3,155,114	± 100.0	7.0	40.7	+ 74.5
Resource Sectors										
Metro-Large	872,662	9.1	- 366,414	- 2,642,692	+ 2,113,799	+ 162,416	+ 59.0	18.6	7.7	- 42.0
Metro-Small	121,005	1.3	- 51,000	- 117,389	+ 45,613	+ 20,776	+ 7.5	17.2	45.5	- 42.1
Whol/Ret Large	1,011,328	10.6	- 542,499	- 860,937	+ 353,932	+ 70,709	+ 25.7	7.0	20.0	- 53.6
Whol/Ret Small	168,084	1.8	- 94,538	- 92,070	- 13,718	+ 11,250	+ 4.1	6.7	82.0	- 56.2
Whol/Ret Out.	305,373	3.2	- 186,007	- 203,300	+ 6,946	+ 10,347	+ 3.8	3.4	149.0	- 60.9
Comp. Shop.	3,542,534	37.0	- 2,336,668	- 1,208,298	- 1,026,046	- 102,324	- 38.5	2.9	10.0	- 66.0
Part. Shop.	1,714,788	17.9	- 1,160,726	- 408,531	- 674,772	- 77,423	- 29.1	4.5	11.5	- 67.7
Full Conv.	1,004,208	10.5	- 683,855	- 225,863	- 427,879	- 30,413	- 11.4	3.0	7.1	- 68.1
Min Con/Ham.	822,404	8.6	- 585,814	- 171,990	- 357,993	- 55,831	- 21.0	6.8	15.6	- 71.2
Total	9,562,586	100.0	- 6,007,521	- 5,931,070	± 2,510,349	± 270,745	± 100.0	2.8	10.8	- 62.8
Total Manufacturing Minus Printing and Publishing										
Metro-Large	5,281,548	52.4	+ 3,426,148	+ 3,713,640	+ 1,448,148	- 1,735,637	- 93.7	32.9	119.9	+ 59.2
Metro-Small	166,195	1.6	+ 210,622	+ 164,962	- 26,642	+ 73,302	+ 3.9	44.1	275.1	+ 126.7
Whol/Ret Large	2,132,509	21.1	+ 1,698,216	+ 1,350,734	+ 461,275	- 116,433	- 6.3	5.5	25.2	+ 79.6
Whol/Ret Small	114,200	1.1	+ 90,132	+ 129,385	- 48,879	+ 9,626	+ .5	8.4	19.7	+ 78.9
Whol/Ret Out.	426,985	4.2	+ 393,740	+ 285,694	+ 14,158	+ 93,888	+ 5.1	22.0	663.1	+ 92.2
Comp. Shop.	1,471,836	14.6	+ 1,662,072	+ 1,698,005	- 870,524	+ 934,591	+ 50.7	63.5	107.4	+ 112.9
Part. Shop.	271,982	2.7	+ 495,940	+ 574,101	- 467,800	+ 389,669	+ 21.1	143.3	83.3	+ 182.3
Full Conv.	127,501	1.3	+ 190,817	+ 316,980	- 266,540	+ 180,427	+ 9.8	141.5	67.7	+ 149.7
Min Con/Ham.	95,217	.9	+ 158,326	+ 241,697	- 213,862	+ 164,493	+ 8.9	172.8	76.9	+ 166.3
Total	10,087,973	100.0	+ 8,326,013	+ 8,475,198	± 1,908,914	± 1,848,533	± 100.0	18.3	96.8	+ 82.5

APPENDIX II-C Panel A (*continued*)

Trade Center Category	1940 Sector Employment	Col 1 % of Total Empl.	Employment Change $G_{ij}+k_{ij}+R_{ij}$	G_{ij}	k_{ij}	R_{ij}	% Total ± R_{ij}	R_{ij} % of 1940 Empl.	R_{ij} % of k_{ij}	Total Employ. Growth Rate %
Linkage Sectors										
Metro-Large	3,879,039	59.6	+ 4,005,386	+ 3,088,365	+ 1,438,869	- 522,848	- 96.0	13.5	36.3	+ 103.3
Metro Small	152,496	2.3	+ 245,423	+ 137,189	+ 29,013	+ 79,221	+ 15.5	51.9	273.1	+ 160.9
Whol/Ret Large	979,972	15.1	+ 1,334,544	+ 1,123,009	- 142,996	+ 354,522	+ 69.2	36.2	247.9	+ 136.2
Whol/Ret Small	96,904	1.5	+ 97,625	+ 107,301	- 13,159	+ 3,483	+ .7	3.6	26.5	+ 100.7
Whol/Ret Out.	184,019	2.8	+ 218,038	+ 237,591	- 66,998	+ 47,455	+ 9.3	25.8	70.8	+ 118.5
Comp. Shop.	838,186	12.9	+ 797,147	+ 1,412,106	- 639,605	+ 24,646	+ 4.8	2.9	3.9	+ 95.1
Part. Shop.	207,247	3.2	+ 181,630	+ 477,437	- 285,696	- 10,111	- .9	4.9	3.5	+ 87.6
Full Conv.	100,719	1.5	+ 85,690	+ 263,609	- 165,991	- 11,928	- 2.2	11.8	7.2	+ 85.1
Min Con/Ham.	64,498	1.0	+ 62,289	+ 201,000	- 141,697	+ 2,986	+ .6	4.6	2.1	+ 96.6
Total	6,503,080	100.0	+ 7,027,772	+ 7,047,607	± 1,462,012	± 528,595	± 100.0	8.1	36.2	+ 108.1
Total Retail										
Metro-Large	3,400,554	52.8	+ 2,623,948	+ 2,619,040	+ 562,303	- 557,395	- 97.4	16.4	99.1	+ 77.2
Metro-Small	148,731	2.3	+ 194,701	+ 116,341	+ 24,163	+ 54,197	+ 9.9	36.4	224.3	+ 130.9
Whol/Ret Large	1,036,968	16.1	+ 1,302,619	+ 952,358	+ 3,627	+ 346,634	+ 63.0	33.4	9557.0	+ 125.6
Whol/Ret Small	101,174	1.6	+ 108,565	+ 91,248	+ 4,031	+ 13,286	+ 2.4	13.1	329.6	+ 107.3
Whol/Ret Out.	208,714	3.2	+ 234,267	+ 201,486	- 8,965	+ 41,746	+ 7.6	20.0	465.7	+ 112.2
Comp. Shop.	1,034,906	16.1	+ 1,045,664	+ 1,197,516	- 245,100	+ 93,248	+ 17.0	9.0	38.0	+ 101.0
Part. Shop.	279,822	4.3	+ 245,431	+ 404,886	- 150,488	- 8,967	- 1.6	3.2	6.0	+ 87.7
Full Conv.	141,157	2.2	+ 124,365	+ 223,550	- 93,150	- 6,035	- 1.1	4.3	6.5	+ 88.1
Min Con/Ham.	89,911	1.4	+ 82,214	+ 170,455	- 89,022	+ 781	+ .1	.9	.9	+ 91.4
Total	6,441,955	100.0	+ 5,961,774	+ 5,976,880	± 590,425	± 561,145	± 100.0	8.7	95.0	+ 92.5
Personal Services										
Metro-Large	2,015,041	49.1	- 385,898	- 203,260	+ 44,893	- 227,531	- 100.0	11.3	506.8	- 19.2
Metro-Small	103,447	2.5	+ 8,131	- 9,029	- 3,095	+ 20,255	+ 9.3	19.6	654.4	+ 7.9
Whol/Ret Large	663,659	16.2	+ 14,123	- 73,911	- 5,127	+ 93,161	+ 42.9	14.0	1817.1	+ 2.1
Whol/Ret Small	73,646	1.8	- 2,510	- 7,081	- 3,238	+ 7,809	+ 3.6	10.6	241.2	- 3.4
Whol/Ret Out.	137,611	3.4	- 12,569	- 15,637	- 3,169	+ 6,237	+ 2.9	4.5	196.8	- 9.1
Comp. Shop.	748,101	18.2	- 66,166	- 92,938	- 27,417	+ 54,189	+ 25.0	7.2	197.6	- 8.8
Part. Shop.	201,562	4.9	- 20,389	- 31,422	- 4,321	+ 15,354	+ 7.1	7.6	355.3	- 10.1
Full Conv.	93,865	2.3	- 7,502	- 17,349	+ 1,119	+ 8,728	+ 4.0	9.3	780.0	- 8.0
Min Con/Ham.	67,793	1.7	- 1,913	- 13,228	+ 58	+ 11,257	+ 5.2	16.6	19408.6	- 2.8
Total	4,104,725	100.0	- 474,693	- 463,855	± 46,219	± 222,261	± 100.0	5.4	480.9	- 11.6
Information Services										
Metro-Large	3,184,003	51.8	+ 7,600,553	+ 6,406,010	+ 1,021,092	+ 173,451	+ 19.1	5.4	17.0	+ 238.7
Metro-Small	121,502	2.0	+ 431,343	+ 284,562	+ 4,749	+ 142,032	+ 15.6	116.9	2990.8	+ 355.0
Whol/Ret Large	968,567	15.8	+ 2,929,610	+ 2,329,410	+ 18,856	+ 581,344	+ 63.9	60.0	3083.1	+ 302.5
Whol/Ret Small	92,857	1.5	+ 237,673	+ 223,186	+ 4,521	+ 9,966	+ 1.1	10.7	220.4	+ 256.0
Whol/Ret Out.	185,761	3.0	+ 456,110	+ 492,821	- 39,319	+ 2,608	+ .3	1.4	6.6	+ 245.5
Comp. Chop.	1,017,833	16.6	+ 2,172,698	+ 2,929,050	- 438,252	- 318,100	- 33.5	31.3	76.6	+ 213.5
Part. Shop.	295,473	4.8	+ 410,456	+ 990,323	- 278,129	- 301,738	- 31.8	102.1	108.5	+ 138.9
Full Conv.	161,056	2.6	+ 201,360	+ 546,790	- 152,070	- 193,360	- 20.4	120.1	127.2	+ 125.0
Min Con/Ham.	115,668	1.9	+ 143,682	+ 416,923	- 136,296	- 136,945	- 14.4	118.4	100.5	+ 124.2
Total	6,142,720	100.0	+ 14,583,485	+ 14,619,075	± 1,046,642	± 929,772	± 100.0	15.1	88.8	+ 237.4

(shaded) Industry sector ratios greater than corresponding ratios for all-sector employment

APPENDIX II-C (*continued*)

Panel B: 31-Sector Grouping

Trade Center Category	R_{ij}	% Total $\pm R_{ij}$	R_{ij}	% Total $\pm R_{ij}$	R_{ij}	% Total $\pm R_{ij}$
	All-Sector Employment		Agriculture		Forestry and Fisheries	
Metro-Large	- 3,128,968	- 99.0	+ 126,241	+ 53.3	+ 552	+ 7.6
Metro-Small	+ 405,782	+ 12.9	+ 4,702	+ 2.0	- 103	- 2.1
Whol/Ret Large	+ 1,507,541	+ 47.9	+ 100,079	+ 42.2	+ 4,831	+ 66.8
Whol/Ret Small	+ 47,262	+ 1.5	- 1,458	- .6	+ 231	+ 3.2
Whol/Ret Outside	+ 230,961	+ 7.3	+ 6,018	+ 2.5	+ 1,000	+ 13.8
Complete Shopping	+ 910,473	+ 28.9	- 71,965	- 31.2	+ 618	+ 8.5
Partial Shopping	+ 46,252	+ 1.5	- 67,469	- 29.2	- 2,186	- 45.5
Full Convenience	- 27,105	- .9	- 36,263	- 15.7	- 476	- 9.9
Min. Con./Hamlet	- 5,883	- .2	- 53,794	- 23.3	- 2,035	- 42.4
	Mining		Contract Construction		Total Manufacturing	
Metro-Large	+ 35,623	+ 48.2	- 212,465	- 95.8	- 1,829,446	- 96.4
Metro-Small	+ 16,177	+ 21.9	+ 18,397	+ 8.6	+ 75,430	+ 4.0
Whol/Ret Large	- 34,201	- 46.9	+ 130,844	+ 61.3	- 67,818	- 3.6
Whol/Ret Small	+ 12,477	+ 16.9	+ 4,310	+ 2.0	+ 10,854	+ .6
Whol/Ret Outside	+ 3,329	+ 4.5	+ 9,505	+ 4.5	+ 99,869	+ 5.3
Complete Shopping	- 30,977	- 42.5	+ 36,870	+ 17.3	+ 962,306	+ 50.9
Partial Shopping	- 7,768	- 10.6	- 9,369	- 4.2	+ 394,652	+ 20.9
Full Convenience	+ 6,326	+ 8.6	+ 4,774	+ 2.2	+ 181,618	+ 9.6
Min. Con./Hamlet	- 2	---	+ 8,794	+ 4.1	+ 164,866	+ 8.7
	Food Manufacturing		Textile Manufacturing		Apparel Manufacturing	
Metro-Large	- 174,118	- 98.0	- 123,576	- 55.8	- 327,380	- 99.3
Metro-Small	- 3,607	- 2.0	- 522	- .2	+ 14,210	+ 4.3
Whol/Ret Large	+ 17,657	+ 9.9	- 90,717	- 41.0	+ 18,678	+ 5.7
Whol/Ret Small	+ 3,514	+ 2.0	- 6,660	- 3.0	+ 615	+ .2
Whol/Ret Outside	+ 8,542	+ 4.8	+ 25,023	+ 11.3	- 2,350	- .7
Complete Shopping	+ 81,151	+ 45.5	+ 116,280	+ 52.5	+ 132,408	+ 40.5
Partial Shopping	+ 37,966	+ 21.3	+ 40,886	+ 18.5	+ 69,632	+ 21.3
Full Convenience	+ 17,699	+ 9.9	+ 10,673	+ 4.8	+ 50,651	+ 15.5
Min. Con./Hamlet	+ 11,909	+ 6.7	+ 28,550	+ 12.9	+ 41,079	+ 12.6
	Printing and Publishing		Chemical Manufacturing		Lumber and Wood Products	
Metro-Large	- 93,809	- 100.0	- 88,537	- 91.8	- 12,439	- 38.5
Metro-Small	+ 3,178	+ 3.4	+ 1,648	+ 1.7	- 6,373	- 19.7
Whol/Ret Large	+ 48,615	+ 52.1	+ 45,364	+ 47.1	+ 19,081	+ 62.4
Whol/Ret Small	+ 1,228	+ 1.3	+ 1,731	+ 1.8	- 5,737	- 17.8
Whol/Ret Outside	+ 5,981	+ 6.4	- 7,913	- 8.2	+ 9,418	+ 30.8
Complete Shopping	+ 27,715	+ 29.7	+ 25,034	+ 26.0	+ 829	+ 2.7
Partial Shopping	+ 4,983	+ 5.3	+ 13,643	+ 14.2	- 3,973	- 12.3
Full Convenience	+ 1,191	+ 1.3	+ 5,752	+ 6.0	- 3,957	- 12.3
Min. Con./Hamlet	+ 373	+ .4	+ 3,179	+ 3.3	+ 1,263	+ 4.1

APPENDIX II-C Panel B (*continued*)

Trade Center Category	R_{ij}	% Total $\pm R_{ij}$	R_{ij}	% Total $\pm R_{ij}$	R_{ij}	% Total $\pm R_{ij}$
	Machinery Manufacturing		Motor Vehicle Manufacturing		Transportation Equipment Mfg.	
Metro-Large	- 336,149	- 85.7	- 165,693	- 98.9	- 148,853	- 99.6
Metro-Small	- 5,517	- 1.4	- 425	- .3	+ 28,295	+ 18.9
Whol/Ret Large	- 50,642	- 12.9	+ 56,153	+ 33.5	+ 23,742	+ 15.9
Whol/Ret Small	+ 2,672	+ .7	- 1,405	- .8	+ 3,493	+ 2.3
Whol/Ret Outside	+ 36,476	+ 9.3	+ 17,126	+ 10.2	- 598	- .4
Complete Shopping	+ 230,428	+ 58.9	+ 58,993	+ 35.2	+ 51,594	+ 34.5
Partial Shopping	+ 70,915	+ 18.1	+ 22,878	+ 13.7	+ 20,889	+ 14.0
Full Convenience	+ 27,849	+ 7.1	+ 7,390	+ 4.4	+ 12,453	+ 8.3
Min. Con./Hamlet	+ 23,186	+ 5.9	+ 4,940	+ 3.0	+ 9,067	+ 6.1
	Other Manufacturing		Railroad Transportation		Trucking and Warehousing	
Metro-Large	- 358,895	- 69.7	+ 8,026	+ 56.1	+ 27,680	+ 39.2
Metro-Small	+ 44,593	+ 8.7	+ 3,293	+ 23.0	+ 6,560	+ 9.3
Whol/Ret Large	- 155,809	- 30.3	+ 1,171	+ 8.2	+ 29,322	+ 41.6
Whol/Ret Small	+ 11,403	+ 2.2	+ 427	+ 3.0	- 436	- .6
Whol/Ret Outside	+ 8,164	+ 1.6	+ 1,392	+ 9.7	+ 7,002	+ 9.9
Complete Shopping	+ 237,324	+ 46.4	- 11,892	- 83.4	- 32,626	- 45.6
Partial Shopping	+ 116,833	+ 22.8	- 1,442	- 10.1	- 17,923	- 25.1
Full Convenience	+ 51,917	+ 10.1	- 412	- 2.9	- 11,771	- 16.5
Min. Con./Hamlet	+ 41,320	+ 8.1	- 512	- 3.6	- 8,725	- 12.2
	Other Transportation		Communications		Utilities	
Metro-Large	- 51,284	- 98.0	- 46,907	- 72.3	- 96.965	- 100.0
Metro-Small	+ 2,887	+ 6.3	+ 4,845	+ 8.1	+ 8,404	+ 8.8
Whol/Ret Large	+ 5,284	+ 11.4	+ 48,047	+ 80.3	+ 8,649	+ 9.1
Whol/Ret Small	- 1,049	- 2.0	+ 2,476	+ 4.1	+ 862	+ .9
Whol/Ret Outside	+ 4,121	+ 8.9	+ 4,181	+ 7.0	+ 4,448	+ 4.7
Complete Shopping	+ 18,955	+ 41.1	+ 301	+ .5	+ 35,156	+ 36.8
Partial Shopping	+ 5,359	+ 11.6	- 7,921	- 12.2	+ 19,288	+ 20.2
Full Convenience	+ 4,349	+ 9.4	- 7,385	- 11.4	+ 10,287	+ 10.8
Min. Con./Hamlet	+ 5,197	+ 11.3	- 2,681	- 4.1	+ 8,383	+ 8.8
	Wholesale Trade		Total Retail		Eating and Drinking	
Metro-Large	+ 28,975	+ 24.8	- 557,395	- 97.4	- 195,335	- 99.6
Metro-Small	+ 23,987	+ 20.5	+ 54,197	+ 9.9	+ 10,719	+ 5.7
Whol/Ret Large	+ 63,051	+ 53.9	+ 346,634	+ 63.0	+ 106,231	+ 56.4
Whol/Ret Small	- 6,414	- 5.2	+ 13,286	+ 2.4	+ 4,634	+ 2.5
Whol/Ret Outside	+ 909	+ .8	+ 41,764	+ 7.6	+ 16,197	+ 8.6
Complete Shopping	- 73,258	- 59.2	+ 93,248	+ 17.0	+ 46,774	+ 24.9
Partial Shopping	- 24,556	- 19.8	- 8,967	- 1.6	- 692	- .4
Full Convenience	- 12,884	- 10.4	- 6,035	- 1.1	+ 821	+ .4
Min. Con./Hamlet	- 6,626	- 5.4	+ 781	+ .1	+ 2,810	+ 1.5

APPENDIX II-C Panel B (*continued*)

Trade Center Category	R_{ij}	% Total $\pm R_{ij}$	R_{ij}	% Total $\pm R_{ij}$	R_{ij}	% Total $\pm R_{ij}$
	Food and Dairy		Other Retail		Finance, Insurance, Real Estate	
Metro-Large	- 306,652	- 95.0	- 55,408	- 97.9	- 298,564	- 100.0
Metro-Small	+ 33,260	+ 10.7	+ 10,218	+ 18.8	+ 26,067	+ 9.1
Whol/Ret Large	+ 204,083	+ 65.7	+ 36,320	+ 66.8	+ 150,323	+ 52.4
Whol/Ret Small	+ 7,206	+ 2.3	+ 1,446	+ 2.7	+ 6,389	+ 2.2
Whol/Ret Outside	+ 21,170	+ 6.8	+ 4,379	+ 8.1	+ 19,411	+ 6.8
Complete Shopping	+ 44,760	+ 14.4	+ 1,714	+ 3.2	+ 60,295	+ 21.0
Partial Shopping	- 8,415	- 2.6	+ 140	+ .3	+ 12,101	+ 4.2
Full Convenience	- 5,696	- 1.8	- 1,160	- 2.1	+ 4,697	+ 1.6
Min. Con./Hamlet	- 2,161	- .7	+ 132	+ .2	+ 7,577	+ 2.6
	Total Services		Lodging and Personal		Business and Repair	
Metro-Large	- 1,318	- .2	- 147,708	- 100.0	+ 192,632	+ 73.0
Metro-Small	+ 128,957	+ 18.0	+ 11,362	+ 8.3	+ 15,646	+ 5.9
Whol/Ret Large	+ 572,291	+ 80.0	+ 77,523	+ 56.9	+ 55,512	+ 21.0
Whol/Ret Small	+ 11,127	+ 1.6	+ 2,779	+ 2.0	- 2,744	- 1.0
Whol/Ret Outside	+ 3,171	+ .4	+ 4,576	+ 3.4	- 7,529	- 2.8
Complete Shopping	- 236,323	- 31.7	+ 26,369	+ 19.7	- 139,025	- 52.2
Partial Shopping	- 244,896	- 32.9	+ 4,976	+ 3.7	- 60,163	- 22.6
Full Convenience	- 153,590	- 20.6	+ 2,468	+ 1.8	- 34,251	- 12.9
Min. Con./Hamlet	- 108,866	- 14.6	+ 5,597	+ 4.1	- 22,489	- 8.4
	Amusement and Recreation		Private Households		Professional Services	
Metro-Large	- 34,650	- 78.5	- 79,823	- 100.0	+ 68,231	+ 12.3
Metro-Small	+ 2,863	+ 6.7	+ 8,893	+ 11.0	+ 89,860	+ 16.3
Whol/Ret Large	+ 37,812	+ 89.1	+ 15,638	+ 19.3	+ 385,806	+ 69.8
Whol/Ret Small	+ 686	+ 1.6	+ 5,030	+ 6.2	+ 5,376	+ 1.0
Whol/Ret Outside	+ 1,058	+ 2.5	+ 1,661	+ 2.1	+ 3,405	+ .6
Complete Shopping	- 2,696	- 6.1	+ 27,320	+ 33.8	- 148,791	- 26.2
Partial Shopping	- 3,451	- 7.8	+ 10,378	+ 12.8	- 196,636	- 34.6
Full Convenience	- 2,907	- 6.6	+ 6,260	+ 7.7	- 125,160	- 22.0
Min. Con./Hamlet	- 456	- 1.0	+ 5,660	+ 7.0	- 97,178	- 17.1
	Civilian Government		Armed Forces			
Metro-Large	- 52,792	- 31.1	- 208,926	- 93.2		
Metro-Small	+ 33,690	+ 22.7	- 1,398	- .6		
Whol/Ret Large	+ 102,214	+ 69.0	+ 46,820	+ 14.5		
Whol/Ret Small	+ 6,648	+ 4.5	- 12,468	- 5.6		
Whol/Ret Outside	+ 5,674	+ 3.8	+ 19,185	+ 5.9		
Complete Shopping	- 27,588	- 16.3	+ 187,353	+ 58.0		
Partial Shopping	- 41,488	- 24.4	+ 43,837	+ 15.1		
Full Convenience	- 31,042	- 18.3	+ 20,702	+ 6.4		
Min. Con./Hamlet	- 16,822	- 9.9	- 1,418	- .6		

(shaded) Industry sector ratios greater than corresponding ratios for all-sector employment.

* See note at end of Appendix B, Panel B.

APPENDIX II-D. Shift-Share Computations by Industry Sector For Transaction-Field Synthetic Regions

Panel A: Six Sector Grouping

Transaction Field Category	1940 Sector Employment	Col 1 % of Total Empl.	Employment Change $G_{ij}+k_{ij}+R_{ij}$	G_{ij}	k_{ij}	R_{ij}	% Total $\pm R_{ij}$	R_{ij} % of 1940 Empl.	R_{ij} % of k_{ij}	Total Employ. Growth Rate %
All-Sector Totals										
Urb Cen Large	16,161,212	35.7	+ 15,083,607	+ 12,085,360	+ 6,101,399	- 3,103,152	- 89.8	19.2	50.9	+ 93.3
Urb Cen Med.	5,930,312	13.1	+ 7,074,035	+ 4,426,505	+ 1,384,108	+ 1,263,422	+ 36.7	21.3	91.3	+ 119.3
Urb Cen Small	4,784,975	10.6	+ 4,765,426	+ 3,578,205	+ 326,277	+ 860,944	+ 25.0	18.0	263.9	+ 99.6
P.L.F. Large	2,037,303	4.5	+ 1,408,911	+ 1,523,502	- 285,204	+ 170,613	+ 5.0	8.4	59.8	+ 69.2
P.L.F. Medium	1,749,393	3.9	+ 1,052,149	+ 1,308,198	- 604,712	+ 348,663	+ 10.1	19.9	57.7	+ 60.1
P.L.F. Small	2,735,741	6.0	+ 1,118,437	+ 2,022,928	- 1,420,901	+ 516,410	+ 15.0	18.9	36.3	+ 40.9
S.L.F. Large	1,176,918	2.6	+ 527,700	+ 880,104	- 412,443	+ 60,039	+ 1.7	5.1	14.6	+ 44.8
S.L.F. Medium	1,843,371	4.1	+ 743,877	+ 1,378,473	- 839,758	+ 205,162	+ 6.0	11.1	24.4	+ 40.4
S.L.F. Small	2,991,300	6.6	+ 596,384	+ 2,236,894	- 1,656,790	+ 16,280	+ .5	.5	1.0	+ 19.9
Outside	5,810,659	12.8	+ 1,311,461	+ 4,335,051	- 2,671,516	- 352,074	- 10.2	6.1	13.2	+ 22.6
Total	45,221,184	100.0	+ 33,681,987	+ 33,775,220	± 7,851,554	± 3,448,380	± 100.0	7.6	43.9	+ 74.5
Resource Sectors										
Urb Cen Large	541,749	5.7	- 182,678	- 2,157,888	+ 1,835,425	+ 139,785	+ 44.0	25.8	7.6	- 33.7
Urb Cen Med.	503,996	5.3	- 197,932	- 790,369	+ 479,576	+ 113,461	+ 35.7	22.5	23.7	- 39.3
Urb Cen Small	727,320	7.6	- 387,131	- 638,902	+ 187,522	+ 64,249	+ 20.2	8.8	34.3	- 53.2
P.L.F. Large	546,687	5.7	- 370,677	- 272,026	- 60,438	- 38,213	- 12.4	7.0	63.2	- 67.8
P.L.F. Medium	663,500	6.9	- 462,642	- 233,583	- 198,016	- 31,043	- 10.1	4.7	15.7	- 69.7
P.L.F. Small	1,237,424	12.9	- 873,650	- 361,202	- 432,353	- 80,095	- 26.0	6.5	18.5	- 70.6
S.L.F. Large	455,607	4.8	- 285,397	- 157,145	- 127,296	- 956	- .3	.2	.8	- 62.6
S.L.F. Medium	805,828	8.4	- 529,239	- 246,132	- 271,612	- 11,495	- 3.7	1.4	4.2	- 65.7
S.L.F. Small	1,428,282	14.9	- 999,112	- 399,406	- 500,238	- 99,468	- 32.3	7.0	19.9	- 70.0
Outside	2,651,984	27.7	- 1,719,964	- 774,041	- 898,904	- 47,019	- 15.3	1.8	5.2	- 64.8
Total	9,562,377	100.0	- 6,008,422	- 6,030,694	± 2,495,690	± 312,892	± 100.0	3.3	12.5	- 62.8
Total Manufacturing Minus Printing and Publishing										
Urb Cen Large	4,298,238	42.6	+ 2,840,948	+ 3,032,447	+ 1,285,384	- 1,476,883	- 80.1	34.4	114.9	+ 66.0
Urb Cen Med.	1,706,033	16.9	+ 1,307,639	+ 1,110,695	+ 480,589	- 283,645	- 15.4	16.6	59.0	+ 76.6
Urb Cen Small	1,272,670	12.6	+ 909,228	+ 897,837	+ 94,081	- 82,690	- 4.5	6.5	87.9	+ 71.4
P.L.F. Large	493,603	4.9	+ 489,976	+ 382,276	- 34,801	+ 142,501	+ 7.8	28.9	409.5	+ 99.3
P.L.F. Medium	349,777	3.5	+ 481,206	+ 328,251	- 104,280	+ 257,235	+ 14.0	73.5	246.7	+ 137.6
P.L.F. Small	457,950	4.5	+ 708,227	+ 507,589	- 304,309	+ 504,947	+ 27.5	110.3	165.9	+ 154.7
S.L.F. Large	198,538	2.0	+ 202,874	+ 220,836	- 105,746	+ 87,784	+ 4.8	44.2	83.0	+ 102.2
S.L.F. Medium	259,821	2.6	+ 361,440	+ 345,883	- 179,713	+ 195,270	+ 10.6	75.2	108.7	+ 139.1
S.L.F. Small	408,076	4.0	+ 504,726	+ 561,279	- 380,529	+ 323,976	+ 17.6	79.4	85.1	+ 123.7
Outside	643,267	6.4	+ 690,766	+ 1,087,745	- 721,336	+ 324,367	+ 17.7	50.4	45.0	+ 107.4
Total	10,087,973	100.0	+ 8,497,030	+ 8,474,838	± 1,845,384	± 1,839,649	± 100.0	18.2	99.7	+ 84.2

Industry sector ratios greater than corresponding ratios for all-sector employment

APPENDIX II-D Panel A (*continued*)

Transaction Field Category	1940 Sector Employment	Col 1 % of Total Empl.	Employment Change $G_{ij}+k_{ij}+R_{ij}$	G_{ij}	k_{ij}	R_{ij}	% Total ± R_{ij}	R_{ij} % of 1940 Empl.	R_{ij} % of k_{ij}	Total Employ. Growth Rate %
Linkage Sectors										
Urb Cen Large	3,254,483	50.0	+ 3,266,771	+ 2,521,869	+ 1,332,799	- 587,897	- 82.8	18.1	44.1	+ 100.4
Urb Cen Med.	983,563	15.1	+ 1,400,939	+ 923,686	+ 132,575	+ 344,678	+ 50.9	35.0	260.0	+ 142.4
Urb Cen Small	672,073	10.3	+ 823,290	+ 744,669	- 83,569	+ 162,190	+ 24.0	24.1	194.1	+ 122.5
P.L.F. Large	220,729	3.4	+ 275,687	+ 317,910	- 105,733	+ 63,510	+ 9.4	28.8	60.1	+ 124.9
P.L.F. Medium	146,056	2.2	+ 202,281	+ 272,984	- 126,335	+ 55,632	+ 8.2	38.1	44.0	+ 138.5
P.L.F. Small	200,605	3.1	+ 255,722	+ 422,126	- 212,928	+ 46,524	+ 6.9	23.2	21.8	+ 127.5
S.L.F. Large	103,589	1.6	+ 110,937	+ 183,653	- 77,203	+ 4,487	+ .7	4.3	5.8	+ 107.1
S.L.F. Medium	163,658	2.5	+ 152,205	+ 287,648	- 134,605	- 838	- .1	.5	.6	+ 93.0
S.L.F. Small	223,110	3.4	+ 174,337	+ 466,777	- 260,824	- 31,616	- 4.5	14.2	12.1	+ 78.1
Outside	535,214	8.2	+ 385,726	+ 904,600	- 429,620	- 89,254	- 12.6	16.7	20.8	+ 72.1
Total	6,503,080	100.0	+ 7,047,895	+ 7,046,222	± 1,448,096	± 693,313	± 100.0	10.7	47.9	+ 108.3
Total Retail										
Urb Cen Large	2,818,755	43.8	+ 2,064,816	+ 2,138,631	+ 499,973	- 573,788	- 87.9	20.4	114.8	+ 73.3
Urb Cen Med.	940,982	14.6	+ 1,168,225	+ 783,316	+ 91,094	+ 293,815	+ 46.6	31.2	322.5	+ 124.1
Urb Cen Small	702,098	10.9	+ 814,380	+ 633,200	+ 18,830	+ 162,350	+ 25.8	23.1	862.2	+ 116.0
P.L.F. Large	259,153	4.0	+ 266,395	+ 269,599	- 33,787	+ 30,583	+ 4.9	11.8	90.4	+ 102.8
P.L.F. Medium	190,287	3.0	+ 225,183	+ 231,499	- 57,220	+ 50,904	+ 8.1	26.8	89.0	+ 118.3
P.L.F. Small	261,289	4.1	+ 285,381	+ 357,979	- 121,842	+ 49,244	+ 7.8	18.8	40.4	+ 109.2
S.L.F. Large	136,327	2.1	+ 137,881	+ 155,743	- 30,103	+ 12,241	+ 1.9	9.0	40.7	+ 101.1
S.L.F. Medium	201,325	3.1	+ 216,569	+ 243,936	- 58,606	+ 31,239	+ 5.0	15.5	53.3	+ 107.6
S.L.F. Small	296,755	4.6	+ 242,936	+ 395,842	- 121,695	- 31,211	- 4.8	10.5	25.6	+ 81.9
Outside	634,984	9.9	+ 540,001	+ 767,134	- 179,247	- 47,886	- 7.3	7.5	26.7	+ 85.0
Total	6,441,955	100.0	+ 5,961,767	+ 5,970,879	± 606,199	± 641,631	± 100.0	10.0	105.8	+ 92.5
Personal Services										
Urb Cen Large	1,645,239	40.1	- 336,781	- 165,976	+ 46,138	- 216,943	- 98.3	13.2	470.2	- 20.5
Urb Cen Med.	588,381	14.3	- 16	- 60,792	+ 207	+ 60,569	+ 28.8	10.3	29260.4	- .0
Urb Cen Small	486,225	11.8	- 4,197	- 49,141	- 16,148	+ 61,092	+ 29.1	12.6	378.3	- .9
P.L.F. Large	164,517	4.0	- 25,116	- 20,923	- 495	- 3,698	- 1.7	2.2	747.1	- 15.3
P.L.F. Medium	125,570	3.1	- 3,117	- 17,967	- 2,971	+ 17,821	+ 8.5	14.2	599.8	- 2.5
P.L.F. Small	197,492	4.8	- 8,725	- 27,782	- 9,295	+ 28,352	+ 13.5	14.4	305.0	- 4.4
S.L.F. Large	90,233	2.2	- 9,495	- 12,087	- 1,404	+ 3,996	+ 1.9	4.4	284.6	- 10.5
S.L.F. Medium	142,665	3.5	- 2,760	- 18,931	- 3,305	+ 19,476	+ 9.3	13.7	589.3	- 1.9
S.L.F. Small	229,023	5.6	- 38,206	- 30,721	- 11,894	+ 4,409	+ 2.1	1.9	37.1	- 16.7
Outside	435,380	10.6	- 46,280	- 59,536	- 1,127	+ 14,383	+ 6.8	3.3	1276.2	- 10.6
Total	4,104,725	100.0	- 474,693	- 463,856	± 46,492	± 215,370	± 100.0	5.2	463.2	- 11.6
Information Services										
Urb Cen Large	2,654,387	43.2	+ 6,196,019	+ 5,230,961	+ 936,760	+ 28,298	+ 2.8	1.1	3.0	+ 233.4
Urb Cen Med.	858,453	14.0	+ 2,679,738	+ 1,915,942	+ 131,033	+ 632,763	+ 62.7	73.7	482.9	+ 312.2
Urb Cen Small	641,708	10.4	+ 1,897,893	+ 1,548,770	+ 508	+ 348,615	+ 34.5	54.3	68625.0	+ 295.8
P.L.F. Large	246,302	4.0	+ 581,693	+ 659,422	- 52,649	- 25,080	- 2.4	10.2	47.6	+ 236.2
P.L.F. Medium	190,363	3.1	+ 431,350	+ 566,234	- 98,495	- 36,389	- 3.5	19.1	36.9	+ 226.6
P.L.F. Small	268,737	4.4	+ 539,193	+ 875,595	- 221,510	- 114,892	- 10.9	42.8	51.9	+ 200.6
S.L.F. Large	133,774	2.2	+ 276,854	+ 380,937	- 55,577	- 48,506	- 4.6	36.3	87.3	+ 207.0
S.L.F. Medium	195,133	3.2	+ 414,108	+ 596,651	- 120,505	- 62,038	- 5.9	31.8	51.5	+ 212.2
S.L.F. Small	289,977	4.7	+ 469,676	+ 968,206	- 255,384	- 243,146	- 23.1	83.9	95.2	+ 162.0
Outside	663,886	10.8	+ 1,097,034	+ 1,876,361	- 258,933	- 520,394	- 49.5	78.4	201.0	+ 165.2
Total	6,142,720	100.0	+ 14,583,558	+ 14,619,079	± 1,065,677	± 1,030,061	± 100.0	16.8	96.7	+ 237.4

APPENDIX II-D (*continued*)

Panel B: 31-Sector Grouping

Transaction Field Category	R_{ij}	% Total $\pm R_{ij}$	R_{ij}	% Total $\pm R_{ij}$	R_{ij}	% Total $\pm R_{ij}$
	All-Sector Employment		Agriculture		Forestry and Fisheries	
Urb Cen Large	- 3,103,152	- 89.8	+ 105,110	+ 41.8	- 851	- 12.5
Urb Cen Medium	+ 1,263,422	+ 36.7	+ 84,992	+ 33.8	+ 2,673	+ 28.9
Urb Cen Small	+ 860,944	+ 25.0	+ 47,355	+ 18.8	+ 2,299	+ 24.9
P.L.F. Large	+ 170,613	+ 5.0	- 5,045	- 2.1	- 2,630	- 38.6
P.L.F. Medium	+ 348,663	+ 10.1	- 27,995	- 11.4	- 1,394	- 20.5
P.L.F. Small	+ 516,410	+ 15.0	- 72,304	- 29.5	+ 468	+ 5.1
S.L.F. Large	+ 60,039	+ 1.7	+ 13,848	+ 5.5	+ 433	+ 4.7
S.L.F. Medium	+ 205,162	+ 6.0	- 15,058	- 6.1	- 1,938	- 28.4
S.L.F. Small	+ 16,280	+ .5	- 84,286	- 34.4	+ 31	+ .3
Outside	- 352,074	- 10.2	- 40,527	- 16.5	+ 3,339	+ 36.1
	Mining		Contract Construction		Total Manufacturing	
Urb Cen Large	+ 35,526	+ 43.6	- 211,683	- 84.5	- 1,580,542	- 83.6
Urb Cen Medium	+ 25,796	+ 31.7	+ 103,673	+ 42.9	- 242,397	- 12.8
Urb Cen Small	+ 14,595	+ 17.9	+ 53,256	+ 22.0	- 68,037	- 3.6
P.L.F. Large	- 30,538	- 38.0	+ 27,563	+ 11.4	+ 159,523	+ 8.5
P.L.F. Medium	- 1,654	- 2.1	+ 24,650	+ 10.2	+ 270,933	+ 14.4
P.L.F. Small	- 7,959	- 9.9	+ 23,718	+ 9.8	+ 509,712	+ 27.1
S.L.F. Large	- 15,237	- 18.9	+ 2,581	+ 1.1	+ 93,876	+ 5.0
S.L.F. Medium	+ 5,501	+ 6.8	+ 6,647	+ 2.7	+ 198,246	+ 10.5
S.L.F. Small	- 15,213	- 18.9	- 12,426	- 5.0	+ 325,096	+ 17.3
Outside	- 9,831	- 12.2	- 26,520	- 10.6	+ 325,968	+ 17.3
	Food Manufacturing		Textile Manufacturing		Apparel Manufacturing	
Urb Cen Large	- 159,586	- 97.0	- 60,709	- 26.0	- 320,005	- 92.6
Urb Cen Medium	- 4,937	- 3.0	- 74,642	- 32.0	- 25,643	- 7.4
Urb Cen Small	+ 10,780	+ 6.5	- 61,523	- 26.4	+ 21,637	+ 6.3
P.L.F. Large	+ 9,153	+ 5.5	- 36,360	- 15.6	+ 20,383	+ 5.9
P.L.F. Medium	+ 16,886	+ 10.2	+ 13,547	+ 5.8	+ 11,429	+ 3.3
P.L.F. Small	+ 31,146	+ 18.8	+ 87,277	+ 37.4	+ 77,262	+ 22.5
S.L.F. Large	+ 12,802	+ 7.7	+ 310	+ .1	+ 13,850	+ 4.0
S.L.F. Medium	+ 13,058	+ 7.9	+ 15,104	+ 6.5	+ 39,899	+ 11.6
S.L.F. Small	+ 30,494	+ 18.5	+ 92,302	+ 39.6	+ 71,227	+ 20.8
Outside	+ 40,917	+ 24.8	+ 24,631	+ 10.6	+ 87,502	+ 25.5
	Printing and Publishing		Chemical Manufacturing		Lumber and Wood Products	
Urb Cen Large	- 103,659	- 100.0	- 82,759	- 81.3	- 6,039	- 15.5
Urb Cen Medium	+ 41,248	+ 40.0	+ 8,844	+ 8.7	+ 2,545	+ 6.8
Urb Cen Small	+ 14,653	+ 14.2	+ 22,833	+ 22.4	- 6,406	- 16.4
P.L.F. Large	+ 17,022	+ 16.5	+ 27,294	+ 26.8	+ 2,073	+ 5.6
P.L.F. Medium	+ 13,698	+ 13.3	+ 13,022	+ 12.8	+ 6,274	+ 16.9
P.L.F. Small	+ 4,765	+ 4.6	+ 24,402	+ 24.0	+ 26,271	+ 70.7
S.L.F. Large	+ 6,092	+ 5.9	- 1,012	- 1.0	- 7,269	- 18.6
S.L.F. Medium	+ 2,976	+ 2.9	+ 5,353	+ 5.3	- 7,635	- 19.6
S.L.F. Small	+ 1,120	+ 1.1	- 1,546	- 1.5	- 5,314	- 13.6
Outside	+ 1,601	+ 1.6	- 16,478	- 16.2	- 6,390	- 16.4

APPENDIX II-D Panel B (*continued*)

Transaction Field Category	R_{ij}	% Total $\pm R_{ij}$	R_{ij}	% Total $\pm R_{ij}$	R_{ij}	% Total $\pm R_{ij}$
	Machinery Manufacturing		Motor Vehicle Manufacturing		Transportation Equipment Mfg.	
Urb Cen Large	- 216,664	- 51.1	- 184,365	- 100.0	- 168,159	- 99.8
Urb Cen Medium	- 152,118	- 35.9	+ 22,819	+ 12.4	+ 56,152	+ 33.3
Urb Cen Small	- 55,207	- 13.0	+ 35,553	+ 19.3	+ 5,887	+ 3.5
P.L.F. Large	+ 67,733	+ 16.0	+ 26,002	+ 14.1	+ 15,258	+ 9.0
P.L.F. Medium	+ 75,480	+ 17.8	+ 32,673	+ 17.7	+ 34,581	+ 20.5
P.L.F. Small	+ 89,937	+ 21.3	+ 23,695	+ 12.9	+ 5,593	+ 3.3
S.L.F. Large	+ 40,905	+ 9.7	+ 4,328	+ 2.3	- 384	- .2
S.L.F. Medium	+ 38,836	+ 9.2	+ 12,194	+ 6.6	+ 17,088	+ 10.1
S.L.F. Small	+ 38,273	+ 9.0	+ 13,970	+ 7.6	+ 10,718	+ 6.4
Outside	+ 72,041	+ 17.0	+ 13,089	+ 7.1	+ 23,350	+ 13.8
	Other Manufacturing		Railroad Transportation		Trucking and Warehousing	
Urb Cen Large	- 278,597	- 61.7	+ 3,075	+ 16.0	+ 5,254	+ 7.3
Urb Cen Medium	- 116,665	- 25.8	+ 9,586	+ 50.0	+ 43,552	+ 60.5
Urb Cen Small	- 56,244	- 12.5	+ 5,541	+ 28.9	+ 15,294	+ 21.3
P.L.F. Large	+ 10,965	+ 2.4	- 5,950	- 31.1	+ 4,762	+ 6.6
P.L.F. Medium	+ 53,343	+ 11.9	+ 340	+ 1.8	+ 3,106	+ 4.3
P.L.F. Small	+ 139,364	+ 31.0	- 394	- 2.1	- 3,338	- 4.6
S.L.F. Large	+ 24,254	+ 5.4	- 625	- 3.3	- 4,318	- 5.9
S.L.F. Medium	+ 61,373	+ 13.7	+ 646	+ 3.4	- 8,723	- 12.0
S.L.F. Small	+ 73,852	+ 16.5	- 2,039	- 10.7	- 18,112	- 24.8
Outside	+ 85,705	+ 19.1	- 10,128	- 52.9	- 38,396	- 52.7
	Other Transportation		Communications		Utilities	
Urb Cen Large	- 30,768	- 73.0	- 44,377	- 70.2	- 101,255	- 100.0
Urb Cen Medium	- 3,162	- 7.5	+ 25,675	+ 44.1	+ 15,292	+ 15.3
Urb Cen Small	- 8,234	- 19.5	+ 25,377	+ 43.6	+ 8,450	+ 8.5
P.L.F. Large	+ 12,559	+ 34.9	+ 6,642	+ 11.4	+ 5,205	+ 5.2
P.L.F. Medium	+ 6,459	+ 18.0	+ 469	+ .8	+ 8,127	+ 8.1
P.L.F. Small	+ 5,408	+ 15.0	- 241	- .4	+ 16,059	+ 16.1
S.L.F. Large	+ 2,985	+ 8.3	- 694	- 1.1	+ 3,007	+ 3.0
S.L.F. Medium	+ 4,042	+ 11.2	- 613	- 1.0	+ 9,698	+ 9.7
S.L.F. Small	+ 876	+ 2.4	- 3,566	- 5.6	+ 12,101	+ 12.1
Outside	+ 3,653	+ 10.2	- 13,716	- 21.7	+ 21,829	+ 21.9
	Wholesale Trade		Total Retail		Eating and Drinking	
Urb Cen Large	- 2,100	- 1.6	- 573,788	- 87.9	- 204,688	- 98.2
Urb Cen Medium	+ 96,662	+ 77.5	+ 293,815	+ 46.6	+ 80,508	+ 40.1
Urb Cen Small	+ 22,856	+ 18.3	+ 162,350	+ 25.8	+ 49,072	+ 24.5
P.L.F. Large	+ 2,265	+ 1.8	+ 30,583	+ 4.9	+ 12,655	+ 6.3
P.L.F. Medium	+ 2,898	+ 2.3	+ 50,904	+ 8.1	+ 13,596	+ 9.3
P.L.F. Small	+ 85	-0-	+ 49,244	+ 7.8	+ 14,223	+ 7.1
S.L.F. Large	- 11,352	- 8.6	+ 12,241	+ 1.9	+ 7,953	+ 4.0
S.L.F. Medium	- 22,254	- 16.9	+ 31.239	+ 5.0	+ 14,230	+ 7.1
S.L.F. Small	- 26,224	- 19.9	- 31,211	- 4.8	- 3,836	- 1.8
Outside	- 69,651	- 52.9	- 47,886	- 7.3	+ 3,444	+ 1.7

APPENDIX II-D Panel B (*continued*)

Transaction Field Category	R_{ij}	% Total $\pm R_{ij}$	R_{ij}	% Total $\pm R_{ij}$	R_{ij}	% Total $\pm R_{ij}$
	Food and Dairy		Other Retail		Finance, Insurance, Real Estate	
Urb Cen Large	- 306,606	- 83.5	- 62,494	- 77.7	- 314,067	- 100.0
Urb Cen Medium	+ 168,080	+ 47.4	+ 45,227	+ 57.9	+ 115,825	+ 38.3
Urb Cen Small	+ 96,983	+ 27.3	+ 16,295	+ 20.8	+ 78,253	+ 25.9
P.L.F. Large	+ 16,163	+ 4.6	+ 1,765	+ 2.3	+ 21,005	+ 6.9
P.L.F. Medium	+ 25,897	+ 7.3	+ 6,411	+ 8.2	+ 20,535	+ 6.8
P.L.F. Small	+ 28,742	+ 8.1	+ 6,279	+ 8.0	+ 24,180	+ 8.0
S.L.F. Large	+ 2,578	+ .7	+ 1,710	+ 2.2	+ 9,392	+ 3.1
S.L.F. Medium	+ 16,520	+ 4.7	+ 489	+ .6	+ 13,390	+ 4.4
S.L.F. Small	- 22,871	- 6.2	- 4,504	- 5.6	+ 4,228	+ 1.4
Outside	- 37,933	- 10.3	- 13,397	- 16.7	+ 15,554	+ 5.1
	Total Services		Lodging and Personal		Business and Repair	
Urb Cen Large	- 77,869	- 8.4	- 148,342	- 97.2	+ 190,830	+ 68.0
Urb Cen Medium	+ 563,249	+ 63.0	+ 48,900	+ 34.7	+ 85,502	+ 30.5
Urb Cen Small	+ 331,058	+ 37.0	+ 49,348	+ 35.0	+ 4,350	+ 1.5
P.L.F. Large	- 51,935	- 5.6	- 553	- .4	- 12,986	- 4.6
P.L.F. Medium	- 20,677	- 2.2	+ 12,054	+ 8.5	- 23,409	- 8.3
P.L.F. Small	- 84,565	- 9.2	+ 16,087	+ 11.4	- 37,956	- 13.4
S.L.F. Large	- 43,797	- 4.7	+ 2,340	+ 1.7	- 21,267	- 7.5
S.L.F. Medium	- 41,333	- 4.5	+ 9,261	+ 6.6	- 21,144	- 7.5
S.L.F. Small	- 211,637	- 22.9	- 3,660	- 2.4	- 52,747	- 18.6
Outside	- 392,302	- 42.5	+ 3,007	+ 2.1	- 113,583	- 40.1
	Amusement and Recreation		Private Households		Professional Services	
Urb Cen Large	- 33,731	- 71.7	- 68,601	- 95.6	- 18,025	- 2.7
Urb Cen Medium	+ 23,073	+ 51.0	+ 11,669	+ 16.0	+ 394,105	+ 61.5
Urb Cen Small	+ 19,198	+ 42.4	+ 11,744	+ 16.1	+ 246,418	+ 38.5
P.L.F. Large	+ 1,094	+ 2.4	- 3,145	- 4.4	- 36,345	- 5.5
P.L.F. Medium	+ 1,618	+ 3.6	+ 5,767	+ 7.9	- 16,707	- 2.5
P.L.F. Small	+ 283	+ .6	+ 12,265	+ 16.9	- 75,244	- 11.5
S.L.F. Large	+ 1	-0-	+ 1,656	+ 2.3	- 26,526	- 4.0
S.L.F. Medium	- 857	- 1.8	+ 10,215	+ 14.0	- 38,808	- 5.9
S.L.F. Small	- 3,659	- 7.8	+ 8,069	+ 11.1	- 159,640	- 24.3
Outside	- 8,787	- 18.7	+ 11,376	+ 15.6	- 284,315	- 43.4
	Civilian Government		Armed Forces			
Urb Cen Large	- 110,776	- 43.4	- 204,041	- 87.1		
Urb Cen Medium	+ 130,083	+ 55.6	- 2,092	- .9		
Urb Cen Small	+ 78,649	+ 33.6	+ 91,882	+ 27.6		
P.L.F. Large	+ 23,157	+ 9.9	- 26,553	- 11.3		
P.L.F. Medium	+ 2,109	+ .9	+ 9,853	+ 3.0		
P.L.F. Small	- 1,975	- .8	+ 58,312	+ 17.5		
S.L.F. Large	- 714	- .3	- 1,587	- .7		
S.L.F. Medium	- 1,229	- .5	+ 26,901	+ 8.1		
S.L.F. Small	- 27,100	- 10.6	+ 105,762	+ 31.8		
Outside	- 113,709	- 44.5	+ 40,249	+ 12.1		

(shaded) Industry sector ratios greater than corresponding ratios for all-sector employment.

* See note at end of Appendix B, Panel B.

APPENDIX II-H. Leading and Lagging Industry-Sector Competitive Shifts for Eight Synthetic Regions Based Upon the B Code, 1940–70

(Reproduced from Table 40, Vol. I)

Code B1 Region $+k_{ij}$, $+R_{ij}$ Industry	Rank	*	Percent Shift #
Bus. & Rep.	Leading Gainers	S	+ 76.6
Other Trans.		S	+ 65.0
Total Serv.		S	+ 64.6
Whol. Trade		S	+ 64.4
Prof. Serv.		S	+ 63.9
Civ. Gov.		S	+ 63.1
Commun.		S	+ 61.8
Pr. & Pub.		S	+ 60.3
Amus. & Rec.		S	+ 60.0
Other Ret.		S	+ 59.3
F.I.R.E.		S	+ 59.0
Tot Ret Tr.		S	+ 58.9
Truck & Whs.		S	+ 58.6
Food Ret.		S	+ 58.3
R.R. Trans.		S	+ 57.8
Total R_{ij}			+ 56.4
Lodg. & Per.	Lagging Gainers	S	+ 55.4
Eat & Drink		S	+ 54.1
Trans. Equip.		S	+ 50.8
Construc.		S	+ 49.4
Mach. Mfg.		U	+ 49.0
Chem. Mfg.		S	+ 46.7
Utilities		S	+ 43.5
Other Mfg.		U	+ 42.0
Total Mfg.		U	+ 41.5
Pvt. Hshld.		S	+ 39.5
Agric.		U	+ 38.7
Lum. & Wood		S	+ 38.6
Mining		U	+ 37.8
For. & Fish		S	+ 37.4
Armed For.		S	+ 35.4
Mot Veh Mfg.		S	+ 32.3
Food Mfg.		S	+ 27.7
Apparel Mfg.		U	+ 16.4
Textile Mfg.		U	+ .5

Code B2 Region $+k_{ij}$, $+R_{ij}$ Industry	Rank	*	Percent Shift #
R.R. Trans.	Leading Gainers	S	+ 7.4
Civ. Gov.		S	+ 7.1
Truck & Whs.		S	+ 7.0
Prof. Serv.		S	+ 6.7
Mot Veh Mfg.		S	+ 6.3
Total Serv.		S	+ 6.1
Whol. Trade		S	+ 6.0
Amus. & Rec.		S	+ 6.0
Pr. & Pub.		S	+ 5.3
Eat & Drink		S	+ 5.2
Bus. & Rep.		S	+ 5.1
Tot Ret Tr.		S	+ 4.7
Agric.		U	+ 4.5
Food Ret.		S	+ 4.5
Pvt. Hsld.		U	+ 4.3
Other Ret.		S	+ 3.7
Lodg. & Per.		S	+ 3.5
F.I.R.E.		S	+ 3.2
Communic.		S	+ 2.4
Total R_{ij}			+ 2.2
Construc.	Lagging Gainers	S	+ 1.8
Other Trans.		S	+ 1.7
Mining		U	+ 1.2
Tran. Equip.		S	+ 1.1
Mach. Mfg.		U	+ .4
Total Mfg.		S	+ .1
Utilities	Counter Trend	S	- .1
Other Mfg.		S	- .6
Apparel Mfg.		U	- 1.1
Food Mfg.		S	- 1.5
Chem. Mfg.		S	- 1.5
Textile Mfg.		U	- 3.7
Lum. & Wood		S	- 5.0
For. & Fish		U	- 10.2
Armed For.		S	- 24.7

Code B3 Region $-k_{ij}$, $+R_{ij}$ Industry	Rank	*	Percent Shift #
Armed For.	Leading Gainers	U	+ 63.9
Lumb. & Wood		S	+ 48.3
For. & Fish.		S	+ 46.9
Mining		U	+ 40.5
Agric.		S	+ 37.7
Pvt. Hshld.		S	+ 37.0
Construct.		S	+ 36.4
Chem. Mfg.		U	+ 35.7
Utilities		U	+ 34.5
Truck & Whs.		U	+ 33.7
Total R_{ij}			+ 32.6
Amus. & Rec.	Lagging Gainers	U	+ 31.9
Tot Ret Tr.		U	+ 31.5
Communic.		U	+ 31.3
Eat & Drink		U	+ 31.3
Food Ret.		U	+ 31.2
Lodg. & Per.		U	+ 30.9
F.I.R.E.		U	+ 30.3
Food Mfg.		U	+ 29.7
R.R. Trans.		U	+ 29.7
Prof. Serv.		U	+ 29.1
Total Serv.		U	+ 28.9
Civ. Gov.		U	+ 28.7
Other Ret.		U	+ 28.3
Textile Mfg.		S	+ 27.6
Whol. Tr.		U	+ 27.5
Pr. & Pub.		U	+ 27.4
Other Trans.		U	+ 26.8
Tran. Equip.		U	+ 26.3
Total Mfg.		U	+ 25.9
Other Mfg.		U	+ 24.7
Mot Veh Mfg.		U	+ 23.5
Mach. Mfg.		U	+ 22.8
Bus. & Rep.		U	+ 18.5
Apparel Mfg.		U	+ 14.3

Code B4 Region $+k_{ij}$, $-R_{ij}$ Industry	Rank	*	Percent Shift #
Agric.	Counter Trend	U	+ 6.5
For. & Fish		U	+ 6.2
Mot Veh Mfg.		S	+ 4.9
Mining		U	+ 3.8
Bus. & Rep.		S	+ 2.6
Eat & Drink		S	+ 1.9
Whol. Trade		S	+ 1.4
Other Ret.		S	+ 1.4
Amus. & Rec.		U	+ 1.1
Truck & Whs.		S	+ .6
Chem. Mfg.		S	+ .4
Prof. Serv.	Lagging Decliners	S	- .4
Tot Ret Tr.		S	- .4
Tot. Serv.		S	- .6
Pr. & Pub.		S	- .9
Food Ret.		S	- 1.6
Lodg. & Per.		S	- 1.9
Civ. Gov.		S	- 3.2
Construc.		S	- 3.3
Communic.		S	- 3.8
R.R. Trans.		S	- 4.3
Other Trans.		S	- 5.2
Total R_{ij}			- 5.4
F.I.R.E.	Leading Decliners	S	- 5.9
Other Mfg.		S	- 6.0
Utilities		S	- 7.1
Food Mfg.		S	- 8.6
Apparel Mfg.		U	- 9.1
Lum. & Wood		U	- 9.3
Total Mfg.		S	- 10.6
Pvt. Hshld.		S	- 10.7
Textile Mfg.		U	- 12.3
Mach. Mfg.		S	- 16.5
Armed For.		S	- 21.6
Tran. Equip.		S	- 26.7

APPENDIX II-H (*continued*)

Code B5 Region $+k_{ij}$, $-R_{ij}$

Industry Rank	Percent * Shift #	Group
Agric.	U + 11.8	
Mining	U - .3	Lagging Decliners
For. & Fish	U - 20.8	Lagging Decliners
Lum. & Wood	U - 41.0	Lagging Decliners
Bus. & Rep.	S - 41.2	Lagging Decliners
Armed For.	U - 42.3	Lagging Decliners
Civ. Gov.	S - 54.7	Lagging Decliners
Truck & Whs.	S - 56.7	Lagging Decliners
Prof. Serv.	S - 58.2	Lagging Decliners
R.R. Trans.	S - 58.2	Lagging Decliners
Textile Mfg.	U - 60.8	Lagging Decliners
Total Serv.	S - 61.3	Lagging Decliners
Whole. Tr.	S - 70.1	Lagging Decliners
Communic.	S - 71.5	Lagging Decliners
Tran. Equip.	S - 73.3	Lagging Decliners
Amus. & Rec.	S - 74.1	Lagging Decliners
Construc.	U - 74.6	Lagging Decliners
Pvt. Hshld.	U - 75.2	Lagging Decliners
Total R_{ij}	- 75.6	
Other Ret.	S - 76.7	Leading Decliners
Food Ret.	S - 76.9	Leading Decliners
Tot Ret Tr.	S - 80.5	Leading Decliners
Lodg. & Per.	S - 81.5	Leading Decliners
Food Mfg.	S - 83.2	Leading Decliners
Mach. Mfg.	S - 83.5	Leading Decliners
Other Mfg.	S - 83.8	Leading Decliners
Other Trans.	S - 84.8	Leading Decliners
F.I.R.E.	S - 85.2	Leading Decliners
Eat & Drink	S - 85.4	Leading Decliners
Total Mfg.	S - 86.2	Leading Decliners
Apparel Mfg.	S - 90.1	Leading Decliners
Pr. & Pub.	S - 91.6	Leading Decliners
Chem. Mfg.	S - 92.4	Leading Decliners
Utilities	S - 93.0	Leading Decliners
Mot Veh Mfg.	S -100.0	Leading Decliners

Code B6 Region $-k_{ij}$, $+R_{ij}$

Industry Rank	Percent * Shift #	Group
Textile Mfg.	S + 69.0	Leading Gainers
Apparel Mfg.	U + 42.7	Leading Gainers
Food Mfg.	U + 29.8	Leading Gainers
Total Mfg.	U + 24.7	Leading Gainers
Other Mfg.	U + 24.2	Leading Gainers
Utilities	U + 21.4	Leading Gainers
Mot Veh Mfg.	U + 19.7	Leading Gainers
Pvt. Hshld.	U + 19.5	Leading Gainers
Chem. Mfg.	U + 17.2	Leading Gainers
Mining	U + 17.0	Leading Gainers
Mach. Mfg.	U + 15.9	Leading Gainers
Tran. Equip.	U + 14.8	Leading Gainers
Construc.	U + 12.5	Leading Gainers
Lum. & Wood	S + 12.3	Leading Gainers
Lodg. & Per.	U + 8.8	Leading Gainers
Total R_{ij}	+ 8.8	
Pr. & Pub.	U + 6.9	Lagging Gainers
Other Ret.	U + 6.8	Lagging Gainers
F.I.R.E.	U + 6.8	Lagging Gainers
Eat & Drink	U + 6.7	Lagging Gainers
Tot Ret Tr.	U + 6.1	Lagging Gainers
Armed For.	U + 5.8	Lagging Gainers
R.R. Trans.	U + 5.7	Lagging Gainers
Food Ret.	U + 5.5	Lagging Gainers
Other Trans.	U + 5.4	Lagging Gainers
Communic.	U + 3.5	Lagging Gainers
Amus. & Rec.	U + .4	Lagging Gainers
Whol. Tr.	U - 1.1	Counter Trend
Truck & Whs.	U - 1.2	Counter Trend
Total Serv.	U - 2.2	Counter Trend
Civ. Gov.	U - 2.9	Counter Trend
Prof. Serv.	U - 4.3	Counter Trend
Bus. & Rep.	U - 14.6	Counter Trend
For. & Fish	S - 32.6	Counter Trend
Agric.	S - 55.3	Counter Trend

Code B7 Region $-k_{ij}$, $-R_{ij}$

Industry Rank	Percent * Shift #	Group
For. & Fish	U + 22.5	Counter Trend
Agric.	U + 17.2	Counter Trend
Utilities	S + 9.9	Counter Trend
Apparel Mfg.	U + 9.1	Counter Trend
Mot Veh Mfg.	U + 4.5	Counter Trend
Mach. Mfg.	U + 3.6	Counter Trend
Tran. Equip.	U + .9	Counter Trend
Total Mfg.	U - 3.3	Lagging Losses
Armed For.	U - 4.2	Lagging Losses
Chem. Mfg.	U - 5.7	Lagging Losses
Food Mfg.	U - 6.6	Lagging Losses
F.I.R.E.	U - 7.2	Lagging Losses
Pr. & Pub.	U - 7.2	Lagging Losses
Eat & Drink	U - 8.6	Lagging Losses
Other Trans.	U - 9.1	Lagging Losses
Other Mfg.	S - 9.8	Lagging Losses
Amus. & Rec.	U - 10.9	Lagging Losses
Lodg. & Per.	U - 11.0	Lagging Losses
Total R_{ij}	- 11.2	
Communic.	U - 11.2	Leading Losses
Whol. Tr.	U - 11.3	Leading Losses
Construc.	U - 11.8	Leading Losses
Tot Ret Tr.	U - 12.3	Leading Losses
Food Ret.	U - 12.7	Leading Losses
Pvt. Hshld.	S - 13.4	Leading Losses
Other Ret.	S - 13.8	Leading Losses
Truck & Whs.	U - 14.4	Leading Losses
Lum. & Wood	S - 14.5	Leading Losses
Total Serv.	U - 15.2	Leading Losses
Prof. Serv.	S - 15.4	Leading Losses
Bus. & Rep.	U - 17.5	Leading Losses
Textile Mfg.	S - 23.1	Leading Losses
R.R. Trans.	U - 24.2	Leading Losses
Civ. Gov.	S - 26.1	Leading Losses
Mining	S - 75.2	Leading Losses

Code B8 Region $-k_{ij}$, $-R_{ij}$

Industry Rank	Percent * Shift #	Group
Apparel Mfg.	U + 17.3	Counter Trend
Food Mfg.	U + 12.9	Counter Trend
Utilities	U + 9.8	Counter Trend
Other Mfg.	U + 9.5	Counter Trend
Mot Veh Mfg.	U + 8.7	Counter Trend
Mach. Mfg.	U + 8.3	Counter Trend
Total Mfg.	U + 7.7	Counter Trend
Tran. Equip.	U + 6.0	Counter Trend
Textile Mfg.	U + 2.8	Counter Trend
Armed For.	U + 2.2	Counter Trend
Pvt. Hshld.	U - .3	Lagging Losses
Chem. Mfg.	U - .3	Lagging Losses
Pr. & Pub.	U - .5	Lagging Losses
Other Trans.	U - 1.9	Lagging Losses
F.I.R.E.	U - 2.4	Lagging Losses
Eat & Drink	U - 6.8	Lagging Losses
Lodg. & Per.	U - 7.0	Lagging Losses
Total R_{ij}	- 7.6	
Tot Ret Tr.	U - 9.0	Leading Losses
Food Ret.	U - 9.3	Leading Losses
R.R. Trans.	U - 9.3	Leading Losses
Other Ret.	U - 9.7	Leading Losses
Construc.	U - 11.5	Leading Losses
Civ. Gov.	U - 14.0	Leading Losses
Communic.	U - 14.6	Leading Losses
Amus. & Rec.	U - 15.8	Leading Losses
Whol. Tr.	U - 18.3	Leading Losses
Total Serv.	U - 20.5	Leading Losses
Prof. Serv.	U - 22.0	Leading Losses
For. & Fish	S - 23.4	Leading Losses
Mining	S - 24.2	Leading Losses
Truck & Whs.	U - 28.1	Leading Losses
Bus. & Rep.	U - 30.6	Leading Losses
Lum. & Wood	S - 30.9	Leading Losses
Agric.	S - 43.9	Leading Losses

* S = Specialized, U = Unspecialized

$\frac{\text{Regional competitive shift}}{\text{All-region competitive shift}}$ for summary line and each industry line

APPENDIX II-I. Comparison of Proportion of Total Competitive Gains or Losses ($\pm R_{ij}$) Contributed by Four Lower Order Trade Centers Depending on the Household Commuting Transaction Field in Which They Were Located, 1940–70

Note: Appendix II-I is produced in the same way as the base tables from which text tables II-8 and II-9 were produced. The 3,065 counties were grouped into 90 synthetic regions defined by the cross-tabulation of the trade-center and transaction-field classifications. (Some of these cross-classifications were nul sets, of course.) The competitive gains and losses for each of the 31 industry sectors were computed for each of the 90 regions. The competitive gains and losses for each industry were then converted to percentages of the total *plus and minus* competitive shifts between all 90 synthetic regions. these percentage competitive shifts are recorded in Appendix II-I for 31 of the 90 synthetic regions formed by the lower order trade centers identified with the transaction fields where they are located. The remaining sets made up the core transaction fields, and the higher order trade-center classifications were aggregated into a single column of appendix II-I headed "core composite." The percentages are to be read horizontally by rows, but the sum of each row is no longer ± 100% because of the netting involved in generating the core composite column. Though they are not arranged here in the same manner as in tables II-8 and II-9, a comparison of the column percentages can be employed tó identify the leading and lagging sectors of each synthetic region.

Note: The algebraic sum of all complete shopping centers (partial shopping centers, etc.) across all transaction fields does not correspond directly with the complete shopping shift patterns presented in table II-8. In computing table II-8, all 3,065 counties were first aggregated to the 9 trade center categories before the shift-share algorithm was applied. In appendix II-I the algorithm was applied to the 90 synthetic regions thus aggregated. The difference in the sequence generates a different order of netting so that the two patterns do not match. Nevertheless, appendix II-I can be employed to learn something about the pattern variations within trade center groupings.

::::::: The gain (or loss) displayed by the industry is greater than (or less than) that displayed by the total employment of the synthetic region.

* Each industry sector competitive gains (or losses) characteristic of each trade-center/transaction-field synthetic region is greater than (or less than) the average of all centers of a type (e.g., complete shopping, etc.).

APPENDIX II-I. Comparison of Proportion of Total Competitive Gains or Losses ($\pm R_{ij}$) Contributed by Four Lower Order Trade Centers Depending on the Household Commuting Transaction Field in Which They Were Located, 1940–70

Ind. #	Industry Sector	Core Composite	Complete Shopping							
			Core	PLF-L	PLF-M	PLF-S	SLF-L	SLF-M	SLF-S	Outside
	Total Employment	- 73.02	+ 5.59	+ 12.32*	+ 14.46*	+ 18.85*	+ 3.52	+ 18.60*	+ 3.84	- 5.94
1	Agriculture	+ 87.75	+ 3.06*	+ .74*	- 3.98	- 7.65	+ 1.64*	+ 5.30*	- 13.57	- 11.78
2	Forest. & Fisheries	+ 55.89	- 1.06	- 7.61	- 5.43	+ 10.97*	+ 1.15*	- 2.04	- 12.41	+ 15.95*
3	Mining	+ 59.15	+ 3.47*	+ 1.22*	- 1.69*	- 9.56	- 32.14	+ 9.28*	- 8.20	- 23.99
4	Contract Construction	- 57.69	+ .94	+ 18.62*	+ 11.41*	+ 14.14*	+ 5.99	+ 10.82*	- 7.51	- 4.45
	Total Manufacturing	- 99.97	+ .15	+ 5.49	+ 8.04	+ 15.17	+ 2.66	+ 7.59	+ 8.58	+ 8.72
5	Food Mfg.	- 100.00	+ 1.15	+ 3.90	+ 4.45	+ 10.01*	+ 3.07	+ 5.47	+ 9.99*	+ 16.34*
6	Textile Mfg.	- 95.59	+ .16	- .47	+ 4.57	+ 21.35*	- .79	+ 5.22	+ 20.74*	+ 5.73
7	Apparel Mfg.	- 100.00	+ .06	+ 2.02	+ .51	+ 11.53*	+ 4.28	+ 4.37	+ 12.11*	+ 10.36*
8	Print. & Publishing	- 94.94	+ .81	+ 17.03*	+ 27.39*	+ 5.00	+ 10.45*	+ 8.47	+ 1.08	+ 6.62
9	Chemical Mfg.	- 79.85	+ 1.28	+ 23.58*	+ 12.36*	+ 14.93*	+ 1.35	+ 7.43*	- 8.70	- 9.96
10	Lumber & Wood Products	+ 13.39	+ .17	- 1.00	+ 8.59*	+ 51.86*	- 7.78	- 25.08	- 5.06	- 17.24
11	Machinery Mfg.	- 98.99	+ .15	+ 8.21*	+ 13.14*	+ 13.45*	+ 6.05	+ 9.41*	+ 3.49	+ 10.76*
12	Motor Veh. Mfg.	- 100.16	+ .03	+ 9.50*	+ 16.62*	+ 14.43*	+ 1.67	+ 5.71	+ 6.16	+ 8.36*
13	Other Trans. Equip.	- 93.57	+ .25	+ 3.20	+ 23.10*	- 1.30	- 5.11	+ 12.91*	+ 6.21	+ 11.98*
14	Other Manufacturing	- 99.55	- .37	+ 4.79	+ 3.05	+ 17.26*	+ 2.20	+ 10.42*	+ 7.89*	+ 7.41*
	Total Trans., Comm., Util.	- 14.26	+ 4.24	+ 16.73	+ 9.71	+ 8.92	+ 3.05	+ 12.62	- 3.94	- 28.81
15	Railroad Transp.	+ 78.56	+ .94*	- 7.26*	- 4.08*	- 16.81	- 3.38*	+ 4.54*	- 5.10	- 36.31
16	Trucking & Warehousing	+ 95.82	+ .16*	+ 2.28*	- 1.08*	- 1.75*	- 3.69*	- 6.98	- 11.93	- 20.94
17	Other Transport.	- 99.49	+ 2.09	+ 12.57*	+ 10.42*	+ 7.14*	+ 8.96*	+ 6.80	+ 3.22	+ 4.39
18	Communications	+ 71.54	+ 3.38*	+ 7.38*	+ .52	+ .41	+ 1.76*	+ 8.48*	- .24	- 16.65
19	Utilities	- 100.00	+ .64	+ 3.24	+ 3.94	+ 8.63*	+ 1.87	+ 9.24*	+ 8.88*	+ 11.71*
20	Wholesale Trade	+ 95.03	- 1.54*	+ .23*	- 1.88*	- 2.66*	- 3.35	- 12.91	- 10.64	- 26.53
	Total Retail Trade	- 52.92	+ 4.92	+ 15.32	+ 16.66	+ 10.54	+ 7.10	+ 19.94	- 6.95	- 7.01
21	Eating & Drinking	- 85.76	+ 2.10	+ 12.21*	+ 18.33*	+ 10.49*	+ 8.59	+ 19.07*	- .94	+ 10.25*
22	Other Retail	- 9.25	+ 5.80*	+ 20.52*	+ 10.39*	+ 2.69*	+ 7.04*	+ 8.90*	- 9.51	- 34.19
23	Food & Dairy	- 35.59	+ 6.19	+ 14.94*	+ 15.41*	+ 11.33*	+ 5.49	+ 21.14*	- 9.82	- 12.14
24	Fin., Ins. Real Est.	- 99.87	+ 2.09	+ 11.09*	+ 12.60*	+ 11.80*	+ 7.48	+ 14.12*	+ 3.11	+ 8.75
	Total Services	+ 95.50	+ 1.50	+ 1.02	+ .19	- 5.21	- 1.50	+ 1.61	- 11.63	- 16.10
25	Lodging & Personal	- 93.82	+ 4.09	+ 8.91*	+ 13.23*	+ 13.59*	+ 3.87	+ 15.80*	- 1.20	+ 4.76
26	Business & Repair	+ 99.88	+ .12	- 2.30	- 5.41	- 8.99	- 4.22	- 2.88	- 9.90	- 20.56
27	Amusement & Recreation	+ 67.15	+ 1.97*	+ 9.53*	- .08*	- .19*	+ 2.69*	- 1.11*	- 16.17	- 14.61
28	Private Households	- 98.74	+ 3.09	- 1.26	+ 5.60	+ 10.95*	+ .24	+ 15.06*	+ 10.30*	+ 9.84*
29	Professional Services	+ 95.28	+ 1.27*	+ 1.52*	+ 1.07*	- 4.88	- .53*	+ .86*	- 11.29	- 12.99
	Total Government									
30	Civil Government	+ 71.73	+ 4.67*	+ 5.97*	+ 4.42*	- 4.55	+ 1.76*	+ 7.17*	- 3.62	- 29.72
31	Armed Forces	- 91.89	+ 11.53*	- 4.29	+ 1.47	+ 6.14	+ .70	+ 9.68*	+ 26.17*	+ 15.27*

APPENDIX II-I (*continued*)

Ind. #	Industry Sector	Full Convenience							
		Core	PLF-L	PLF-M	PLF-S	SLF-L	SLF-M	SLF-S	Outside
	Total Employment	+ .15*	+ 2.59*	+ .50*	+ .04*	- .01*	- .75	+ .09*	- 4.89
1	Agriculture	- .12*	- 2.34	- 1.48*	- 2.37	+ .16*	- 2.18	- 2.96	- 4.62
2	Forest. & Fisheries	+ .07*	- 2.51	+ .03*	+ .99*	+ 1.20*	- 8.62	+ .41*	+ 1.67*
3	Mining	- .02	+ .66	- 2.11	- .94	+ .60	+ 1.24	+ 2.17*	+ 9.87*
4	Contract Construction	+ .26	+ 4.63*	+ 1.70*	+ 3.07*	- .04	+ .40	+ 1.00*	- 4.84
	Total Manufacturing	+ .09	+ 1.28	+ .79	+ 1.80	+ .85	+ 1.01	+ 2.00	+ 2.89
5	Food Manufacturing	+ .14	+ 2.18*	+ .93	+ 1.50*	+ .78	+ 1.46	+ 2.67*	+ 2.25*
6	Textile Manufacturing	- 0 -	+ .24	- 2.86	+ 1.94*	+ .44	+ .54	+ 3.10*	+ 1.87*
7	Apparel Manufacturing	+ .08	+ .96	+ .73	+ 1.90	+ .53	+ 3.56*	+ 3.61*	+ 5.99*
8	Printing & Publishing	+ .11	+ 2.86*	+ 1.15*	+ .09	+ .75*	- .67	+ .20	- 1.05
9	Chemical Manufacturing	- 0 -	+ .52	- .13	+ 3.66*	- .02	+ .75	+ 1.08	+ 3.79*
10	Lumber & Wood Products	+ .33*	- .16*	+ 3.95*	- 3.33	+ 1.05*	- 1.80	- 2.13	- 9.38
11	Machinery Manufacturing	+ .16	+ 1.39*	+ 1.61*	+ 2.36*	+ .57	- 1.01	+ .76	+ 2.03*
12	Motor Vehicle Mfg.	+ .01	+ 1.44*	+ 1.04*	+ .66	+ 1.13*	+ 1.19*	+ 1.17*	+ 1.26*
13	Other Transport. Equip.	- .01	+ 3.36*	+ 1.99*	+ 1.11	+ 1.55*	+ .58	+ 1.56*	+ 2.28*
14	Other Manufacturing	+ .09	+ .94	+ 1.20	+ 1.72*	+ 1.25	+ 1.29	+ 1.75*	+ 3.38*
	Total Trans., Comm., Util.	+ .20	+ 7.23	+ 1.68	+ .27	- 2.02	- 2.11	- 3.05	- 10.80
15	Railroad Transportation	+ .29*	+ .71*	+ .84*	+ .29*	- .54	+ .90*	- .31*	- 4.69
16	Trucking & Warehousing	+ .01*	+ .97*	+ .03*	- 1.81*	- 1.40*	- 1.64*	- 3.08	- 8.87
17	Other Transportation	+ .03	+ 2.97*	+ 1.49	+ 1.24	+ .23	+ 1.68*	+ .23	+ 4.71*
18	Communication	- .02*	+ 3.04*	- .75*	- 3.21*	- 2.16*	- 6.13	- 4.99	- 17.14
19	Utilities	+ .06	+ 1.74	+ .52	+ 2.37*	+ .64	+ 1.02	+ 2.42*	+ 5.50*
20	Wholesale Trade	+ .13*	+ .67*	+ 1.10*	- 1.07*	- 1.33	- 1.09*	- 1.92	- 6.87
	Total Retail Trade	+ .16	+ 3.95	+ .14	+ .72	- .74	- .20	+ .10	- 7.22
21	Eating and Drinking	+ .21	+ 1.37*	+ .42*	- .28	- .04	+ .97*	+ .52*	- 1.37
22	Other Retail	+ .05*	+ 6.11*	- 1.19	+ 1.48*	+ .70*	+ .14*	+ 1.32*	- 13.99
23	Food and Dairy	+ .15*	+ 4.87*	+ .22*	+ 1.15*	- 1.46	- 1.04	- .45*	- 9.05
24	Finance, Ins., Real Est.	+ .09	+ 1.69*	+ .42	+ 1.92*	+ .39	+ .14	+ .77*	+ .32
	Total Services	- .01	+ .07	- .75	- 2.20	- 1.31	- 2.01	- 2.91	- 10.40
25	Lodging & Personal	+ .15	+ 2.01*	+ .08	+ 2.20*	- .27	+ .62	+ .17	+ 1.13*
26	Business & Repair	- .01*	- .17*	- .39*	- 1.53*	- 1.04*	- 1.45*	- 2.27	- 6.48
27	Amusement & Recreation	+ .08*	+ 1.04*	+ .06*	- .76*	- 1.23	- 1.47	- 3.45	- 15.85
28	Private Households	+ .02	+ 1.80*	+ 1.27	+ 2.56*	+ .67	+ 1.15	+ 2.88*	+ 2.08*
29	Professional Services	- .02*	- .17*	- .92*	- 2.57*	- 1.26*	- 2.10*	- 2.98	- 10.64
	Total Government								
30	Civil Government	- .04	+ .56	- .28	- 1.54	- 1.19	- 2.06	- 3.40	- 12.03
31	Armed Forces	- 0 -	- 0 -	- 0 -	- 3.15	- 0 -	- 0 -	+ 1.28	+ 8.25

APPENDIX II-I (*continued*)

Ind. #	Industry Sector	Partial Shopping							
		Core	PLF-L	PLF-M	PLF-S	SLF-L	SLF-M	SLF-S	Outside
	Total Employment	+ .12	+ 4.48*	+ 4.38*	+ 4.50*	+ .72	- 1.01	- 1.93	- 7.37
1	Agriculture	+ .40*	- 1.11*	- 2.08*	- 6.49	+ .45	- 6.80	- 11.37	+ .50*
2	Forest. & Fisheries	+ .16*	- 4.15	- 5.24	- 5.31	+ .53	- 5.88	+ 6.98*	- 12.80
3	Mining	- .21*	+ 4.92*	+ 2.53*	+ .03*	+ 1.72	- 2.33	- 11.26	- 4.73
4	Contract Construction	+ 2.88*	+ 5.09*	+ 7.76*	- 1.61	+ .80	- 3.25	- 3.52	- 16.67
	Total Manufacturing	- .03	+ 2.36	+ 2.64	+ 5.14	+ 1.10	+ 2.77	+ 3.95	+ 5.37
5	Food Manufacturing	+ .02	+ .65	+ 2.86	+ 5.35*	+ 2.59	+ 1.34	+ 5.91*	+ 7.03*
6	Textile Manufacturing	- .05	- .25	+ .41	+ 5.02*	+ 1.21	+ 1.21	+ 8.69*	+ 3.85*
7	Apparel Manufacturing	- 0 -	+ .99	+ .95	+ 4.98*	+ .98	+ 4.38*	+ 4.57*	+ 6.95*
8	Printing & Publishing	- .25	+ 4.17*	+ 1.34	+ 2.52*	+ 4.24	- 1.11	+ .81	+ 1.95*
9	Chemical Manufacturing	+ .03	+ 6.59*	+ 3.11*	+ 6.70*	+ .42	+ .81	- .56	+ 5.90*
10	Lumber & Wood Products	- .01*	+ 3.04*	+ 1.80*	- 3.57	- 2.50	+ 6.03*	- 12.22	- 3.24
11	Machinery Manufacturing	- 0 -	+ 3.04*	+ 2.81	+ 4.59*	+ .72	+ 2.45	+ 2.18	+ 4.25*
12	Motor Vehicle Mfg.	- 0 -	+ 5.40*	+ 4.64*	+ 4.90*	+ .80	+ 1.98	+ 2.71	+ 4.08*
13	Other Transport. Equip.	- .01	+ 2.59	+ 3.75*	+ 3.19*	+ 2.04	+ 2.96*	+ 2.07	+ 4.26*
14	Other Manufacturing	- .08	+ 2.63	+ 3.56*	+ 5.97*	+ .73	+ 3.16	+ 4.26*	+ 5.88*
	Total Trans., Comm., Util.	+ .52	+ 9.07	+ 7.68	+ 3.89	- 1.75	- 1.81	- 5.61	- 14.81
15	Railroad Transportation	+ .43*	- .77	+ 1.32*	+ 5.84*	- 1.41	- 1.69	+ .95*	- 10.52
16	Trucking & Warehousing	+ .06*	+ .66*	- .11*	- 3.03	- 1.38	- 2.28*	- 5.37	- 12.65
17	Other Transportation	+ .18	+ 6.92*	+ 4.38*	+ 2.09*	+ .05	+ 1.86	- .50	+ 1.22
18	Communication	+ .28*	+ .26*	+ .68*	- 4.20*	- 2.78	- 5.55	- 4.57	- 17.81
19	Utilities	+ .05	+ 2.72	+ 3.08	+ 4.84*	+ 1.30	+ 2.23	+ 2.78	+ 9.43*
20	Wholesale Trade	- .11*	+ 1.33*	+ .24*	- 1.53*	- 1.72	- 2.58	- 3.53	- 12.08
	Total Retail Trade	- .09	+ 4.38	+ 5.46	+ 3.12	- .04	- 1.64	- 7.17	- 9.03
21	Eating and Drinking	- .04*	+ 2.33*	+ 4.69*	+ 2.41*	- .07	- .80	- 4.70	- 4.72
22	Other Retail	- .03	+ 5.95*	+ 9.39*	+ 6.58*	+ .62	- 3.92	- 5.58	- 10.99
23	Food & Dairy	- .13	+ 5.03*	+ 4.65*	+ 2.58*	- .16	- 1.57	- 8.54	- 10.70
24	Finance, Ins. Real Est.	- .12	+ 3.06*	+ 3.72*	+ 3.56*	+ .30	+ .31	+ .61	+ 2.89*
	Total Services	- .06	- .18	- .87	- 4.03	- 1.46	- 3.52	- 7.27	- 14.26
25	Lodging & Personal	+ .10	+ 2.21*	+ 7.26*	+ 5.26*	+ .61	- .28	- 4.43	+ 1.43
26	Business & Repair	- .02*	- .55*	- 1.61*	- 3.28	- 1.34	- 2.52*	- 4.36	- 9.87
27	Amusement & Recreation	+ .02*	+ .63*	+ 10.90*	- 2.47*	- 1.06	- 4.25	- 8.24	- 20.19
28	Private Households	+ .60	+ 1.30	+ 2.52	+ 6.45*	+ 2.36	+ 2.88*	+ 1.75	+ 3.43*
29	Professional Services	- .13*	- .29*	- 1.45*	- 4.72	- 1.55	- 3.62*	- 7.20	- 14.23
	Total Government								
30	Civil Government	- .44*	- .31*	+ .16*	- 2.68*	- 1.33	- 2.58*	- 4.30	- 15.59
31	Armed Forces	- 0 -	- 0 -	- 0 -	+ 6.15*	+ 1.50	- .17	+ 9.94*	- .72

APPENDIX II-I (*continued*)

Ind. #	Industry Sector	Hamlet and Minimum Convenience						
		PLF-L	PLF-M	PLF-S	SLF-L	SLF-M	SLF-S	Outside
	Total Employment	+ 1.31*	+ .96*	+ 2.46*	+ .12*	- .12	- .29	- 5.04
1	Agriculture	- .71*	- 2.82	- 5.42	- 1.11*	- 3.63	- 3.22	- 2.18*
2	Forest. & Fisheries	- 12.04	- 4.20	- 3.24*	+ .57*	- 7.45	+ 2.63*	+ .80*
3	Mining	- .72	+ .74*	- 1.44	+ .47*	- .35	- .31	+ 1.93*
4	Contract Construction	+ 3.31*	+ .90	+ 4.51*	+ .20	+ 1.24	- .41	+ .31
	Total Manufacturing	+ .45	+ .94	+ 2.46	+ .40	+ .81	+ 1.90	+ 2.58
5	Food Manufacturing	+ 1.04	+ .87	+ 1.63*	+ .43	+ .58	+ 1.29*	+ 2.11*
6	Textile Manufacturing	+ .14	+ .31	+ 3.89*	+ .55	+ .33	+ 6.85*	+ 1.66
7	Apparel Manufacturing	+ .10	+ .83	+ 3.11*	+ .65	+ 1.96*	+ 2.37*	+ 4.56*
8	Printing & Publishing	+ .90*	+ 1.09*	+ .83*	+ .01	- .16	+ .08	- 1.77
9	Chemical Manufacturing	- .81	+ 1.26*	+ 2.19*	+ .05	+ .50	+ .63	+ 1.04*
10	Lumber & Wood Products	- 3.25	- .11	+ 6.59*	- .61	+ .69*	- 1.54	+ 2.51*
11	Machinery Manufacturing	+ .25	+ .95*	+ 1.46*	+ .13	+ .49	+ 1.06*	+ 2.06*
12	Motor Vehicle Mfg.	+ 1.04*	+ .71	+ 1.21*	+ .16	+ .44	+ .62	+ 1.12*
13	Other Transport. Equip.	+ 1.50*	+ 2.05*	+ 1.86*	+ .52	+ .30	+ .96	+ 1.87*
14	Other Manufacturing	+ .76	+ 1.00	+ 2.30*	+ .49	+ .81	+ .93	+ 2.88*
	Total Trans., Comm., Util.	+ 4.33	+ 2.31	+ 5.89	+ .62	+ 1.03	- 1.66	- 9.38
15	Railroad Transportation	+ .23*	- .23*	+ 4.17*	- .30*	- .16*	- 1.77	- 4.70
16	Trucking & Warehousing	- .68*	+ .03*	- .03*	- .24*	- .91*	- 2.83	- 7.32
17	Other Transportation	+ 2.61*	+ 1.58	+ 3.17*	+ .47	+ .71	+ 2.39*	+ 4.20*
18	Communications	+ 1.25*	+ .38*	- .35*	+ .45*	+ .19*	- 2.12	- 11.32
19	Utilities	+ 2.14*	+ .83	+ 1.93*	+ .40	+ 1.30	+ 1.58	+ 3.19*
20	Wholesale Trade	- 1.29	+ .21*	+ .83*	+ .01*	+ .21*	- 1.02	- 4.35
	Total Retail Trade	+ 2.32	+ 1.22	+ 3.03	+ .53	+ .39	- 1.06	- 5.92
21	Eating & Drinking	+ 1.38*	+ 1.17*	+ 2.09*	+ .84*	+ .58	- .10	- 1.18
22	Other Retail	+ 3.35*	+ 2.44*	+ 5.02*	+ 1.51*	- .48	- 1.79	- 9.08
23	Food and Dairy	+ 2.53*	+ .89*	+ 2.97*	+ .06*	+ .41	- 1.45	- 7.90
24	Finance, Ins., Real Est.	+ 1.89*	+ 1.18	+ 2.72*	+ .29	+ .42	+ .99	+ 1.29*
	Total Services	+ .12	- .18	- 1.17	- .29	- .87	- 2.70	- 9.10
25	Lodging & Personal	+ 1.95*	+ 1.77	+ 3.67*	+ .94	+ 1.66	+ .66	+ 1.89*
26	Business & Repair	- .37*	- .46*	- .78*	- .22*	- .74*	- 1.59	- 4.65
27	Amusement & Recreation	+ .46*	+ .12*	- .84	+ .78*	- .79	+ 4.57*	- 7.24
28	Private Households	+ 2.53*	+ 2.77*	+ 1.84*	+ .60	+ .66	+ 1.70*	+ 1.10
29	Professional Services	- .05*	- .41*	- 1.60*	- .42*	- .98*	- 3.12	- 9.90
	Total Government							
30	Civil Government	+ 3.23*	- .03*	- .66*	+ .32*	- .78*	- 2.31	- 10.54
31	Armed Forces	- .69	- 0 -*	- 0 -*	- .92	- 0 -*	- 0 -*	+ .09*

APPENDIX II-J. County Code-C Frequency Tabulations by Industry Sector and Trade-Center Category

Panel A
Percentage of Industry and Trade-Center Frequencies Recording Total Competitive Gains (R_{ij}) Between 1940 and 1970

Industry Sectors	Metro. Large	Metro. Small	Whol/Ret Large	Whol/Ret Small	Whol/Ret Outside	Complete Shopping	Partial Shopping	Full Conven.	Hamlet & Min Conv.	All Counties
Agriculture	@72.9*	@72.0*	@66.4*	@65.1*	58.6*	50.1	50.6	52.6	50.5	53.8
Forest. & Fish.	@71.3	68.0	@71.0	@74.4	@67.1	@75.0	@77.8*	@82.4*	@83.2*	@77.3
Mining	@89.5*	@80.0	@75.2	@76.6	@77.1	@77.3	@81.2*	@85.2*	@84.7*	@81.1
Contract Const.	68.9*	@84.0*	57.0	62.8*	60.0	55.4	56.3	62.3*	77.2*	61.7
Total Manufact.	@73.4	@80.0	63.1	@76.1	@64.3	@86.3	@95.0*	@96.5*	@98.5*	@88.4
Food Manufact.	62.0	48.0	61.7	@69.8	@61.4	@66.1	@82.0*	@90.1*	@94.8*	@76.8
Textile Manufact.	63.5	@72.0	@65.9	@86.0	@72.9	@86.7	@95.3*	@97.6*	@99.2*	@88.7
Apparel Manufact.	66.1	@88.0	@70.1	@79.1	@74.3	@87.6	@95.5*	@98.7*	@98.3*	@89.6
Print. & Pub.	@71.4	64.0	@71.5	@67.4	52.9	@67.3	@75.1	@82.2*	@90.7*	@75.2
Chem. Manufact.	66.1	52.0	@69.2	@65.1	@61.4	@74.9	@84.7*	@91.4*	@92.8*	@80.7
Lumber & Wood	63.5	68.0*	53.3	51.2	57.1	63.5	@70.1*	@76.7*	73.3*	67.4
Mach. Manufact.	@78.7	@80.0	@75.7	@74.4	@75.7	@91.9	@98.3*	@99.3*	@100.0*	@93.0
Motor Veh. Mfg.	@79.7	@88.0	@84.6	@90.7	@94.3	@96.4*	@99.8*	@99.6*	@99.8*	@96.1
Tran. Equip. Mfg.	@75.5	@96.0*	@78.5	@86.0	@77.1	@93.8*	@98.3*	@98.9*	@99.2*	@93.7
Other Manufact.	@71.4	@88.0*	@65.9	@69.8	@64.3	@82.9	@93.8*	@96.3*	@98.3*	@87.1
Railroad Transp.	62.0*	@80.0*	53.3	53.5	45.7	44.5	51.9	59.7*	69.6*	54.6
Truck. & Warehsg.	@76.5*	64.0*	60.3*	44.2*	54.3*	38.8	36.8	37.4	43.9*	43.6
Other Transp.	69.3	60.0	58.4	53.5	58.6	@68.5	@82.0*	@87.9*	@92.1*	@76.8
Communications	70.3*	64.0*	@66.4*	@65.1*	45.7	50.8	49.2	49.8	67.7*	55.7
Utilities	68.2	@72.0	55.6	58.1	57.1	@70.2	@86.2*	@87.9*	@90.7*	@77.8
Wholesale Trade	@75.0*	@76.0*	63.6*	32.6	42.9	43.0	53.3	54.4	77.4*	56.1
Total Retail	@72.9*	@76.0*	63.6	62.8	58.0	57.1	62.4	68.5*	@85.6*	66.0
Eating & Drinking	@74.5*	56.0	@71.5*	@65.1	@68.6*	61.4	64.9	69.4*	@81.6*	68.4
Other Retail	@73.0*	@72.0*	56.5	62.8	57.1	52.6	58.0	61.9	74.1*	60.6
Food & Dairy	@72.4*	@76.0*	62.1*	62.8*	57.1	56.8	58.7	68.1*	@82.0*	64.7
F.I.R.E.	@75.0	@76.0	@72.4	@65.1	@65.7	@72.3	@80.2*	@88.1*	@96.7	@80.2
Total Services	68.2*	@76.0*	59.3*	53.5*	51.4*	37.4	31.8	31.5	50.5*	42.0
Lodging & Pers.	@73.4*	@72.0*	@65.0	62.8	57.1	60.0	63.5	69.2*	@82.4*	67.1
Business & Repair	65.6*	56.0*	43.0*	34.9*	30.0*	20.1	17.8	20.9	42.0*	28.6
Entertain. & Rec.	@73.0*	60.0*	62.1*	51.2	48.6	49.1	44.9	50.4	68.9*	54.3
Private Hsehlds.	56.8	@76.0*	52.8	@79.1*	50.0	@64.6	@69.9*	@73.1*	@80.3*	68.2
Prof. Services	67.2*	@72.0*	59.8*	58.1*	54.3*	38.2	28.2	29.1	41.4*	39.7
Civil Govern.	64.1*	60.0*	43.5*	55.8*	37.1	35.7	33.3	37.9	53.4*	41.4
Military	@78.1	@76.0	@86.9	@86.0	@91.4	@95.9*	@98.2*	@98.5*	@98.6*	@95.0
Total	70.9*	71.5*	64.5	64.8	60.5	64.2	68.9	72.8*	80.2*	69.5

APPENDIX II-J (*continued*)

Panel B
Percentage of Industry and Trade-Center Frequencies Recording Leading Competitive Gains Between 1940 and 1970

Industry Sectors	Metro. Large	Metro. Small	Whol/Ret Large	Whol/Ret Small	Whol/Ret Outside	Complete Shopping	Partial Shopping	Full Conven.	Hamlet & Min Conv.	All Counties
Agriculture	@31.2	32.0	@46.7*	@55.8*	@45.7*	@41.0*	@41.8*	@45.2*	@36.0	@41.0
Forest. & Fish.	23.0	32.0	@39.2	30.2	@35.7	@49.9*	@49.8*	@50.6*	@41.0	@45.3
Mining	@35.9	@40.0	@37.8	@46.5*	@38.6	@43.0*	@42.9*	@48.7*	@29.2	@40.6
Contract Const.	@36.0*	@40.0	@34.6*	23.3	28.5	33.3*	30.6	@35.4*	@32.5*	@32.4
Total Manufact.	@31.3	@40.0	@35.5	@37.2	@37.2	@64.1*	@71.7*	@63.0*	@43.5	@56.7
Food Manufact.	19.8	20.0	@34.5	@41.8	@38.5	@42.4*	@52.8*	@50.5*	@34.2	@41.9
Textile Manufact.	13.0	28.0	27.1	30.1	@45.7*	@48.0*	@47.1*	@43.3*	@32.7	40.5
Apparel Manufact.	16.1	@36.0	@37.3	30.2	@51.4*	@56.4*	@60.0*	@61.3*	@43.9	@51.2
Print. & Publish.	@34.4*	20.0	@34.6*	25.6	21.4	29.2*	28.4*	26.2	17.2	27.0
Chem. Manufact.	25.0	16.0	@36.4	30.2	@38.6*	@41.4*	@41.7*	@40.7*	24.2	@36.6
Lumber & Wood	15.6	28.0	31.3	23.3	@34.3	@41.6*	@48.1*	@47.4*	@32.1	@39.2
Mach. Manufact.	@36.5	20.0	@41.5	@37.2	@47.2*	@55.5*	@52.4*	@45.4	@27.3	@45.8
Mot. Veh. Mfg.	@37.0	32.0	@41.1	30.2	@52.9*	@50.2*	@48.7*	@42.5	@25.0	@42.7
Tran. Equip. Mfg.	@30.7	@48.0*	@37.4	30.2	@37.1	@50.1*	@45.1*	@39.2	@25.5	@40.7
Other Manufact.	@29.2	@40.0	@35.5	@34.9	@41.4	@57.0*	@61.5*	@54.0*	@36.2	@49.9
Railroad Transp.	@30.7	32.0*	28.5*	30.2*	27.1*	25.9	28.7*	29.1*	21.7	26.8
Truck. & Warehsg.	@43.3*	28.0*	30.8*	23.2*	@34.3*	17.8	16.0	13.9	11.6	18.8
Other Transp.	@31.8	20.0	18.7	20.9	25.7	32.9	@36.9*	@42.5*	@32.5	@33.5
Communications	28.7*	20.0	@41.1*	@39.6*	25.7*	23.4*	17.3	10.4	13.7	20.4
Utilities	25.0	@56.0*	24.7	@32.6	@40.0	@50.4*	@65.1*	@62.1*	@41.9	@49.7
Wholesale Trade	@47.4*	@48.0*	@35.0*	11.6	22.8*	13.8	17.3	17.6	15.5	19.4
Total Retail	@31.3*	32.0*	29.9*	30.3*	30.0*	16.9	14.6	14.7	13.9	18.1
Eating & Drinking	@30.8*	24.0	@42.6*	@39.5*	@42.9*	31.8*	26.7	30.6*	21.7	29.9
Other Retail	@31.3*	28.0*	24.3*	27.9*	22.8	22.4	27.2*	24.9*	20.9	24.3
Food & Dairy	@32.8*	@40.0*	27.6*	@32.6*	25.7*	18.4	15.8	15.8	13.6	18.8
F.I.R.E.	@33.3*	@48.0*	@40.7*	@32.6*	@32.9*	27.6	27.7	27.6	21.3	28.2
Total Services	@30.2*	@52.0*	32.3*	25.6*	17.2*	10.3*	2.3	2.6	3.7	9.9
Lodging & Pers.	22.4	@36.0*	32.2*	30.2*	22.8	29.8*	29.1*	26.4	@24.5	27.9
Business & Repair	26.0*	20.0*	15.0*	11.7*	7.2*	2.5	1.5	2.2	4.3	5.3
Entertain. & Rec.	@31.3*	28.0*	30.8*	@34.9*	20.0	21.3*	17.1	19.2	15.9	20.7
Private Hsehlds.	14.6	@48.0*	33.2	@55.8*	@32.8	@47.1*	@47.9*	@48.5*	@36.4	@42.5
Prof. Services	@30.2*	@60.0*	32.8*	30.2*	14.3*	12.1*	2.7	2.9	1.9	10.3
Civil Govern.	25.5*	28.0*	18.2*	27.9*	12.9*	12.2*	9.9	8.2	8.9	12.2
Military	@30.2	@40.0*	@45.8*	@51.2*	@50.0*	@44.2*	@36.3*	32.2	16.6	@35.7
Total	29.0	33.4*	33.5*	32.3*	32.8*	34.5*	34.6*	33.4*	24.5	32.2

APPENDIX II-J (*continued*)

Panel C
Percentage of Industry and Trade-Center Frequencies Recording Leading Competitive Losses Between 1940 and 1970

Industry Sectors	Metro. Large	Metro. Small	Whol/Ret Large	Whol/Ret Small	Whol/Ret Outside	Complete Shopping	Partial Shopping	Full Conven.	Hamlet & Min Conv.	All Counties
Agriculture	@25.0	@24.0	@26.7	@32.6	@34.3	@42.8*	@45.5*	@45.0*	@47.6*	@41.7
Forest. & Fish.	16.7	@24.0*	18.7*	11.7	21.4*	18.6*	19.1*	16.1	15.2	17.7
Mining	9.4	16.0	20.1*	18.7*	14.3	19.5*	16.2*	12.3	14.3	16.2
Contract Const.	15.6	12.0	@24.8	20.9	25.8	@30.9*	@32.3*	@25.8	@17.2	@26.3
Total Manufact.	@18.7*	16.0*	@29.0*	11.6*	24.3*	7.0*	1.6	1.7	.4	6.9
Food Manufact.	@25.0*	@44.0*	@23.8*	20.9*	@31.4*	20.6*	10.3	5.5	3.7	14.5
Textile Manufact.	@25.0*	@24.0*	@24.3*	11.6*	24.3*	11.1*	4.1	2.0	.6	8.8
Apparel Manufact.	@20.8*	8.0*	19.6*	11.7*	21.5*	9.4*	4.2	1.1	1.8	7.6
Print. & Publish.	@18.2*	@28.0*	12.6*	20.9*	24.3*	15.8*	11.1	8.1	5.2	12.3
Chem. Manufact.	@20.3*	@32.0*	18.7*	@30.2*	@28.6*	18.3*	10.8	6.6	6.0	13.7
Lumber & Wood	@21.9	@32.0*	@32.7*	@41.9*	25.7	@31.8*	@27.7	@21.4	@25.1	@27.8
Mach. Manufact.	12.0*	12.0*	18.2*	16.3*	17.1*	5.6*	.7	.4	--	4.7
Mot. Veh. Mfg.	8.3*	8.0*	8.4*	7.0*	2.8*	2.7*	--	.4	.2	2.2
Tran. Equip. Mfg.	13.1*	4.0*	11.7*	2.3	12.8*	4.2*	1.0	.7	.8	3.7
Other Manufact.	@20.4*	4.0	@25.7*	21.0*	25.7*	11.3*	4.4	2.2	1.6	8.9
Railroad Transp.	@23.9	16.0	@37.9*	@41.9*	@44.3*	@45.4*	@38.5*	@29.3	@26.7	@36.4
Truck. & Warehsg.	9.9	@32.0	@24.8	@44.2	@32.9	@51.4*	@54.3*	@53.8*	@50.3*	@46.9
Other Transp.	@20.3*	@36.0*	@26.1*	@30.3*	22.8*	17.5*	11.4	7.7	5.8	14.1
Communications	@17.7	@32.0	20.0	23.3	@40.0*	@35.1*	@39.6*	@39.6*	@25.5	@32.8
Utilities	@20.3*	16.0*	@29.4*	@30.3*	25.7*	17.8*	8.6	5.1	6.0	13.3
Wholesale Trade	13.0	20.0	@24.3	@60.5*	@42.9*	@44.2*	@35.8*	@33.4*	@18.6	@33.3
Total Retail	14.0	@24.0*	17.8*	21.0*	18.6*	21.9*	16.1*	11.0	7.4	15.9
Eating & Drinking	9.9	@36.0*	11.2	20.9*	10.0	21.2*	17.5*	17.8*	11.6	16.8
Other Retail	14.6	16.0	@28.0*	23.3	@27.2*	@32.6*	@26.4*	@22.7	@20.3	@26.0
Food & Dairy	15.1	@24.0*	21.5*	23.3*	@27.1*	25.4*	19.8*	12.4	8.3	18.6
F.I.R.E.	14.1*	16.0*	8.4*	18.7*	7.1*	7.6*	5.5	1.3	1.0	5.8
Total Services	11.0	20.0	@24.8	@30.2	@32.8	@52.9*	@60.0	@58.8	@43.3	@47.9
Lodging & Pers.	13.5	20.0*	19.1*	21.0*	24.3*	23.2*	20.2*	12.8	9.3	17.8
Business & Repair	15.6	@44.0	@43.9	@55.9	@57.1	@73.7*	@72.9*	@72.6*	@52.2	@63.2
Entertain. & Rec.	10.9	@32.0*	18.2	@32.5*	@30.0	@36.4*	@39.0*	@35.7*	@23.4	@31.5
Private Hsehlds.	@30.8*	20.0	@34.1*	11.6	@28.6*	23.8*	20.0	17.6	14.7	21.7
Prof. Services	11.5	20.0	@22.9	@27.9	@28.6	@51.9*	@64.9*	@64.1*	@53.6*	@50.8
Civil Govern.	@19.8	@32.0	@37.4	@30.2	@45.8*	@46.1*	@47.6	@44.9*	@37.3	@42.1
Military	@18.2*	@24.0*	9.8	13.9*	7.2*	3.7	1.5	1.5	1.4	4.3
Total	17.1	22.8*	22.7*	25.1*	26.2*	25.8*	22.9*	20.0*	16.3	22.0

APPENDIX II-J *(continued)*

Panel D
The Excess (or Deficit) of Leading Gains Relative to Leading Losses (Panel B Minus Panel C)

Industry Sectors	Metro Large	Metro Small	Whol/Ret Large	Whol/Ret Small	Whol/Ret Outside	Complete Shopping	Partial Shopping	Full Conven.	Hamlet & Min Conv.	All Counties
Agriculture	+ 6.2*	+ 8.0*	-20.0	@+23.2*	@+11.4*	- 1.8	- 3.7	+ .2*	-11.6	- .7
Forest. & Fish.	+ 6.3	+ 8.0	@+20.5	@+18.5	@+14.3	@+31.3*	@+30.7*	@+34.5	@+25.8	@+27.6
Mining	@+26.5*	@+24.0	@+17.7	@+27.8*	@+24.3	@+23.5	@+26.7*	@+36.4*	@+14.9	@+24.4
Contract Const.	@+20.4	@+28.0*	+ 9.0	+ 2.4	+ 2.7	+ 2.4	- 1.3	+ 9.6	@+15.3	@+25.5
Total Manufact.	@+12.6	@+28.0	+ 6.5	@+25.6	@+12.9	@+57.1*	@+70.1*	@+61.3*	@+43.1	@+49.8
Food Manufact.	- 5.2	-24.0	@+10.7	@+20.9	@+ 7.1	@+21.8	@+42.2*	@+45.0*	@+30.5*	@+27.4
Textile Manufact.	-12.0	- 4.0	+ 2.8	@+18.5	@+21.4	@+36.9*	@+43.0*	@+41.3*	@+32.1*	@+31.7
Apparel Manufact.	- 4.7	@+28.0	@+17.7	@+18.5	@+29.9	@+47.0*	@+55.8*	@+60.2*	@+42.1	@+43.6
Print. & Publish.	@+16.2*	- 8.0	+ 2.2	+ 4.7	- 2.9	@+13.4	@+17.3*	@+18.1*	@+12.0	@+14.7
Chem. Manufact.	+ 4.7	-16.0	@+17.7	- 0 -	+ 1.0	@+23.1*	@+30.9*	@+34.1*	@+18.2	@+22.9
Lumber & Wood	- 6.3	- 4.0	- 1.4	-18.6	@+ 8.6	@+ 9.8	@+20.4*	@+26.0*	+ 7.0	@+11.4
Mach. Manufact.	@+24.5	+ 8.0	@+23.3	@+20.9	@+30.1	@+49.9*	@+51.7*	@+45.0*	@+27.3	@+41.1
Mot. Veh. Mfg.	@+29.7	@+24.0	@+32.7	@+23.2	@+50.1*	@+47.5*	@+48.7*	@+42.1*	@+24.8	@+40.5
Tran. Equip. Mfg.	@+17.5	@+44.0*	@+25.7	@+27.9	@+24.3	@+46.0*	@+44.1*	@+38.5*	@+24.7	@+37.0
Other Manufact.	+ 8.8	@+36.0	@+ 9.8	@+13.9	@+15.7	@+45.7*	@+57.1*	@+51.8*	@+34.6	@+41.0
Railroad Transp.	+ 6.8*	@+16.0*	- 9.4*	-11.7	-17.2	-19.5	- 9.8	- .2*	- 5.0*	- 9.6
Truck. & Warehsg.	@+33.4*	- 4.0*	+ 6.0*	-21.0*	+ 1.4*	-33.6	-38.3	-39.9	-38.7	-28.1
Other Transp.	+11.5	-16.0	- 7.4	- 9.4	+ 2.9	@+15.4	@+25.5*	@+34.8*	@+26.7*	@+19.4
Communications	+10.0*	-12.0*	@+21.1*	@+16.3*	-14.3	-11.7	-22.3	-29.2	-11.8*	-12.4
Utilities	+ 4.7	@+40.0*	- 4.7	+ 2.3	@+14.3	@+35.6	@+56.5*	@+57.0*	@+45.9*	@+36.4
Wholesale Trade	@+34.4*	@+28.0*	@+10.6*	-48.9	-20.1	-30.4	-18.5	-15.8	- 3.1*	-13.6
Total Retail	@+17.3*	+ 8.0*	@+12.1*	@+ 9.3*	@+11.4*	- 5.0	- 1.5	- 3.7	+ 6.5*	+ 2.2
Eating & Drinking	@+20.9*	-12.0	@+31.4*	@+18.6*	@+32.9*	@+10.6	+ 9.2	+13.1*	@+10.0	@+13.1
Other Retail	@+16.7*	@+12.0*	- 3.7*	+ 4.6*	- 4.4*	-10.2	+ .8*	+ 2.2*	+ .6*	- 7.1
Food & Dairy	@+17.7*	@+16.0*	+ 6.1*	@+ 9.3*	- 1.4	- 7.0	- 4.0	+ 3.4*	+ 5.3*	+ .2
F.I.R.E.	@+19.2	@+32.0*	@+32.3*	@+13.9	@+25.8*	@+20.0	@+22.2	@+26.5*	@+20.3	@+22.4
Total Services	@+19.2*	@+32.0*	+ 7.5*	- 4.6*	-15.6*	-42.6	-57.7	-56.2	-39.6	-38.0
Lodging & Pers.	+ 8.9	@+16.0	@+13.1	@+ 9.2	- 1.5	+ 6.6	+ 8.9	-13.6	@+15.2*	+10.1
Business & Repair	+10.4*	-24.0*	-28.9*	-44.2*	-49.9*	-71.2	-71.4	-70.4	-47.9*	-57.9
Entertain. & Rec.	@+20.4*	- 4.0*	@+12.6*	+ 2.4*	-10.0*	-15.1	-21.9	-16.5	- 7.5*	-10.8
Private Hsehlds.	-16.2	@+48.0*	- .9	-44.2	+ 4.2	@+23.3	@+27.9*	@+30.9*	@+21.7*	@+20.8
Prof. Services	@+18.7*	@+40.0*	@+19.9*	+ 2.3*	-14.3*	-39.8*	-62.2	-61.2	-51.7	- 40.5
Civil Govern.	+ 5.7*	- 4.0*	-19.2*	- 2.3*	-32.9	-33.9	-37.5	-36.7	-28.4*	-29.9
Military	@+12.0	@+16.0	@+36.0*	@+37.3*	@+42.8*	@+40.5*	@+34.8*	@+30.7*	@+15.2	@+31.4
Total	+11.9*	+10.6*	+ 9.6	+ 7.2	+ 6.6	+ 8.7	+11.7*	+13.7*	+ 8.2	+10.2

@ = above synthetic region average
* = above industry-sector average
░ = above both region and sector average

APPENDIX II-K. County, Code-C Frequency Tabulations by Industry Sector and Transaction-Field Category

Panel A

Percentage of Industry and Transaction-Field Frequencies Recording Total Competitive Gains ($+R_{ij}$) Between 1940 and 1970

Industry Sectors	Urban Core Large	Urban Core Medium	Urban Core Small	Primary Labor Field Large	Primary Labor Field Medium	Primary Labor Field Small	Second. Labor Field Large	Second. Labor Field Medium	Second. Labor Field Small	Outside	All Counties
Agriculture	@78.1*	@77.5*	63.3*	47.3	42.7	37.2	59.2*	49.2	45.3	59.7*	53.8
Forest. & Fish.	68.4	@72.1	@74.7	65.3	69.9	@79.2*	@78.2*	@76.6	@80.6*	@80.1*	@77.3
Mining	@90.4*	@82.0*	@80.1	@84.7*	@82.5*	@79.4	81.0	@78.1	@78.6	@81.8*	@81.1
Contract Const.	67.5*	@69.4*	65.1*	@72.7*	68.0*	67.0*	61.3	55.9	58.1	58.3	61.7
Total Manufact.	68.4	64.9	@69.3	@87.3*	@91.7*	@94.9*	@88.7*	@92.2*	@92.2*	@90.7*	@88.4
Food Manufact.	61.4	56.8	61.4	70.0	@75.7	@86.5*	@79.6*	@77.0*	@78.4*	@79.7*	@76.8
Textile Manufact.	60.5	61.3	@74.1	@76.7	@84.5	@93.2*	@86.6	@93.8*	@94.0*	@94.5*	@88.7
Apparel Manufact.	64.9	@69.4	@74.1	@82.7	@85.9	@91.3*	@91.5*	@90.6*	@95.1*	@94.8*	@89.6
Print. & Publish.	@70.2	@70.3	@71.1	@78.7*	@79.6*	@79.2*	@74.6	@72.3	@73.3	@75.8*	@75.2
Chem. Manufact.	64.0	67.6	67.5	@81.3	@83.5	@84.8	@79.6	@81.6*	@75.6	@85.9*	@80.7
Lumber & Wood	67.5*	66.7*	46.4	63.3	68.0*	62.5	66.9	66.0	65.4	@73.8*	67.4
Mach. Manufact.	@75.4	@74.8	@76.5	@93.3*	@94.2*	@95.2*	@97.2*	@94.5*	@95.7*	@96.0*	@93.0
Motor Veh. Mfg.	@76.3	@77.5	@88.6	@96.7*	@97.6*	@96.9*	@98.6*	@96.1*	@99.1*	@98.8*	@96.1
Tran. Equip. Mfg.	66.7	@76.6	@84.9	@84.0	@94.7*	@96.9*	@95.1*	@95.3*	@97.9*	@97.3*	@93.7
Other Manufact.	69.3	65.8	@71.1	@84.7	@86.9	@94.4*	@85.2	@89.1*	@90.2*	@90.1*	@87.1
Railroad Transp.	62.3*	63.1*	57.8*	57.3*	55.3*	52.1	48.6	52.3	53.0	54.7*	54.6
Truck. & Warehsg.	@76.3*	@70.3*	60.8*	54.0*	54.4*	45.1*	34.5	39.8	36.1	36.2	43.6
Other Transp.	@71.1	61.3	57.2	@76.0	@82.5*	@81.4*	@69.7	@78.1*	@76.5	@80.2*	@76.8
Communications	68.4*	@69.4*	@71.1*	65.3*	56.3*	56.9*	45.1	54.7	57.1*	49.9	55.7
Utilities	66.7	57.7	62.7	@81.3*	@76.7	@80.6*	@76.8	@77.7	@83.3*	@79.9*	@77.8
Wholesale Trade	@75.4*	@73.9*	62.7*	64.0*	63.1*	60.8*	46.5	52.7	52.6	50.8	56.1
Total Retail	@71.1*	@71.2*	@68.7*	@73.3*	@78.6*	71.9*	59.2	64.5	61.1	62.5	66.0
Eating & Drinking	69.3*	@75.7*	@69.9*	@77.3*	@79.6*	71.8*	64.1	@72.3*	61.1	65.5	68.4
Other Retail	@70.2*	@69.4*	62.0	68.0*	68.9*	66.2*	65.5*	53.1	56.2	57.1	60.6
Food & Dairy	@72.8*	@69.4*	65.7*	@74.0*	@75.2*	69.6	59.2	62.1*	59.8	61.7*	64.7
F.I.R.E.	@71.1	@73.9	@77.1	@80.0	@85.4*	@87.6*	@79.6	@77.7	@80.3*	@79.6	80.2
Total Services	@70.2*	65.8*	@69.9*	52.7*	49.0*	46.2*	34.5	37.1	32.9	34.2	42.0
Lodging & Pers.	@72.8*	@69.4*	@71.7*	@74.0*	@75.2*	@77.5*	60.6	63.7	58.8	64.9	67.1
Business & Repair	@71.1*	59.5*	47.0*	36.0*	29.6*	29.3*	22.5	20.7	20.9	22.9	28.6
Entertain. & Rec.	@75.4*	66.7*	67.5*	59.3*	61.2*	57.5*	54.9*	51.6	48.1	49.1	54.3
Private Hsehlds.	57.9	53.2	63.3	61.3	@73.8*	@73.0*	66.2	@75.0*	64.7	@70.0*	68.2
Prof. Services	68.4*	65.8*	@69.9*	52.7*	44.7	39.7	34.5	37.1	31.6	31.5	39.7
Civil Government	69.3*	55.0*	50.6*	61.3*	49.0*	46.8*	42.3*	44.5*	35.7	31.4	41.4
Military	@72.8	@82.0	@86.7	@94.0	@96.1*	@97.7*	@94.4	@98.4*	@98.5*	@96.8*	@95.0
Total	70.1*	68.5	67.8*	71.5*	72.3*	72.2*	67.7	68.6	67.8	69.3	69.5

APPENDIX II-K. *(continued)*

Panel B

Percentage of Industry and Transaction-Field Frequencies Recording Leading Competitive Gains Between 1940 and 1970

Industry Sectors	Urban Core Large	Urban Core Medium	Urban Core Small	Primary Labor Field Large	Primary Labor Field Medium	Primary Labor Field Small	Second. Labor Field Large	Second. Labor Field Medium	Second. Labor Field Small	Outside	All Counties
Agriculture	@33.0	@42.3*	@42.8*	29.3	29.1	29.3	@47.1*	@39.5	@37.4	@50.0*	@41.0
Forest. & Fish.	21.1	@34.2	@36.1	25.3	31.1	@41.1	@52.2*	@51.6*	@54.9*	@50.7*	@45.3
Mining	@37.7	@36.9	@39.7	@32.7	31.1	@35.0	@38.0	@40.3	@42.9*	@45.0*	40.6
Contract Const.	@38.6*	@34.2*	@33.2*	@43.3*	@37.4*	@36.6*	@38.0*	30.1	30.1	28.4	@32.4
Total Manufact.	27.8	26.1	@33.7	@54.0	@70.8*	@72.9*	@63.4*	@66.4*	@67.3*	@51.6	@56.7
Food Manufact.	14.9	21.6	@33.8	@35.4	@44.7*	@51.5*	@58.5*	@38.3	@46.3*	@42.1*	@41.9
Textile Manufact.	9.6	16.2	28.3	22.0	30.1	@48.7*	@45.0*	@44.1*	@54.0*	@42.4*	@40.5
Apparel Manufact.	13.2	21.6	@34.9	@36.7	@39.8	@61.4*	@62.7*	@60.9*	@63.5*	@52.6*	@51.2
Print. & Publish.	@39.5*	27.9*	28.3*	@31.3*	@33.0*	23.4	@36.6*	19.9	24.6	26.3	27.0
Chem. Manufact.	21.1	30.6	@33.7	@39.3	@38.3*	@42.5*	33.8	@37.1*	@34.8	@37.7*	@36.6
Lumber & Wood	14.0	28.8	22.9	@32.7	@43.7*	@37.2	@47.2*	@50.0*	@41.9*	@41.4*	@39.2
Mach. Manufact.	@33.3	32.4	@36.1	@41.3	@55.8*	@51.0*	@54.9*	@49.2*	@45.3	@45.1	@45.8
Motor Veh. Mfg.	@32.5	@36.9	@34.9	@52.7*	@47.5*	@40.9	@52.8*	@44.6*	@43.8*	@41.7	@42.7
Tran. Equip. Mfg.	@27.2	31.5	@34.9	@41.4*	@47.5*	@37.8	@47.2*	@41.0*	@46.3*	@40.2	@40.7
Other Manufact.	21.9	27.9	@36.7	@47.3	@67.0*	@62.2*	@56.3*	@57.0*	@54.7*	@45.5	@49.9
Railroad Transp.	27.2*	32.4*	30.1*	22.6	28.6*	28.8*	27.4*	23.8	29.7*	24.8	26.8
Truck. & Warehsg.	@36.0*	@40.5*	31.9*	26.7*	29.1*	20.9*	15.5	14.1	14.9	12.5	18.8
Other Transp.	@36.8*	21.6	19.3	@39.3*	@33.5	27.0	36.6*	@34.0*	@33.9*	@37.1*	@33.5
Communications	25.4*	@36.0*	@40.9*	24.0*	16.5	14.6	21.8*	17.6	21.6*	17.4	20.4
Utilities	15.7	27.0	30.1	@53.4*	@48.5	@53.5*	@53.5*	@52.0*	@59.4*	@51.9*	@49.7
Wholesale Trade	@49.1*	@47.7*	30.7*	22.6*	21.9*	22.3*	11.3	12.9	16.5	13.8	19.4
Total Retail	@32.5*	31.5*	30.1*	16.0	22.8*	15.2	19.7*	15.3	13.3	16.2	18.1
Eating & Drinking	21.9	@45.0*	@39.7*	@32.6*	@37.3*	25.3	35.2*	@32.8*	24.8	28.2	29.9
Other Retail	@29.8*	27.9*	25.9*	17.4	28.2*	24.8*	31.0*	19.6	25.8*	22.7	24.3
Food & Dairy	@37.8*	30.6*	28.3*	20.7*	19.9*	17.1	19.7*	16.8	14.5	16.4	18.8
F.I.R.E.	@27.1	@44.1*	@40.9*	21.4	30.1*	26.5	31.7*	20.7	26.7	27.9	28.2
Total Services	@27.1*	@42.3*	@36.8*	7.4	7.7	7.0	9.1	7.0	4.0	5.9	9.9
Lodging & Pers.	14.9	32.4*	@33.7*	24.0	29.2*	29.6*	32.4*	29.7*	24.0	28.3*	27.9
Business & Repair	@34.2	23.4*	13.8*	6.7*	2.9	3.7	1.4	2.8	2.1	1.9	5.3
Entertain. & Rec.	@32.8*	@35.1*	@33.1*	20.7	18.5	20.9*	23.9*	18.8	18.2	17.7	20.7
Private Househlds.	10.5	26.1	@41.6	@38.0	@43.2*	@46.8*	@43.0*	@50.0*	@46.8*	@42.8*	@42.5
Prof. Services	@27.2*	@42.3*	@38.6*	9.3	8.3	7.6	10.5*	7.1	4.5	6.0	10.4
Civil Government	24.5*	27.0*	24.7*	18.0*	13.6*	13.5*	14.8*	10.1	11.5	6.6	12.2
Military	25.5	@45.0*	@44.0*	28.6	25.7	27.6	@38.7*	@35.2	@39.1*	@38.2*	@35.7
Total	26.9	32.5*	33.0*	30.2	32.6*	32.5*	36.1*	32.3	33.4*	31.8	32.2

APPENDIX II-K. *(continued)*

Panel C

Percentage of Industry and Transaction-Field Frequencies Recording Leading Competitive Losses Between 1940 and 1970

Industry Sectors	Urban Core Large	Urban Core Medium	Urban Core Small	Primary Labor Field Large	Primary Labor Field Medium	Primary Labor Field Small	Second. Labor Field Large	Second. Labor Field Medium	Second. Labor Field Small	Outside	All Counties
Agriculture	@18.4	18.9	@32.6	@52.3*	@55.9*	@60.3*	@35.9	@45.7*	@49.6*	@34.4	@41.7
Forest. & Fish.	@16.7	17.1	18.6*	@28.6*	@26.2*	17.2	17.6	21.1*	15.4	14.9	17.7
Mining	7.9	13.5	17.4*	12.0	16.6*	18.8*	14.8	18.3*	18.6*	15.3	16.2
Contract Const.	14.0	13.5	21.1	16.0	@26.7*	27.6*	@28.9*	@34.4*	@28.6*	@27.4*	@26.3
Total Manufact.	@21.9*	@30.6*	@23.5*	9.3*	4.9	2.8	5.6	4.7	3.9	3.8	6.9
Food Manufact.	@22.8*	@27.9*	@28.4*	@22.0*	18.4*	9.0	14.1	14.1	12.2	11.3	14.5
Textile Manufact.	@22.8*	@29.7*	19.3*	19.3*	13.6*	6.4	12.7*	5.5	5.1	4.0	8.8
Apparel Manufact.	@18.4*	@21.6*	16.8*	10.7*	11.2*	8.5*	7.0	8.2*	3.4	4.0	7.6
Print. & Publish.	@19.3*	15.3*	17.5*	12.0	12.6*	11.8	12.0	12.9*	13.9*	9.8	12.3
Chem. Manufact.	@18.4*	@20.7*	@24.1*	14.0*	12.6	12.1	14.8*	12.9	17.7*	9.9	13.7
Lumber & Wood	11.4	@25.2	@42.2*	@33.3*	@28.6*	@34.9*	@26.8	@30.1*	@32.1*	@22.2	@27.8
Mach. Manufact.	11.4*	@19.8*	16.8*	5.3*	4.4	4.5	2.1	3.5	3.2	1.9	4.7
Motor Veh. Mfg.	7.0*	13.5*	8.4	1.3	1.5	2.2	.7	3.2*	.6	.7	2.2
Tran. Equip. Mfg.	@18.4*	9.9*	8.4*	11.3*	3.4	2.6	3.5	1.6	1.7	1.6	3.7
Other Manufact.	@19.3*	@24.3*	22.9*	13.3*	11.2*	5.1	11.2*	7.1	5.6	6.0	8.9
Railroad Transp.	@20.2	@24.3	@36.2	@39.3*	@40.8*	@43.1*	@42.3*	@37.9*	@36.1	@34.8	@36.4
Truck. & Warehsg.	7.9	15.3	@27.1	@37.4	@40.2	@49.3*	@57.7*	@53.6*	@56.0*	@52.3*	@46.9
Other Transp.	@16.7*	@27.9*	@31.3*	14.7*	12.6	10.4	16.9*	13.3	15.2*	10.6	14.1
Communications	@14.9	@22.5	18.6	@26.7	@38.4*	@35.0*	@38.7*	@36.4*	@31.2	@36.1*	@32.8
Utilities	@16.7*	@27.0*	@26.5*	11.3	18.4*	12.6	16.9*	12.1	10.5	10.1	13.3
Wholesale Trade	7.9	17.1	@30.1	@27.4	@30.5	@32.6	@45.0*	@39.1*	@34.8*	@36.1*	@33.0
Total Retail	14.1	15.3	17.5*	10.0	13.6	16.3*	20.4*	16.0*	18.1*	15.3	15.9
Eating & Drinking	12.3	7.2	18.1*	10.0	11.1	17.2*	19.7*	13.7	@24.0*	17.2*	16.8
Other Retail	@15.8	17.1	@25.3	20.0	@26.2*	23.9	21.8	@32.8*	@29.5*	@26.9*	@26.0
Food & Dairy	14.1	16.2	21.7*	12.7	17.5	19.1*	@26.0*	20.7*	20.5*	17.4	18.6
F.I.R.E.	@16.7*	8.1*	9.0*	8.0*	4.9	4.8	5.6	4.7	5.3	4.8	5.8
Total Services	4.4	15.3	18.0	@42.0	@48.1*	@48.5*	@57.0*	@53.5*	@56.9*	@54.6*	@47.9
Lodging & Pers.	10.6	17.1	17.5	16.0	15.5	10.7	@24.6*	20.7*	@24.4*	17.3	17.8
Business & Repair	7.1	@24.3	@43.4	@58.0	@67.5*	@67.0*	@71.2*	73.8*	@70.8*	@67.9*	63.2
Entertain. & Rec.	6.1	16.2	19.2	@26.7	@32.1*	@32.4*	@28.1	@32.8*	@36.3*	@35.9*	@31.5
Private Hsehlds.	@24.6*	@34.2*	@28.4*	@32.0*	20.8	21.4	23.9*	16.0	@24.2*	17.8	21.7
Prof. Services	4.4	15.3	16.8	@42.0	@53.4*	@54.9*	@57.8*	@57.4*	@60.1*	@57.4*	@50.8
Civil Government	10.5	@30.6	@33.8	@28.7	@42.8*	@40.9	@43.6*	@40.6	@42.9*	@49.8*	@42.1
Military	@21.0*	@15.3*	11.4*	5.3*	3.4	2.2	5.6*	1.6	1.5	2.8	4.3
Total	14.6	19.6	22.9*	21.5	23.2*	27.6*	24.1*	23.4*	23.6*	21.2	22.0

APPENDIX II-K. ***(continued)***

Panel D

The Excess (or Deficit) of Leading Gains Relative to Leading Losses (Panel B Minus Panel C)

Industry Sectors	Urban Core Large	Urban Core Medium	Urban Core Small	Primary Labor Field Large	Primary Labor Field Medium	Primary Labor Field Small	Second. Labor Field Large	Second. Labor Field Medium	Second. Labor Field Small	Outside	All Counties
Agriculture	@+14.9*	@+28.4*	@+10.2*	-23.0	-26.8	-31.0	+11.2*	- 6.2	-12.2	@+15.6*	- .7
Forest. & Fish.	+ 4.4	@+17.1	@+17.5	- 3.3	+ 4.9	@+23.9	@+34.6*	@+30.5*	@+39.5*	@+35.8*	@+27.6
Mining	@+29.8*	@+23.4	@+22.3	@+20.7	@+14.5	@+16.2	@+13.2	@+27.0	@+24.3	@+29.7*	@+24.4
Contract Const.	@+24.6	@+20.7	@+12.1	@+27.3*	@+10.7	+ 9.0	+ 9.1	- 4.3	+ 1.5	+ 1.0	@+25.5
Total Manufact.	+ .9	- 4.5	@+10.2	@+44.7	@+65.9*	@+70.1*	@+57.8*	@+61.7*	@+63.4*	@+47.8	@+49.8
Food Manufact.	- 7.9	- 6.3	+ 5.4	@+13.4	@+26.3	@+42.5*	@+44.4*	@+24.2	@+34.1*	@+30.8*	@+27.4
Textile Manufact.	-13.2	-13.5	+ 9.0	+ 2.7	@+16.5	@+42.3*	@+32.3*	@+38.6*	@+48.9*	@+38.4	@+31.7
Apparel Manufact.	- 5.2	- 0 -	@+18.1	@+26.0	@+28.6	@+52.9*	@+55.7*	@+52.7*	@+60.1*	@+48.6	@+43.6
Print. & Publish.	@+20.2*	+12.6	@+10.5	@+19.3*	@+20.4*	@+11.6	@+24.6*	+ 7.0	+10.7	@+16.5*	@+14.7
Chem. Manufact.	+ 2.7	+ 9.9	+ 9.6	@+25.3*	@+25.7*	@+30.4*	@+19.0	@+24.2*	@+17.1	@+27.8*	@+22.9
Lumber & Wood	+ 2.6	+ 3.6	-19.3	- .6	@+15.1*	+ 2.3	@+20.4*	@+19.9*	+ 9.8	@+19.2*	@+11.4
Mach. Manufact.	@+21.9	+12.6	@+19.3	@+36.0	@+51.4*	@+46.5*	@+52.8*	@+45.7*	@+42.1*	@+43.2*	@+41.1
Motor Veh. Mfg.	@+30.5	@+23.4	@+26.5	@+51.4*	@+46.0*	+@38.7	@+52.1*	@+41.4*	@+43.2*	@+41.0*	@+40.5
Tran. Equip. Mfg.	+ 8.8	@+21.6	@+26.5	@+30.1	@+44.1*	@+35.2	@+43.7*	@+39.4*	@+44.6*	@+38.6	@+37.0
Other Manufact.	+ 2.6	+ 3.6	@+13.8	@+34.0	@+55.8*	@+57.1*	@+45.1*	@+49.9*	@+49.1*	@+39.5	@+41.0
Railroad Trans.	+ 7.0*	+ 8.1*	- 6.1*	-16.7	-12.2	-14.3	-14.9	-14.1	- 6.4*	-10.0	- 9.6
Truck. & Wrehsg.	@+28.1*	@+25.2*	+ 4.8*	-10.7*	-11.1*	-28.4	-37.2	-39.5	-41.1	-39.3	-28.1
Other Transp.	@+20.1*	- 6.3	@+12.0	@+24.6*	@+20.9*	@+17.0	@+19.7*	@+20.7*	@+18.7	@+26.5*	@+19.4
Communications	+10.5*	@+13.5*	@+22.3*	- 2.7*	-21.9	-20.4	-16.9	-18.8	- 9.6*	-18.7	-12.4
Utilities	- 1.0	- 0 -	+ 3.6	@+42.1*	@+36.1	@+30.9	@+36.6*	@+39.9*	@+48.9*	@+41.8*	@+36.4
Wholesale Trade	@+41.2*	@+30.6*	+ .6*	- 4.8*	- 8.6*	-10.3*	-33.7	-26.2	-18.3	-22.3	-13.6
Total Retail	@+18.4*	@+15.9*	@+12.6*	+ 6.0*	+ 9.2*	- 1.1	- .7	- .7	- 4.8	+ .9	+ 2.2
Eating & Drinking	+ 9.6	@+37.8*	@+21.6*	@+22.6*	@+26.2*	@+11.1	@+15.5*	@+19.1*	+ .8	@+11.0	@+13.1
Other Retail	@+14.0*	@+10.8*	+ .6*	- 2.6	+ 2.0*	+ .9*	+ 9.2*	-13.2	- 3.7	- 4.2	- 1.7
Food & Dairy	@+23.7*	@+14.4*	+ 6.6*	@+ 8.0*	+ 2.4*	- 2.0	- 6.3	- 3.9	- 6.0	- 1.0	+ .2
F.I.R.E.	+10.4	@+36.0*	@+31.9*	@+13.4	@+25.2*	@+21.7	@+26.1*	@+16.0	@+21.4	@+23.1*	@+22.4
Total Services	@+22.7*	@+27.0*	@+18.8*	-34.6*	-40.4	-41.5	-47.9	-46.5	-52.9	-48.7	-38.0
Lodging & Pers.	+ 4.3	@+15.3*	@+16.2*	+ 8.0	@+13.7*	@+18.9*	- 7.8	@+ 9.0	- .4	@+11.0*	+10.1
Business & Repair	@+27.1*	- .9*	-29.6*	-51.3*	-64.6	-63.3	-69.8	-71.0	-68.7	-66.0	-57.9
Entertain. & Rec.	@+26.4*	@+18.9*	@+13.9*	- 6.0*	-13.6	-11.5	- 4.2*	-14.0	-18.1	-18.2	-10.8
Private Hsehlds.	-14.1	- 8.1	@+13.2	+ 6.0	@+22.4*	@+25.4*	@+19.1	@+34.0*	@+22.6*	@+25.0*	@+20.8
Prof. Services	@+22.8*	@+27.0*	@+21.8*	-32.7*	-45.1	-47.3	-47.3	-50.3	-55.6	-51.4	-40.4
Civil Government	@+14.0*	- 3.6*	- 9.1*	-10.7*	-29.2*	-27.4*	-28.8*	-32.8	-31.4	-43.2	-29.9
Military	+ 4.5	@+29.7	@+32.6*	@+23.3	@+22.3	@+25.4	@+33.1*	@+33.7*	@+37.6*	@+35.4	@+31.4
Total	+12.3*	+12.9*	+10.1	+ 8.7	+ 9.4	+ 9.9	+12.0*	+ 8.7	+12.2*	+10.6*	+10.2

@ = above synthetic region average

* = above industry-sector average

(shaded) = above both region and sector average

Glossary

CODE A. The summary code. A four-digit classifying code summarizing the relationship between the national growth effect and the total differential effect for each region. See p. 117 in volume I or the code diagram on the front endpaper of either volume.

CODE B. The differential code. An eight-digit code classifying the relationship between the industrial mix effect and regional-share (competitive) effect for each region. See p. 117 in volume I or the code diagram on the front endpaper of either volume.

CODE C. The developmental code. An eight-digit code classifying the developmental role that industries play in different localities by identifying those that lead, lag behind, or counter the competitive-developmental tendencies of the region taken as a whole.

DEVELOPMENT(AL). Changes in the way behavioral entities do things and value things that are born of technological change and extraordinary environmental challenges (as distinct from growth, see pp. 14, 34–35 in volume I).

DEVELOPMENTAL CODE. *See:* CODE C.

DEVELOPMENTAL EPOCHS IN U.S. ECONOMIC HISTORY.

Epochs	*Important Characteristics*
First—before 1870	Colonial mercantilism.
Second—1780–1840	Transmontaine spread.
Third—1840–1870	A national transport system, and the new urban hierarchy.
Fourth—1870–1910	Industrialization and interurban transport reorganization.
Fifth—1910–1940	Industrialization, and reorganization of intra-urban transport.
Sixth—1940–1970	The second interurban transport reorganization, and the "birth" of the information society—the study period.
Seventh—1970–?	The developing information society involving a phase-shift in problems and technologies.

DEVELOPMENTAL PROBLEM TYPOLOGY. An attempt to characterize problems and developmental responses by systemic traits independent of specific historical manifestations. See "More About Developmental Sequences," in chapter 9, p. 101.

Type one: Those generic developmental problems that involve some defect in the design of physical performance processes (production processes and the like). Identifiable at the second level of observation (see chapter 1 in volume I).
Type two: Those generic developmental problems that reflect some inadequacy in the types and sources of energy available to drive physical processes. Identifiable at the second level of observation (see chapter 1 in volume I).
Type three: Those generic developmental problems that reflect some limitation imposed on physical processes by the characteristics of the materials that embody them (or are subject to transformation by them). Identifiable at the second level of observation (see chapter 1 in volume I).
Type four: Those generic developmental problems that reflect some inadequacy in the managerial or cybernetic information processes that coordinate physical process activities. Identifiable at the third level of observation (see chapter 1 in volume I).
Type five: Those generic developmental problems that reflect a limitation in the learning or self-reorganizational capacity of an activity system under stress. Identifiable at the fourth level of observation (see chapter 1 in volume I).

DIFFERENTIAL CODE. *See:* CODE B.

DIFFERENTIAL EFFECT. A derived or constructed component of the shift-share technique (D_{ij}). The algebraic sum of the industrial mix and regional share effects ($K_{ij} + R_{ij}$). The total interregional shift in employment.

D_{ij}. *See:* DIFFERENTIAL EFFECT.

G_{ij}. *See:* NATIONAL GROWTH EFFECT.

GROSS SHIFTS. The size of the shift in employment across urban-region boundaries in a given time period. Also, the summation of the mix, share (competitive), or differential shifts across all regions for each industry sector (and for the all-industry line) without the netting implied in the gains and losses.

GROWTH. Changes in the scale and mix of established and preexisting modes of activity and physical output of the behavioral entities under observation. (As distinct from development, see pp. 14, 34–35 in volume I.)

INDEX OF INDUSTRIAL CONCENTRATION. The proportion of the total initial-period employment in an activity sector that would have to be redistributed among regions (in this study 171 urban regions) before they would all contain the same share of the sector's employment. Sometimes referred to as the index of regional localization.

INDEX OF REGIONAL LOCALIZATION. *See*: INDEX OF INDUSTRIAL CONCENTRATION.

INDEX OF REGIONAL SPECIALIZATION. The proportion of the total initial-period employment of a region that would have to be redistributed between industry sectors to give the region the same activity profile as the nation.

INDUSTRIAL MIX EFFECT. One of the components of the shift-share technique (K_{ij}). The degree to which a region augments or diminishes its share of total national employment because its activity structure places it in a position to share disproportionately in national growth.

LEVELS OF BEHAVIORAL OBSERVATION. 1. *Physical objects*—observing the physical product or output of the activity of behavioral entities (such as individuals, households, organized establishments, and the like); that is, observing what has been done. 2. *Physical activities*—observing the activity processes that transform physical object inputs into physical object outputs; that is, observing how the results are achieved. 3. *Managerial or programmatic activities*—observing behavior at the level of information process controls; that is, observing how physical activities are regulated. 4. *Developmental activities*—observing the sources of behavioral change, the reprogramming of managerial and physical activities; that is, observing how and why new behavior is instituted (see chapter 1 and figure 1 in volume I).

MODES OF OBSERVATION. 1. *Classificational*—the differentiation of observational entities into common descriptive groupings yielding boundary network representations. 2. *Relational*—the identification of linkages that connect observational entities to form holistic patterns and processes seen as tree and circuit network representations (see chapter 1 and figure 1 in volume I).

NATIONAL GROWTH EFFECT. One of the components of the shift-share technique (G_{ij}). The change in employment a region would experience if it were a "micronation," that is, if all component industries were distributed in the same proportions regionally as nationally and each sector grew in each region at the national all-sector industry growth rate.

REGIONAL SHARE EFFECT (COMPETITIVE EFFECT). One of the components of the shift-share technique (R_{ij}). Commonly referred to as the "competitive effect." Reflects the difference between the regional and national dynamics manifest in the difference between national and regional industry-sector growth rates.

R_{ij}. *See*: REGIONAL SHARE EFFECT.

SHIFT-SHARE. A statistical-computational technique designed to identify differentiated components of the changing structure of the activities and outputs of regions (see chapter 9 in volume I for a detailed explanation).

SUMMARIZING CODE. *See*: CODE A.

TRADE-CENTER TYPE. A classification of urban centers created by Borchert and Adams in accordance with the kinds of retail and wholesale establishments they contain (see chapter 5, figure 5 in volume I). The types used in the study are: hamlet, minimum convenience, partial shopping, complete shopping, wholesale-retail, and metropolitan (listed in order from the smallest and least complex to the largest and most complex).

TRANSACTION FIELDS (COMMUTING FIELDS). Bounded zones surrounding the dominant center of a broad urban region based primarily on commuting data. Four zones: urban-region core, primary, secondary, and other (that is, beyond the transaction dominance of the urban core).

References and Index

References

Airov, Joseph. 1959. *The Location of the Synthetic-Fiber Industry* (Cambridge, Mass., M.I.T. Press).

American Trucking Association. 1963. *Highways, Trucks, and New Industries: A Study of Changing Patterns in Plant Location* (Washington, D.C.).

Berry, Brian J. L., and Quenton Gillard. 1977. *The Changing Shape of Metropolitan America* (Cambridge, Mass., Ballinger).

Bohi, Douglas R., and Milton Russell. 1978. *Limiting Oil Imports: An Economic History and Analysis* (Baltimore, Johns Hopkins University Press for Resources for the Future).

Bohm, Robert A., and David A. Patterson. 1972. "Interstate Highway Location and County Population Growth," in Oak Ridge National Laboratory, *Urban Growth Patterns,* ORNL-4784 (Oak Ridge, Tenn., Oak Ridge National Laboratory).

Bolton, Roger E. 1966. *Defense Purchases and Regional Growth* (Washington, D.C., The Brookings Institution).

Borchert, John R. 1967. "American Metropolitan Evolution," *Geographical Review,* vol. 57, pp. 301–302.

Brown, David L. 1981. "Spatial Aspects of Post-1970 Work Force Migration in the United States," *Growth and Change* (January).

Business Week. 1974. "Making Money with Air Freight," November 2, p. 105.

________. 1978. "Corporate Flying," February 6, p. 62.

________. 1979. "More Gloom for the Textile Industries," April 9, p. 66.

Bylinski, Gene. 1974. "California's Great Breeding Ground for Industry," *Fortune* (June) p. 129.

Carter, Anne P. 1970. *Structural Change in the American Economy* (Cambridge, Mass., Harvard University Press).

Carter, Luther J. 1974. *The Florida Experience* (Baltimore, Johns Hopkins University Press for Resources for the Future).

Clawson, Marion, and R. Burnell Held. 1957. *The Federal Lands: Their Use and Management* (Baltimore, Johns Hopkins University Press for Resources for the Future).

Cochrane, Willard W. 1979. *The Development of American Agriculture: A Historical Analysis* (Minneapolis, University of Minnesota Press).

Craig, Paul. 1957. "Location Factors in the Development of Steel Centers," *Papers and Proceedings of the Regional Science Association,* vol. 3.

de Sola Pool, Ithiel, ed. 1977. *The Social Impact of the Telephone* (Cambridge, Mass., M.I.T. Press).

Duncan, Otis Dudley, 1959. "Manufacturing As an Urban Function: The Regional Viewpoint," *Sociological Quarterly.*

Dunn, Edgar S., Jr. 1971. *Economic and Social Development: A Process of Social Learning* (Baltimore, Johns Hopkins University Press for Resources for the Future).

Ebeling, Walter. 1979. *The Fruited Plain: The Story of American Agriculture* (Berkeley, Calif., University of California Press).

Filani, Michael O. 1972. "Changing Patterns of Central Places and Functional Regions" (Ph.D. dissertation, Pennsylvania State University).

Fuchs, Victor R. 1962. *Changes in the Location of Manufacturing in the United States Since 1929* (New Haven, Conn., Yale University Press).

Hall, Max, ed. 1959. *Made in New York: Case Studies in Metropolitan Manufacturing* (Cambridge, Mass., Harvard University Press).

Hartshorne, Richard. 1928. "Location Factors in the Iron and Steel Industry," *Economic Geography* vol. 4 (July).

Helfgott, Roy B., W. Eric Gustafson, and James M. Hund. 1959. "Women's and Children's Apparel," in Max Hall, ed. *Made in New York: Case Studies in American Manufacturing* (Cambridge, Mass., Harvard University Press).

Hirt, Francis L. 1961. "Light on Patterns of Output Growth," *Survey of Current Business* (September).

Hoch, Irving. 1980. "The Role of Energy in the Regional Distribution of Economic Activity," in Victor L. Arnold, ed. *Alternatives to Confrontation: A National Policy Toward Regional Change* (Lexington, Mass., D. C. Heath).

Hodge, Gerald. 1965. "The Prediction of Trade Center Viability in the Great Plains," in *Papers and Proceedings of the Regional Science Association,* vol. 15, pp. 87–115.

Hoover, Edgar M., Jr. 1937. *Location Theory and the Shoe and Leather Industry* (Cambridge, Mass., Harvard University Press).

Hunter, Helen. 1955. "Innovation, Competition and Locational Change in the Pulp and Paper Industry, 1880–1950," *Land Economics* (November).

Isard, Walter. 1948. "Some Location Factors in the Iron and Steel Industry Since the Early 19th Century," *Journal of Political Economy,* vol. 56 (June).

Kaniss, Phyllis C. n.d. "The Role of Regional Decline in Adaptive Transformation," in Walter Buhr and Peter Friedrich, eds., *Regional Development Under Stagnation* (Baden-Baden, Nomos Verlagsgesellschaft).

Lindsay, Robert. 1956. "Regional Advantage in Oil Refining," *Papers and Proceedings of the Regional Science Association,* vol. 2.

Meyer, J. Alan. 1977. "Urban Growth and Development of the Telephone," in Ithiel de Sola Pool, ed. *The Social Impact of the Telephone* (Cambridge, Mass., M.I.T. Press).

Miernyk, William H. 1952. "Labor Costs and Labor Supply as Determinants of Industrial Location" (Ph.D. dissertation, Harvard University).

Noble, Stedman. 1981. "Particularizing the Generality of Economic Analysis," in Harvey V. Greenberg and John S. Maybee, eds., *Computer Assisted Analysis and Model Simplification* (New York, Academic Press).

Olsen, Richard J., and G. W. Westley. 1974. "Regional Differences in the Growth of Overnight Truck Transport Markets, 1950–1970," *The Review of Regional Studies,* vol. 4.

———, and ———. 1975. *Synthetic Measures of Truck Operating Times Between the Metropolitan Centers of B.E.A. Economic Areas: 1950, 1960 and 1970, with Projections* (Oak Ridge, Tenn., Oak Ridge National Laboratory).

Olsen, Richard J., L. G. Bray, and G. W. Westley. 1974. "The Location of Manufacturing Employment in BEA Economic Areas" (Oak Ridge, Tenn., Oak Ridge National Laboratory, February).

Paradiso, Lois J., and Francis L. Hirt. 1953. "Growth Trends in the Economy" *Survey of Current Business* (January).

Perloff, Harvey., Edgar S. Dunn, Jr., Eric S. Lampard, and Richard H. Muth. 1960. *Regions, Resources, and Economic Growth* (Baltimore, Johns Hopkins University Press for Resources for the Future).

Polenske, Karen R. 1969. "Shifts in the Regional and Industrial Impact of Federal Government Spending," an Economic Development Administration Report (Washington, D.C.).

Pred, Allan R. 1966. *The Spatial Dynamics of U.S. Urban-Industrial Growth, 1800–1914* (Cambridge, Mass., M.I.T. Press).

———. 1977. *City-Systems in Advanced Economies* (New York, Wiley, A Holsted Press Book).

Rae, John Bell. 1971. *The Road and Car in American Life* (Cambridge, Mass., M.I.T. Press).

Rodgers, Allan. 1952. "Industrial Inertia—A Major Factor in the Location of the Steel Industry in the United States," *Geographical Review,* vol. 42 (January).

Spiegelman, Robert G. 1961. *Factors Determining the Location of the Precision Instrument Industry* (Menlo Park, Calif., Stanford Research Institute, prepared for the Area Redevelopment Administration).

Sundquist, James L. 1975. *Dispersing Population: What Americans Can Learn from Europe* (Washington, D.C., Brookings Institution).

U.S. Department of Agriculture. 1977. *Changes in Farm Production and Efficiency,* Economics, Statistics and Cooperative Service, Statistical Bulletin No. 612.

U.S. Department of Commerce, Bureau of the Census. 1966. *Shipments of Defense Oriented Industries,* Special Report MC63(s) = 2 (Washington, D.C.).

———. Various dates. *U.S. Census of Manufactures* (Washington, D.C., U.S. Government Printing Office).

U.S. Department of Transportation. 1977. *National Transportation Trends and Choices* (Washington, D.C., U.S. Government Printing Office).

Vance, James E. 1970. *The Merchant's World: The Geography of Wholesaling* (Englewood Cliffs, N.J., Prentice-Hall).

Wall Street Journal. 1979. "Tracking a Trend," December 21, p. 36.

Index

The book was designed by Herbert C. Morton. It was set in Times Roman by Monotype Composition Company, Baltimore, Maryland. The color plates were printed on 80 lb. Mead Black and White Enamel Dull Finish and the text was printed on 60 lb. Mohawk vellum by French/Bray Printing Company, Glen Burnie, Maryland.

Library of Congress Cataloging in Publication Data
(Revised for vol. 2)

Dunn, Edgar Streeter.
The development of the U.S. urban system.

Includes bibliographies and indexes.
CONTENTS: v. 1. Concepts, structures, regional shifts.
—v. 2. Industrial shifts, implications.
1. Cities and towns—United States—Collected works.
2. Urban economics—Collected works. I. Title.
HT123.D83 307.7'64'0973 79-2180
ISBN 0-8018-2196-7 (v. 1)
ISBN 0-8018-2638-1 (v. 2)